WOMEN AND GENDER
Transforming Psychology

Janice D. Yoder

University of Akron

Prentice Hall
Upper Saddle River, New Jersey 07458

Library of Congress Cataloging-in-Publication Data

Yoder, Janice D.
    Women and gender : transforming psychology / Janice D. Yoder.
        p.   cm.
    Includes bibliographical references and index.
    ISBN 0-13-644600-0 (pbk.)
    1. Feminist psychology.   I. Title.
BF201.4.Y63   1999
155.3'33—dc21   98-8124
                                                          CIP

Editor in chief: Nancy Roberts
Executive editor: Bill Webber
Assistant editor: Jennifer Cohen
Editorial/production supervision
    and interior design: Mary Araneo
Buyer: Lynn Pearlman
Editorial assistant: Tamsen Adams
Cover photo: "Faces V"
Cover photographer: Diana Ong/
    SuperStock, Inc.

Line art coordinator: Guy Ruggiero
Line art creation: Maria Piper
Photo researcher: Beth Boyd
Photo research supervisor: Melinda Reo
Image permission supervisor: Kay Dellosa
Cover art director: Jayne Conte
Cover designer: Joe Sengotta
Director, Image Resource Center:
    Lori Morris-Nantz

Photo credits appear beginning on page 434, which constitutes a continuation of this page.

This book was set in 10/12 New Baskerville by A & A Publishing
Services, Inc. and was printed and bound by R.R. Donnelly & Co.
The cover was printed by Phoenix Color Corp.

 © 1999 by Prentice-Hall, Inc.
Simon & Schuster/A Viacom Company
Upper Saddle River, New Jersey 07458

Printed in the United States of America

10   9   8   7   6   5   4   3   2   1

ISBN 0-13-644600-0

PRENTICE-HALL INTERNATIONAL (UK) LIMITED, *London*
PRENTICE-HALL OF AUSTRALIA PTY. LIMITED, *Sydney*
PRENTICE-HALL CANADA INC., *Toronto*
PRENTICE-HALL HISPANOAMERICANA, S.A., *Mexico*
PRENTICE-HALL OF INDIA PRIVATE LIMITED, *New Delhi*
PRENTICE-HALL OF JAPAN, INC., *Tokyo*
SIMON & SCHUSTER ASIA PTE. LTD., *Singapore*
EDITORA PRENTICE-HALL DO BRASIL, LTDA., *Rio de Janeiro*

To My Family

John, Kate, and Dan

CONTENTS

CHAPTER FIVE
Gender Comparisons: Questioning the Significance of Difference   111

CHAPTER SIX
Sexism: Sexist Prejudice, Stereotyping, and Discrimination   147

CHAPTER SEVEN
Women's Multiple Roles: Achieving Satisfaction in Close Relationships   176

CHAPTER EIGHT
Multiple Roles Continued: Work, Wages, and Closing the Gap   209

CHAPTER TWELVE
Making a Difference: Transforming Ourselves, Our Relationships, and Our Society   335

PREFACE

I am excited about this book and want to share with you the reasons for my enthusiasm. In the 20 years since I taught my first course, I have watched feminist psychologists transform the field of psychology by creating a legitimate specialty area focused on women and gender and by infusing all other specialty areas within the field with new understandings. This transformation is far from finished, yet this book acknowledges the progress that has been made.

This progress is reflected in the breadth with which we now approach problems in psychology, recognizing that although we are fundamentally psychologists in *how* we do our work, our work is more useful if it draws upon a broader array of perspectives relevant to a problem. In this text, I will bring in a multitude of social and biological scientists to explicate a topic.

Progress also is evident in where we focus our attention. The debate over whether we study women or gender is made moot by an overarching feminist approach, an approach that works to end sexist oppression whether that oppression unjustly disadvantages or privileges women or men, girls or boys. This book is not just for women, or for psychologists only, or for scholars interested in women and gender; it is a book for anyone interested in social justice. Although my focus is primarily on gender, I recognize throughout this book that gender does not exist in isolation from other aspects of our personal identities such as our race and ethnicity, sexual orientation, socioeconomic class, age, physical ability, religion, and so on.

There are two potentially disastrous pitfalls to wanting to reach such a diverse audience. On the one hand, feminist psychology often is marginalized in academic circles; the very courses that are likely to adopt this text typically fall outside departments' "core" curriculum. A common response to this is to assert one's legitimacy by assuming the trappings of "hard science": developing elaborate jargon, detaching one's self from the materials to give them an aura of objectivity, etc. At the other extreme, pop psychology books claiming to understand women and men (even by associating them with different planets or opposing sides of the brain) make bestseller lists but are not well grounded in systematic research. These books are very appealing to broad audiences, but fail to make research-based arguments.

I have worked hard to avoid both pitfalls with this text. On the one hand, I myself have taught in a wide variety of academic settings including a very formal, authoritarian structure at West Point; innovative, highly student-oriented settings at Webster University in St. Louis and Alverno College; a highly competitive institution at Washington University in St. Louis; and large, public, mostly commuter campuses at the University of Wisconsin-Milwaukee and University of Akron. Each location exposed me to a diversity of students with differing needs, questions, expectations, and views of the world from whom I've expanded my approaches to teaching. At UWM, I won two teaching awards. My confidence in how this book will work with students doesn't just rest on my teaching laurels. I spent a semester benefiting from intensive feedback from 13 honors students at UWM who painstakingly reviewed each and every chapter of this book, discussed it openly with me in weekly "roast-Jan" sessions, and tried out revisions. There are pieces of each and every one of them in this book. They were a tough audience, but I am grateful for all I learned with them.

On the other hand, this text is academically rigorous in that it encourages readers to think critically and is well grounded in an extensive body of research drawing on over 1700 references. I sought out comments from topical experts who generously shared their expertise with me and oftentimes took my presentation to the cutting-edge. I purposively rejected a "scientific" style that is jargon-y and depersonalized. I use personal examples where appropriate and may even embarrass my children beyond what parents commonly do. I opted to integrate the research that I read so that each chapter develops around clear themes, rather than simply cataloguing findings or providing outlines of disjointed, opposing viewpoints. Students often reported reading chapters in one sitting because the "story" flowed.

How should you read this book? I encourage you to work interactively with this book; interspersed throughout it are brief exercises to get you thinking about the points being discussed. Also, think about what you are reading within the context of your own life—does it resonate; spur you to see the world differently; etc? I have drawn on the most up-to-date materials; this is one area where critical readers readily reject a piece of research because "it's too old." Pre-1990s research that shows linkages among factors is still very useful and I use these materials extensively, but most research reported here that describes ongoing processes (e.g., socialization practices) was published in the 1990s.

What should you do with this book? I think you'll find this to be a book that you'll want to talk about with others. Take advantage of your class to do this. You probably will talk to people in your everyday life about it as well. As we will see in the last chapter, most readers of these kinds of texts and students in these classes come away from the semester seeing the world through different lenses. This book should engender feelings, challenge opinions, and change behaviors. A common mistake for an author is to fail to acknowledge these effects and to leave readers groping for something to do with these. I sincerely hope that you'll find the last chapter of this book helpful in this regard so that it won't decay on your bookshelf or go into a used-book pile without having an impact on you and how you think. To fail in this way would be the most devastating indictment of my feminist approach.

ACKNOWLEDGMENTS

I am indebted to so many people who helped challenge, refine, and expand my thinking for this book, although in all fairness to them, I'm ultimately responsible for what appears in these pages. I am very grateful to the members of my Fall 1997 honors seminar on "Feminist Approaches in Psychology": Shannon Ahrndt, Fran Chaney, Elizabeth Costabile, Roxie Guenther, Jenny Konrad, Lisa Mahan, Becky Murphy, Iolanda Olivia, Angela Rich, Valerie Richter, Sarah Stuebner, Jen Trimble, and Juliet Warner. Your openness, honesty, and hard work shines through in every chapter of this book. I also sincerely appreciate the voluntary efforts of my "dream team" of topical experts who commented on select chapters: Deb Padgett (Ch. 1); Linda Bernardine (Ch. 2); Stacey Oliker (Ch. 3); Mary Gergen and Dale Jaffe (Ch. 4); Kathryn Dindia and Alice Eagly (Ch. 5); Peter Glick (Ch. 6); Suzanna Rose (Ch. 7); Sue Rosenberg Zalk and John Zipp (Ch. 8); Diane Reddy (Ch. 9); Paula Caplan (Ch. 10); Mary Koss and Lenore Walker (Ch. 11); and Celia Kitzinger (Ch. 12). I also thank Lynne Berendsen, Carole Hoefs, Sue Lima, Tedd McDonald, Kat Quina, Diane Clark, Kate Conway-Turner, Anne Peplau, Arnie Kahn, Linda See, Carie Forden, Maggie Madden, Jennifer Aube, Laurel Wainwright, and Anne Marie Orza for their general reviews and helpful comments.

The beginning groundwork for this book was facilitated by the independent study work completed by Jennifer Bednarek, Danielle Birdeau, Emily Dallmann, Dennis Eckrich, Beth Ann Felch, Micheline Jozefiak, Nicole Kucavich, Michele Lintonen, Sammy Nelson, Elizabeth Schmidt, Mary Smits, Bridget Sweeney, and Mark Zbikowski. The initial impetus for this book was Wayne Spohr of Prentice Hall, still the master of Missouri float trips. I also deeply appreciate the patience, encouragement, and assistance of Jennifer Cohen and Bill Webber at Prentice Hall as well as Mary Araneo. Last but certainly not least, my family came through with support and "free" time to get me through a very intense period of writing. Thanks John, Kate, and Dan. (Bosco and Emma, my dog and cat companions, saw me through many days and nights of isolated writing!)

Jan Yoder

ABOUT THE AUTHOR

Jan Yoder earned her doctorate in psychology in 1979 from the State University of New York at Buffalo. Her interests in women, gender, and feminism developed professionally through her observations of the first women cadets at West Point and personally through her own struggles with sexual harassment, dual-career challenges, work-family juggling, and women's universal exposure to sexism. Her job paths traveled a circuitous but enlightening route through West Point, where she stood out as

one of the first two civilian women to teach there; through a small student-centered college in St. Louis, Webster University; through an exhilarating foray into the world of advertising and marketing research in Chicago at DDB Needham Worldwide; to large research-oriented universities in Milwaukee and finally Akron. The wealth of these diverse experiences comes through in this book as she blends a strong research base with her sensitivity to women's and men's everyday lives and with an engaging style that comes from teaching for over 20 years in a variety of college and university settings. She now lives in Akron, Ohio with her awesome children, Kate and Dan, her soul-mate husband, sociologist John Zipp, and her working-late cat companion, Emma. She remembers enjoying reading, gardening, hiking, weight-lifting, cooking, and needlework, but with kids, job, this book . . . they seem like distant memories. If you'd like to contact her, e-mail is a good bet: janyoder@uakron.edu.

ONE

FEMINIST TRANSFORMATIONS OF PSYCHOLOGY
There's No Turning Back

A father brings his 18-year-old daughter, Dora, to a male therapist, complaining that she is defiant and willful. The young woman's family is distressed by Dora's annoying behaviors, and the father beseeches the therapist to "bring her to reason."

Over the next three months, Dora's story unfolds as she describes her beliefs that her father and a friend of the family, Mrs. K, are having an affair. Mrs. K's husband exhibits an attraction to Dora, buying her expensive gifts and taking long, unchaperoned walks with her since she was 7 or 8. Dora's growing uneasiness with Mr. K was validated when she was 14. She was invited to watch a festival from Mr. K's office window. Expecting her family to attend, she was surprised to arrive to a darkened room, alone with Mr. K. He kissed her deeply, she felt his erection, and she pulled away. Dora marks this as the starting point of her "symptoms." Other more serious incidents followed, and Dora's "symptoms" worsened. Dora is convinced that her father and her abuser have made a pact, either implicit or open, compensating Mr. K for his unfaithful wife with her lover's daughter (Dora).

Although the therapist acknowledges that Dora's perceptions are valid, he withholds his affirmation from her, fearing that this will encourage her disruptive, "neurotic" behavior. Instead, he suggests that Dora is sexually attracted to Mrs. K and offended by the therapist's failure to be sexually attracted to her. Dora terminates therapy after three months, and we never learn how her problems were resolved.

This soap-opera-like story was told in 1899 by the treating therapist, Sigmund Freud (Hare-Mustin, 1983; Lakoff, 1990). With 100 years hindsight, many of us would be quick to identify Dora's case as an example of childhood sexual abuse, complete with the family betrayal that characterizes this insidious form of abuse. In this light, Dora's "symptoms" take on a less pathological look and instead seem adaptive by helping her to resist an abnormal situation. We recognize her powerlessness as a child and the invalidation of her experiences by more powerful others, including her parents and her therapist.

This case and our reaction to it capture the transformation of psychology across its past 100-plus years as an academic and applied discipline. The male-centered perspective that victimized Dora twice (first by sexually abusing her and second by invalidating that abuse) is replaced by an understanding that affirms her experiences and reactions and works toward empowering her. Psychology today has been transformed to its very core by the questions, probing, analyses, and alternatives offered by a feminist perspective. Whether we openly acknowledge the role feminism has played in this transformation or not, it is clear that there is no turning back—psychology and the way we approach women and gender have been altered irrevocably. The purpose of this text is to describe this new (improved and improving) psychology, knowing full well that psychologists 100 years from now may look with hindsight at some of what we are doing with the same incredulity with which we view Freud's analysis of Dora's case.

Psychology has come a long way since the days of Dora and Freud. One purpose of this chapter is to document this historic shift. Are we there yet? This question assumes a definable, static endpoint—a goal to be reached like the peak of a mountain. Our goal is unlikely to be so simple or concrete. We should expect an ongoing series of transformations as psychology becomes increasingly useful to women and men, girls and boys. How do we keep working at this transforming process? A good place to start is with questions.

Even our images of women in the future have changed from sex object (left) to captain of a starship (right).

QUESTIONING QUESTIONS

Questions. The cornerstone of all psychology is questions. Theorists propose models to suggest answers to questions. Researchers conduct studies to seek answers to questions. Therapists approach every diagnosis and treatment plan with questions. The art and science done by psychologists centers around questions. What questions might we ask of a psychology that helps us understand women and gender?

Lots of questions immediately come to mind: Do we need a separate psychology of women (not people)? Who are the women in psychology's history? Do women and men think differently, act differently, talk differently, and have different personalities? Why do women live longer than men? Are women mentally "sicker" than men? Why don't battered women leave? Why are most famous people men? Why do women earn less than men? Why do many women feel fat? Should mothers, not day care providers, care for children? Does women's employment hurt families? Why do boys gather around the basketball hoop while girls gather in the housekeeping corner? This list goes on and on, as does our fascination with these questions. These questions, and many more, will be addressed throughout this book.

We all have opinions about answers to these questions. We've heard the opinions of others, expressed with varying degrees of confidence, in our daily conversations with family members, friends, acquaintances, and even strangers. We've heard answers bantered about on talk shows from Oprah to Geraldo, "60 Minutes" to "20/20." Psychologists are not exceptions.

Although psychologists indeed share the populace's enthusiasm with these questions, it is our approach to understanding women and gender that ultimately distinguishes our answers from the opinions of the general public. We pursue questions with scientific inquiry, using systematic methods that can take us beyond the realm of unexplored, simple opinion. Does this make us objective or mean we give factual answers? I'm not convinced. But I do know that systematic inquiry can make the answers more complex, and certainly more useful and defensible, than mere opinion.

The purpose of this book is to explore these types of questions. You may already realize that there rarely are simple answers. On the other hand, we never will be groping in the dark. As the field of the psychology of women and gender burgeons, what we do know is becoming more and more sophisticated. This book will introduce you to an accumulation of questions, research findings, theory, and thought. *Always question.* Some of your opinions may be challenged—question them. Some of your own experiences may suddenly make sense—think about them. Read a newspaper, watch television, talk to your friends, watch kids at play, look around work and school—ask questions and think about what's happening. You'll know that you're getting somewhere if you're questioning and thinking from a better informed base.

The Role of Values

We value some questions more than others. My research focuses on women in nontraditional occupations—military cadets at West Point and firefighters. I ask these women questions about their work-group climate, about sexual harassment, about promotion opportunities, and so on. Why these women and why these questions?

Whenever researchers choose to pursue one research project, we necessarily disregard a whole array of potential other questions. Similarly, whenever instructors elect to cover one topic and to focus on certain theory and research related to that topic, we ignore other possible topics and other approaches to discussing the selected topic.[1] These choices may reflect funding opportunities (some research attracts grants more readily than others), whether or not results are likely to be published in highly ranked journals, researchers' particular interests, and so on. Underlying all of these choices, whether apparent or not, whether explored or not, are **values**.

Let me come clean then with *my* values. With no apologies for using the f-word, I am a feminist. This raises an obvious question: What is a feminist? We all know the images the media has created—man-hating, bra-less, unhappy women. In reality, feminists come in all shapes and sizes—I happen to be married, have two neat kids, a dog, and a cat, live in a sleepy suburb, and own a station wagon (no van!). Much of what I study as a feminist psychologist seeps into my personal life (and vice versa), so you'll come to know my family somewhat in some of the examples I use. My husband, John Zipp, also is an academic (sociology), my daughter Kate was born in 1986 and Dan in 1991. When I first wrote this, Kate was 11 and Dan, 6.

I am open about my feminist values. It's important for you to be forthcoming with your own. You may find that much of the research described throughout this book resonates with your own experiences or helps you to understand those experiences. What is more challenging to explore is those times when scholarship diverges

---

[1] For a discussion of teaching as a political act, see Kinsler and Zalk (1996).

from your experiences or from widely held folk wisdom. Rather than discount the research, ask new questions that may reconcile your experiences with the general patterns supported by the research. Recognize that "bandwagon concepts" supported by folk wisdom may be intuitively obvious, simple, and basically satisfying but rooted in unquestioned myth rather than researched evidence (Mednick, 1989). Also consider how the research itself may be narrow or flawed. It is in this way that we move beyond the limits of what we know so far. To me this is the excitement of psychology—the challenge of asking questions, thinking, and going beyond one's own view of the world. The exploration will be frustrating at times; but it will be compelling and well worth your investment.

Looking beyond our own personal values, there is scholarship exploring the role of values in understanding women and gender (Riger, 1992). At an ideological level, there are a variety of **feminisms**, and these shape the work psychologists and others do in a myriad of ways. Ellen Kimmel (1989) surveyed 51 distinguished members of Division 35 (Psychology of Women) of the American Psychological Association and asked them to describe their feminist values. For them, as for me, feminism means valuing women and their experiences, a concern for equality of power, the need for change and activism, and the belief that gender is created and defined by our culture. I have no doubts that my values and the values of others in this field who generate the scholarship we'll examine will guide what and how I present materials. Given this, it is critical to consider the value base from which we'll be working in this book.

Feminism offers a filter for bringing research and personal experience together. Sociologists describe feminism as a **social movement**, and social movements are characterized by organizations and leadership, change strategies, and ideology. In general, there are two types of social movements: **reforms** (which work within existing systems to more effectively serve disenfranchised groups) and **revolutions** (which seek to restructure social and/or political institutions). The most visible form of feminism in the contemporary United States is a liberal, reform movement with organizations like the National Organization for Women; leaders like Gloria Steinem, Betty Friedan, and Susan Faludi; change strategies like electing supportive candidates and sponsoring legislation; and an ideology of equal opportunities for women and men.

This is not the only strand of feminism out there (Jaggar, 1983; Lorber, 1994). Other feminists argue that the sexual and reproductive oppression of women is part of a global system of patriarchal domination; they call for revolutionary social changes in broad social institutions, especially the family (MacKinnon, 1982). Still others emphasize the gendered division of labor and the interaction of gender oppression with class oppression (Barrett, 1988; Hartmann, 1976). Others add the influence of race and heterosexuality to the mix, asking liberal feminists a very simple question about equal opportunity: Equal to whom?—certainly not poor men or African American men or gay men (Collins, 1989; Connell, 1987; hooks, 1984). Sociologist Judith Lorber (1994) thinks of gender as a social institution

> that establishes patterns of expectations for individuals, orders the social processes of everyday life, is built into the major social organizations of society, such as the economy, ideology, the family, and politics, and is also an entity in and of itself (p. 1).

Obviously, there's a lot more to feminism than not wearing a bra (on the trivial side) or, more seriously, wanting to share equally in the privileges afforded some men in our culture. It's really more representative of the ideology underlying the feminist social movement to talk about *feminisms*. Despite differences in definitions of feminism, there is some common ground: all views value women and women's lives and all call for social changes designed to end **sexism** (unjust treatment resulting from one's sex and gender). It is these commonalties that tie feminism to psychology and that make feminism fundamental to our understanding of women and gender.

Feminism gives psychology meaning and purpose. Research, theory, teaching, and practice in feminist psychology all contribute to the feminist goal of social change to end sexism in our own thinking, in our relationships with others, and in larger organizations and social institutions. This is the ultimate use to which our work will be put, and it provides the litmus tests from which we can judge the value of our work (Unger, 1982). The theory and research of feminist psychology becomes a contributor to the ideology of feminism as a social movement. In turn, feminism gives the psychology of women and gender direction. The goal of feminist psychology as a perspective within the overall field of psychology is to *create a psychology opposed to sexist oppression* (Kahn & Yoder, 1989).

Framing and Choosing Our Questions

In addition to thinking about the blatant and hidden values involved in the questions we ask, we need to consider how we frame the questions themselves. Again, our values can play a role. How we ask a question can shape the approaches we take toward answering it.

For example, a whole literature in developmental psychology evolved around the implied question: Is day care bad for children? As we'll see in Chapter 7, researchers measured "maternal separation anxiety," aggressive displays by children in day care, defiance, sociability, intellectual achievement, and so on. Even when positive outcomes were found, they often were presented as compensations for the "obvious" drawbacks of other-than-mother care. The overarching question of this research came to influence both what measures were taken and how findings were regarded.

Louise Silverstein (1991) approaches this same area of study with a differently framed question. She argues that given trends in the employment of mothers, it is unlikely that day care will disappear as an option. She then suggests that we explore how to make day care *more effective* for children and their families. This new question inspires a very different, proactive approach to doing research on the effects of day care.

Sometimes our initial question raises new, more refined questions. Another example will illustrate this. Consider a study by Catriona Llewellyn (1981). A bank engaged her to explain why it was promoting women less than men. The data were clear: few women were being promoted. Further data collection revealed that the aspirations of current women employees were lower than those of men; that there was higher turnover among the women, 90% of whom left the bank before they reached age 30; that the women, as a group, were less educated than their male counterparts; and that the women infrequently took an exam that was critical for promotion. These data clearly answer the implied research question: What's wrong with these women? They also strongly suggest a solution: "fix" the women.

Llewellyn did not end her analysis here. Rather, she refined her beginning question and asked: Why are women's aspirations low; why are they leaving; why aren't they as well educated; and why don't they take the exam? The focus of her analysis shifted from the women themselves to their surrounding context within the bank. She began by exploring the recruiting procedures followed by the bank, reporting her findings that typically men were recruited for careers with long-term growth potential. In contrast, most women were recruited for *jobs*. Career-oriented recruitment attracted candidates with better educational credentials, that is, better educated men.

On the job, it didn't take women long to notice that few women were being promoted. Although we generally think that workers' aspirations influence their chances for promotion, it also is true that perceived opportunities for promotion affect aspirations (Kanter, 1977). When workers believe that their jobs are deadend positions, one response is to lower their aspirations; another is to leave the job. Certainly, they don't bother to do the kinds of arduous things (like study for and take exams) that seem unlikely to pay off.

Notice how the focus has shifted. In Llewellyn's beginning analysis, the women took center stage, and her data convincingly described them as deficient relative to the men. In her subsequent analysis, a different focus emerges. The women no longer appear inadequate; rather, the work setting seems fundamentally different for the women and men employed in it. Notice too how the solutions have changed. The first analysis ends with a frustrated plea from the bank for competent women: "If we could find women as qualified as men, we'd promote them!" The second analysis calls for serious reconsideration of bank procedures to make them fairer.

In sum then, we will question our questions. (1) *Look for and consider the values underlying the questions asked and not asked.* Why does this question get lots of attention and money when another doesn't? Why is this question of interest to me?

(2) *Think about how the question is framed.* Does it imply negativity and deficiency, all too often directed at women? Realize that these sentiments frequently are subtle, but influential and pervasive. Few people overtly ask: "Are women with children in day care bad mothers?" Yet this could be the underlying assumption of some research.

(3) *Consider additional questions.* Sometimes, these are complementary questions. For example, Michele Fine (1989) refused to consider the costs of creating a rape-crisis center without also factoring in the costs, both economic and psychological, of *not* having such a facility. Sometimes they are follow-up questions, as in the example with Llewellyn (1981) at the bank. These further questions refine and redirect the original question, potentially shifting the focus of our work and shaping the solutions we propose.

THE POWER OF LANGUAGE

Sex, Sexuality, and Gender

Language provides the medium through which we think and share our ideas with others. When Freud analyzed the case of Dora, he didn't have access to some terms and concepts, such as recovered memories and male violence against women we readily use today and, to his credit, he offered some of his own (e.g., unconscious). The terms we use to talk about feminism, psychology, women, and gender will affect how we think about these concepts—so it is important to clarify their meaning up front.

When we want to talk about a difference between women and men, girls and boys, what terms should we use? This seems like a pretty simple question and maybe even a bit picky, but our discourse can subtly shape our thinking. Do we want to imply that a difference is rooted in biology and therefore is part of the essential natures of women and girls, men and boys? To avoid such unscrutinized biological essentialism (as well as its political implications for unrealistic, unnatural change), some feminists restrict usage of the term "sex" to discussions which find or assume biological determinants (Unger, 1979). An alternative is to speak in terms of "gender" to imply psychologically, socially, and culturally based differences between women and men.

However, there are drawbacks with relying on this simple sex (biology) and gender (social) dichotomy. Sex gets mixed up with sexuality which itself is more than a biological activity, and semantics get even more confusing when we confound biology and culture in combinations like "sex roles." More importantly, the distinction between sex and gender sets up a nature-versus-nurture duality (Unger & Crawford, 1993) that doesn't allow for their interaction (Deaux, 1993; Hyde, 1994a). Much of what we do and who we are probably reflects both our bodies (nature) and our socialization (nurture). Furthermore, if we think only of social gendered causes we might ignore biological influences and vice versa; who's to say when we start studying one particular female-male difference that it is going to turn out to be socially and/or biologically rooted (Eagly, 1994)? For a science, this is tantamount to putting the cart before the horse. Finally, framing matters in terms of nature and/or nurture ignores a third contributor: **context**. Some psychologists have gone so far as to contend that everything we do is mired in a specific social and cultural context (Rosnow & Rosenthal, 1989). The terms sex and gender, both of which root differences inside individuals, fail to capture the impact of forces that are external to the person emanating from social and cultural settings.

I know of no completely satisfactory accommodations to our dilemma at this time. However, I do think that for most of us who are not immersed in this field, the term "sex" carries with it the day-to-day connotations of sexuality and anatomy. When we talk about "sex differences," most of us automatically will conjure up images of sexual or biological causes. In keeping with this expectation, usage of "**sexuality**" will be restricted to discussions about reproductive structures and functions and of "**sex**" to clearly narrow reviews of biological explorations (mostly in Chapter 2). Certainly our thinking should not be limited to these domains. To avoid this, I like the term "gender" because it isn't used as commonly as "sex" and thus carries less baggage. This use of **gender** may inspire a fresh look and encourage you to think more broadly by considering the confluence of biology, socialization, and social context.

Doing Gender

You are: ☐ Female   ☐ Male

How many surveys and forms have you completed, mindlessly checking one of the above boxes? This approach to measuring sex (or is it gender?) assumes that there are two and only two choices (a dichotomy); that everyone fits in one of the two classifications (all-inconclusive); and that we each fall into one and only one category (mutually exclusive). These same sentiments underlie our descriptions of the "opposite" sexes (rather than simply referring to the "other" sex). This approach also suggests that being female or male is something we *are*—something static, immutable, and essential to our natures.

An alternative approach is offered by social constructionists who view gender as something we do, create, or construct with the consensus of others (Gergen, 1985; West & Zimmerman, 1987). **Doing gender** refers to a dynamic process of enacting femaleness and maleness in relation to others, not a static, unchanging state of being. Think how disturbing it is not to know the sex of a person with whom we are dealing. We go to great lengths in our everyday lives to broadcast our sex to others through our names, the clothes we wear, the pitch of our voices, etc. We construct gender—something that becomes even clearer when we look across cultures and find places where others do it differently. How we construct gender is not an individualized thing; rather we do it within the dictates of our culture, both reflecting and reproducing that social structure. This perspective will permeate this book.

The character, Pat, from the television show, "Saturday Night Live," is both disturbing and comic because we never really know what gender s/he is.

TOWARD A FEMINIST PSYCHOLOGY

Moving toward a transformed, feminist psychology is a slow, painstaking process and, we shall see, different areas of psychology are farther along than others. Typically, this progression moves through three phases, but the progression may not be smooth and clear-cut (Crawford & Marecek, 1989; Lerner, 1992). In the early phases, questions are raised about **androcentric bias**—a perspective that places men at its core. In the next compensatory phase, women are "discovered," both as doers and objects of study, and are re-placed in the field's history. At the next level, an ongoing process of transformation begins that irrevocably alters the field and how its work is approached. I have argued here that feminism provides the value base toward such transformations in a psychology focused on women and gender.

Androcentric Bias

A brief look at the history of psychology suggests that androcentric bias has appeared throughout it and may even persist to some degree today. Women's participation in this history often is overlooked. Examine your textbook from your Introductory Psychology class; are there any women pictured in the history section (usually in the first chapter of the book)? While women did not have opportunities equal to those of men at the time (Furumoto & Scarborough, 1986), there were indeed some very influential women. Despite their presence, how many women are visible in this history? How many of the following psychologists can you identify? (If you need some help, consult footnote 2.)

Christine Ladd Franklin	Mary Whiton Calkins
Margaret Floy Washburn	Leona Tyler
Florence Denmark	Janet Taylor Spence
Bonnie Strickland	Dorothy Cantor
Leta Stetter Hollingworth	Ruth Howard (Beckham)
Martha Bernal	Maime Phipps Clark[2]

Not only were women psychologists and their work overlooked, but women often were excluded as research participants. Kathleen Grady (1981) counted twice as many men as women in psychological studies. Time and time again, theories and

---

[2] Ladd-Franklin, Calkins, and Washburn were the only 3 women among 50 psychologists listed by James McKeen Cattell in 1903 as the most famous psychologists in the United States. Ladd-Franklin developed an influential theory of color vision; Calkins invented the paired associate technique (not Freud), and Washburn, the first woman to earn her Ph.D. in psychology, wrote "The Animal Mind" which has been cited as a precursor and impetus to behaviorism. The seven women from Calkins through Cantor are the only women APA presidents from 1892-1998: Calkins (1905), Washburn (1921), Tyler (1973), Denmark (1980), Spence (1984), Strickland (1989), and Cantor (1996). Hollingworth, often declared the "mother" of the psychology of women, debunked myths that menstruation adversely affects women's performance and that women are intellectually inferior to men. Howard and Bernal were the first African American and Chicana women, respectively, to earn Ph.D.s in psychology. And, Clark's work with her often-cited husband, Kenneth Clark, spurred the Supreme Court's desegregation decision in *Brown v. the Board of Education* (Russo & Denmark, 1987). For more about women in psychology, also see Furumoto and Scarborough (1987), O'Connell & Russo (1990), and Paludi (1992).

research on life cycle development (critiqued by Gilligan, 1979), achievement motivation (Kahn & Yoder, 1989), leadership (Hollander & Yoder, 1980), structure (Shields, 1975) and utilization (Sherman, 1978) of the hemispheres of the brain, and, believe it or not, even breast cancer[3] involved only men—mostly white, college men. A singular but striking example is reported by Mary Brown Parlee and Jayalakshmi Rajagopol (1974, in footnote 2) who note that an often-cited secondary source, presumed to support the conclusion that women and men differ in spatial abilities, cites a study that included only men.

A major problem with all of this single-gender research is that psychologists did not stay within the confines of what they studied. Rather, having studied only men, they all-too-often generalized their results to women (Holmes & Jorgensen, 1971; Reardon & Prescott, 1977; Schwabacher, 1972). This exclusive concentration of researchers and theorists on being male-centered is part of what defines androcentric bias.

Even the inclusion of men in research was not inclusive of *all* men; psychologists uncritically relied on readily available white, educated, upper class, heterosexual, male college students (Lykes & Stewart, 1986; Sears, 1986). For example, Robert Guthrie (1976) exposed psychology's exclusion of people of color in his acclaimed book, *Even the Rat Was White*. There certainly is a place for single-gender research. The mistake is not in doing it, but in extending conclusions to unstudied groups and letting those excluded groups go unstudied.

When psychologists studied women, it often was in politically "safe" areas stereotyped as appropriate for women—and men were excluded. However, some aspects of women's lives were neglected by psychologists who historically ignored domestic work (Chapter 7), wage disparities (Chapter 8), women's physical health (Chapter 9), and male violence against women (Chapter 11). These areas of special interest to women need to be added to psychology as deserving areas for future research and funding (Epstein, 1988; McHugh, Koeske, & Frieze, 1986; Smith, 1987).

Studies focused on women as mothers (critiqued by Eyer, 1992), self-disclosers (Dindia & Allen, 1992), and neurotics and depressives (Lerman, 1986) abound, while research on men in these areas is sparse. We need to learn more about men who are the primary caregivers for their children ("mothers?") (Chapter 7), how men self-disclose in friendships (Chapter 7), and how men express depression (Chapter 10). Although the focus is mainly on women in this text, some of these gender issues as they extend to men will be included as well.

We are calling for a psychology that is inclusive of all women and all men. However, **androcentric bias** involves more than including only men—it refers to being male-centered. There have been times in psychology's history when women were studied, but their actions were considered only as deviations from what "normal" participants (i.e., men) do. For example, when women gave others equal

---

[3]Unbelievable as it may seem, Congressional Representative Olympia Snowe (Republican, ME) described a pilot study done at Rockefeller University to study the relationship between obesity and the development of cancer in breasts or uterine lining that used only men as participants (Jaschik, 1990). This example was part of a broader study of the National Institutes of Health (NIH) charging that women's needs were being underserved. In response to this charge, the first woman director of NIH announced a new $500 million program of research on women's health (Eckholm, 1991).

rewards, ignoring the unequal contributions of group members, rather than distributing more to people who did more as predicted by equity theory's research with men, women's choices were declared artifactual (reviewed in Kahn and Gaeddert, 1985). When women realistically identified how they'd do on a test in contrast to men who overestimated their performance, women were said to lack confidence, rather than men being deemed unrealistically overconfident (Ryujin & Herrold, 1989). Even men's bodies are considered normative, with women's bodies viewed as a deviation from this norm in Supreme Court cases where "pregnancy-related disabilities constitute an *additional* risk, unique to women" (*General Electric v. Gilbert*, cited in Bem, 1993, p. 75). Research suggesting differing effects of antidepressants on women was actively suppressed because it called into question the adequacy of drug testing (Hamilton, 1992). The point is that what men do is considered normative for all human beings;[4] what women do is regarded as a deficient or irrelevant deviation from that standard.

Granted, the history of psychology was biased, but we've learned from it. Does androcentric bias still exist in psychology? One very basic indicator of equity would be the full inclusion of women in psychological research. Deborah Adler and Suzanne Johnson (1994) analyzed the contents of two issues of every APA journal published in 1990, selecting every article that involved human participants, for a total of 801 studies in 506 articles across 26 journals. There's some encouraging news: 60% included women and men, averaging 52.5% women. Combine this with the findings of Linda Gannon and her colleagues (1992) who report that the proportion of male-only studies has been declining since the 1970s, and a more promising picture emerges.

Still, there's some cause for continued vigilance. Adler and Johnson (1994) go on to find that only 14% of the 484 studies reporting the sex of their participants actually discussed gender, and only 35% analyzed their data to check for possible differences in how women and men responded. Fully 30% of the studies failed to mention the sex of their participants. The most negligent offenders were in the areas of cognition, perception, and learning, suggesting that women and men continue to be regarded as interchangeable in these core experimental specialties.

The remaining 10% of the studies sampled by Adler and Johnson (1994) included only one sex, and 67% of these studied only women. Of the single-sex studies, 41% made it clear in the title that only one sex was included, and 54% noted this in the opening abstract which summarizes the paper. Only 11% warned that generalizability of the findings to all people was limited to the sex studied. Most interestingly, an indication in the title or abstract that the study included a single sex was clearer when the participants were female than when they were male. In sum, there has been progress with the inclusion of women, but psychology is far from being satisfactorily transformed.

---

[4] Ironically, the equation of maleness with generic humanness misses the essential nature of masculinity—of what men are like as men. A corrective to this oversight is offered by profeminist approaches to men's studies (Brod, 1987b).

Re-placing Women

An obvious corrective to the exclusion and misinterpretation of women and women's lives in psychology has been the development of a women-centered psychology. There is no doubt but that the psychology of women has been entrenched as a legitimate area of study within the discipline. There are college courses like the one you're taking: 50% of colleges and universities in the United States and Canada offer at least one undergraduate or graduate course on the psychology of women or gender roles (Women's Programs Office, 1993).[5] In 1994, 61.5% of all new doctorates in psychology in the United States were earned by women, and in 1995, 44.9% of members of the American Psychological Association were women (Women's Program Office, 1995).[6] Women first-year undergraduates are three times more likely than men to plan to pursue psychology majors (Clay, 1996), and women earned fully 73% of bachelors degrees in psychology in 1992–93 (Murray, 1996). There are recognized organizations within psychology: Division 35: Psychology of Women [established in 1973; the fourth largest division within the American Psychological Association (APA)][7]; the Association for Women in Psychology (est. 1969)[8]; and the Women's Program Office (est. 1977) and Office of Lesbian and Gay Concerns[9] (both in the Public Interest Directorate of APA). There are journals devoted exclusively to research and theory in the field: *Sex Roles* (published since 1975), *Psychology of Women Quarterly* (1977), *Women & Therapy* (1982), and *Feminism & Psychology* (1991). In sum, the area has all the trappings of other specialties within the discipline, like developmental, personality, and clinical psychologies.

Unlike these other areas, the psychology of women cuts across the field emerging in everything from experimental and cognitive to developmental, clinical, counseling, social, history, testing, and health psychologies (O'Connell & Russo, 1991). The core focus that ties this all together is women; women and women's lives are put at the center of what we do in order to create a psychology for women.

---

[5] Contact the Women's Program Office within the Public Interest Directorate of the American Psychological Association for a free listing of "Graduate Faculty Interested in the Psychology of Women" (see footnote #9).

[6] For more information about the gender composition of psychology, request a free copy of the October 1995 report on the "Changing Gender Composition of Psychology" from the Women's Program Office of the American Psychological Association (see footnote #9).

[7] To join Div. 35 as a student member and receive the quarterly newsletter and *Psychology of Women Quarterly*, just send your name, address, and the annual fee of $15 to: Division 35 Central Office, 919 W. Marshall Ave., Phoenix, AZ 85013.

[8] To learn more about AWP, including how to join, explore their home page on the world wide web at: www.iup.edu/counsl/awpac/.

[9] APA offices can be reached by contacting the American Psychological Association at 750 First St., NE, Washington, DC 20002-4242, (202) 336-5500, e-mail: publicinterest@apa.org or visit APA's home page at http://www.apa.org/. More information about the Women's Programs Office can be found in their 1995 publication, "Women in the American Psychological Association."

Can women be studied simply as women? Think of a woman. Jot down a few descriptions of her in the space below before you read on. Feel free to stereotype!

This is the typical procedure of stereotyping studies—give raters a stimulus and ask them to describe that person. Usually, "a woman" is described, among other things, as being neat, talkative, vain, gentle, passive, dependent, and tender (Broverman et al., 1970). Who is this woman? Is she an African American woman? Hope Landrine (1985) finds that these women were rated as dirty, hostile, and superstitious; another study reports a mixed bag of descriptors: loud, talkative, aggressive, intelligent, straightforward, and argumentative (Weitz & Gordon, 1993). Is she a working class woman? Landrine (1985) finds that these women were evaluated as confused, dirty, hostile, illogical, impulsive, incoherent, inconsiderate, irresponsible, and superstitious. Furthermore, Landrine's data show that stereotypes of the "typical" woman overlapped with those of white, middle class women. In other words, the "typical" woman we described at the start of this section is not typical at all. Rather, she is a specific kind of woman, a woman who is white and middle class (and probably a lot of other things we assumed, like heterosexual, young, and physically able).

Divisions among women have been fostered by the assumption that sex and gender can be studied in isolation of other ascribed social statuses, such as race, class, religion, sexual orientation, and so on (Reid & Comas-Díaz, 1990; Spelman, 1988). Sometimes the work in the field reflects and maintains this faulty assumption. For example, Michelle Fine's (1985) content analysis of articles published in *Psychology of Women Quarterly* from 1978 to 1981 found that 51% included only college students, only 9% mentioned respondents of color, and information about social class was not reported. Even our textbooks were faulted for not being inclusive of African American women (Brown, Goodwin, Hall, & Jackson-Lowman, 1985).[10] Certainly a women-centered psychology cannot include only white, middle-class women nor can it assume that by ignoring other social statuses defined by race, class, religion, sexual orientation, age, physical ability, and so on, that gender alone can be studied. A women-centered psychology must be inclusive of *all* women, recognizing both commonalties and diversity.

Candace West and Sarah Fenstermaker (1995) describe how to "**do difference**" from the perspective of social constructionists. Just like gender, other social indicators (such as race and ethnicity, sexual orientation, age, physical ability, religion, socioeconomic class, and so on), are often checked off on surveys in seemingly all-inconclusive, mutually exclusive, defined categories. However, each is constructed, day-in and day-out, through interactions with other people. Each defines us within our

---

[10] Both *Psychology of Women Quarterly* (see Luce and Russo, 1996) and textbooks in the area (see Kahn and Gibson, 1993, and Yoder and Winegarden, 1993) have been proactive about responding to these shortcomings.

Which of these women is the *real* woman?

society: our race (Anzaldua, 1987; Higginbotham, 1992), socioeconomic class (Reid, 1993), age (Lorde, 1984; Pohl & Boyd, 1993; Whitbourne & Hulicka, 1990), physical ability (Appleby, 1994; Fine & Asch, 1988), sexual orientation (L.S. Brown, 1989; Kitzinger, 1987; Pharr, 1988), religion (Siegel, Choldin, & Orost, 1995), and so on. We "do" these too. Most importantly, we don't enact each alone; rather, they are constructed in unison. When I, as a white, middle-class, heterosexual, physically able, 40-something woman, raised as a Catholic, do gender, I do it with my own special twist; all these factors operate *simultaneously* and *interactively*. Furthermore, all these factors are **omnirelevant**, that is, they never go away; they always work to shape how we enact gender in our everyday lives.

Is my way or your way the only way to "do" gender? Of course not. Is there a way that is better than others? Of course not, again. A women-centered psychology must stress the plurality of "women." Women are diverse; no singular, generic woman exists—although we may be misled to think so by conjuring up our culture's mainstream assumptions for women (white, middle class, heterosexual, Protestant, physically able, young, mother . . .). One core goal for this book is that we not lose track of this diversity as we review the research of the psychology of women and that we don't stereotypically include some groups of women only when the topic "fits."

Transforming Psychology

As we have seen, a women-centered psychology offers a needed corrective to an androcentric psychology. Is this enough? Do we really need two psychologies: one for women and girls and another for men and boys? Obviously not.

We have seen that the mistakes of an androcentric psychology rested in overgeneralizing findings from (a select group of) men to all people and in value judgments that regarded women as deficient relative to men. A women-centered area of psychology must not repeat these mistakes. Furthermore, a psychology that seeks to end sexism as its goal ultimately includes all people regardless of, and with full recognition of, their gender and its consequences.

It is this approach to psychology that goes beyond a women-centered perspective to a transformative, feminist one. This approach is emerging more and more in the journals, organizations, courses, and books that compose this area of exploration into women, women's lives, and gender. This is not a psychology just by, for, and about women, but rather a psychology that is informed by and rooted in feminist goals and ideology.

How do men contribute to this feminist psychology? A ready example is provided by the men who are contributing to this literature.[11] But, women have contributed to sexist psychology, so the simple sex of psychologists is no assurance that their approach will be consistent with the one discussed here. This is not a story of women versus men. This is a story about an approach to psychology that is inclusive and that values women and the things women do (even when the things women traditionally do are done by men). Such an approach is not guaranteed by being female, nor does being male negate it. It comes from being feminist.

In addition to wanting psychologists (both women and men) to adopt a feminist approach, we should examine how men will be treated by a feminist psychology aimed at ending sexism. A frequent claim leveled against women feminists is that we engage in "male bashing" (the denigration of men and boys for being male). Remember that our goal is to end sexism, not hate men. Sue Cataldi (1995) writes a thoughtful analysis of the discourse used to talk about "male bashing" and how charges of man hating serve to undermine women's solidarity as feminists. She concludes: "One can be against sexism without hating men, just as one can be against racism without hating whites or against homophobia without hating heterosexuals" (p. 77).

---

[11] For discussions of men teaching feminist courses, see Heller (1996) and Johnson et al. (1996).

Many benefits of ending sexism are obvious for women, but how would ending sexism affect men? Some feminists suggest that ending sexism will free men from oppressive forces that limit their lives. One often-cited oppression of men and boys is sanctions against expressing deep emotions, for example, by crying. However, these assurances that men too will be liberated by the elimination of sexism seem overly simplistic and patronizing to me. Further exploration of the crying example clarifies my hesitancy with this superficial analysis. Jack Sattel (1976) points out that expressing hurt (by crying, etc.) makes one vulnerable by showcasing one's deepest emotions. In contrast, refusal to express what one is feeling can be empowering—it not only avoids exposure but also keeps outsiders at bay. This analysis raises serious questions about the role **power** plays in maintaining sexism in our society.

Sexism unjustly empowers people. By preferring men for certain jobs, male candidates are privileged. By preferring women as the caretakers of their children, mothers are privileged over fathers. Both women and men can be unfairly empowered and devalued by sexism. The bottom line though is that men are privileged by sexism more often and in more valued areas than women (Frye, 1992). "However much men are hurt by sex roles in this country, the fact remains that they are *not* systematically denied power simply because of being born a certain sex, as women are" (Blood, Tuttle, & Lakey, 1995, p. 159). To put this more concretely, are two people equally privileged if one gets to change more dirty diapers because of her gender while the other gets to chair business meetings because of his? Although ending sexism could hurt women in a few ways, feminists find the potential gains worth it. Although ending sexism could benefit men in a few ways, how does one enlist men to give up privileges?

Tough question. The obvious answer is because it's fair. There's little satisfaction in getting ahead on a tilted playing field. Also, oppressions sustain each other (Pharr, 1988), so that men who are devalued because of their race, age, sexual orientation, etc. are indirectly oppressed by sexism as well (Blood, Tuttle, & Lakey, 1995). I think there's another reason if we look beyond ourselves to the other significant people in our lives. What about mothers, and daughters, and wives and partners, and friends? Shouldn't they get a fair shot? And who better to enlist than men who don't seem self-serving in their feminist efforts? When my husband refuses to attend a breakfast meeting because he wants to be involved in getting the kids off to school, this speaks volumes beyond the same stance when I espouse it. Feminism isn't about male bashing; it's about **social justice**—something we all have a stake in pursuing.

Social justice doesn't seem to be such a radical goal to pursue. So why are feminists negatively stereotyped? Historically, feminists were described as "mannish in temperament," found children to be "more or less a bore," and disparaged "men's sex-passion" as a "mere impertinence" (Carpenter, 1896, quoted in Jeffreys, 1985, p. 107). Today, they are stereotyped less favorably than "housewives" (Haddock & Zanna, 1994). Antifeminist rhetoric portrays feminism as women's "worst enemy. All this freedom is making you miserable, unmarriageable, infertile, unstable. Go home, bake a cake, quit pounding on the doors of public life, and all your troubles will go away" (Gibbs, 1992, summarizing Susan Faludi's 1991 book on *Backlash*). Antifeminist "lesbian baiting" draws on homophobia to dissuade women (and men) from identifying as feminists (Garnets, 1996):

> The lesson of my experience . . . is that sooner or later, all nonconforming women are likely to be labeled lesbians. True, we start out with smaller punishments of being called "pushy" or "aggressive," "man-hating" or "unfeminine." But it's only a small step from those adjectives, whether bestowed by men or other women, to the full-fledged epithet of "lesbian" (Steinem, 1978, p. 267).

Studies repeatedly show that women support the agenda of the women's movement and even feminism itself (Jackson et al., 1996), yet they shirk the feminist label (Griffin, 1989; Kamen, 1991; Renzetti, 1987) [even in other countries, like Ireland (Percy & Kremer, 1995)]. Let's face it: who'd volunteer to be stereotyped negatively? Making feminism a dirty, demeaning "f-word" discourages people from uniting to bring about social change (Stimpson, 1987). It is no accident that attacks on feminists become most aggressive when gains are being made (Faludi, 1991).

DOING FEMINIST PSYCHOLOGY

As we have seen, we need to do more to "fix" psychology than "add women and stir" (Bohan, 1990; 1993; Crawford & Marecek, 1989). We are talking about transforming psychology—about questioning our basic values, assumptions, and normative practices. Because research is the cornerstone of the field, a feminist transformation of how we design, execute, and interpret research is critical. **Systematic research** defines our scholarship and underlies the therapies we practice, the courses we teach, and the consulting work we do as expert legal witnesses, in business, in education, and in government as well. One of the most pervasive influences feminist psychology has had on psychology is its critique of the presumed objectivity of research.

It is tempting to regard anything published as absolute truth, especially if lots of numbers and sophisticated statistical analyses accompany the work. Paradoxically, it also is tempting to write off research in favor of personal experiences that seem to contradict the data. Faced with mountains of data a student may conjure up a friend of a friend whose opposing experience presumably invalidates a carefully constructed thesis. I argue for something between these two extremes: *the critical usage of triangulated research.* We should be critical, questioning how research is done and interpreted. And, we should think of research as a process, not an outcome—akin to putting together a very complicated puzzle. Well-crafted research offers findings that add pieces to an intricate puzzle; it is the **triangulation** or bringing together of these pieces that gives us a coherent argument. This is my goal for this book: to integrate masses of well-done and up-to-date research to give us a picture of a feminist psychology of women and gender. More often than not, the picture will be a work-in-progress rather than a finished work. This is both the frustration and the challenge of *doing* psychology.

If research is the cornerstone of the discipline, the next question seems to be: What makes a piece of research sound? The traditional approach in psychology drew on the philosophy of **positivism**, the belief that there is an objective truth out there and the job of scientists is to discover it. In psychology, we isolate a variable (the independent variable), manipulate it in the laboratory with a group of similar participants (human or not), control all extraneous (outside) influences, then precisely measure an outcome (the dependent variable). Underlying this process are assumptions that research is value-free and objective; if we simplify and isolate a variable, we can understand it better (atomism); and that being observed doesn't affect participants (Unger, 1983).

I believe that there is no set formula for doing any piece of research. Instead, a researcher makes many decisions along the way that can affect the outcomes of the study. The first often invisible decision is to do the study itself. Why that particular study (Wallston & Grady, 1985)? Because grant money was available (Useem, 1976); because a business wanted it done; because one's colleagues would value both it and the researcher and thus look favorably on her or him for tenure; because it forwards a theory or ideological cause near-and-dear to the heart of the researcher? . . . There are lots of reasons, some better than others, but better according to whom? What one (and others) value seems inextricably entangled in such decisions (Denmark, Russo, Frieze, & Sechzer, 1988).

Even after this initial decision is made, there are lots of decisions left. Consider studies of maternal attachment. Who will participate? Until recently (Deater-Deckard, Scarr, McCartney, & Eisenberg, 1994), no one studied paternal separation. What will be measured (Marecek, 1989)? Many psychologists settled on measuring "separation anxiety." Why anxiety? Why not relief after a weekend of sibling fights, facing stacks of work to do on the job, with the security that providers are caring and well trained, and with kids happy to see their friends? Will mothers who are asked if they are anxious become anxious (or guilty for not being as anxious as "good" mothers are expected to be)? Where will we study them? In high-quality day-care centers, in laboratories, in homes with relatives as providers, in institutions or foster homes? . . . Who will study them (Basow & Howe, 1987)? Imposing men in lab coats, government agents pushing work-fare, graduate student novices, people hostile to employed mothers? . . . Decisions, decisions. Is this process as *objective* and *value-free* as planting crops in different soils and recording crop yields—the agricultural research that spawned the experimental method adopted by positivists? I think not (along with others like Prilleltensky, 1989 and Sampson, 1978).

Turning to the assumption of *atomism,* do we learn more by studying less? The tendency to break down behaviors and then study those simple components also tends to ignore history and context (Sherif, 1979). Returning to our day care example, no doubt there are Moms who are anxious about dropping off their kids, and some days are worse than others. Was the child coughing through the night, are there family members who disapprove, does the woman like her job, is the child care arrangement stable and enriched, is there a broad public outcry that discourages separation before kindergarten but lauds it afterwards? . . . These are questions about culture, and history, and context—questions often unanswered when we narrowly observe "maternal separation anxiety" in contrived, laboratory settings.

Finally, does being observed make a difference in how research participants act? One of my favorite demonstrations of participants' *reactivity* is a little known study with psychology students like you. When they took their required methods course, half were assigned rats declared to be "maze-bright" rats bred from quick-study parents. The other half were told their rats were "maze-dull," bargain-basement breeds. In reality, rats were randomly assigned to students; there were no differences among them. By the end of the semester, the "maze-bright" rats were outperforming their "maze-dull" counterparts, presumably responding to the differing expectations of their observers. The standard remedy for this unwanted influence is for psychologists to keep those who interact with research participants unaware of the actual hypotheses of the study or to give observers opposing expectations in order to measure these **experimenter effects**. This is not so easy when studying gender; we all feel very uncomfortable if we don't know the gender of a person with whom we are interacting, and we have lots of gendered hypotheses about how we expect women and men to behave.

Thus we call into question the standard psychology experiment; is it a dinosaur soon to be extinct? Is it better to rely on that friend of a friend's experience? I think not (as do others like Peplau and Conrad, 1989).[12] Both personal experience and controlled experimentation have some value. But they aren't the only resources we have. There are surveys, interviews, case histories, archival records, biographies, experiments done in real-life field settings, observations, and ethnographies. Furthermore, there are more social and physical scientists than just psychologists addressing a question; there are historians, sociologists, anthropologists, political scientists, biologists, economists, etc. A feminist psychology of women and gender offers us an approach to doing research that is *problem-centered* by being both *multimethodological* and *multidisciplinary*. No one study in any one discipline stands alone to answer a question. Rather, it is the triangulation, the bringing together, of the pieces that helps us formulate an answer.

A feminist approach toward understanding psychology does not discount personal experiences (Unger, 1988), but rather these experiences contribute only one piece to the process of inquiry. Differences between our experiences and our research findings suggest new questions that can further refine our understanding. Feel free to consider what is presented in this book in light of how it feels to you. When it doesn't feel right, don't shrug it off. Questioning is how we expand our thinking. Probe the data, challenge the method, consider other studies, and bring it all together.

OVERVIEW OF THE BOOK

Now that we know where we are going and how I propose to take us, it's time to ask some specific questions of our feminist psychology of women and gender. We'll begin by looking at the roles our bodies play in shaping our sex, rejecting the idea that we are controlled by our physical bodies (Chapter 2). We'll then turn to examine our socialization, that is, how we learned to be girls and boys, women and men (Chapter 3). In Chapter 4, we'll see that development doesn't end with childhood, but rather is a life-long process. Next, we'll explore some frequently made gender comparisons, looking at ways in which women and men are similar and different (Chapter 5).

---

[12] Some recent resources to read about feminist approaches to doing research include McHugh, Koeske, and Frieze (1986); Rabinowitz and Sechzer (1993); and Reinharz (1992).

We'll go on to examine how societal images of women shape how we see ourselves and others in gendered ways (Chapter 6).

In Chapter 7, we'll describe women's relationships and include men who engage in activities (e.g., mothering) that are traditionally associated with women. We'll tackle some pressing issues of contemporary life such as how families juggle the demands made by their relationships and employment. Next, we'll move to the workplace where we'll explore the meaning of work in women's lives as well as a variety of reasons for the persistent gap between women's and men's wages proffered by social scientists (Chapter 8). The next block of three chapters will concentrate on issues of women's well-being: physical health (Chapter 9), mental health (Chapter 10), and violence as one of the most significant threats to women's well-being (Chapter 11). In the final chapter, we'll consider how each of us can use what we've learned to make a difference (Chapter 12).

During our odyssey through this feminist approach to psychology, there undoubtedly will be times when we become frustrated, overwhelmed, and angry. This course hits too close to home to be approached dispassionately. It is not uncommon for folks to approach this course with feelings of apprehension, wariness, and suspicion. You may find yourself disturbed by what you'll read, motivating you to dismiss some conclusions or argue vehemently against them. You also may be disturbed by events and people in your everyday life that you hadn't noticed or cared about before reading this text. These are critical moments—try not to let them pass without exploration of what you're feeling and why. You may seek out additional readings or others to talk with at these points. Remember through these times that being aware of this work is better than ignoring it, for awareness is the first step toward realizing the social justice we all deserve.

CHAPTER SUMMARY

We have seen in this chapter that the processes through which we frame our questions and how we choose which questions to explore and which to ignore are influenced by our basic values. I offered feminist values, including the valuing of women and their experiences, a concern for equality of power, the need for change and activism, and the belief that gender (and other forms of social categorization) are socially constructed, as the foundation for building a transformed psychology of women and gender. We saw that androcentric bias permeated some of psychology's history and persists at some levels and in subtle forms today. A women-centered psychology that includes a full diversity of women has emerged as a corrective and is transforming into a feminist approach to women and gender that is inconclusive of all people: women and men, girls and boys. This feminist approach to doing psychology calls for an expanded view of systematic research that is responsive to people's experiences, that draws on a variety of methodologies and research participants, and that works toward the elimination of sexist oppression. It is clear that psychology has been transformed by feminists and feminist theories, research, and practice, and that this process continues. There truly is no turning back.

Before you move on from this chapter, take some time to complete the scale on the next two pages. We'll revisit it in the final chapter at the end of the course. By comparing your responses now to those you'll give at the end of this book, you will have some sense of how you are affected by this book and course you are taking. My greatest hope for this book is that its impact will not end for you when you turn the final page.

1. I think that most women will feel most fulfilled by being a wife and a mother.

   strongly disagree   disagree   neither agree nor disagree   agree   strongly agree

2. I used to think that there isn't a lot of sex discrimination, but now I know how much there really is.

   strongly disagree   disagree   neither agree nor disagree   agree   strongly agree

3. Being a part of a women's community is important to me.

   strongly disagree   disagree   neither agree nor disagree   agree   strongly agree

4. Some of the men I know are more feminist than some of the women I know.

   strongly disagree   disagree   neither agree nor disagree   agree   strongly agree

5. I want to work to improve women's studies.

   strongly disagree   disagree   neither agree nor disagree   agree   strongly agree

6. I've never really worried or thought about what it means to be a woman in this society.

   strongly disagree   disagree   neither agree nor disagree   agree   strongly agree

7. It only recently occurred to me that I think it's unfair that men have the privileges they have in this society simply because they are men.

   strongly disagree   disagree   neither agree nor disagree   agree   strongly agree

8. My social life is mainly with women these days, but there are a few men I wouldn't mind having a nonsexual friendship with.

   strongly disagree   disagree   neither agree nor disagree   agree   strongly agree

9. While I am concerned that women be treated fairly in life, I do not see men as the enemy.

   strongly disagree   disagree   neither agree nor disagree   agree   strongly agree

10. I have a lifetime commitment to working for social, economic, and political equality for women.

    strongly disagree   disagree   neither agree nor disagree   agree   strongly agree

11. If I were married to a man and my husband was offered a job in another state, it would be my obligation to move in support of his career.

    strongly disagree   disagree   neither agree nor disagree   agree   strongly agree

12. It makes me really upset to think about how women have been treated so unfairly in this society for so long.

    strongly agree   disagree   neither agree nor disagree   agree   strongly agree

13. I share most of my social time with a few close women friends who share my feminist values.

    strongly disagree   disagree   neither agree nor disagree   agree   strongly agree

14. I feel that some men are sensitive to women's issues.

    strongly disagree   disagree   neither agree nor disagree   agree   strongly agree

15. I feel that I am a very powerful and effective spokesperson for the women's issues I am concerned with right now.

    strongly disagree   disagree   neither agree nor disagree   agree   strongly agree

16. I am not sure what is meant by the phrase "women are oppressed under patri-archy."

    strongly disagree   disagree   neither agree nor disagree   agree   strongly agree

17. When I see the way most men treat women, it makes me so angry.

    strongly disagree   disagree   neither agree nor disagree   agree   strongly agree

18. Especially now, I feel that the other women around me give me strength.

    strongly disagree   disagree   neither agree nor disagree   agree   strongly agree

19. Although many men are sexist, I have found that some men are supportive of women and feminism.

    strongly disagree   disagree   neither agree nor disagree   agree   strongly agree

20. I am very committed to a cause that I believe contributes to a more fair and just world for all people.

    strongly disagree   disagree   neither agree nor disagree   agree   strongly agree

21. I think that rape is sometimes the woman's fault.

    strongly disagree   disagree   neither agree nor disagree   agree   strongly agree

22. When you think about most of the problems in the world—the threat of nuclear war, pollution, discrimination—it seems to me that most of them are caused by men.

    strongly disagree   disagree   neither agree nor disagree   agree   strongly agree

23. If I were to paint a picture or write a poem, it would probably be about women or women's issues.

    strongly disagree   disagree   neither agree nor disagree   agree   strongly agree

24. I evaluate men as individuals, not as members of a group of oppressors.

    strongly disagree   disagree   neither agree nor disagree   agree   strongly agree

25. I am willing to make certain sacrifices to effect change in this society in order to create a nonsexist, peaceful place where all people have equal opportunities.

    strongly disagree   disagree   neither agree nor disagree   agree   strongly agree

Source: A. Bargad and J. S. Hyde, Women't Studies: A study of feminist identity development in women. *Psychology of Women Quarterly,* 15, 181–201. Reprinted with the permission of Cambridge University Press.

TWO

BIOLOGICAL ESSENTIALISM
Our Bodies, Ourselves?

Answer each of the following questions:

1. When the sexes differ in some way, how likely is it that the difference is due to the ways boys/men and girls/women are socialized (how they are treated by parents and others)?

1	2	3	4	5	6	7
not at all likely						very likely

2. When the sexes differ in some way, how likely is it that the difference is due to biological factors (hormones, chromosomes, etc.)?

1	2	3	4	5	6	7
not at all likely						very likely

3. When the sexes differ in some way, how likely is it that the difference is due to the kinds of opportunities they've had?

1	2	3	4	5	6	7
not at all likely						very likely

4. When the sexes differ in some way, how likely is it that the difference can be eliminated?

1	2	3	4	5	6	7
not at all likely						very likely

Carol Lynn Martin and Sandra Parker (1995) asked these questions of undergraduate students to explore **folk wisdom** about sex and gender differences. The first three questions tap our general beliefs about what causes differences between women/girls and men/boys: socialization, biology, and opportunities. They found that students most strongly endorsed socialization as a cause for gender differences, with biology scoring a close second, and opportunities a significantly less likely third. Parallel questions were asked of the same students to explore their racial assumptions. Striking differences between presumed sex/gender and racial causes emerged. Racial differences were attributed more to opportunities; sex differences, more to biology. Furthermore, the more respondents believed that sex/gender or racial differences were rooted in biology, the more difficult they thought it would be to eliminate those differences. These findings highlight both the strength of public acceptance of biological explanations of sex differences and the political consequences of this acceptance for inhibiting social change. How did you score?

The focus of this chapter is on biological explanations for sex[1] differences. The subtitle, "Our Bodies, Ourselves?," comes from an excellent resource for women about their health that was first published in 1969 by the Boston Women's Health Collective. My intent in using it (with the added question mark) is to discuss **biological essentialism**—the belief that what we do, think, and feel is rooted in our bodies (Bem, 1993). The three theories presented in this chapter (theories of brain development, sociobiology, and Freudian psychoanalysis) are linked by a fundamental belief that

---

[1] I will use the term "sex" throughout this chapter to highlight the common assumption of biological determinants, even though most psychologists believe that much of what is discussed here includes at least some social and cultural influences indicative of "gender."

women and men are naturally and inevitably different because of our intrinsically different biological natures. Our overriding question for this chapter is: Are our bodies the building blocks of who we are? Put concisely, are our bodies ourselves?

We typically think of sex as **dimorphic**, that is, as having two forms which are mutually exclusive and all-inclusive so that everyone fits, without question, in one and only one of two categories: female or male. In reality, our sex is not that clear-cut; determining if a person is female or male takes into consideration chromosomes, gonads, gonadal hormones, internal accessory organs, external genitalia, sex label, and gender of rearing (Money & Ehrhardt, 1972). To be consistently female, one needs two X chromosomes; ovaries; more estrogens and less androgens; Fallopian tubes and a uterus; a clitoris, labia minora, and vagina; to be labeled as a female; and to be raised as a girl (see Table 2.1). To be consistently male, a child needs a Y chromosome (usually with one X chromosome); testes; more androgens (like testosterone) and less estrogens; seminal vesicles; a penis and scrotum; to be labeled as a male; and to be reared as a boy. For most of us, we "fit" consistently into one of these two classifications.

This isn't always the case, however. People with Turner's syndrome (usually identified as female) have one unmatched X chromosome and thus fail to develop breasts, have ovaries and a uterus that are underdeveloped so they do not menstruate (thus they are infertile), and are unusually short (usually under 4'6") (Hartl, 1983). Men with an extra Y chromosome are taller than average and suffer moderate mental impairment (conclusions that these men are unusually violent have been debunked) (Witkin et al., 1976). Genetic females, whose adrenal glands malfunction so that large amounts of androgens (testosterone) were produced, are born with masculinized external genitals so that they can be mislabeled as boys [congenital adrenal hyperplasia (CAH) or adrenogenital syndrome] (Hines & Kaufman, 1994). There are other types of **pseudohermaphrodites**, people who have a mixture of female and male reproductive structures. Although each of these combinations is atypical relative to the consistent female and male patterns, these anomalies become interesting case studies for researchers wanting to explore how biology and environment interact.

TABLE 2.1   All seven elements combine to determine our sex and gender.

	Female	Male
Chromosomes	XX	XY
Gonads	Ovaries	Testes
Gonadal Hormones	More estrogens	More androgens
	Less androgens	Less estrogens
Internal Accessory	Fallopian tubes	Vas deferens
Organs	Uterus	Seminal vesicles
External Genitalia	Clitoris	Penis
	Labia minora	Scrotum
	Vaginal orifice	
Sex Label	Girl; Woman	Boy; Man
Gender of Rearing	Feminine	Masculine

Source: Complied from J. Money and A. Ehrhardt (1972). *Man & woman: Boy & girl.* © 1972. The John Hopkins University Press.

Clearly, our biologies contribute to who we are, so understanding how our sex affects us is a good place to start. However, I will argue that this is only part of the story. Biological essentialism goes too far by taking away our abilities to actively shape our bodies, rather than be limited by them.

Before we proceed, a brief note on the generalizability of animal studies to humans is warranted. Much biological research reported in this chapter is restricted to naturalistic studies because it generally is unethical to experimentally manipulate or interfere with biological processes.[2] Controversy rages over which animals are evolutionarily, genetically, sexually, anatomically, etc., closest to humans, and all kinds of cases can be constructed to justify experimentation with certain animals. Naomi Weisstein (1971) sagely warns that:

> The most general and serious problem is that there are no grounds to assume that anything primates do is necessary, natural, or desirable in humans, for the simple reason that humans are not nonhumans. For instance, it is found that male chimpanzees placed alone with infants will not "mother" them. Jumping from hard data to ideological speculation researchers conclude from this information that *human* females are necessary for the safe growth of human infants. Following this logic, it would be reasonable to conclude that it is quite useless to teach human infants to speak since it has been tried with chimpanzees and it does not work (p. 141).

Heeding this warning, I will stick mostly with evidence derived from studies with human beings.

SOURCES OF BIOLOGICAL DIFFERENCE

Where have we looked for biological differences? A good place to start is by looking at how women's and men's bodies were viewed at various times in history (Schiebinger, 1992). Aristotle concluded that women are cold and moist in contrast to men who are warm and dry. Because women do not generate sufficient heat to "cook" their blood, they do not purify their souls so that their power of reasoning is deficient. Craniologists of the 18th and 19th centuries assumed that the larger male skull is equipped with a heavier and more powerful brain. In 1879, Gustave Le Bon, considered the founder of social psychology, pontificated:

> . . . there are a large number of women whose brains are closer in size to those of gorillas than to the most developed male brains. This inferiority is so obvious that no one can contest it for a moment; only its degree is worthy of discussion. All psychologists who have studied the intelligence of women . . . recognize today that they represent the most inferior forms of human evolution and that they are closer to children and savages than to an adult, civilized man. They excel in fickleness, inconstancy, absence of thought and logic, and incapacity to reason. Without doubt there exist some distinguished women, very superior to the average man, but they are as exceptional as the birth of any monstrosity, as, for example, of a gorilla with two heads; consequently, we may neglect them entirely (quoted in Gould, 1981, pp. 104–105).

---

[2]We do alter biology at times. For example, CAH girls often are surgically "fixed" to conform to our expectation that genes and genitals match. Some question this as an attempt to force nature into an "unnatural" sexual duality (Fausto-Sterling, 1993).

(How will today's "truths," considered "beyond dispute," be regarded by our progeny 100 years from now?)

Le Bon's drivel did not go unheeded. In the late 19th century, Edward Clark, one of the leading educators of his day, argued that if women exercised their brains by pursuing education, their ovaries would shrivel.[3] Consider this nonsense in relation to a more contemporary perspective on women in combat. Guess who said the following (if you need help, see footnote #4):

> If combat means being in a ditch, females have biological problems staying in a ditch for 30 days because they get infections, and they don't have upper body strength. I mean some do, but they are relatively rare. On the other hand, men are basically little piglets, you drop them in the ditch, they roll around in it. . . .
>
> On the other hand, if combat means being on an Aegis-class cruiser managing the computer controls for 12 ships and their rockets, a female again may be dramatically better than a male who gets very, very frustrated sitting in a chair all the time because males are biologically driven to go out and hunt giraffes.[4]

As we get closer to modern times, scientists' interests coalesced around the brain. Franz Joseph Gall declared unequivocally that he could distinguish a woman's brain from a man's through gross anatomical observation (Walker, 1850 cited by Shields, 1975). Arguments raged about differences in the size of the overall brain and development of various brain centers. Regarding size, more brain meant better/smarter brain, so controversy centered on how to measure size: as absolute brain size, as a ratio of brain surface to body surface (both of which "favored" men), or as a ratio of brain weight to body weight (which "favored" women) (Shields, 1975).[5]

Turning to brain development, when the frontal lobes were deemed the seat of the highest mental capacities, researchers reported that men's were noticeably larger and better developed than women's. When interest shifted to the parietal lobes as the repository of intellect, researchers reported that men's were bigger and better (Shields, 1975). Keep this history in mind as we review contemporary beliefs about women's and men's brains. Does history repeat itself?

Theories of Brain Development

Is there a woman's brain and a man's brain? The best place to start our inquiry is at our beginnings, exploring the embryonic development of the reproductive structures and the typical brain. Every cell of the developing embryo contains 22 pairs of chromosomes called **autosomes** and one pair of **sex chromosomes**. Every chromosome carries a large number of genes, up to thousands, depending on its size. The sex chromosomes initiate the development of the embryo's reproductive structures as follows: female if the child receives an X chromosome from both her parents (XX);

---

[3]Note that this fear for women's reproductive capacity was limited to certain types of women—those affluent women likely to be exposed to education—so that this prediction is not only sexist, but classist and racist as well (S.L. Bem, 1996).

[4]Then Speaker of the U.S. House of Representatives, Newt Gingrich ("Newt sticks neck out . . ." 1995).

[5]Similar measurements historically were taken to "prove" the intellectual inferiority of various races (Gould, 1981). However, even this approach hasn't died. For example, a 1992 study reported largest average cranial capacities for "Mongoloids," followed by "Caucasoids," and finally, trailed by "Negroids" (Rushton, 1992).

male if the child receives an X chromosome from his mother and a Y chromosome from his father (XY). Over 300 genes are located on the X chromosome, compared to the Y chromosome which appears to be specialized primarily for the development of the male sex organs.

What does all this have to do with brain development? For the first six weeks, the fetus has a sexual **bipotential**: XX and XY embryos' gonads are anatomically identical (Fausto-Sterling, 1992, pp. 77–85). Each develops an embryonic gonad named the "indifferent gonad" because of its sameness in both XX and XY embryos. During the sixth week, the Y chromosome is activated in the male embryo, promoting a protein called H-Y antigen. It appears that this antigen plays a role in helping the tissues of the indifferent gonad to organize into an embryonic testis. This testis contains sperm-producing tubules and synthesizes two hormones: one to block further female development and the other (testosterone) to promote further male development.

Testosterone, one of a group of chemically interrelated hormones called **androgens**, stimulates growth of the male duct system. As many as 19 different genetic loci on the X chromosome and scattered over many of the autosomes (but not involving the Y chromosome) are implicated in the process of producing more hormones, both androgens and **estrogens** (typically and deceptively referred to as the female hormones). Women and men produce both androgens and estrogens, but the balance differs so that women have more estrogens and men have more androgens.

The basic pattern then is that embryos with the potential to develop as female or male differentiate during the sixth week of development. The Y chromosome activates prenatal hormones that stimulate male organ development (see Figure 2.1).

But, what happens with the XX embryo? What we know about female development is obscure (Fausto-Sterling, 1992). Many scientists have implied that females develop passively; if the Y chromosome isn't present, the male pattern is not triggered and a girl is produced. This view presents female development as something of a default option—what happens if nothing intervenes. Anne Fausto-Sterling (1992) observes that female development is less studied

> . . . due both to technical difficulties and to the willingness of researchers to accept at face value the idea of passive female development. Because it is in the nature of research in developmental biology to always look for underlying causes, failure to probe beyond the "testosterone equals male"—"absence of testosterone equals female" hypothesis is a lapse which is at first difficult to understand. If, however, one notes the pervasiveness throughout all layers of our culture of the notion of "female as lack," then one learns from this account that such rock-bottom cultural ideas can intrude unnoticed even into the scientist's laboratory (p. 81).

Recent work suggests that estrogen may play a parallel role in female development as

FIGURE 2.1 A simple schematic of the chain of events leading to embryonic development of the female and male reproductive structures.

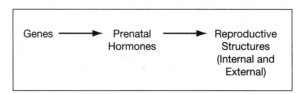

testosterone plays in male, although this still is being debated (Micevych & Ulibarri, 1992). Obviously, further research is warranted.

We've looked at how genes activate prenatal hormones that stimulate growth of the internal reproductive structures (again, see Figure 2.1). A similar pattern describes development of the external genitalia. But what do ovaries and testes have to do with brain development? Ovaries and testes secrete hormones, and these influence brain development. First, let's take a look at these hormones.

As we have seen, estrogen is secreted by the ovaries which also produce progesterone. Androgens are the general name for the "male" sex hormones secreted by the testes, which include several types of testosterone. The tendency to label these as "female" and "male" hormones, respectively, ignores the fact that the adrenal cortex produces androgens in women (as do the ovaries in small amounts) and estrogens in men (as do the testes in small amounts) (Becker & Breedlove, 1992). Androgens can even be converted to estrogens in a woman's body, further blurring this distinction between these two types of hormones.

What does differentiate women and men, girls and boys, is the *concentrations* of each of these hormones. But even this blurs at times. Examining amniotic fluid surrounding the embryo at 14–20 weeks gestation, 25% of the males and 9% of the females have overlapping levels of testosterone (Finegan, Bartleman, & Wong, 1989). Only at puberty is there no overlap between girls' and boys' testosterone levels (Hoyenga & Hoyenga, 1993). Furthermore, there are large amounts of overlap in the ranges of estrogens found in adult women and men depending on the stage of the woman's menstrual cycle. In sum, *both women and men possess both estrogen and testosterone;* women generally have more of the former and men more of the latter.

Prenatal hormone theory posits that exposure of the developing embryo to hormones, in part, organizes the development of the human brain (see Figure 2.2). In addition to triggering the development of reproductive structures, prenatal hormones "irreversibly organize mammalian brains into a male or female pattern, and these hormonally organized brains, in turn, organize mammalian hormone function and mammalian behavior into a male or female pattern" (Bem, 1993, p. 23). Two different brains allegedly result: one, female and the other, male. A cycle that begins with prenatal hormones affecting brain development comes full circle.

At least three assumptions underlie this belief in the organization of the brain:

FIGURE 2.2   This is a grossly simplified schematic. Fausto-Sterling presents a much more complex diagram involving over 40 components, linked through a myriad of nonlinear connections, much of which we do not yet understand (1993, p. 73).

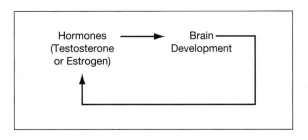

(1) brain structures, once organized, are permanent and unchangeable; (2) there are two types of (dimorphic) brains: female and male; and (3) these two brain types contain structures that do not overlap so that they clearly distinguish women from men (Hoyenga & Hoyenga, 1993). As we shall see, each of these assumptions can and *should* be questioned.

In essence then, because brain development is linked to hormones and the amounts of these vary by sex, brain development is expected to be different in some ways for women and men. (We'll see that because of this predicted sex difference, researchers will speculate about differences according to sexual orientation as well.) Contemporary researchers looking for brain differences have concentrated in three areas: (1) brain size, (2) brain asymmetry, and (3) the hypothalamus. It is important to note that not all biologists find value in searching for differences in women's and men's brains; many believe that a brain simply is a brain regardless of the sex of its owner. However, reputable scientists have made the following arguments in legitimate publications, and each is relevant to our study of women and gender.

Brain size.   Interest in brain size never died. I must admit that I was stunned to see debates raging in the *1990s* literature on how to measure brain size and declaring definitive linkages between brain size and intelligence. Researchers still calculate "cranial capacities from external head measurements" (Rushton, 1994), measure "total forebrain volume" (Steinmetz, Staiger, & Schlaug, 1995), and weigh and compare brains of women and men (Ankney, 1995). One researcher went so far as to relate cranial capacity to sex, military rank, and race (Rushton, 1992). Moreover, bigger still is deemed better. Richard Lynn (1994) does not waver:

> Because men's brains are larger than women's by approximately 100 g. even when corrected for body size, and because brain size is positively correlated with intelligence, men have a higher mean IQ than women by approximately 4 points (p. 257).

Brain size is even used to affirm the spatial and mathematical superiority of men (Ankney, 1995).

This continued interest in brain size and intelligence raises red flags about the presumed objectivity of science. We discovered this in Chapter 1, but I think many of us are more willing to concede that psychology is socially constructed, but not the "hard" sciences. This confidence in scientific "fact" dates back to the enlightenment era of the 18th century (Schiebinger, 1992) and is difficult to abandon. I encourage you to set aside this assumption as you read this chapter and instead challenge this science. Ask questions like: What is the value of finding sex differences in the brain? Will we give up educating some people because of proven brain deficiencies or does biology just dictate a range of possible outcomes? Will we intervene in brain development to "fix" inadequacies? Which gets more media attention: brain differences in women and men or the gender gap in pay? (See Box 2.1 for some examples of headlines in popular magazines and newspapers linking brain and sex differences). I am not suggesting that biology is unrelated to what we are and can become; but I am asking how much biology can we, or do we, want to control?

Be wary of a propensity to think in terms of scientific givens. Much of what the brain is and does remains unknown (Fausto-Sterling, 1992). Furthermore, much of

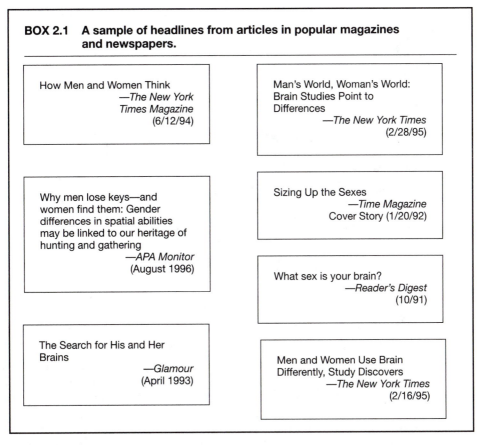

BOX 2.1   A sample of headlines from articles in popular magazines and newspapers.

How Men and Women Think
—*The New York Times Magazine*
(6/12/94)

Man's World, Woman's World: Brain Studies Point to Differences
—*The New York Times*
(2/28/95)

Why men lose keys—and women find them: Gender differences in spatial abilities may be linked to our heritage of hunting and gathering
—*APA Monitor*
(August 1996)

Sizing Up the Sexes
—*Time Magazine*
Cover Story (1/20/92)

What sex is your brain?
—*Reader's Digest*
(10/91)

The Search for His and Her Brains
—*Glamour*
(April 1993)

Men and Women Use Brain Differently, Study Discovers
—*The New York Times*
(2/16/95)

what is presented here is a "work-in-progress." Lines of research being actively pursued today may lead down deadends and ultimately be abandoned. It seems absurd today to think of intelligent women's brains as analogous to those of mutated gorillas and to believe that educating women will lead to infertility and eventual "race suicide." It may become similarly far-fetched to equate lesbians' brains with those of heterosexual men (presumably because both share a "masculinized" orientation).

Brain asymmetry.   The human brain is divided into two structurally similar halves (**hemispheres**), popularly referred to as the left and right brains (see Figure 2.3). Each hemisphere controls the opposite side of the body so that what we do with our left hand is controlled by our right hemisphere; with our right hand, by our left hemisphere. The two cerebral hemispheres are connected by the **corpus callosum**, a huge mass of nerve fibers. Anne Fausto-Sterling (1992, p. 228) draws an analogy between the corpus callosum and a phone cable connecting all the United States with Europe. Thousands of connections run through this cable; we might cut a few to see what happens, but we'd be lucky to link a general region in one country with another vague location in another. This depicts the needle-in-the-haystack task faced by neuroanatomists trying to understand the functions of the corpus callosum.

The corpus callosum attracted attention because it is big, easy to find, and can

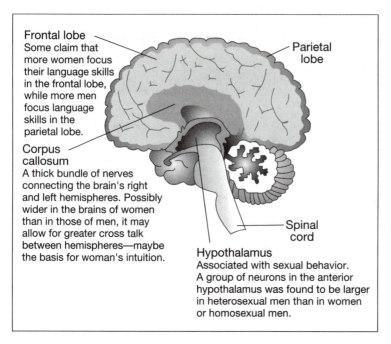

Frontal lobe
Some claim that
more women focus
their language skills
in the frontal lobe,
while more men
focus language
skills in the
parietal lobe.

Corpus
callosum
A thick bundle of nerves
connecting the brain's right
and left hemispheres. Possibly
wider in the brains of women
than in those of men, it may
allow for greater cross talk
between hemispheres—maybe
the basis for woman's intuition.

Parietal
lobe

Spinal
cord

Hypothalamus
Associated with sexual behavior.
A group of neurons in the anterior
hypothalamus was found to be larger
in heterosexual men than in women
or homosexual men.

FIGURE 2.3
The hemispheres of the
brain and the critical
structures implicated in
possible sex differences.

be studied noninvasively in living people (Fausto-Sterling, 1992, p. 229). In 1908, E.A. Spitzka argued that great men had great corpora collosa. Another researcher reported that the last fifth of the corpus callosum located at the back of the head, called the **splenium**, was smaller in African Americans and accounted for the mental superiority of whites. This latter assertion was refuted, and interest in the corpus callosum lay dormant until 1982 when a cell biologist, Christine de Lacoste, and a physical anthropologist, Ralph Holloway, published a paper in *Science*, the official publication of the American Association for the Advancement of Science.

de Lacoste and Holloway (1982) made three claims. (1) The shape of the splenium is dramatically different between the sexes, such that females have a bulbous, as compared to the male cylindrical, splenium (which eventually lead to the development of a statistic dubbed, somewhat humorously, the "bulbosity coefficient"). (2) The width of the splenium is so distinctively different that even a novice can identify the sex of any brain. (In fact, the only clearer sex difference, they suggested, is in the reproductive organs.) (3) There is a sizable sex difference in splenial surface area (even though this difference [p =.08] didn't even reach statistical significance in their own data). With a sample of only 5 female and 9 male brains, all obtained at autopsy (so disease was not controlled) and of varying ages (even though age is known to change the brain, including the corpus callosum), de Lacoste and Holloway heralded the significance of their data. They claimed that their finding "has widespread implications for students of human evolution and comparative neuroanatomy, as well as for neuropsychologists in search of *an anatomical basis for possible gender differences in the degree of cerebral lateralization*" (quoted in Bleier, 1986, p. 155, italics added).

Anne Fausto-Sterling (1992, pp. 233–39) cites 16 follow-up studies attempting to confirm this presumed sex difference only to find significant methodological differences among the studies and seriously conflicting results. The major impact of this "finding" may not be in the veracity of the finding itself, but rather in its linkage to cerebral lateralization made by the original authors (see the highlighted portion of their quote above). This shifts our focus away from the structure of the splenium itself to how we use the two hemispheres of the brain.

Hemispheric functionality.   Is there a left brain and a right brain? Pop psychology books purport to teach us how to balance the energies of our left and right brains (Turgeon, 1993), to use our right brains to enhance sexual pleasure (Wells, 1991), to reach our unconscious through our right brains (Joseph, 1992), and even to manage our "left-brain finances" (Monroe, 1996). The scientific basis for these dubious claims is grounded in the notion that the two hemispheres of the brain, although structurally parallel, process information differently, with the left (dominant) side being verbal (that is, controlling language, speech, reading, and writing) and the right side being visuospatial (and musical). This difference in functionality is referred to as **brain lateralization**.

What do left and right brains have to do with women's and men's brains? Differences between females' and males' hemispheres have been described as displaying both volumetric (size) and functional (use) asymmetries. Some researchers have suggested that the right hemisphere of the brain in the developing male fetus may be larger in volume than the left (de Lacoste, Horvath, & Woodward, 1991). In contrast, in the female brain, hemispheres may be more alike or the left is slightly larger. Although this size difference has yet to be fully substantiated, it is consistent with the logic of those studying purported sex differences in hemispheric utilization.

These researchers propose functional differences in how women and men *use* their left and right hemispheres. It is argued that typically men show greater **specialization**, with the left side handling verbal processes and the right hemisphere, visuospatial processing. In contrast, it is hypothesized that women can use both hemispheres to engage in both forms of cognitive processing, referred to as **bilateralization**. Generally, the assumption that runs through this literature is that the more specialization (being an expert) the better. This is true even though brain damage to one side of the specialized brain (for example, as the result of a stroke) could result in loss of functionality since the other hemisphere is not equipped to pick up where the damaged hemisphere left off (Bleier, 1986).[6] This presumed difference also has been extended to explain the purported spatial and mathematical superiority of men, arguing that men's greater specialization produces more expert processing (see Chapter 5 for an extensive discussion of this supposition). Because women's cognitive processing is presumably diffused across both hemispheres, less expert development is expected to result.

Extensive literature reviews have challenged the notion that there are sex differences in brain lateralization of cognitive functions (Alper, 1985; Caplan, MacPherson, & Tobin, 1985; Kimball, 1981; McGlone, 1980). Additionally, Ruth Bleier (1991),

---

[6]It is interesting that recent research has begun to co-opt this presumed advantage of bilateralization for men. Desmond and his colleagues (1994) argue that many men afflicted by right-side stroke avoid disruptions of their visuospatial processing, unlike the women he studied, because the *men* are visuospatially bilateral. Can researchers really have it both ways?

like Anne Fausto-Sterling (1992), concludes that there is no truth to structural differences in the splenium of the corpus callosum connecting the two brain hemispheres. However, Bleier jadedly predicts that because this has become entrenched as assumed "neuroscience fact," it is likely to remain for at least the next 10 years, and some recent research confirms her pessimistic prediction.

Functional magnetic resonance imaging (fMRI) allows researchers to chart blood flow in various brain regions, arguing that increased flow indicates utilization of the areas mapped. In one study, men doing spelling tasks appeared to activate two expectedly related verbal centers in the brain: Broca's area, responsible for language production, and Wernicke's area, responsible for language and understanding (Wood, Flowers, & Naylor, 1991). These two areas were activated independently in women, and activation of one area in one hemisphere was associated with parallel activation in the other hemisphere, suggesting bilateralization. In a second study, differential activation of the frontal lobes of the brain while performing rhyming tasks also is interpreted as suggesting bilateralization by women (Shaywitz, et al., 1995).

But the picture remains much murkier than these most recent studies suggest. Handedness plays a role in lateralization (remember that the hemispheres control opposite sides of the body and hence the opposite hand) (see for example, Goldberg, Podell, Harner, Riggio, & Lovell, 1994). And, more men than women are left-handed. Even the menstrual cycle has been implicated such that during menstruation, right-hemisphere superiority has been found for women's face perception (Heister, Landis, Regard, & Schroeder-Heister, 1989). Anne Fausto-Sterling (1992) points to wider *intrasexual* (within groups of women and within groups of men) than intersexual (between women and men) differences. In other words, an individual woman is just as likely to differ from another woman as from a man, and there are women and men who are alike. All this argues for some real skepticism concerning presumed differences in both structure and functions of the brain.

Hypothalamus. Why the hypothalamus? The hypothalamus becomes a likely suspect in our search for sex differences in the brain because it plays a role in regulating the amounts of hormones, including sex hormones, circulating in our bodies. In women, estrogen from the ovaries activates the hypothalamus which stimulates the pituitary gland to release a LH-surge (luteinizing hormone), triggering ovulation. In contrast to this LH-surge, men's hypothalamus produces a steady flow of LH (necessary for sperm formation). The involvement of the hypothalamus in reproductive activities is clear and different for women and men. When different functions are discovered, the natural inclination of physiologists is to look for structural correlates (Fausto-Sterling, 1992, pp. 241–245).

Roger Gorski and his collaborators (1978) found a cluster of cells in the hypothalamus that was 5 to 8 times larger in male *rats* than in female. They called this area the sexually dimorphic nucleus (SDN). Again, Anne Fausto-Sterling (1992, pp. 244–247) reviews the research on the SDN, concluding that there is no solid evidence for its existence in humans (or mice, for that matter), just rats.

Others focus on an area of the hypothalamus (INAH-3) that may be about 2.5 times larger in volume for male than female humans (Allen, Hines, Shryne, & Gorski,

1989). However, Fausto-Sterling (1992) points out there is a ten-fold variation in volumes within each sex (intrasex) that dwarfs the between-sexes difference (intersex) and that there is a large amount of overlap such that many women are similar to many men. Again, an individual woman may differ from other women and be similar to some men. Despite this overlap, interest in finding sex differences related to the hypothalamus persists and recently has extended to a search for a "gay gene."

Genes. We've been talking about the hypothalamus, brain structures and functions, and hormones. Where do genes come in? Recall that we began this chapter by linking the brain's development to genes (or more specifically, the XX and XY chromosomes). We were discussing comparisons of women with men, not gays and lesbians with heterosexuals. There is a questionable connection being assumed here between maleness and being lesbian and femaleness and male homosexuality. Keep this in mind. As we'll see, the debate about the "gay gene" began with searches for sex differences in the hypothalamus, splintered off onto a tangent considering homosexuality, came to concentrate on an area of the hypothalamus referred to as INAH-3, then extended to exposure to prenatal hormones and ultimately, genes. This is a rather convoluted series of connections, and the links from one focus to another are not above questioning.

Simon LeVay (1991), a British neuroanatomist, himself openly gay, considered all that we have been discussing about sexual dimorphism in the hypothalamus (see Burr, 1996, for a very understandable presentation of both sides of the debate).[7] He then compared the INAH-3 regions of the hypothalamus of deceased people including 19 gay men who died of AIDS, 16 presumed heterosexual men (6 of whom died of AIDS as drug-users), and 6 presumed heterosexual women. (He wrote that he excluded lesbians because he could think of no disease he could use to unquestionably identify lesbians.) He concluded that the volume of INAH-3 was twice as large in heterosexual men as in gay men.

Why genes, we might ask? As an interim part of the story, Chandler Burr (1996, pp. 29–35) provides a rather humorous account of genetically mutated "fruitless" fruit flies which engage in homosexual-like behaviors. However, the next major piece of the human puzzle came from researchers of twins. Monozygotic (identical) twins share identical genes because they came from one fertilized egg and sperm. In contrast, dizygotic (fraternal) twins share the same prenatal environment, but no more genes than any pair of siblings, because they developed from two independently fertilized eggs. If genes are involved, we would expect those who share more genes to be more likely to share their sexual orientation (in other words, we'd expect **concordance** between these two variables).

Pursuing this logic, researchers found that fully 52% of 56 monozygotic gay men had a gay twin brother compared to only 22% of 54 dizygotic twin gay men and 11% of 57 nongenetically related adopted brothers (Bailey & Pillard, 1991). A similar pattern emerged for lesbians: 48% of monozygotic twins were both lesbian, 16% of dizygotic twins, and only 6% of adoptive sisters (Bailey, Pillard, Neale, & Agyei,

---

[7] For an alternative theory that blends both the biological data with a social constructionist point of view, see Daryl Bem's (1996) paper.

1993). Although not all genetically identical women and men shared their sexual orientation (leaving room for some environmental influences), the pattern is consistent with a genetic *component:* the stronger the genetic link, the more concordance there is with sexual orientation.

Many believe the ideal test of biology (nature) versus environment (nurture) is to find twins reared apart—they share nature but no nurture. A study of two such monozygotic male twins found that in both pairs both were homosexual (Eckert, Bouchard, Bohlen, & Heston, 1986). This evidence supports a genetic link. On the other hand, of the four sets of female twins in the study, each pair included one lesbian and one heterosexual sister. Surprisingly, these data are presented without apology in an article arguing for "the innateness of homosexuality" (Bailey & Pillard, 1997).

Then, there's the presumed hormonal link. What if a developing embryo is exposed to the "wrong" "feminizing" (estrogen) or "masculinizing" (testosterone) hormones? An assumption here is that part of being "feminized" encompasses choosing men sexually and being "masculinized" includes pursuing women. Continuing with this questionable logic, those who select women (lesbians and heterosexual men) must have been masculinized in contrast to those who seek men (gay men and heterosexual women). Much of this work has been done with animals, but there are some naturally occurring human examples.

Remember those CAH (cogenital adrenal hyperplasia) women we briefly mentioned at the beginning of this chapter? Their adrenal glands produced high levels of testosterone prenatally. They were born with masculinized external genitals, typically corrected surgically today. Researchers asked if this masculinization extends to other outcomes, including personality characteristics and sexual orientation.

John Money and Anke Ehrhardt (1972) describe a pattern of "tomboyism" with CAH girls who exhibit high activity levels, interest in "boys'" toys, less fascination with dolls and infant care, less interest in marriage, and a stronger career orientation. Others have argued that parents' awareness of the "masculinization" of their daughters (they saw their original enlarged, penis-like clitoris) affected their treatment, expectations for, and acceptance of these daughters (Bem, 1993). Most pointedly for our discussion, there is no pattern of disproportionate lesbianism among CAH girls and women (Banks & Gartrell, 1995; Ehrhardt & Meyer-Bahlburg, 1981). Parallel arguments can be made for XY boys shielded from prenatal testosterone exposure by a rare enzyme deficiency (see Bem, 1993, pp. 27–29).

What's the answer? This is one of those times when there is no ready answer. But, there are lots of questions challenging the assumptions underlying much of the research on brain differences between women and men. Do different brain functions reflect differing brain structures? A common, and often unchallenged, assumption among anatomists is that differing structures *cause* differing functions (Fausto-Sterling, 1992). But, as every beginning statistics student knows, correlation does not imply causation. It also is possible that different uses of the brain lead to changes in its structure.

Brain development does not stop at birth, although the total number of nerve cells may be established during the first half of gestation. Rather, glial cells (which are involved in making myelin, the electrical insulation for nerve fibers) and neural pathways continue to multiply across about the first four years of life (Fautso-Sterling, 1992, pp. 73–74). Even the shape and size of structures, like the corpus callosum (Burke & Yeo, 1994), change with age (Driesen & Raz, 1995; Murphy, et al., 1996) and disease (Fausto-Sterling, 1992, p. 239).

We also tend to think of brain growth as something that happens through addition, and indeed this is true prenatally. The brain starts as a hollow tube, gradually adding new nerve cells (estimated at a mind-boggling rate of a quarter of a million neurons per minute) that migrate out to their proper locations, until the brain assumes the adult shape we are accustomed to seeing (Kolb, 1989). At this point, the brain "overproduces" neurons and synaptic connections, both by as much as a factor of two. Much of brain development after birth involves the chiseling away of unused, excess cells and connections—something of a "use-it-or-lose-it" process. Such cell death and synaptic loss can continue at a slowed rate throughout adulthood, although most occurs throughout childhood. Brain development after birth then is more of a *subtraction* of cells and connections, paradoxically at the same time that functions are expanding.

We might expect then that if the brain is damaged, some cells and connections that otherwise might have decayed may be retained and thus recover at least some of the functionality lost to the damage, especially for young children (Kolb, 1989). This ability to pick up lost functionality refers to the brain's **plasticity**. Furthermore, drawing on results that are far from conclusive, Mukerjee (1995) proposes that "sexual and other abuses may alter a brain region," specifically the hippocampus (also see Teicher et al., 1993). Across all this evidence, the pattern is clear: *brains are not immutable and unreceptive to experiences* (also see Halpern, 1997):

> The brain's final "wiring diagram" as so many writers like to call it, is not a printed circuit, stamped out in accordance with a great genetic blueprint. It resembles more the weaving of an untutored artisan who, starting out with a general plan in mind, modifies it in the course of his or her work, using the available material and yes, while covering up or making creative use of mistakes in pattern (Fausto-Sterling, 1992, p. 77).

Are there two distinctive sexes? Atypical developmental patterns of CAH girls, pseudohermaphrodites, and others blur the lines between female and male. If there are not strictly dimorphic reproductive structures and these play a critical role in brain development, can there be strictly dimorphic brains? Anne Fausto-Sterling (1993) controversially challenges the duality of the sexes in her article titled, "The five sexes." Indeed, there are cultures where more than two sexes are considered normal (Imperato-McGinley, Peterson, Gautier, & Sturla, 1979; Herdt & Davidson, 1988).

Relatedly, our conceptualization of sex and sexuality as dimorphic implies that there is little to no overlap in the ranges of female and male, homosexual and heterosexual. We will challenge this assumption in detail in Chapter 5. Throughout the present discussion we have seen that there is lots of overlap (sometimes more overlap than difference). Even the "female" (estrogen) and "male" (testosterone) hormones are deceptively misnamed.

So . . . is there a female brain and a male brain? We've reviewed a quite complicated body of research and have come away with no clear answer. Even the simplest evidence, expected differences in structures we literally can see, has eluded scientists. Instead, we are left better informed by our review, but no more convinced that differences indeed exist.

But even if we assume that definitive differences eventually are documented, does this mean that some behavioral differences between women and men are permanently fixed in our biological wiring? We already have seen that brain development is a life-long, changeable process that may be affected by environmental experiences (e.g., exposure to long-term childhood abuse). But even granting this, does biology control us or can we shape our biologies?

A fascinating study of the menstrual cycles of college women living in dormatories is suggestive of the latter proposition (McClintock, 1971). The cycles of roommates and close friends (defined as women who mutually reported spending lots of time together) synchronized across the first four months of dorm life such that proximal women's cycles converged. Similar menstrual synchrony has been documented among lesbian couples (Weller & Weller, 1992). Thus close social interaction among women may alter their menstrual cycles, suggesting that environment can change biology. Pursuing this reasoning further, even if sex differences in human brains are established, we still will be left with the proverbial chicken-or-egg question. Do brain differences cause variability in the behaviors of women and men *or* do the variable experiences of women and men produce different brains?

Sociobiology: Evolution

Sociobiologists propose that human social behavior and social organization are encoded in our genes. They argue that adaptive genes are targeted through evolution for natural selection and are thus reproduced, while nonadaptive genes are selectively lost from the pool. The arguments of sociobiologists achieved notoriety in the late 1970s with the appearance of five interrelated books: Edward O. Wilson's (1978) *On Human Nature;* David Barash's (1979) *The Whisperings Within;* Richard Dawkins' (1976) *The Selfish Gene;* John MacKinnon's (1978) *The Ape Within Us;* and Donald Symons' (1979) *The Evolution of Human Sexuality* (Bem, 1993, pp. 14–23).

Although this sociobiological argument allows for environmental influences to determine what is and isn't adaptive through time, the bottom line is what humans now are is believed to be *universally* dictated by our genes. Like those advocating sex differences in brain development, sociobiologists fundamentally accept biological essentialism. Although sociobiologists purport to explain a vast array of human behaviors, the most relevant arguments for us in the psychology of women deal with sexual selection, sex differences, and the inequitable treatment of women and men.

Much of sociobiologists' analyses is rooted in what Wilson (1978, p. 124) called "the conflict of interest between the sexes." This conflict is detailed by Barash (1979) to explain the double standard of women's and men's sexuality:

> Sperm are cheap. Eggs are expensive. . . . For males, reproduction is easy, a small amount of time, a small amount of semen, and the potential evolutionary return is very great if offspring are produced. On the other hand, a female who makes a "bad" choice may be in real evolutionary trouble. If fertilization occurs, a baby is begun, and the ensuring process is not only inexorable but immensely demanding. . . . The evolutionary mechanism should be clear. Genes that allow females to accept the sorts of mates who make lesser contributions to their reproductive success will leave fewer copies of themselves than will genes that influence the female to be more selective. Accordingly, genes inducing selectivity will increase at the expense of those that are less discriminating. For males, a very different strategy applies. The maximum advantage goes to individuals with fewer inhibitions. A genetically influenced tendency to "play fast and loose"—love 'em and leave 'em"—may well reflect more biological reality than most of us care to admit (p. 48).

More generally, "evolutionary selection enables certain behaviorally specific genes to leave many more copies of themselves than other behaviorally specific genes; as a result, the human species now has a genetic makeup that predisposes it to behave in more or less the same way in all cultures" (Bem, 1993, p. 20).

"Evolutionary psychologists" have related the above reasoning to sexual selection—how humans choose mates (Buss, 1995). They argue that men are motivated by needs to be assured that children legitimately are theirs (men can never be as sure of paternity as women are of maternity); by desires to identify reproductively valuable women (unclear because fertility is virtually unknowable); and by gaining sexual access to women. Women, in contrast, are genetically driven to find men who are willing and able to invest in their offspring—men who will not "love 'em and leave 'em." David Buss (1995) goes on to relate each of these motivations for sexual selection to the actual dating and mating behaviors of women and men.[8]

Whatever the veracity of the above linkages (can you think of social explanations for why there is a "double standard" promoting men's and restricting women's sexuality?), sociobiologists go on to associate genes with both sex differences and inequities. They link the above evolutionary logic with what they claim are universal patterns in male dominance and in the division of labor along sex lines (such that women take care of home and hearth and men venture into the public sphere).

Consistent with the thinking of sociobiologists, we hear all kinds of discussion about height and strength differences between women and men and the implications of these. When we consider that the overall variability in human heights spans over two feet, the average difference between women and men of 3–5 inches doesn't seem so large (Hubbard, 1990). Furthermore, size disparities vary within cultures. Concerns about women's deficient upper-body strength permeate athletics as well as policy and access of women to nontraditional careers in the military, fire service, police, mining, the trades, etc. Studies conducted by U.S. Army researchers recently concluded that with sufficient strength training, many women can load trucks, fix heavy equipment, and march with loaded packs as well as most men ("Army says . . . ,"

---

[8] Highlighting the impact of social factors on sexual attitudes and behaviors, Mary Beth Oliver and Janet Hyde (1993) report that many gender differences narrowed from the 1960s to the 1980s.

Contemporary women athletes are challenging folk wisdom about women's physical fragility.[9]

1996). Some physical abilities tests have been criticized for their irrelevance to on-the-job duties and their overrepresentation of selected aspects of job requirements, such as upper-body strength. For example, a test of grip strength for police officers both disadvantaged women and had dubious job relevance (Arvey, Landon, Nutting, & Maxwell, 1992). In addition, the gap between women and men athletes has been narrowing as women's access and participation in sports is increasing. For example, within 20 years, women runners in the Boston marathon narrowed the gender gap in times from 80 minutes in 1963 to just 15 (Fausto-Sterling, 1992). Even if genes play a role in setting a range of size and strength potentials, it is clear that training, exercise, diet, attitudes, and so on can make a big difference in what each individual achieves (Hubbard, 1990).

Sandra Bem (1993) summarizes three feminist responses to these sociobiologists (taken from Bleier, 1984; Fausto-Sterling, 1992; and Sayers, 1982) and adds a fourth

---

[9] For an excellent overview of women in sports, see Hall (1996).

"Okay...Heads, *I* hunt animals and you raise the kids. Tails..."

Sociobiologists never tell us how it happened that men became the hunters and women, the child-raisers.

of her own.[10] First, feminists have attacked the presumption of universality. There is a vastly wide range of behaviors exhibited across cultures and across species. Second, they have noted that no specific linkages between particular genes and human behaviors have been established. Clearly, the burden of providing such proof falls onto the shoulders of sociobiologists. Third, critics have highlighted some circular reasoning used by sociobiologists. Speculating that a behavior has a genetic base, some sociobiologists create a story to illustrate their speculation, then they use this story to argue for the existence of the originating gene. The argument is circular with only speculation to tie the pieces of the argument together.

An example of such tautological thinking appeared in a *Time* magazine cover story (Gorman, 1992). Speculating that because it *was* adaptive for women as gatherers to remember where foods were located, women today are expected to be better than men at recalling objects scattered on a tabletop. Finding that indeed women list not only more items but more of their locations than men, this evidence is used to support the original contention that women's memory is genetically shaped by their past roles as gatherers. The logic has come full circle: assuming women's genes are programmed by long-dead generations of women gatherers, they should remember locations in today's world better; finding this to be true, "proves" somehow that indeed women are so genetically programmed. A giant leap is made from historical speculation to a contemporary finding, then back again, with little to test the veracity of the presumed genetic link (Halpern, 1997). Given this logic, wouldn't it be similarly adaptive for men as hunters to remember where a cliff was? Wouldn't those who forgot be more vulnerable to taking a fatal dive in the heat of a hunter's chase?

Finally, Bem (1993, pp. 21–23) argues that cultural invention, itself a human

---

[10] Some sociobiologists blend evolution with feminism—see a newspaper report of a conference on "Evolutionary Biology and Feminism" by Angier (1994).

endeavor, can overshadow these presumed genetic limitations. For example, she notes how airplanes have overcome our biological limitation of being without wings, how antibiotics challenge our susceptibility to infections, and how plumbing and refrigeration have negated our primitive needs to live as survivalists. By focusing on evolutionary adaptation alone, sociobiologists ignore the roles culture, history, and technology play in influencing both how we, as a species, have come to be what we are and how we, as individuals, currently can express ourselves.

Freud: Anatomy Is Destiny

Unlike the theories of brain development and sociobiology, Sigmund Freud developed a comprehensive theory of normal personality development. The thread that links Freudian thinking to these other two approaches is biological essentialism. Although many of Freud's successors abandoned his claim that "anatomy is destiny" (as we shall see in Chapter 3), biological essentialism lies at the core of Freud's original analysis. I quote Freud himself extensively throughout this section because I think his wording will give you the best feel for his argument as he constructed it.[11]

We all are familiar with Freud's basic tenets of personality development. Adult personality is fully formed through the resolution of three developmental stages encountered during the first 5–6 years of life. Every stage is characterized by different erogenous zones—areas that give pleasure to the basically hedonistic child (who is motivated to seek pleasure and avoid pain). For our purposes, the stage of interest is the **phallic** stage, the third stage in a fixed, chronological sequence, with its focus on the genitals as the child's source of pleasure. Just as brain development theorists stress the role of the internal reproductive structures, Freud emphasizes the importance of external reproductive structures (i.e., the clitoris and penis).

There's a second similarity between Freudian thinking and theorizing about brain development that takes us to the "bipotential" beginnings of the phallic stage. Freud (1990, p. 99) describes girls and boys emerging from the first two phases of psychosexual development (oral then anal) "with a bisexual disposition"—that is, encompassing feminine as well as masculine elements but with varying degrees of each. Furthermore, "with their entry into the phallic phase the differences between the sexes are completely eclipsed by their agreements. We are now obligated to recognize that the little girl is a little man" (Freud, 1990, p. 100). In other words, girls and boys at around ages 3–6 enter the phallic stage with similar backgrounds and with similar potentialities (presumed to be masculine: "little man").

As erotic attention shifts in all children to their genitals (the penis for boys and the clitoris for girls), the object of their affection is the mother. Development diverges for girls and boys at this point. The boy derives pleasure by masturbating, and his mother, as the object of his affection, symbolically becomes his lover (paralleling the Greek myth of Oedipus the King, hence, the **Oedipal complex**). His mother, becoming aware that "his sexual excitation relates to herself" (Freud, 1969, p. 46), bans such activity. At about the same time, the boy discovers that girls do not possess his

---

[11] See Freud's lecture on "Femininity," originally published around 1933, and Chapter VII of his "Outline of Psychoanalysis," published posthumously in 1940.

"supremely valued part" (Freud, 1969, p. 47), and he begins to fear that his mother will call upon his sexual rival for her, his father, to castrate him. He resolves his **castration anxiety** by identifying with his father, rather than by competing with him. He vicariously attains his mother, and by modeling his father, develops his own heterosexuality as well as the third and final structure of his personality, his **superego** (essentially, his moral conscience). With the penis as the central player in this developmental series, the stage is dutifully dubbed "phallic."

But what about girls? That central player in the story, "the boy's far superior equipment" (Freud, 1990, p. 104), is missing. In its stead, girls possess a woefully inadequate penis-substitute, a clitoris. In contrast to boys who retain their erogenous zone (their penis) and the object of their sexuality (their mother, ultimately generalized to women), girls confront two unique, difficult, and complicated tasks: to change from clitoral to vaginal gratification and to regard men as the objects of their sexuality.

In a blatant display of androcentrism, Freud extends the reasoning of the Oedipal complex to girls (grudgingly considering the name, **Electra**, to distinguish this process) (Freud, 1969, p. 51). Like boys, a girl enters the phallic stage strongly attached to her mother. This attachment turns to contempt when the girl sees the genitals of the other sex. First, "girls hold their mother responsible for their lack of a penis and do not forgive her for being thus put at a disadvantage" (Freud, 1990, p. 103). Second, she comes to devalue her mother: "with the discovery that her mother is castrated it becomes possible to drop her as an object" (Freud, 1990, p. 104). Replacing her wish for a penis (**penis envy**) with the symbolic equivalent of a baby (especially a baby with his own penis), the girl shifts the object of her fantasized sexuality to her father. She, like the boy, desires the other-sex parent and regards the same-sex parent as a rival. The girl comes to resent her mother for a third reason, parallel to a boy's, as they each vie for the affection of the other-sex parent.

To resolve this rivalry, the girl is stuck having to identify with and model a person, her mother, whom she despises and regards as inadequate. She develops her heterosexuality and superego, but her complete resolution of this stage is compromised:

> In the absence of fear of castration the chief motive is lacking which leads boys to surmount the Oedipus complex. Girls remain in it for an indeterminate length of time; they demolish it late and, even so, incompletely. In these circumstances the formation of the super-ego must suffer; it cannot attain the strength and independence which gives its cultural significance. . . . (Freud, 1990, p. 105).

What about homosexuality? How does a girl develop a lesbian identity? Another possible

> reaction to the discovery of female castration [is] the development of a powerful **masculinity complex**. . . . [The girl] exaggerates her previous masculinity, clings to her clitoral activity and takes refuge in an identification with her phallic mother or her father. What can it be that decides in favour of this outcome? We can only suppose that it is a constitutional factor. . . . The extreme achievement of such a masculinity complex would appear to be the influencing of the choice of an object in the sense of manifest homosexuality. Analytic experience teaches us, to be sure, that female homosexuality is sel-

dom or never a direct continuation of infantile masculinity. Even for a girl of this kind it seems necessary that she should take her father as an object for some time and enter the Oedipus situation. But afterwards, as a result of her inevitable disappointments from her father, she is driven to regress into her earlier masculinity complex (Freud, 1990, p. 105, highlighting added).

Freud, like his successors in brain development we discussed at the start of this chapter, clearly links masculinity to the development of a lesbian sexual identity and orientation.

The biological essentialism that underlies Freud's projections for the development of "normal femininity" extends to his discussions of homosexuality. Furthermore, Freud (1990, p. 103) outlines "three possible lines of development" from a girl's discovery of her own castration: "normal femininity," "sexual inhibition or neurosis," and "masculinity complex." In comparing these options, an implicit value judgment emerges, implying that the last two outcomes are deviations from "normal."[12]

Recent analyses of psychoanalytic work conclude that much of the homophobic denigration of homosexuality as a disease developed in the theories of Freud's followers, not from Freud himself (Bem, 1993, p. 87–92). Writing in a Viennese newspaper in 1903, Freud outlined his more subtly heterosexist[13] position:

> I am . . . of the firm conviction that homosexuals must not be treated as sick people, for a perverse orientation is far from being a sickness. Would that not oblige us to characterize as sick many great thinkers and scholars of all times, whose perverse orientation we know for a fact and whom we admire precisely because of their mental health? Homosexual persons are not sick (quoted in Bem, 1993, p. 90).

One of the most harmful consequences of Freudian theory for women may be in the dismissal of women's claims of sexual abuse as psychosexual fantasy. Freud himself (1990, p. 101) admits that "almost all my women patients told me that they had been seduced by their father," and analysts indeed have argued that Freud was aware of both the prevalence and violence associated with actual childhood sexual abuse (Masson, 1985). The case of Dora, which opened this book, is a good example; Freud believed Dora's claims but failed to acknowledge and act upon this. Freud (1990) reports:

> I was driven[14] to recognize in the end that these reports were untrue and so came to understand that hysterical symptoms are derived from phantasies and not from real occurrences. It was only later that I was able to recognize in this phantasy of being seduced by the father the expression of the typical Oedipal complex in women (p. 101).

---

[12] For a recent review of psychoanalytic views of women's homosexuality, see Magee and Miller (1992).

[13] **Homophobia** reflects a fear of and hatred towards gays and lesbians. **Heterosexism** assumes that the standard is heterosexual, and that homosexuality is a difference (or more typically, a negative deviation) from that norm. Paralleling his androcentricism which puts men and boys at the center, Freud's heterosexist analysis suggests that "normal" development is heterosexual. Declaring that homosexuality is a disease, in contrast, would be indicative of homophobia, and Freud himself does not do this. For a good resource for teaching about heterosexism, see Simoni (1996).

[14] Jeffrey Moussaieff Masson (1985) paints a less-than-flattering picture of why Freud was "driven" to such a reformulation of his original thesis that women were victims of very real abuse. He points to the rejection of these early claims by the medical community, Freud's reluctance to blame men, and his protection of a possibly abusive and professionally incompetent personal friend.

If indeed Freud's clients were survivors of sexual abuse, then their original abuse was multiplied by a therapist who insisted that their experiences were concocted "from phantasies." This tendency to pathologize survivors of childhood abuse in clinical psychology may have started with Freud, but it certainly hasn't stopped there (Caplan, 1995).

Psychoanalytic theory did not end with Freud, but rather has been actively expanded, refined, and reformulated over the past 60 years. We will continue our discussion of contemporary psychoanalysis in Chapter 3. Two key points for us in this chapter are the biological essentialism and androcentrism (putting men at the center) of Freud's analysis. To highlight these, Gloria Steinem (1994), somewhat tongue-in-cheek, turned the tables by introducing the fictional "Dr. Phyllis Freud" who purportedly developed a theory of masculinity as a deviation from female anatomy.

Steinem's article is full of humor as well as stinging truths that highlight the misogyny and androcentrism that runs through Freud's contentions. For example, Phyllis argues that women's natural *superiority* rests in women's "life-giving wombs" which are the very seat of creativity; in women's "sustenance-giving breasts" which destine women to be the great chefs of the world; in women's menstruation because "only women could bleed without injury or death"; in women's "envelopment" as part of women's heterosexuality (as opposed to men's "penetration"); and in the absorption of the man's sperm by the woman's egg. Steinem takes much of Freud's thinking on women and turns it on its head, using women as the starting point for her analysis. Her technique of using **absurd statements** is a good way to bring out underlying sexism in an argument (see Garnets, 1996, for further discussion of this technique).

"Dr. Phyllis Freud," complements of Ms. Gloria Steinem.

It's difficult to read Freud's writings, especially in his own words, and not share Steinem's contempt.[15] However, Freud's proposals that childhood development is important and that parents play a central role in this have permeated our culture, becoming widely accepted folk wisdom. Although Freudian thinking is firmly rooted in biology, specifically anatomy, by considering familial relationships, Freud also opened the door to consideration of environmental forces. Some of this more social psychoanalytic theory will be considered in the next chapter.

FEMINISM AND BIOLOGY

What role does biology play in a feminist psychology? It's tempting to say "none," but most psychologists would agree that this is too simplistic a solution. An alternative is to consider some feminist approaches to science and biology (for example, see Bleier,1984, 1986; Harding, 1986; and Hubbard, 1990). Feminists need not dismiss biology as something that is beyond our control and can be used only to oppress women. Rather a feminist approach can transform the study of our bodies from a science in search of immutable scientific truths toward a social construction aimed at understanding women's and men's bodies and the roles these play in our lives.

Ruth Hubbard (1990) considers three ways to think about the relationship between nature (biology) and nurture (environment). The simplest is additive: biology contributes a specified amount and then environment adds the rest. For example, an additive psychologist would conclude from the finding, discussed earlier, that 48% of lesbian monozygotic twins had lesbian twin sisters, that 48% of women's sexual orientation is inherited and the remainder is learned.

Others argue that "nature and nurture interact in ways that cannot be quantified that easily because they are not additive but act simultaneously and affect each other" interactively (Hubbard, 1990, p. 114). Although both biology and environment act on each other, they still are, at least conceptually, distinct. We conceivably could isolate some aspect of each of these, manipulate it, and seek to understand its singular contribution.

A third approach, a **dialectical** model, regards nature and nurture as so interdependent that their influences are always intertwined and inseparable. (A similar argument was made for the intertwining of race, class, gender, etc., in Chapter 1.) Consider Hubbard's (1990) example:

> If a society puts half its children in dresses and skirts but warns them not to move in ways that reveal their underpants, while putting the other half in jeans and overalls and encouraging them to climb trees and play ball and other active outdoor games; if later, during adolescence, the half that has worn trousers is exhorted to "eat like a growing boy," while the half in skirts is warned to watch its weight and not get fat; if the half in jeans trots around in sneakers or boots, while the half in skirts totters about on spike heels, then these two groups of people will be biologically as well as socially different. Their muscles will be different, as will their reflexes, posture, arms, legs and feet, hand-eye coordination, spatial perception, and so on. They will also be biologically different if, as adults,

---

[15] In addition to his degrading depiction of women, Freud himself was receptive neither to feminists who, he predicted, would not be "pleased" with his revelations nor to his "excellent women colleagues" whom he assured: "This doesn't apply to *you.* You're the exception; on this point, you're more masculine than feminine" (Freud, 1990, p. 99).

they spend eight hours a day sitting in front of a visual display terminal or work on a construction job or in a mine. . . . There is no way to sort out the biological and social components that produce these differences, therefore no way to sort nature from nurture, when we confront sex differences or other group differences in societies in which people, as groups, do not have equal access to resources and power and hence live in different environments (pp. 115–116).

Biology is inconsequential outside the social context in which it develops and is expressed. Sandra Bem (1993), in her rejection of biological essentialism, sums this up concisely:

No matter how many subtle biological differences between the sexes there may someday prove to be, both the size and the significance of those biological differences will depend, in every single instance, on the situational context in which women and men live their lives (p. 38).

CHAPTER SUMMARY

Now that you have read this chapter, please answer the following question:

When the sexes differ in some way, how likely is it that the difference is due to biological factors (hormones, chromosomes, etc.)?

1	2	3	4	5	6	7
not at all likely						very likely

How does your answer compare to your opinion at the start of this chapter?

We have explored three approaches to understanding women's and men's bodies: biological, sociobiological, and Freudian psychoanalytic. All share an assumption of biological essentialism—the belief that our bodies determine who we are. We saw at the beginning of this chapter that there is widely held folk wisdom accepting biology as a cause of sex differences and that these beliefs get in the way of actions aimed at social change. The evidence we reviewed in this chapter challenges these assumptions.

Although a complete dismissal of biological influences certainly would ignore part of each of us, we have seen that an exclusively biological perspective is inadequate not only because the evidence presented here is far from definitive, but also because the ultimate meaning and utility of biologically rooted sex differences are dubious. A feminist approach to understanding the impact of our biology on who we are (physically, sexually, psychologically, and interpersonally) regards biology as only a piece of the puzzle that has no meaning separate from the full puzzle itself. Are our bodies, ourselves, such that women and men are indisputably, fundamentally, and immutably different by virtue of our differing bodies? A feminist approach to psychophysiology offers a resounding "no" at the same time that it does not dismiss the omnirelevant role our body does play in contributing to who we each are and can become.

THREE

SOCIALIZATION PRACTICES
Learning to Be Ourselves in a Gender-Polarized World

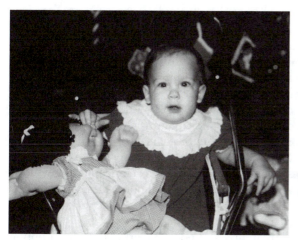

Jot down a few words below each picture to describe each 9-month-old child. How strong, cute, sturdy, cuddly, confident, and fragile is each baby?

You just participated in a "baby X" study—you know nothing about the babies pictured, but you have a first impression similar to any initial reaction when you first meet someone. A unique thing about babies is that it's hard to tell their sex, so we look for clues in dress and in their surroundings to make these judgments. The girl on the left is clothed in her holiday finery and is sitting in one of her presents, a sled, with her new Cabbage Patch doll. Pretty cute and cuddly. The boy on the right is dressed for some serious play in overalls and Nikes and is about to throw that ball. He looks sturdy and ready for action. Do your descriptions capture these gender-related differences? Do they come from each child's surroundings or do they emanate from within the child? How often have we heard the old adage: "Girls will be girls; and boys will be boys?"

In Chapter 2, we saw that assumptions of biological essentialism argue for the latter—biology dictates what girls and boys do. However powerful biological influences may prove to be, there's more to growing up female and male than biology can explain. The central question in this chapter asks, *How do we learn to be girls and boys, women and men?* In part, we are exploring how we each develop our own **gender identity**—how we perceive ourselves as female and male. Our gender identity includes how we label ourselves (woman or man), how we view our activities and interests (e.g., being a mother and liking football), how we perceive our own personality characteristics (e.g., caring and being assertive), and how we regard our social relationships, including our friendships and sexual orientation (Mussen, Conger, Kagan, & Huston, 1990). We also are questioning how we enact our **gender roles**—what we do that identifies us as women and men. Gender identity involves how we think and feel about our gender, and gender roles influence how we behave. Each reflects and reinforces the other.

The process by which we acquire our gender identity and our gender roles is called **gender-typing**. Gender-typing involves both biological contributions and specific indicators which are constructed by our culture and passed on to us through the process of **socialization**. Thus, socialization practices teach us how to get along within our culture, including how to properly enact our gender roles. We will focus our attention here on research and theory outlining just how we are socialized to be appropriate girls and boys, women and men in American culture.

You may respond, "Don't we treat girls and boys similarly, giving both opportunities to become whatever best suits their individuals desires and talents? Prior generations may have constricted their children's choices along gendered lines, but we've moved beyond that." Reconsider your descriptions of those photos at the start of this chapter. Both pictures are of my daughter, Kate. She is cute and cuddly, sturdy and ready-for-action; in sum, she is Kate. However, I question whether she will be treated with open expectations covering a full range of possible characteristics when she is dressed as the girl she is. In a series of 23 "baby X" studies similar to this one,[1] people repeatedly described the "girl" as more feminine and the "boy" as more masculine (Stern & Karraker, 1989). (If you guessed that the photos were of the same baby, note that different people responded to the differently dressed child in the "baby X" studies. What we did here does not parallel their method in an important way. but at the very minimum, you get the gist of what they did in these studies.)

Four theories dominate psychologists' explanations for such gendered socialization: **psychoanalytic** (Neo-Freudian), **social learning**, **cognitive developmental**, and **gender schema** theories. Each offers a different perspective on how gender identity develops. Fundamental assumptions that link all four theories together are the beliefs that basic gendered personality development occurs in childhood and that the resulting personality traits that emerge from this process are somewhat stable and enduring so that they shape our adult thoughts, feelings, and actions. To some extent, we are what we learned to be as children.

PSYCHOANALYSIS

My experience with teaching the following materials is that students cavalierly write off psychoanalysis as something too far-fetched to be viable today. I ask you not to be too quick to dismiss this perspective. It still is a very influential view within psychology; a survey of the theoretical orientations of faculty in APA-accredited clinical

---

[1] Only two of these 23 studies used photographs; the remainder used either videotapes of or direct interactions with "baby X."

doctoral programs reported that fully 28.4% identified their primary orientation as "psychodynamic/ psychoanalytic" (Mayne, Norcross, & Sayette, 1994). Freudian thinking has infiltrated our basic cultural assumptions in many ways. We take for granted the beliefs that we can be influenced by unconscious forces, that children aren't just little adults, and that mothers are responsible for the psychological development of their children mostly because of Freud's work (Jacklin & McBride-Chang, 1991).[2] For better or for worse, these basic Freudian assumptions have been accepted almost as unquestioned folk wisdom.

As we saw in Chapter 2, Freudian psychoanalysis describes women's and girls' development as a deviation from a male model (androcentrism), is rooted in the assumption that anatomy is destiny (biological essentialism), and envisions women's superego (moral) development as inadequate relative to that of men. Many of Freud's successors in psychoanalysis digressed from the original theory by rejecting his androcentrism and/or biological essentialism. Instead, they posited a variety of social influences associated with anatomical differences between girls and boys to explain, among other things, how gender identity is learned. The common threads linking these Neo-Freudian theories to psychoanalysis are fundamental beliefs in the stages of psychosexual development and the primacy of childhood relationships with parents (mostly mothers) for personality development. Additionally, cognitive psychologists (not psychoanalytic in their orientation) have compiled empirical evidence to challenge Freud's contention that women's superego development is lacking.

Psychoanalytic Responses to Androcentrism

Reacting to the androcentrism of "penis envy," Karen Horney suggests that "womb envy," arising from men's inability to bear children, affects masculine development (Horney, 1926; 1966). Erik Erikson (1968) argues that the foundation of female identity development is not the absence of a penis but rather the presence of a uterus. It is women's "inner space" that is the basis for women's "biological, psychological, and ethical commitment to take care of human infancy" (p. 266).

Others consider the symbolic rather than biological implications of penis envy. Kate Millet (1969) observes:

> Girls are fully cognizant of male supremacy long before they see their brother's penis. It is so much a part of their culture, so entirely present in the favoritism of school and family, in the image of each sex presented to them by all media, religion, and in every model of the adult world they perceive, that to associate it with a boy's distinguishing genital would, since they have learned a thousand other distinguishing sexual marks by now, be either redundant or irrelevant. Confronted with so much concrete evidence of the male's superior status, sensing on all sides the depreciation in which they are held, *girls envy not the penis, but only what the penis gives one social pretensions to* (pp. 264–265, italics added).

Clara Thompson (1964) similarly speculates that the penis symbolizes men's privilege in a patriarchal society and that women's envy is a healthy response to their

---

[2] Taken to its logical extreme, parents (especially mothers) are being charged for the crimes committed by their children (Eagan, 1995).

own undervaluation within a competitive society. She proposes three *normal* responses to such devaluation: proving one's self through attempts to successfully compete with men, revenge, and withdrawal from competition, for example, by striving for success in nonthreatening areas separate from male dominance (e.g, being the best mother possible).

A Psychoanalytic Response to Biological Essentialism

Various Neo-Freudians have replaced Freud's biological essentialism with theories that root personality development in social interaction. One contemporary, feminist, psychoanalytic reformulation of the phallic stage of development is offered by Nancy Chodorow in her widely acclaimed book, *The Reproduction of Mothering* (1978). Chodorow begins her analysis with the Western cultural norm for families composed of an employed father, nonemployed mother, and children. (Chodorow realizes that this does not describe the majority of families today, but it is what we think of as the "ideal" family.) She agrees with Freud that prior to entering the phallic stage, girls and boys are privy to an ideal emotional relationship with their mother (at least from the child's perspective) that is exclusive, intense, and characterized by boundary confusion such that the child does not feel separate from the mother. In other words, the mother is there to meet the child's every need—and selflessly does so.

With the onset of the phallic stage, mothers come to treat their sons as sexual objects (psychologically, not physically) because: (1) the father is distant and less affectionate (i.e., he's off at his job a lot) and (2) she, like the rest of society, overvalues males. This sets up the classic Freudian Oedipal complex such that the boy, who also sexually desires his mother, wants to be rid of his father. (Remember, Chodorow is a psychoanalyst.) This stage is successfully resolved when the boy shifts his identification with his mother to his father, thus, developing his own heterosexuality and masculinity. An essential part of his masculinity involves his rejection of the mother, symbolically generalizing to all that is feminine. In addition, since his father is away a lot, the masculinity that the boy develops does not come from direct contact with his father but rather is culled from the culture as a whole. Thus boys' masculinity is more *stereotyped* than directly modeled (Lynn, 1966). In addition, as part of the masculine stereotype, the boy adopts a **logical, rational orientation** so that he thinks as a detached, analytic problem-solver. This orientation encourages him to strive for autonomy and be anxious about forming emotional ties with others.

A girl also enters the phallic stage having been in an ideal pre-Oedipal relationship with her mother. Freud believes that the Electra complex is triggered for a girl when she realizes that she has no penis. However, Chodorow points out that Freud never explains why a girl suddenly comes to "miss" her "lost" organ. Chodorow argues that what a girl does come to realize at this stage is *not* that her mother castrated her, but that boys are preferred by mothers (and society as a whole) and that boys are granted greater independence than girls. This creates ambivalence for the girl in her relationship with her mother: on the one hand, she wants to retain her warm, fuzzy attachment to her mother. On the other hand, she'd like to be both independent and loved like a son. All is achieved to some degree by identifying with her mother so that the girl develops her own heterosexuality and femininity. In contrast to the boy's masculinity, the girl's femininity is learned *in direct interaction* with her mother so that she develops a hands-on gender identity (that is not undermined by the girl's resentment that her mother castrated her as Freud believed). As part of her femininity and in relations with her mother, the girl develops a strong **relational, nurturing orientation**.

Chodorow then plays out the maturation of these children. Both have become heterosexual so they form adult relationships with the other sex. If they pursue the norm of the "ideal" family, the rational man will be employed, the relational woman will turn to her sons to fill the emotional gap left by the distant, logical/rational father, and the whole cycle will reproduce itself. (Note again the title of her book: *The Reproduction of Mothering.*)

How do we break this cycle? Chodorow calls for dual-parenting. If fathers, as well as mothers, participate in the raising of their children, then boys will develop a version of masculinity that is hands-on and that includes the care and nurturing of children. (It seems logical to extend this reasoning to dual-employment so that girls incorporate the independent, rational aspects of their employed mothers into their directly acquired version of femininity—but this goes beyond Chodorow's speculation.) A potential catch-22 of this argument is that the work of parenting may not be compatible with men's rational, nonrelational orientation. Despite this limitation, the main point for us is that Chodorow offers a version of psychoanalytic reasoning that is true to the major underpinnings of psychosexual development without relying on biological determinants of personality development.

Nancy Chodorow's theory lacks the extensive empirical grounding we'll see underlying the next three socialization theories, and her model is rooted in a European-American framework.[3] However, Chodorow makes at least three important points. First and foremost, change is possible. Personality development is not slavishly attached to whether or not an individual possesses a penis. Second, she links intrapsychic development to broad social structures. It is society's framing of families as employed men with dependent wives and children that underlies and maintains the cycle of mothering. And third, Chodorow's analysis strikes a resonant chord with feminist activists who advocate equal sharing of childrearing responsibilities.

An Empirical Test of Moral Reasoning

Chodorow's theorizing coalesces with the work of cognitive psychologists interested in **moral reasoning.** The latter researchers study how we reason about ethical choices defining right and wrong. Much of this research presents a moral dilemma to participants who are asked to describe what they would do if they themselves faced the dilemma and why. What research participants decide to do is not important. Rather, *why* they make their choices is critical to understanding their level of moral *reasoning.*

At the most rudimentary level, **preconventional** reasoning is egocentric, so that what's regarded as moral is what gets rewarded and/or avoids punishments. At the next, **conventional** level, societal conventions become important so that approval

---

[3] Chodorow's model has been extended to development of gender identity in Chicana/Chicano families (Segura & Pierce, 1993).

and disapproval of others influence the decision. At the most advanced, **postconventional** stage, abstract principles are considered that move beyond the individual and what others regard as moral. As we move from preconventional to postconventional reasoning, the complexity of participants' thinking increases, shifting from consideration of just one's self, to thinking about others, to grappling with abstract concepts.

Much of this theorizing was done by Lawrence Kohlberg using the following case. What you would do if you found yourself in Heinz's shoes? Be sure to note not just your solution (to steal or not), but your justifications for your choice.

> In Europe, a woman was near death from a very bad disease, a special kind of cancer. There was one drug that the doctors thought might save her. It was a form of radium that a druggist in the same town had recently discovered. The drug was expensive to make, but the druggist was charging ten times what the drug cost him to make. He paid $200 for the radium and charged $2,000 for a small dose of the drug. The sick woman's husband, Heinz, went to everyone he knew to borrow the money, but he could only get together about $1,000, which was half of what it cost. He told the druggist that his wife was dying and asked him to sell it cheaper or let him pay later. But the druggist said, "No, I discovered the drug and I'm going to make money from it." So Heinz gets desperate and considers breaking into the man's store to steal the drug for his wife (Kohlberg, 1981).

Revisiting the three stages and assuming a decision to steal, at the preconventional level, we might argue that Heinz should steal the drug because he'd miss his wife if she died. At the conventional stage, we might suggest that Heinz should steal the drug because others would think he was a rotten husband if he failed his dying wife. At the postconventional level, we might persuade Heinz to steal the drug because life is more important than another's property. Arguments fitting each stage can be constructed for the choice not to steal; remember that it is the rationale, not the decision itself, that Kohlberg analyzes. Does your own reasoning fit into one of these levels?

Don't be discouraged if your reasoning doesn't fit as neatly as Kohlberg would want. This is exactly what some researchers found for many women and some men. When this coding scheme was used, women's responses overall ended up being coded at lower levels than men's, confirming Freud's speculation about women's inadequate superego development. In response to this conclusion, Carol Gilligan presented an alternative line of reasoning for resolving the Heinz dilemma in her widely cited book, *In a Different Voice* (1982).

Balanced throughout Gilligan's reasoning are concerns about caring and hurt. At the lowest level, only our own hurt is considered—we (as Heinz) would be hurt and lonely if our wife died or if we were put in jail for stealing. Conventional reasoning takes into account not only our own hurt (as Heinz) but also that of immediate others (e.g., the wife who might die and the pharmacist who'd lose money). Our concerns here center on being responsible, with our caring extending beyond ourselves to others. At the postconventional stage, caring moves beyond the immediate actors to broader principles of caring and our responsibility to enact those abstract principles. Consistent with the original formulation, each stage is characterized by increasing levels of cognitive complexity. These two orientations are diagrammed in Table 3.1

TABLE 3.1   Kohlberg's and Gilligan's Perspectives on Moral Reasoning

Stages of Moral Development	Kohlberg's Rights Perspective	Gilligan's Caring Perspective
Postconventional	The right to life is more important than the right to property	Principles of caring extend to all people. Money must not take priority over our responsibility to preserve life.
Conventional	Others would approve if I saved my wife.	I am responsible for caring for my wife. It would hurt her and others if she died.
Preconventional	Stealing lets me keep my wife.	It would hurt me to lose my wife.

Increasing Cognitive Complexity ↑

In essence, Gilligan offers a **caring rationale** as an alternative to the **rights reasoning** constructed by Kohlberg and his colleagues. Sometimes, elements of each perspective are blended in our reasoning. At other times, the two approaches lead to opposed solutions (as in the example in Box 3.1). At these times, it's almost like having two different voices, with one voice stressing rights; the other, caring and responsibility.

BOX 3.1   Another Look at Moral Reasoning

Although I like to use the Heinz case to present the evolution of Carol Gilligan's thinking because this represents what happened, I also sense that it doesn't as clearly distinguish between the rights and caring perspectives as much as I would like. An example in which the two perspectives are in conflict may be more illuminating.

The Los Angeles Fire Department was at the center of a controversy over the display of a poster of John Wayne ("Duke at center," 1996). White supporters of the poster stress their right to free expression to support their claims to keep the poster prominently displayed. They see the dilemma from a rights perspective, and they argue that the owner of the poster has a right to free expression by posting the picture.

On the other hand, some African American firefighters find the poster deeply offensive. To them, John Wayne symbolizes white supremacy because of blatantly racist comments he made and because of the strongly individualistic message implied by his cowboy-as-hero movies. Arguing for the removal of the poster, detractors balance the harm done by displaying the poster (it seriously upsets people) with the harm done by removing it (a minor inconvenience, at most). Their caring perspective argues for the removal of the poster, even if its removal is involuntary. In this case, and in parallel ones questioning whether sexually explicit postings constitute sexual harassment, the two perspectives come to opposing resolutions.

Gilligan offers the caring approach as a woman's alternative to the male-oriented justice approach. It fits well with Chodorow's supposition that women acquire a nurturing, caring orientation through the resolution of their Electra complex as opposed to boys' rational, rights orientation. Both theorists assume that the caring perspective is used more often by women, in contrast to the justice perspective preferred by men.

However, subsequent research does not support this claim of a clear-cut gender difference (Friedman, Robinson, & Friedman 1987; Mednick, 1989; Stack, 1986; L.J. Walker, 1984), even across different cultures (e.g., the U.S. and Brazil [Carlo, et al., 1996]). For example, when parents considered both hypothetical and real-life moral dilemmas involving a physically disabled child, mothers and fathers responded similarly (Clopton & Sorell, 1993). Furthermore, these views romanticize women's presumed nurturance (Kerber, 1986) and limit caring to the domain of women and girls. Even if caring arguments are constructed more frequently by women than men, a caring orientation is not exclusive to women's thinking, just as a rights perspective is not exclusive to men's. Although Gilligan's caring perspective adds an important extension to a theory of moral development that had been overlooked, it does not support the notion that women's moral reasoning is deficient or superior in relations to men's.

SOCIAL LEARNING THEORY

Social learning theory is rooted in B.F. Skinner's behaviorism with its emphasis on **operant conditioning**. Quite simply, we learn and repeat behaviors that are rewarded, and we extinguish those that are punished or ignored. In his revolutionary book, *Walden Two*, Skinner (1948) describes a utopian society based on behaviorist principles in which children's behaviors are incrementally shaped to conform to the ideals of the society and to maximize the individual talents of each child. This is done through group rather than family care:

> If your boys don't want to "be like Daddy" or, less happily, "like Mama," how are their personalities built up?
> We know very little about what happens in identification. . . . All we really know is that children tend to imitate adults, in gestures and mannerisms, and in personal attitudes and relations. They do that here, too, but since the family structure is changed, the effect is very different.
> Our children are cared for by many different people. It isn't institutional care, but genuine affection. Our members aren't overworked, and they haven't been forced into a job for which they have no talent or inclination. . . .
> Remember that the adults who care for our children are of both sexes. We have broken down prejudices regarding the occupations of the sexes. . . . (Skinner, 1948, pp. 144–145).

Skinner's remarks about the centrality of imitation for childhood identification are expanded upon by social learning theorists. Albert Bandura and Richard Walters (1963) describe the importance of indirect learning—learning by doing what other people do (**imitation or modeling**) and learning by simply watching others

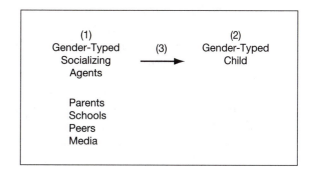

FIGURE 3.1
A simple schematic of social
learning theory.

(**observational learning**). Applying all this to the development of our gender identities, social learning theorists stress the role other people (**socializing agents**) play in modeling, rewarding, and punishing gender appropriate and inappropriate behaviors (Lott & Maluso, 1993).

Fundamentally, social learning theorists propose that *socializing agents produce gender-typed children* . To support this formula, three questions must be answered: (1) Do socializing agents treat girls and boys differently? (2) Are children gender-typed? and (3) Do these agents *cause* children to be gender-typed? (See Figure 3.1 for a representation of these questions.) We shall see that making this final causal connection will prove to be the most difficult part of the theory to support definitively, yet it is the critical test of social learning theory.

Gender-Typed Socializing Agents?

Generally, researchers have studied four groups of socializing agents: parents, schools, peers, and the media (books, television, etc). Much of this research was conducted in the 1970s, coinciding with the resurgence of the women's movement during that time.[4] One could argue that much has changed since then, although it also is possible to argue that a lot has stayed the same. For example, analyzing 172 studies published since the 1950s, Hugh Lytton and David Romney (1991) find no evidence to support the claim that general parental practices have changed across the past 40 years. Whatever you believe, I will provide the most recent references to support the claims made by these theorists. I will not rely on research that one easily could write off as outdated.

Remember as you read that researchers look for general patterns across many individuals—not all parents, schools, peers, and media conform to these overall trends. But overall trends speak volumes about what we all encounter repeatedly and persistently throughout our lives.

---

[4] A good overview of that research, and the social learning perspective that dominated at that time, is captured in the video, "Pinks and Blues" (57 minutes), 1980, from Time-Life Film & Video. An implicit theme that runs through this video is the assumption that if sexism in socialization is exposed, that itself will somehow end it.

Parents.   Although parents believe that they treat girls and boys comparably, there's reason to question this assertion. Parents of newborn girls described their daughters as finer featured, less strong, more delicate, and more feminine than the parents of newborn boys rated their sons (Karraker, Vogel, & Lake, 1995). Similarly, first-time mothers reported that their newborn sons, not their daughters, had broad, wide hands; looked tall, large, and athletic; and were serious (not smiling but not crying) (Reid, 1994). Similar stereotyping has been found among both British and Polish mothers (Bielawska-Batorowicz, 1993). And don't forget those "baby X" studies like the one that opened this chapter (Stern & Karraker, 1989).

Parents dress girls and boys differently, and this contributes to differences in how children are perceived. Observing 1- to 3-month-olds at a suburban shopping center, researchers found that fully 75% of girls (and no boys) wore pink or were surrounded by pink toys and blankets and 79% of the boys (compared to only 8% of the girls) were identified by blue (Shakin, Shakin, & Sternglanz, 1985). Interestingly, parents were unaware of their choices. (In defense of parents, if you visit the children's departments in your local stores, you'll find it awfully hard to avoid pink or blue choices.) But do clothes make the baby? The same 11-month-old girl dressed in a ruffled dress, as compared to being clothed in blue or yellow shorts, is less frequently described as strong, heavy, hard, and large and is more often regarded as happy and good (Leone & Robertson, 1989).

Parental gender-typing with toys is more complex than "boy" toys for boys and "girl" toys for girls (although I urge you to take a walk through any toy store and see if you can identify the "girls'" and the "boys'" sections). As expected, parents completing the "Toy Desirability Scale" stated gender-typed preferences, rating feminine toys (e.g., kitchen sets, dolls, and sewing machines) more desirable for their daughters and masculine toys (e.g., guns, bats and balls, and trucks) for their sons. However, when these same parents were given a chance to play with their children, selecting from a range of toys (masculine, feminine, and neutral), choices were less stereotyped. Parents more often presented masculine and neutral toys to both their daughters and sons, and they actually spent more time playing with these toys than with feminine ones (Idle, Wood, & Desmarais, 1993).

These data suggest two conclusions. First, parents prefer gender-appropriate toys for their children. In fact, researchers find that parents are more likely to honor both girls' and boys' requests for gender-congruent toys (Etaugh & Liss, 1992). In all honesty, I found it much more difficult to fulfill my son's Christmas request for a Barbie bubble gum press than my daughter's typical requests for "boys'" toys. Some of this has to do with my second point: "boys'" toys are more fun. When parents choose toys to actually play with, like their children they gravitate toward the "boys'" toys. This makes life simple for sons: parents prefer and actually play with masculine toys. For daughters, the message is mixed: many "boys'" toys are more engaging, but parents don't desire them for their daughters. Not surprisingly then, boys' toy choices are more consistently stereotypic than girls' (Carter & Levy, 1988). You can do your own inventory of any children's toy boxes and see what you find (then see Rost & Hanses, 1994).

I can see this ambivalence played out in some of my own daughter's choices of toys. When Kate was 8 years old, I watched her struggle to stock games for her "Game

Boy," a hand-held video-game player. She shied away from the many violent cartridges that dominate the electronics shelves (Cesarone, 1994), but found the programs designed specifically for girls "boring." Even the product name bothered her to a point where she and a friend "liberated" their casings by replacing the product name with a sticker christening them "Game Girl." It is no wonder, given this tailoring of toys toward the presumed interests of boys, that a "computer gap" is emerging that short-changes girls (Sutton, 1991).

Even the language parents use in interaction with their children varies by gen-der of the child. Parents doing jigsaw puzzles and memory tasks encouraged inde-pendent problem solving from their sons but suggested specific solutions to their daughters (Frankel & Rollins, 1983). Parents more often directed specific negative eval-uations of puzzle-solving skills to daughters (for example by saying, "You're not very good at puzzles.") (Alessandri & Lewis, 1993). Traditional mothers used more ques-tions, numbers, verbal teaching, and action verbs with their sons than with their daughters (Weitzman, Birns, & Friend, 1985). There even are some differences in what emotions mothers discuss with their preschoolers: moms stressed positive over negative emotions with daughters (they talked about these equally with sons), never mentioning anger with their daughters (Fivush, 1989).

How mothers and their children communicate when doing gender-typed play is consistent with predictions that mothers encourage gender-appropriate play (Leaper, Leve, Strasser, & Schwartz, 1995). Researchers analyzed the speech patterns of moth-ers and their children playing at home with three sets of toys: neutral (zoo animals), feminine (plastic kitchenware), and masculine (a plastic car track). Mothers more fre-quently reciprocated supportive statements from daughters (e.g., "That's a good idea.") than from their sons when they were playing with feminine toys. With both their daughters and sons, mothers responded to collaborative speech acts with control-ling statements when the toys were gender inappropriate. For example, when build-ing the car track, a mother might respond to her daughter's request to work together to connect the pieces (a collaborative act) by commanding her not to touch pieces (a controlling act). Both patterns suggest that mothers subtly, and probably inad-vertently, support gender-congruent play through their speech.

What parents themselves do and say everyday to each other may send differ-ent messages to girls and boys. What does a child learn when dad drives whenever the family is in the car, when mom makes all the meals, etc.? Even among employed moms and dads, there are differences in how much childcare is done by each (Jump & Haas, 1987). Furthermore, children are astute observers of how parents interact with each other, picking up gendered stereotypes (Meyer, Murphy, Cascardi, & Birns, 1991). For example, when my son was 4 years old, he declared that he would only do "boy" jobs. I was stunned. Deciding to play this out, I asked him just what "boy" jobs he intended to do. Defiantly he retorted: "Laundry—just like Dad!" I just smiled. . . .

Much of the above research included only white families, and many of these families comprised parents who were heterosexual and in intact marriages. Recent studies present a more diverse view of families that vary according to composition, liv-ing arrangements, race, ethnicity, class, geography, and sexual orientation (Davenport & Yurich, 1991). For example, fewer African American families are gender polar-ized; more of them value independence training for their daughters (Reid, 1985); and

What's odd about this picture?

most successfully teach children about racism (Greene, 1990a). The myth of the sharply gender-polarized Hispanic family has been debunked in a comprehensive review of research involving Puerto Rican, Mexican, and Cuban American families (Vazquez-Nuttall, Romero-Garcia, & De Leon, 1987). Asian American parents are characterized as stressing achievement in both daughters and sons, but there is a gap between what Asian American women are taught to strive for and what they realistically achieve within a discriminatory society (Woo, 1995).

It has been suggested that more rural, as compared to urban, families enact gender polarization (Bushy, 1990). Overall, the attitudes and behaviors of children of lesbian and heterosexual mothers are more alike than different (Falk, 1993; Patterson, 1992). Families with lesbian and heterosexual daughters do not differ in their enforcement of gender-role rules (Dancey, 1990). Children raised in lesbian families are no more likely than other children to be homosexual, although the former may more readily explore same-sex relationships (Golombok & Tasker, 1996). A study of African American lesbian mothers suggests that they treat their children with even less gender polarization than other mothers (Hill, 1987).

Schools.   The central socializing agents for children in school are teachers, but the educational context extends beyond just teachers. The lessons children learn at school about their gender identities and roles come from how teachers treat them, from how schools are structured, from counselors and other specialists, and from the materials to which they are exposed. All come together to produce an educational climate that two long-time researchers, reviewing research spanning over 20 years, conclude "shortchanges girls" (Sadker & Sadker, 1994).

Myra and David Sadker (1994) describe the gendered lessons taught at school: girls learn to speak quietly, to defer to boys, to avoid math and science, to value neatness over innovation, and to stress appearance over intelligence. Girls also experience an erosion of their achievement so that their tendency to outperform boys when they first start school degenerates to a point where they lag behind boys by high school graduation. Other studies add that girls learn to present themselves as modest, self-deprecating, passive, and obedient compared to boys who learn to be self-assertive and self-promoting (Ellis, 1993).

As for teachers themselves, teachers generally pay more attention to boys (Ellis, 1993) and have lower expectations for girls (Vandell & Dempsey, 1991). When boys make mistakes, teachers are likely to give them constructive feedback and encouragement to try again; girls are likely to be counseled not to worry (Sadker & Sadker, 1994). Girls who violate gender stereotypes by being less compliant (Gold, Crombie, & Noble, 1987) and physically tall and/or heavy (Villimez, Eisenberg, & Carroll, 1986) are evaluated as less competent by teachers. One study observed toddlers with play-group teachers at two points (Fagot, Hagen, Leinbach, & Kronsberg, 1985). Initially, girls and boys communicated similarly, but over time, teachers unknowingly reinforced girls for communicating politely and boys for assertiveness so that they displayed dramatically divergent styles during the researchers' follow-up observations (also see Maccoby, 1990).

Some educators argue that gender-segregated education avoids the generally chilly climate of the coeducational classroom and instead fosters girls' learning and development (Coats, 1994; Ransome, 1993). However, the research data on single-sex education is, at best, mixed. On the one hand, more junior and senior high school girls in Louisiana enrolled in chemistry, advanced biology, and advanced math classes in an all-girl parochial school than in public coed schools (Campbell & Evans, 1993), and single-sex schooling has been linked to less gender stereotyping (Lawrie & Brown, 1992). On the other hand, few differences between the career pursuits of thousands of alumnae from coed and all-girl high schools were found (Shmurak, 1993). Home background appears to be a better predictor of girls' achievement in physics than the gender composition of girls' schools (Young & Fraser, 1992).

Arguments for segregated education become even more complex when we consider both gender and race. For example, many African American women in predominately white colleges develop strong survival skills including articulateness, heightened racial consciousness, and assertiveness yet experience lowered academic performance and more dissatisfaction with college (reviewed in Gillem, 1996). These latter disadvantages disappear in Black colleges but are accompanied by reduced assertiveness and increased passivity and shyness. Neither setting offers a chance for African American women to develop both academically and in their relationships with men.

Other educators focus on making changes within existing school systems. For example, the Sadkers (1994) recommend over 250 books with strong female characters. Others recommend teacher-training reform that makes teachers aware of subtle, and often unintended, gender-biased practices (Vandell & Dempsey, 1991). Two leading organizations pursuing such reforms are the American Association of University Women (AAUW) and the Association of American Colleges and Universities.[5] For example, the AAUW published a report and video exploring such schoolwide

---

[5] To obtain materials from these organizations, contact the AAUW at 1111 Sixteenth St, NW, Washington, DC 20036 and the Association of American Colleges and Universities at 1818 R St., NW, Washington, DC 20009.

reforms as team teaching and cooperative learning and their impact on girls in middle schools (AAUW, 1996).

Peers.   As early as preschool, other children punish violations of gender prescriptions, with girls patrolling girls and boys monitoring boys (Fagot, 1985). For example, when my son at age 2 borrowed his big sister's barrettes to "look pretty" for a parade, his most vocal critics were other boys; the girls and the teachers acted nonchalant. Interestingly, more children in an ethnically diverse group of third-to-sixth graders wanted to be friends with a fictitious child who behaved in gender-traditional ways than with a "deviant" child (Zucker et al., 1995). Middle class, mostly white girls and boys, ages 7 to 12, positively evaluated the performance of a videotaped fifth-grade girl exhibiting masculine stereotyped behavior, but denigrated her personality (McAninch, Milich, Crumbo, & Funtowicz, 1996).

Sisters and brothers also play a role in socializing younger children. My son who is younger than his sister has ample opportunities to play with her Barbies, polly-pockets (miniature dollhouses), and other "girl" toys. Research shows that the older child dictates what kinds of toys are played with, and that children with older other-gender siblings engage in less gender stereotyping than those with same-gender siblings (Stoneman, Brody, & MacKinnon, 1986).

Media.   Check out birth announcement and congratulations cards at a store. Do they tell you anything about what we expect infants to be like? Judith Bridges (1993) systematically analyzed these cards and found intriguing differences in both visual images and verbal messages. Images indicative of physical activity, such as action toys and active babies, appeared on cards for boys, and verbal messages of sweetness and sharing were dominant themes on cards for girls. Most strikingly, more boy than girl cards heralded a message of happiness for both the parents and the baby.

"Dick" and "Jane" tend to get equal time in children's school readers, but animal characters are male in three of every four stories and boys appear in two of every three illustrations (Purcell & Stewart, 1990). Looking beyond simple representation to what characters do, female humans and animals are more likely to need to be rescued, are less adventurous, engage in fewer occupations, and espouse a caring morality based in connection with others as opposed to a rights morality stressing individuality. Men also are depicted in far more occupations than women (Tognoli, Pullen, & Lieber, 1994). Not surprisingly, "Dick" and "Jane" are very likely to be white (Reid & Paludi, 1993).

There have been some changes in storybooks over the years, but the representation of female and male characters largely has remained unchanged. In both storybooks (Turner-Bowker, 1996) and comics (Brabant & Mooney, 1997), men and boys continue to dominate in titles and pictures, and they play more potent and active roles. Analyzing Caldecott award-winning books published between 1937 and 1989, a large proportion of female characters was shown using household items in contrast to male characters who disproportionately used nondomestic production items, such as construction, agricultural, and transportation objects (Crabb & Bielawski, 1994). Over time, the proportion of women and girls engaged in household activities has remained stable, but there has been an increase in men's and boys' household involvement. In other words, women's and girls' roles remain confined to the home while men's and boys' roles recently have expanded into the home (also see Tognoli, Pullen, & Lieber, 1994). Similarly, girls in children's picture books have become increasingly instrumental across the past 50 years, yet have remained consistently passive and dependent (Kortenhaus & Demarest, 1993). The moral decision making of storybook characters parallels gendered stereotypes with girls being more caring and connected in contrast to individualistic, rights-oriented boys (Tetenbaum & Pearson, 1989). Does all this matter? The link between strong same-gender characters and children's self-esteem has been established empirically (Ochman, 1996).

Children average 133 minutes of television viewing each day (that's over 2 hours); 35% of this time they watch alone (Frances & Wozniak, 1989). Researchers videotaped the programs 24 5-year-old children watched over a ten-day period and found a much greater percentage of male than female characters portrayed (Luecke, Anderson, Collins, & Schmitt, 1995). This pattern extends to Japanese television as well (Rolandelli, 1991). Two types of programs targeted specifically toward children are cartoons and educational programming. Neither forum does an admirable job of dispelling gender stereotypes.

Saturday morning is prime time for children to tune into cartoons. Analyzing cartoons aired on two Saturdays, one morning in 1990 and the other in 1992, cartoon characters were overwhelming male—82% and 76%, respectively (Swan, 1995). Children's favorite cartoons are continuing adventure series (much to my chagrin, my son at 5 years old was addicted to "Power Rangers"), and these cartoons are strongly steeped in traditional masculine stereotypes, although less so in the 1980s than previously (Thompson & Zerbinos, 1995). Not surprisingly to anyone who has watched cartoons, violence clearly is associated with masculine stereotypes and characters; even the commercials aired during cartoons stress the linkage between masculinity and violence (Palmerton & Judas, 1994). Most relevant to our argument here, not only are cartoons gender-biased, but a majority of 4- to 9-year-olds are aware of this (Thompson & Zerbinos, 1997).

What is surprising is that educational television has not done the job one would expect regarding gender-stereotyping. Think of "Sesame Street," the most celebrated and long-running exemplar of educational programming. How many muppets are female? An analysis of 15 randomly selected segments aired between November 1992 and May 1993 revealed that male characters appeared on the show twice as often as female characters (Jones, et al., 1994). More disturbing, those male characters disproportionately dominated primary roles. Examining the roles these characters played, most were gender-stereotyped; characters were ten times more likely to appear in stereotyped than in nonstereotyped roles.

"Sesame Street" is not the only culprit. Another study explored five episodes of four children's educational science programs ("Mr. Wizard's World," "Beakman's World," "Bill Nye the Science Guy," and "Newton's Apple") (Steinke & Long, 1995). Two of every three adult scientists was a man, and three times as many male as female characters appeared on these shows. Fully 84% of the female characters were relegated to the secondary roles of students, laboratory assistants, and science writers.

The marketing of toys to children also is highly gender specific. Advertisers know that children prefer children as the spokespersons for products pitched toward them, and fully 98% of toy ads depict ordinary children in the act of play (Kline, 1993). Toys aimed at boys are pitched by boys; "girls'" toys by girls. Children of color are largely invisible in children's commercials (O'Connor, 1989). Furthermore, most toy ads are gender segregated; only 23% of ads include characters of both sexes, and these ads are almost exclusively for traditional toys (e.g., pogo sticks and slinky) (Kline, 1993). This is true for the packaging and cataloguing of toys as well (Schwartz & Markham, 1985)—look through a toy catalogue and note how often you see girls with power rangers and boys with Barbies (Smith, 1992). The kinds of fantasy play promoted for boys' and girls' toys also differ, with boys' ads stressing the stereotyped activities of working, building, managing, and battling and girls' commercials depicting nurturance, grooming, mothering, and theatrics (Kline, 1993).

The gender-specific audience for ads is so clear that children can identify an ad as appropriate or inappropriate for their own gender without knowing the product being pitched. Advertisements aimed at girls rely on fades and dissolves, background music, and female narration. In contrast, commercials targeted toward boys include rapid action, frequent cuts, loud music, sound effects, and quick scene changes (Welch, Huston-Stein, Wright, & Plehal, 1979). When children as young as 6 are exposed to these differing presentational forms, even without the inclusion of gender-typed products, they know whether or not the ad is designed for their gender (Huston, Greer, Wright, Welch, & Ross, 1984). Knowing of this research, I am now much less amazed when I watch my children, playing in front of an unwatched tv set, suddenly stop their play and become engrossed in a commercial for a gender-congruent toy.

Summing up, there is substantial research evidence, even through the 1980s and into the 1990s, supporting the contention that socializing agents, in general, treat girls and boys differently, with boys typically being advantaged relative to girls. Of course, there are exceptions to this rule, but remember that most of us are unaware of all the messages we send and receive everyday through the barrage of "little things" we do and see. Furthermore, as a parent, I am becoming increasingly cognizant that as my children age, I have less and less control over what they encounter. Socialization clearly is a process spread throughout our entire culture.

Gender-Typed Children?

I believe that I've offered a compelling case in support of the social learning theorists' supposition that girls and boys are treated differently by socialization agents, even into the 1990s. Turning to their second claim, do girls and boys think and act differently? If they are treated differently, we would expect them to turn out differently. Are there recent data to confirm this predicted outcome?

Differences in the interests, preferences, and activities of children begin early. During their first year of life, children begin to be aware that there are two distinct gender roles (Poulin-Dubois, Serbin, Kenyon, & Derbyshire, 1994). This understanding becomes more stable and expansive through the preschool years as even 3-year-olds, especially boys, prefer to imitate same-sex models more than other-sex ones (Bussey & Bandura, 1984). Preschoolers describe infants and animals in line with gender stereotypes: girl babies, dogs, and horses are depicted as smaller, slower, weaker, quieter, and softer than their male counterparts (Cowan & Hoffman, 1986; Fagot & Leinbach, 1995). Children as young as 2- to 3-years old prefer gender-typed games and toys (O'Keefe & Hyde, 1983). This is true for both African American and white 4- to 8-year-olds (Emmerich & Shepard, 1984) and for children in both England and Hungary (Turner, Gervai, & Hinde, 1993).

When children enter school and begin to write stories of their own, subtle gender-typed patterns emerge. Their stories show a preference for males. Although girls write about more female characters than do boys, male protagonists dominate for both sexes (Trepanier & Romatowski, 1985). Furthermore, male characters do more: 87% of the 127 different occupations assigned to characters in children's made-up stories went to males including doctor, astronaut, dentist, clown, professor, and police officer. Those few occupations assigned to girls also fit gendered occupational stereotypes: for example, princess, cook, nurse, babysitter, and teacher. (Somehow, I don't regard princess as a realistic occupational choice.)

The dominant pattern among over 800 children, aged 5 to 15, who were asked to note how moms and dads differ, associated fathers with discipline and mothers with child care, housework, being loving, and traditional jobs (e.g., hairdressing and typing) (Goldman & Goldman, 1983). It's not surprising then that even as kindergartners, girls tend to aspire to traditional female careers (Stroeher, 1994). Finally, children, including both African Americans and whites (Emmerich & Shepard, 1984), prefer same-sex over other-sex playmates (Maccoby, 1990). Overall, two different types of children emerge: girls and boys.

The Causal Link

The evidence that socializing agents treat girls and boys differently and that they indeed act differently seems incontrovertible. But the key supposition of social learning theory is that it is the agents themselves who *cause* these gender-typing differences to be manifest. Since we ethically and practically can't randomly assign children to different forms of socialization, the critical experimental test of this linkage cannot be conducted. However, two types of studies can inform our understanding: (1) short-term experiments exposing participants to stereotyped images and measuring their impact and (2) correlational studies exploring the amount of exposure a child has to gender-typed socializing agents. The latter approach predicts that the more experience a child has with gender-typing agents, the more she or he will exhibit gender-typed behavior. Across both types of studies, *exposure* is the key element.

A few short-term experiments do find a link between exposure to sexist displays and responses from adult audiences. In one experiment, women watched one of four replicas of ongoing television commercials, either as actually shown on tv or with gender roles reversed. Women exposed to the traditional ads wrote essays imagining their lives 10 years in the future that de-emphasized achievement relative to those who viewed the counter-stereotyped ads (Geis, Brown, Jennings, & Porter, 1984). A parallel experiment exposed undergraduates to actual rock videos that portrayed women as sex objects or neutral videos. Again, the first perpetuated gender stereotypes, this time involving chivalry (Hansen & Hansen, 1988).

Turning to correlational studies, age should be indicative of greater exposure.

TABLE 3.2   Percentage of Children Assigning Each Occupation to a Male Doll

Occupation	2- and 3-year-olds	4- and 5-year-olds	6- and 7-year-olds
Doctor	67	79	84
Police	67	90	92
Mayor	61	79	91
Basketball player	83	90	99
Construction worker	78	98	97
Secretary	33	34	04
Teacher	22	10	06
Dancer	39	10	09
Model	33	28	34
Librarian	56	16	03

Source: L. D. Gettys and A. Cann, *Sex Roles,* 7, pps. 301–308, 1981. Table 3.2, p. 31. Printed with permission of Plenum Publishing Corp.

Arguably, older children have had more chances to be influenced by gender-typed agents than younger ones. One common procedure asks children to assign occupations to either a female or male doll. As we can see in Table 3.2, even the majority of 2-year-olds point to the male doll as a basketball player and construction worker. Children's stereotypes of occupational gender-typing persist in 1994 and are consistent with actual gender-typing in the labor force (Reid, 1995). My daughter, Kate, at age 3 argued that women couldn't play basketball, citing the fact that she had never seen them play on television. By 6 to 7 years old, these occupational gender stereotypes are even more solidly entrenched (Gettys & Cann, 1981). Subsequent research looking at other gendered activities found a similar pattern until about fifth grade when children were more likely to insist that activities could be done by either sex (Archer, 1984). Overall, the general pattern through the early school years is that gender-typing increases as children age (Carter & Levy, 1988; Martin, 1993; Martin, Wood, & Little, 1990).

Another indicator of exposure is amount of television viewing. We might expect heavy viewers of this gender-typed medium to hold more stereotyped attitudes than light viewers. Heavy viewing is related to more sexist views of women's roles in society (Signorielli, 1989) and to children's attitudes toward the gender-typing of household chores as well as what they themselves report doing (Signorielli & Lears, 1992). In addition, which television shows children watch is important; those who watch more stereotyped programs tend to describe themselves in more traditional terms (Ross, Anderson, & Wisocki, 1982). Although these findings are consistent with what we would expect based on social learning theory, it also is possible that parents who do less gender-typing themselves discourage television viewing or that children who are less gender-typed themselves choose less stereotypic programming or find television less interesting, especially when it clashes with their view of the world. Clearly television viewing and gender stereotyping are related, but determining the causal pattern is difficult.

Finally, researchers have examined maternal employment arguing that children, especially girls, exposed to nontraditional parents, especially mothers, will be less gender-typed. Indeed, young girls with employed mothers make fewer gender-typed activity attributions and aspire to less traditional occupations for themselves, especially if their mothers are nontraditionally employed (Barak, Feldman, & Noy, 1991; Selkow, 1984), compared to girls with full-time homemakers for moms (Hoffman, 1989). Adolescents whose mothers supervise employees report more egalitarian attitudes than adolescents whose moms are committed primarily to homemaking (Tuck, Rolfe, & Adair, 1994). Children whose mothers model nontraditional activities in the home (e.g., mow the lawn) (Serbin, Powlishta, & Gulko, 1993) or who hold egalitarian attitudes (Steele & Barling, 1996) are less likely to show gender-typed preferences for themselves. Analyzing daily phone interviews with 9- to 11-year-olds, fathers in single-earner families spend more time with their sons, in contrast to fathers in dual-earner couples who spend equal amounts of time with their daughters and sons (Crouter & Crowley, 1990). Not surprisingly, nontraditional families include nontraditional children.

The bottom line is that the causal link between what we know socializing agents do and what children think and do is tenuous. There is ample evidence that socializing agents do not treat girls and boys similarly and also evidence that girls and boys are gender-typed. It seems logical that the former causes the latter, but other possibilities exist. Maybe children themselves act differently (because of their biologies or how they think), and socializing agents are simply picking up on those differences. Maybe there are outside factors that simultaneously affect both children and these socializing agents. The safest conclusion proposes a circular pattern: socializing agents influence what children think, feel, and do (as social learning theory posits) *and* these children, in turn, affect how socializing agents respond to them (see Figure 3.2).

The second half of this circular causal pattern (whereby children influence agents) points to the active role that most psychologists assume children play in their own socialization. A shortcoming of social learning theory is that it conceives of children as passive receptors of what others do to them, similar to rats pressing a lever for food. On the other hand, by rooting gender-typing in agents outside the child, social learning theorists open up realistic prospects for social change aimed at changing socializing agents. It is at least theoretically conceivable that if we eliminate sexism in socializing agents, sexism in our children would disappear.

FIGURE 3.2
A likely circular causal pattern exists between gender-typed socializing agents and gender-typed children.

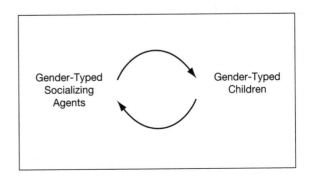

COGNITIVE DEVELOPMENTAL THEORY

The central concept for cognitive developmental theorists is **schema**—an internal cognitive framework that organizes and helps us understand the world (Bem, 1981). Schemas spontaneously develop as we need them, that is, whenever we encounter new information that doesn't fit into our existing view of the world. Once formed, schemas are shaped through two processes: **assimilation** and **accommodation**. New information is assimilated into an existing schema without changing the original schema. In contrast, schemas themselves can be adjusted to accommodate new, discordant information.

For example, a child's schema that four-legged animals are dogs would assimilate that child's first exposure to a German Shepard; the obviously limited schema would remain unchanged. However, when that child points to a sheep, wrongly declares that it is a dog (sheepdog?), and is informed otherwise, she may accommodate this discrepant information by refining her original schema to note that dogs are four-legged animals that bark and sheep are four-legged animals that baah. Her animal schema thus is expanded and refined. Schemas change in response to environmental and social stimuli, and children play an active role in creating and shaping their schemas (Piaget, 1954). Furthermore, cognitive developmental theorists believe that development occurs in **stages**. Children can only accommodate and assimilate information they are maturationally ready to handle.

Applying cognitive developmental theory to our topic, gender is conceptualized as one kind of schema (Kohlberg, 1966). In the first stage, children begin to form ideas about their own gender identity around 18 months to 2 years, first by identifying themselves as a girl or boy, then turning to others around them (Slaby & Frey, 1975). However, gender identity is not yet stable. In the second stage, lasting from about 2- to 5-years old, children become more accurate at gender differentiation and labeling (Etaugh & Duits, 1990), but still make errors that adults find memorable. For example, my son, Dan, at age 3 declared that he wanted to be a mom when he grew up (undaunted by the fact that he'd have to change his sex). When we challenged him on this, he thought for a moment and conceded that if he couldn't be a mother, he'd settle for being a lion. Who knew where to go with that one!

In the final stage at around 6- to 7-years old, children will not make my son's mistake; they have achieved **gender constancy**—the understanding that gender is a permanent part of one's identity. Clothes, haircuts, names, earrings, etc. cannot alter one's sex. With the mastery of gender constancy, cognitive developmental theorists assert that children develop a gender-based cognitive system that supports gender-congruent activities, attributes, and peers. For example, a girl who has achieved gender constancy also might prefer dolls over trucks, being nice over rough, and playing with girls rather than boys because these patterns fit nicely into her salient gender schema. The same evidence used by social learning theorists to support the prediction that children are gender-typed is interpreted by cognitive developmentalists to confirm the existence of a coherent gender schema.

Given that achievement of gender constancy is necessary for a child to make consistent gender-typed choices and attributions, the age at which gender-typed behaviors emerge is important to cognitive developmentalists. If the stagewise assumptions of cognitive developmental theory are correct, children should show consistent patterns of gender-typing only after ages 6 to 7 (the age at which they have mastered gender constancy). But, the timing of such gendered thinking does not fit as well with the data as cognitive developmentalists might like (see for example Levy & Carter, 1989; Martin & Little, 1990). We have seen that gendered preferences and activities appear in children as young as 2- to 3-years old, presumably before they have acquired gender constancy.

Cognitive developmental theory avoids the criticism of social learning theory's assumed passivity by describing children who actively think about, construct, and refine their own views of the world. They propose that the gender-typing we find in children's behavior emanates from within children themselves, rather than being foisted upon them by external socializing agents. Although both cognitive developmental and social learning theorists draw on much of the same empirical body of research to support their claims that children are gender-typed, the critical difference between them resides in the role played by the child. There is little disagreement among psychologists that children actively participate in their own socialization, a key contribution of cognitive developmental theorists.

GENDER SCHEMA THEORY

Social learning theory highlights the importance of socializing agents, and cognitive developmental theory proposes that children actively think about and organize their worlds. As we have seen, each alone has shortcomings. Socializing agents seem to represent only part of the picture as all frustrated parents, who watch their children come home with ideas they never heard at home, know. Further, children come up with ways of seeing things we never imagined because they do more than passively take in what they see others do. Sandra Bem's (1981) theory fills in some of these gaps by combining the best of both theories.

Why do children have a gender schema? Why not an eye-color schema or a shoe-size schema? Bem's simple answer is because gender is so salient and pervasive in our culture: "gender has come to have cognitive primacy over many other social categories because the culture has made it so" (Bem, 1985, p. 212). We all have learned what characteristics are appropriate for women (e.g., caring) and men (e.g., assertiveness), what activities are female-defined (sewing) and male-defined (football), what jobs belong to women (nursing) and men (engineering), and what physical features describe women (frail) and men (strong) (Deaux & Lewis, 1984). Consistent with this reasoning, degree of acculturation of Asian American women is associated with gender-typing; those more in tune with American culture display more Americanized gender stereotyping (Gue, 1985). Considering the role of culture more broadly, gender schema theory is the most useful approach for bringing in multicultural elements beyond gender such as the impact of race and ethnicity, class, religion, etc., on socialization processes (Reid et al., 1995). Because the importance of gender is socially constructed, its centrality can be altered by social change—an important point to which we'll return.

Fundamentally, Sandra Bem argues that gender-typing takes place within a specific cultural context so that femininity and masculinity are expressed in ways unique to that context. In Western culture, our social context is **gender polarized**, that is, we tend to regard gender as something that comes in only two forms (female and male) and we think that these two types are both inclusive of everyone and mutually exclusive (nonoverlapping) (Bem, 1993). Although we often think of this duality as obvious and "natural," we saw in Chapter 2 that some other cultures consider a multiplicity of sexes.[6]

However, within our culture, gender polarization defines "mutually exclusive scripts for being male and female" and "any person or behavior that deviates from these scripts as problematic" (Bem, 1993, pp. 80–81). It dichotomizes not only people, but also what people do. Furthermore, gender polarization, by stressing differences between women and men, girls and boys, glosses over differences within these groups, that is differences among women, among girls, among men, and among boys. It also pressures all of us to exaggerate our femaleness or maleness so that we prove ourselves as "real" women and men. (This readily can be extended to challenges to gender identity for lesbians, stereotyped as "butch," and gay men, stereotyped as effeminate.)

Because society stresses gender, children pick up on it and learn to develop a schema around it. In other words, *children develop a gender schema by internalizing the gender polarization of our culture* (Bem, 1993, p. 125). This schema reflects children's culture and, in turn, guides their perceptions of both themselves and their social worlds. This schema functions as an anticipatory structure in that it is ready to search for and assimilate information to fit into its existing framework. Gender-schematic children interpret their perceptions against their schema. They don't need external socializing agents to shape their gendered behavior, rather they do it themselves. Conforming to the specific dictates of their schema, children themselves begin to act in gender-congruent ways. Thus the cycle is complete: the sociocultural gender-typing that began the process is reaffirmed through the gender-appropriate behavior of gender-typed children (see Figure 3.3).

A clever study showed how powerfully our gender schema can shape what we perceive. Five- and six-year-old children were shown line drawings of children engaged in activities that were either consistent with gender stereotypes (e.g., a girl baking) or inconsistent (e.g., a girl boxing) (Martin & Halverson, 1983). A week later, they were asked to describe the pictures they had seen. Many children distorted their recall of the gender-inconsistent pictures, for example, by incorrectly reporting that a boy was boxing.

Because of individual variations in how rigidly gender socialized we are, we all differ in how strong our gender schema is. Read through the following list of 14 words, look away, then write down as many as you can recall:

---

[6] To further stretch your imagination here, check out Ursula LeGuin's (1994) science-fiction novel, *The Left Hand of Darkness*, which describes a society where people routinely switch sexes.

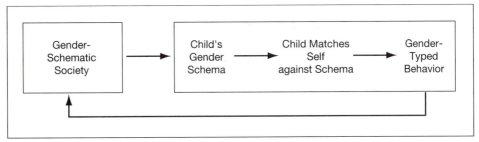

FIGURE 3.3 A diagram of gender-identity development according to gender schema theory. *Source:* Developed from S. L. Bem (1981). Gender schema theory: A cognitive account of sex typing. *Psychological Review*, 88, 354–364. Copyright © 1981 by the American Psychological Association. Adapted with permission.

James, butterfly, trousers, Mary, ant, Peter, blushing, gorilla, stepping, Christine, hurling, pig, sweater, blouse

Bem (1981) presented 61 words like these in random order to students. Those who described themselves in gender-traditional terms listed the words they recalled in clusters defined by gender: masculine words (James, trousers, Peter, gorilla, hurling), feminine words (butterfly, Mary, blushing, Christine, blouse), and gender-neutral words (ant, stepping, pig, sweater) appeared together on their answer sheets. Those who described themselves in ways that did not conform to gendered patterns (for example, women· who thought of themselves as both assertive and caring) also listed the words they recalled in clusters, but clusters defined by commonalties other than gender (e.g., names, clothes, animals, verbs). Both groups remembered the same number of words; the difference was in how they linked them together to organize their memories. Bem referred to the former group who drew heavily upon gender connections as **gender-schematic** as opposed to the latter **gender-*a*schematic** people. Similar patterns of recall have been found with children as young as preschoolers (Carter & Levy, 1991; Levy, 1994) and in other tests with adults (Frable & Bem, 1985).

My daughter, Kate, encountered a most amazing example of gender-schematic thinking when she was in kindergarten. Every week a different "letter person" visited her classroom. When Mr. T came, they learned that Mr. T liked lots of things starting with the letter "t": tomatoes, turquoise, turtles, etc. Kate excitedly reported on the interests of each character: Mr. T, Mr. B., Mr. M, etc., becoming increasingly agitated that no "girl" characters had shown up. Needless to say, she was ecstatic when "Miss A" appeared, soon followed by "Miss E." Unbelievably, someone had gendered the alphabet: consonants were boys and vowels were girls! (The school told me that this was part of a nationwide program, not the machination of some clueless teacher.) No matter how important we claimed vowels to be ("You can't make a word without one"), Kate was crushed that there were fully 21 boy-letters and only 5 girls. (I can't help but wonder if the school would have been as tolerant of this system if racial or class dualities had been used. It's easy and instructive to consider these kinds of absurd statements here.)

REMAINING QUESTIONS

Having examined these four major theories of gender-identity development (psychoanalysis, social learning, cognitive developmental, and gender schema), some basic questions emerge. Which of these four theories is right? Is sexist socialization the same for girls and boys? And most practically, how do we break the cycle of sexist socialization?

Which Theory?

Which theory is right? The seemingly simple answer to this question is that they all are. Each theory adds a few pieces to a not-so-simple puzzle. Chodorow highlights familial relationships stressing sexuality and *affect,* that is, how feelings become associated with our gender identities. Social learning theorists focus on what we do as women and men, girls and boys, explaining how we learn gendered *behaviors.* Cognitive developmentalists stress our thoughts about gender noting how *cognitive* processes construct our gender identities. Gender schema theory combines cognitive and behavioral elements and brings in a broader *societal* view of socialization processes. Each tells part of the story of gender identity and role development, and each may help us understand certain aspects of ourselves better than the others. Together these theories create a holistic human psychology that helps us understand all three core aspects of who we are: how we think, feel, and act—all within the context of our culture.

At least four common perspectives are shared by these four theories. First, each posits that gender identity and roles are *learned* as opposed to being biologically determined. Second, learning occurs through human interaction. Third, each assumes that how we think, feel, and act occurs within a specific social context; using the terms we discussed in Chapter 1, gender identity and roles are *socially constructed.* Childhood socialization does not take place in a vacuum; rather, it takes place in relation to others. Furthermore, social institutions or contexts shape our relationships with others. Fourth, each emphasizes the importance of *childhood* as a formative stage in personality development.

Same for Girls and Boys?

Is sexist socialization the same for girls and boys? Everyday experience tells us that boy "sissies" are sanctioned more harshly than girl "tomboys," and researchers have confirmed this observation (Fagot, 1985; Stoddart & Turiel, 1985). But, why? Some developmental psychologists point to the overall tendency in our society to prize masculine and devalue feminine activities. When girls seek out masculine activities, they understandably are going for what our society values. When boys participate in the feminine sphere, they are both rejecting their valuable birthright and settling for less (Bem, 1993, pp. 149–151).

Homophobic fears also may underlie this difference, with socializing agents anxious that masculine interests by girls and feminine leanings in boys may be early signs of adult homosexuality. This speculation is consistent with the combination of findings that more fathers insist that sons do not violate gender-role dictates for play

(Lytton & Romney, 1991; Martin, 1990; Turner & Gervai, 1995) and that more men are homophobic than women (Herek, 1988). In general, parental homophobia and traditional gender-role attitudes go hand-in-hand (Holtzen & Agresti, 1990). These fears are aggravated when researchers link feminine toy choices with adult male homosexuality in fundamentally flawed research (e.g., Bailey & Zucker, 1995). It is common for researchers to forward these kinds of conclusions based on retrospective accounts from parents who, knowing that their adult child is gay, understandably may look back at that child's past through a distorted lens, recalling and exaggerating cross-gender acts to the exclusion of same-gender behaviors. For example, it is plausible that parents may "remember" that their gay son played with dolls more often than their heterosexual son, not because their play actually differed, but because parents' hindsight is distorted by their knowledge that their sons "turned out" differently.

When we think about conformity to gender-role expectations, we may want to consider who has the most to gain from adhering to these norms. Would I benefit my son as much as my daughter by following rigid gendered dictates in American culture? Given our valuation of those traits and behaviors that accompany the masculine role, clearly my son has more to gain by sticking to them. When we factor in other forms of oppression, it becomes more and more understandable that women and girls, as well as those subordinated based on other statuses (such as race and sexual orientation), would have even less to gain by promoting gender polarization.

Breaking the Cycle?

How then do we break the cycle of sexist socialization? All four theorists talk about a self-perpetuating cycle that serves to maintain the gender-typing of generation after generation of children. Chodorow argues that we can break this cycle by engaging in dual-parenting so that children have both female and male models of nurturing (be they parents or other significant people). Cognitive developmental theorists call for changing gender schemas, and social learning theorists focus on changing socializing agents. But for those of us who are parents, we know that we control an ever-shrinking portion of our children's socialization. There are powerful forces out there (schools, friends, and the media) that seem to effortlessly derail even our most dedicated efforts.

If socialization is confined to childhood, then activists might question why we should forsake generations of adults, whose socialization is complete, in hopes that the next generation will transcend our culture. Indeed, this is the catch-22 of turning to socialization for broad social changes toward nonsexism: *How do we socialize children to be nonsexist within a sexist context?* Isn't socialization the *passing on* of one's culture to the next generation (Barry, Bacon, & Child, 1957; Parsons & Bales, 1955; Whiting & Edwards, 1988)? How do we do that within a sexist culture? And, even if we are successful with a few children, aren't we condemning them to being regarded as social deviates or at least as being somehow basically different from others? How do these children cope with being out of synchrony with the majority in their culture?

Sandra Bem's (1983) gender schema theory helps us tackle at least some of these questions by giving us some pointers on how to "raise gender-aschematic children in a gender-schematic society." First, Bem suggests that we teach our children that the only differences between women and men, girls and boys are *anatomical* and *reproductive*. My favorite Berenstain Bears book for young children does this with poetic flair (Berenstain & Berenstain, 1974, pp. 2–11):

> Every single bear we see is a he bear or a she.
> Every single bear we see has lots of things to do and be.
> I'm a father. I'm a he. A *father's* something *you* [pointing to Brother bear] could be.
> I'm a mother. I'm a she. A *mother's* something *you* [pointing to Sister bear] could be...
> But there are other things to be. . . .
> We could . . . fix a clock, paint a door, build a house, have a store.
> Drive a dump truck, drive a crane, bulldoze roads, drive a train. . . .

The litany of jobs goes on and on, picturing women and men bears doing all sorts of gender-typical and atypical activities. The point is obvious to any preschooler: beyond our reproductive options, our potentials are unbounded by our gender. They also are not dictated by the clothes we wear, the length of our hair, what we like and dislike, who our friends are, etc.

Two lessons are forwarded by this approach: (1) What makes us female and male is limited to scant anatomical and reproductive differences; and (2) These differences have very little real bearing on our opportunities, our identities, and so on. This second point is critical to avoid regressing to biological essentialism and the reassertion that "anatomy is destiny" (Lott, 1997). (Let me warn you that this makes for some interesting trips to the zoo with young children who insist on correctly identifying the sex of every animal and on broadcasting their discoveries.)

Teaching anatomical difference as the defining, but not constraining, feature of sex counters the pervasive tendency for most children to learn to distinguish the sexes by relying on external indicators such as clothing, interests, and hairstyles. Bem (1989) illustrated how persistently some children overrely on exterior signs of gender. She showed children pictures of a nude toddler, followed by pictures of the same toddler outfitted to look like a boy or a girl. Gender-schematic children misidentified the anatomically known boy as a girl when he wore a cheap wig with ponytails (see the photo of a toddler boy on the next page). Bem (1993) concluded:

> . . . although fully 80 percent of American two-year-olds can readily distinguish males from females on the basis of purely cultural cues like hairstyle and clothing, as many as 50 percent of American three- and four-year-olds still fail to distinguish males from females if all they have to go on are biologically natural cues like genitalia and body physique (p. 114).

Teaching children to rely on external cues to determine gender can lead to some humorous, but telling declarations by children. Bem (1993, p. 149) relates the story of her son who wore barrettes in his hair to nursery school where he was hounded by another boy to a point where her son exposed his genitals to "prove" his maleness. Undeterred by what should have been the definitive proof, the other boy persisted: "Everybody has a penis; only girls wear barrettes."

Furthermore, relying on external, changeable cues to determine another's sex conveys a message that "being male or female is something to work at, to accomplish, and to be sure not to lose, rather than something one *is* biologically" (Bem,

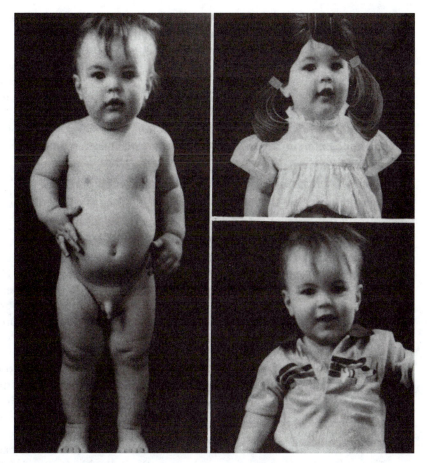

Some children insist that the coifed child is a girl, even after having seen the boy nude.

1993, p. 148). Bem argues that such fear of gender bending (confusing one's gender) contributes to adults' attempts to prove that they are "real" women and men by limiting their choices to those deemed gender appropriate, thus reinforcing rather than challenging stereotypes. My 6'6" husband claims that his height liberates him from demands to prove his masculinity so that many traditional men accept his feminism without questioning his masculinity.

In contrast, children who define sex by anatomical differences avoid relying on restrictive stereotypes to define another's gender (Bem, 1989). Only about half the 3- through early 5-year-olds tested could correctly identify the sex of toddlers who were nude from the waist down. But of the children who made correct identifications, fully 74% showed gender constancy as they accurately named the sex of a child they had seen nude, even when that child was dressed or coifed to look like the other sex.

A second positive strategy caregivers can adopt is to provide children with **alternative schemas** to a gender schema. One such alternative is an **individual-differences schema**. This schema is constructed around the idea that individuals are unique so that what defines them is their own interests, preferences, and activities, not necessarily those dictated by their gender. Accordingly, Billy likes football because Billy likes football, not because he is a boy. Similarly, Billy likes cooking because Billy likes cooking, not because Billy is a sissy. (My kids have even discovered advantages from adopting this perspective. They tell me that they don't like zucchini because it doesn't taste good to them; just because I like it, doesn't mean they should like it too. Different strokes for different folks.)

A **cultural-relativism schema** helps children understand that people in different cultures and different historical times held different beliefs about what was appropriate for women and men, girls and boys to do. My daughter is stunned by videos like "Anne of Green Gables," which shows orphaned Anne being shunted from family to family to help with the housework, and "League of Their Own," where women baseball players are trivialized with makeup and skirted uniforms that offer no protection against severe bruises from sliding into base (Randle, 1992). The lesson such exposure to variety teaches is that no one point of view is sacrosanct.

A third alternative schema helps children deal with their difference from more strongly gender-typed peers, teachers, and others: a **sexism schema**. Having a sexism schema, a way to label unfair treatment as sexist, discourages children from internalizing sexist ideas. For example, a substitute gym teacher told my fourth-grade daughter's class that boys were good at many sports because they had more experience playing them; in contrast, girls' expertise was limited to jumping rope. Combine this with the fact that much more attention is afforded male than female athletes, and my daughter eventually could believe this to be true. This stereotype would be reinforced by her not participating in sports, thus becoming incompetent at them. Instead Kate's fine-tuned sexism antenna went up, she discussed the situation with us at home that night, and the next day she complained to her teacher. Having a wonderfully sensitive teacher, her teacher soon discovered that other girls were disturbed by the comment and invited the gym teacher to talk to the class. This of course opened up a whole discussion about women and sports. Similarly, Sandra Bem's son didn't discard his barrettes just because another boy was being sexist about it. The bottom line is that, by having a well-developed sexism schema, my daughter (and I hope my son also) will not assimilate into a gender schema all the sexist things out there I can't stop them from being exposed to.[7]

CHAPTER SUMMARY

We reviewed a lot of compelling evidence in this chapter that writes two different scripts for growing up female and male in American culture. Chodorow's psychoanalytic approach describes two different personality configurations resulting from parent-child socialization practices: a girls' version that stresses nurturance and relational thinking and a boys' version that emphasizes autonomy, detachment, and

---

[7] For an interesting discussion by feminists and their sons about raising nonsexist sons, see *Ms.* magazine, November/ December, 1993. Also see Audre Lorde's (1995) essay on raising her son from the perspective of an African American, lesbian mother.

rational thinking. Social learning theorists highlight the roles socialization agents (including parents, schools, peers, and the media) play in creating gender-typed children, that is, girls who engage in feminine behaviors and boys who exhibit masculine ones. Cognitive developmental theorists assign children a more active role in their own socialization, arguing that a cognitive schema focused on gender writes different scripts for girls and boys. Gender schema theory considers the social context in which socialization occurs, suggesting that gender schemas are formed and used by children because our society polarizes people along gendered lines. A holistic approach to understanding the role of socialization in shaping both gender identity and gender roles draws on all four of these theories.

We also saw that sexist and homophobic values influence these processes and that deviations by boys are tolerated less than cross-gender behaviors by girls. We considered some of the challenges to feminists interested in changing socialization practices by grappling with the dilemma of eliminating sexist socialization when socialization itself is reflective of and surrounded by a sexist culture. Potential remedies inferred from this thinking include confining difference to minimized anatomical and reproductive distinctions and developing alternative schemas, such as a sexism schema.

On a personal note, people often smile at me knowingly and assert: "Now that you have a boy and a girl, you must realize that there's something about girls that makes them different from boys," implying a presumably undeniable and immutable biological difference. Recognizing that my own children are temperamentally quite different and that biology must have played some role in this, I always smile back and conclude: "Yes, Kate is Kate and Dan is Dan." Gendering children to me is like gendering the alphabet—why do it? Rather let each child be whatever she or he becomes, neither restricted by nor promoted by their sex.

Take a moment to answer the following question once more.

> When the sexes differ in some way, how likely is it that the difference is due to the ways boys/men and girls/women are socialized (how they are treated by parents and others)?
>
> | 1 | 2 | 3 | 4 | 5 | 6 | 7 |
> |---|---|---|---|---|---|---|
> | not at all likely | | | | | | very likely |

Now turn back to the first page of Chapter 2 to compare your answers. Whether your answer changed or not, at least this chapter provided some ways to think about socialization processes as well as research evidence showing the influence of these processes on all of us.

Before we move on in this book, I want to point out that there is a third possible explanation for differences between women and girls, men and boys that Chapters 2 and 3 overlook. While it is common to frame this discussion in terms of nature (biology) or nurture (socialization), a third possibility, *opportunities,* was included in the questions at the start of Chapter 2. Everything we've learned did not happen in our childhood. Everything that influenced and is influencing us is not rooted in our past. Rather, opportunities in our present lives set a stage for us as we continue to learn and grow. This life-long developmental process is the focus of the next chapter. In Chapter 4 and beyond, we'll see the influence of this third factor whenever we talk about the impact of **social context** and opportunities, that is, factors in our present social environment that affect how we think, feel, and act now as adult women and men. In Chapter 5, we'll take a closer look at some examples of how social context sets the stage for apparent gender differences.

FOUR

CHANGES ACROSS THE LIFE COURSE

Women's Lives from Adolescence through Old Age

- Do you enjoy doing things for old people?
- Do you expect to feel good about yourself when you're old?
- Do you ever dread looking old?
- Do you fear that when you're old all your friends will be gone?

Each of these questions explores your attitudes about getting older. Is it something you look forward to, accept as inevitable, or actively dread? Attitudes toward aging fall into four categories represented by each of the questions above: fear of old people, psychological concerns about growing older, dread of changes in physical appearance, and fear of loss, respectively (Lasher & Faulkender, 1993). Despite all the folk lore suggesting that growing older is more threatening for women, women actually answer questions like these (and the 16 others that make up the Anxiety toward Aging Scale) more favorably than do men (Lasher & Faulkender, 1993).

My goals in this chapter are twofold: (1) to examine how gender identity changes across women's and men's lives and (2) to explore the life work women do across the course of their lives. For too long, psychologists focused on development across childhood and into adolescence without considering life processes that span our entire lives. In contrast, a **lifespan** perspective regards aging as an active and individualized process. Each of us will work out our own life paths in response to our own interests and desires, to the opportunities that present themselves, and to our broader culture (George, 1996). We'll make choices that will move us along certain trajectories and away from others, sometimes in patterns that are neither linear nor progressive. This variability across individuals and across generations doesn't fit with a pattern of clear development whereby people move through an invariant progression of stages toward some higher goal. Understanding how others have worked through their own aging may give us a fuller picture of what our present choices may lead to and what our future options may be.

Two conceptually distinct influences are intermeshed in discussions of age-related change. How people grapple with their life's work may be affected by their chronological age (the effects of **age** itself) and by their experiences because they matured during a specific time period (the effects of a specific **cohort** or generation with its own unique history). Emphasizing one over the other possibility may lead to very different expectations. For example, if a change is indeed related to age, then we would expect most people around that age to experience similar changes. If, in contrast, change is bound to cohort, we would expect the change being studied to result only for those with shared historical experiences.

For example, women in their late 60s recorded retrospective accounts of their work lives. None of the married women studied described uninterrupted, continuous career paths compared to fully 55% of the never married women (Keating & Jeffrey, 1983). These women's work lives spanned across a world war and the baby boom of the late 1940s through 1960s. Do you think their work patterns will parallel those of current high-school girls who expect to combine career and family (Bybee, Glick, & Zigler, 1990) or currently employed women, the majority of whom are employed even when they have preschoolers? Probably not. To extrapolate from this cohort of women born in the 1920s to successive cohorts of women would likely lead to faulty overgeneralizations about the continuity of women's work-force participation. Even women who share some of the same major life events, like a world war, may be affected differently depending on where they were in their life course at the time of the event (Stewart & Healy, 1989). Such are the challenges and consequences of disentangling age-related and cohort-limited effects.

Is aging then an unpredictable, individualistic process that defies generalizations? There is a socially constructed, normative pattern expected for aging. This is captured in the concept of the **life course**, a cultural ideal of an age-related progression or sequence of roles and group memberships that an individual is expected to follow as she or he matures (Atchley, 1994). Clearly, we each forge our own unique path through life; following a national sample of high-school graduates across eight years, researchers found that it took fully 1,827 different sequences to capture the experiences of 7,095 women (Rindfuss, Swicegood, & Rosenfeld, 1987). Still, we share common expectations about when and in what order we do certain things. We even have laws dictating some of these, like when we can stop attending school, start drinking alcohol, get married, etc. A **time line** describing general life course periods appears in Figure 4.1. Additionally, we tend to hold expectations about when in the life course we will tackle various issues related to education, employment, and relationships. Try filling in your own paths, both what you have accomplished so far and projecting ahead to your future plans, by completing the three blank time lines in Figure 4.1.

FIGURE 4.1 Time lines of the life course. Note that thinner vertical lines indicate that the timing is discretionary. Fill in your own time lines for your education, employment, and relationships using both past actual experiences and projections for the future.

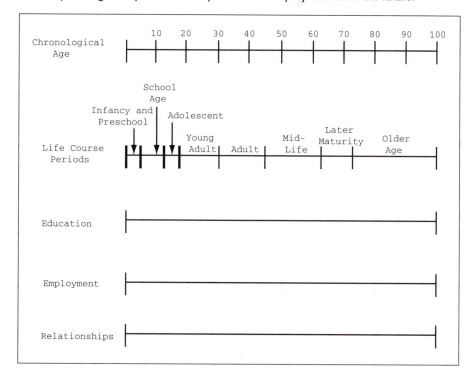

You may find some future projections in your time line hard to consider. I myself found it easy to project my goals for the next ten years, but was lost thinking about retirement and being without children in the house. Generally, adolescents make projections that carry them to about age 30; thinking beyond that becomes vague (Nurmi, 1991). For those at older ages, we tend to think concretely for about ten years into the future.

Although many concepts have been studied across the life course, we have spent a lot of time in Chapter 3 exploring the childhood development of gender identity (how we regard ourselves as female and male). Because of the centrality of this concept to a feminist psychology, I have chosen to explore this concept across the life courses of women and men. We'll then examine selected issues likely to involve women at certain periods of the life course.

GENDER IDENTITY ACROSS THE LIFE COURSE

In Chapter 3, we defined the gender identity of children as encompassing their gender label (e.g., I'm a girl, I'm a boy), their activities and interests (e.g., I like cooking/football), their personality characteristics (e.g., caring and assertiveness), and social relationships (e.g., I prefer to play with girls/boys). For adults, gender identity measures typically have focused on one of these (most often, personality attributions). *Does gender identity change across the life cycle?* First, let's consider how it is measured.

Measuring Gender Identity

One of the first measures of femininity and masculinity was the Mf subscale (Scale 5) of the Minnesota Multiphasic Personality Inventory (MMPI), a widely used personality inventory. The Mf scale conceptualizes masculinity and femininity as opposing endpoints on the same scale so that a very masculine person is, by definition, low in femininity. Items were selected based on differential endorsement of gender-linked activities; for example, the item, "I read sports magazines," was identified as masculine because more men than women said they engaged in this activity (Lachar, 1974). Arguing, without any solid evidence, that cross-gender characteristics are pathological, this scale originally was validated using 13 gay men to determine the feminine pole of the scale. Developed in 1943 and nominally updated in the 1990s, the Mf scale was the most commonly used measure of femininity and masculinity until the mid-1970s (Beere, 1990).

In the 1970s, many conventional assumptions about gender and gender roles were called into question by psychologists, leading to the independent development of two new scales. Sandra Bem introduced the *Bem Sex Role Inventory* (BSRI) in 1974, and it has become the most widely used measure.[1] At the conceptual heart of the BSRI is the assumption that masculinity and femininity are separate and unrelated dimensions so that an individual can score high on both, low on one and high on

---

[1] Beere (1990) lists 795 articles published across 12 years that used this scale.

the other, etc. To create the BSRI, college students rated traits according to how desirable they felt each was for women and for men in American society. Twenty items considered significantly more desirable for men defined masculinity; 20 items regarded as more desirable for women described femininity; and 20 filler items were rated as equally desirable. Masculine items include aggressive, ambitious, dominant, independent, self-reliant, and competitive; examples of feminine items are affectionate, childlike, flatterable, sympathetic, warm, and yielding. Are both sets equally flattering?

To complete the BSRI, respondents simply indicate if each trait is "never or almost never true" to "always or almost always true" of themselves on 7-point scales. Those who describe themselves more strongly on the masculine items than the feminine ones are considered masculine in their gender identity; feminine scorers do the reverse. To label those who describe themselves equally strongly as both masculine and feminine, Bem introduced to psychology the concept of **androgyny**. This measure defines androgyny then as the equal blending of masculine and feminine traits.

Simple to score and also widely used[2] is the *Personal Attributes Questionnaire* (PAQ) developed by Janet Spence and Robert Helmreich in 1974 to measure femininity and masculinity. The PAQ comprises eight masculine and eight feminine items.

Masculine	*Feminine*
independent	emotional
active	able to devote self completely to others
competitive	gentle
can make decisions easily	helpful to others
never gives up easily	kind
confident	aware of the feelings of others
feels superior	understanding of others
stands up well under pressure	warm in relations with others

Like the BSRI, separate feminine and masculine scores are calculated, and these are used together to categorize individuals as feminine, masculine, or androgynous (where androgyny involves *high* levels of both feminine and masculine characteristics).

When the PAQ was developed, all items were considered socially desirable in both genders. (For example, you don't see those demeaning items, like childlike, in the PAQ). When the scale was being constructed, items were chosen to represent the feminine scale because raters thought these characteristics were more common in women; masculine items, in men. However, when women and men actually completed the scale, some women scored high on the masculine items; some women scored low on the feminine items; some men scored high on the feminine items; and so on. Masculinity, although stereotyped as occurring more frequently in men, was not confined to men nor femininity to women. Reflecting the dispersion of masculinity and femininity across women and men, the difference between the scores

---

[2] Beere (1990) lists 238 articles published across 12 years that used this scale.

of women as a group and men as a group was small, and may even be shrinking over time. Furthermore, dispelling the assumptions of the MMPI, PAQ classifications are unrelated to sexual orientation; lesbians may be stereotyped as masculine, but there's nothing in the data to support this myth (Dancey, 1992). There is some evidence that African American women, on average, score high on the masculine items (Binion, 1990; deLeon, 1993).

The concept of androgyny took off through the late 1970s and into the 1980s. Androgynous people were expected to be more behaviorally flexible—for example, they played with kittens (a "feminine" task) and did not conform under pressure (a "masculine" task) (Bem, 1975). They were high in self-esteem and psychologically well-adjusted (Bem, 1977; Spence & Helmreich, 1978). Although it hasn't disappeared, the construct of androgyny has faded because of many serious measurement and conceptual problems. For example, the validity of the BSRI as a measure of femininity and masculinity among both Latina/Latino American and African American respondents (A.C. Harris, 1994) and across world cultures (Murphy-Bermer, Berman, Singh, & Pandy, 1992) has been questioned.

Just what the BSRI and PAQ measure is open to debate. In Chapter 3, we saw that Sandra Bem (1985) conceptualized gender identity in terms of **gender-schematicity** rather than masculinity-femininity. Gender-schematic people see themselves in gendered terms, such that gender-schematic men score high on the masculine items and low on the feminine ones; gender-schematic women do the opposite. In contrast, gender-*a*schematic women and men use a variety of adjectives to describe themselves, rather than relying on gender stereotypes. Differing from Bem, Janet Spence and Robert Helmreich (1980) have come to think of the PAQ as a measure of **instrumentality** (those who score high on the M items take charge and actively do things) and **expressiveness** (the F items measure caring and nurturing tendencies). Alice Eagly (1987) considers the same dichotomy in terms of **agentic** (people who are independent, active agents) and **communal** (people who work with others) orientations. You may want to reexamine the items of the PAQ to see if you think they fit with these reconceptualizations.

Whatever the interpretation, these scales remain rooted in their original construction—*they measure gender stereotypes* (i.e., what people in the 1970s thought were desirable characteristics for women and men) (Morawski, 1987). Thus they may be useful to the extent that they measure how much we stereotype ourselves along gender lines; they may not be so useful as presumed measures of true "inner" femininity or masculinity (Morawski, 1987). Furthermore, these concepts may be inextricably linked to values; for example, recent research finds that being communal is associated with low status (being female?) and being agentic, with high status (being male?) (Conway, Pizzamiglio, & Mount, 1996). We will see that these concepts and their measures will crop up a lot in research discussed throughout the rest of this book so it is important that you clearly understand what we know and don't know about these elusive, but ubiquitous constructs.

These scales should be used with caution. A message that comes through repeatedly in this literature is that masculine traits, alone or in combination with feminine ones, are better. As J.G. Morawski (1987, p. 58) points out, "androgyny research overlooked a crucial component of gender—that of social power." For example, is decisiveness (a "masculine" trait) really a better trait than warmth (a "feminine" trait), or is one more closely connected to what we regard as powerful in our culture?

"Androgynous" Aging?

Having said all this about the BSRI and PAQ, let's return to our original question focused on changes across the lifespan. A generally accepted truism about gender identity is that it passes through phases (James, Lewkowicz, Libhaber, & Lachman, 1995; Pleck, 1975). In early childhood, gender identity is thought to be vague and unorganized, becoming rigid during adolescence, and slowly gaining in flexibility through adulthood until an androgynous conceptualization emerges in old age. To reach androgyny, a *cross-over* occurs for women and men such that women gain in masculinity as they age in contrast to men who add feminine traits (Gutmann, 1987). Others have extended this model across the life course into old age when **gender-role transcendence** appears in the more similar lifestyles of retired women and men

Research suggests that gender roles have become more flexible in the 1990s.

so that they appear to move beyond, or transcend, gendered dictates (Rebecca, Hefner, & Oleshansky, 1976).

Folk wisdom tends to support the cross-over model. Undergraduates asked to project PAQ ratings for themselves into the future, and retirees asked to complete the scale retrospectively, described their older selves as both more masculine *and* more feminine than their younger selves (McCreary, 1990). (I watch my father, who never changed a diaper nor located a can opener throughout my childhood, make his own suppers when my mother is visiting us; diapers remain off limits.) Such transcendence or co-presence of gendered attributes has been linked to psychological well-being (Stewart & Malley, 1987).

However, is this move toward similar gender identities the result of simple aging? Maybe not. Few studies have followed people longitudinally as they age so that changes in societal attitudes may play a role in such cross-over. (Is my retired dad more self-sufficient domestically because he's older, as predicted by cross-over theory, or because this is an expectation for men in the 1990s?) A recent longitudinal study finds that (1) a majority (54%) of older people remained in the same gender-identity category over the past ten years and that (2) the largest proportion of men labeled feminine appear in the *youngest* age group (Hyde, Krajnik, & Skuldt-Niederberger, 1991). The first finding suggests limited change across the age span (contrary to the predictions of cross-over theory for this age period). The second finding is consistent with our speculation about changing times—in the 1990s, young men's descriptions are more likely to include "feminine" terms. Another study with older participants finds limited evidence of cross-over, and much of what little is found is restricted to women and men who have lived traditional lives (James et al., 1995). (Thus, my father may exhibit more "feminine" traits and roles as he ages because he played the traditional role of sole breadwinner and, in essence, had the longest way to go to catch up to the more "androgynous" expectations of the 1990s.)

PERIODS IN WOMEN'S LIFE COURSES

Are life course changes the same for women and men? Asked another way: Is the life's work constructed by women and men similar? The most obvious differences are those readily identified by biological changes specific to women: menarche (the onset of menstruation), child bearing, and menopause (the end of menstruation). Overemphasis on biological events in women's lives readily can lead to biological essentialism (an over-reliance on biological explanations). When women's life course centers on attractiveness, fertility, and youth, aging becomes the loss of these defining womanly functions (Gergen, 1990). Mary Gergen (1990) argues that a feminist approach to studying aging across women's lives must debunk the myths surrounding such "biologizing" of the life course.

Does this mean that aging for women is completely different from aging for men? Mary Gergen (1990, p. 483) asks us to question whether such a "permanent bisection does more harm than good." Certainly, there is *human* development across the lifespan. However, Gergen also notes that by moving beyond biology, we can construct women's lives in richer and more diverse ways, thus opening up avenues for exploration that previously have been ignored. Until recently an androcentric, male-centered bias has fostered the assumption that understanding men's life course will inform us equally about women's (Wine, 1985). When we studied men's retirement patterns, for example, women were expected to either follow the same trends or be irrelevant because they didn't participate in the workforce. Correctives to this exclusionary pattern are just beginning. Although I'll try to fill in some gaps by reviewing what we know about different periods across women's life course, much more research needs to be done. This leads to two goals for our upcoming review: (1) to debunk biologizing myths about women's life course and (2) to sketch a richer picture of developmental issues central to women's lives.

Through the remainder of this chapter, we will explore a sampling of life-course challenges that are typically confronted by women at certain periods of their life course. The list is by no means exhaustive. Some issues are exclusive to women (e.g., menarche); most are not. However, all may be approached somewhat differently by girls and women, boys and men. By presenting mostly descriptive materials of these times, I avoid comparing women's life paths to those of men (an approach that we have seen often succumbs to androcentrism).

Furthermore, I'll try to avoid thinking in terms of "development" which assumes a linear progression such that decisions made at earlier stages limit later choices. Life is not that restrictive. For example, women who forego college during the traditional years certainly can assume this role, with a different orientation, later in life. Not having children in one's twenties does not preclude having children in one's forties. However, our culture dictates normative periods for making these decisions, and these will be vaguely followed here, with the understanding that each individual's life cycle is flexible. The following discussion is framed using each of these normative periods: adolescence, young adulthood, mid-life, and old age. (Note that I skip adulthood, and only look at the choice to be a mother in young adulthood, because these two periods are assumed by much of the subsequent research in this book.)

Adolescence

A clear biological marker of adolescence is the onset of puberty; but a more social indicator of adolescence tied to progression through the school system is simple chronological age, typically the second decade of life (Petersen, 1988). Folk wisdom alleges that this developmental period is stormy (the "terrible teens") as adolescents struggle to control their "raging" hormones (Offer & Schonert-Reichl, 1992). This assessment is believed to be especially true for adolescent girls[3] whose progression through adolescence is unmistakably distinguished by the onset of menstruation (or **menarche**), on average at 12.8 years in the United States.

Are hormones the critical denominator of girls' adolescent development? Christy Buchanan, Jacquelynne Eccles, and Jill Becker (1992) conclude that indeed

---

[3] Some writers regard menarche as the defining feature of womanhood and thus refer to menstruating "women," not "girls." In keeping with my premise that gender is socially, not biologically, constructed, I use a social marker, graduation from high school, to distinguish between girls and women.

when we compare adolescents to both younger children and adults, teenagers do experience more mood swings, more intense moods, lower or more variable energy levels, more restlessness, higher anxiety, and heightened self-consciousness. But, there's a lot of variability across individuals and within genders. Little evidence exists to support the myths that adolescence is stormier for girls and that changes in mood are linked to hormonal fluctuations.

Even when hormonal linkages are found, they do not take control of adolescents' behavior. For example, high levels of testosterone in girls have been associated with greater sexual activity and interest. However, among girls who participate in sports, the relationship disappears (Udry, 1988). This suggests that hormones do not ravage adolescents' lives, but rather their impact can be modified by environmental influences. In all, the myth of the "terrible teens" is generally just that—a socially constructed exaggeration reflective of biological essentialism.

Moving beyond the biological changes that too often dominate discussions of adolescence, what is the major life work for girls during this phase of their life cycle? Adolescence itself presents a variety of challenges for girls including maintenance of self-esteem, identity formation, social development, and future planning.

Self-esteem.   In 1990, the American Association of University Women (AAUW), a national organization open to all graduates of regionally accredited colleges and universities, commissioned the Wellesley College Center for Research on Women to prepare a comprehensive report for educators and policymakers on the educational experiences of girls. This 128-page report, "How Schools Shortchange Girls," challenges the common assumption that girls and boys are treated equally in our schools (AAUW, 1992; also see Orenstein, 1994).[4] Looking at girls' classroom experiences, these researchers conclude that girls attract less attention from teachers than boys; that African American girls, despite more frequent attempts, interact even less with teachers than white girls; and that gender harassment of girls by their male classmates is rising. Regarding the curriculum, they report that the contributions and experiences of girls and women are marginalized or ignored in texts; that education on sexuality and healthy development is largely inadequate; and that violence against girls, a reality for many, is rarely discussed.

For us, one of the most stunning findings to come from this large-scale survey centers on the self-esteem of girls and boys. The percentage of girls who reported that it's "always true" that "I'm good at a lot of things" fell precipitously from elementary to middle school (see Table 4.1). In contrast, esteem ratings of boys stayed constant across their school years. A similar pattern emerged from the question: "I'm happy the way I am." Something was happening to girls between elementary and middle schools that did not affect boys to the same extent.[5] These patterns were replicated in an even larger study of 3,586 girls and 3,162 boys in grades 5–12 conducted by the Commonwealth Fund in 1997 (Brody, 1997). The AAUW with its focus

---

[4] This report can be ordered from the AAUW Sales Office, P.O. Box 251, Annapolis Junction, MD 20701-0251, (800) 225-9998.

[5] Other studies further specify this conclusion by noting that self-esteem is affected not only by gender but also by minority status (Martinez & Dukes, 1991).

Table 4.1 Girls' and Boys' Self-Esteem Across Their School Years

	Percentage responding "always true"		
	Elementary School	Middle School	High School
"I'm good at a lot of things."			
Girls	55	29	23
Boys	45	48	42
"I'm happy the way I am."			
Girls	60	37	39
Boys	67	56	46

Source: Extracted from *The AAUW report: How schools shortchange girls.* (1992). Washington, DC: American Association of University Women Educational Foundation. Printed with permission.

on school experiences concluded that schools were shortchanging girls, often in subtle ways, and ultimately undermining their self-esteem.

The AAUW identifies two potential inoculations against this drop in girls' self-esteem: high interest in science and math and participation in sports. Girls who take a variety of math and science courses throughout middle and high school typically maintain higher levels of self-esteem (AAUW, 1992). Also, physically active high school girls have a more positive self-image than inactive girls (Covey & Feltz, 1991).

The AAUW's (1992) report outlines 40 steps toward the reform of our schools, including further implementation of Title IX of the Education Amendments of 1972. Title IX, passed on June 23, 1972, with a compliance date of 1978, simply states:

> No person in the United States shall, on the basis of sex, be excluded from participation in, be denied the benefits of, or be subjected to discrimination under any educational program or activity receiving federal financial assistance.

Title IX extends to all academic and other school-related activities, including sexual harassment, financial aid, pregnancy discrimination, employment, career guidance and counseling, and sports.

Despite the known benefits of participation in physical activities for girls, the 25th anniversary report of the AAUW on sports suggests that full compliance with Title IX has a long way to go (Sklover, 1997). The good news is that since 1972, girls' participation in interscholastic sports has shown an eightfold increase, and the number of intercollegiate women athletes has shot up 300%. Discouragingly, the proportion of women coaches has fallen from 58.2% in 1978 to 47.7% in 1996 (despite sizable increases in the absolute number of such positions), and coaches of women's teams continue to command lower salaries. The few women coaches of men's teams tend to be ghettoized in less prestigious sports (Kane & Stangl, 1991). Male college athletes benefit from $179 million more in athletic scholarships than female students. It seems that sports affects not only self-image, but opportunities as well.

In sum, a key issue for girls through their middle and high school years is to maintain self-esteem. "Fixing" the schools and providing better opportunities for girls, especially in math, science, and sports, can facilitate how girls handle this issue. Research testing additional interventions is sorely needed.

Identity formation.   Erik Erikson (1959), in one of the earliest theories of development across the lifespan, regards identity development as the primary life work of adolescence. The type of identity Erikson envisions is one of autonomy and individualism—learning to be one's self, independent of others. He views this as a necessary task to be accomplished before intimate relationships can be established. According to Carol Gilligan and other researchers associated with the Harvard Project on Women's Psychology and Girls' Development, this view of identity formation conflicts with girls' relational leanings, that is, with girls' desires for intimacy with other people.

Researchers conducted intensive workshops and interviews with adolescent, mostly white girls in an elite private school (Brown & Gilligan, 1993) and with a racially and ethnically diverse group of girls considered "at risk" for completing their high-school degrees (Taylor, Gilligan, & Sullivan, 1995). They concluded that girls all too often are *silenced* by an androcentric culture that glorifies autonomy. This may be especially true for Asian American women (Gratch, Bassett, & Attra, 1995). Annie Rogers (1993) compares the authentic and outspoken relationships of younger girls to the more restrained relationships of adolescents who lose clarity, self-confidence, courage, and their "voice" (their ability to communicate and be heard). These data are consistent with the AAUW's findings about declining self-esteem in middle and high-school girls.

Jean Baker Miller (1986) offers a fusion of what seem to be competing, irreconcilable pressures: the push to develop an independent identity versus the pull to join in relationships with others. She argues that it is possible both to feel effective and free *and* to form intense connections with others. In essence, Miller describes the development of a sense of **personal empowerment**—the possibility of simultaneously enhancing one's own and others' power (Griscom, 1992). This suggests that one goal for girls in a male-dominated culture is to develop, not an autonomous, individualistic identity, but rather an identity enriched by personal empowerment in connection with others.

Social development.   Jane Loevinger (1976) defines social maturity as a progression through stages of increasingly complex perceptions of ourselves and others. (This parallels the logic of moral development by cognitive developmental theorists we saw in Chapter 3.) As we mature, we become increasingly aware of our own motivations, moving from concrete to abstract thinking and from an orientation rooted in the immediate present to considerations for the future. For both girls and boys, dramatic personality advances occur between 7th and 12th grades, with girls forging ahead at a faster rate of development. Pulling together data from 65 studies, Lawrence Cohn (1991) finds that by adolescence, moderately large differences between girls and boys appear. Through beginning adulthood, this difference is slight then disappears in the thirties. Thus gender differences in social maturity at one phase of the life course (adolescence) fade at later periods (young adulthood).

Another expression of adolescents' social development revolves around how prestige is achieved. Research with high-school graduates of the early 1980s (1979–1982) and late 1980s (1988–1989) shows that gender norms defining social status for girls and boys remain different and basically constant across the decade (Suitor & Reavis, 1995). Girls acquire prestige mainly through physical appearance, sociability, and school achievement.[6] Boys achieve status through sports, grades, and intelligence. There were a few changes for girls that reflect less traditionalism across the decade: girls' acquisition of prestige through both sports and sexual activity increased while the importance of cheerleading declined. This is a pattern we'll see often in gender research—things change a bit, but basically remain unaltered.

Future planning. Future planning is a central issue for adolescents because choices made here mark the beginnings of certain trajectories and the rejection of others. Jari-Erik Nurmi (1991, p. 34) concludes that "studies show unexpected similarity in adolescents' interests across cultures: they all seem to be most interested in two main domains of their future life, work and education." What are the educational and vocational aspirations of adolescent girls?

We might begin our answer to this question by ticking off differences between girls and boys. Summarizing these findings, Jacquelynne Eccles (1994) reports:

> Despite recent efforts to increase the participation of women in advanced educational training and high-status professional fields, women and men are still concentrated in different occupations and educational programs, and women are still underrepresented in many high-status occupational fields—particularly those associated with physical science, engineering, and applied mathematics. . . . These differences in educational and occupational attainment are evident even among highly gifted individuals in this country. . . . For example, among a national sample of youth gifted in both mathematics and language, only 20% of the girls, compared to 40% of the boys, planned to pursue careers in mathematics or science. . . . These differences are still evident in the occupational aspirations and plans of contemporary high-school students. . . . (p. 586).

An androcentric assumption running through this approach envisions boys' and men's aspirations as appropriate in contrast to women's, which appear deficient. "Why aren't women making the same occupational choices as men?" is one potential question. But, underlying this question is an acceptance of a general truism of occupations—higher prestige and better paying occupations tend to be male dominated (we'll discuss this in Chapter 8). When we accept this, we define an ideal standard of achievement based in both androcentric and classist values (Eccles, 1994). If we reject this bias, we'll stop concentrating on why women are less likely to become engineers, for example, and consider as well why men avoid nursing. We might also ask why women are underrepresented in less prestigious, but similarly male-dominated occupations like electricians and coal miners. My point is that we need to consider a whole range of occupational possibilities for *both* women and men, broadening our question to: *Why do women (and men) pursue particular occupations?*

Do adolescent girls and boys consider a full range of potential occupations? I believe not. Who we see doing certain jobs, the language we use to describe those workers, and how jobs are presented all can shape whether or not some jobs are even

---

[6] Eisenhart and Holland (1992) in an intensive study of the college experiences of 12 African American and 11 white women report that attractiveness to men was the main indicator and source of women's prestige.

considered viable. When we see mostly men as firefighters, when we call these workers "firemen," and when recruiters pursue men, not women, we are strengthening the viability of this option for boys, and at the same time, we are diminishing it for girls. There is evidence that each of these three processes occurs.

As we'll see in Chapter 8, much of the U.S. labor force is segregated along gender lines; women and men typically are employed in different occupations. Potential explanations for this gender-typing of work have been offered focusing on job content, occupational demands, and gender ratios. The arguments centered on *job content* suggest that women and men bring different personality characteristics with them to employment; in other words, they are cut out for different occupations. For example, women are more likely to be nurses because women's nurturing qualities draw them toward this work.

The reasoning regarding *occupational demands* reverses this logic: the work demands of the occupations themselves necessitate differential hiring. In other words, because nursing requires caring, people high in caring (mostly women) are recruited for this work. Finally, the logic of **gender ratios** simply suggests that who does a job predicts future candidates. Because most nurses are women, women are likely to be the nurses of the future. Research teasing apart these three possibilities is consistent with the gender ratios explanation (Krefting, Berger, & Wallace, 1978). In sum, who we see engaged in a specific occupation cues us as to the appropriateness of that occupation for ourselves.

It is possible that **language** also plays a role in this process, so that by restricting our descriptions of workers to one gender, we shape how people gender-type that occupation. Alternatively, it is possible that the language we use may simply reflect the gender ratio of who *is* doing certain work—nothing more. For example, we realistically may say "fire*men*" because over 95% of professional firefighters are men. The first argument frames language as playing an active role in maintaining gender segregation; the second line of reasoning views language as reflecting, not influencing, existing gender dichotomies. Those who believe language reflects existing reality often criticize advocates of the first position and mockingly refer to them as the "pc police" (politically correct) for making much ado about nothing.

To tease apart the roles of language and of gender ratios, Janet Hyde (1984a) created a fictional job, "wudgemaking:"

> Few people have heard of a job in factories, being a wudgemaker. Wudges are made of plastic, oddly shaped, and are an important part of video games. The wudgemaker works from a plan or pattern posted at eye level as he puts together the pieces at a table while he is sitting down. Eleven plastic pieces must be snapped together. Some of the pieces are tiny, so that he must have good coordination in his fingers. Once all eleven pieces are put together, he must test out the wudge to make sure that all of the moving pieces move properly. The wudgemaker is well paid, and must be a high school graduate, but he does not have to have gone to college to get the job (p. 702).

Hyde read the description of wudgemakers to elementary school children, one-quarter of whom heard the exact description reprinted above. For the others, the pronouns used to describe wudgemakers were varied so that one-quarter heard about workers described as "she" while others heard "they" or "he or she." All children

Is this who we picture when we think of a "fireman"?

then were asked to rate the competence of women and men as wudgemakers—imaginary workers they could never have seen in action. (In this way, language was cleverly separated from gender ratios.)

Children thought men would be fine wudgemakers regardless of the pronoun used (even she!). However, the pronoun definitely affected their projections for women. Both girls and boys who heard wudgemakers described with "he" evaluated women as "just OK" potential wudgemakers. Children's ratings of women wudgemakers became more positive in response to both gender-neutral (they) and gender-inclusive (he or she) versions. Women were considered the best at wudgemaking when the description used the feminine pronoun, "she." These data lead me to speculate that when we hear about firemen and the "nurse, she . . . ," these contribute to our views about the gender-appropriateness of firefighting and nursing. These findings support the feminist contention that language itself plays an active role in shaping how we think about things, including the gender-appropriateness of occupations. Add to this the reality that gender ratios indeed vary in many real-life occupations, and the lesson becomes even more ingrained.

In addition to gender ratios and language, **how jobs are presented** can make various vocations more or less viable for each gender. In a dated but fascinating study, Sandra and Daryl Bem (1973) presented graduating high-school seniors with differently worded advertisements for jobs regarded as appropriate for the other gender: telephone operators for boys and line-maintenance workers for girls. The ads were worded in one of three formats: gender-biased (the actual form of the ad), gender-inclusive, or gender-reversed. For example, one-third of the boys read the following biased ad for a telephone operator:

> Who says it's a man's world? Behind every man's telephone call, there's a woman. She is a smart woman. She's efficient. She has to be. She places the complex long distance calls people cannot place themselves or helps them locate telephone numbers. Hers is a demanding job. But we make it worth her while. We can make it worth your while too. Not only do we pay a good salary to start, but also offer group life insurance.... (p. 8).

The gender-inclusive version called for "calm, coolheaded men and women with clear friendly voices," etc. Finally, the gender-reversed ads were transformed to recruit the gender atypical for the job: "We need calm, coolheaded men with clear masculine voices...."

Parallel versions of an ad for a maintenance worker for telephone lines were presented to girls recruiting linemen (gender-biased), women and men lineworkers (gender-inclusive), and linewomen (gender-reversed). After reading one of these ads, seniors were asked to note whether or not they'd be interested in applying for the job. Remember, both girls and boys were reading about gender-atypical work. For both, interest rose significantly from the biased to the unbiased ads. Girls' willingness to apply for the masculine job of lineman rose from a low of 30% when the gender-biased ad specified line*men*, to 75% when gender-inclusive recruitment included

FIGURE. 4.2   Two actual job ads: from the 1970s (left) and from the 1990s (right). What does each imply about who does each job?

both women and men, and to 65% when the gender-reversed ad specifically addressed women. For men applying for the stereotyped job of telephone operator, the more recruitment targeted them, the more interest they showed, rising from a low of 5% in response to the gender-biased ad, to 25% for the gender-inclusive ad, and to a high of 45% for the gender-reversed ad.

One rightly might object that ads can't be this blatantly biased any more. Indeed, classified ads in newspapers no longer can be divided along gender lines. Are they as gender-neutral as we might like? Contrast the gender-reversed ad run in *Ms.* magazine in 1972 with the ad run on the back cover of the *American Psychologist* in July 1995 (see Figure 4.2). What does the latter ad imply about who fills the roles of psychologist and client? Which type of ad are we likely to see over and over again? You might peruse the classified ads in your local paper with a keener eye.

Gender ratios, language, and recruiting strategies all conspire to limit the field of viable occupational choices considered by girls and boys. In fact, in my own studies with women firefighters, we began our interviews by asking women how they decided to pursue firefighting. Most said that they never even contemplated firefighting—it was not one of the options they considered viable. Then, someone in firefighting (typically a husband, relative, or friend) told them of openings for women, or they saw a woman firefighter, or they chanced upon some recruitment campaign specifically aimed at women. In other words, a person or event had to challenge their long-held perception of firefighting as closed to women. Similar stereotyping of occupations has been shown to limit the set of viable options considered by lesbians (Morrow, Gore, & Campbell, 1996).

Gender ratios, language, and how occupations are presented all work to limit the set of occupations girls and boys consider viable. How do they choose among the options left? Jacquelynne Eccles and her colleagues (1983) present a rather complicated model describing how such choices are made (see Figure 4.3), and Eccles (1994) reviews an extensive research program supporting this model. In essence, there are two lines of influence leading up to our vocational choice involving: (1) expectations and (2) values. To pursue an occupation, we need to feel that we can succeed at it (expectations) and we need to value that type of work.

What influences our **expectations**? Working backwards in the model (looking from right to left in Figure 4.4), we can see the complex experiences that help shape our confidence. Whatever the causes, are girls less confident than boys? Is this why girls shy away from more prestigious (and presumably demanding) occupations? Evidence can be found to both debunk and support such a gender difference. However, Eccles (1994) points out that the critical comparison is confidence levels for various choices *within*, not across, individuals. For example, in one study of gifted children, girls were more confident about their reading abilities than their math abilities, even though their confidence in math was equal to that of the boys (Eccles & Harold, 1992). Should these gifted girls choose careers demanding reading over math skills, it would be misinformed to say that they rejected math-related fields because of lack of confidence in math. It would be more accurate to note that they simply had higher expectations for success in reading than in math.

Turning to **values**, what makes a chosen task more valuable than those rejected? Again, the model outlines these influences. Most critical for us, are there differences

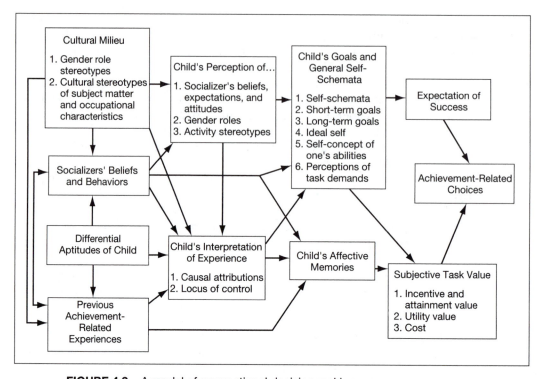

FIGURE 4.3   A model of occupational decision making.

Source: J. S. Eccles (1994). "Understanding Women's Educational and Occupational Choices: Applying the Eccles et. al. Model of Achievement-Related Choices," *Psychology of Women Quarterly,* vol. 18, pp. 585–609. Reprinted with permission of Cambridge University Press.

in what girls and boys value? Eccles (1994) describes four components that define the value of a given task: perceived utility, intrinsic interest, attainment value, and projected costs of doing the task. For example, an ethnography of 12 African American college women concludes that some women perceive little **utility** in obtaining a college degree because they consider the content of schoolwork irrelevant and doubt the link between getting a degree and getting a job (Eisenhart & Holland, 1992). **Intrinsic interests** also can vary by gender. For example, gifted girls both like and report doing activities involving arts and crafts, domestic skills, and drama in contrast to gifted boys who engage in scientific, math-related, and/or electronic hobbies (Dauber & Benbow, 1990; Eccles, 1994).

Attainment value has to do with how much engaging in the task is consistent with our self-image. Does our job fit with how we see ourselves? Again, more specific to our interests here, do girls and boys, women and men, have different work values? No and yes. No, girls and boys do not differ in the value they attach to doing their best at work and wanting to do creative and/or intellectually stimulating work (Jozefowicz, Barber, & Eccles, 1993). However, these researchers also find that high-school girls were more willing to make occupational sacrifices for family, and they valued doing something helpful for others and worthwhile for society more highly than boys.

Eccles (1994) argues that this gender difference in attainment values is rooted in differing family/work mandates for women and men. Men can fulfill their family role through successful employment; for women, work and family are separate, and sometimes conflicting, spheres. Consistent with this reasoning, men are more likely than women to report single-minded devotion to one specific goal. In contrast, women seem to value competence in a wider range of activities.

Finally, as to how **perceived costs** influence values, there is evidence that people perceive costs associated with nontraditional occupational choices for women that may make these options less attractive than others. In my own research, we asked undergraduates to describe a successful woman or man in a nontraditional or traditional occupation (nursing, engineering, day-care provider, or electrician) (Yoder & Schleicher, 1996). Students rated a woman in the male-dominated occupations as less positively feminine, likeable, and attractive.[7] Furthermore, they socially distanced themselves from her by not wanting to befriend her. Other researchers also found that women in nontraditional occupations were least preferred as heterosexual romantic partners (Pfost & Fiore, 1990). These are potentially nasty consequences that can make such an occupational choice less appealing.

In sum, we have seen that the vocational and educational choices of adolescent girls and boys differ, and that this difference arises from the options they consider viable, their expectations for success, and their values. These factors have been shown to affect career development patterns of white women, African American women (Hackett & Byars, 1966) and Latinas (Gomez & Fassinger, 1994). Although we each exercise some choice in what future plans we elect to pursue, there are many external forces channeling us away from some options and encouraging others. To focus exclusively on "choices" tends to root differences within girls and boys, women and men, and can support the androcentric conclusion that girls and women, because of deficiencies within (e.g., lack of confidence), make less lucrative choices. Eccles's model blends influences both within and outside individuals leading up to vocational pursuits. Her analysis also encourages us to ask why some career options are more socially valued than others.

Young Adulthood: Choosing Motherhood?

Vocational and educational decisions are not limited to adolescence, although they typically begin to take form during this period. Also, progression is not always linear—people return to school, change occupations, etc., throughout their lives. The same can be said for relationship choices. Additionally, many of the transitions of adolescence and young adulthood are not discretionary. Rather, **decision demands** force us to work within social systems to find our own slot. We are required to make choices about education, employment, and relationships. We have explored educational and occupational pursuits, and we will discuss other relationship processes in Chapter 7. One critical decision demand often encountered in young adulthood concerns mothering.

---

[7] Men doing "women's work" were evaluated similarly to traditionally employed men, except that the former were regarded as more positively feminine (i.e., as sensitive men).

An overwhelming majority of women have or will have[8] a baby sometime during their lives. Why do women choose to be mothers? As we have seen, sociobiologists concoct a biological imperative for women to reproduce ("maternal instinct"), and even a few feminist activists discuss how women can be driven by the ticking of their "biological clocks" (Schwartz, 1989). Freudian psychoanalysts speak of the need to replace women's lost penis with the production of a baby. However, these biologizing perspectives ignore the social pressures that both encourage motherhood and discourage being childfree—pressures that are so forceful that Nancy Russo (1979) referred to a "motherhood mandate." One telling exception to this general mandate may be expectations for physically disabled women who may face opposition to or even restriction of their reproductive freedom (Lonsdale, 1992).

Oftentimes, the clearest way to see a norm in operation is to watch what happens when one violates it. If there is a mandate requiring motherhood for women, then remaining *voluntarily* childfree should be regarded as deviant, and as such, should be denigrated. In my own research, we found that childfree women, even if happily employed, were projected by undergraduates to lead less fulfilling and rewarding lives, to be unhappy at age 65,[9] and to be less acceptable role models than mothers (Mueller & Yoder, 1997). Indeed, women are more willing to take medical risks to pursue pregnancy than are their spouses, at times taking medical treatments to extremes (Becker & Nachtigall, 1994).

Deciding whether or not to become a mother is intimately intertwined today with decisions about employment. Statistically, the normative woman is employed, even if she has preschool children (U.S. Bureau of the Census, 1995, pp. 399, 406). Furthermore, many college students aspire to combine both employment and motherhood in their lives (Baber & Monaghan, 1988; Florentine, 1988; Weathers, Thompson, Robert, & Rodriguez, 1994).

What influences women's decisions to have or not to have children, with or without a career? Kathleen Gerson (1985) interviewed three groups of heterosexual women (homemakers, childfree career women, and combiners) about how they made their decisions.[10] Surprisingly, she found that homemakers and careerists were the most attitudinally similar: they shared the assumption that motherhood and careers are incompatible—they simply made the opposite choices. She also found that what these adult women thought they would do when they themselves were children (their aspirations) were often unrelated to what they did as adults. Fully 67% of those who aspired to be homemakers when they grew up veered toward employment as adults; 60% of those who expected employment ended up as homemakers. What was more closely related to adult choices were largely unanticipated present pushes and pulls. For example, some women were pushed out of the work force by dead-

---

[8] The U.S. Bureau of the Census (1995, p. 81) estimates that only 9.3% of all women between 18- to 34-years old will not give birth across their lifetimes.

[9] Recent research challenges the popular wisdom that having children is a hedge against loneliness in old age (Connidis & McMullin, 1993). Life satisfaction and happiness of women and men over 55 were comparable for those who had close relationships with their children and for those who were childfree by choice. Those who described their relationships with their children as distant reported the lowest levels of satisfaction and happiness.

[10] For information about lesbians' decision to mother, see Pies (1989).

end, unstimulating jobs and pulled into the domestic sphere by a spouse who looked askance at employed mothers. Others were pulled into the work force by financial pressures resulting from a divorce or fulfilling work successes and pushed away from domestic activities by the isolation of homemaking.

All women describe costs and benefits associated with their decisions, but the three groups weighed these differently. All thought that having children would be fulfilling, but careerists oftentimes dismissed this and/or found themselves in positions where their spouses either didn't want children or made it clear that they would not participate sufficiently in their care. They highlighted the costs children would exact on their careers. Some homemakers described deadend jobs that pushed them from the work force and spousal attitudes and comfortable finances that pulled them toward home. Combiners reported failed marriages or egalitarian fathers who shared in domestic responsibilities as well as enthusiasm for their employment. Woven throughout these stories were "pushes" and "pulls"—pressures that made mothering and/or career more or less attractive.

Strategies for combining career and family include limiting family size and interrupting employment. (The possibility of sharing child rearing with a partner is explored in Chapter 7.) The stigma of the single-child family may be less in the 1990s (Mueller & Yoder, 1997) than in the 1970s when only-children were belittled as spoiled brats (Polit, 1978). In the more recent study, one-child mothers, whether employed or not, were regarded as positively as normative two-child mothers.

Research exploring the combination of employment and motherhood has found that continuously employed mothers are denigrated as compared to those who interrupted their careers (Bridges & Etaugh, 1995). Also, employed mothers are regarded as less well adjusted (Etaugh & Poertner, 1991) and dedicated to their families (Etaugh & Study, 1989; Etaugh & Nekolny, 1990) than nonemployed mothers. A survey of college women found that a majority plan to interrupt their careers when their children are young (Schroeder, Blood, & Maluso, 1992). Although the interrupted career may represent the ideal of many college women of the 1990s, the realities of employment with limited maternity leave (current U.S. law mandates only 12 weeks of *unpaid* leave—for employers with over 50 workers) may limit the realization of such an ideal. (We'll explore this further in Chapters 7 and 8.)

Mid-life: Ups and Downs

A student working on a team of undergraduates doing some research for this book approached her charge to find studies about "what it's like to be an older woman" with a very simple question: "What's old?" This seemingly simple question may lie at the crux of what psychologists have theorized and studied about women and aging.

At what age are we old? Age, like beauty, may be in the eye of the beholder: my son at age 5 considered his then 10-year-old sister old, wise, and over-privileged by her age. When researchers ask people to designate ages for different life events and stages, a general consensus does emerge. For example, 462 women and men aged 16–70 generally agreed that women are middle-aged at about 42 (45 for men), old at about 65 (70 for men), best looking at approximately 25 (30 for men), and in their prime around 35 (38 for men) (Zepplin, Sills, & Heath, 1987). The pattern of consistently younger ages for women than men is statistically significant, suggesting that women "age" earlier than men.

There's an old adage that you're as old as you feel. Not surprisingly, white professional women and men report that they feel younger than they appear on the outside to both others and themselves (Karp, 1988). Seven related markers remind us of our age: body signals (e.g., more frequent aches and pains); time markers (e.g., birthdays and anniversaries); generational reminders (e.g., being a senior member of one's work group and watching parents age); contextual reminders (e.g., as not being fully welcomed in certain places and with people of different ages); mortality reminders (e.g., the death of friends and others one's age); human development reminders (e.g., being aware of the wisdom of one's judgment); and life-course reminders (e.g., becoming a grandparent). We all encounter such enlightening moments in our day-to-day lives that make us stop and become increasingly sensitive to our own aging.

Biological decline?   Sociobiologists and psychoanalysts, who link women's psychology to reproduction, regard **menopause** (the end of menstruation and hence fertility) as *the* defining time marker of mid-life (Gergen, 1990). Early signs of menopause can begin as early as 35, with the average age of menopause (defined as one full year without menstruating) at 50 (Leiblum, 1990). The most consistently reported sign[11] of menopause is the hot flash, a sensation of heat, typically restricted to the face and upper torso, that lasts for a few minutes. Estimates of the prevalence of hot flashes range from 30–93% of menopausal women, but anywhere between 16–80% of women report experiencing no menopausal indicators (Woods, 1982). Previously dismissed as figments of women's imaginations (Travis, 1992), hot flashes have been linked to reductions in estrogen,[12] although no clear relationship has been established between estrogen levels and the frequency and intensity of hot flashes (Gannon, 1985). Furthermore, variations across cultures have been noted (Barnett, 1988; Flint & Samil, 1990; Kaufert, 1990).

In popular lore, psychological consequences have been associated with menopause including depression, irritability, and mood swings. There is no solid evidence that these or other psychological indicators are more prevalent in menopausal women than other women (Etaugh, 1993; Lennon, 1987). Even if individual women seem to experience elevated levels of psychological distress during menopause, there are a host of other, nonbiological factors that could play a role. For many women, menopause coincides with other life events such as children leaving home, changes in identity and body image, possible divorce or widowhood, career changes, illness of parents or partners, and so on. Focusing on menopause as the single or most critical

---

[11] Typically, the term "symptom" is used to designate a sign or indicator of menopause, implying that menopause is a disease rather than a normal stage of female physiological development (Cole & Rothblum, 1990). This perception of menopause as related to disease is promoted by discussions of menopause that use terms to pathologize it (Tavris, 1992) and is shared by many adult women whose primary sources of information are friends and popular books and magazines (Mansfield & Voda, 1993).

[12] Controversy surrounds a common "treatment" for menopause, estrogen-replacement therapy. Although useful for some women (women whose ovaries have been removed, who experience severe discomfort, and who are at high risk for bone fractures), it is not recommended for all women and should not be adopted cavalierly (National Women's Health Network, 1989).

contributor to psychological distress in the midst of such a long list of social possibilities is simply another example of misplaced biological essentialism (Rostosky & Travis, 1996). In fact, middle-aged women themselves generally report positive attitudes toward menopause (Black & Hill, 1984; Etaugh, 1993; Standing & Glazer, 1992).

Do mothers fall apart when their children leave home? Related to women's waning fertility is the life-course reminder of the **passage of children** from their parental home, presumably leaving women with an "empty nest." Folk lore links "empty nest syndrome" to a variety of maladies for mid-life women, most notably, depression (Raup & Myers, 1989). But are these dire outcomes more myth than reality? Studies of marital satisfaction indeed do record changes associated with the presence and ages of children (Etaugh, 1993), such that satisfaction peaks before the birth of the first child and hits lows when children are preschoolers and teenagers. However, satisfaction levels grow with the passage of children from the home, almost returning to the peak of the "honeymoon" years. Clearly this pattern is inconsistent with the dire prospects portended by "empty nest" speculation. This does not mean that all women follow this general trend. A few women indeed react negatively to the departure of their children, but these women were extremely child centered and developed few extrafamilial interests or activities during their lives (Lehr, 1984). Certainly these few exceptions do not "prove" the rule.

The biologizing of women's aging has challenged their **sexuality** as well by using some frightful and fatalistic terminology, such as "vaginal atrophy" (Cole & Rothblum, 1990). Although clitoral response does not seem to change with age, less muscle tension can develop during sexual arousal, vaginal secretions can decrease, and orgasmic contractions can decline in number and intensity (Etaugh, 1993). Yet, some psychologists point out that increased marital satisfaction at this age and freedom from fears of pregnancy contribute to heightened sexual desire and pleasure (Williams, 1987). Ellen Cole and Esther Rothblum (1990) report that lesbian sexuality at mid-life can be "as good or better than ever."

The role of biology in determining psychological outcomes (biological essentialism) is overemphasized throughout this discussion of women at mid-life, painting an overall picture of decline and degeneration. As we have seen so far, much of this is debunked by feminist research with mid-life women. One area that attracts much attention about women's aging (possibly because it is linked with sexuality and fertility?) is **physical attractiveness**. Indeed, there are a variety of body signals associated with aging for women (Whitbourne, 1985). Typically, hair becomes thinner and grayer; weight increases until about age 50 and redistributes to the abdomen, buttocks, and upper arms; wrinkles and age spots may appear; and even height may shrink an inch or two. Personally, I don't find it coincidental that as my generation of baby boomers ages, there's a new-found interest in tight "abs" (abdominal muscles)—our surest sign of aging. Mary Gergen (1990) sums up this forecast of decline with the title of her rejoinder to it: "Finished at 40."

Many mid-life and older women feel that they virtually disappear; this sense is even more pronounced for those with physical disabilities (Luborsky, 1994). The scarcity and stereotyping of older women in the media is consistent with this perception of declining importance. From 1927 through 1990, only 27% of the nominations for best movie actress included actors over 39 compared to fully 67% of the nominations for best actor (Markson & Taylor, 1993). The 100 top-grossing movies from 1940 through the 1980s underrepresented older women characters relative to men and portrayed the former more negatively (Bazzini et al., 1997). On prime-time television, only 3% of the characters are older actors, and men are portrayed more favorably than women (Vernon, Williams, Phillips, & Wilson, 1991). A viewer would have to watch 4 to 5 hours to see an older woman, but only 22 minutes to encounter an older man (Kehl, 1985). Editors of women's magazines acknowledge that shots of older women are routinely airbrushed to reduce signs of aging (Chrisler & Ghiz, 1993). In advertising, older women are ignored or are dredged up to give advice about cooking, dentures, and laxatives (Grambs, 1989) or to need medical attention (Bailey, Harrell, & Anderson, 1993).

No wonder then that it is perceptions of women's physical attractiveness that most consistently decline with age. In general, older targets are rated as less physically attractive than younger ones, regardless of targets' gender (Kite & Johnson, 1988). However, this decline is more precipitous for women. Both 18- to 22-year-old undergraduates and seniors over 60 consider a stimulus person over 60 to be least attractive if she is a woman (Deutsch, Zalenski, & Clark, 1986). Although not finding evidence of a double standard of aging for women and men in other areas, researchers found that 35 year-old women targets were thought to possess more feminine physical characteristics than 65-year-old women (Kite, Deaux, & Miele, 1991).

We have been exploring the intertwined effects of both ageism and sexism in women's lives. **Ageism** refers to prejudicial attitudes and discriminatory practices directed toward the aged and the process of aging (Schaie, 1988). If we move beyond visions of women rooted in their reproductive capacities, then images of older women become more balanced. When we view women as more than physically attractive mechanisms for reproduction, even physical aging need not be regarded as declining. In fact, liberation from cultural demands to be physically attractive can spark greater independence (Niemela & Lento, 1993) and self-confidence (Grambs, 1989; Helson & Wink, 1992).

Not finished at 40.   This fuller view of mid-life and older women encourages us to take another look at life beyond age 40.[13] Valory Mitchell and Ravenna Helson (1990) review data from a sample of 700 college alumnae, aged 26–80, and conclude that many women in their fifties seem to be in the "prime of life." Fully half of the 51 year-old women in their longitudinal study describe their lives as "first-rate," the most favorable endorsement of any age group tested. These women describe themselves as financially comfortable, as healthier than women in their forties, as less concerned about loneliness, as engaged in politics and social issues, as valuing friendships, as autonomous, and as having high levels of life satisfaction. Life for these affluent, college-educated women is far from finished!

These positive patterns of aging ring true for lesbian women as well. A study of 110 mid-life lesbians found that the majority reported feeling fulfilled, self-confident, self-accepting, and self-directed (Sang, 1993). They describe heightened desires to have fun and lowered achievement orientation.

---

[13] For a refreshing example of this approach, see Gullette (1997).

In a second analysis with the college alumnae described above who are now in their fifties, Ravenna Helson (1992) reviewed 88 written accounts in which they recounted a "time of personal difficulty" during different periods of their adult lives. The majority were in stable heterosexual relationships, and most were employed at least part-time. Different themes dominated their stories at different ages. Although these themes were not restricted to any one age, they did tend to cluster across women at certain age periods.

Stories attributed to ages 21–26 oftentimes described these young women as lonely, isolated, unattractive, and inferior. A second theme focused on a bad partner—someone who possessed an unknown and undesirable characteristic (e.g., being alcoholic), or who developed a serious weakness (e.g., being suicidal), or who was a neglectful workaholic. Around both age 30 and 40, their most common struggle centered on a search for independent identity, typically separate from that of a spouse. The sequel of this search for independence appeared in the stories describing events around ages 36–46. These critical periods generally took one of two forms: grappling with discrimination at work or dealing with a partner's abandonment. Finally, two themes dominated the years from 47–53 focusing on destructive relationships with partner, parents, or children or overload—pressure from work, parental care, and so on. Although themes changed with age, nothing in these women's stories suggests that life at 50 is any more or less difficult than any other time period.

Many of our misconceptions about aging come from misleading media representations and our own ignorance; researchers find that both younger and older people are largely uninformed about the normal changes that accompany aging (Bailey, 1991). Until recently, psychologists have provided little to fill in the gaps, but this is changing. Balanced views of a full range of changes across this point in our life cycles are appearing (see for example, Bergquist, Greenberg, & Klaum, 1993; Coyle, 1989; Grambs, 1989; L. Jackson, 1992; Markson, 1983; Rountree, 1993).

Later Maturity and Older Women: Ups and Downs

If life isn't over at 40, it's certainly not over when women reach 60 and beyond. With life expectancies creeping upward, more and more women and men will be grappling with the issues associated with being elderly. Women tend to face different retirement and financial circumstances than men, a greater likelihood of widowhood, and challenges to their well-being.

Retirement and financial security. We tend to think of retirement as the cessation of employment—pretty simple. However, for many people retirement is not such an all-or-nothing proposition. Some older people "retire" from a long-term job, then they go on to accept "bridge" employment that is part- or even full-time (Feldman, 1994). This is especially true for working-class women who have had less opportunity to save for a financially secure retirement (Perkins, 1993). Consequently, researchers define retirement in a variety of ways, including self-attributed (the person reports that she or he is retired), pension (receiving Social Security and/or other pension arrangements), and degree of retirement (measured by reported number of hours employed per week) (Talaga & Beehr, 1995).

Exploring the factors that influence women's and men's decisions to retire, interesting similarities and differences are found (Talaga & Beehr, 1995). Folk wisdom contends that women retire when their spouses do, but when we look at degree of retirement, women actually work for pay for more hours each week when their spouses are retired than when they were employed. Women describe themselves as retired more often when their spouse reports ill health, but they work as many hours as women with a healthy spouse. The former may be in keeping with gender-role expectations that women *should* retire when their husband needs them, but the latter speaks to the reality of these women's working lives. Again, as we'd predict given women's expected caretaker role, women are more likely to report retirement and actually work for pay less often when they have dependents in the home. When couples were both employed during childrearing, they tend to retire together; in couples where the woman reentered the work force after childrearing, women retire more slowly (Henretta, O'Rand, & Chan, 1993). Thus the decision to retire for a woman is complexly linked to her work history and familial obligations and expectations.

Turning to adjustment to retirement, four individualistic modes of experiencing retirement have been described (Hornstein & Wapner, 1985). People who regard retirement as a **transition to old age** think of retirement as a time to wind down—to reflect, to rest, and to put life in order. Others think of retirement as a **new beginning**—a time to embark on new projects and please themselves. Others barely acknowledge their retirement, seeing it as a **continuation** of what they were doing before. Finally, some view retirement as an **imposed disruption**, feeling that part of themselves is lost in this unwanted transition. A very small sample of self-attributed retirees suggests that women fall disproportionately into the continuation category (Hanson & Wapner, 1994). A key point is that retirement is neither uniformly perceived nor experienced.

One of the clearest obstacles differentially impacting women and men retirees is financial. In 1980, women's chances to retire with a private pension were less than men's, and when women did have such resources, their income averaged only 59% of men's (Arber & Ginn, 1994). Financial insecurity tends to be even more severe for African American women (Logue, 1991). Not surprisingly, older women report experiencing more psychological distress related to finances than men (Keith, 1993). These gender differences have been attributed to women's typically shorter employment histories, greater likelihood of interruptions, and lower wages. Consequently, women constitute 75% of the elderly poor, although they represent only 59% of all elderly people (Arber & Ginn, 1994). This linkage between poverty and gender among the elderly holds across African American, Latina, and white women (Hardy & Hazelrigg, 1995).

Widowhood. Because women tend to marry older men and because women's average life expectancy is longer, widowhood is a more likely prospect for women than men. The likelihood of being widowed is even greater for African American and Latina women than for white women (Markides, 1989). In fact, in 1988, widows outnumbered widowers 5 to 1 so that there were 27 unmarried men for every 100 unmarried women (Etaugh, 1993). In a study of women and men over 85, women averaged 25 years of widowhood as opposed to 10 years for men (Barer, 1994).

Studies comparing the physical and mental health of widows with married women of the same age generally find no differences between the two groups (Etaugh, 1993). A critical factor in how well a woman adjusts to widowhood may be the expectedness of her husband's death. Younger widows typically experience more distress than older women, possibly because they did not anticipate the death of their spouse. Additionally, younger widows are less likely to be financially secure, to be free of child-rearing responsibilities, and to have friends in similar circumstances.

Loneliness is thought to be one of the most pressing difficulties of widowhood. Researchers find that older women tend to expand their social support networks more so than older men. These friendships and community ties serve as buffers against loneliness and even bolster physical health (Arber & Ginn, 1994; Hessler, Jia, Madsen, & Pazaki, 1995; Shumaker & Hill, 1991; Shye, Mullooly, Freeborn, & Pope, 1995). With years of experience as the social planners for their families, women report less loneliness and more connection to an active social network. For many African American women, religious participation provides strong social supports (Hatch, 1991; Nye, 1993), as does involvement in the gay community for older lesbians (Quam & Whitford, 1992). Although living alone is related to depression among both elderly women and men, women report less depressive symptomology than men (Dean, Kolody, Wood, & Matt, 1992). More active day-to-day socializing may be a key to women's positive adjustment (Barer, 1994).

Those children perceived by their parents as supportive also play an important role. However, children are more likely to regard a widowed mother as self-sufficient than a widowed father, and thus they offer fewer supports to their mother. Similarly, older women report more positive beliefs about their own self-efficacy than do men (Bosscher et al., 1995). These attitudes often combine to leave women to face more caretaking responsibilities than similarly situated men.

Well-being.   Physical and psychological well-being are obviously connected, especially so for the elderly. Although women, on average, live longer than men, elderly women are prone toward nonlethal disabilities, especially those associated with musculoskeletal disorders (Arber & Ginn, 1994). This leaves more surviving women in need of physical caretaking. Unlike men, women's feelings of positive well-being are not compromised by reliance on others for personal assistance (Penning & Strain, 1994). In fact, women are more likely than men to increase their feelings of personal control by entering into reciprocal helping relationships where they both give and receive assistance (Krause & Keith, 1989; Silverstein & Waite, 1993).

Not surprisingly, the major concerns of older women focus on health maintenance, household management, budgeting, and limitations of their own activities (Heidrich & Ryff, 1992). Because men generally remain more physically capable, men's daily routines include higher activity levels, more involvement in hobbies and household maintenance, more participation in organizational activities, and consequently greater independence (Barer, 1994). In contrast, more women describe a more passive approach to their daily schedules. A 90-year-old woman reports: "What used to take me three hours to do, now takes me three days. And then I need a two hour nap in the middle of the day, so I lose those hours" (Barer, 1994, p. 35). Other women cope successfully by focusing on social comparisons with those less well off than

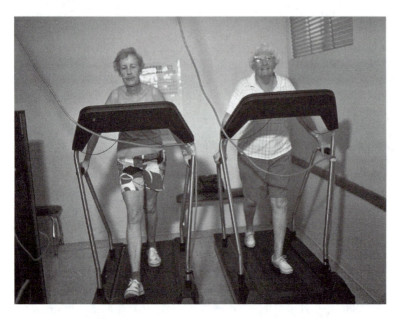

Physical activity and social networks are key ingredients for health and happiness for older women.

themselves (Heidrich, 1993), by engaging in physical activity such as walking or gymnastics (Dan, Wilbur, Hedricks, O'Connor, & Holm, 1990; Ruuskanen & Ruoppila, 1994), and by maintaining a future orientation (Whitbourne & Powers, 1994).

When younger people read the literature describing late maturity and older ages, it is easy to be discouraged about one's own prospects. Visions of the elderly, decaying and abandoned in nursing homes, seep into one's consciousness because this phase of the life course often is stereotyped as a struggle to hold on to health, dignity, and well-being. I think Mary Gergen's reassessment of assumptions underlying research on mid-life development readily can be extended to older ages. As we have seen, recent research on women in mid-life has challenged notions of women as infertile, useless empty-nesters, instead suggesting a period of self-satisfaction and liberation. Might future researchers offer an alternative picture of older ages?

Balanced accounts by and with elderly women highlight both the positive and negative experiences associated with older ages (see for example Adolph, 1993; Brody, 1990; Harris, Begay, & Page, 1989; Healey, 1993; Paradise, 1993; Tijerina-Jim, 1993). Interviews with 56 women in their 60s indeed describe fears of declining health, misinformation about approaching senility, and laments about feeling invisible and inconsequential to others (Siegel, 1993). But they also detail evidence of new opportunities—chances to tackle new projects or work as volunteers, to travel, to write poetry, and to take classes for fun. Knowing that future options may be limited, these women report urges to seek what is most important in life, to compromise, and to look for true intimacy. Coming to terms with one's own convictions and preferences, instead of conforming to others' expectations, reflects growing independence and self-confidence in these women. "Call it wisdom, or call it life experience; our late life learning adds to an inner sense of knowledge about ourselves and about our place in the universe" (Siegel, 1993, p. 184). Although the women interviewed for this study shared health and financial resources that are not assured to all older women, their balanced stories do contradict the presumed inevitability of dire consequences for the elderly. Their sense of liberation from oppressive societal dictates comes through clearly in Jenny Joseph's (1987) poetic "Warning":

When I am an old woman I shall wear purple
With a red hat which doesn't go, and doesn't suit me.
And I shall spend my pension on brandy and summer gloves
And satin sandals, and say we've no money for butter.
I shall sit down on the pavement when I'm tired
And gobble up samples in shops and press alarm bells
And run my stick along the public railings
And make up for the sobriety of my youth.
I shall go out in my slippers in the rain
And pick the flowers in other people's gardens
And learn to spit.

You can wear terrible shirts and grow more fat
And eat three pounds of sausages at a go
Or only bread and pickle for a week
And hoard pens and pencils and beermats and things in boxes.

But now we must have clothes that keep us dry
And pay our rent and not swear in the street
And set a good example for the children.
We must have friends to dinner and read the papers.

But maybe I ought to practise a little now?
So people who know me are not too shocked and surprised
When suddenly I am old, and start to wear purple.[14]

CHAPTER SUMMARY

We explored two approaches to studying aging. First, we followed measures of gender identity across the life course, noting that when gender roles begin to merge in old age and retirement, gender attitudes may follow suit. Second, we described the issues that typically confront girls and women at different periods in the life course. Past attempts to restrict our understanding of women's life courses to unique biological markers, like menarche and menopause, have been replaced by feminist reconceptualizations of these biological markers as well as by a broadening of our focus to encompass psychological and sociological indicators of how women generally live their lives. This transformed view of human development moves beyond childhood to explore change across the life course and to describe women's lives independent from the patterns of men's lives.

In adolescence, key issues for girls focus on maintaining high levels of self-esteem, forming an identity, developing socially, and planning for the future, including educational and vocational values and expectancies. For example, we saw that

---

[14] *Source:* WARNING by Jenny Joseph from SELECTED POEMS, Bloodaxe/Dufour, 1992. Reprinted with permission of John Johnson Ltd.

who does certain jobs (gender ratios), the language that is used to describe workers, and how jobs are presented all contribute to whether or not girls and women
will even consider pursuing a given occupational trajectory. In young adulthood,
one decision demand often focuses our attention on relationships, one of which
involves the decision to be a mother.

A balanced view of women at mid-life includes prejudicial attitudes and discriminatory practices (ageism) that diminish women's aging, as well as close friendships, feelings of autonomy, and high levels of life satisfaction that enhance it. A
similar balance of minuses and pluses emerges from the life stories of older women.
On the one hand, these women are especially vulnerable to financial shortfalls and
chronic, nonfatal illnesses. On the other hand, many older women nurture rich networks of social and physical supports as well as the freedoms to deviate from social dictates and to explore new opportunities. We also saw that the anxieties surrounding
aging that opened this chapter may skew the focus of our explorations. As a result we
overlook evidence from women's real lives—evidence that suggests that we need not
be finished at 40, or 60, or beyond. *Live long and prosper.*

FIVE

GENDER COMPARISONS
Questioning the Significance
of Difference

Consider the two photographs above. Both actors are showing strong emotions in their facial expressions. Can you identify what they are feeling? Given our interest in women and men, the most fundamental question we might ask is: Do women and men differ in the accuracy of their judgments of facial expressiveness? Say we do one study and find that women's judgments, on average, are more accurate than men's. Does this lead us to conclude that we've found a basic gender difference? Certainly we wouldn't form so rash a conclusion based on a single study. But, when is the evidence compelling enough to be considered conclusive?

In this chapter, we'll see that meta-analysis gives us a statistical tool for combining findings across multiple studies so that evidence can be summarized. However, even if a difference is found consistently across studies, does it mean that all women are better than all men on this sensitivity task? In other words, how do we judge the *meaning* of this difference? A closer look at what meta-analysis does and doesn't do will help us make these judgments about the meaning and utility of our research findings. Even after considering all this, are we sure that sex or gender underlie differences found between women and men? In other words, is there something specific to women that makes them better judges of others' emotions or are there contextual factors or circumstances that can enhance or diminish women's accuracy in comparison to men's?

The series of questions posed above outline the logic of this chapter. Our first task will be to determine when we have sufficient research evidence to believe differences exist between women and men. We'll spend some time taking an in-depth look at meta-analysis so that we understand both its usefulness and limitations. Meta-analysts summarize research findings so that we can base our conclusions on more than a handful of studies. We'll see though that meta-analysis only begins to answer our questions by identifying areas where women, on average, differ from men, on average, knowing full well that this pattern may even reverse itself for some individuals. After we identify areas where consistent differences have been found between groups of women and men, we'll consider the reasons underlying some of the most commonly cited gender differences in both cognitive and social abilities.

Are women and men different? Most people would not hesitate to say "yes," and most readily proceed to describe just how we differ. We all know the litany of accepted folk wisdom: men are independent, aggressive, dominant—in sum, masculine; women are caring, warm, expressive—in sum, feminine. Are these presumed differences real in that women and men, girls and boys, indeed are different, or do they reflect stereotyped images of females and males? We will discus stereotypes and their effects in Chapter 6. Our goal here is to see if our folk wisdom about differences between women and men will hold up under systematic investigation and, if so, why.

THE MEASUREMENT OF DIFFERENCE

I am going to talk about some statistical issues in this section. It has been my experience that some students, both women and men, tune me out when I do this. Whether or not you have had statistics or feel comfortable with statistical jargon, the conceptual logic of the following reasoning will come through. Understanding the conceptual underpinnings and limitations of meta-analysis will help us critically consider the findings of meta-analysts in this chapter as well as in subsequent presentations in this book.

Defining Difference

How do we measure differences between women and men? Generally, we create tests to measure one or more psychological functions, directly observe women and men in action, or ask individuals to rate how they think of themselves using a variety of adjectives (self-report measures). We then compare the responses of groups of women with groups of men, statistically analyze the data, and declare that women and men are different whenever their mean scores fall far enough apart to meet our statistical criterion. This seems simple enough.

However, there are at least two serious problems with this comparative approach. I find it easiest to think about these problems if I visualize gender comparisons graphically. If we graph the scores from a large group of women in a frequency distribution and do the same with the scores from a large group of men, we can compare the two distributions according to (1) the mean (arithmetic average) or median (fiftieth percentile) scores, (2) how dispersed or spread out the scores are (the standard deviation), and (3) how much the two distributions overlap each other. Some possible configurations appear in Figure 5.1.

Although mean (or median) differences between two groups, such as women and men, do indicate that the groups, on average, differ, they do not automatically mean that all members of one group outscore the other. In other words, two groups'

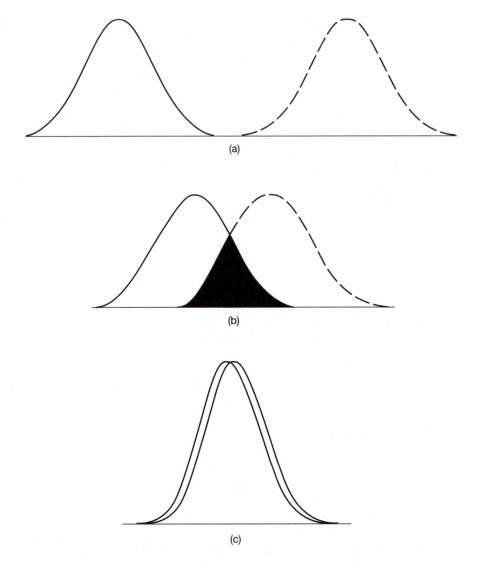

FIGURE 5.1 Line graphs of three combinations: (a) two frequency distributions with no overlap; (b) two distributions showing that 98% of girls throw a ball slower than the average boy; and (c) overlapping curves illustrating women's and men's math abilities (Hyde, 1994a).

scores can overlap substantially even when their averages differ significantly (Lott, 1997). Expressed graphically, the distributions in Fig. 5.1(a) illustrate an average difference *and* no overlap (psychologists never have found a difference between women and men such that all members of one group outscored all members of the other group). Yet, when we assert that women and men are the *opposite* sexes, we imply that there is no overlap between their distributions of scores. (Referring to the "other" sex or gender avoids this erroneous connotation.)

Contrast, the graph in Figure 5.1(a) with the way even relatively huge, *real* average differences overlap in Figure 5.1(b). By far, one of the largest differences between girls and boys, across childhood and adolescence, found to date involves simple throwing velocity—how fast each can throw a ball. Assuming that both distributions are normal and equal, graphs of these distributions and their overlap appear as Figure 5.1(b). Although about 98% of all girls throw slower than the average boy at the mean, there still is some overlap between their speeds as indicated by the shaded area. Furthermore, a few fast-throwing girls outperform some boys. In sum, when one compares an individual girl with an individual boy, it is likely that he will throw a ball faster than she, but there will be notable exceptions to this rule. As we'll see, no psychological differences, nor most motor differences for that matter, come even close to the size of this difference in throwing speed. The overlap between girls' and boys', men's and women's, cognitive and social scores will be more like Figure 5.1(c) which shows the gender distributions for women's and men's math abilities (Hyde, 1994a). Here, there is not much difference.

Our analysis so far assumes that the distribution of scores for women is similar in shape to the distribution for men. Often we think of this shape in terms of a "normal" bell-curve and of distributions that are similarly dispersed or spread out (as indicated by the standard deviation). However, distributions can vary in both their shape and dispersion. For example, there could be a handful of exceptionally high scorers in one group who pull up the group's mean score, although most women and men score similarly.

In sum, the first problem with how psychologists' study gender differences involves how we define difference—is it an average difference, a difference in dispersion, or a notable degree of nonoverlap? I think all three pieces of the puzzle are important to examine.

Overlooking Similarity

A second problem with this comparative approach is that it encourages a search for difference and a complementary tendency to overlook similarity. The foundation of statistical comparisons is a desire to reject the null hypothesis (the null is rejected when a statistically significant difference is found between two or more groups). In a fundamental experimental design for psychologists, we start with the assumption that two groups are similar; we treat one but not the other, control group; we compare the two groups; and if we find a statistically significant difference, we conclude that the difference was caused by our treatment. Failure to find a difference (that is, a decision to accept the null hypothesis) can mean that the treatment didn't "work," that our measures weren't sensitive enough to detect the difference that really does exist, or that we messed up our procedure in some uncontrolled way. Even finding a significant difference doesn't necessarily mean that our treatment was effective or very powerful. The groups may have been different before we did anything to them. Random assignment of research participants to experimental conditions became a hallmark of scientific research because it assures us, to some degree, that our groups were similar before they were treated.

Comparing women and men raises serious questions about several of these assumptions. First, we can't randomly assign people to be women and men; they come as one or the other. Second, it's hard to disguise our gender when we meet others, so that even in the most well-controlled experiment, we know when we are dealing with women or men. Third, when we find no statistically significant differences between a group of women and a group of men, our measures might be faulted for being too gross to detect differences, and/or our methods may be flawed. When we find statistically significant differences, we feel more confident that our findings are valid (though we still might question whether or not statistical differences are meaningful). There is a growing movement in psychology to look beyond tests of statistical significance to judge the merit of a finding.

Given this reasoning, studies finding differences are more likely to highlight these results than studies finding similarities. Researchers indeed may test to see if an effect holds for both women and men, and if it does, this similarity simply is reported in the results of the study. It is uncommon for these similarities to make their way into the title or even the summarizing abstract of the study. Furthermore, when we find similarities, it's hard to be sure that the groups are indeed similar (that is, that the null hypothesis is correct), because it's also conceivable that our study was not done well enough to detect differences that are really there. Finally, consider which finding is more exciting and likely to make newspaper headlines: "Women and Men Read Maps Similarly" or "Men Are Better at Reading Maps than Women." Gender differences are more appealing to read about and to study than gender similarities, and they oftentimes fit with our folk wisdom about women and men. All of this conspires to fill psychology journals with studies touting gender differences rather than similarities which then make their way into the popular press.

A quick scan of recent publications in PsycLIT (a CD-ROM listing of articles and chapters in psychology publications) confirms this pattern. From 1991 through September 1997, 2,681 articles and 656 chapters and books referred to gender differences in their abstracts and an additional 9,654 articles and 1,691 chapters and books referred to sex differences. In marked contrast, only 27 articles and 9 books mentioned gender similarities, and 12 articles and no chapters and books dealt with sex similarities.[1]

Summarizing Data: Meta-Analysis

Acknowledging all these warnings, we still should be able to collect data to answer the question, "Do women and men differ?" Stated more precisely, do the research data support the conclusion that differences exist? As you might have guessed, there's no simple answer. There's an abundance of data in the psychology literature. Given the diversity of cognitive and social variables measured by psychologists, no one study can be comprehensive enough to answer our overriding question. However, there are ways to combine data from a large number of studies so as to fit together the pieces of a bigger puzzle. From such a confluence of data from a variety of sources, a meaningful pattern may emerge.

---

[1] Entries for this search were "gender diff*," "sex diff*," "gender simil*," and "sex simil*," respectively.

How then do psychologists summarize research data? Traditionally, psychologists wrote **narrative** reviews of an area of research (Hyde, 1990). Quite simply, the author(s) of a review read all the relevant research on a topic and reported their impressions and conclusions. More recently, computerized abstracts (such as PsycLIT) have helped to identify the work that's been done in an area, including references to some unpublished works that are too often lost to readers. A second approach takes the review process a step further and provides a list of publications and their conclusions so that studies showing (1) no differences, (2) differences favoring women, and (3) differences favoring men can be **counted** or tallied. In counting reviews, a difference is declared when the scales tip toward one of these three patterns.

The most recent development in the area of literature reviews is a statistical technique called **meta-analysis**. Essentially, meta-analysis pools data from a large number of studies (sometimes 100 or more). In a typical research study, a researcher combines data from a sizable sample of individual research participants. In meta-analysis, the units of analysis are not individual research participants, but rather are individual studies, each weighted for the number of participants involved in it. When large numbers of women and men are compared in a typical study, a z-score may be calculated to capture the dispersion of scores around the mean of zero. When studies involving women and men are compared in a meta-analysis, a d statistic (also referred to as an **effect size**) is computed that tells us the degree of difference between the two groups. The d statistic tells us how far apart the means for women and men are in standard deviation units.[2]

If you think about this, a $d = 0$ would indicate that two groups scored identically. When can we conclude that the difference between two groups is greater than zero? Remember that a large number of studies, each involving a substantial number of research participants, is summarized in these calculations so that it doesn't take much for a d to be statistically significant—but what is meaningful? The general convention in psychology is to consider a d around .20, small; around .50, moderate; and around .80, large (Cohen, 1977). What do these mean? Moderate effect sizes (around .50) correspond to group differences that people would normally notice in their day-to-day lives and large differences (around .80) are "grossly perceptible" (Cohen, 1977, p. 27). Note that small differences defy detection, but they still can have meaningful consequences (Rosenthal, 1991). Thus, if we find $d = -.50$ for aggression, we should notice in our everyday interactions that one gender (in this case, men) is more aggressive, on average, than the other.

The numeric size of a d also tells us about the degree of overlap in the distributions of the scores for the two groups being compared. For a small effect size of about ±.2, the distributions will overlap by 85% (Eagly, 1995a). As we have seen earlier, overlap means not only that a large majority of people have similar scores, but also that a few members of the group that generally scores lower actually outscore most of the other group. For example, although adolescent and adult women exhibit more democratic leadership as a group than do men as a group ($d = +.22$) (Eagly & Johnson, 1990), about 85% share comparable degrees of democratic leadership, and a few men are more democratic than many women. Even with larger ds, there are

---

[2] For a clear, step-by-step overview of meta-analysis, see Hyde & Frost (1993).

TABLE 5.1   Interpreting Effect Sizes

$d = \pm.20$	small	overlap = 85 percent	not detectable, but potentially important
$d = \pm.50$	moderate	overlap = 67 percent	detectable
$d = \pm.80$	large	overlap = 53 percent	grossly perceptible

substantial degrees of overlap: 67% for moderate ds of about ±.50; 53% overlap for large differences of about ±.80. (Eagly, 1995a).

Note that ds can be positive or negative depending on which mean is entered first. This decision is arbitrary, and if you read meta-analyses, you will discover that what researchers decide varies. To avoid confusion here, I'll always report an effect size as positive (+d) to indicate that women typically outscore men on the variable tested. A negative d (−d) will indicate that men's scores averaged higher.

All of this information about ds is captured in Table 5.1; if you understand this table, this is most of what you'll need to know about meta-analysis. A d score tells us three things: (1) its size and how detectable a difference is in everyday life; (2) the degree of overlap of the two distributions; and (3) which group's mean outscored the other's, as indicated by the sign (+ or −) of the score.

AN OVERVIEW OF META-ANALYTIC FINDINGS

Meta-analysis has developed as a review technique throughout the 1980s so that a large number of meta-analyses exist comparing the cognitive and social characteristics of women and men. Janet Hyde and Laurie Frost (1993, pp. 72-75) compiled a list of meta-analyses making gender comparisons and the overall ds they found (see Table 5.2). This list may look imposing at first, but I think you will find it a handy reference. A word of caution however: Don't expect this table to give you ready answers about gender differences. As we'll see later in this chapter, d statistics are only a first step toward understanding gender comparisons.

TABLE 5.2   A Summary of Gender Comparisons Done By Meta-Analysts

Study	Variable	Age	Number of Reports	d
COGNITIVE VARIABLES				
Hyde (1981)	Verbal ability	11 and older	12	+.24
	Quantitative ability	11 and older	7	−.43
	Visual-spatial ability	11 and older	8	−.45
	Field articulation	12 and older	14	−.51
Rosenthal & Rubin (1982a)	Verbal ability	11 and older	12	+.30
	Quantitative ability	11 and older	7	−.35
	Visual-spatial ability	11 and older	7	−.50
	Field articulation	12 and older	14	−.51
Meehan (1984)	Propositional logic	All ages	15	−.22
	Combinatorial reasoning	All ages	23	−.10
	Proportional reasoning	All ages	35	−.48

TABLE 5.2   continued

Study	Variable	Age	Number of Reports	*d*
Linn & Petersen (1985)	Spatial perception	All ages	62	−.44
	Mental rotation	All ages	29	−.73
	Spatial visualization	All ages	81	−.13
Whitley et al. (1986)	Attribution of success to ability	Adolescents and adults	29	−.13
	Attribution of success to effort	Adolescents and adults	29	+.04
	Attribution of success to task	Adolescents and adults	29	+.01
	Attribution of success to luck	Adolescents and adults	29	+.07
	Attribution of failure to ability	Adolescents and adults	29	−.16
	Attribution of failure to effort	Adolescents and adults	29	−.15
	Attribution of failure to task	Adolescents and adults	29	+.08
	Attribution of failure to luck	Adolescents and adults	29	+.15
Hyde & Linn (1988)	Vocabulary	All ages	40	+.02
	Analogies	All ages	5	−.16
	Reading Comprehension	All ages	18	+.03
	Speech Production	All ages	12	+.33
	Essay writing	All ages	5	+.09
	Anagrams	All ages	5	+.22
	General verbal ability	All ages	25	+.20
	SAT-Verbal	All ages	4	−.03
Feingold (1988)	DAT verbal reasoning	Adolescents	20	−.05
	DAT spelling	Adolescents	20	+.50
	DAT language	Adolescents	20	+.43
	DAT space relations	Adolescents	20	−.15
	DAT numerical ability	Adolescents	20	−.05
	PSAT-verbal	High school juniors/seniors	6	+.12 to −.01
	PSAT-math	High school juniors/seniors	6	−.12 to −.49
	SAT-verbal	High school juniors/seniors	7	+.06 to −.11
	SAT-math	High school juniors/seniors	7	−.37 to −.51
Hyde et al. (1990)	Computation	All ages	45	+.14
	Understanding math concepts	All ages	41	+.03
	Complex problem solving	All ages	48	−.08

SOCIAL VARIABLES
Influenceability and conformity

Cooper (1979)	Group Pressure	Adolescents and adults	11	+.28
	Fictitious norm group	Adolescents and adults	3	+.01
	Persuasion	Adolescents and adults	2	+.02

TABLE 5.2   continued

Study	Variable	Age	Number of Reports	d
Eagly & Carli (1981)	Group Pressure	Adolescents and adults	46	+.32
	Persuasion	Adolescents and adults	33	+.16
	Other conformity	Adolescents and adults	11	+.28
Becker (1986)	Group Pressure	Adolescents and adults	35	+.28
	Persuasion	Adolescents and adults	33	+.11
	Other conformity	Adolescents and adults	10	+.13
Aggression Hyde (1984,1986)	Aggression (all reports)	All ages	69	−.50
	Mixed aggression	All ages	16	−.43
	Physical aggression	All ages	26	−.60
	Verbal aggression	All ages	6	−.43
	Fantasy	All ages	1	−.84
	Willingness to shock, hurt	All ages	8	−.39
	Imitative	All ages	5	−.49
	Hostility scale	All ages	2	−.02
	Other	All ages	5	−.43
Eagly & Steffen (1986)	Aggression (all reports)	14 and older	50	−.29
	Physical aggression	14 and older	30	−.40
	Psychological aggression	14 and older	20	−.18
	Laboratory studies	14 and older	37	−.35
	Field studies	14 and older	13	−.21
Helping behavior Eagly & Crowley (1986)	Helping behavior	14 and older	99	−.34
Small-group behavior Carli (cited in Eagly, 1987)	Task behavior	Adults	10	−.59
	Positive socioemotional behavior	Adults	9	+.59
Wood (1987)	Individual performance	Adults	19	−.38
	Group performance	Adults	45	−.39
Leadership behavior Dobbins & Platz (1986)	Initiating structure	Adults	8	+.03
	Consideration	Adults	8	+.05
	Subordinate satisfaction	Adults	7	+.08
	Leadership effectiveness	Adults	11	−.18
Eagly & Johnson (1989)	Task style	Adolescents and adults	136	+.04
	Interpersonal style	Adolescents and adults	139	.00
	Democratic vs. autocratic style	Adolescents and adults	23	+.22

TABLE 5.2   continued

Study	Variable	Age	Number of Reports	*d*
Nonverbal behavior				
Hall (1978)	Decoding	All ages	46	+.46
Eisenberg & Lennon (1983)	Empathy (reflexive crying)	Infants	5	+.34
	Empathy to pictures/ stories	Children	14	+.11
	Self-report empathy	Children and adults	17	+.91
Stier & Hall (1984)	Initiate touch	All ages	6	+.09
	Receive touch	All ages	5	−.02
Hall (1984)	Decoding skill	All ages	64	+.43
	Face recognition skill	Children and adolescents	5	+.30
		Adults	12	+.35
	Expression skill	All ages	35	+.52
	Facial expressiveness	Adults	5	+1.01
	Social smiling	Children	5	−.04
		Adults	15	+.63
	Gaze	Infants	8	+.41
		Children	10	+.39
		Adults	30	+.68
	Receipt of gaze	Adults	6	+.65
	Distance approach to others:			
	naturalistic	Adults	17	−.56
	staged	Adults	8	−.12
	projective	Adults	11	−.14
	Distance approach by others:			
	naturalistic	Infants	5	−.98
		Adults	9	−.95
	staged	Adults	5	−.63
	projective	Adults	7	−.85
	Body movement and position:			
	restlessness	Adults	6	−.72
	expansiveness	Adults	6	−1.04
	involvement	Adults	7	+.32
	expressiveness	Adults	7	+.58
	self-consciousness	Adults	5	+.45
	Vocal behavior:			
	speech errors	Adolescents and adults	6	−.70
	filled pauses	Adolescents and adults	6	−1.19
	total speech	Adults	12	−.10
Hall & Halberstadt (1986)	Social smiling	Children	5	−.04
	Social smiling	Adults	15	+.42
	Social gazing	Children	11	+.48
	Social gazing	Adults	30	+.69
PSYCHOLOGICAL WELL-BEING				
Hattie (1979)	Self-actualization	Adults	6	+.15

TABLE 5.2   continued

Study	Variable	Age	Number of Reports	*d*
Wood (1987)	Well-being (all reports)	Adults	85	+.01
	Life satisfaction	Adults	17	+.03
	Happiness	Adults	22	+.07
	Positive affect	Adults	6	+.07
	General evaluation	Adults	40	−.06
MOTOR BEHAVIORS				
Thomas & French (1985)	Balance	Children and adolescents	67	−.09
	Catching	Children and adolescents	23	−.43
	Grip strength	Children and adolescents	37	−.66
	Pursuit rotor	Children and adolescents	14	−.11
	Shuttle run	Children and adolescents	28	−.32
	Tapping	Children and adolescents	34	−.13
	Throw velocity	Children and adolescents	12	−2.18
	Vertical jump	Children and adolescents	20	−.18
	Dash	Children and adolescents	66	−.63
	Long jump	Children and adolescents	68	−.54
	Sit-ups	Children and adolescents	29	−.64
	Throw distance	Children and adolescents	47	−1.98
	Agility	Children and adolescents	19	−.21
	Anticipation timing	Children and adolescents	23	−.38
	Arm hang	Children and adolescents	16	−.01
	Fine eye-motor	Children and adolescents	30	+.21
	Flexibility	Children and adolescents	13	+.29
	Reaction time	Children and adolescents	42	−.18
	Throw accuracy	Children and adolescents	14	−.96
	Wall volley	Children and adolescents	32	−.83
Eaton & Enns (1986)	Motor activity level	Prenatal	6	−.33
		Infants	14	−.29
		Preschoolers	58	−.44
		Older children	49	−.64

Source: J. S. Hyde and L. A. Frost, Meta-analysis in the psychology of women. In *Psychology of Women: A Handbook of Issues and Theories,* F. L. Denmark and M. A. Paludi (eds.). Copyright © 1993, Westport, CT: Greenwood Publishing Group. Reproduced with permission of Greenwood Publishing Group, Inc., Westport. CT.

Janet Hyde and Laurie Frost (1993) clustered meta-analyses on gender differences into four major categories: cognitive variables, social variables, psychological well-being, and motor behaviors. We will explore specific cognitive and social/personality variables later in this chapter and differences in psychological well-being (or mental health) in Chapter 10. For now, notice the general patterns.

Cognitive abilities yield some noteworthy differences, especially regarding spatial abilities which favor men. Looking at social variables, effect sizes for influenceability and leadership are relatively small; the pattern for aggressiveness is all negative indicating greater male aggressiveness; and nonverbal behavior shows some large effects, mostly indicating that women are more socially adept than men. Differences in well-being are remarkably small. Some of the largest ds appear in a few select motor behaviors of children and adolescents: $d = -2.18$ for throwing velocity and $d = -1.98$ for throwing distance indicating that boys can throw a ball faster and farther than girls, on average (Thomas & French, 1985). Even within motor abilities, these are very large differences, and, as we saw in Figure 5.1(b), there still is overlap between girls and boys for throwing velocity. Across all these meta-analyses, ds rarely exceed ±1.0. Finally, although many areas have attracted the attention of meta-analysts and have a substantial base of research from which to conduct such analyses, not all possible gender comparisons are represented here. (This bias probably is skewed toward measures that are expected to produce differences rather than similarities.)

INTERPRETING META-ANALYSES

Table 5.2 presents numbers, but what exactly do these numbers mean? The criteria we laid out in Table 5.1 to judge the size of ds helps us see that some noteworthy differences emerge. But do these numbers paint an overall picture of women and men as generally similar or different?

Similar or Different?

Even the meta-analysts disagree here. On the one hand, Janet Hyde and Elizabeth Plant (1995) argue that women are more similar to, than different from, men. Hyde and Plant (1995) tabulated ds from 171 meta-analyses focused on gender and 302 meta-analyses of various psychological, educational, and behavioral treatments.[3] They grouped the effects into five categories (see Table 5.3).

Summarizing Table 5.3, Hyde and Plant (1995, p. 160) conclude "that there really are a lot of close-to-zero gender differences"; fully one of every four gender studies (25%) yielded ds that are virtually zero. In contrast to other treatment comparisons made by psychologists, which find nonexistent differences only about 6% of the time, psychological gender differences appear relatively infrequently.

Alice Eagly (1995a and b) looks at the same reviews as Hyde and Plant (1995), agrees somewhat, but comes to a very different conclusion. Both meta-analysts agree

---

[3] The meta-analyses focusing on gender were reviewed in Hyde and Frost (1993) and Ashmore (1990); the meta-analyses of various psychological, educational, and behavioral treatments were reviewed by Lipsey & Wilson (1993).

TABLE 5.3　　Effect Sizes for Psychological Gender Differences and Other Effects in Psychology, Falling into Different Ranges of Magnitude

Measure	Effect size				
	No Difference 0-0.10	Small 0.11-0.35	Moderate 0.36-0.65	Large 0.65-1.0	Extra Large Over 1.0
Gender differences	43	60	46	17	5
($n = 171$)	25%	35%	27%	10%	3%
Other effects in psychology	17	89	116	60	20
($n = 302$)	6%	29%	38%	20%	7%

Note: $x^2 = 47 37$, p < .0001
Source: J. S. Hyde and E. A. Plant, Magnitude of psychological gender differences: Another side of the story. *American Psychologist,* 50, 159–160. Copyright © 1995 by the American Psychological Association. Adapted with permission.

that there is a large degree of overlap between the distributions of women's and men's scores. However, Eagly (1995a and b) concludes that gender differences are comparable to those often talked about by psychologists in our textbooks. Looking at Table 5.3 again, fully 40% of the gender comparisons done show moderate or greater effect sizes such that these differences between women and men as groups should be observable in our daily lives. Janet Swim (1994) compared meta-analytic findings with college students' judgments about the size of gender differences. She concluded that students in introductory psychology classes were pretty accurate in their assessments; in other words, their judgments of gender differences often paralleled the findings of meta-analysts (and if anything, students underestimated differences). This is consistent with Cohen's (1977) contention that moderate and larger effects will be detected in our everyday interactions.

So where are we? On the one hand, it's easy to feel rather frustrated. We've done all these studies, used the sophisticated statistical technique of meta-analysis to bring together large numbers of related studies, and we still can't reach consensus about our overriding question: *Are there substantial psychological differences between women and men?*

On the other hand, Table 5.2 offers a jumping-off point to further exploration. In the upcoming sections on cognitive and social comparisons, we'll bring Table 5.2 to life by exploring the meaning and consequences of the comparisons highlighted there. Some of this can be done by focusing on key individual pieces of research and some can be accomplished within meta-analysis itself. In addition to calculating an overall effect size, meta-analysts can code their entries to test for the effects of moderator variables. Moderators may either enhance or limit the conditions under which a reliable gender comparison is found. One indicator that moderators may be at work comes from a finding that an effect is not homogeneous or uniform—another statistical test available to meta-analysts. It suggests that the data being combined in the meta-analysis don't fit together too well—a signal that we might be trying to combine apples and oranges.

For example, if we find a small difference between women and men, such as somewhat higher rates of self-disclosure by women, might there be circumstances where this difference is exacerbated, such as when women disclose to women friends, and others where it is minimized, such as when women and men talk with strangers? Similarly, if we find a larger difference, say in spatial perception that favors men, might there be settings in which women typically outperform men? If gender was the sole influence, the pattern of difference between women and men would be invariant. In contrast, these limiting and enhancing patterns, found through analyses of moderators, suggest that there's more than a stable gender difference at work.

In sum, even when we find reliable differences between women and men across a substantial number of studies, this doesn't mean that women and men are fundamentally different. Similarly, finding little difference may not rule out differences across some specific contexts. Listing effect sizes (*d*s) then is only a first step. Our next step is to probe cognitive and social comparisons of women and men more deeply than can be realized from a table of effect sizes. When we do explore cognitive and social comparisons, we need to do so with our eyes open for indicators of the causes of found differences. Thus we need to digress one last time to consider what might cause a gender difference.

Potential Causes of Difference

When considering the possible causes of a reliable gender difference, two possibilities immediately come to mind: biology and socialization (experiences from childhood). Let's focus on one difference confirmed by the meta-analysts: more women are sensitive to the emotional expressions of others than are men ($d = +.43$) (Hall, 1984). Why is this? A biological explanation might suggest that women are better at reading the emotions behind the expressions of others because of some better developed regions of their brains (biology), perhaps evolved through thousands of years of rearing children (sociobiology). Another explanation might be that women possess this social advantage because they have been rewarded as children for being sensitive to the feelings of others (social learning theory). More recent psychobiosocial models focus on the interplay of biology and socialization such that the effects of each are so intertwined that they become functionally inseparable (Halpern, 1997). Whatever the approach, the assumption is that many women possess this ability because of something within them—something that is a part of them and that is relatively permanent. Similarly, the implication is that many men lack this capability, so that they either need remedial training to compensate for their insufficient socialization or can never make up for their biological or evolutionary inadequacy.

Think of the ramifications of this analysis. If sensitivity to others' feelings is something we value in our culture, men are viewed as severely handicapped in this arena. If we assume that men's lack of sensitivity resides exclusively in their biologies (or evolutionary histories), then change becomes virtually impossible (or frighteningly surrealistic). As we have seen, Carol Martin and Sandra Parker (1995) found that the more college students regard gender differences as biologically caused, the more difficult they think it would be to eliminate those differences.

Even if we assume that differences in sensitivity are learned, fully or in part, isn't childhood socialization over for adults, and we are stuck with whatever we have become? Or we might ask, since socialization explanations acknowledge the role of learning, can adults unlearn and/or relearn? When we speak of such remedies for a gender difference, aren't we implying that the sex/gender to be changed is deficient? Are we blaming members of one gender for their "inadequacies" (Halpern, 1997)?

This last process has been dubbed "**blaming the victim**" (Ryan, 1972). How this process works is illustrated by an intriguing study from the social psychological literature on cognitive dissonance (Glass, 1964). In this study, college students were induced to shock another innocent student (actually an accomplice of the experimenter who wasn't really shocked). According to dissonance theory, this should create inconsistent cognitions for those delivering shocks: "I shocked an innocent person" contrasts with their perceptions of themselves as nice people. How could they resolve this inconsistency? The shock has been done publicly, so it cannot be denied. However, it can be justified if one concludes that the victim really deserved it. In a classic illustration of the process of "blaming the victim," shockers denigrated the victim, and when they were given an opportunity to shock the same victim again, many did.

We've seen examples of this process used in everyday justifications for misfortune: women are raped because they dress provocatively, and welfare recipients are poor because they are lazy. This process has at least two noteworthy side effects. First, it serves an ego protective function—if I avoid doing whatever the victim presumably did, I will avoid her or his fate. A deplorable example of this logic was offered by Phyllis Shaffly, an antifeminist favorite of the popular media. Shaffly suggested that women could avoid sexual harassment at work by wearing a button pronouncing them "ladies." Although this charm was meant to ward off harassers, it implied that women who experienced harassment provoked it through their "unlady-like" behavior.

Second, blaming the victim deflects criticism away from larger social forces by pinning the blame squarely on the shoulders of presumably defective individuals. Whatever the reasons for engaging in victim-blaming, the result is a victim who may be victimized multiple times. Consider the recipients of shocks in Glass's (1964) study—first they are shocked, then they are blamed for it, then they are shocked again. They lose repeatedly!

There's a possible explanation beyond biology and socialization that we haven't yet considered and that avoids the pitfalls of victim-blaming.[4] What could make women and men appear different is the social circumstances in which they find themselves. Continuing with our example of sensitivity to the feelings of others, people in subordinated positions may need to think more about the feelings of their superiors than do people in more powerful positions. In our society, as well as in most globally, women are more often in subordinated positions than men so that women may rely on these skills more than men. Think about your bosses, teachers, parents, and so on. How much time have you spent at work talking about the personal life and moods of your boss? On the other hand, how often have you talked about the personal lives of those below you in the hierarchy, such as the custodian or the person who drops off the mail?

---

[4] For a good overview of the philosophical position taken here that supports constructionism (looking for social forces) over essentialism (looking within individuals), see Janis Bohan, 1993.

The relationship between gender and status as they relate to interpersonal sensitivity (also popularly known as "women's intuition") was probed in a series of studies conducted by Sara Snodgrass (1985; 1992). In the earlier study, one member of 36 female-female, male-male, and female-male dyads was randomly selected to teach the partner sign language spelling and to test and grade her or him. (The later study used a boss-employee role-playing procedure.) This set-up empowered one member, the teacher, relative to the subordinated learner. After the lesson and test, the partners played two competitive games: Blockhead (a block-stacking game) and Password (a word game). Throughout these activities, the dyadic exchange was interrupted so that each partner could complete a questionnaire privately describing (1) their own feelings and thoughts, as well as (2) those projected for their partner. By comparing what each person reported (question 1) with what her or his partner believed their reaction to be (question 2), Snodgrass measured the accuracy of each partner's perceptions of the other. As you might have guessed, learners were more accurate than teachers regardless of gender. When both women and men were in subordinated roles, they were more interpersonally sensitive, suggesting that status, not gender per se, underlies differences found between women and men.[5]

Notice how our focus has shifted. We have moved away from considering internal, dispositional characteristics of women and men to think about the social circumstances in which they find themselves. The key to doing this type of analysis is to identify a contextual factor that is **confounded** with gender, that is, a factor that occurs differently for women than for men (e.g., status). The critical test is to vary this factor in such a way that men are exposed to what typically occurs for women and vice versa. If we find that men act "like women" when exposed to the circumstances that typically impact women, and that women act "like men" when placed in men's typical circumstances, then what seemed to have been a "gender difference" has disappeared. It is now better regarded as a difference in contextual factors. The way we do this is to probe gender comparisons for **moderator** variables (e.g., social status).

This logic is diagrammed in Figure 5.2. Hypothesis 1 assumes that there is something about women that makes them produce Behavior A, and something about men that evokes Behavior B. Hypothesis 2 proposes that a contextual factor (Factor 1) typically associated with women causes women to do Behavior A while a different contextual factor (Factor 2), generally impinging on men, produces Behavior B. Hypothesis 2 is supported if the results show the hypothetical pattern diagrammed in Figure 5.2(c). When women and men are exposed to Contextual factor 1, they *both* do Behavior A; similarly, when they are influenced by Contextual factor 2, they both exhibit Behavior B. Thus Behavior A is not a "women's reaction," but rather is a reaction created by a contextual factor (Factor 1) more typically encountered by women.[6]

---

[5] Judith Hall and Amy Halberstadt (1997) cite a still unpublished follow-up study by Snodgrass and her colleagues (1995) reportedly showing that this effect results from the expressivity of higher status people rather than the sensitivity of lower-status observers. If this is so, status, not gender, remains the important ingredient, shifting our focus to explorations of why higher status people might be less guarded with their feelings (possibly because they are not as fearful of misuses by lower-status others?).

[6] For a good example of this logic and its evolution, see Rosalind Barnett's (1997) discussion of the effects of family and work relationships on women's and men's mental and physical health.

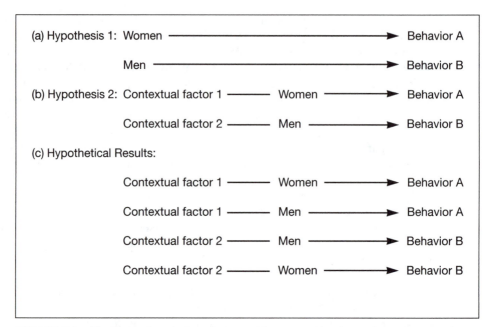

FIGURE 5.2   The logic of exploring contextual factor explanations of apparent gender differences.

The overriding point here is that finding a gender difference may be just the start of one's exploration, not the end. To say simply that sex or gender is the cause of the difference ignores other possibilities (James, 1997). The next step should be to explore *why* the "difference" exists. All too often, we psychologists have limited our explorations to possibilities internal to women and men, that is, to biology and to past learning (socialization). Some of this may be because focusing on the presumed internal dispositions of others is a general psychological tendency, referred to by social psychologists as the **fundamental attribution error** (Ross, 1977). One way to avoid this tendency is to think about how you yourself might act and why, because we tend to regard surrounding, circumstantial factors as more salient when we think about ourselves (Taylor & Fiske, 1975). Overall, a complete understanding of what we think, feel, and do must take into account a combination of biology, socialization (and other historical experiences), as well as present social context (Riger, 1997).

As we turn to the core of this chapter (an exploration of cognitive and social comparisons of women and men), we'll do so with an eye toward going beyond simple evidence of similarity or difference to probe the circumstances under which differences are magnified and minimized. Understanding the role of such moderating contextual factors raises fundamental questions about whether what appear to be gender differences truly are accounted for by gender (whether created by biology or socialization) or other factors related to gender (such as different life experiences and differences in status or power). We'll see that *how* a difference is interpreted can play a major role in shaping the implications of that finding.

COGNITIVE COMPARISONS

In 1974, Eleanor Maccoby and Carol Nagy Jacklin published a book, *The Psychology of Sex Differences,* that is now considered a classic in the field of the psychology of women. In over 600 densely-packed pages, they presented a *counting* review of research comparing women and men on (1) intellect and achievement involving perception, learning, and memory; intellectual abilities and cognitive styles; and achievement motivation and self-concept and (2) social behavior focused on temperament; social approach-avoidance; and power relationships. Probably the most frequently cited conclusions from this review involve cognitive differences between women and men. Specifically, Maccoby and Jacklin (1974) concluded that:

- More women score better on some tests of **verbal ability** than do men. Interestingly, this difference emerges around ages 10–11 so that through high school and college, girls and women tend to outscore boys and men.
- More men score better on tests of **math ability** than do women. Again, this difference seems to emerge such that at ages 9–13, boys start to outdistance girls, although the degree to which boys and men outscore girls and women varies in magnitude.
- More men and boys score better on tests of **visual-spatial ability** than do women and girls.

These three areas of cognitive processing have taken center stage when psychologists ask questions about gender comparisons in how women and men *think.*

Meta-Analytic Evidence

Each of these areas of study has generated large bodies of research findings, and each has been reviewed by meta-analysts. We'll start our discussion by looking at the meta-analyses to discover exactly if and where these differences exist. We have seen that meta-analysis serves only as the first step in our probing; effect sizes tell us little about the meaning of differences. For this, we'll go on to explore possible explanations for why these differences exist, as well as consider the implications of each potential cause.

Verbal abilities.   Janet Hyde and Marcia Linn (1988) reviewed 165 studies comparing the verbal abilities of women and men. Looking across various measures of verbal skills, they found a virtually nonexistent relationship between gender and verbal performance ($d = +.11$).[7] However, there are a myriad of ways to test verbal performance including vocabulary tests, analogies, anagrams, reading comprehension, essay writing, and speech production (the quality of speech, not the quantity). If you consider your own aptitudes, you probably are better at some of these than others; try some examples in Box 5.1. Looking at these separate skills, women seem to show a small advantage over men in two areas: quality of speech production ($d = +.33$) and

---

[7] A similar conclusion was reached by Feingold (1988) using different measures of verbal aptitude.

Box 5.1   Test Your Verbal Skills*

---

(1) Vocabulary
Define each of the following:
(a) exogenous
(b) androcentric
(c) androgynous

(2) Similarities (or analogies)
In what way are each of the following pairs of items alike?
(a) lion - tiger
(b) circle - triangle
(c) hour - week

(3) Anagrams
Unscramble the letters to form a word:
F S E E F D E C R I N

Answers: (1a) originating from external causes; (1b) male-centered; (1c) blending "feminine" and "masculine" qualities; (2a) animals (felines); (2b) shapes; (2c) units of time; (3) differences.

---

anagrams ($d = +.22$). Note that both are small given Cohen's (1977) criteria so that neither should be detected in our everyday lives. One area where there may be a strong ($d = +1.2$) female advantage involves verbal fluency, but this finding is based on a much smaller literature (Hines, 1990, cited in Halpern, 1997).

There is one notable exception to the above findings: the verbal scale of the Scholastic Aptitude Test (SAT) (the college entrance exam) (Hyde & Linn, 1988). Beginning in 1972, the traditional superiority of women on this subtest reversed. In 1985, the d of $-.11$ favored men (Ramist & Arbeiter, 1986). Although this is a very small effect, given the hundreds of thousands of students who take the SATs each year and the uses of this score for getting into college, the implications of this difference are not small. For example, a study at the University of California at Berkeley concluded if SAT scores projected women's college grades without bias, fully 5% more women would have been admitted to their university (that's 200–300 students) (Leonard & Jiang, 1995).

Hyde and Linn (1988) consider two possible explanations for the SAT's reversal of the previous pattern of no difference or differences favoring women. First, there is reason to believe that the content of the verbal portion of the SAT has become more technical in ways that favor men.[8] The second possibility involves sampling.

---

[8] The current movement to take the SATs via computer may make the test even less "women-friendly" because of gender differences in women's and girls' experiences with computers.

Because more women than men tend to take the SATs, the smaller samples of men may be more selective and thus reflect a narrower, higher ability group of test-takers. Still, we might reflect on why it is that when verbal tests have meaningful consequences, gender patterns reverse to favor men.

Math abilities. Moving to math ability, a meta-analysis of 100 studies by Janet Hyde, Elizabeth Fennema, and Susan Lamon (1990) calculated an overall d of $-.15$— a stunningly small effect size that should defy detection in everyday life, but that has attracted far-reaching popular attention. Again, breaking math ability into areas generally tested, three separate skills emerge: computation (e.g., adding numbers), understanding concepts (e.g., the concept of limits in calculus), and problem solving (e.g., those wonderful word problems that we all remember from grade school: If a train going 50 mph travels 50 miles east . . .). Surprisingly, there were no significant gender differences for these specific measures—the "largest" effect was a $d = +.14$ for computation suggesting slight female superiority.

Why all the hubbub about male math superiority? Looking at **problem solving** alone, a gender difference emerges with age. In elementary school (ages 5-10 years), there is no gender difference ($d = .00$) and this holds through middle school (ages 11–14 years; $d = +.02$). However, the pattern changes when children enter high school: a small, but significant effect emerges between ages 15-18 ($d = -.29$) and remains into college (ages 19–25; $d = -.32$). Does the size of the adult effect look familiar? The effect size for quality of speech production, favoring women, was $+.33$. About which difference do we hear more?

Again, the math section of the SAT deserves separate consideration. Using data from the 1985 administration of the SAT, Ramist and Arbeiter (1986) report a $d = -.40$ for the math portion of the test. This is a considerably larger difference than the overall $d = -.15$ found by Hyde, Fennema, and Lamon (1990) using standardized math tests other than the SAT. The same concerns about sampling and content arise here as for the SAT-verbal, and given the size of the difference, its effects are even more far-reaching. Most troubling about these tests is evidence that although these standardized tests are designed to predict college scores and men do perform better on them, women earn higher grades in college and graduate school (Bridgeman & Lewis, 1995; Stricker, Rock, & Burton, 1993).

Although the effect size for gender differences in non-SAT math abilities is small to moderate and is concentrated in one area of math skills (problem solving), the consequences of this difference are extensive. An eye-opening report written by Clifford Adelman (1991), issued by the Department of Education, suggests some intriguing possible consequences of girls' and women's exclusion from math experiences. Almost 20,000 high-school graduates in the Class of 1972 were periodically surveyed beginning with their graduation until 1986 when they reached 32 years of age. Women's academic performance exceeded men's in both high school and college, no matter what college field of study they pursued. This pattern was repeated in individual college courses including statistics and calculus.

Despite their academic success, those women who remained childfree failed to achieve pay equity with childfree men in 26 of 33 major occupations. Most interestingly for our present discussion, in five occupations (four of which were in business-related fields), women who took more than eight credits of college-level math achieved pay equity. Although far from conclusive, these longitudinal data suggest that exposure to math literally pays! Thus the consequences of a relatively small effect size (d = −.32 for math problem solving) may be quite far-reaching.

Spatial abilities.   Turning to visual-spatial skills, a meta-analysis involving 172 studies conducted by Marcia Linn and Anne Petersen (1985) found that a homogenous effect could not be calculated, suggesting that spatial abilities be broken into three different aspects. On **spatial perception** tasks, research participants are asked to determine spatial relationships with respect to the orientation of their own bodies. **Mental rotation** tasks involve the ability to rotate a two- or three-dimensional figure rapidly and accurately. Finally, **spatial visualization** tasks include complicated, multistep manipulations of spatially presented information. Try doing examples of each of these in Box 5.2.

Here we find the largest and most consistent sex or gender differences. A $d = -.64$ was found for spatial perception, and $d = -.73$ for mental rotation (reported elsewhere as −.90; Masters & Sanders, 1993). Both effects are in the moderate to large range and favor men and boys. While mental rotation consistently favors males, the gap in spatial perception widens considerably around age 18 ($d = -.37$ for children and adolescents under 18; $d = -.64$ for adults). There is virtually no gender difference on spatial visualization tasks ($d = -.13$).[9] Although these are the most widely used spatial abilities tasks, there are some spatial tasks, such as mirror tracing, in which women typically outscore men (Halpern, 1997).

Causes of Cognitive Differences

Now that we have reviewed the meta-analytic findings, our global question about women's and men's thinking can be narrowed to explorations of specific math and spatial differences between women and men. We know that we should concentrate on problem solving skills in math and spatial perception and mental rotation tasks. Our narrowed question becomes: Why do women and men differ on these three cognitive tasks? As we noted earlier, there are three possible causal explanations to explore: biology, socialization, and contextual factors.

Biology.   A direct link between a biological mechanism and math and spatial abilities has been elusive. Researchers have ruled out the possibility of a sex-linked math gene and spatial gene (Sherman & Fennema, 1978). A direct link between the onset of puberty and increased spatial ability also has been discounted (Linn & Petersen, 1985). Yet, the widely reported reviews of Camilla Benbow and Julian Stanley (1980) continue to fuel speculation about the role of physiology in creating cognitive sex differences (also see Benbow, 1988). The most compelling evidence to date is coming from an innovation in brain scanning called functional magnetic resonance imaging (fMRI). In beginning work with 38 right-handed participants, Bennett and Sally Shaywitz and their colleagues (1995) have reported that different areas of women's and men's brains appear to be activated when they work on word problems involving

---

[9]Using another test of spatial visualization, Feingold (1988) comes to a similar conclusion.

Box 5.2   Test Your Spatial Abilities

Spatial Perception
Which of the following four tilted glasses has a horizontal water line?

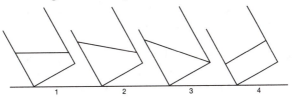

Mental Rotation
Which two of the four choices below show the standard in a different orientation?

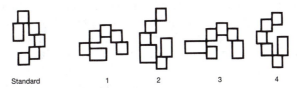

Spatial Visualization: Embedded Figures
Find the simple shape above within the more complex pattern below.

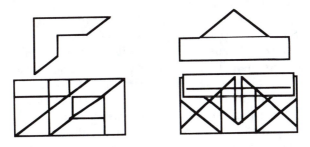

Answers: 1. glass #1. 2. Figures #1 and #4.

Source: M. C. Linn and A. C. Petersen (1985). Emergence and Characterization of Sex Differences in Spatial Ability: A Meta-Analysis. *Child Development,* 56, 1479–1498. University of Chicago Press. Reprinted with permission.

rhyming. Their work made headlines in *The New York Times* (Kolata, 1995), and it is likely that we will hear more about this procedure as it is adapted to these kinds of research projects.

If there is a biological component to doing math and spatial tasks, does this mean that girls will be lost hopelessly on these tasks? The data suggest not. When women elect to take four semesters or more of high-school math, their math scores parallel those of men on the Scholastic Aptitude Test (SAT) for college (Adelman, 1991). Similarly, reviews of research relating spatially relevant experiences to spatial ability found significant relationships between exposure and performance (Baenninger & Newcombe, 1989) and between training and scores on the water-level task (Vasta, Knott, & Gaze, 1996). Studies such as these suggest that giving girls the experiences more frequently available to boys can close the gap in their math and spatial performances. At best, biology can fill in only part of the puzzle.

Socialization.   There is clear evidence that girls and boys, as groups, are exposed to differing amounts of relevant math, science, and spatial experiences. The American Association of University Women (AAUW) (1992) reports that 31% of elementary school girls surveyed and 49% of boys believe that they are good in math, but by middle school these figures drop to 18% and 31%, respectively. Not surprisingly, when math courses become elective in high school, girls begin taking fewer of them (Chipman & Thomas, 1985). This pattern continues through college where women again generally take fewer math courses than men (Adelman, 1991).

A parallel pattern emerges with computers. More boys attend computer camps, have access to a computer at home, grab prime seats in computer labs, work on computers before and after school, and take computer classes (Kramer & Lehman, 1990; Nelson & Watson, 1990–91). Educators have begun to intervene to actively encourage girls' participation with computers by organizing computer clubs for girls and scheduling periods of "girls only" access; in some trial schools, girls' usage has surpassed boys' (Fish, Gross, & Sanders, 1986).

Finally, the spatial skills of boys are more likely to be honed as they venture farther from home (Bryant, 1985; Feiring & Lewis, 1987) and dominate video arcades and computer clubs heavily designed around the interests of boys (Kantrowitz, 1994; Kiesler, Sproull, & Eccles, 1985). In fact, a frequently used list of activities judged to promote the development of spatial skills (the Spatial Activities Questionnaire developed by Newcombe, Bandura, & Taylor, 1983) readily can be clustered along gender lines. Of the 81 experiences listed, fully 40 are masculine-typed and are more accessible to men and boys (21 are feminine-typed and 20 are neutral). Complete the checklist in Box 5.3. How many of these activities have you done? (Note that the 24 entries in that table alternate beginning with a masculine [tackle football], then neutral [bowling], then feminine [figure skating] example, and so on.)

Why are experiences of girls and women in math and science courses and in spatial activities different from those of boys and men? Reviewing research on math and science experiences, Jacquelynne Eccles (1989) concludes that:

- girls are less confident about their math and science skills and attach less value to activities involving math and the physical sciences than do boys;
- teachers treat girls and boys differently in math and science, allowing boys to dominate these classes while girls sit silent;
- parents have different expectations about the abilities of girls and boys such that many *expect* girls to do poorly and to have to work extra hard to get by.

BOX 5.3   Put a check next to each activity that you have done.

Tackle football _____   Skateboarding _____
Bowling _____   Frisbee _____
Figure skating _____   Pottery (wheel) _____
Basketball _____   Air hockey _____
Softball _____   Sculpting _____
Baton twirling _____   Embroidery _____
Darts _____   Car repair _____
Volleyball _____   Marching band _____
Gymnastics _____   Touch typing _____
Hunting _____   Juggling _____
Jewelry (mounting stones) _____   Drawing (three-dimensional) _____
Tap dance _____   Knitting _____

Source: Adapted from N. Newcombe, M. M. Bandura, and D. G. Taylor, (1983). Sex differences in spatial activities. *Sex Roles*, 9, 377–386. Plenum Press. Reprinted with permission.

Maybe each of the above outcomes occur because most girls and women simply don't have an aptitude for math and science. Contrary to this speculation, Jacquelynne Eccles and Janis Jacobs (1986) conclude that the types of social and attitudinal factors mentioned above influence junior- and high-school students' grades and enrollment in math courses *more* than individual variations in math aptitude. It is the experiences of girls and women that are deficient, not girls and women themselves.

If there is a socialization component, are adult women hopelessly lost in science and math because they have been deprived of fundamental childhood experiences with relevant tasks? Asked a different way, can "lost experiences" be replaced by concentrated training in an area? A meta-analysis of the effects of spatial training concludes that training indeed can improve the spatial performance of women and men so that their final performances become comparable (Baenninger & Newcombe, 1989). This pattern holds true for first graders (Conner, Schackman, & Serbin, 1978), high-school students (Conner & Serbin, 1985), college students (Koslow, 1987), and even for the elderly with an average age of 73 years (Willis & Schaie, 1988). It seems that people are never too old to improve their spatial abilities.

Social context.   A third strand of research on spatial performance focuses on contextual factors. For example, Matthew Sharps, Jana Price, and John Williams (1994) simply varied women's and men's expectations about a spatial task. Before doing a standard test of mental rotation, women and men college students were given different impressions about the uses of the task they were about to do. Half were told that the task was used to test skills necessary for the navigation of naval vessels, the flying of military aircraft, and the engineering of aircraft and propulsion systems. These uses were chosen because they are plausible and because they paint a picture of the task as one designed to test skills generally regarded as more appropriately masculine. The remaining participants were given a stereotypic feminine task description. Here the task was presented as measuring skills necessary for handicrafts and interior decoration and design. Remember, all students went on to complete the same mental image rotation (MIR) task.

The performance of participants was affected by the *interaction of their gender with their expectations*. When men believed that the task tested "masculine" skills, they outperformed every other group. The instructions did not influence the scores of women, and men who believed the task tested "feminine" competencies scored similarly to women participants. A growing body of parallel research evidence indicates that the gap in women's and men's mental image rotation (Sharps, Welton, & Price, 1993) and college math scores (Steele, 1996) can be reduced, or even eliminated, through instructional manipulations.

These data confirm the existence of influential contextual factors that differentially affect women and men. There is growing evidence from educators that girls' math and science skills can thrive when they learn in classrooms that emphasize and support girls' competencies (Martinez, 1992; Mason & Kahle, 1988; Smith & Erb, 1986). Now that we have pinpointed the areas of reliable difference (math problem solving and two spatial tasks—mental rotation and spatial perception), we need to continue to more fully explore the causes and consequences of these differences.

Do women and men think differently? Yes, there is evidence that more men outscore women in math problem solving and on some spatial tasks. I know I typically perform terribly on those spatial tests where I'm given a picture of an unfolded box and am told to mentally fold it and match it to one of a series of folded choices. But I also know that when the dishwasher is over-loaded, my husband, who usually does the after-dinner clean-up, steps aside and let's me, the "spatial expert," take over. I can cram that last pot in with the best of them! On the one hand, I test as a spatial spastic; on the other hand, I rule supreme on a daily spatial task. I cannot help but think that my exposure to specialized spatial experiences and my expectations about what I can and cannot do shape my abilities here.

In sum, I contend that a full answer to our question about comparisons of the ways women and men think will coalesce only when we combine the findings from research focused on biology, socialization, and, last but certainly not least, contextual factors (also see Riger, 1997). The challenge to future researchers, and to you as you think about cognitive similarities and differences, is to remember contextual factors. It certainly would be disappointing to miss out on major advances in math or science because the persons with the aptitudes to make them were not the "right" sex or were not exposed to relevant experiences.

SOCIAL COMPARISONS

If you refer back to Table 5.2 summarizing meta-analytic findings, meta-analysts have had something to say about various social variables, most notably social influence, aggression, helping behavior, and verbal and nonverbal communication (or what may better be subsumed under sociability). Each of these has been seriously affected by moderator variables that raise questions about whether or not these apparent differences between women and men emanate from gender itself or from exogenous factors related to gender. You'll see in the next section that gender comparisons involving each of these social variables cannot readily be reduced to a single, summarizing effect size (d).

Social Influence

In a classic social-psychological experiment, Solomon Asch (1956) lined up 7–9 white college men in two rows of seats and simply asked them to publicly indicate which of three lines was the same length as a fourth standard. The correct answer was obvious and indisputable—erroneous alternatives differed from the standard by ¾ to 1¾ inches and, when men made judgments privately, they were correct 99% of the time. However, when a lone man announced a judgment in the context of 6–8 others (who had been secretly recruited by Asch to give wrong answers on some designated trials), on average, the only true participant conformed to the obviously faulty group consensus fully one-third of the time.

As you might have guessed, it didn't take long for researchers to compare women's and men's rates of conformity. These social influence studies evolved into three forms: (1) **group pressure** studies like Asch's; (2) **persuasion experiments** where an influencing agent expressed her or his position on an issue and gave supporting arguments, and (3) **nonsurveillance procedures** where participants were exposed to arguments discrepant with their own position but the influencing person was not present.

In a meta-analysis comparing women and men in each of these three kinds of conformity settings, Alice Eagly and Linda Carli (1981) found small effect sizes ranging from +.16 to +.32 such that women conformed more than men. Follow-up analyses focused on both the gender congeniality of the topic/task and the gender of the studies' authors. Although masculine, feminine, and neutral content was used across these studies, more masculine topics (such as sports, the military, and technology) produced greater female influenceability. Interestingly, greater female conformity was found in studies that had high percentages of male authors. While studies authored by a majority of women found no gender differences, women's conformity was higher than men's in studies authored by a majority of men. Both follow-up findings hint at factors beyond gender as contributors to a small gender difference in conformity patterns (also see Bond & Smith, 1996).

Research continues to show gender differences in conformity. For example, in a clever observational study, women were more likely than men to take a dessert in a cafeteria line if their dining partner ahead of them indulged first, especially if their partner was a woman (Guarino, Fridrich, & Sitton, 1994; also see Collin, DiSano, & Malik, 1994; Larsen, 1990). However, some variability in conformity rates within groups of women suggest that power differences may play a role. Samuel Roll and his colleagues (1996) asked 30 mixed and matched pairs of Mexican American and Anglo women to record privately their three best responses to projective Rorschach cards (inkblots) and then share their answers. They measured the influence of the partner by asking each participant to add two more responses to their initial list and to note something they hadn't seen originally. Mexican American and white women were similarly influenced by their same-ethnicity partner, but when Mexican American women were paired with an Anglo partner, their susceptibility to influence increased. This finding might help explain Eagly and Carli's (1981) puzzling finding about the influence of the gender of a study's author(s). Might women conform more in the presence of higher-status male experimenters, just as Mexican American women did when relating to higher-status white women?

Aggression

Picture two kindergarten boys, outfitted with plastic shields, helmets, and swords, sword-fighting. Nothing odd about this. Now replace those boys with two girls outfitted in pink frilly dresses. Jarring? Aggression, especially physical aggression, is something we expect to distinguish girls from boys and women from men. Indeed, meta-analysts find moderate effects across various measures of aggression ($d = -.50$) indicating greater aggression in males (Hyde, 1984b). Throughout these studies, aggression is defined as behavior intended to inflict harm (as opposed to accidental injury).

For our purposes here, we'll concentrate on adults' aggressiveness. The results reported above were influenced heavily by numerous studies with children. It's laughable to picture two plastic-outfitted adults sword-fighting; obviously forms of aggression vary with age. Generally, adults' aggression comes in two varieties: **physical aggression** (including delivering shocks and noxious noise in the laboratory as well as outright assault) and **psychological aggression** (including verbal, nonverbal, and written forms). It is these variations in aggression by aggressors 14 years and older

that were studied with meta-analysis by Alice Eagly and Valerie Steffen (1986). They found only a small difference between women and men on psychological aggression ($d = -.18$) as well as a moderate effect for physical aggressiveness ($d = -.40$). Interestingly, they reported a stronger effect in the laboratory ($d = -.35$) than in field studies ($d = -.21$), suggesting that the laboratory setting may elicit more stereotyped behavior. Note that these studies observed aggression between strangers so that this literature is not relevant to our discussion of male partner abuse in Chapter 11.

Recent reviews subdivide psychological aggression into two forms. **Direct** psychological aggression is what we typically imagine; for example, yelling at someone. **Indirect** aggression, such as gossiping and excluding others, involves social manipulation, taking a more circuitous route that often protects the identity of attackers as well as shields them from retaliation (Björkqvist, 1994). This additional approach to defining aggression has just begun to influence research on aggression.

Eagly and Steffen also found that women and men have different beliefs about the consequences of their own aggression. Women reported higher fears that their aggressiveness will pose dangers to themselves, perhaps reflecting their awareness that such behavior violates gendered expectations as well as attracts retaliation. Women also expected to feel more anxiety and guilt than men as a consequence of behaving aggressively. Thus women may exercise more control over their expression of aggression because they anticipate more negative consequences (Harris, 1995), or they may seek more indirect outlets.

Are women more inhibited from aggressing than men? What would happen if we equalized their inhibitions by lowering women's. College women and men played a violent videogame under anonymous conditions; the experimenters' expectation was that being unidentifiable would make women feel just as comfortable to aggress as men (Lightdale & Prentice, 1994). Indeed, under these circumstances, women opted to drop as many bombs as men. However, women's and men's reports of their own aggressiveness differed— women described significantly less aggressive self-behavior. This pattern is consistent with an explanation based on inhibitions: when inhibitions are lifted, women aggress like men, but being aware of societal inhibitions against female aggression, women fail to acknowledge their own aggressiveness. This reasoning also is consistent with findings of a positive association between alcohol consumption and aggressive behavior in women indicating that drinking may lower inhibitions (Dougherty, Cherek, & Bennett, 1996).

All this argues that a stereotype of nonaggressive women exists (see White & Kowalski, 1994, for a review). This stereotype comes up as one of five traits believed to distinguish between women and men by respondents from 30 different countries (Williams & Best, 1982).[10] Does this mean that women really are nonaggressive? Jacquelyn White and Robin Kowalski (1994) state that an affirmative conclusion would be misleading because it implies that women never aggress, a finding countermanded by research evidence. Instead, a better summary of this literature is that *women will aggress given the appropriate circumstances.* The myth of women's nonaggressiveness sustains men's power by encouraging women's dependence on more powerful men; by bolstering the preconception that women always will lose out to a man's greater strength (misleading women to believe that "resistance is futile"—see Chapter 11); by discounting the potential of assertiveness and competitiveness (believed to be related to aggressiveness); by labeling aggressiveness by women as deviant; and by deflecting exploration away from understanding the conditions under which women will act aggressively.

What does it take to provoke aggressive behavior in women? Physical attacks, verbal insults, and frustrations (such as cutting ahead in line, losing a competitive game, blockage by a stopped car, and difficult puzzles) all reduce the difference in aggressive responses between women and men (Bettencourt & Miller, 1996).[11] Even when provoked, women engage in less aggression than men, although the difference narrows. Trained women and men coders rated the procedures used in research studies

---

[10] The others are dominance, autonomy, achievement, and endurance.

[11] Bogus negative feedback seems to make women, but not men, feel unhappy instead of aggressive. Using this as a means to provoke aggression in women thus is invalid.

according to the intensity of provocation used and the likelihood of retaliation. Women perceived less provocation in the procedures and felt more endangered by retaliation. These findings suggest that it may take more to induce aggression in women and that women may exercise greater control over their own aggressiveness because of fears of retaliation. Extrapolating these findings beyond what is traditionally done in social psychological experiments of aggression, it seems that with significant provocation and reduction of women's stronger inhibitions against aggression, the gap between women's and men's aggressiveness might be closed. (A preferable alternative might be to understand the factors which reduce men's provocation and enhance fears of retaliation in men and thus close the gap by reducing the aggressiveness exhibited by men.)

Helping Behavior

A hitchhiker stands on the side of a highway (Pomazal & Clore, 1973), a man collapses on a subway (Piliavin, Piliavin, & Rodin, 1975), a brutal fight breaks out (Borofsky, Stollak, & Messé, 1971)—who comes to the rescue? In all likelihood, it's a man (the huge effect sizes for these three comparisons are –1.42, –1.44, –1.23, respectively). When we look across a variety of helping studies, there is a small-to-moderate tendency for men to offer help more than women ($d = -.34$) and for women to receive help more than men ($d = +.46$) (Eagly & Crowley, 1986). Given that the nurturing role is typically ascribed to women, and as we'll see in Chapter 7, more caregiving is done by women, the first finding seems odd.

Who helps others more: women or men?

As you might have guessed, context matters. Much of the social-psychological literature on helping behavior relies on settings involving interactions with strangers in short-term relationships. Of course, it is these circumstances that provoke wariness in women and that are likely to reduce their willingness to intervene (Erdle, Sansom, Cole, & Heapy, 1992). As women's comfort levels go up, so does their helpfulness. For example, in studies conducted on campus, a presumably safer-feeling environment for women, the gender difference virtually disappears ($d = +.04$) (Eagly & Crowley, 1986). The difference also evaporates when the appeal for help comes in the form of a direct request ($d = -.07$). Finally, much of this literature construes helpfulness in terms of rescuing and chivalry between strangers, behaviors that are congruent with the masculine stereotype. We might expect people to be more responsive to stereotyped expectancies when they are watched than when they act unnoticed by others. Consistent with this reasoning, the gender gap in helping fades when potential helpers feel unobserved ($d = +.02$).

Sociability

We expect women to be more sociable: to talk about themselves (self-disclosure), to smile, to stand closer, to be sensitive to what others feel and want, to openly express their emotions, and so on. Indeed, in many families, women are responsible for scheduling the family's leisure time (Shaw, 1992). As with all stereotypes, a clear way to become aware of their operation is to see what happens when they are violated. When photographed women are not smiling, for example, evaluators rate them negatively, describing nonsmilers as less happy, warm, relaxed, and carefree than the average woman (Deutsch, LeBaron, & Fryer, 1987). How accurate is this stereotype of women's actual sociable behaviors?

Which woman is happier, warmer, more relaxed, and more carefree?

One clear example of sociability involves verbal self-disclosure.[12] Kathryn Dindia and Mike Allen (1992) conducted a meta-analysis using 205 studies and found a small overall gender difference in self-disclosure indicating greater disclosure by women ($d = +.18$). As has become the pattern in our review, the effect was not uniform (homogeneous), indicating that moderator variables were at work. The gender difference almost disappears when disclosers are engaged in conversations with strangers ($d = +.07$) and vanishes altogether when the listener is a man ($d = .00$). The conditions that inspire the largest gender differences involve female ($d = +.35$) and same-sex targets ($d = +.37$), exchanges with friends ($d = +.28$), and measures of disclosure that rely on partners' assessments ($d = +.44$) rather than self-assessments or observations of behaviors. These latter conditions all are congruent with the sociability stereotype for women: women are disclosed to, women talk confidentially to other women, women are more intimate with their friends, and others expect women to disclose more than men. Thus it is hard to distinguish real gender differences from differences created by gender-related expectations.

A second, extensive body of research explores gender similarities and differences in nonverbal communication. In an influential narrative review of gender differences in nonverbal communication, Nancy Henley (1977) described "body politics," such that women and lower-status others stake out less territory, wait more, are touched more and touch less, seek eye contact, and smile more in nonintimate relationships. All indicate greater sociability on the part of women. Through a detailed meta-analysis of nonverbal skills and behaviors, Judith Hall (1984) confirmed this conclusion, finding small to moderate adult gender differences in decoding skills (being sensitive to the feelings of others) ($d = +.21$); recognizing faces ($d = +.17$); accurately expressing emotions ($d = +.25$); social smiling ($d = +.30$); distance maintained from others ($d = -.27$) and by others ($d = -.43$); and expansiveness ($d = -.46$). There is certain agreement among these researchers that gender differences in nonverbal communication are reliable and form a pattern indicating the greater social skills and closeness of women.

Nancy Henley offers a **power** explanation, maintaining that what appear to be gender differences reflect differential access to and expression of perceived status in our culture (see Henley & Freeman, 1989, for a good overview). Henley brings together an extensive literature with her analysis, and two recent studies support her reasoning.

In the first, John Dovidio and his colleagues (1988) assigned women and men college students to female-male dyads. These pairs engaged in three distinct discussions: (1) an open baseline condition, followed by (2) a discussion in which one member was empowered to evaluate her/his partner and to award extra credit points, followed by (3) a final interaction in which the evaluator role was exchanged. In this way, both partners had a chance to evaluate the other. In the baseline condition, the typical gendered pattern of visually dominant men prevailed, that is, men looked at their partner more while speaking and looked away while listening. Because looking while speaking is associated with power and looking while listening with subor-

---

[12] The stereotype of the talkative woman is debunked in task-related settings where researchers find that men take up more air time than women (Swacker, 1975).

Body language gives powerful clues about which of these is a woman and which is a man.

Source: From WOMEN AND SEX ROLES: A Social Psychological Perspective by Irene H. Frieze, et al. Copyright © 1978 by W.W. Norton & Company, Inc. Reprinted by permission of W.W. Norton & Company, Inc.

dination, we'd expect the empowered partner to look while talking, regardless of gender, in the remaining exchanges. This is what happened. When women were empowered to evaluate and reward their partner, they became visually dominant, that is, they made more eye contact when speaking than when listening. Dominance, not gender per se, predicted visual patterns.

In a second study, power or social status was related to how communal and agentic targets are expected to be. Michael Conway and his colleagues (1996) asked college students to rate hypothetical characters, "Mary Smith" and "Robert Jones," along the dimensions of the Personal Attributes Questionnaire indicating communal (e.g., warm and able to devote self to others) and agentic (e.g., aggressive and independent) attributes. Some students read about targets in gender-traditional jobs (e.g., Mary as a filing clerk); others, about nontraditional employees (e.g., Robert as a filing clerk). The jobs varied by status: high (e.g., surgeon) and low (e.g., nurse on a surgical ward). The job status of both Mary and Robert made a difference: high-status workers were regarded as more agentic and less communal than low-status workers.

Jobs in the real world are not neatly dispersed for researchers; higher-status jobs tend to be dominated by white men and jobs vary according to how much agency and communality they connote (for example, our expectations that high-status surgeons will help people are unlike our expectations for high-status stockbrokers). Conway and his colleagues (1996) got around these problems in follow-up studies in which they described *fictitious* people whose status was varied with social cues such as clothing and access to resources. The pattern noted above persisted: low-status individuals were described using communal/sociable terms in contrast to agentic high-status people. Combined with the study by Dovidio and his associates (1998), these data suggest a link between status or power and sociability such that lower-status people (typically women) are expected to be, and actually are, more sociable.

All this takes us back to the bottom line question: Why are women more sociable than men? Does it have something to do with women's natures? If so, then why do contextual differences emerge such that the gap between women and men closes or widens depending on various outside circumstances, such as to whom one is disclosing or the status of the role one is enacting? Questions such as these emerge throughout all areas of research reviewed here. It is clear that *context plays a role as a moderator of apparent gender differences*. The next question we then might ask concerns the consequences of finding gender-related differences.

THE CONSEQUENCES OF DIFFERENCE

Is it more useful to think about women and men as basically similar or different? Quite simply, we can either assume that we are fundamentally different or assume that we are basically the same. Rachel Hare-Mustin and Jeanne Marecek (1988) have labeled these views alpha bias and beta bias, respectively. Psychologists who believe in **alpha bias** assume that females and males are opposites and thus have mutually exclusive and nonoverlapping traits (like the frequency distributions graphed in Figure 5.1[a]). We can see this in the way we stereotype women and men. Women are soft, dependent, and irrational; men are hard, independent, and logical; in essence, men are not feminine; women are not masculine. In contrast, people holding **beta bias** believe that differences should be ignored or are indeed minimal. Theorists and researchers assuming beta bias tend to look for gender similarities rather than differences.

It's impossible to say which set of assumptions is "unbiased," that is, true or valid. As we have seen, an empirical approach has not produced consensus—even the meta-analysts disagree about whether or not the data support a general pattern of similarity or difference. I think this is because what we are dealing with here is an approach to viewing the world. Philosophers of science refer to this as one's **world view**—a set of implicit assumptions that shape how we think about, and then go about, exploring the world (Pepper, 1970). It can be argued that these views defy empirical testing. Rather, we need to be up-front with our values and assumptions and to evaluate them for their utility (Hare-Mustin & Marecek, 1988). Now the important question is: What are the consequences of being alpha biased versus beta biased?

As we have seen, assuming and finding differences frequently have serious practical costs, especially for women. Often, differences are viewed as deficiencies, and solutions take the form of fixing the defective party. This is especially true for women for whom androcentric bias dictates that the male way is the better way. How many of the gender differences documented in Table 5.2 imply that women need to catch up to men? What I am getting at here is that intrinsic to gender comparisons are assumptions about what is valued in our society.

Consider two of the differences we examined: aggressiveness, with more men being aggressive than women, and interpersonal sensitivity, with more women being sensitive than men. Do we value these characteristics equally in our society? How do we deal with the lower-scoring group? For example, since more men are aggressive than women, should we try to remedy women's deficiency in aggressiveness? This will sound less absurd if we rethink it in terms of "assertiveness." Assertiveness training has long been touted as a way to further women's opportunities in the workforce, especially in management. Is our response to differences in interpersonal sensitivity parallel? Has sensitivity training for men been pursued to the same degree as assertiveness training for women? Whether outcomes are valued or devalued may play a large role in determining how much energy is put into understanding how and why a gender difference occurs, who is considered "normal," and who is declared "deficient."

This gets even more complicated when we consider women's apparently stronger nonverbal skills, including their interpersonal sensitivity and visual subordination. We have seen that both are negatively related to power and status. What we might value as important social skills (e.g., being sensitive to others) is devalued by its association with subordinated status. Do we suggest that women avoid sociable behaviors in order to enhance their status, for example, by calling for a "smile boycott" (Deutsch, LeBaron, & Fryer, 1987)? Might such an approach smack of androcentrism—the assumption that what is male-defined is unquestionably normative and more valuable? Rather than rejecting the positive aspects of feminine behavior as disempowering, might it be better to work toward enhancing the value of these skills and the people who master them? If this were to become our goal, then men too might have to work to develop their interpersonal skills to the benefit of us all. Maybe men need a "smile-athon" even more than women would benefit from a "smile boycott."

Another piece of our analysis focuses on presumed cause. When we concentrate exclusively on causes internal to women as the roots of gender differences, we fail to challenge external forces (such as schools, businesses, and social norms, each of which contributes to the differential treatment of women, men, girls, and boys). This has lead Arnie Kahn and me (1989) to advocate an assumption of beta bias. For us and others like us (e.g., Lott, 1991), it fits our social-psychological and feminist frameworks because it stresses contextual factors as moderators.

We do not say that women and men are identical (nor should they be treated identically), but that individual differences among women and among men are far greater than any group differences between us. I do not espouse a minimalist, feminist partyline that limits research on gender differences.[13] I simply propose that we ask questions whenever we find gender differences that explore contextual factors as well as dispositional factors. The major advantage of finding contextual factors is that these can be changed so that if women and men are disadvantaged by a presumed gender difference, we can alter their circumstances. In this way, we can allow both women and men to express their individuality without being constrained by limitations imposed by gender.

CHAPTER SUMMARY

In this chapter, we have questioned the significance of difference by looking beyond simple summaries of studies that have compared women and girls with men and boys. The measurement of difference is complicated by statistical and interpretive issues inherent in how we measure difference and by our research methodology

---

[13]For a detailed discussion of whether or not psychologists should study sex and gender differences, see the special feature in *Feminism & Psychology*, November 1994, vol. 4(4), for articles by Celia Kitzinger, Janet Shibley Hyde, Alice Eagly, Diane Halpern, Rachel Hare-Mustin and Jeanne Marecek, and Wendy Holloway.

itself, which defines success as the confirmation of differences. Meta-analysis has been developed as a useful tool for combining data across a large number of studies on a topic, but even it cannot give us definitive answers about whether or not women and men are basically different. Rather, meta-analysis is only a first step toward a fully informed understanding.

The next step is interpreting meta-analytic findings, leading us to probe the causes underlying potential differences. Are differences rooted within individuals (in our biologies or socialized learning) or does social context play a role such that contextual factors external to the individual can both exaggerate and limit differences? Although biology, socialization, and social context probably come together to influence us, I have argued that contextual factors often are overlooked, despite the possibility that they may contribute substantially and in ways that are consistent with a feminist orientation. We reviewed contextual alternatives as they play out in research on cognitive differences, including verbal, math, and spatial abilities, and on social differences, such as social influence, aggression, helping behavior, and sociability. Are women truly from Venus and men from Mars? I suspect not. Rather, we need to question the significance of difference: "We're for difference, for respecting difference, for allowing difference, until difference doesn't make any difference."[14]

---

[14]Johnnetta B. Cole, President of Spelman College, quoted in James, 1997, p. 213.

SIX

SEXISM
Sexist Prejudice, Stereotyping, and Discrimination

A boy and his father were in a major car accident. The father was pronounced dead at the scene; meanwhile, the boy was rushed to the nearest hospital. A prominent surgeon was called to perform a life-saving operation. As the boy was being prepared for the surgery, the surgeon saw him and declared: "I can't operate. He's my son." How can this be?

This brain-teaser was widely circulated in the 1970s and baffled many people. Some suggested that the surgeon was a stepfather, an unknown biological father (as opposed to the adoptive father who died in the crash), a reincarnation of the dead father, mistaken about the identity of the boy, and so on. A simple solution eluded many.[1] Yet this simple riddle speaks volumes about how deep-seated sexism can be; we are likely to consider all sorts of outlandish possibilities before we challenge the misleading assumption that the surgeon is male.

Sexism directed against women is the *oppression* or "inhibition" of women[2] "through a vast network of everyday practices, attitudes, assumptions, behaviors, and institutional rules" (Young, 1992, p. 180). If we look at sexism through the eyes of a social psychologist, we see that it has three interrelated, but conceptually distinct, parts: prejudice, stereotyping, and discrimination (Lott, 1995). **Sexist prejudice** refers to negative as well as apparently positive attitudes toward women and girls that serve to oppress them. **Sexist stereotypes** refer to the ascription of both positive and negative traits which characterize women and girls as well suited to restricted, less powerful and/or disliked roles. **Sexist discrimination** describes overt negative acts directed toward women and girls as well as patronizing acts that assert male superiority.[3] The typical triumvirate of psychological conceptualization (affect or feelings, cognitions or beliefs, and behavior, respectively) are subsumed into this definition of sexism.

We are accustomed to thinking about prejudice, stereotyping, and discrimination in completely negative terms. When discussing the sexist versions of these, we often are confused by blatantly sexist people who have strong, loving relationships with women and girls. As one arguably misogynist man declared emphatically to me, "How can I hate women; I married one!" As we shall see in this chapter, sexism paradoxically may encompass feelings, beliefs, and even actions that on the surface appear benevolent. The fundamental point that ties seemingly benevolent attitudes with overtly hostile ones is their consequences, regardless of intent—*feelings, thoughts and actions are sexist whenever they serve to oppress women and girls* by keeping them "in their place" (Glick, 1997).

We usually think of these three components of sexism as being interrelated; prejudiced chauvinists stereotype women and discriminate against them. However, we shall see that sometimes things aren't this clear-cut. Even the most ardent feminists get caught every now and then stereotyping or acting discriminatory. I remember my first encounter with the opening riddle (it was the central focus of an "All in the Family" television segment); the solution was not all that apparent. Sometimes sexism is so ingrained in our thinking that we aren't even aware of it until we confront ambi-

---

[1] The surgeon is the boy's mom.

[2] I do not mean to dismiss sexism directed against men as inconsequential (see Chapter 1); however, women will take center stage in the present discussion of sexism.

[3] These definitions were influenced heavily by comments from Peter Glick.

guities such as those in the surgeon riddle. At other times, we realize that something is sexist but we let it slide; it is exhausting to charge every windmill (and one can become ineffective as well). It's difficult to discern where to draw the line between silent tolerance and complicity. In this chapter, we'll explore prejudice, stereotypes, and discrimination both individually and in relation to each other.

SEXIST PREJUDICE

Personality theorists have devoted much energy toward developing measures of a "prejudiced personality," and prejudice expressed as sexism is no exception. The long-standing measure of attitudes toward the rights, roles, and privileges of women in American society is the *Attitudes toward Women Scale* (AWS) introduced by Janet Spence and Robert Helmreich in 1972. There are three versions of the AWS, varying in length (Spence & Helmreich, 1978), and it is the most widely used measure of sexist prejudice (Beere, 1990).[4]

The AWS has been criticized for its transparency; it is easy to know the socially desirable answer for some of the items (e.g., "Swearing and obscenity are more repulsive in the speech of a woman than a man"). If you think the questioner wants nonsexist answers (or if you wanted to annoy such a surveyor), it would be easy to frame your answers to give off the impression you wanted. Consistent with this reasoning, there is little variability in the responses of contemporary respondents, especially with well-educated samples (Cota, 1990, cited in Cota, Reid, & Dion, 1991). Furthermore, overall scoring, suggesting that white women are more egalitarian than African American (Clark, 1986; Gackenbach, 1978; Zuckerman, 1980; 1981) and Japanese American, Chinese, and Hawaiian women (Ullman, Freedland, & Warmsun, 1978), has been challenged as inconsistent with other measures that find no racial differences in gender attitudes (Berendsen & Yoder, 1997).

If people indeed are scoring as more egalitarian on the AWS (Spence & Hahn, 1997), does that mean sexist prejudice is on the decline? Unfortunately, there's another possibility. Recent theorists have argued that sexist, as well as racist prejudices, have become more subtle in the 1990s so that few people make openly hostile comments (Dovidio & Gaertner, 1986). The Modern Sexism Scale has been introduced to tap these subtleties (Swim, Aikin, Hall, & Hunter, 1995). Look over the items of this scale in Box 6.1. Items cluster together to measure three distinct aspects of subtle sexism: denial of continuing discrimination, antagonism toward women's demands, and special favors for women.

SEXIST STEREOTYPING: IMAGES OF WOMEN

Stereotypes are used whenever we classify others according to some categorical membership. **Gender stereotypes** simply are consensual beliefs about the characteristics of women and men (Deaux & Kite, 1993). They may be sexist in that they oppress

---

[4] Beere (1990) lists 270 studies using the AWS from 1979–1990; 101 other references were counted prior to 1979. The March 1997 issue of *Psychology of Women Quarterly* is devoted to exploration of this scale and similar measures (Frieze & McHugh, 1997).

BOX 6.1   Modern Sexism Scale

Denial of Continuing Discrimination
1. Discrimination against women is no longer a problem in the United States.*
2. Women often miss out on good jobs due to sexual discrimination.
3. It is rare to see women treated in a sexist manner on television.*
4. On average, people in our society treat husbands and wives equally.*
5. Society has reached the point where women and men have equal opportunities for achievement.*

Antagonism toward Women's Demands
6. It is easy to understand the anger of women's groups in America.*
7. It is easy to understand why women's groups are still concerned about societal limitations on women's opportunities.

Resentment about Special Favors for Women
8. Over the past few years, the government and news media have been showing more concern about the treatment of women than is warranted by women's actual experiences.*

Note: Items are numbered in the order they appear in the scale. Each item is rated on 5-point scales where 5 = disagreement. Starred (*) items are reverse coded so that higher sums indicate higher levels of *sexism*. *Source*: J. K. Swim, K. J. Aikin, W. S. Hall, and B. A. Hunter (1995). Sexism and racism: Old-fashioned and modern prejudices. *Journal of Personality and Social Psychology*, 68, 199–214. Copyright © 1995 by the American Psychological Association. Reprinted with permission.

---

women and men, or not. Before we tackle the question of whether or not gender stereotypes are sexist (in that they serve to oppress women and girls), let's explore what gender stereotypes are like.

Gender Stereotypes

Read the following narrative, picture Chris and Pat, and at each question mark, jot down the sex of each.[5]

> At a singles bar, Pat watches Chris shoot pool across the room. Chris is an obviously aggressive player, taking tough shots and talking trash. Chris has a tall, athletic build, and other players seem awed by Chris's play.
> ?
>
> As the game ends, Chris moves toward the bar for a beer. Pat approaches Chris, pays for Chris's beer, and asks Chris to dance. Chris doesn't know Pat and is a bit wary, but hesitantly agrees.
> ?
>
> As they dance, they chat a bit. They discover that they went to the same high school

---

[5] A similar approach was used by John and Sussman (1989).

but Chris graduated a few years ahead of Pat. Pat now teaches at a local elementary school, and Chris is a firefighter.

?

As you read, was it hard not to add pronouns to the story? Did you ache to refer to Chris's beer as *his* beer? But wait, Pat paid and asked to dance? Is Pat the guy? But, Pat's a school teacher? The story mixes stereotypes of women and men, drawing on four different aspects of gender stereotypes: **traits** (e.g., aggressiveness and passively watching); **role behaviors** (e.g., the dating roles defining who pays and who asks whom to dance); **occupations** (e.g., teacher and firefighter); and **physical characteristics** (e.g., being tall and athletic). Kay Deaux and Laurie Lewis (1983) identified these four components of gender stereotypes, and they argue that these components can best be viewed as distinct factors.

Traits. This seems easy enough. We looked at the Bem Sex Role Inventory (BSRI) in Chapter 3 and saw a list of personality characteristics ascribed to women and men: sensitive, kind, assertive, confident, etc. But, who are these women and men? Remember that the BSRI specified "typical" women and men when it was constructed. But, who is typical? And, what about our "ideal" woman and man? Each of these questions further complicates our exploration of gender-stereotyped traits.

What traits are used to describe *typical* women and men? When almost 3,000 graduate and undergraduate students in academic year 1991-92 were asked to describe "most women," they reported traits associated with compassion (e.g., caring, sensitive, loving, able to cry, emotional, gentle, and sentimental) (Street, Kimmel, & Kromrey, 1995). These attributions are consistent with other research concluding that a "niceness-nurturance" dimension defines the core traits of typical women (De Lisi & Soundranayagam, 1990) and that women's nicknames connote beauty/goodness (Phillips, 1990) and affection (De Klerk & Bosch, 1996). In contrast, "most men" were rated as high in three clusters of masculine-typed traits: power (e.g., achievement-oriented, competitive, assertive), sexuality (e.g., sexually aggressive and skilled lover), and intellect (e.g., self-disciplined, logical, and analytical). The three clusters of traits most descriptive of typical men are regarded as the least descriptive characteristics of typical women. In other words, being masculine implies anti-femininity and vice versa.

Both women and men describe typical women and men in gender-typed terms. However, ratings diverge from typical to ideal targets and from women to men raters describing ideal men. Women stereotype the *ideal* man as combining clusters of intellectual and compassionate traits; deference is the trait women least like in the ideal man (Street et al., 1995). Men most highly value intellect in the ideal man, followed by power, compassion, and sexuality. The ideal woman combines compassion and intellect—sound familiar? Women's and men's ratings of the ideal woman diverge on only one trait, deference, with men (not surprisingly) preferring higher levels.[6] This combining of intellectual traits, typically regarded as more masculine in their ori-

---

[6] Participants descriptions of themselves conform to the ideals. For women's self-ratings, this means blending intellect and compassion; for men's, the ideal men of women and men is amalgamated so that intellect, power, compassion, and sexuality combine in their self-descriptions (and deference is denied).

entation, with compassionate characteristics, typically regarded as more feminine, fits with other research describing the female and male ideal in androgynous terms (Lindner, Ryckman, Gold, & Stone, 1995).

Consider the eight clusters of traits in Box 6.2. First, review each cluster and rate on the 7-point scales how much you'd like someone with that combination of traits and how competent you think they'd be. Next, look at the eight clusters themselves, and fill in blanks (A), (B), (C), and (D) with African American, Mexican American, Asian American, and Anglo American—one for women and one for men.

We saw in Chapter 1 that stereotypes of presumably generic women and men actually assume other demographic characteristics such as race (white) and class (middle) (Landrine, 1985). What are the trait stereotypes for specific subgroups of women and men? An ethnically diverse sample of 259 students was asked to simply list the first 10 adjectives that came to mind for each of eight groups of African American, Anglo-American, Mexican American, and Asian American women and men (Niemann, Jennings, Rozelle, Baxter, & Sullivan, 1994). Box 6.2 lists the top 20% of synonyms applied to each target group. How accurately did you fill in the blanks? (See footnote #7 for the findings.)[7]

The first point that should emerge from Box 6.2 is that trait stereotypes do not come in one size that fits all. Second, we are pretty accurate at identifying stereotypes even if we don't espouse them ourselves. Third, the valence (or affective tone) of trait stereotypes varies according to the social status of each ethnic group. Anglos are the dominant group and thus sport the most favorable traits. Asian Americans are oftentimes viewed as a "model minority"—high in competence but disliked for their perceived lack of amicability (Lin & Fiske, 1997, cited in Glick & Fiske, 1999). African and Mexican Americans are afforded the least status and are stereotyped accordingly (Glick & Fiske, 1999). There is growing consensus among stereotyping theorists that the content of stereotypes is inextricably linked to social status (Glick, 1997).

Role behaviors.   A second component of gender stereotypes is role behaviors, that is, what women and men do. (Note that employment splinters off from this category to form its own component of gender stereotyping.) Stereotypes of women and men vary not only according to targets' race/ethnicity but also according to what role they are playing. For example, consider your own images of housewives and career women, male athletes and businessmen. Are they different?

Six distinct role clusters emerge for men when mostly white students were asked to "name as many different types of men as you can" (Edwards, 1992). Follow-up research fills in the defining characteristics for each role: **businessman** (educated, busy, aggressive, achieving, and dressed in a suit); **loser** (underachieving, unhappy, pessimistic quitter); **blue-collar worker** (hardworking, high school educated, tv-watching, family-caring, union member); **athlete** (physically fit and health conscious); **family man** (dedicated, responsible, employed father, husband, and breadwinner); and **womanizer** (attractive, confident, vain, self-centered). These subcategories of men are consistent with both prior (Deaux, Winton, Crowley, & Lewis, 1985) and more recent research (England, 1992).

---

[7] Findings for Box 6.3: (A) African American; (B) Anglo American; (C) Asian American; (D) Mexican American.

BOX 6.2 Trait Stereotypes of Eight Different Subgroups of Women and Men

- Complete the scales for each cluster.
- Fill in (A), (B), (C), and (D) in each column with:
  - * African American
  - * Mexican American
  - * Asian American
  - * Anglo American

Women

(A) _____

    speak loudly
    dark skin
    antagonistic
    athletic
    pleasant/friendly
    unmannerly
    sociable/socially active

1	2	3	4	5	6	7
dislike						like
1	2	3	4	5	6	7
incompetent						competent

(B) _____

    attractive
    intelligent
    egotistical
    pleasant/friendly
    blond/light hair
    sociable/socially active

1	2	3	4	5	6	7
dislike						like
1	2	3	4	5	6	7
incompetent						competent

(C) _____

    intelligent
    speak softly
    pleasant/friendly
    short

1	2	3	4	5	6	7
dislike						like
1	2	3	4	5	6	7
incompetent						competent

(D) _____

    black/brown/dark hair
    attractive
    pleasant/friendly
    dark skin
    lower class
    overweight
    baby makers
    family-oriented

1	2	3	4	5	6	7
dislike						like
1	2	3	4	5	6	7
incompetent						competent

Men

(A) _____

    athletic
    antagonistic
    dark skin
    muscular appearance
    criminal activities
    speak loudly

1	2	3	4	5	6	7
dislike						like
1	2	3	4	5	6	7
incompetent						competent

(B) _____

    intelligent
    egotistical
    upper class
    pleasant/friendly
    racist
    achievement oriented

1	2	3	4	5	6	7
dislike						like
1	2	3	4	5	6	7
incompetent						competent

(C) _____

    intelligent
    short
    achievement oriented
    speak softly
    hard workers

1	2	3	4	5	6	7
dislike						like
1	2	3	4	5	6	7
incompetent						competent

(D) _____

    lower class
    hard workers
    antagonistic
    dark skin
    non-college educated
    pleasant/friendly
    black/brown/dark hair
    ambitionless

1	2	3	4	5	6	7
dislike						like
1	2	3	4	5	6	7
incompetent						competent

Source: Adapted from Y. F. Niemann, et al., Use of free responses and cluster analysis to determine stereotypes of eight groups. *Personality and Social Psychology Bulletin, 20,* 379–390, copyright © 1994 by Sage Publications, Inc. Reprinted by Permission of Sage Publications, Inc.

Five subcategories of gender stereotypes emerge for women: housewife/mother, sexy woman, athlete, career woman, and feminist (Deaux et al., 1985; Eckes, 1994). The **housewife/mother** stereotype is characterized as nondemanding, selfless, longing for security, and focused on family affairs (Eckes, 1994).[8] Most notably, it is this stereotype that most overlaps with the stereotype of the typical woman, suggesting that the typical woman is not only white and middle class as Hope Landrine (1985) indicated, but also fulfills the roles of housewife and mother. The role of mother is especially steeped in femininity: there is much more overlap between descriptions of mother and parent (41%) than between father and parent (15%) (Deaux et al., 1985).

But are all mothers stereotyped similarly? Does race and ethnicity make a difference? Consider, for example, the stereotype of African American mothers which brings in conflicting images of mammies, welfare, promiscuity, matriarchy, and superwomen (Sparks, 1996). Also consider married mothers, stepmothers, divorced mothers, and never married mothers. Stereotypes of these groups differ as well. Graduate students in nursing and child development generated quite different stereotypes of these four types of mothers (Ganong & Coleman, 1995). Married mothers fit the cultural stereotype of presumably generic mothers. Not surprisingly, virtually all of the attributes extended to them are indisputably positive (e.g., forgiving, generous, protective, warm, and caring); the only possible exceptions are "tired" and "willing to give up her career for family," both of which are extensions of selflessness.

Contrast this with the stereotype for stepmothers, for example, the stepmother in Cinderella (and other Disney classics). Stepmothers are portrayed as lacking many of the positive characteristics of biological mothers and as possessing several undesirable personality traits (e.g., being unkind and unreasonable). They are depicted as less family oriented, uninterested and unskilled in raising children, and less successful in their marriages.

Stereotypes also are unforgiving for divorced and never married mothers. Divorced mothers are characterized as lonely, unhappy, stressed, financially poor, and with bleak futures. Never married mothers are portrayed as unpleasant people with many negative and few favorable traits. They are expected to be deficient in their childrearing skills, failures as marital partners, and products of dysfunctional families. The mother stereotype is rosy only if the mom is married and biologically related to her child(ren).

The subtype of **sexy woman** conjures up a well-dressed woman with a good figure, pretty face, long hair, and nail polish (Deaux et al., 1985). The stereotype of women as erotic sex objects is especially pronounced for Asian and Asian American women (Chan, 1987). This stereotype emerges as the dominant image of women, both sought after and seeking, in heterosexual personals ads. Not surprisingly, most men desire physical attractiveness: "Single white male looking for thin, very attractive. . . ." (Feingold, 1990; Smith, Waldorf, & Trembath, 1990; Willis & Carlson, 1993). Understanding the market, women typically described themselves using physical descriptors (Davis, 1990). Although women also look for physical attractiveness in

---

[8] A good review of societal images of motherhood and how these effect daughters' perceptions of mothers, as well as an assignment to confront and change these stereotyped views, is presented by Howe (1989).

The five different subtypes of women:
(a) housewife/mother; (b) sexy woman; (c) athlete; (d) career woman; and (e) feminist.[9]

---

[9] In keeping with Landrine's (1985) findings, I purposively used all white women as examples. Each subtype has its own version for women of color.

their sought-after dates, financial security and interpersonal understanding generally dominate women's expressed desires.

The third subcategory of role stereotypes for women describes **athletes**, women with good bodies who are muscular, strong, aggressive, and masculine (Deaux et al., 1985). This stereotype often envelopes stereotypes of lesbianism, hence my selection of Matina Navartolva on page 155, who is openly lesbian (Blinde & Taub, 1992). The stereotype of lesbians includes myths about lesbians' seduction of heterosexual women, lesbian boasting, and a masculine aura (Eliason, Donelan, & Randall, 1992). It is noteworthy that this configuration does not emerge from general stereotyping studies of women; none of the above studies found a cluster of traits associated with lesbian women. Do you think a different list of traits would distinguish stereotypes of a lesbian from those for a "typical" woman?[10] Would these lists of adjectives overlap much?

The **career woman** is independent, educated, and unconventional, and she occupies high social status (Eckes, 1994). There is evidence that this role stereotype can clash with the feminine stereotype, especially for some occupations like manager. A long-standing series of studies has asked raters, typically middle managers themselves, to rate the characteristics of *successful* middle managers (no sex specified), as well as women and men in general. In 1973, Virginia Schein found that there was a lot of overlap between the descriptions of middle managers and men, and little overlap between the ratings of managers and women. In other words, successful managers were stereotyped using masculine terms, presumably setting up a conflict for women: How can they be successful managers and women at the same time? Subsequent research has replicated this pattern using men as raters (both managers and students); however, women raters describe successful managers in terms that blend masculine and feminine characteristics (Brenner, Tomkiewicz, & Schein, 1989; Dodge, Gilroy, & Fenzel, 1995; Schein, Mueller, & Jacobson, 1989). Cross-culturally, both women and men persist in gender-typing managers in Germany; British women do less gender-typing (Schein & Mueller, 1992); and Nigerian men are especially harsh gender-typers (Tomkiewicz & Adeyemi-Bello, 1995).

Generally, studies uncover two separate clusters of characteristics: one for career women and another for housewives/mothers (Eckes, 1994). They also find considerable overlap between the housewife/mother stereotype and "typical" woman stereotype, suggesting that presumably global stereotypes of women narrowly assume the housewife/mother subtype. Relatedly, "typical" women are *not* career women.

If the career woman is not like a "typical" woman or like a male manager, what type of woman is she? The traits that characterize the role stereotype of the career woman are related to the **feminist** stereotype (Eckes, 1994). A feminist stereotypically is judged to be critical of society, ideologically minded, politically committed, and rebellious-aggressive. Both career women and feminists score high on a potency dimension, being regarded as independent, self-confident, and dominant. This pattern is consistent with images associated with the use of Ms. as a title of address (Dion & Cota, 1991). Students rated a successful woman manager addressed with the title Ms. as closer to the presumably generic image of a successful middle manager than the same woman using a traditional title (Mrs. or Miss) (Dion & Schuller, 1990).

---

[10] Linda Garnets (1996, pp. 139–140) describes an interesting class exercise for comparing and contrasting stereotypes of feminine and masculine people with those for lesbians and gay men.

"Ms. Manager" evoked expectations of competence, leadership, and stereotypic masculinity.

Roles are dependent on social contexts, and gender roles are no exceptions. The five role-based stereotypes for women (housewife/mother, sexy woman, athlete, career woman, and feminist) all depend on the social context in which they are evoked. For example, consider a business setting. It is unlikely that, upon seeing a woman at a desk with a computer terminal, the housewife/mother stereotype will be activated. "Career woman" fits better . . . but manager? Secretary is a more likely bet. We generally look for a good situation-role fit to determine which subtype of role stereotyping to use (Eckes, 1996).

Occupations. Try the stereotyping exercise in Box 6.3.

BOX 6.3

On a distant planet, two different species, Orinthians and Ackmians live together. There are no sexes on this planet; any individual can mate with anyone else, causing both to reproduce.

Orinthians function primarily as *child raisers.* Orinthians spend most of their time at the group home, where they take responsibility for the care and teaching of the group's young. Orinthians typically are adventurous, compassionate, charming, forceful, patient, creative, outspoken, warm, and likeable.

Ackmians are *city workers,* working in the nearby cities, where all the business, industry, technology, and higher education are concentrated. Ackmians travel to the city each day and return to the group home in the evening. Ackmians generally are assertive, considerate, imaginative, intellectual, sensitive, responsible, opinionated, helpful, and happy.

Describe Orinthians:

Describe Ackmians:

Source: Adapted from C. Hoffman and N. Hurst (1990). Gender stereotypes: Perceptions or rationalization? *Journal of Personality and Social Psychology, 58,* 197–208. Copyright © 1990 by the American Psychological Association. Adapted with permission.

Curt Hoffman and Nancy Hurst (1990) asked students to consider a variety of different and more complicated scenarios than the one you read above. The key though is what they varied in these vignettes—the highlighted roles of child raiser and city worker. The traits listed as characterizing each "species" are purposively diverse. I list three sets of three traits whereby the first trait in each set is masculine/agentic (e.g., outspoken and opinionated), the second is feminine/communal (e.g., warm and helpful), and the third is neutral (e.g., likeable and happy). Note that Orinthians and Ackmians both are described using three traits from each gender-typed category. These researchers found that student raters relied on the occupations of the two species to describe them so that the child-rearing Orinthians were described in feminine/communal terms and the city-working Ackmians in masculine/agentic terms. Furthermore, students recalled more role-congruent (e.g., Orinthians are patient, warm, and compassionate) traits than inconsistent ones (e.g., Orinthians are adventurous, forceful, and outspoken). These findings are even more pronounced when the two groups are distinguished as biologically distinct (as species) rather than as culturally different (as subcultures).

Obviously for us, Orinthians parallel women and Ackmians represent men on planet Earth. By using fictitious groups, the researchers avoided any preconceptions that might have contaminated their study. Their findings highlight the importance of occupational cues—we expect "child raisers" to differ from "city workers" even when these occupations are stripped of their gender cues and even when those filling each role manifest both stereotypic and counterstereotypic traits.

What about other gender-typed occupations like miner and manicurist? Joyce Beggs and Dorothy Doolittle (1993) document a continuum of occupations that are perceived as being masculine on one end (with miner as the most extreme) to feminine on the other (manicurist). Of the 129 occupations included, all but five[11] retained the same classification as masculine, feminine, or neutral in the 1990s that previous researchers had established in 1975. Overall, women's ratings in the 1990s are less gender-typed than men's. Of the 56 occupations that in real-life saw increases in the proportion of women actually doing the job, fully 46 were rated as less masculine in the 1990s than in the mid-1970s. Again, this suggests that who does a job (i.e., gender ratios) makes a difference in how it is perceived. Returning to our interaction in the singles bar between our sex-indeterminate friends, Pat and Chris, when Pat says she(?) is a school teacher and Chris reveals that he(?) is a firefighter, this muddies our prior conviction that Pat is a man and Chris is a woman.

Physical characteristics. One of the dominant physical stereotypes for women centers on attractiveness. Women's bodies attract a lot of attention in our culture, and there seems to be at least two different views of them—one from women and another from men. Consider the silhouettes of women's and men's bodies in Figure 6.1. Indicate where you think you fall on the scale; where the ideal woman and ideal man are; and where you think the ideals of other peers would be.

Where women place themselves on the scale is pretty accurate; in a study with 87 white college women, trained observers' ratings and self-ratings overlapped by 72-85% (Cohn & Adler, 1992). As expected, women do tend to underreport their weight and to think of themselves as overweight (Betz, Mintz, & Speakmon, 1994). And not surprisingly, white women's ideal was thinner than themselves; about half the women selected an ideal that was fully one silhouette thinner than themselves (Cohn & Adler, 1992). The preference expected by peers was even thinner.

---

[11] The five exceptions were: sales manager which moved from masculine to neutral; taxidermist which shifted from neutral to masculine; and social worker, florist supply sales, and file clerk which went from neutral to feminine.

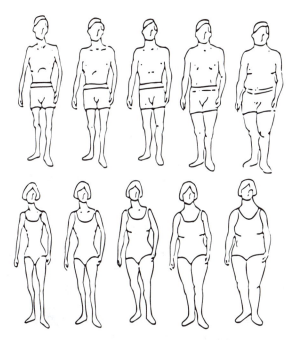

FIGURE 6.1

Needless to say, this differential between perceived and ideal body sizes is consistent with reports of women's body dissatisfaction. In a 1993 survey of 803 adult women across the United States, nearly half reported globally negative evaluations of their appearance and a preoccupation with being or becoming overweight (Cash & Henry, 1995). Most of this dissatisfaction was directed at general weight as well as at the lower- (hips, buttocks, thighs, and legs) and mid-torso (waist and stomach). Less than 20% expressed discontent with their face, height, or hair. Overall, more women than men hold negative attitudes toward their body parts (Franzoi, 1995).

Do women set these standards of thinness for themselves or do men play a role? It is commonly believed that white women are stricter critics of women's bodies than white men (Furnham, Hester, & Weir, 1990). Fully 69% of women considered the thinnest silhouettes as most attractive to men; only 25% of men actually selected these options (Cohn & Adler, 1992). However, more white than African American men reported both a low desire to date a woman with a heavier-than-ideal body size and fears of ridicule (Powell & Kahn, 1995). Combine this with heterosexual men's personals ads emphasizing the physical attractiveness of prospects, and one is left to contemplate that women's perceptions of men's preferences for thinness may be firmly grounded.

Body dissatisfaction is not felt universally by women, although some authors have overgeneralized from studies with white women to all women (Trepagnier, 1994). Comparisons of African American and white women find that more African American women are satisfied with their bodies (S. Harris, 1994; Stevens, Sumanyika, & Keil, 1994) and hold less strict criteria for defining fatness (Cunningham, Roberts, & Barbee, 1995; Rucker & Cash, 1992); this may be especially true among African American women of lower socioeconomic status (Allan, Mayo, & Michel, 1993). More

Ghanaian than U.S. women rated larger body sizes as ideal (Cogan, Bhalla, & Sefa-Dedeh, 1996), as did Ugandan as compared to British women (Furnham & Baguma, 1994). Possibly related to this pattern is the finding that African American men prefer a larger woman's silhouette than do white men (Rosen et al., 1993; Thompson, Sargent, & Kemper, 1996); although substantially overweight figures continue to be undesirable (Singh, 1994), they are not actively disparaged (Jackson & McGill, 1996). On a related note, African American college women generally are satisfied with their own skin tone, but among those who desire a different color, lighter is considered better (Bond & Cash, 1992).

Body dissatisfaction rates for Asian American women are more similar to those of African American women than to white women's (Akan & Grilo, 1995). Women holding feminist attitudes toward physical attractiveness also have lower rates of body dissatisfaction (Dionne, Davis, Fox, & Gurevich, 1995). Body esteem and overall self-esteem are more closely related in lesbian than in heterosexual women (Striegel-Moore, Tucker, & Hsu, 1990), but there is some evidence that fewer lesbians feel pressured to conform to unrealistic standards of thinness or to value small body sizes (Herzog, Newman, Yeh, & Warshaw, 1992; Root, 1990). Conflict between mainstream valuing of thinness and lesbians' acceptance of women's bodies is a recurring theme in interviews with young lesbian women (Beren et al., 1997). More older than younger women prefer larger figures (Lamb, Jackson, Cassiday, & Priest, 1993).

All of this research on women's body image stands in contrast to findings for men. Overall, women's bodies are viewed as objects of beauty, in contrast to men's which are regarded as instruments of action (Franzoi, 1996, p. 316). According to theorists stressing **objectified body consciousness**, the tendency to treat women's bodies as objects causes women themselves to view their bodies as if they are outside observers (McKinley & Hyde, 1996; Spitzack, 1990). Constant self-surveillance is necessary to comply with cultural standards and to avoid negative judgments. Responsibility for reaching the bodily ideal falls squarely on the shoulders of women; with enough effort, it is believed they can control their appearance. Diet and exercise regimens all imply that everyone who tries can achieve the approved bodily look. Furthermore, cultural body standards are internalized by women so that they themselves appear to be the sources of their body dissatisfaction. The external, cultural sources of women's body dissatisfaction become lost as women seemingly freely choose to pursue the ideal body. All this is exemplified by the woman who endured 18 operations to transform herself into the cultural ideal— a "Barbie" doll (see photo on page 161).

In conclusion, we have seen that gender stereotypes encompass expectations about women's traits, role behaviors, occupations, and physical characteristics. How do these interrelate? Kay Deaux and Laurie Lewis (1984) described a target using one component of gender stereotypes; then they asked students to note the probability that the target would display other stereotypic characteristics consistent and inconsistent with the initial information. When they described targets' physiques as masculine (tall, strong, sturdy, and broad-shouldered), raters were confident that those targets possessed masculine traits, filled masculine roles (e.g., financial provider and head of household), and worked in masculine occupations. The same pattern emerged when targets were described as possessing a feminine body type (soft voice, dainty, graceful, and soft). These researchers concluded that (1) stereotypes come in

Would a man endure all this to look like "Ken"?

homogeneous packages in which the components are consistent and (2) physical characteristics, more than any other single component (traits, role behaviors, and occupations), generate the most consistent package of descriptions (also see Larose, Tracy, & McKelvie, 1993). Considering that physical information is garnered within the first one-tenth of a second of meeting someone (Locher, Unger, Sociedade, & Wahl, 1993), we convey a lot to others simply by the way we look.

Along these lines, I know someone who is convinced that she can spot gays and lesbians by sight. Unbeknownst to her, I tested her powers by asking her which of four friends of mine is lesbian. In reality, three are lesbian and only one heterosexual (so her odds of being correct were excellent). But, I knew that the heterosexual woman best fit the lesbian stereotype because she possesses "masculine" features. Not surprisingly, my spotter immediately declared the lone heterosexual woman to be the indisputable lesbian, confirming the strength of physical stereotypes as well as findings about the stereotyping of lesbians (Dunkle & Francis, 1990; Rothblum, 1994a).

Sexist Stereotypes

When do gender stereotypes go from being valid descriptions of women and girls to being sexist? Regarding gender stereotypes as true descriptions assumes that there is a "kernel of truth" in them. Indeed, gender stereotypes are pretty stable across cultures and time. A study involving 30 nations found some common stereotypes such that women are regarded as sentimental, submissive, and superstitious in contrast to men who are seen as adventurous, forceful, and independent (Williams & Best, 1990). Looking across time, comparisons of findings from 1972 with 1988 (Bergen & Williams, 1991) and from 1957 with 1978 (Werner & LaRussa, 1985) conclude that gender stereotypes generally are stable. All this appears to support a conclusion that gender stereotypes indeed reflect true differences between and among women and men.

However, at the heart of our exploration of the veracity of stereotypes are concerns about the evaluative meaning of specific stereotypes. Let's face it—no one will balk if they are stereotyped favorably in ways that enhance their status and likeability. For example, what's wrong with women being regarded as nurturant and as claiming the moral high ground? The key question that concerns us here focuses on the **evaluative meaning** of gender stereotypes. Simply asked, do gender stereotypes oppress women so that they indeed are sexist stereotypes?

Consider the five subtypes of gender-role stereotypes: housewife/mother (specifically, biological and married mothers), sexy woman, athlete/lesbian, career woman, and feminist. Each of these is quite different from the others, just as the stereotypes for different ethnic groups of women and men vary. This in itself flies in the face of "kernel-of-truth" reasoning which promotes a singular, cross-cultural image of women. It also fundamentally reflects the responsiveness of stereotyping to social changes. The athlete/lesbian, career woman, and feminist stereotypes capture contemporary images of women. The stability across time that "kernel-of-truth" researchers find is confined to one subtype: housewife/mother. The responsiveness of stereotypes to social changes contradicts what one would expect if stereotypes simply described characteristics that are part of women's "natures."

Competent or likeable.   Stereotypes involve two conceptually distinct dimensions: competence and likeability[12] (Glick & Fiske, 1999). The **competence** dimension focuses on respect, achievement, and status; the **likeability** aspect, on social qualities like warmth and being affable. These two dimensions occur differently in the subtypes of gender-role stereotypes: housewives/mothers and sexy women are liked, albeit in different ways, but incompetent, fitting traditional stereotypes, fulfilling heterosexual needs, and accepting a subordinated power position. In contrast, the athlete/lesbian, career woman, and feminist lose out on the likeability side of the formula, but they achieve some level of respect and status. They deviate from traditional gender expectancies, do not fulfill heterosexual needs, and challenge societal power relations. Thus these five subtypes filter into two categories of women: traditional and nontraditional, respectively. Note that neither has both competence and likeability so that both stereotypes remain fundamentally sexist. This logic readily extends to ethnic groups, as we demonstrated in Box 6.2. (You might go back and check your competence and likeability ratings.)

Ambivalent sexism.   These prejudicial and ultimately discriminatory effects of sex-

---

[12] This distinction parallels and fits well with the instrumental/expressive and agentic/communal dichotomies for gender roles we reviewed in Chapter 4.

ist stereotyping are captured in the Ambivalent Sexism Inventory (ASI) developed by Peter Glick and Susan Fiske (1996). The ASI points to the **ambivalence** of sexist prejudice. Because women and men are intimately connected, sexism is unlike other forms of prejudice (Fiske & Stevens, 1993). And, because of this connection, sexist prejudice can evoke both expectedly negative images as well as arguably benign or even revered ones (Glick & Fiske, 1996). These contrasting images are captured in the ASI with two subscales measuring "**hostile**" and "**benevolent**" sexism. Note that benevolent sexism is indeed sexist in that it views women stereotypically and in restricted roles (e.g., standing by her man). But, the benevolent items, in contrast to the open negativity of the hostile ones, are subjectivity positive in tone and describe behaviors that are prosocial (e.g., caring). In fact, some of these items might be embraced by women as well-intentioned and even flattering, but they all share a limited and limiting view of women and women's roles. The common bond between the two subscales is that: "both hostile and benevolent sexism serve to justify men's structural power" (Glick & Fiske, 1996, p. 492).

Look over the items of the ASI in Box 6.4. The items that compose the hostile subscale conform to what we typically think of when we consider prejudice: a position advocating these items is demeaning to women. These attitudes typically are reserved for nontraditional women. In contrast, a benevolent sexist supports items that, at least from the sexist's point of view, appear benign or even complimentary. However endorsement of these items functions to keep women "in their place"—to maintain a status quo wherein women are dependent on men. These items go beyond simple descriptions of women to **prescribe** what women *ought* to do—be traditional (Glick & Fiske, 1999). Because women have close ties to men (who may rely on them for economic support, for heterosexual fulfillment, and for child rearing), benevolent sexists have a stake in keeping things the way they are by limiting women to traditional roles. It is not the roles themselves that are oppressive, but the you-just-can't-have-it-all nature of sexist stereotypes. In sum, sexist stereotypes, whether hostile or benevolent, do not allow for competent *and* likeable women.

The role of values.   As we have seen before in this book, such reasoning encourages us to question our values. Alice Eagly and Antonio Mladinic (1989) assessed the favorability of undergraduates' free-response descriptions of "women" and "men." They found that significantly more favorable traits were ascribed to women than men, especially by women raters. On the face of it, this suggests that gender stereotypes are not degrading of women. However this conclusion becomes shaky when we examine the content of the stereotypes generated for women and men. Women were evaluated more positively on feminine-positive (e.g. caring) and masculine-negative (e.g., aggressive) traits; in other words, women were described as more caring and less aggressive than men. In contrast, men were rated more positively on masculine-positive (e.g., decisive) and feminine-negative (e.g., fickle) subscales. There is no question but that the overall tone of the stereotypes of women is favorable, but are these the qualities valued by our society?

It is nice to be considered warm, caring, and nonaggressive; without question, it is honorable to be a nurse; and fulfilling the roles of housewife and mother obviously are important to the development of the next generation. But, are these as well rewarded as being assertive and decisive; as being a surgeon; and as being a busi-

---

BOX 6.4 **The Ambivalent Sexism Inventory (ASI)**

Hostile Sexism

2. Many women are actually seeking special favors, such as hiring policies that favor them over men, under the guise of asking for "equality."
4. Most women interpret innocent remarks or acts as being sexist.
5. Women are too easily offended.
7. Feminists are not seeking for women to have more power than men.*
10. Most women fail to appreciate fully all that men do for them.
11. Women seek to gain power by getting control over men.
14. Women exaggerate problems they have at work.
15. Once a woman gets a man to commit to her, she usually tries to put him on a tight leash.
16. When women lose to men in a fair competition, they typically complain about being discriminated against.
18. There are actually very few women who get a kick out of teasing men by seeming sexually available and then refusing male advances.*
21. Feminists are making entirely reasonable demands of men.*

Benevolent Sexism

1. No matter how accomplished he is, a man is not truly complete as a person unless he has the love of a woman.
3. In a disaster, women ought not necessarily be rescued before men.*
6. People are often truly happy in life without being romantically involved with a member of the other sex.*
8. Many women have a quality of purity that few men possess.
9. Women should be cherished and protected by men.
12. Every man ought to have a woman whom he adores.
13. Men are complete without women.*
17. A good woman should be set on a pedestal by her man.
19. Women, compared to men, tend to have a superior moral sensibility.
20. Men should be willing to sacrifice their own well being in order to provide financially for the women in their lives.
22. Women, as compared to men, tend to have a more refined sense of culture and good taste.

Note. Items are numbered in the order they appear in the scale. Each item is rated on a 5-point scale where 5 = agree strongly. Starred (*) items are reverse coded so that higher sums indicate higher levels of *sexism*.
Source: P. Glick and S. T. Fiske (1996). The Ambivalent Sexism Inventory: Differentiating hostile and benevolent sexism. *Journal of Personality and Social Psychology, 70,* 491–512. Copyright © 1996 by the American Psychological Association. Reprinted with permission.

---

nessman? Being described positively does not necessarily mean that one is being described in socially valued and important ways. I do not mean to imply that being caring is objectively less valuable than being decisive, but it does seem that our culture rewards one more than the other. The key then to understanding sexism in stereotypes may not be in the positive tone or valence of the stereotype, but in the way our culture values and rewards those qualities attributed differentially to women and men. Another way to think about this is to ask *who has more power:* a caring person (woman?) or a decisive one (man?)?

Consider what happens to "feminine" men and "masculine" women (Helgeson, 1994). Included in the top 20 characteristics generated for the cue, "feminine male," are homosexual, thin, insecure, emotional, likes art, caring, shy, delicate, weak, and soft-spoken. Contrast these with some of the top 20 for "masculine females": likes sports, muscular, short hair, dresses causally, self-confident, aggressive, dominant, tall, and ugly. Both are far from flattering caricatures, and other researchers find that "a masculine woman" and "a feminine man" are the least liked of their targets (Leaper, 1995; Lobel, 1994). Most relevant though to my argument here is the question: Is one portrayal more powerful than the other? I think the aura of power that is attached to the masculine stereotype extends, but with some costs (e.g., being ugly), to the masculine woman. Similarly, the disempowerment that accompanies the feminine label undermines the power associated with being male for the feminine man. Again, choose your poison: incompetent or disliked?

The role of power in shaping what we value in women and men comes across in who is identified as "most admired" in an annual Gallup/Good Housekeeping survey (Young & Harris, 1996). Women are more likely than men to be *liked* because they belong to a royal or political family, work as activists and reformers, or are entertainers. Most men are *respected* for service in the military, politics, religion, and economics. Overall, nominated women tend to be dependent, but likeable in contrast to competent men. Summing up, it seems reasonable to conclude that gender stereotypes are affectively sexist.

Links to sexist prejudice. There are clear linkages between sexist prejudice and sexist stereotyping. For example, women and men in the community who scored high in hostile sexism on the Ambivalent Sexism Inventory (sexist prejudice) also ascribed negative traits to women (sexist stereotyping) (Glick & Fiske, 1996). Specifically, these hostile attitudes predicted negative evaluations of nontraditional career women. In contrast, benevolent attitudes were associated with favorable ratings of traditional women homemakers (Glick et al., 1997). The less favorably respondents felt about women's roles (as measured by the Attitudes toward Women Scale), the more narrow were the categories of stereotypes attributed to women (Innes, Dormer, & Lukins, 1993). The more traditional one's attitudes are, the more constrained is one's view of women's attributes.

Sexist prejudice and sexist stereotyping go hand-in-hand, such that sexist stereotypes both reflect and confirm sexist prejudices in a mutually reinforcing cycle. Even as stereotypes change or new ones develop, sexist prejudice assumes that competence and likeability cannot be achieved in tandem. Thus, sexist prejudice and sexist stereotyping work together to insure the continued oppression of subordinated groups.

Perpetuating Sexist Stereotypes

There is an amazing consistency to sexist stereotypes. It is not hard for us to tick off a list of stereotypes for women and men, girls and boys, and to elicit a lot of agreement among people. Where do these stereotypes come from? How are they maintained?

Why do we all seem to know them? Rather than suggesting a "kernel of truth" in these seemingly universal stereotypes, might they have sources that are so pervasive that most, if not all, of us have been exposed to them? Three likely sources and perpetuators of stereotypes are (1) the media, (2) language, and (3) expectancies and behaviors.

Media. We probably aren't taken aback by the assertion that the media presents sexist images of women, but the extent and the recency of the data may be surprising.[13] Portrayals of women's traits, roles, occupations, and physical appearance all tend to conform to sexist stereotypes in the sampling of studies presented here. Analyses of MTV's music videos found that more men were engaged in aggressive and dominant behavior in contrast to women who were more often portrayed as sexual objects displaying subservient behavior (Sommers-Flanagan, Sommers-Flanagan, & Davis, 1993). Stories in teen magazines present female characters as dependent on others to solve their problems, almost half of which revolve around relationships with boys (Peirce, 1993).

The role of the authority in television commercials is enacted through "voice-overs": the narrator of the commercial. From 1982–89, 91% of voice-overs were done by men (Allan & Coltrane, 1996). In three California newspapers, women were most likely to be portrayed as victims and men as experts or rescuers (DeLouth, Pirson, & Hitchcock, 1995). Women were stereotyped in the role of caregiver ("Dr. Mom") in a sample of television ads for over-the-counter drugs (Craig, 1992).

Turning to occupations, 79% of women in tv ads between 1982-89 had no identifiable occupation compared to 62% of men (Allan & Coltrane, 1996). Unlike commercials from the late 1950s and 1960s, employed women were distributed across 6 of the 7 major occupational categories (none were laborers). Still, men were proportionally better represented in every occupational category except one—clerical. Analyzing print ads in medical journals, physicians were disproportionately represented by white men (Hawkins & Aber, 1993).

Most women will agree that fashion models are unrealistically thin, but even knowing this, the figures are jarring. In the 1960s, models averaged 15 pounds less than the typical American woman; in the 1990s, models average 35 pounds less and 4 inches taller (Cheever, 1996). A disproportionate number are blonde (Rich & Cash, 1993). Body measurements of *Playboy* centerfolds and Miss America contestants from 1979–1988 indicate body weights that are 13-19% below those of normative women in their age group, and the latter get thinner across this time period (Wiseman et al., 1992).

A subtle measure of how women are portrayed in print, called **face-ism**, takes a ratio of the distance from the top of the head to chin (face) to the distance from the top of the head to the lowest part of the body shown (body). If only face is shown, this ratio will be 1.00; if no face is included, this ratio will be .00. The more face, the higher the index (Archer, Iritani, Kimes, & Barrios, 1983). Using this face-ism measure and 1,750 photographs from *Time, Newsweek, Ms,* and one large- and one small-

---

[13] A noteworthy exception to these generally negative trends is the *Oprah Winfrey Show,* the most-watched daytime talk show, which works to empower women (Squire, 1994).

city newspaper, the facial index for men was .65 compared to .45 for women, indicating that women's faces were shown less. (Examples illustrating approximations of these two ratios appear in the photos below). Follow-up content analyses of news magazines, women's magazines, and newspapers continue to find that men receive greater facial prominence than women (Nigro, Hill, Gelbein, & Clark, 1988; Zuckerman & Kieffer, 1994). Additionally, women are more likely than men to be photographed with their mouths open, a pose suggestive of less seriousness (Dodd, Harcar, Foerch, & Anderson, 1989). Face-ism declines even farther for African American fashion models (Jackson & Ervin, 1991) and for women in television beer commercials (Hall & Crum, 1994).

This is only a small sampling of an extensive body of media analyses available, and it seems quite clear that sexist stereotyping pervades a variety of media. This stereotyping extends to portrayals of African, Latina/Latino, and Asian Americans (Taylor, Lee, & Stern, 1995) and cuts across cultures, including British (Furnham & Bitar, 1993), Kenyan (Mwangi, 1996), and Australian television (Mazzella, Durkin, Cerini, & Buralli, 1992).

Granting that sexist stereotyping exists, the next question asks, "So what?" When I worked as a research associate in advertising for a top-ten agency, the pervasive feeling was that ads simply reflect a sexist society. Advertisers argue that they shape their ads to their audience, and indeed they do. Commercials aired during the daytime soaps are more traditionally stereotypic than those offered to a presumably more sophisticated prime-time audience (Craig, 1992). Advertisers argue that the point is to sell products, not challenge people's stereotypes.

However, some clear linkages have been established between media portrayals and viewers' attitudes. Heavy television watchers tend to hold more stereotyped views of women and men (Signorielli, 1989). Even clearer evidence comes from the face-ism studies. When raters were shown pictures of women and men with varying degrees of face-ism, the more facial prominence, the more ambitious, intelligent, and physically attractive the person pictured was expected to be (Archer et al, 1983). When

The picture of the woman has a face-ism score of about .45 in contrast to the man with an index of .65. Who looks more imposing?

women's faces are shown less than men's in news magazines and newspapers (not just fashion magazines), photographers are doing more than reflecting cultural values; they are subtly shaping values as well.

Exposure to sexist advertising can lead to serious consequences for women who are evaluated by men. Laurie Rudman and Eugene Borgida (1995) primed one group of college men with sexist television ads. These men then prepared for and participated in a simulated job interview with a woman candidate. Their behaviors were compared to those of a control group of men who had not been exposed to sexist ads. Men who had seen the sexist ads selected more sexist and inappropriate questions to ask the woman job candidate, sat closer to her, rated her as more friendly but less competent, and afterwards remembered more about her physical appearance and less about her biographical background. In sum, more primed men stereotyped the woman applicant as a traditional sex object (likeable but incompetent) and they acted accordingly. These findings suggest that sexist media portrayals of women encourage sexist prejudices and stereotypes that can lead to discriminatory behavior.

Language.   Language and gender stereotypes are intertwined in a variety of ways (Graham, 1975). Often we delimit what is considered to be the **exception** to the rule (e.g., the *woman* engineer and the *male* nurse). We also use gender forms that tend to **trivialize** women, such as girl for adult women, actress, suffragette (instead of suffragist—watch "Mary Poppins" from the vantage of an adult), and my "favorite" local high school girls' basketball team, the "Lady Popes." Some of this deprecation of women is done by association, for example, by sexualizing terms (e.g., madam). This is overtly illustrated by the American Sign Language system which signs references to men, masculine pronouns, and intelligence around the top portion of the head in contrast to women, feminine pronouns, and emotions assigned to the lower part of the face (Jolly & O'Kelly, 1980). Probably the most pervasive form of sexist language is the **exclusion** of women, sometimes subtly and other times blatantly (when "all men are created equal" was written, the vote was not extended to women—or nonlandholding men for that matter).

A good example of subtle exclusion is the case of the presumably generic "he." Grammatically, we use the pronoun, "he," to refer both specifically to an individual man or boy or more generally to any person. Sometimes this produces ambiguities: does "all men created equal" mean just men or all people? What happens *psychologically* is clear: both *male = people* and *people = male* (Hamilton, 1991; Merritt & Kok, 1995). Students were more likely to refer back to a male protagonist in a story as a "person" (male = person), and an imagined "typical person" was more likely to be construed as a man (person = male). Reviewing across 20 studies, masculine forms (e.g., he or his) may be grammatically generic in that it is correct to subsume women and girls under their usage, but this does not extend to psychological usage where masculine forms connote men and boys only (Henley, 1989). Gender-neutral plurals (e.g., they and their) are perceived as true generic pronouns for both women and men (Gastil, 1990).

But isn't this much ado about nothing? Feminists who point to inequities in language usage have been accused of being overly sensitive and of nit-picking. Some people mock efforts to eliminate exclusionary language by suggesting awkward terms (such as "person-hole," instead of manhole, cover) and by warning of overly vigilant "pc police" (political correctness). Not surprisingly, women are more concerned about sexist language, are more likely to evaluate it negatively, and make greater efforts to avoid using it (Rubin & Greene, 1991). There's some compelling research evidence arguing that these concerns are not misplaced or frivolous. Remember those children in Chapter 4 who thought women would be better wudgemakers when they heard a description of the fictional job of wudgemaking that used "she" instead of "he" (Hyde, 1984a). Parallel results are found for women undergraduates reading job descriptions using masculine pronouns (Stericker, 1981). In Chapter 4, we also saw that high school seniors were more likely to apply for gender-atypical jobs (as linewomen and as male telephone operators) when the ads avoided gender-biased language (Bem & Bem, 1973). Similarly, more students who read the "Ethical Standards of Psychologists," altered to use masculine-typed language, thought psychology was a less attractive career option for women compared to undergraduates who read gender-neutral versions (Briere & Lanktree, 1983). These studies combine to suggest that language can shape our perceptions of the gender-appropriateness of occupations—certainly not frivolous stuff!

Gender biases in language can even influence how women perform on comprehension and memory tests. Women remembered more of a science fiction story when it was read using unbiased language compared to masculine forms (Hamilton & Henley, 1982). A similar outcome was found when women were tested 48 hours after reading written essays (Crawford & English, 1984).

Mykol Hamilton (1988) examined how AIDS transmission was discussed in two newspapers and two news magazines. She found that from 1983–85, most of the headlines and text used generic terms like "homosexual" or "gay" to describe at-risk groups. Interestingly, if you think about AIDS transmission, lesbians are in a low-risk group for the *sexual transmission* of AIDS. Hamilton speculated, however, that if readers overgeneralized from the generic terms to women, they would be likely to mistake lesbians as a high-risk group. Indeed this is what she found.

A methodologically similar study was conducted by Sharon Lamb and Susan Keon (1995), but this time focused on language used to describe male partner abuse. Consider the following descriptions of the same events: (1) "Elizabeth Jones' husband beat her, raped her, and committed gross sexual abuse against her" versus (2) "Elizabeth and Charles Jones had an abusive relationship, in which there were beatings, rapes, and gross acts of sexual abuse." The first version uses the active voice as opposed to shared responsibility in the second. Lamb and Keon found that the second form dominated newspaper reports of battering and that students assigned the most lenient penalties to the abuser when the shared-responsibility form was used.

The bottom line in all this is that *language makes a difference.* Become sensitive to and avoid sexist language. In 1982, the American Psychological Association (APA) mandated that all publications and presentations *must* avoid sexist language. The "Publication Manual of the APA" (1994, pp. 50–51) provides some helpful hints, such as avoiding the use of masculine pronouns as generic, of exclusionary occupational titles (e.g., fireman), and of gendered stereotypes. The APA also has issued useful guidelines for avoiding heterosexual bias in language (Committee on Lesbian and Gay Concerns, 1991).

Expectancies and behavior.   In addition to media and language, sexist stereo-types can be perpetuated by the actual behaviors of women and men. This takes us back to our recurring discussion about a possible "kernel of truth" to stereotypes. Inherent in this reasoning is the assumption that when women and men act in stereo-typic ways, the root cause of their behavior is something internal to them. This assumes that there is something about women and about men that makes them act stereo-typically so that their behavior, in turn, verifies the stereotype.

In Chapter 5, we explored explanations that look to external factors which dif-ferentially impact women and men (i.e., social context). A parallel logic is pursued here. According to the **self-fulfilling prophecy**, expectations can make anticipated events come true (Jussim, 1986; Merton, 1957; Miller & Turnbull, 1986). A classic example points to runs on banks during the Depression of the 1930s: when people feared that their bank would close, they rushed to withdraw their money, panic spread, and the bank eventually closed. What people expected to happen, happened.

Extending this logic to gender stereotypes, Berna Skrypnek and Mark Snyder (1982) conducted a clever study. Because the design is complicated, it helps to under-stand the findings first and then consider the procedure. Skrypnek and Snyder showed that when a man expected to be interacting with a woman, the woman acted like women are supposed to act. When another man thought he was interacting with another man (but his partner was really a woman), the woman acted in line with her partner's expectations by responding in masculine ways. The man's expectations were fulfilled by his partner's behaviors, even when those expectations and behav-iors were at variance with the partner's true gender. In the end, the partner's behav-iors confirmed the stereotyped *expectations* of the other partner.

Turning to Skrypnek and Snyder's (1982) procedure, male-female pairs arrived separately at the lab and were kept away from each other. For some of the men, they were told that their partner was a man; others were led to believe that their partner was a woman. The pairings always included one man and one woman so that *some men were misinformed about the gender of their partner.* Which men were misinformed was determined randomly. Each partnered pair was given 12 pairs of tasks to do. The tasks were masculine (e.g., bait a hook), feminine (e.g., ice a cake), or neutral (e.g., score tests), and the task pairs included all combinations. The participants' job was to agree on who would do each task in a pair. They communicated their preferred task through lights so that the partners never interacted directly.

In the first round, the man selected first, and he understandably treated his partner in accordance with his expectations. For example, he might prefer to bait the hook and leave his partner to frost the cake when he believed his partner to be a woman. On the other hand, for those men informed that their partner was a man, some agreed to ice the cake. All men used stereotypes to initiate their interactions with their partner—something we'd expect because the only concrete information these men had about their partner was the gender they were told.

The really interesting findings came in the second round of 12 different task pairs when the woman chose first. Women whose partner believed them to be women made feminine task selections; in contrast, women whose partner believed them to be men chose masculine tasks. These women's seemingly free choices were influ-enced by their partners' expectations which must have been subtly conveyed to them

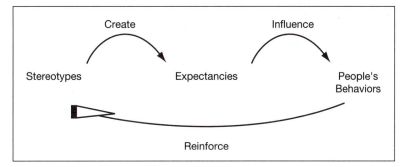

FIGURE 6.2   The circular relationships among stereotypes, expectancies, and behaviors.

through their exchanges in the first round. These women displayed gender-consistent, stereotypic behaviors, not because they were women (in that case, all women would have made feminine selections),[14] but because of what their partners expected. The man's prophecy was fulfilled.

Summing up, even finding apparent confirmations in women's and men's stereotyped behaviors doesn't necessarily verify that stereotypes are true, that is, reflective of genuine, internal characteristics of women and men. When women and men act in concert with sexist stereotypes, it may be because that is what is *expected* of them, not because there's a "kernel of truth" in these stereotypes. In other words, people's stereotypic behaviors may be as much the products of stereotypes themselves as the cause of them. A circular pattern that is mutually reinforcing may be established (see Figure 6.2).

Reducing Stereotypes

Stereotypes are attempts to find meaning in unknown circumstances (Fiske, 1993). Sifting individuals into categories provides some background so that we can interact appropriately. The less we know about the categories in question, the more uniform the stereotype. For example, if we don't interact much with feminists, we are likely to regard feminists as a homogeneous group. The more exposure we have, the more we learn that feminists come in many shapes, sizes, ideologies, and lifestyles. A key toward reducing stereotyping of an individual is to have **individuating** information, that is, knowledge about the specific traits, role behaviors, occupation, and physical characteristics unique to that person (Fiske & Von Hendy, 1992). Other hedges against relying on stereotypes are for the evaluator to be held publicly accountable for her or his judgment (Tetlock, 1992) and for standards of evaluation to be clearly delineated (Fiske & Taylor, 1991). The more objectively verifiable the standards of assessment are, the less subjective are the judgments, the less they draw on stereotypes.

---

[14] If women and men made their choices based solely on what they like to do, their choices would be idiosyncratic and no patterns related to gender would have been found in the data. However, gendered patterns were found, thus ruling out this explanation.

SEXIST DISCRIMINATION

What we have seen so far is that individuals vary in their attitudes toward the roles and rights of women (prejudice) and that there are different beliefs about women and girls (stereotypes) involving their traits, role behaviors, occupations, and physical characteristics. We have argued that what makes these prejudices and stereotypes sexist is that they work to oppress women and girls. To harbor sexist feelings and thoughts about categories of people is one issue. A key point in our argument requires that we link these sexist prejudices and sexist stereotypes to overt *behaviors with meaningful consequences*. This is where sexist discrimination comes in. As we discussed at the beginning of this chapter, **sexist discrimination** refers to acts that serve to oppress women and girls. Sexist discrimination can take a myriad of forms but for our purposes we'll explore three: interpersonal, physical, and occupational discrimination.

Interpersonal Sexist Discrimination

Bernice Lott (1995) describes **interpersonal sexist discrimination** as attempts to separate from women through exclusion, avoidance, and physical distancing. These processes have been documented in studies of attorneys who believe that judges pay more attention to the opinions and arguments of male counselors (MacCorquodale & Jensen, 1993); in observations of grocery clerks who are treated more favorably by customers if they are men (Rafaeli, 1989); in experiments where high performing men allocate more rewards to male partners than to women (Griffith, Sell, & Parker, 1993); in observations of prime-time television shows where men more often move away and separate from women (Lott, 1989); and in memory tests where participants remembered the names of more famous men than famous women (Banaji & Greenwald, 1994) and recalled negative counter-stereotypic information better than positive (Cann, 1993). The link between discrimination and stereotyping becomes very clear in a study of hypothetical interactions with photographed women (Lott, Lott, & Fernald, 1990). Those men who adhered to stereotyped beliefs about gender roles also socially distanced themselves most from the pictured women.

Much controversy has surrounded claims that women's work is evaluated more harshly than men's, and two large-scale reviews concluded that this claim is unfounded (Swim, Borgida, Maruyama, & Myers, 1989; Top, 1991). However, most of the studies reviewed involved students doing simulated tasks or evaluators who knew the targets being assessed (Lott, 1995). A narrative review of this extensive literature concluded that evaluation bias negatively affects women under only some circumstances like the following: when the setting is real, not simulated; when the person being rated is unknown to the evaluator; and when there are potential consequences for the evaluator (Lott, 1985). An example of an evaluative setting that includes these three characteristics is the hiring of employees—not an inconsequential scenario. As we will see in Chapter 8 on work, "occupational suitability" studies conclude that women can be severely disadvantaged.

Physical Discrimination

Physical discrimination becomes clearest when we observe the consequences of deviating from stereotyped perceptions of women's bodies including social pressures to be thin and able-bodied. Stigmatization of obesity is evidenced as early as the first

Is this what you picture when you consider a "disabled" woman?

grade (Goldfield & Chrisler, 1995) and carries with it strict proscriptions about women's eating behaviors. Women who eat smaller meals are considered more physically desirable (Bock & Kanarek, 1995), interpersonally attractive (Mooney & Lorenz, 1997), and socially appealing (Basow & Kobrynowicz, 1993). Passers-by at a summer fair rated silhouettes of overweight women more negatively than those of men (Spigelman & Schultz, 1981). Weight may even play into hiring decisions. Actors of normal weight who were dressed in theatrical prostheses to appear overweight were videotaped during a mock employment interview; hiring preferences were biased against the "job applicants" when they appeared overweight (Pingitore, Dugoni, Tindale, & Spring, 1994).

Theorists argue that a "myth of bodily perfection" dominates American culture and creates misperceptions of those who deviate from this standard by virtue of physical disabilities (Stone, 1995). The stereotype of physically challenged people includes victimization, dependence, helplessness, and social isolation—stereotypes that are exaggerated for women (Hanna & Rogovsky, 1991). The stereotype of dependence can translate into overt discrimination as in the case of physicians who are more likely to advise physically challenged women than men to retire from paid employment (Russell, 1985). Women also are less likely to be offered post-disability employment than men (Fine, 1991; Fulton & Sabornie, 1994) and are more likely to be targeted as victims of sexual assault (Furey, 1994). Physically challenged African American women average lower socioeconomic status than would be predicted by their gender, race, or disability status alone (Hanna & Rogovsky, 1992). In response to findings such as these, a feminist model of (dis)ability is beginning to emerge (Lloyd, 1992; Morris, 1992).

Occupational Discrimination

Occupational discrimination is reflected in who is considered for certain jobs (occupational suitability) and in on-the-job treatment. (More will be said about both of these in Chapter 8 on work.) Psychological testimony in the Supreme Court case involving *Price Waterhouse v. Hopkins* directly linked sexist stereotypes to sexist discrimination (Fiske, Bersoff, Borgida, Deaux, & Heilman, 1991). Price Waterhouse, a nationally recognized accounting firm, denied promotion of Ann Hopkins to partner because this "lady partner candidate" was "macho," "overcompensated for being a woman," and needed a "course at charm school." (I actually met Ann and found her both gracious and charming—but this is not the point.) She was advised by her supporters to "walk more femininely, talk more femininely, dress more femininely, wear make-up, have her hair styled, and wear jewelry." All this was said to a woman who distinguished herself by logging more billable hours than any of the other 87 *all-male* candidates considered for promotion in 1982, bringing in business valued at $25 million. A judge ultimately ruled that an "employer that treats [a] woman with [an] assertive personality in a different manner than if she had been a man is guilty of sex discrimination" (*Hopkins v. Price Waterhouse*, 1985, quoted in Fiske at al., 1991, p. 1052).

Sexist prejudice, stereotyping, and discrimination appear interrelated and mutually supportive such that discriminatory treatment may result from both prejudicial attitudes and stereotypic beliefs. However, the form each of these takes may not always be intentionally hostile. For example, prejudicial attitudes toward women include protective paternalism and desires for heterosexual intimacy (labeled "benevolent sexism"). These may combine with stereotypes of women as sexy to promote sexually harassing behaviors (sexist discrimination) (Fiske & Glick, 1995). The perpetrator may be genuinely supportive of women, or at least those women who play roles consistent with traditional stereotypes, but the resulting behavior, harassment, is unques-

Ann Hopkins in 1990.

tionably discriminatory. In other words, not only the most obvious traditionalists may discriminate at times, illustrating that nonsexist attitudes and beliefs don't always guarantee nondiscriminatory actions. As we have seen throughout this chapter, prejudice, stereotyping, and discrimination all contribute to the perpetuation of sexism.

CHAPTER SUMMARY

Sexism includes sexist prejudice, stereotyping, and discrimination, all of which operate to oppress women and girls. Sexist prejudice appears less blatant in the 1990s, taking more subtle forms like denial of continuing discrimination, antagonism toward women's demands, and resentment about special "favors" for women.

Gender stereotypes focus on traits, role behaviors, occupations, and physical characteristics which combine to form consistent clusters of women. These clusters may be traditional (comprising housewives/mothers and sexy women) or nontraditional (athletes/lesbians, career women, and feminists). Looking at two fundamental dimensions of stereotypes (competence and likeability), nontraditional women are viewed as competent but unlikeable and are targets of hostile sexism. In contrast, traditional women are regarded as likeable but incompetent, and this evaluation may engender "benevolent" sexism—attitudes that appear benign from the viewpoint of the sexist but which, like hostile sexism, perpetuate the oppression of women and girls. It is the evaluative meaning of stereotypes that moves gender stereotypes away from simple descriptions containing a "kernel of truth" to instruments of sexism. Sexist stereotypes are perpetuated by the media, language, and even our own behaviors which are responsive to others' expectancies in a cycle of self-fulfilling prophecies. Researchers have shown that sexist stereotypes can be reduced by individuating targets, by making evaluators publicly accountable for their actions, and by standardizing assessments.

Sexist discrimination can take a variety of forms including interpersonal sexist discrimination, physical discrimination, and occupational discrimination. Although sexist prejudice, stereotyping, and discrimination are not perfectly related so that only the most blatant sexists exhibit all of these aspects of sexism, they generally are mutually supporting. The common link among them, whether they appear on the surface as hostile or benevolent, is that they work together to oppress women and girls. In Chapter 1 we defined feminism as a movement to end sexist oppression. Thus the elements of sexism discussed in this chapter become critical targets for feminist activism.

SEVEN

WOMEN'S MULTIPLE ROLES
Achieving Satisfaction in Close Relationships

Janet is 32-years old, married with two children ages three- and five-years old, and employed full-time. She lives with her family in a moderate-sized city in the Midwest.

Rate her on the following scales:

1	2	3	4	5	6	7
unhappy						happy

1	2	3	4	5	6	7
incompetent						competent

1	2	3	4	5	6	7
not likeable						likeable

1	2	3	4	5	6	7
overworked						not overworked

1	2	3	4	5	6	7
not at all independent						independent

1	2	3	4	5	6	7
not devoted to others						devoted to others

Linda Jackson and Linda Sullivan (1990) asked 331 undergraduates to rate one of 16 targets, either Janet or John, just like you did. Eight different role combinations were described varying the marital status (married or single), parental status (with children or childfree), and employment status (employed or homemaker) of the target. The "Janet" described above occupies the most roles in the design: spouse, parent, and worker (Crosby, 1987). The 42 questions that the researchers asked about the target clustered into six categories, represented by each of the scales you completed: adjustment, competence, likeability, role overload, instrumentality, and expressiveness, respectively.

In this chapter, we will explore a diverse array of roles in women's and men's lives focusing on friendships, romantic attachments, and caregiving. In Chapter 8 we will shift our interests to the public sphere of our lives to look at employment roles. We'll start here by considering the costs and benefits of holding multiple roles, their quality and meaning, and both individual and structural ways to cope with multiple role demands.

MULTIPLE ROLES

How did students regard the combination of roles held by Janet in the vignette that started this chapter? In general, *the more roles, the better.* Combining work and family roles enhanced perceptions of adjustment, competence, instrumentality, and expressiveness for *both* Janet and John (Jackson & Sullivan, 1990). In fact, Janet's competence and instrumentality were regarded even more favorably than John's when they both enacted all three roles. Nontraditional role combinations, such as single mothers

BOX 7.1   Real-life negative images of women holding multiple roles.

And Shoes for the Kids, and Groceries, and a Roof Over Their Heads . . . The First Baptist Church in Berryville, Arkansas, has closed its day care center, informing parents in a letter that mothers should not be out at work, since by so doing they "neglect their children, damage their marriages, and set a bad example." Local families can do fine on one salary, the letter argues, if they decide to forgo such luxuries as "big TVs, a microwave, new clothes, eating out, and nice vacations."

Source: New Woman, August 1997, p. 150.

Headline: "Mom loses custody over use of day care"
—Milwaukee *Journal*
(7/27/94)

Photo caption: "The case of Louise Woodward, a 19-year-old nanny accused of killing a child in her care, has also prompted criticism of working mothers."
—*The New York Times*
(10/24/97)

Headline: "Proof that women are achieving greater equality in the workplace." Text: "As women climb the corporate ladder, there's one thing that's also rising. Their heart disease fatality rate . . ."
—Advertisement in
The New York Times
(10/24/97)

Headline: "Custody fight in capital: A working mother loses"
—*The New York Times*
(9/20/94)

and male homemakers, were perceived least favorably. Not surprisingly, students described the parental role as most responsible for role overload. In opposition to reports from real-life mothers who report more role overload than fathers, undergraduates believed that the parental role was just as demanding for women and men. (This may reflect an ideal of equal sharing in the home that we will see later in this chapter is challenged by evidence from everyday settings.) Given these findings, your ratings of Janet at the start of this chapter were likely to be pretty positive.

On the other hand, we have seen negative images of women who "have it all" (see Box 7.1). Women who are spouses, mothers, and workers often are described as harried, overloaded, tired, and burned out. They are vulnerable to the custodial loss of their children in divorce proceedings (Chesler, 1991). These contradictory images reflect a tension between two competing views of **multiple roles**. On the one hand, the **scarcity hypothesis** predicts that holders of multiple roles will be vulnerable to role conflict and role overload. **Role overload** results from a build up of pressures from multiple sources, and **role conflict** arises from the competing demands of multiple roles. On the other hand, the **enhancement hypothesis** contends that multiple roles serve as buffers against undesirable consequences in any subset of roles. For example, if things get rough at work, it is argued that folks who can go home and find solace in strong family ties will be less seriously affected (Baruch & Barnett, 1986).

Burnout or Enhancement?

Which is it? Are multiple roles good or bad for you? In support of the scarcity hypothesis, employed mothers report more role overload than employed fathers (Cooke & Rousseau, 1984; Crosby, 1991; Pleck, 1985). (This won't be surprising after we review who's doing the housework later in this chapter.) More recently, multiple role demands have been linked to psychophysiological arousal both on and off work (Lundberg, 1996). Simultaneously attending to the demands of two different roles has been shown to detract from employed mothers' task enjoyment and mood (Williams, Suls, Alliger, Learner, & Wan, 1991).

On the other hand, Faye Crosby (1991) concludes that at least three benefits may accrue from holding multiple roles, supporting the enhancement hypothesis. True variety, not just interruptions, provided by various roles is associated with stronger psychological well-being. Multiple roles provide multiple audiences—a variety of people to talk to and get feedback from. Additionally, multiple roles can serve as buffers by providing other places to escape to when things go bad.[1] Although each of these benefits may be realized by multiple-role holders, the likelihood of doing so is reduced if one does not control her or his own time.

Crosby's observations fit with other research evidence. For example, multiple roles have been associated with longevity (Moen, Dempster-McClain, & Williams, 1989) and, relatedly, physical health (Adelmann, 1994a; Hibbard & Pope, 1991) for both African American and white women (Waldron & Jacobs, 1989). This relationship extends to psychological well-being (Vandewater, Ostrove, & Stewart, 1997) and a sense of self-efficacy (Adelmann, 1994b), as well as mental health outcomes (Barnett, 1997). Women returning to school at a community college were found to be happier if they occupied the three roles of partner, mother, and paid employee than if they filled none or only one of these (Kopp & Ruzicka, 1993).[2] Finally, employment has been shown to buffer against family strain (Barnett & Marshall, 1992); sin-

---

[1] On the other hand, bad moods derived from work can spill over into home life and vice versa so that the more roles one holds, the greater is the possibility for such spillover. This pattern has been shown for both women and men, but more strongly for employed women (Williams & Alliger, 1994).

[2] A good resource of college experiences for women over 40 and physically challenged women is Holcomb and Giesen (1995).

gle and childfree women experienced more distress as their job-role quality declined than did similarly job-disillusioned partnered women and mothers (Barnett, Marshall, & Singer, 1992). This last relationship is moderated by how challenging employment is—parental distress is lowered only for women employed in challenging jobs (Barnett, Marshall, & Sayer, 1992).

This combination of perspectives and findings merges in a single study of 118 employed mothers of preschoolers aged 23–43 months (Rankin, 1993). Of the 100 mothers who described their lives as stressful, fully 62% reported high levels of stress. The major sources of their stress were lack of time, child-related problems, and maternal guilt. At the same time, these women reported rewards including personal benefits, financial rewards, and improved family lives as emanating from their various roles.

There is no ready answer to the question about the consequences of multiple roles; rather, there is evidence of *both* burnout and enhancement. It seems that "it depends" is the answer most true to the research evidence. Given this, let's reframe our question to ask under what conditions enhancement is a more likely outcome than burnout. To explore this question, we need to look at roles themselves, who is enacting them, and the context in which they are played.

Role Quality and Meaning

Beginning with roles themselves, it is obvious that not all roles are created equal. Employment may be high-pressured or humdrum; parenting may be physically demanding at certain times (e.g., infancy) and emotionally demanding at others (e.g., adolescence); and so on. Researchers find no differences in the number of roles reported by 421 women and 397 men aged 58–64; furthermore, simple role accumulation is not related to self-esteem, but role commitment is (Reitzes & Multran, 1994). A key factor then may not be the number of roles per se, but rather **role quality**. Grace Baruch and Rosalind Barnett (1986) define role quality as the balance of pluses and minuses associated with how one sees a given role. For example, children may be "black holes" for parents' time and energy, always able to absorb more, but on balance, most parents feel they are well worth it. It is favorable role quality that Baruch and Barnett find to be positively associated with psychological well-being.

Turning to whose roles we are discussing, individual differences influence what people want from the roles they enact. Sharon Rae Jenkins (1996) tracked a sample of 118 women college seniors over the next 14 years of their lives. Those who were autonomous in defining their roles, and thus were less bound by conventional dictates, sought excellence in multiple roles with less role conflict. Feeling capable to handle one's roles also is important: women caregivers who felt competent to handle task demands reported less role-related stress (Franks & Stephens, 1992). Similarly, those whose attitudes support their role enactments exhibit enhanced well-being. Employed single mothers of preschool children report strong psychological well-being when they believe that maternal employment does not harm children and perceive their childcare arrangements as high quality (Goldberg, Greenberger, Hamill, & O'Neil, 1992).

How people define their roles is important. For example, work and family roles have different *meanings* for women and men. Robin Simon (1995) interviewed 40 employed and married mothers and fathers of children under 18 in dual-earner families. The meaning of work and family roles to them was probed by asking them to describe a "good" mother or father. Whereas men believed that providing economic support was a central part of being a "good father," all but a handful of women viewed employment as an added responsibility separate from their primary obligations to family.

This is consistent with findings linking nonwork stressors to burnout for employed women, but not for employed men (Aryee, 1993). If work is considered part of men's family role, engaging in it produces little to no conflict and hence no burnout. As expected, Simon found more work-parent conflict from women (75%) than from men (40%). Moreover, the nature of the conflict they reported differed. Whereas women's conflict was diffuse, nonspecific, and pervasive, men's was limited in scope and specific. Given this, which of the following quotes came from a woman and which from a man? (The answer is in footnote #3.)

> I'm not here. I'm not watching my kids grow. I'm just getting pieces of their lives. I tell them I love them and hug and kiss them all the time, but I don't think that's enough. Maybe it's just being in the living room when they come in.

> I've missed a lot of my daughter's after-school activities due to my work hours. For me it is stressful. I'm sure that it's important to my daughter that both of us show up to these things, and a lot of times I'm just not able to (Simon, 1995, p. 187).[3]

Individual and Structural Coping

There are individual differences in how people cope with multiple roles. Douglas Hall (1972) describes three different **coping strategies**. Women who use **personal role redefinition** change their own expectations and perceptions of their own behavior. For example, women employing this strategy in response to work-family conflict may explore time management techniques to be more efficient; try to minimize simultaneous overlap of roles (e.g., soccer on weekends only); reduce their standards (e.g., living with unmade beds); eliminate roles; and rotate their attention. The way they cope is by adapting themselves.

In contrast, **structural role redefinition** focuses outward on changing structurally imposed expectations. Women employing this strategy may redefine a role by changing the activities required (e.g., reduce tasks at work); seeking support from sources beyond themselves, including outsiders (e.g., housekeepers) and insiders to the role (e.g., one's spouse and children); collaborating with role senders to redefine roles (e.g., encouraging children to accept sending store-bought, not homemade, cookies to school); and integrating roles so that activities for one role contribute to another. The third strategy, **reactive role behavior**, doesn't really cope at all as the user attempts to "do it all" ("superwoman").

The type of coping strategy used by women was related to their satisfaction with their career (Hall, 1972). Although most women used combinations of strategies, those who relied most heavily on reactive role behaviors were the least satisfied.

---

[3] The first is from a woman; notice how diffuse her sense of "missing out" is. The second is from a man who delineates exactly what he misses—after-school activities.

Those who used strategies involving structural role redefinition were the most satisfied. But, is it better to restructure work or family demands?

Tamao Matsui, Takeshi Ohsawa, and Mary-Lou Onglatco (1995) explored the structural role redefinition strategies used by 131 Japanese married, employed women. They separated this coping strategy into two components: **work-role redefinition**, which involves altering work activities and expectations to meet family-role demands, and **family-role redefinition**, which focuses on changes in the family. Family-role redefinition was more typical of these women's coping than work-role redefinition, and spillover of work into family was more common than from family to work. This is consistent with other research concluding that work interferes more with family life than vice versa (Bolger, DeLongis, Kessler, & Wethington, 1989; Gutek, Repetti, & Silver, 1988).

Are role conflict and overload inevitable for some roles and some people? This is where context comes in. Multiple roles do not lead inevitably to negative consequences if **social supports** are strong. Women over 35-years old returning to college experienced less strain when they had high grade-point averages *and* the support of their children (Novak & Thacker, 1991). Elizabeth Ozer (1995) found a woman's belief in her capacity to enlist the help of her spouse for childcare predicted both well-being and reduced distress. Actual responsibility for greater childcare produced the opposite outcomes. Real support from husbands buffers the effects of parental demands on work-family conflict (Matsui, Ohsawa, & Onglatco, 1995). The influence of family supports extends beyond immediate partners to a full array of family members (Poole & Langan-Fox, 1992). For example, an unpredictable and ever-present stress for many families involves arrangements for sick children, and African American kin are more likely than white to provide this safety net (Benin & Keith, 1995).

Looking beyond these interpersonal and individual supports, **structural supports** also can moderate the relationships between roles and strain. Abridged maternity leave of less than six weeks can combine with existing marital stress to put new mothers at risk for depression (Hyde, Klein, Essex, & Clark, 1995; also see Gjerdingen, Froberg, & Fontaine, 1990). The 1993 U.S. Family and Medical Leave Act, which guarantees a minimum of 12 weeks of *unpaid* leave for childbirth, adoption, or sick dependents, from businesses employing over 50 people, is woefully behind what other industrialized countries offer women and men. European countries routinely provide four months to three years of leave that is fully or partially paid (Kamerman & Kahn, 1995). At the most generous extreme, Sweden offers parents of a newborn 12 months of leave at 90% pay (to be split or shared) with additional increments at reduced pay until 18 months, at which time the child is eligible for placement in a childcare center. Parents then are entitled to work part time (75% time at 75% pay) until the child reaches 8-years old.

Is part-time employment a structural solution for women juggling work-family demands? Kathleen Barker (1993) surveyed 315 employed women and did not find the expected linkage between part-time employment and reduced role conflict and overload. What she did find was a mixed bag of costs and benefits. Benefits accrue in increased happiness and satisfaction at both home and work. The costs of part-time employment are felt at work where part timers reported exclusion from organizational (e.g., promotion), interpersonal, and skill-enhancement opportunities as well as heightened job insecurity. What structural supports might employers provide to reduce these costs?

There is compelling evidence that structural supports from employers, however limited, do help out. Inflexible employment schedules aggravate role strain for women (Galambos & Walters, 1992); alternatively, flexible schedules reduce such stress (Matsui, Ohsawa, & Onglatco, 1995). A critical part of flexibility may be the autonomy to be absent (Moen & Forest, 1990). Wage-earning and salaried parents with less stress and better coping were found to have jobs with greater autonomy, more schedule control in their own hands, fewer demands, greater security, and more support, including supportive supervisors, workplace cultures, and opportunities for advancement (Galinsky, Bond, & Friedman, 1996). The provision by employers of on-site childcare has been linked to improved attitudes about managing work and family (Kossek & Nichol, 1992), and it is widely supported by workers (Mize & Freeman, 1989). How does one encourage employers to make such provisions? Researchers find that companies with the most family-friendly benefits are those with substantial percentages of women in their workforce (Auerbach, 1990; Seyler, Monroe, & Garand, 1995). This may be a factor to bear in mind in a job search.

In conclusion, multiple roles themselves do not guarantee either role burnout or enhancement. Differences exist in what individuals value and need, in the quality of their roles, in the meaning of roles in the context of their full lives, in how individuals cope with role demands, in the social supports that either value or devalue roles, and in structural supports that either facilitate or inhibit role enactment. It is these variations that ultimately determine whether women's multiple roles work smoothly together or interfere with each other.

CLOSE RELATIONSHIPS

Understanding this overview about women's general role patterns, we move on to explore specific roles in women's close relationships: friendships, romantic attachments, and caregiving.

Defining Close Relationships

Judith Worell (1988) describes the defining features of a **close relationship**: it is *expected* to endure over time and to provide an individual with respect, intimacy, caring, concern, support, and affection. **Romantic attachments** include all this plus sexual passion, exclusiveness, and commitment. **Relationship satisfaction** refers to the degree to which we think and feel a relationship is living up to our expectations, preferences, and conceptualization of what a good, close relationship should be. Thus how satisfied we are with a relationship depends, to a large extent, on what we *expect* from a relationship and how well we think the actual, enacted relationship measures up.

Why are psychologists interested in close relationships? There is a substantial body of evidence that relationship satisfaction is positively associated with psychological and physical well-being (Worell, 1988). Supportive relationships enhance our responses to stress, our self-esteem, our feelings of self-efficacy, and our resistance to loneliness, depression, serious illness, and disability. The state of our close relationships also aligns with our general feelings toward life—happy people report having close and supportive relationships.

Gender or Stereotypes?

Consider the conversation below between a women and man trying to make plans for a dinner party. Which one is the woman, M or P, and which is the man?

> M: The only weekend we seem to have free is October tenth.
> P: That's the weekend of the tennis tournament.
> M: Well, let's do it Saturday or Sunday evening.
> P: Okay, make it Saturday.
> M: Wouldn't you want to be free to go the tournament on Saturday?
> P: [Annoyed] I *said* Saturday, so obviously that's the day I prefer.
> M: [Now also annoyed] I was just trying to be considerate of you. You didn't give a reason for choosing Saturday.
> P: I'm taking off Thursday and Friday to go to the tournament, so I figure I'll have had enough by Saturday night.
> M: Well, why didn't you say that?
> P: I didn't see why I had to. Why do I have to explain every detail? (adapted from Tannen, 1990, pp. 158–159).

Exchanges like this one seem to dominate discussions of close relationships. They paint a picture of irreconcilable differences between women and men and describe two kinds of language, women's and men's (Henley, 1995), ultimately supporting arguments that women and men are from completely different planets. Gendered analyses of the conversation above attribute M's statements to a woman and P's to a man, concluding that men maintain autonomy (and hence avoid accountability) in relationships in contrast to women who seek consideration and understanding.

Does M's style reflect that of all (or even most) women and P's, men, or do we each have a style that is unique to who we are regardless of our gender? Is it inconceivable that the woman and the man might exchange places in this dialogue? Personally, I can put myself in P's shoes and recount plenty of examples when I am annoyed that people ask me to justify my actions—I know what I'm doing and find the intrusion annoying! I also have had experiences like M's when a little more information would have made the other person's position immediately understandable. Is the pattern in the conversation reflective of genuine gender differences or does it simply fit gendered stereotypes? Separating stereotypes from true gender differences is a major problem for researchers of friendships.

FRIENDSHIPS

Gender Differences?

The popular wisdom used to be that women's friendships were inferior to those of men. In addition to being shallow, women were expected to abandon their friends when opportunities to be with men arose (Wright, 1982). Throughout the 1970s and

1980s, the opposite image evolved, portraying women's friendships as superior to men's. In a widely cited study, women and men reported the same number of friendships and similarly valued intimacy in them, but women emphasized emotional sharing and talking in contrast to men, whose friendships revolved around shared activities (Caldwell & Peplau, 1982). Two divergent pictures emerged of women's and men's same-gender friendships: women talking heart-to-heart and men, meeting to engage in activities, oblivious to the emotional ups and downs of their partners. These different images fit well with stereotypes of women seeking communal or expressive outcomes in their friendships in contrast to men's agentic or instrumental desires (Orosan & Schilling, 1992), of women desiring connection, and of men wanting separation (Lang-Takac & Osterweil, 1992). Consistent with this reasoning, researchers found that women's friendships with women were evaluated as more rewarding, reciprocal, disclosing, and close than those between men (Dolgin, Meyer, & Schwartz, 1991; Parker & de Vries, 1993; Reisman, 1990; Wright & Scanlon, 1991).

All of this tends to romanticize women's friendships as exemplars of feminist sisterhood (Bank, 1995). But, does it truly describe women's, as well as men's, same-gender friendships? In a recent study, Karen Walker (1994) conducted 52 in-depth interviews with working-class and professional women and men. She replicated the prior patterns in her own data: women described sharing intimate feelings with women friends and men reported bonding through shared activities. These findings are even in line with her interviewees' perceptions—they believed that their relationships differed along these gendered lines.

When Walker (1994) elicited specific experiences in friendships, a different picture emerged. Fully 75% of the men she interviewed detailed counterstereotypic interactions. For example, one man described how he had exchanged details with his closest friend at work about their wives' sexual "courtship" preferences—one liked to be wined-and-dined and the other valued spontaneity. Furthermore, there was

Are there women's friendships where women share feelings and men's, where men share activities? Or, are these really just stereotypes?

a wide discrepancy between the activities they said they engaged in with their friends and how much they actually did. Similarly, about 65% of the women's actual friendship scripts did not conform to what they had recounted previously. These findings raise serious questions: (1) How much does what we expect for friendships shape our perceptions; and (2) To what extent are our expectancies influenced by gendered beliefs—in this case beliefs that women's and men's friendships are qualitatively different (also see Sherrod, 1987)?

A laboratory study of women's and men's exchanges furthers this argument. Harry Reis, Marilyn Senchak, and Beth Solomon (1985) found that undergraduate men described social interactions that were less intimate than those reported by women. This difference held when participants were asked to write down narratives of two recent exchanges. Even when other raters didn't know the gender of the people involved in the written narratives, the men's narratives were deemed less intimate than the women's. So far, this fits with the stereotypic pattern. However, when participants and their best friends were asked to engage in an intimate conversation in the lab, both self-ratings and ratings by external judges showed no gender differences in the intimacy of the taped conversations. When the setting expressly called for intimacy, men were just as capable of being intimate as women.

This leads me to believe that women don't corner the market on intimacy in their friendships. Does this mean then that women's and men's friendships are the same? Judith Worell (1988) cites women's disproportionate interest in popular self-help books devoted to understanding relationships and her own and others' experiences in psychotherapeutic practice as evidence that women hunger for information about close relationships. Differential interest, just like differences in stereotypes, does not necessarily signify differences in how relationships are realized, however. The bottom line question may be: What is the value in finding similarity or difference?

In the remainder of this chapter, we'll take a fresh look at women's close relationships. Although it would be a disservice to both women and men to ignore differences in what they want from and how they enact their day-to-day relationships, we'll explore women's *relationships as they are* (rather than looking at how they contrast with those of men) and with an eye toward understanding how women's satisfaction through their relationships can be maximized.

Friendships between Women

What do women friends do? They most frequently get together to talk, less often to work on a task, and least often to deal with a relationship issue pertinent to the friendship itself (Duck & Wright, 1993). Talk is the centerpiece of most women's friendships (Rose, 1995), and friends may offer a safe haven for less inhibited expression. Women were videotaped while they viewed emotionally stimulating slides in the presence of either a stranger or a close friend. External judges, identifying the emotions expressed on the videotapes, were more accurate for women viewing with friends, suggesting that women were more freely expressive in the presence of friends than strangers (Wagner & Smith, 1991). Women veer away from few topics in friendships, although this varies cross-culturally (for example, British disclosers regard fewer topics as taboo than Chinese) (Goodwin & Lee, 1994). Women tend to discuss family life, disclose political and religious disagreement, and be demonstrative by hugging or crying with a close friend.

What do women want in their friendships with women? Two factors are prominent in contributing to women's satisfaction with women friends: **intimacy** and **equality** (Worell, 1988). Although anywhere from 7–57% of women report not having a close friend at some point in their lives (Ratcliff & Bogdan, 1988; Goodenow & Gaier, 1990), the pattern of having a few close friendships, rather than gangs of acquaintances, tends to begin early for girls (Bank, 1994; Rose, 1995) and persist into old age (Johnson & Troll, 1994). Women generally look for all-purpose friends with whom they can relate across a variety of dimensions rather than different friends for different needs (Barth & Kinder, 1988). Women seek connection with other women through cooperation and egalitarian exchange (Parker & de Vries, 1993). Literary depictions of women's friendships portray them as rich in intimacy, respect, mutual help, and even confrontation (Contarello & Volpato, 1991).

Women's friendships hardly come in "one size that fits all." Heterosexual relationships can interfere with women's friendships by replacing them, as well as extend women's friendships when the man's friends become incorporated into the couple's network (Fischer & Oliker, 1983; Rose & Serafica, 1986). Never-marrieds tend to fall at one of two extremes in their friendships, being either isolated or very active, and never-married women generally interact frequently with relatives (Seccombe & Ishii-Kuntz, 1994). Differences in the sexual orientations of women friends can be disruptive until both parties come to define and accept their own and each other's sexualities (Palladino & Stephenson, 1990). Class differences can shape the form of women's friendships: working-class women seek reciprocity and interdependence with respect to material goods and services compared to middle-class women who are more likely to celebrate shared leisure time (K. Walker, 1995). African American professional women seek social companionship, task help, emotional support, commitment to each other, and encouragement from Black women friends (Denton, 1990). African American women's relationship networks typically encompass more kin, related and unrelated, than friends (Stack & Burton, 1993). Chicana single-mothers initially rely on family for support, but become increasingly interdependent with friends over time (Wagner, 1987). Relationships between physically challenged and able women often exchange the latter's physical help for the former's emotional support (Fisher & Galler, 1988).

"Cross" Friendships

"Cross" friendships involve people of different types, such as cross-gender and cross-racial bonds. These relationships openly violate a fundamental characteristic of most close friendships—similarity (Floyd, 1995). Given this, cross friendships are expected to challenge their participants.

Theorists have speculated that four challenges may confront women and men in close friendships: determining the type of emotional bond to be experienced in the relationship; confronting the issue of sexuality; dealing with equality within a cultural context of inequality; and presenting the friendship as just that, friendship (not romantic involvement), to relevant audiences (O'Meara, 1989). However, research with existing casual and close cross-gender friends concludes that few of these, or any other, challenges are reported by actual cross-gender friends (Monsour, Harris, Kurzwell, & Beard, 1994). Still, fully 43% of cross-gender friends did mention concerns about defining their emotional bonds in the relationship; 20% of the men and 10% of the women noted sexual tensions; and 5–22% reported problems dealing with outsiders. The difference in women's and men's perceptions of sexual tension is consistent with other research showing that more men than women interpret ambiguous behaviors as sexual in intent (Shotland & Craig, 1988). Although these challenges may be more fiction than fact in ongoing, cross-gender friendships, the fiction itself may inhibit some women and men from initiating these friendships.

Suzanna Rose (1996) explored obstacles to the formation of friendships between women of color and white women. Rose first notes that although anyone can be prejudiced, only whites in our culture can be **racist** because only whites can both believe that their race is superior *and* enforce their beliefs. She cites a telling example from a white woman server who complained to her boss about a derogatory racial comment from an African American male cook. The cook was forced to apologize to the student by the owner who told him, "You picked the wrong white girl to mess with." The student came to realize that the cook's comment, although racial, was not racist:

> It made me realize that racism really is prejudice + institutional power. The cook may have been prejudiced against me or even angry with all whites. However, I realized that he couldn't have been racist even if he wanted to. He was "put in his place" and made to apologize, not because of our argument, but because he is black and I am white. It was no longer "our" argument. It had become bigger than that and I began to feel like the one to blame. I felt that something had been turned around and I was on the wrong side (Rose, 1996, p. 224).

How do cross-racial friendships develop? Rose suggests that they require a thorough analysis of racism (grappling with issues like those above) as well as well-developed racial identities so that each party is secure in her own identity and open to exploring and valuing differences in that of another. Her research with a handful of existing cross-race friendships suggests that most are initiated by white women and that work must be actively done to engender trust (Hall & Rose, 1996). Parallel patterns are found for friendships between physically challenged and able women (Fisher & Galler, 1988). The implications of successfully forging such bonds can be extended to diverse groups of women who may learn from these interpersonal exchanges how to unite at a broader level.

ROMANTIC ATTACHMENTS

As we noted at the beginning of this chapter, romantic attachments encompass the same features as close friendships plus sexual passion, exclusiveness, and commitment. Judith Worell (1988) abstracted three themes from popular self-help books devoted to women's relationships. Presumably women don't know what will make them happy in relationships (ignorance); women lack the skills or savvy to initiate and maintain satisfying liaisons (incompetence); and in heterosexual relationships, a polarity between women and men creates a rift between them that is difficult, if not impossible, to bridge (illusion). Interestingly, researchers find that the more exposed adults are to this popular media, the more dysfunctional and unrealistic are their beliefs about intimate relationships (Shapiro & Kroeger, 1991). Although Worell goes on to debunk each of these relationship myths, their residuals often float in our understandings of relationships. As you read about how romantic attachments are formed and realized, it is important to be aware of each of these myths.

Becoming Partnered: Dating

What do heterosexual women look for in romantic partners? Stephan Desrochers (1995) asked a diverse group of undergraduate women to evaluate different profiles of men according to their romantic attractiveness. Men who were evaluated most favorably were portrayed as positively expressive (using the traits from the Personal Attributes Questionnaire, such as helpful, gentle, and understanding). Interestingly, when income was added to the mix, women looked for desirable personality traits first, then considered earnings. These findings fit with studies showing that women value quality of communication in dates (Sprecher & Duck, 1994) and delineating the qualities that older couples identify as keeping their marriages intact (Lauer, Lauer, & Kerr, 1990). They also contradict folk wisdom that women generally give highest priority to men's economic status.

How do women and men go about establishing romantic attachments? Many of these relationships are forged through the courtship process of dating, so psychologists have studied the dating expectancies and behaviors of women and men. Suzanna Rose and Irene Hanson Frieze (1993) detailed both the actual and hypothetical (expected) **dating scripts** of 135 mostly white undergraduates. From the perspective of your *own* gender, try out the following task:

> List the actions which a woman (man) would typically do as she (he) prepared for a first date with someone new, then met her (his) date, spent time during the date, and ended the date. Include at least 20 actions or events which would occur in a routine first date, putting them in the order in which they would occur (Rose & Frieze, 1993, p. 502).

Our cultural expectations about dating construct our hypothetical dating scripts, so that these scripts turn out to be very similar to what students actually report doing on dates. Some of the core elements of a dating script are shared by women and men: worrying about one's own appearance, talking, joking, laughing, eating, kissing goodnight, and going to a movie, a show, or a party. Beyond these basics, dating scripts reflect gender-typed roles: men play active roles by initiating the date, choosing the activity (Surra & Longstreth, 1990), controlling the public domain (e.g., driving and opening doors), and initiating sexual interactions (O'Sullivan & Byers, 1992). The corollary is women's reactivity, focused on the private domain (e.g., her appearance and enjoyment), in the structure of the activities (e.g., being picked up), and in her sexual responses. Women tend to present their first date as something that evolved according to the plans of the man, in contrast to men who focus on

First dates typically follow prescribed, gender-typed scripts so that men play active roles and women are reactive.

their own planning. Thus men tend to bear the burden of shaping the date (hence their anxiety?) in comparison to the less powerful and passively reactive woman.[4]

What happens to dating scripts when gender roles are not applicable? Interestingly, there is a substantial amount of overlap between the actual dating scripts of lesbian and heterosexual women (Klinkenberg & Rose, 1994). The most glaring differences point to closer equality in power, more affective/evaluative consideration, and a balance of active and reactive behaviors. Like heterosexual women, lesbians are nervous about their first date, but their preparation focuses more on cleaning up and meal preparation than on appearance. They are likely to engage in the same activities (talking, movies, etc.), but throughout the script, lesbians are more likely to contemplate how they are feeling and assess how things are going. Lesbians also note that they sometimes initiate sexual contact and assume the responsibility for enacting the date (e.g., picking up their partner).

Heterosexual identity development in our culture is relatively easy—it's what's expected of us. But, how does a woman develop a lesbian or bisexual identity? There are at least two approaches to this question (Kitzinger & Wilkinson, 1995). The **essentialist** position assumes that homosexuality is part of one's true nature so that the "coming out" process is simply a series of stages through which one must pass in order to accept the inevitable. Indeed, this often is how gays describe their identity development (Epstein, 1987). On the other hand, there is evidence that the development of our sexual identities does not follow a progressive, stage-wise pattern (Rust, 1993).

---

[4] Even though women today do more of what are considered the "masculine" activities, gendered patterns are far from extinct (McNamara & Grossman, 1991; Lottes, 1993).

On April 30, 1997, Ellen DeGeneres educated television audiences about lesbian "coming out" processes.

A **social constructionist** position, in contrast, argues that lesbian identity is pieced together from scraps of evidence interpreted as indicative of one's own lesbianism. Celia Kitzinger and Sue Wilkinson (1995) describe many barriers that illustrate lesbians' resistance to claiming a lesbian identity. For example, although most lesbians report having heterosexual experiences, the myth that lesbians feel no heterosexual attraction keeps some women from interpreting even direct sexual experience as lesbianism: "It's just sex—I was only experimenting, and anyway I'm sexually attracted to men, too" (Kitzinger & Wilkinson, 1995, p. 99). These authors go on to detail how women make the transition to a lesbian identity and how, even after claiming this identity, lesbians continue to work at constructing it, often by becoming involved in lesbian communities.

Being Partnered

Significant others in women's lives are not limited to romantic attachments. For example, never-married women, especially African American women (Raley, 1995), tend to be in frequent contact with relatives (Seccombe & Ishii-Kuntz, 1994). Furthermore, romantic attachments are not limited to marital arrangements, although this is by far the most frequently studied bond. Here, we'll explore relationship satisfaction in two types of bonds, lesbian and marital, recognizing that marriage is not the only context in which heterosexual romantic attachments are enacted. What do women want in their romantic attachments? Judith Worell (1988) concludes that women are far from ignorant—they want what they desire in friendships: **intimacy** and **equality**. We'll see that relationship satisfaction is high to the extent that both these desires are met.

Lesbian relationships. Natalie Eldridge and Lucia Gilbert (1990) conducted an extensive nationwide survey of 275 lesbian couples where both partners were employed full time. Several patterns emerge from their data. First, although these women had been in their current relationship for an average of over five years, most lived with their partner, and 15% were raising children together, their relationship was largely **invisible** to outsiders. Sizable numbers did *not* tell employers (65%),[5] coworkers (35%), fathers (over half), mothers (one-third), or neighbors and strangers (three-quarters). Partly because of this secrecy, other researchers find that lesbian women are less satisfied with their social relationships with coworkers and employers than heterosexual women (Peters & Cantrell, 1993).

Second, despite lack of public acknowledgment of their bond, Eldridge and Gilbert (1990) found that *lesbian relationships were stable, enduring, and committed* and that the women in them displayed high levels of self-esteem and life satisfaction. These data dispel myths that lesbian relationships are fleeting, debilitating, and only sexual in nature. Although sexual intimacy is related to relationship satisfaction for lesbian couples, we will see that it is not the foremost bond of intimacy.

Third, fully 13 of 14 psychological factors studied were associated with relationship satisfaction. The one exception was career commitment: when partners had divergent career commitments, relationship satisfaction was low. Couples satisfied with their relationship reported high levels of both attachment to their partner and personal autonomy. Relationships generally were characterized by heightened intimacy (see also Hurlbert & Apt, 1993), especially *recreational* (common interests) and *intellectual* intimacy, with social intimacy lagging last (another potential cost of secrecy). Couples also reported a clear sense of power or influence in their relationship.

Equality of influence is a central feature of satisfied lesbian couples. Lesbian partners value ideal equality more than gay men, even though both partnerships are exempted from gender-role disparities (Kurdek, 1995). Compared to heterosexual couples, lesbians are more likely to use bilateral influence strategies where both partners participate, and it is these strategies which are associated with more favorable intimacy in both types of relationships (Rosenbluth & Steil, 1995). Given these values, it is not surprising that lesbian couples tend to perform an equal number of household tasks, unlike both gay male and heterosexual partners (Kurdek, 1993).

Marital relationships.   A long-standing conclusion, supported even by the most recent data, asserts that men report higher levels of marital satisfaction than women (Fowers, 1991; Kaslow, Hansson, & Lundblad, 1994; Ying, 1991). Although love or intimacy may be the cornerstone of marriage, at least in Western, individualistic societies (Levine, Sato, Hshimoto, & Verma, 1995), women's second desire in relationships, *equality,* may be the force that underlies marital satisfaction. In dating relationships, fewer than half of the 413 heterosexual couples studied reported an equal distribution of power; in the majority, men were twice as likely as women to be named the more powerful partner (Felmlee, 1994). Inequality in both attitudes and behaviors is related to lower marital satisfaction for women.

Women generally endorse more egalitarian roles in marriage than do men (Fowers, 1991). Women who see themselves as equal partners in their marriage are more satisfied, in general, than traditional pairings and are less likely to use power

---

[5] For an excellent resource for people seeking information on coming out at work, see Rasi and Rodriguez-Nogues (1995).

strategies to get their way (Yukie & Falbo, 1991). Relatedly, the more liberal the husband's gender attitudes are, the more marital satisfaction is reported by both spouses (Shacher, 1991). In older couples, perceptions of social support are strongly related to both the marital satisfaction and the general well-being of women (Acitelli & Antonucci, 1994). All this is consistent with an equal-sharing standard for marriage projected by college-aged women (Schroeder, Blood, & Maluso, 1992).

This all seems quite simple: women want equality, and positive attitudes about equality are associated with strong marital satisfaction. But what about behaviors? It's one thing to value equality; another to realize it. Let's look at **household tasks** (not including childcare) to see how close we get to this 50–50 ideal. There is an extensive body of data using all kinds of measures that comes to the same conclusion: *women perform a disproportionate share of household labor* (for example, see Baxter, 1992; Beckwith, 1992; Biernat & Wortman, 1991; Moore, 1995; Starrels, 1994). This holds regardless of socioeconomic class (Wright, Shire, Hwang, Dolan, & Baxter, 1992) and regardless of race/ethnicity (John & Shelton, 1997).

How much time do women and men spend on household tasks? It depends on what household tasks we're talking about. Some are more time-demanding than others and require repeated and time-specified attention. Mowing the lawn or painting can be put off more easily than making dinner, and dinner has to be made within a specified time range. The gendered division of labor generally splits along such time lines, with those tasks with the greatest time demands (meal preparation, clean-up, grocery shopping, housecleaning, and laundry) being designated as "women's work" (Beckwith, 1992). These are the chores on which we'll concentrate our attention. The general pattern illustrated in Table 7.1, indicates that men typically do about 20% of the female-typed tasks; this percentage holds across Anglo, African Ameri-

TABLE 7.1   Mean Hours per *Week* Spent on Household Chores

	Women		Men	
	Hours	Percent	Hours	Percent
Cooking	9.49	81%	2.27	19%
Clean-up	5.66	77%	1.73	23%
Shopping	2.89	69%	1.31	31%
Laundry	4.11	88%	0.58	12%
Cleaning	7.56	84%	1.48	16%
Subtotal of female-typed tasks	29.71	80%	7.37	20%
Outdoor Jobs	1.70	28%	4.45	72%
Auto	0.14	9%	1.43	91%
Bills	1.55	57%	1.19	43%
Subtotal of male-typed tasks	3.39	32%	7.07	68%
TOTAL	33.10	70%	14.44	30%

Note. Percentages reflect the proportion reported by each gender. Data come from self-reports of 3,190 married or cohabitating couples completing the 1988 National Survey of Families and Households (Blair & Lichter, 1991).
Source: Adapted from S. L. Blair and D. T. Lichter (1991). Measuring the division of household labor: Gender segregation of housework among American couples. *Journal of Family Issues,* 12, 91–113. Copyright © 1991 by Sage Publications, inc. Reprinted by Permission of Sage Publications, Inc.

can, and Latina/Latino couples (John, Shelton, & Luschen, 1995) and across many developed countries (United Nations, 1995).

Hold on a minute—we've heard lots about how men are doing more at home, and certainly my husband does more than my father did. How can there be such a wide gap between what women and men are doing today? The answer is that both perceptions are right: a wide gap persists, but it has narrowed. Men went from doing only 8% of the housework in 1965 to 20% in 1985 (Robinson, 1988)—a significant increase but still quite distant from that 50% "ideal." It is no wonder then that recently married couples report being less traditional in their household division of labor than their parents, but still not on par with their stated ideals (Findlay & Lawrence, 1991).

Why do women do more? Maybe it has to do with who has more *time* for such responsibilities. In this case, we might predict that men would contribute more if women had less time or men had more. Surely, women have less time for housework if they are employed, but researchers find little to no overall increases in men's participation when comparing dual-earner to male-earner families (Baxter, 1992; Bittman & Lovejoy, 1993; Douthitt, 1989; Shelton, 1990) or women's part-time to full-time employment (Hossain & Roopnarine, 1993) (for a review, see Coverman, 1989). When women's employment is added to the mix we find that, although men put in the same number of hours, women's time contributions shrink so that household tasks are either done more efficiently, less elaborately, or not at all (Baxter, 1992; Douthitt, 1989; Robinson, 1988). As for decreasing men's time at work, even with the time savings afforded work-at-home men over commuters, household contributions did not change (Silver, 1993). In light of these data, the time available is not a plausible explanation of unequal sharing of household chores.

What about *attitudes*? Indeed, men's attitudes have become increasingly egalitarian from 1972 to 1989, but only in regard to shared workload, not the responsibility for it (Wilkie, 1993). We might predict that couples who believe in egalitarian sharing would be more likely to share closer to their ideal of equality than traditionalists. However, this prediction is *not* supported by research; researchers often find a disjunction between attitudes and behaviors (Bittman & Lovejoy, 1993). Arlie Hochschild (1989) carefully detailed this inconsistency through intensive interviews and observations of dual-earning families. Based on their comments and actions, Hochschild classified each partner's *attitudes* and *behaviors* as **traditional**, **transitional** (moving from traditional toward egalitarian), or **egalitarian**. On the positive side, a few couples in her sample shared and realized egalitarian ideals.

Two cases exhibit some fascinating mixes. Nancy Holt believes in an egalitarian ideal and reports that she has attained it by dividing the house, 50/50, into upstairs (her portion) and downstairs (his). In reality, downstairs is the basement, which contains her husband's hobby shop, in contrast to the upstairs living area which demands most of the routine household labor. Although Nancy denies inequities obvious to Hochschild as a detached observer, their effects are felt by Nancy, who reports being very troubled in her marriage.

In contrast, the Delacortes hold traditional attitudes, but financial constraints force the wife, Carmen, to provide in-home childcare. Their shared belief is that Frank "helps out" around the house; for example, he makes spaghetti sauce because his is better. In reality, Frank doesn't just "help out"; he contributes significantly. This family is, paradoxically, both attitudinally traditional and behaviorally egalitarian, and the Delacortes seem to have a stable and happy marriage. Two points emerge from Hochschild's stories: (1) attitudes and behaviors about household contributions are not necessarily consistent and (2) couples go to great lengths to find satisfaction in the arrangements they construct.

The balance of *power* in a relationship may make a difference, but the evidence is mixed. On the one hand, one study of women earning at least one-third more than their spouses found they still performed more than their equal share of domestic labor, but had more say in decision-making (Steil & Weltman, 1991; see also, Biernat & Wortman, 1991; Kamo, 1994). On the other hand, enhanced earnings were associated with more household sharing in other studies (Izraeli, 1994; Pyke & Coltrane, 1996; Starrels, 1994). One provocative finding concerns remarried men who contributed more to household chores than first-marrieds (Ishii-Kuntz & Coltrane, 1992). Might remarriage somehow shift the balance of power by sending a message that "bad" marriages can be dissolved? Other researchers find that women who have fewer alternatives to marriage because of limited economic resources, in contrast to more independent women, are more likely to view unequal divisions of labor as just (Lennon & Rosenfield, 1994).

The widening unequal sex ratio in the African American community has far-reaching effects on relationships between Black women and men (Dickson, 1993). In 1985, there were 78 Black men for every 100 Black women, and men's availability for commitment in relationships was further compromised by disproportionately high rates of imprisonment, drug and alcohol abuse, unemployment, poverty, and homicide. Because women can be readily replaced, men oftentimes hold the balance of emotional and domestic power in these relationships.

What are the consequences of such inequality on marital satisfaction? Much of this has to do with feelings of unfairness (**entitlement**), not necessarily objective inequity. Brenda Major (1993) grapples with the paradox that although women contribute a disproportionate share of the housework, they often report contentment with this inequity (Biernat & Wortman, 1991; Stohs, 1995). One explanation involves choices for comparison: women are doing more compared to whom? If the **comparison group** considered is other women, then the answer may be "no." If the comparison is to normative standards (what women are supposed to do), then some women may even feel inadequate. What if the comparison is to other arrangements, like staying home full-time or being employed? It may be better to accept what one has rather than consider switching to an undesired alternative. And, what about comparing one's spouse's contributions to those of other men? Not surprisingly, women who compared their husband's level of participation to their own inputs, rather than those of other men, have husbands who contribute more (Hawkins, Marshall, & Meiners, 1995).

Although women generally may feel less unfairly treated than we might objectively predict, those who do perceive inequities suffer in terms of heightened distress and marital dissatisfaction (Golding, 1990; Robinson & Spitze, 1992). We might speculate that this is one reason why women try to deny, rationalize away (Blain, 1994), or work out ways to juggle excessive demands (Hessing, 1994) rather than admit that unfairness threatens their marriage. Looking at this through a rosier lens, women exhibit a stronger sense of fairness if they feel their labor is appreciated, if the couple actively decides together how to allocate chores, and if men participate (Hawkins, Marshall, & Meiners, 1995).

Our discussion implies that men are essentially lazy "cads," relaxing while their harried wives do all the disagreeable chores (Johnson & Hayes, 1993). Surely this does not describe all men. What does spur men's participation? Arlie Hochschild (1989) describes two equal-contributing men, Art Winfield and Michael Sherman. Both come to this position for less-than-inspiring reasons: one seeks to avoid the dissolution of his marriage, and the other wants to redress the neglect of his own father. Interviews with couples who do share provide some insights into how they negotiate such an exchange (see Goodnow & Bowes, 1994).

An encouraging portrayal of *egalitarian men* is provided by Kathleen Gerson's (1993) study of 138 men from diverse social backgrounds. One-third of these men are with work-committed women with whom they share economic and domestic responsibilities. How did this happen? Half these sharing men expressed egalitarian attitudes before becoming committed to their wives; the remainder developed these attitudes as a result of their commitments. But we know that attitudes can take us only so far. The rest evolved: some sharing men voluntarily veered away from high-pressure careers; others hit an occupational deadend. As work became less central in their lives, unlike the primary breadwinners in Gerson's sample, these men became more involved at home. Involvement spawned further involvement because these men reaped benefits from sharing, including a strengthened marriage, bonding with children, increased influence at home, development of expressive qualities, and enhanced personal pride. An upward spiral of participation developed:

> Her going to work was a help in a lot of different ways, not just financially. I think it strengthened things between the two of us. It made her realize that I cared enough to share responsibilities, and made me realize that there were responsibilities that needed to be shared. We're sharing more, and I really enjoy doing it. We're buying a new stove, and I now have a say in what color comes into the kitchen since I'm here a good portion of the time (Gerson, 1993, p. 170).

Lauren Weitzman (1994) reviews research on multiple-role realism and concludes that, although many college women desire to combine work and family in their own future projections and are aware of the existence of multiple-role conflict, they don't expect it to be problematic in their own lives. Research on multiple-role planning finds that it is not enough to be aware of what we discussed in this chapter. Personal, relationship, and even financial satisfaction is enhanced to the extent that women and men directly confront these issues (Weitzman, 1994). Egalitarian sharing does not just happen in relationships; rather, it is actively constructed by committed and vigilant partners (we'll discuss this further in Chapter 12) (Blaisure & Allen, 1995). Sandra Tangri and Sharon Rae Jenkins (1997) found that women who expect work-family conflict and prepare accordingly—by asserting their career intentions with their spouse, by postponing childbearing, and by having fewer children—experience less marital conflict than those who fail to acknowledge potential problems.

CAREGIVING

One of the most fundamental roles to the image of women is that of caregiver, especially to children.[6] In all likelihood, most women will assume the role of caregiver across their lifetimes—as a caregiver to children, partners, parents, friends, and neighbors, or through volunteer work. Women are expected to be the caregivers of last resort, whenever public services and other sources of caretaking break down. Women who feel obligated to care for elderly relatives remark, somewhat guiltily and certainly with ambivalence: "But who else is going to do it?" (Aronson, 1992). After we briefly explore general patterns in caregiving, we will turn to childcare, including images of mothers and the still evolving image of the employed supermom and her use of nonparental childcare.

General Patterns

With increasing life spans and with the balance of young to older people likely to tip in the direction of more elderly (Himes, 1992), caretaking needs for the elderly are on the rise (Kaye & Applegate, 1990). A report by the Older Women's League found that women average 18 years caring for elderly parents, a year more than they average in childcare (Robinson, 1989). The expected 17–18 year commitment of children in the home is expanding: one of every three single men as well as one of every five single women, aged 25–34, were living with their parents in 1990 (Gerstel & Gallagher, 1993; Gross, 1991). To get a sense of the time commitments we are talking about, review Table 7.2 for the monthly averages reported in 1990 by 179 married women and 94 of their husbands (Gerstel & Gallagher, 1994). The kinds of help given included practical tasks (e.g., providing a meal or mowing the lawn), material tasks (e.g., giving or lending money or goods), and personal services (e.g., giving advice).

Some interesting patterns emerge from the data in Table 7.2. The most obvious conclusion is that women give about twice as much help in a month as men. Women provide about equally for their friends and parents; adult children command as much caregiving as these two groups combined. Men contribute to more volunteer groups, but this difference disappears for local community groups suggesting that men have more official memberships than women, but women give more time to local groups. Further probing of these data, designed to explore the effects of the wife's employment, finds that employed women and homemakers perform practical, labor-intensive caregiving chores equally. Employed husbands help fewer relatives and friends and spend fewer hours than their similarly employed female counterparts. In sum, caregiving, even outside of childcare, is expected to be, and is, "women's work."

Images of Mothers

Turning to caregiving for children, childcare is considered so much a part of women's nature that the word we most frequently use to describe it is gender-specific: "moth-

---

[6] An overview of different theoretical approaches to studying women as caregivers is provided by Stoller (1994).

TABLE 7.2   Mean Number of People and Hours Helped per *Month*

	Wives		Husbands	
	Number	Hours/Mo.	Number	Hours/Mo.
Informal Caregiving				
Kin[a]	5.25	42.77	4.02*	15.06
Parents		11.52		3.76*
Parents-in-law		6.20		3.95
Adult Children		20.79		4.60*
Friends	3.44	10.93	2.26*	6.35*
Formal Caregiving				
Volunteer Groups	2.08	8.09	3.14*	9.41
Local Groups	1.07	.54	.84	.33*
TOTAL		61.79		30.82*

[a] Other kin include siblings, grandparents, aunts and uncles, etc.

Note. Starred items indicate that the comparison of wives and husbands for that measure is significantly different.

Source: Adapted from N. Gerstel and S. Gallagher (1994). Caring for kith and kin: Gender employment, and the privatization of care. © 1994 *by The Society for the Study of Social Problems.* Reprinted from *Social Problems,* Vol. 41, No. 4, pp. 519–539.

ering."[7] Stop for a moment and picture a "mother." Jot down some characteristics that you think are essential to describe her and what she does.

    The dominant cultural images of a "mother" are embodied in two configurations: (1) the traditional, full-time, domestic mother whose sole job is her family and (2) the employed mom with multiple roles—job, self, and family (Thurer, 1994). A defining difference between the two images focuses on caregiving for children. Caregiving for children involves both **caring for** (serving the needs of or caretaking) and **caring about** (loving) children (Traustadottir, 1991). Two features define the traditional mom who provides both forms of caregiving for her children: she is (1) **continually present** and (2) **all-powerful** in that she is expected to be the primary, if not sole, childcare provider (Uttal, 1996). The "supermom" differs from the traditional one along both of these dimensions.

    Both images shown above, like other global cultural stereotypes, incorporate class and racial/ethnic biases by assuming middle-class and white statuses. Very different images of mothering emerge within African American communities (Collins, 1994). Here, motherhood involves shared and sharing responsibility as African American mothers assume the mothering of others' children and their community, as well as engage others in the mothering of their own biological offspring. The privatized

---

[7] A quick glance through Psychological Abstracts (PsycLIT) soon reveals that some research purporting to study "parenting" actually includes only mothers so that what really is being studied is "mothering." I have found no reversal of this pattern—"fathering" is clearly meant to be gender-specific.

Two different images of mothers: (1) traditional, still epitomized by the character June Cleaver on the tv show "Leave It to Beaver," and (2) "supermom," combining employment and children as parts of women's family responsibilities.

view of mother described by the dominant culture is contrasted with this more collective orientation in the African American community.

Images of family structure in Latina/Latino families often exaggerate traditional images of mothers. These questionable stereotypes rely on simplified explanations involving machismo and submissive roles for women that fail to consider the flexibility of gender roles within families in response to outside forces (e.g., degree of acculturation, specific country of origin, and the availability and need for dual employment) (Vega, 1990). Keeping these variations in mind, we will consider the work of mothering, the social construction of mothering, and the role of nonparental care on the evolving image of the employed mother.

Who mothers? In part, this basic question asks who does the *caretaking* chores for children in the home. The answer is obvious, but the data are illuminating. In the National Survey of Families and Households conducted in 1987–88, 640 parents in two-parent households with children under age 5 were asked, "About how many hours in a typical day do you spend taking care of your child's physical needs, including feeding, bathing, dressing, and putting him/her to bed?" On average, men reported contributing about 26% of the total hours spent in direct caretaking activities (Ishii-Kuntz & Coltrane, 1992). Fathers were more likely to play with children than do the nitty-gritty tasks of caretaking, such as getting up at night (Tiedje & Darling-Fisher, 1993).

What encourages some fathers to participate more than others? Men who share in housework are more likely to share with childcare. These fathers also are more likely to be employed fewer hours and to hold egalitarian attitudes toward maternal employment. Mothers' higher relative earnings, longer hours of employment, and elevated acceptance of maternal employment are associated with closer sharing of caretaking (Ishii-Kuntz & Coltrane, 1992). Interestingly, fathers of younger children are more likely to pitch in with housework, not childcare, in contrast to fathers of older children who supplement the available pool of household workers. Looking beyond basic caretaking, there is some evidence that as housework load increases, husbands are likely to assist wives by doing the "nicer" tasks, such as playing with the kids while mom makes dinner (Coleman, 1988).

If we move beyond simple caretaking to the full responsibility of caring for and caring about, we ask: Can men mother? As we saw in Chapter 2, sociobiologists regard caring for children as the essential evolutionary contribution of women. When we talk about "maternal instinct," women's presumed "biological clocks," and "mother-infant bonding," we are implying that being a mother is biologically programmed in women and specific to them. The same is true when we talk about how women are socialized to be "relational," "communal," or "nurturing." All this implies that the "caring about" part of mothering is exclusive to women. Another view, however, sees this essential part of mothering as emerging from the role itself, so that men who are the primary caregivers for their children look more like "mothers" than fathers in dual-parent families.

Barbara Risman (1987) tested this hypothesis by surveying 55 single fathers of children under 13 whose full-time caretaking resulted from widowhood, desertion, or the mother's disinterest in shared responsibility. Each single father, most of whom were white, was compared to a single mother, a married two-paycheck mother and father, and a married traditional mother and father, all of whom had a youngest child of about the same age. The dual-paycheck families were the most affluent; men tended to work in professional and blue-collar jobs and women, in clerical and sales positions.

Single fathering increased personal household responsibility dramatically; more generally, primary parents (whether women or men) contributed more. Single mothers as well as traditional fathers, regardless of maternal employment, reported fewer affectionate displays with their children in contrast to sharing parents of *both* genders. The best predictor of parent-child intimacy across all groups was expressiveness as measured by the Bem Sex Role Inventory: more expressive women *and* men were more intimate.

Risman's point is that "mothering" does not always break down along gender lines—not only women (nor all women) are capable of caregiving. Single fathers "mothered" in the sense that they did the same caretaking work as women mothers, and sharing fathers "mothered" in that they provided the same intimacy as sharing mothers. Also note that not all women mothered in the sense of caring about (intimacy). Similar patterns emerge when we consider caregiving to elderly spouses (Applegate & Kaye, 1993; Chang & White-Means, 1991) and caregiving to parents (Kaye & Applegate, 1990). Thus *caregiving may best be conceptualized as a role we enact*, rather than as a predilection that we are either born with or are socialized to develop.

The Supermom and Nonparental Childcare

The notion that men can "mother" challenges both primary dimensions of traditional images of women who are expected to be (1) present at all times and (2) primarily responsible. This leads us to consider the second, still evolving image of the employed supermom and the role nonparental childcare plays in the lives of employed mothers and their children. We will begin with data on the prevalence of nonparental childcare then go on to explore its meaning in women's lives and the psychological debate and findings about its effects on children.

Prevalence.   In our society, care outside the family is almost universal—what varies is the initial timing. Almost all children are in the care of nonfamily members by the time they reach school age at about six, and fully two of every three 3- to 5-year-olds in the United States in 1990 were in some form of nonmaternal care (Kamerman & Kahn, 1995).[8] Fewer preschoolers experience some form of nonparental care (see Figure 7.1). Latina/Latino preschoolers (46%) are cared for by nonparents less than both African American (66%) and white (62%) children. Overall though, nonparental care is statistically normative so that the often heated debate about the impact of such care has more to do with timing than with its ultimate inevitability for all but a handful of children.

What are these other childcare arrangements for preschoolers? We generally think of nonparental care as occurring in a group center, and indeed 31% of children under age 6 are enrolled in preschools, day-care centers, Head Start programs, and the like (West, Wright, & Hausken, 1995).[9] Other arrangements involve care by relatives (21%) or nonrelatives (18%), both in the home (i.e., a "nanny"—4%) or in the provider's home (i.e., "family childcare"—14%). Of course, these arrangements vary by the child's age with infants under one rarely being cared for in centers (7%) compared to by relatives (24%) or by nonrelatives (17%). Not surprisingly, nonparental care is more common among children with full-time (88%) as opposed to part-time (75%) employed mothers and with better educated mothers (high school—56%; college grads—70%; advanced degrees—78%).

The meaning of nonparental care.   Stop for a moment and think about what childcare means in general and in your life, if you use it. Oftentimes, childcare is conceptualized as a service that provides a location for children while their parents pursue employment (as opposed to "babysitting"). We often assume that women feel guilty for using these services, relying on a traditional image of mothers. However, as the supermom image of mothers evolves, employment becomes a part of a woman's family responsibilities so that we'd expect guilt to diminish (Segura, 1994). Indeed, researchers find that middle- and upper-income married women in white collar and professional occupations are not experiencing high degrees of separation anxiety (Erdwins & Buffardi, 1994).

How do women who are forging a new image of mothers that includes employment think about nonparental childcare? An insightful exploration of the meaning of childcare in employed women's lives is offered by Lynet Uttal (1996) who conducted in-depth interviews with a purposively diverse sample of 31 employed women

---

[8] Kamerman and Kahn (1995) report that out-of-home care for 3- to 5-year-olds is almost universal in Europe where day care is more fully subsidized. In contrast, the relationship between childcare issues and women's choices in the United States was made blatantly clear in Little Rock, Arkansas, in April of 1997, when a Baptist church closed its day care facility to encourage mothers to stay home because employed mothers "neglect their children, damage their marriages and set a bad example" (Dodds, 1997).

[9] The percentages reported here include those in parental care so that the base is all 21+ million preschoolers across the United States. Percentages that don't sum to 100% reflect multiple arrangements for some children.

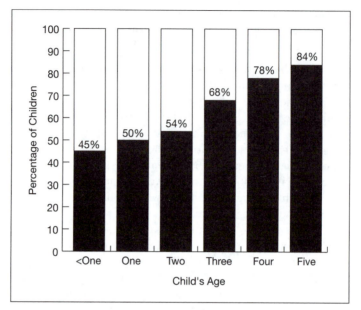

FIGURE 7.1   Percentage of children in the United States experiencing some form of routine nonparental care.

Source: U.S. Department of Education. National Center for Education Statistics. Child Care and Early Educational Program Participation of Infants, Toddlers, and Preschoolers, NCES 95-824, by J. West, D. Wright, and E. G. Hausken, Washington, DC: 1995.

with preschoolers, toddlers, and infants. She identified three distinct patterns, each of which challenges at least one of the core dimensions of traditional mothers' childcare, that is, (1) continued presence and (2) primary/sole responsibility.

Women who regard childcare as **custodial care** separate mothering (caring about) from custodial care (caring for) and retain the exclusive rights to the former. They set sharp limits on what providers can and can't do regarding the child's physical, social, and moral development. They often check in throughout the day to give specific directions and to make caregiving decisions. As a home-employed mother explained:

> I'm leaving my children in the care of somebody, but it's like I'm overwatching the whole time, making sure my kids are all right, making sure they're safe. And I feel like I'm in control the whole time of what's going on (Uttal, 1996, p. 301).

In this way, these mothers retain sole responsibility for mothering their children, like traditional mothers, but relinquish the traditional mother's provision of continued presence.

A small minority of women who view their childcare as **surrogate care** surrender care to another because the conditions of their employment demand more separation from their children than they deem appropriate or because they feel inadequate as mothers. For these mothers, the provider becomes the child's "real," preferred mother. These mothers challenge the traditional assumption that only biological mothers can "mother" but they embrace the traditional belief that continued presence is needed to fulfill the demands of true motherhood.

Mothers who embrace **coordinated care** regard childcare providers as joint contributors to a child's development and well-being. Unlike custodial arrangements wherein mothers micromanage their child's day and surrogate arrangements where mothers abdicate their responsibilities, coordinated arrangements evolve around continuing discussions that seek to synchronize philosophies, values, and practices. Both parties learn from each other and enact child rearing that is coordinated and consistent. In essence, they develop a cooperative alliance that challenges both dictates of traditional mothering, rejecting notions that mothers must be constantly present and exclusively responsible. This approach is reflected in the statement of a Mexican American full-time receptionist whose 3-year-old is cared for by a family provider:

> I understand that I am the mother and she's the care provider, [and] at the same time I never feel jealous because she's taking more care of Grego than I do. . . . I feel that she's helping me in some way through my problems, and I appreciate that a lot from her. Time that I don't have for Grego, somebody else will do it for me. It's not easy, but life is not easy. And I had to let go my feelings in a way [by] saying let go, let this person help Grego to grow. And *both of us* will probably do a good job (Uttal, 1996, p. 304).

Summing up, we have seen that nonparental care of preschoolers is becoming statistically normative and that nonmaternal care, both by fathers and by childcare providers, challenges basic tenets of the image of traditional mothers as the always present and exclusive providers of both care for and care about their children. When fathers provide both custodial and emotional care for their children, their similarity to women who mother discredits biological explanations of women as mothers, instead regarding motherhood as a socially constructed role that can be assumed (and rejected) by anyone. Similarly, when childcare providers act as extensions of parents in children's lives, traditional images of mothers are reframed and a more realistic picture of a "supermom" develops. One obstacle to the further development of this alternative image of mothers is the often heated debate about the effects of nonparental care on children.

Effects of nonparental care on children. How have psychologists studied the effects of day care? Sandra Scarr and Marlene Eisenberg (1993) review this literature, and they conclude that research can be clustered into three waves. In the 1970s, the first wave concentrated on comparing maternal versus nonmaternal care, implicitly asking "How much damage is done to infants and young children by working mothers?" (Also see Silverstein, 1991.) The second wave went beyond this simple question to consider that children's individual responses to day care may vary. In the 1980s, researchers directly observed day care in progress, evaluated the quality of care, and assessed children individually. The most recent wave takes a much more complicated look at day care, considering the impact of a broad array of factors including the characteristics of each child, the quality of the care as well as home life, parental happiness and stressors, and various support systems. Although the welfare of the child is paramount, researchers have come to understand that if day care helps parents, these parents will be better for their children. Two basic facts of child rearing are that all children, even those who attend day care, are being raised primarily by their families and that virtually every child experiences some kinds of extrafamily care, even if this is confined to an occasional babysitter.

Scarr and Eisenberg (1993, p. 623) note that, "No one has proposed that preschool children over the age of 3 years are likely to be harmed by good quality, non-maternal care." Nearly all the debate in psychology about the "risks" associated with day care swirls around infant and toddler care. There is solid evidence that children from socioecomonically disadvantaged families benefit from quality day care (Scarr & Eisenberg, 1993; Feagans, Fendt, & Farran, 1995; Hagekull & Bohlin, 1995; Mindel, 1995) and also from after-school care (Posner & Vandell, 1994). Additionally, children without strong parental attachments appear to benefit from attachments to other caregivers (Goossens & van Ijzendoorn, 1990). It also is clear that the quality of care makes a big difference. Evaluations of the quality of day care include caregiver stability (Barnas & Cummings, 1994), group size (Dunn, 1993), as well as caregiver-child ratio, caregiver training, health and safety requirements, responsive and warm interaction between staff and children, developmentally appropriate curriculum, and adequate indoor and outdoor space (Scarr, Eisenberg, & Deater-Deckard, 1994). Not surprisingly, those centers which serve affluent children are, on the whole, of higher quality than other centers (Phillips et al., 1994). All this confirms the reasoning of the third wave of research: it is a mix of factors that influence whether day care is beneficial or not for a given child and for her or his family.

Researchers have explored the effects of day care on infants' and toddlers' emotional, social, and intellectual development. Probably the most heated part of this debate centers on emotional development, specifically **maternal attachment**.[10] A widely used measure of maternal attachment, developed by Mary Ainsworth and her colleagues (1978), is referred to as the **"strange situation."** This laboratory procedure involves a mother, her toddler, and a woman stranger and includes eight episodes. The strange situation takes place in a room filled with toys and a chair for an adult, and it is viewed by trained observers through a one-way mirror (so even when the toddler is alone, s/he is being monitored). The sequence introduces the mother and child to the room (Episode 1) and doesn't begin until the toddler is playing comfortably (Episode 2). The stranger, always a woman, enters the room and sits quietly in a chair (Episode 3). When the child is playing comfortably, the mother is cued to leave the room (Episode 4). In the first critical episode the mother returns (Episode 5), and the stranger leaves. When the child is again comfortable, the mother is signaled to leave, and the toddler is left alone (Episode 6). In Episode 7, the stranger enters, then the child and mother are reunited a second time in Episode 8.

Data are collected during episodes 5 and 8, during which the mother and child are reunited. Although some children may fuss when their mother leaves, observations of the *reunion* are central for classifying a relationship as secure or not. **Securely attached** toddlers greet the returning mother, then resume their play. **Insecurely attached** children (1) cling and/or are hostile to the returning mother or (2) ignore her return (labeled as **avoidant**).

In 1988, Jay Belsky and Michael Rovine pulled together data from five studies involving 491 children in the strange situation. They concluded that rates of inse-

---

[10] Only a handful of studies has explored father-child attachment. Lois Hoffman (1989, p. 288) describes three, but the combination of findings is confusing and inconsistent. A recently introduced measure of paternal separation anxiety (Deater-Deckard, Scarr, McCartney, & Eisenberg, 1994) may spark further research in this neglected area.

The "strange situation" is enacted daily in the lives of children in day care, raising questions about how strange this situation is for them.

cure attachment were significantly higher in children whose mothers were employed 20 hours or more per week: 36% of these children as opposed to 29% of children with part-time or nonemployed mothers were classified as insecurely attached. They interpreted this difference as indicative of the negative effects of other-than-mother care on toddlers' emotional attachment.

At least three critical concerns call into question this interpretation of the data (Clarke-Stewart, 1989). First, think about this series of events from the perspective of children in day care. The sequence parallels their daily routine. No wonder day-care children in the strange situation seem less disturbed by the mother's absence (Doyle & Somers, 1978). For day-care savvy children, the "strange situation" may not be that strange.

A second problem focuses on the definition of "avoidant" behavior. Toddlers are classified as avoidant (and thus insecurely attached) if they don't seek proximity or interact with their returning mother; if they don't resist contact but, if picked up, don't resist being released; and if they treat the stranger like their mother. Are these children really "avoidant" or are they "independent"? Third, is the difference between 36% (children with employed moms) and 29% (children with part-time and nonemployed mothers) *meaningful*, not just statistically significant?[11] The lesson to take away from all this is to be wary of speculation about maternal attachment derived from the strange situation. However, it is the strange situation that often underlies both professional and mass media reports on maternal attachment (for example, see Eckholm, 1992).

---

[11]Note too that the comparison of children with mothers employed 20+ hours versus mothers employed less than 20 hours really says nothing about day-care experience. Many of the former children, as well as some of the latter children, probably have been exposed to some kinds of nonmaternal care. The relevant measure would be degree of such exposure.

A concern for researchers of attachment that reaches beyond the strange situation has to do with **selection bias**. We can't randomly assign children to day care and home care. The types of parents who select each may be quite different (Clarke-Stewart, 1989). There is repeated evidence that employed mothers value independence in their children and thus foster this (Hoffman, 1989). Citing personal experience, for example, there were days when my children as toddlers greeted me like a returning goddess and there were other days when they were so absorbed in what they were doing that my arrival was treated as an unwanted intrusion. Their independence might have been annoying on days I was in a hurry, but it paid off in easy drop-offs, and it fit with my values for my children.

If we look beyond the strange situation, are there other indicators of the influence of day care on emotional and **social development**? Three recent studies identified by Sandra Scarr and Marlene Eisenberg (1993) integrate issues of context, quality, and family background in their explorations. Carollee Howes (1990) found heightened social competence in children who entered day care early and experienced high quality care. The reverse was true for early entrants exposed to poorer care, although even among these children only 4% fell outside normal ranges. In 1991, Howes found less competence only in early entrants who had been judged to have insecure maternal attachments. Finally, Tiffany Field (1991) positively associated length of day care exposure with number of grade-school friends and activities, leadership, popularity, attractiveness, assertiveness, and nonaggressiveness.

There are mixed data showing and not showing increased levels of aggression and noncompliance in children in day care (reviewed in Scarr and Eisenberg, 1993). When my son was a toddler, I was working on a lecture on this topic and stopped to make dinner. After dinner, Dan was in his high chair savoring his favorite cookie. As my husband and I cleaned up, Dan took advantage of our turned backs and stood up precariously in his high chair. When I saw him, I naturally confronted him and threatened to take away the cookie if he stood up again. A few moments later, I turned to see him grinning from ear to ear as he stood in his high chair with his mouth crammed full of cookie! I knew I was supposed to be enraged by his defiance (and indeed I did scold him about it), but both he and I knew that I couldn't be seriously angry because I was awed by his cleverness. He had his cookie (he got to stand up) and ate it too (literally). This example harkens back to our earlier point about different families valuing and encouraging different behaviors from their children.

Finally, what about **intellectual** consequences? Again, the research is extensive but mixed (see review by Scarr and Eisenberg, 1993). The most consistent finding is enhanced intellectual outcomes for children from disadvantaged families in high quality care (also see Caughy, DiPietro, & Strobino, 1994). For other children, a mix of factors contribute to intellectual outcomes, including the kind of care (Kontos, Hsu, & Dunn, 1994), the child's gender (Medcalf-Davenport, 1993), and family characteristics such as socioeconomic status, parental education, and parental attitudes (Scarr, Phillips, & McCartney, 1989).

We have taken a close-up look at a variety of close relationships central to women's lives. Is there a global recipe for attaining relationship satisfaction that we can take away from this review? As much as I would like to resist falling back on the answer "it depends," it *does* depend. To make blanket statements about what women

---

BOX 7.2   A Checklist for Choosing Quality Day Care

One proactive step toward securing high quality day care is for parents to be choosey consumers. Toward this end, psychologists have been working to devise easy-to-use checklists for parents and guardians searching for high quality care. One 69-item example (Bradbard, Brown & Bischoff, 1992) for parents of school-age children (aged 5-12) focuses on:

- health and safety standards
- adult-child-peer interactions
- home/center coordination
- physical space
- program materials and activities
- making transitions from school to day care to home
- making transitions from day care to self-care.

Source: Extracted from M. R. Bradbard, E. G. Brown, and R. Bischoff. (1992). Developing the day care checklist for parents of school-age children. *Early Child Development and Care,* 83, 77–91. Gordon and Breach Science Publishers. Reprinted with permission.

---

want, need, or should have would be overly simplistic and a disservice to many women. Different friendships, partnerships, and families work in different ways and each needs to find its niche. Rather than disparage those who deviate from what we ourselves live or what we idealize, we need to provide both the social and structural supports to facilitate the pursuit of a wide array of choices.

CHAPTER SUMMARY

In this chapter, we explored a multitude of roles that comprise people's interpersonal lives. We discovered that holding multiple roles can have both overload and enhancement consequences. Role enhancement is facilitated to the extent that each role is of high quality, fulfills needs in an individual's life, and is meaningful and valued. Coping with the demands of multiple roles is enhanced if structural role redefinition is used to redefine otherwise incompatible roles and if social and structural supports are strong.

Close relationships are expected to endure over time and to provide an individual with respect, intimacy, caring, concern, support, and affection. Satisfaction with close relationships is positively associated with psychological and physical well-being. Oftentimes when we consider the role of gender in close relationships, it is difficult to distinguish between genuine gender differences and the self-fulfilling consequences of gendered stereotypes. Although there is no universal recipe for attaining relationship satisfaction, we explored issues involved in working toward such satisfaction in women's friendships, romantic attachments, and caregiving.

An apparent gender difference in friendship patterns evolved in the 1980s suggesting that women share feelings and men share activities with their close friends. Although it is clear that these friendship patterns are consistent with gender stereo-types, the reality of this difference is being challenged by recent research that shows men being as intimate as women in settings that call for intimacy. Turning to women's friendships, women seek intimacy and equality from their friends, although how these are realized varies according to the characteristics of friends, including matches and mismatches in gender, race, and physical ability.

Heterosexual dating scripts reflect gender-typed roles, with men playing the more active and powerful role. Although lesbian dating scripts parallel heterosexual ones in many ways, the former are characterized by more equality of power, less attention to appearance, and more attention to feelings. Lesbian relationships often are invisible to outsiders, yet in contrast to homophobic portrayals, frequently offer intimacy and equality in stable, enduring, and committed relationships.

Marital satisfaction is heavily influenced by issues of equality as women generally continue to shoulder the lion's share of domestic responsibilities. This imbalance spills over into caregiving relationships where women often provide a disproportionate share of care for children and other kin. Recent research suggests that the "caring about" part of caregiving, prototypically referred to as "mothering," is not exclusive or universal to women. Furthermore, a new image of mothers is evolving that combines employment with mothering as parts of women's family responsibilities. This image challenges traditional images of mothers as the always present and exclusive providers of childcare.

Public controversy surrounds debates about "supermom" images and non-parental childcare. Research has become increasingly complex, considering the full array of people involved, individual differences among them, the quality of settings, and the strength of social and structural supports. Broad overgeneralizations about "bad" day care have been replaced by an "it-depends" approach that seeks to understand combinations of factors that best promote an individual woman's satisfaction and health. A clear theme that runs through all of these areas is that relationship satisfaction doesn't come in "one size that fits all" nor is it something that one simply has. People do not just "find happiness"; rather, relationship satisfaction is *achieved* through persistent, everyday work.

EIGHT

MULTIPLE ROLES CONTINUED
Work, Wages, and Closing the Gap

Brian is 20 years old, grew up in Springfield, IL, and worked in a day-care center
last summer. Is he graduating from college
as an engineering or nursing student?

1	2	3	4	5	6
definitely engineering					definitely nursing

Karen is 21 years old, grew up in Lan-
caster, PA, and her hobby is weightlifting.
Is she graduating from college as an
engineering or nursing student?

1	2	3	4	5	6
definitely engineering					definitely nursing

Thomas Nelson and his colleagues (1996) asked college students to make the same judgments you just did for 32 photographed students. We might expect that someone with childcare experience would have the personality characteristics to be a good nurse and a weightlifter to be suited for engineering, but gender overrode such information in students' ratings, especially from those students with more traditional attitudes about the roles of women in American society. Students consistently and with confidence pictured women as nurses and men as engineers, ignoring other information that might be expected to influence their perceptions. Gender stereotypes were reduced, but not eliminated, when raters were held publicly accountable for their responses and were given information to invalidate their occupational stereotypes (e.g., there's a 50:50 ratio of women to men in both nursing and engineering at the targets' university). In this chapter, we will see how a variety of contextual factors, including stereotypes, influences what jobs women pursue, promotion opportunities, and even wages.

THE MEANING OF WORK

Traditionally, social scientists have defined work as the production of goods and services that are of value to others (Fox & Hesse-Biber, 1984). Given this definition, women's "work" monopolizes much of their waking lives, including the caregiving activities we examined in Chapter 7 (Chester & Grossman, 1990). Globally, unpaid work encompasses family-related services (e.g., childcare and housework), subsistence and nonmarket activities (e.g., agricultural production for household consumption), and household enterprises (e.g., keeping the books for a family business) (United Nations, 1995). A disproportionate share of this unpaid and underrecognized work is done by women. In developed countries, if we are asked what we "do," we commonly define work narrowly as our employment status. The purpose of this chapter is to explore the role of *paid* employment in women's lives.

In 1994, women accounted for fully 46% of the workforce in the United States (U.S. Department of Labor, 1995). Looked at another way, nearly six of every ten women over 16-years old (58.8%) were in the labor force—with participation rates of over 70% for women, aged 20 to 54, in their prime employment years. These participation rates vary little by race/ethnicity: 60% of Asian and Pacific Islander women, 58.9% of white women, 58.7% of African American women, 55% of Native American women, and 52.9% of Latinas were employed in 1994 (Herz & Wootton, 1996). This translates into 57 million employed women in the United States, 41 million of whom were employed over 35 hours each week. Of the 16 million women employed part-time, 3.3 million held multiple jobs.

The United Nations measures women's and men's work globally by examining time use to capture both paid and unpaid productivity.

Studies of why women are employed conclude that women work for the same reasons as men: for financial compensation, to fulfill identity needs (James, 1990), and to function as competent and productive members of society (Chester & Grossman, 1990). Striving for competence includes both achievement (goal-oriented) and relational (people-oriented) goals, with individuals stressing these differently (Chester, 1990).

In 1997, the AFL-CIO labor union commissioned telephone interviews and questionnaires returned by over 50,000 union and unrepresented American women to understand the work issues that affect women's lives, both on and off the job. Fully 94% rated "equal pay for equal work" as "very important," making it working women's #1 priority, followed by a safe and healthy work environment (93%); secure, affordable health insurance (87%); paid sick leave for themselves (82%); pension and retirement benefits (79%); punishment of sexual harassers (78%); paid vacation time (76%); protection from layoffs and downsizing (72%); and paid leave to care for sick family members (70%). When women were asked in an open-ended question to describe the "biggest problem facing women at work," 41% cited pay first. The importance of pay is not so surprising when we realize that 64% of the respondents provided at least half their household income: 41% headed their own households and of these, 28% had dependent children.

The economic necessity of work for many women is confirmed by other studies as well. Fully 43% of all women in the United States in 1994 supported themselves, with labor participation rates of 65.1% for never married, 17.3% for widowed, and 73.9% for divorced women (Herz & Wootton, 1996). Families maintained solely by a woman in 1994 accounted for fully one-quarter of families with children (that's more than 8 million families compared to 1.4 million families maintained by solo men). Looking at it another way, 23% of mothers in the workforce were single parents (compared to only 4% of fathers) (Galinsky & Bond, 1996). In 1993, nearly half of all female-headed families with children lived in poverty (versus 25% for parallel male-headed families) (Costello & Krimgold, 1996, Section 4). For women living alone or with nonrelatives, the poverty rate in 1993 was over 25% (compared to 18% for their male counterparts). Wages, by necessity, are of urgent concern to working women.

Given this emphasis, income will be the focal point of this chapter. We'll first take a close look at the wage gap between women and men and among women and then explore a wide range of potential explanations for this gap. Although this list is far from exhaustive, it does review a variety of psychological and sociological approaches to understanding this gap and the role it plays in women's working lives.

THE WAGE GAP

The most fundamental difference between women's and men's participation in the workplace is captured by the differential in their earnings. To gauge this differential, or wage gap, we simply take the ratio of women's to men's earnings and subtract it from 1.0. If women's and men's earnings were identical, this ratio would be 1.00 or, expressed another way, women would earn, on average, 100% of what men earned. In this case, the wage gap would be zero, indicating no difference between their earnings. However, if this ratio is less than 1.00, there is a gap that disadvantages women. In 1995, the earnings ratio in the United States was .714 (or 71.4%) yielding a gap between women's and men's wages of 28.6%.[1]

$$1995 \text{ Earning Ratio} = \frac{\text{median annual earnings of full-time employed women}}{\text{median annual earnings of full-time employed men}} = \frac{\$22,497}{\$31,496} = .714$$

You may have noticed that different sources report different earnings ratios and gaps, although no one has come close to wiping out the gap by manipulating the figures. The U.S. Census Bureau recommends using the median annual earnings of full-time workers as the most representative way to calculate the earnings ratio, and hence the wage gap. (I will use this too unless I state otherwise.) The median, or the 50th percentile, is the best way to represent incomes because large outliers (in this case, those who make millions) deceptively pull arithmetic means upward. Restricting incomes to those of full-time workers assures that we compare similar groups, since women are overrepresented among those employed part-time. Finally, annual earnings give a more accurate picture of income than smaller units of measure which may be affected by vagrancies of overtime and temporary or seasonal work. Smaller time units tend to narrow the gap a bit; for example, the earnings ratio using median *weekly* earnings rises to 75.4% in 1995.

Again, although different ratios are sometimes reported in the media, no one can come close to closing the wage gap by tinkering with the formula. What might close the gap is *the* big question, but before we tackle this question, there are some basic facts about the wage gap we should understand. First, earnings ratios vary by race and ethnicity. Using the incomes of white men as the base (denominator), the earnings ratio for white women is 71.2%; 64.2% for African American women; and 53.4% for Latinas.[2] There are additional earnings gaps by sexual orientation, such that lesbians earn less than heterosexual women (Institute for Gay and Lesbian Strategic Studies, 1996), and by physical ability—disabled women earn 69% of what women in general make (Russo & Jansen, 1988).

Second, the gap has narrowed somewhat recently. From 1955 when the earnings ratio was 63.9% to 1987, the earnings ratio in the United States hovered between 58.8% and 65.2%. In contrast to the stability of the U.S. earnings ratio at this time, the wage gap narrowed in many of the industrialized European countries to which the United States often compares itself (Hewlett, 1986) so that the U.S. today lags behind most of its common comparison groups. The earnings ratio is highest (around 90%) in Tanzania, Iceland, France, and Australia; only Japan (50%), Korea, Cyprus, and Egypt have lower earnings ratios than the United States, according to a 1991 United Nations report (pp. 88–89).

---

[1] The earnings data presented here were compiled by the Institute for Women's Policy Research (1400 20th Street, NW, Suite 104, Washington, DC 20036, (202) 785-5100) in January 1997 from published and unpublished federal data sources produced by the U.S. Census Bureau and Bureau of Labor Statistics.

[2] With white men as the base, the ratios for African American and Latino men are 75.9% and 63.3%, respectively.

The 65% U.S. ceiling was exceeded by the end of the 1980s, creeping into the low 70%s in the early 1990s, but stalled in the mid-1990s (Lewin, 1997). The shattering of the 65% ceiling was greeted with enthusiasm by some until a fuller understanding of the gap's narrowing was accounted for more by declines in men's wages than increases in women's. In fact, if the earnings ratio is calculated in dollars adjusted for inflation, fully 75% of the narrowing of the wage gap from 1979-1995 is accounted for by losses in men's wages. This pattern also holds true within specific occupations (Roos & Reskin, 1992). Although parity can be reached by either advancing women's wages or reducing men's, few labor activists advocate the latter strategy.

Finally, looking at age differentials in earnings between women and men, the news is mixed. The wage gap varies across workers' age such that the 1995 earnings ratio for the youngest workers, aged 25–29, was 82.4% compared to figures in the upper 50% range for workers over 45-years old. Does this portend eventual change as the youngest workers mature in the workforce? This is a plausible possibility because each cohort (or birth group) indeed experiences its own unique history. However, if today's young workers follow in the footsteps of their elders, for whom the wage gap also was narrower when they first entered the workforce, the difference between women's and men's wages will expand throughout their life cycles. The typical lifespan pattern has been for the gap to widen because men's earnings rise substantially until they enter their fifties in contrast to women's wages which remain relatively flat across their work lives. The old patterns may or may not be good predictors of the future.

CAUSES OF THE WAGE GAP

Given this base of information about the wage gap, the most basic and controversial question focuses on what *causes* this differential. Two general explanations have been offered by social scientists (Wittig & Lowe, 1989). The first, **human capital theory**, focuses on differences in qualifications and personal investments arguing, in essence, that because women are deficient in some areas relative to men, they are deservedly compensated at lower levels. These arguments take a *person-centered* approach, looking at women themselves as the causes of their own equitable, but lower, compensation (Riger & Galligan, 1980). The second, **discrimination theory**, turns to outside factors rooted in the contexts of women's lives. This *situation-centered* approach highlights differences in how women and men are treated, sexist stereotypes, hiring biases, differential access to opportunities, and other forms of sexist discrimination.

Often researchers taking one of these two perspectives examine the same topics, but they do so by asking different questions and/or by exploring different aspects of the topic under scrutiny. For example, human capital theorists might argue that women make irrational *choices* when they select low-paying occupations. In contrast, discrimination theorists might argue that women are *channeled* into these less lucrative occupations by biases in hiring and costs associated with deviating from gendered occupational stereotypes. Oftentimes human capital possibilities begin with the phrase, "if only women . . . ," suggesting that if women adopted the work-related strategies of men, they would be paid and promoted like men. Such an approach is incompatible with the feminist orientation we have adopted in this text.

We will discuss 13 possible explanations for the wage gap: job discontinuity, family-work conflict, relocation, turnover, education, achievement motivation, attributions for success, assertiveness, leadership, mentoring, occupational segregation, competence, and discrimination. All but the last of these can be framed in a person-centered form that makes women themselves the objects of our inquiry. We'll start each of the following 12 sections with a human capital statement beginning with "if only women . . . ." We shall see that in many instances, the deficiency model of human capital theorists is contradicted by the evidence; in other cases, an alternative and plausible explanation can be constructed from the discrimination perspective. Although this review is far from exhaustive, the topics I selected to cover here have been painstakingly addressed by psychologists and sociologists.

Job Discontinuity

If only women . . . didn't interrupt their careers. Not surprisingly, interruptions characterize more women's work histories than men's, and in some occupations, such as public school teaching, job discontinuity is almost normative (Singer, 1993). More women's than men's job exits are motivated by family obligations, including child raising (Koenigsberg, Garet, & Rosenbaum, 1994; Li & Currie, 1992) and dual-career conflicts (Tesch et al., 1992). Interruptions are costly to one's salary (Olson, Frieze, & Detlefsen, 1990), as well as self-esteem and sense of accomplishment (Keddy et al., 1993). All this suggests a link between job discontinuity and lower wages that may explain the wage gap, at least in part. The litmus test of this linkage is to compare noninterrupting women's wages to those of noninterrupting men's. If the wage gap narrows, this would argue that noninterrupting makes women's and men's work histories more comparable and thus similarly compensated. However, when statisticians compare the earnings of noninterrupting women to noninterrupting men, the gap in earnings remains unaffected (Rix, 1988).

Noninterrupters do not close the wage gap, but do they do better than those who interrupt or reduce their work hours, in terms of both salary and career advancement? The answer would seem obvious—job discontinuity, and the reductions in work experience it engenders, must incur some work-related costs. It does, adversely affecting both salary (Eliason, 1995; Keddy et al., 1993; Olson et al., 1990) and managerial level (Melamed, 1995a). In Chapter 4 we saw that many college women praise mothers who interrupt their work histories to raise their children and regard this as a preferred work pattern (Bridges & Etaugh, 1995; Schroeder, Blood, & Maluso, 1992). Although employment discontinuity or part-time employment (Olson et al., 1990) may be ideal resolutions to anticipated work-family conflict, the reality is that the pursuit of such a career path is likely to incur work-related costs.

Family-Work Conflict

If only women . . . didn't put family first. We saw in Chapter 7 that domestic responsibilities fall disproportionately onto the shoulders of many women, even if they are employed. Given this, policymakers have argued for structural changes to reduce the work-family conflict experienced by many women (and some men), such as caregiving leave, flex-time, job sharing, on-site childcare, and so on. There is evidence that such provisions reduce work-family conflict (Nelson, Quick, Hitt, & Moesel, 1990). However, these important accommodations carry with them an assumption that domestic responsibilities invariably will impede the workplace effectiveness of some employees, mostly women. Short of voluntary sterilization, almost all women may be suspect to employers who expect the inevitable ticking of the "biological clock" to someday disrupt the full commitment of their women (and possibly a few men) employees.[3]

In a 1989 article in the prestigious *Harvard Business Review*, Felice Schwartz, a respected consultant to businesses about women's workplace participation, proposed a separate and unequal track for women wanting to blend a corporate career with having a family. Her proposal later was dubbed the "Mommy track" in the popular media. Schwartz argues, with little concrete evidence to support her assumptions, that workers with families (read as "mothers," although men theoretically are eligible) cost more to employ because they need family-friendly supports. She proposes that these employees "reimburse" their employers by accepting a second-tier track with lower pay, less promise of advancement, and/or temporary work. This proposal assumes that women are responsible for most childcare (and, ultimately, that this is grounded in biological necessity); that the corporate climate reasonably demands excessive time commitments as well as a masculine milieu; that mothers can afford to accept lower wages; and that full employment and mothering are incompatible. It is all based on the fundamental assumption that family life interferes with employment.

Does it? We think it does: Management students and executives believe that career success negatively impacts on family life (Westman & Etzion, 1990). And of course, it usually is women who are expected to give up their employment should family demands so dictate (Janman, 1989). Indeed, one of the justifications for the wage gap is the assumption that women freely accept lower wages in order to gain family-supportive compensations. I grew up being urged by my parents to be a school teacher so that my work schedule would conform to that of my children. However, this reasoning is fundamentally flawed because predominately female jobs are not necessarily those that accommodate family responsibilities (Glass, 1990). Working even the 7 AM to 3 PM shift as a nurse certainly doesn't fit with the school day (and no job can cope with seemingly endless days off for teacher conferences, clerical days, grading days, winter breaks, spring breaks, and so on.)

The bottom line question is: Are family-committed employees worse workers? The research findings to date are inconsistent. Nancy Betz and Louise Fitzgerald (1987) reviewed this literature and concluded that being married and having children negatively affect career involvement and achievement. This conclusion is supported by recent studies showing lesser time commitment from women business owners (Parasuraman, Purohit, & Godshalk, 1996) and lower earnings among women with disproportionate responsibility for domestic chores (Cannings, 1991). On the other hand, a study of women scientists found no difference in the number of research papers published by married women with children and single women without children (Cole & Zuckerman, 1987). Another study with women personnel professionals

---

[3] In a landmark "fetal-protection" case, the Supreme Court ruled that a company, Johnson Controls, could not discriminate against women by barring them from better-paying jobs in battery production (where exposure to lead is possible) because of fertility without also excluding fertile men (Aukofer & Gunn, 1991).

uncovered no relationship between work-family conflict and career progress (Nelson et al., 1990).

The most direct test of whether family obligations affect wages comes from a survey of 925 women and men who earned their MBAs between 1975 and 1980 (Schneer & Reitman, 1993). Controlling for age, hours worked, experience, employment discontinuities, and field of responsibility, single women without children earned about 12% *less* than married women with children and an employed spouse (the circumstances under which we'd expect the most work-to-family disruption). Furthermore, these family-involved women were at least as satisfied with their careers as women with other familial configurations. Speculating about their findings, Joy Schneer and Freida Reitman suggest that although single, childfree women have been considered the least encumbered employees, they also are the most mobile and thus less attached to an organization. This may translate into greater acceptance of employed mothers as valuable resources (Vanderkolk & Young, 1991).

General employment trends make it clear that employed mothers are not an anomaly, and there is nothing to suggest that mothers' participation in the workforce will decline in the near future.[4] Rather than questioning if mothers are effective workers, both women and employers might be better served if we strive to make the workplace work for women. We have seen that many people expect family demands to interfere with work responsibilities, and we know that expectancies can become self-fulfilling. Might expectations that women will be encumbered by families limit the opportunities some women are given? If so, workplace effectiveness is not being restricted by family itself, but rather by stereotyped expectations. Following this reasoning, we might want to compare family-friendly with family-incompatible workplaces. If we find family-to-work costs in nonsupportive contexts but not in supportive ones, this may help account for some of the inconsistencies in this literature. Certainly more research looking for possible contextual variation is warranted.[5] Recent data suggest that although families add significantly to the work loads of women (and some men), they do not interfere significantly with workplace participation.

An intriguing and consistent finding in this literature is that employed men with employed wives report lower earnings. This finding has been replicated with men MBAs (Schneer & Reitman, 1993) and academic faculty (Bellas, 1992). The literal payoffs of having a nonemployed wife (the "housewife bonus") fit with theories emphasizing the greater economic needs of sole-breadwinner men, fewer distractions for men with homemakers to take care of the domestic front, and the social acceptability of traditional familial arrangements. These data also converge with findings about the relationship between family and work involvement: men (and women) who are more devoted to family also tend to be less committed to work (Tenbrunsel et al., 1995). This pattern of what has been referred to as the "Daddy penalty" (Lewin, 1994) highlights why the wage gap is more than a women's issue.

---

[4] It is easy to find stories in the media about "drop-out moms" who leave the workforce to raise children. Although drop-out rates among women of childbearing age were substantial through the 1970s, since then women's labor force participation rates have been stable among these age groups (Outtz, 1996).

[5] We saw in Chapter 7 that there is an extensive body of research exploring the impact of work on family. Why has there been relative disinterest in family-to-work linkages?

Relocation

If only women . . . would relocate. One commonly held belief about women, especially those with partners and children, is that they are rooted and will not relocate to benefit their careers. It is argued that turning down relocations results in fewer opportunities and thus depressed earnings and advancement. In keeping with this reasoning, the most significant predictor of willingness to relocate for both women and men is spousal agreement (Brett, Stroh, & Reilly, 1993).

Does women's unwillingness to relocate contribute to the wage gap? Further study suggests not. A large-scale study of 1,000 employees from 20 different Fortune 500 companies found that women and racial/ethnic minorities were just as willing to relocate as white men, but that the former were offered fewer opportunities to do so (Brett et al., 1993). In a related study, women and men managers had "all the right stuff": they had comparable levels of education, maintained similar levels of family power, kept their names on transfer lists, and even moved within the past two years for the purpose of career advancement. Despite all this, gendered salary differences remained (Stroh, Brett, & Reilly, 1992).

Turnover

If only women . . . would stay put. If women don't benefit from being willing to relocate or actually doing it, maybe staying put is a plus. Here we face complaints that women's job turnover (leaving for another job) exceeds men's and that "starting over" repeatedly in new jobs depresses salaries. An assumption related to women's turnover is that they leave in response to unmanageable family demands. In the extensive study of women and men managers in Fortune 500 companies, 26% of the women, compared to just 14% of the men, left their employers (Stroh, Brett, & Reilly, 1996). However, women's reasons for leaving were unrelated to either dual-earner status or number of children. Rather, the best predictors of turnover among women were factors that similarly influence men: lack of opportunity for advancement, job dissatisfaction, and discontent with the present employer. Might we now ask why these job shortcomings were more common among women than men? This leads to questions about workplace discrimination that will be addressed later in this chapter.

Education

If only women . . . were as educated as men. It has been argued that some of why the wage gap is narrower among younger workers is because these women and men are more similarly educated in contrast to older generations where women's rates of higher education lagged behind men's. Clearly, the education gap is closing. In 1993-94, women earned 59% of all associates degrees, 54% of all bachelors degrees, 55% of all Masters degrees, 39% of all Ph.D.s, and 41% of all professional degrees (U.S. Department of Education, 1996, Table 239, p. 253).[6] For educational differences to

---

[6] Interestingly, gender segregation by specialty (academic area or field) declined with more advanced degrees: women and men graduated with associates degrees in areas that were most different and doctorates in areas that were least different (Jacobs, 1985). Thus we might expect more occupational integration among workers with advanced degrees and thus less of a wage gap based on differences in training/expertise. However, this does not fit with the stable wage gap across educational levels shown in Table 8.1.

TABLE 8.1 *Mean* Annual Earnings of Women and Men over Age 18, 1995

Education:	High School	College	Masters
All Women	$15,970	$26,841	$34,911
All Men	$26,333	$46,111	$58,302
White Women	$16,196	$26,916	$35,125
White Men	$27,467	$47,016	$58,817
African American Women	$14,473	$25,577	$35,222
African American Men	$19,514	$36,026	$41,777
Latinas	$14,989	$25,338	$33,390
Latinos	$20,882	$35,109	$38,539

Source: Compiled by the Institute for Women's Policy Research, Washington, DC. Reprinted with permission.

contribute to the wage gap, we would expect the differential between women's and men's wages to decline when we compare women with men of equal educational attainment.

This predicted pattern does not emerge from such an analysis; rather, the wage gap remains stable when we compare women and men within educational levels (see Table 8.1). Note that the often quoted, and profoundly depressing, finding that women with college diplomas average earnings close to those of male high-school graduates persists into 1995. Also notice that racial/ethnic minorities are implicated in wider disparities, even within educational levels. Education pays off for both women and men; education is not a plausible explanation for the wage gap.

Achievement Motivation

If only women . . . were as driven as men. Here it is argued that if women possessed the same strong needs for achievement as men, they too would be propelled upward in their careers. One of the first studies of women's achievement motivation introduced a very simple procedure in which women were asked to write stories about "Anne" who was described as topping her medical school class (Horner, 1970). Prior research on achievement motivation relied on projective techniques such as this, as well as cards from the Thematic Apperception Test (TAT), to assess the presumed need for achievement of the individual. The assumption underlying such procedures is that participants project their own drives onto the stimulus, thus revealing information about their own achievement motivation.

In Matina Horner's (1970) dissertation, women wrote negative stories about Anne, describing fears of social rejection, concerns about Anne's normality and femininity, and denial of her success. A particularly pointed story reflects Anne's presumed fears of social isolation and rejection, as follows:

> Anne doesn't want to be number one in her class. She feels she shouldn't rank so high because of social reasons. She drops down to ninth in the class and then marries the boy who graduates number one (Horner, 1970, p. 60).

In keeping with prior assumptions from this literature, Horner interpreted women's negativity toward Anne as reflective of their own confused achievement needs and concluded that, instead of proactively pursuing lofty achievement goals, women are held back by **fear of success**. Thus women themselves became their own greatest obstacles to career achievement.

During the 1970s, two other strands of research called into question Horner's interpretation of her data. First, Rosabeth Moss Kanter (1977) studied the **opportunity** paths open to women and men in a corporate setting. Kanter challenged the causal chain assumed by achievement researchers who believe that individual's achievement aspirations drive them to seek promotions. Kanter argued the reverse: that promotion opportunities influence achievement motives, initiating a reciprocal spiral that could cycle upward or downward. Supporting her speculation, Kanter found that when both women and men thought their career paths were deadend, their aspirations plummeted so that they did little to prepare for and seek advancement, further diminishing their opportunities, and so on, in a downward spiral. Kanter went on to argue that because women are more likely than men to encounter barriers to promotion, depressed achievement motivation is more common among women workers.

A second strand of research continued in the laboratory using Horner's projective procedure. The crowning study in this series extended Horner's procedure to include women and men storywriters, a female and male target (Anne and John), and two occupational settings—one congruent with gendered expectations for men (medical school) and the other consistent with the feminine gender role (nursing) (Cherry & Deaux, 1978). Fully 70% of men raters wrote negative stories about Anne in medical school, even though it is unlikely that they were projecting their own fears of success onto Anne. Along these same lines, only 14% of women raters denigrated Anne when she topped her nursing class, indicating that presumed fear of success didn't generalize to Anne in settings where her success was consistent with gender stereotypes. Across all their data, a clear pattern emerged: both John and Anne were belittled for gender-inappropriate success by both female and male raters. The key to understanding Horner's original findings then was not women's fear of success, but rather costs associated with gendered occupational violations or **deviance**.

Although both these lines of research, conducted within ten years of Horner's original work, should have laid the concept of fear of success to rest, its appeal persists. Research on fear of success as a personality defect in women continues (Piedmont, 1995; Thorne, 1995) and has spawned multiple reincarnations as the "impostor phenomenon" (Clance & O'Toole, 1987; Clance et al., 1995), "Cinderella complex" (Dowling, 1981), and so on.[7] In sum, there is no solid research evidence to support the contention that women are any more or less driven toward success than men, given similar opportunities for advancement (also see Jacobs & McClelland, 1994).

Attributions for Success

If only women . . . internalized success. Psychologists have focused here on causal attributions—how people "explain" success and failure. Think about the reasons you

---

[7] The "impostor phenomenon" proposes that women avoid taking risks that may lead to advancement because they fear being exposed as incompetent fakes (impostors). Similar reasoning underlies the "Cinderella complex" for women who, at some critical point in their careers ("at the stroke of midnight"), revert back to their impoverished, incapable selves.

might give for doing well on an exam: "It was an easy test" (task difficulty); "I lucked out" (luck); "I studied like crazy" (effort); or "I can do this stuff" (ability). The first two, task difficulty and luck, have nothing to do with you, and they do little to predict future success or to encourage you. There's no pride in acing an easy test or making lucky guesses. Effort and ability are inputs you control (that is, they are internal), but only ability is stable—you'll have it across many exams independent of how much time you have to study, how difficult the exam is, and through unlucky times. Ability, as a stable, internal attribution for your success, builds self-confidence and can lead to future success (McFarland & Ross, 1982). If women more rarely attribute their success to ability than men do, this could explain their differential levels of occupational success (reflected hence in wage attainment).

Research in the 1970s documented such a gender difference: women explained their own successes using external causes, such as luck and task ease (McMahan, 1982). The reverse was true for failure: women tended to explain their own failures by internalizing them. Parallel findings emerged regarding how *others* interpreted women's and men's successes and failures. Other women's successes were justified as the consequences of luck (Deaux & Emswiller, 1974), effort (Feldman-Summers & Kiesler, 1974), and simplicity of the task (Feather & Simon, 1975). Lack of ability was more often used to rationalize other women's failures than other men's failures (Feather & Simon, 1975).

Subsequent research on gender differences in causal attributions took on a "now you see it, now you don't" look (Mednick & Thomas, 1993). When findings change across studies, this is a good clue that other factors (moderators) are at work to either suppress or facilitate the effect being studied. When women and men score high in instrumentality, they both are likely to make ability attributions to explain their own behaviors (see Mednick and Thomas, 1993, for a review). Women also make ability attributions similar to those of men when the task is not male linked and when the work group includes only women. Recent research finds ability attributions among women senior public administrators (Russo, Kelly, & Deacon, 1991) and upper-level executives (Gaskill, 1991). This is confirmed by additional research with women and men academics that also adds occupational setting, networks and roles, and academic department as other moderators of the relationship between gender and internal attributions (Fox & Ferri, 1992). Because women and men act similarly under some conditions, it takes more than gender to explain these findings. Personality traits, gender-typing of tasks, the gender congeniality of coworkers, and status all influence attribution choices.

What about gendered expectations about *others'* successes and failures? Research on attributions for others' behaviors also is affected by moderators, such as the gender-appropriateness of a task. A woman's success is most likely to be attributed to luck when she engages in a male-typed task, such as identifying pictures of mechanical objects (Swim & Sanna, 1996). Attributions merge for women and men when the task is neutral, such as identifying everyday household objects. In fact, this line of research raises more questions about *stereotypes* of what is considered appropriate for women and men and how these affect attribution patterns than it provides insights about how attribution deficiencies in women undermine their ambitions and self-confidence.

Assertiveness

If only women . . . were as assertive as men. Another argument considered by psychologists focuses on women's assertiveness and maintains that if women acted as assertively as men, they would command comparable salaries, be eligible for promotions, and enhance their overall job performance. Studies looking for evidence of nonassertiveness in women's language have yielded mixed results, although folk wisdom contends that women use more tentative speech than men, including fewer interruptions, more hedging (using adverbs that weaken claims, like "sort of"), more tag questions ("It's a nice day, *isn't it?*"), disclaimers ("I may be wrong, but . . . "), and intensifiers ("so"; "really"). Consistent with this reasoning, women MBA students report feeling less assertive at work than men do (Goh, 1991).

Linda Carli (1990) argued that the evidence about women's tentative speech is inconclusive because use of tentative speech reflects subordinated status. She proposed that anyone, a woman or a man, who is in a subordinated position will use tentative, as opposed to assertive, speech. Carli tested her hypothesis in two settings. In the first study, 30 pairs of women participants, 30 pairs of men, and 58 mixed-gender pairs were formed on the basis of a pretest so that each pair was composed of members disagreeing about one of two topics—either government-funded day care or lowering of the drinking age to 18. Carli analyzed the speech of each disagreeing pair as they argued their position with each other. Women were not always tentative, as a gendered explanation would predict. Rather, women were more tentative only when they disagreed with men who, arguably, are higher-status others. Most interestingly, women were more influential in changing the attitude of their male partner when they used tentative speech as opposed to assertive speech. In contrast, women were more influential with their female partner when they used assertive speech.

In a second study, raters listened to a contrived audiotape of either a man or a woman arguing in favor of an imposed fare for use of the campus bus, a position that was counterattitudinal for the student raters (Carli, 1990). The speeches were framed using either tentative or assertive speech, and Carli measured both the amount of influence the speech exerted on subsequent audience attitudes as well as ratings of the presenter's knowledge. Women speaking assertively were considered more knowledgeable and competent by both women and men raters. Consistent with this, assertive women were more influential in affecting the attitudes of their female audience. Paradoxically, among male listeners, tentative women were more influential, even though these men evaluated them as less competent.

It is clear that women are capable of using assertive language; they do so spontaneously in contexts with equal-status others (i.e., other women). However, assertiveness presents a double-bind for women when they interact with men; being assertive is perceived as competent, but fails to influence. Other research replicated the finding that assertive women are regarded as competent, but added that assertive women are disliked by many men (Gervasio & Crawford, 1989). We've returned to the catch-22 of sexist stereotypes for women that we saw in Chapter 6—either competent *or* likeable, but not both.

Knowing of these findings doesn't present a clear picture of how and when women should be assertive, but it certainly does explain a common experience of having a suggestion ignored by a group until it is reintroduced by a more powerful other, at which time it is miraculously embraced by the group. I remember clearly making a suggestion at a meeting that I thought would bring closure to the discussion and end the meeting. It was ignored, until a few minutes later when the same point was made by a male friend of mine. This time it had the predicted effect: everyone embraced it and the meeting ended. I felt totally ineffectual and began questioning my own assertiveness until my friend approached me after the meeting and apologized for stealing my point. He said he knew it was the exact point that needed to be made. So much for being assertive and effectual—and who even cares about being liked?

What does it take for a woman to influence her coworkers? A fascinating series of four studies conducted by M.D. Pugh and Ralph Wahrman (1983) suggests a solution, albeit less than ideal. In each study, pairs comprised of a woman and a man completed a task described as a spatial-abilities task. (This procedure sets up an analog to a work setting for women where her colleagues are male and the task is masculine.) Participants viewed 40 slides of green rectangles in which two triangles, one black and the other white, were embedded. The pair's task was to agree on the relative size of each triangle by indicating which was bigger (although they appeared different, in reality, they were the same size so that there was no correct answer). The dependent measure was the change in each partner's discrepant choices, indicating the amount of influence exerted by the partner.

In the baseline condition, men influenced women to change their judgments more than women influenced men. In a second condition, the task was preceded by a verbal disclaimer noting that previous studies found no relationship between task performance and gender. The baseline finding of greater male than female influence persisted. In a third condition, participants individually completed a hidden pictures task which they were led to believe was a good indicator of skill on the subsequent triangles task. Partners were informed that their pre-task scores were similar. Even believing that partners were equally capable, men continued to be more influential than their female counterparts, just as in the baseline condition. In the final, fourth condition, women's pre-task scores indicated that they outperformed their male partner. Given their proven superiority, we would expect men to defer more to these women; in actuality, their rates of influence were equal. Since this last condition was the only one in which women and men were equally influential, it appears that to be influential, women must be proven overcompetent.

Leadership

If only women . . . possessed the leadership qualities of men. Some have argued that women are excluded from top positions because many lack the highly valued and well-compensated leadership skills of men. Much research on gender and leadership has focused on two definitions of leadership **style**. The first argues that women tend to be considerate leaders who care more about feelings of group members (relationship-oriented leaders) than getting the job done (task-oriented). The second envisions women as democratic, participative leaders (vs. autocratic, directive leaders).

In a meta-analysis pooling 370 gender comparisons, Alice Eagly and Blair John-

Do we imagine women as leaders? This photograph of world leaders was taken at a 1995 meeting at the United Nations. Globally, only 24 women have been elected heads of state or government, half since 1990, and women rarely compose more than 1-2% of top business leaders (United Nations, 1995).

son (1990) found very small differences between women and men in leadership style. Although women tended to be more democratic than men, the difference was small (d = +.27). Further probing of these data did show some interesting gender differences within certain settings. For example, more stereotyped gender patterns were found in contrived laboratory than in real-life field studies. Furthermore, the style of leadership enacted by women and men varied according to how well the leadership role fit with gender roles (gender congeniality) and who the followers were. Both women and men tended to be more task oriented when they filled leadership roles compatible with their gender—for example, when women were head librarians and men were military officers. Also, women were more likely to use an autocratic style when they led groups of men, although subsequent meta-analytic work finds that use of such a gender-inappropriate style by women is disliked by male followers (Eagly, Makhijani, & Klonsky, 1992). Combining these findings suggests that women and men leaders rise to whatever the occasion dictates. When conflicts between the demands of leadership and gender are minimal, these leaders can get the task done. In contrast, when conflicts exist, they divert attention away from task completion toward handling members' concerns about gender violations.

Moving beyond leadership style, are men more effective as leaders than women? **Effectiveness** typically is defined as a leader's facilitation of a group's or organization's ability to achieve its stated goals. Alice Eagly, Steven Karau, and Mona Makhijani (1995) meta-analyzed 76 studies and found no differences in the effectiveness of women and men leaders. This pattern held whether the studies were conducted in the laboratory or in the field, with the exception of the military, where men fared significantly better. This final caveat raised questions about the gender congeniality of the leader role and the gender composition of the group, two factors that we have seen affect leadership style. The military involves both a leadership role that is stereotyped as masculine and groups that are often numerically dominated by men. Men were regarded as more effective leaders than women when most leaders in that role were men and when men dominated the group of subordinates. This explains the military exception and extends the findings beyond that setting to any gender-incongenial leadership role and imbalanced group membership. Women were favored only when they served in feminine leadership roles and lead groups of mostly women.

Consider the experiences of the first women cadets to attend the U.S. Military Academy at West Point, a training ground for military leaders. I observed cadets subtly push women aside when they worked on physically demanding tasks like constructing a pontoon bridge (Yoder, 1989). Instead of learning to be the leaders they were training to be during such exercises, women became passive observers who oftentimes were criticized for their noncommand voices and peripheral importance. Almost half these women reported feeling overprotected as cadets, a circumstance incompatible with the leadership role but one that conforms readily to the feminine role. In a setting that defined cadets in masculine terms, these women struggled to create a new role, woman-cadet, and to disassociate themselves from femininity. As an example of the latter, women shunned their skirted uniform and instead tried to blend in by wearing only trousers. Inconsistencies between followers' expectations for leaders and for women seem to mediate women's effectiveness more than anything about women's leadership style per se.

Research on both leadership style and effectiveness emphasizes the importance of *context*: leaders adapt their styles in accordance with contextual cues, like the gender of their followers and the gender-appropriateness of their role, and are most effective when they do so. Despite this variability though, the role of leader continues to be *basically masculine* unless something suggests otherwise. Looking across 74 studies on the emergence of leaders in initially leaderless groups, men come forward more often than women, unless the group task requires complex social interaction (Eagly & Karau, 1991). In a corporate setting, this gendered expectation for leadership translates into a view of "think manager, think male" which appears globally (Schein, Mueller, Lituchy, & Lui, 1996).[8]

The personalities of women leaders don't seem to differ much from those of male leaders. Lynn Offermann and Cheryl Beil (1992) compared women and men college leaders to other undergraduates and found that the achievement profiles of leaders, regardless of gender, were more similar to each other than to those of nonleaders of the same sex. One significant difference between women and men leaders is that men reported enjoying exerting power and influence more than women. These studies conclude that women leaders are similar to men leaders and can lead as effectively as men, although gendered stereotypes about the leadership role that favor men persist, and contextual variations influence how leadership is expressed by both women and men.

---

[8] For an interesting classroom exercise on the emergence of leaders within different contexts, see Hebl (1995).

Mentoring

If only women . . . mentored and were mentored like men. If we expect mentoring to help explain the wage gap, we first must show that having a mentor pays off in better wages as well as other markers related to earnings, such as promotion. George Dreher and Ronald Ash (1990) confirmed this linkage for both women and men. Business-school graduates who experienced extensive mentoring reported more promotions, higher incomes, and greater satisfaction with their pay and benefits than those for whom mentoring was superficial or nonexistent. Other research extends these favorable outcomes to global job satisfaction (Mobley et al., 1994) and to a variety of women in various occupations, such as African American women university administrators (Ramey, 1995).

How is having a mentor linked to better wages (as well as other career outcomes such as promotion)? Kathy Kram (1985) described two ways in which mentoring from senior managers may prove beneficial to the career success of the protégé. First, the mentoring system opens doors into important social networks, which serve as repositories of valuable information often inaccessible through formal communications networks. Indeed, both women and men managers with mentors scored higher on informal and formal communication indicators than did those without mentors (Bahniuk, Dobos, & Hill, 1990). These networks provide the protégé with alliances as well as opportunities to be visible to senior decision-makers. Second, mentors model and they offer vicarious reinforcements—when the mentor is in the limelight, the protégé too may shine on the fringes.

The role-modeling function of women mentors for women protégés may be especially valuable when women are forging new roles in occupations dominated by men (Gilbert & Rossman, 1992). For example in my own research with cadets at the U.S. Military Academy at West Point, women struggled with role conflicts generated by opposing messages sent by the feminine role and the role of macho cadet (Yoder, Adams, & Prince, 1983). Men cadets had long benefited from the active support, as well as role modeling, provided informally by upper-class cadets and officers who were warmly acknowledged as "fairy godfathers." Given the ambiguity of the woman-cadet role, it would seem even more compelling for women cadets to look for senior women to serve as mentors, and indeed researchers find that women display modest preferences for women mentors (Burke & McKeen, 1995).

However, finding a woman to serve as one's mentor may be "easier said than done," at least according to surveys of business women and men (Ragins & Cotton, 1991) and of psychologists (Cohen & Gutek, 1991). One obvious barrier to finding a woman mentor is their simple *scarcity* in male-dominated occupations, especially in senior positions (Ragins & Scandura, 1994). Even when senior women are available, forced mentor-mentee pairings do not automatically enhance protégés' job satisfaction (Mobley et al., 1994). This leaves us with voluntary mentoring initiated by the mentor, which is the typical pattern for mentor-mentee relationship formation (Kram, 1983). The propensity for senior women not to embrace mentoring tasks wholeheartedly lead some critics to talk about a "queen bee syndrome," where successful women kill off competition from junior women by ignoring their pleas for assistance (Staines, Tavris, & Jayaratne, 1974). This woman-blaming explanation has been discounted by subsequent studies, which find high levels of interest in being a mentor among senior women (Ragins & Cotton, 1993), and situational constraints that prevent women from shouldering mentoring responsibilities. For example, at West Point, women coached junior women on their all-women sports teams but not in contexts dominated by men. In those settings, upper-class women felt so stressed and visible as women that they avoided any interactions and behaviors that called unnecessary attention to their gender, including being seen with other women (Yoder et al., 1985).

This leaves cross-gender mentoring. Women express concerns about having a man as a mentor (Burke & McKeen, 1995), and cross-gender protégés are less likely to report engaging in after-hours social activities with their mentors and to view their mentors as role models (Ragins & McFarlin, 1990). In a provocative recent study, George Dreher and Taylor Cox (1996) found that MBA business graduates (including white women, African Americans, and Latina/Latinos) who established mentoring relationships with white men mentors reported an average annual compensation advantage of fully $16,840 over those with mentors with other demographic profiles. Although women and racial/ethnic minority protégés were less likely than their white male counterparts to form mentoring bonds with senior white men, those who did benefited similarly to white male protégés mentored by white men. No compensation differences were found between those without mentors and those with women or minority mentors. This opens up questions about what it is about white men mentors that provides their mentees with better prospects for economic payoffs.

The most probable answer focuses on the power and status of mentors. It seems reasonable to speculate that white men have the strongest links to social networks and are most likely to be rewarded—two processes which we have seen mediate the relationship between having a mentor and favorable outcomes. Simply put, more white men tend to hold positions of status and power. The relationship between a mentor's power and the mentee's outcomes is clear: protégés believe high-ranked mentors can exercise more power (Struthers, 1995) and indeed a mentor's standing in the organizational hierarchy has been associated with her/his effectiveness (Shea, 1994). In sum, mentoring may play a role in closing the wage gap, although it is unlikely that it will close it completely, and its effectiveness may be limited to certain occupations. Much of the research to date on mentoring has been confined to managerial and professional (white collar) settings.

Occupational Segregation

If only women . . . would chose the same jobs as men. Women and men are concentrated in different occupations, in essence, creating a workforce characterized by "women's work" and "men's work," with some gender-neutral occupations. Barbara Reskin and Irene Padavic (1994) describe gender segregation in the U.S. labor force by looking at the gender composition of the 503 occupations, collections of jobs that involve similar activities, detailed by the U.S. Census Bureau. Looking at broad occupational categories gives us a limited sense of job segregation because women and men may be segregated within occupations. For example, male bakers tend to be concentrated as unionized, high-paying processors of mass-produced goods in contrast to women

TABLE 8.2   The Top Ten Occupations for U.S. Women and Men, 1990

Women	Men
Secretary	Salaried manager, administrator
Elementary school teacher	Truck driver
Cashier	Salaried sales supervisor, proprietor
Registered nurse	Janitor, cleaner
Bookkeeper, accounting clerk	Carpenter, except apprentice
Nurse's aide	Sales representative, mining, mfg., wholesale
Salaried manager, administrator	Construction laborer
Sales representative, other commodities	Cook
Waitress	Supervisor, production occupation
Salaried sales supervisor, proprietor	Automobile mechanic

Source: B. Reskin and I. Padavic, *Women and Men at Work,* pp. 34, 37, copyright © 1994 by Pine Forge Press. Reprinted by permission of Pine Forge Press.

who tend to work in retail bakeries where pay is lower (Steiger & Reskin, 1990). Indicators of job segregation are limited to studies within specific occupations, while larger scale overviews of occupational segregation can be gleaned from census data.

When the 1990 census was conducted, fully one-third of the 56 million employed U.S. women were concentrated in just ten of 503 occupations, with secretary topping the list (see Table 8.2). One of every ten employed women was employed in the clerical occupations of secretary, typist, stenographer, and office clerk. Only 11% of employed women worked in occupations that were at least 75% male. Men were more evenly spread across occupations, with one-quarter employed in their top ten occupations. Table 8.2 illustrates how little overlap there is between the top ten lists for women and men.

The top ten list of "women's work" has been amazingly stable: since 1940, the only change in this list has been the recent addition of "miscellaneous salaried managers." We tend to think that more and more women are entering male-dominated occupations like physician and lawyer, and indeed they are, but the grim reality is that for every female lawyer in 1990, there are 101 women doing clerical work, 33 women operating factory machines, 30 sales clerks, 9 nurses aides, and 8 waitresses. In fact, adjusting for the influx of women into the labor force between 1960 and 1980, Natalie Sokoloff (1988) found that the overrepresentation of white men in the prestigious male-dominated occupations actually increased across this 20-year span.

To get an overview of the degree to which occupations are gender segregated, an **index of segregation** is calculated to represent the proportion of all female (or male) workers who would have to change occupations to achieve genuine occupational integration (a state of 50-50 representation in every occupation). Zero would denote a fully integrated workforce in contrast to an index of 100, which would indicate a completely segregated labor force. In 1990, the index of occupational segregation in the United States was 53, meaning that 53% of the female workforce (that's 32 million workers) would have to switch to male-dominated work to achieve full integration. The index does show some favorable changes across time: after hovering between 65 and 69 from 1900 to 1970, the 1970s saw declines in the index into the

TABLE 8.3   The Top Occupations for U.S. Women, 1990

African American Women	Latinas
Cashier	Secretary
Secretary	Cashier
Elementary school teacher	Janitor, cleaner
Cook	Sewing machine operator
Janitor, cleaner	Nurse's aide, orderly
General office clerk	Elementary school teacher
Maid, "houseman"	Maid, "houseman"
Registered nurse	General office clerk

Asian American Women	White Women
Registered nurse	Secretary
Cashier	Elementary school teacher
Secretary	Cashier
Sewing machine operator	Bookkeeper
Accountant, auditor	Registered nurse
Bookkeeper	Salaried manager, administrator
Waitress	Sales, other commodities
General office clerk	Waitress

Source: B. Reskin and I. Padavic, *Women and Men at Work*, pps. 34, 37, copyright © 1994 by Pine Forge Press. Reprinted by permission of Pine Forge Press.

50s (also see Jacobs, 1989; Reskin, 1993).[9] This decline continued but at a slower pace in the 1980s, and it is accounted for more by women moving into "men's work" than by men pursuing nontraditional options (Cotter, DeFiore, & Hermsen, 1995).

Occupational segregation extends within gender to race/ethnicity groupings, and it is not readily explained by differences in the characteristics of workers themselves (Anderson & Shapiro, 1996). Table 8.3 shows the top occupations for a diversity of women. Although these lists illustrate how women are divided along racial/ethnic lines in the workforce, they also reflect major changes toward racial integration, at least within gender. For example, the index of segregation calculated by comparing the integration of African American and white women dropped from 65.4 in 1940 to 29.2 in 1988.

Employment in different occupations wouldn't produce a wage gap if women's work was paid comparably to men's. However, occupations with high concentrations of women and people of color fall at the low end of the pay scale. This uneven distribution of workers into occupations of varying pay focuses our next question: Why do occupations that employ mostly women pay less?

We first might ask why women make such "irrational" choices: if they are qualified for better paying jobs, why do women take jobs that pay less? In Chapter 4, we explored the future planning of adolescents, concentrating on occupational choices. We saw that who does a job (gender ratios), language (the wudgemaker, "he" . . .), and how jobs are presented (as appropriate or inappropriate for women) all affect

[9] During 1960–1980, occupational gender segregation declined in a majority of 56 developed and developing countries (Jacobs & Lim, 1992).

occupational expectations. Combine these with gender differences in values, and it is not surprising that girls are likely to pursue one track; boys, another. Given the significant influence of occupational differences on perpetuating the wage gap, a more proactive question would be: "What happens when women elect to deviate from the proscribed path for their gender by pursuing a male-dominated occupation?"

Tokenism. In 1977, Rosabeth Moss Kanter described the work lives of a few women salesmanagers at a Fortune 500 company. She described these women as **"tokens,"** who comprised less than 15% of their work group and who faced pressures from their constant visibility and difference from the dominant group of men. Subsequent research with all kinds of women doing all kinds of masculine jobs from West Point cadets to lawyers, coal miners, and autoworkers showed that these women faced negative consequences associated with their difference, visibility, role violations, and intrusiveness into masculine domains. Unfavorable outcomes include stress, social isolation, role conflicts, sexual harassment, wage inequities, and blocked upward mobility (see Yoder, 1991, and Zimmer, 1988, for reviews), as well as increased reliance on restrictive gender stereotypes (Ely, 1995).

Some of the most recent work on tokenism processes has expanded definitions of difference to encompass both gender and race, for example, by studying African American women firefighters (Yoder & Aniakudo, 1997), police officers (Martin, 1994), and elite Black leaders (Jackson, Thoits, & Taylor, 1995). This broadened definition of tokenism highlights both the omnirelevance and inseparability of race and gender (see Chapter 1 for this discussion), as well as subordination through exclusion. For African American women in these white- and male-dominated contexts, they saw their exchanges with their colleagues as perpetually being shaped by intertwined racial and gender themes. One African American woman firefighter summed this up: " . . . being a Black female . . . it was like two things needed to be proven" (Yoder & Aniakudo, 1997, p. 336).

African American women firefighters and policewomen report stories of insufficient instruction, coworker hostility, silence, close supervision, lack of support, and stereotyping. All share a common message, sometimes direct, but oftentimes subtle, of exclusion and subordination. For example, a 16-year veteran of firefighting vividly recalled her first encounter with her white male captain:

> . . . the first day I came on, the first day I was in the field, the guy told me he didn't like me. And then he said: "I'm gonna tell you why I don't like you. Number one, I don't like you cuz you're Black. And number two, cuz you're a woman." And that was all he said. He walked away (Yoder & Aniakudo, 1997, p. 329).

Another 40-year-old African American woman firefighter describes what it was like to endure the "silent treatment":

> . . . no one really talked to me. It was difficult the first, I'd say, six months, because I was basically alone. I'd walk in and everything would get quiet. I'd go to eat; everybody leaves the room. Once they saw I was not going anywhere and I was there to stay, slowly guys started coming around, you know, talking. As I said, I've been on the job now seven

years, and there're still guys that don't talk to me. They speak and that's it. Haven't really accepted the fact that yes, we do have women on the department. . . . Yoder & Aniakudo, 1997, p. 330).

All of this would seem to conspire to make occupational deviance something to be avoided, yet these women moved from feminine stereotypic jobs to firefighting because it offered monetary advancements and challenges they found appealing.

"Unsocialized" women.   Does it take a certain breed of woman to meet this challenge? Maybe. Nancy Betz (1993) describes some "unsocialized" facilitators that help women break *away* from prevailing socialization practices typically pressuring girls and women toward traditional occupations. Women who pursue male-dominated occupations tend to exhibit high levels of instrumentality, express egalitarian attitudes toward women's roles in society, and feel self-confident. In addition, they tend to have moms who are employed and well educated. The personality configuration associated with nontraditionally employed women includes high levels of competency traits (e.g., independence and assertiveness), as well as positive aspects of the feminine stereotype (Lemkau, 1979).

The Supreme Court mandated that the Virginia Military Institute open its doors to women in 1997. On the opening day, someone laid out 30 dead lab rats on the parade grounds with a towel bearing the message: "Save the males!"

Hiring bias.   It also is clear that the opportunity to move outside gendered occupational options must be seen as viable before even the most determined women can make such choices. In studies of hiring patterns, raters (typically students or business professionals) review the resumes of job candidates and record their hiring preferences. The general pattern is for women to be preferred for feminine jobs and men for masculine ones (Martinko & Gardner, 1983; Kalin & Hodgins, 1984), with this gendered pattern holding for African American women and men (McRae, 1994). Such gendered preferences extend to the selection of corporate directors (Bilimoria & Piderit, 1994). Obviously, this hiring bias helps maintain a gender-segregated workforce.

What can be done to counter such bias? Women must be given opportunities to toss their resumes into the applicant pool. As we saw in Chapter 4, how job advertisements are framed can influence women's and men's willingness even to apply for a position. In our work with firefighters, women reported that the simple discovery that the profession was open to women was a necessary revelation. Women saw women firefighters in action, were informed by friends and relatives of openings, and saw recruitment ads geared specifically toward women. A key test of the effectiveness of such recruitment efforts may be to see if the gender ratio in the pool of available candidates, that is, all those who qualify for a job, is similar to the applicant pool (Bronstein & Pfenning, 1988).

Once in the pool of eligible candidates, women must be granted fair consideration. The Department of Labor notes that some informal hiring practices, like interviewing candidates in hotels and over dinner, subtly chill women out of participation (U.S. Department of Labor, 1991). Relatedly, other research suggests that formal as opposed to informal job search procedures facilitate women's chances of landing jobs in male-dominated fields (Drentea, 1995). Compelling research with faked applications that are identical in content except for the gender of the applicant finds biases against women (as well as people of color) (Firth, 1982).

To directly counter the tendency to prefer men for masculine and women for feminine jobs, individuating information is helpful, but not fully compensatory. For example, Peter Glick and his colleagues (1988) "masculinized" the fictitious resumes of female and male applicants by giving them summer jobs in a sports store (as opposed to a feminine jewelry store), a work-study job in grounds maintenance (vs. aerobics instructor), and captain of the varsity basketball team (vs. pep squad). They found that masculinizing information about female candidates for a position in sales management in a heavy machinery company enhanced their likelihood of being interviewed, although being male was an even stronger predictor (also see Branscombe & Smith, 1990). In general, candidates who seem to mesh with the gender orientation of a job are considered stronger applicants (Towson, Zanna, & MacDonald, 1989). Sometimes giving the impression of a good fit simply requires some semantic reframing. For example, my husband advised a woman graduate student to list her hobby as a "marathoner," not a "jogger," when she applied for a masculine-typed position.

Job queues, gender queues.   Occupational segregation along gender lines can contribute to the wage gap only if "women's work" is paid less than men's, and indeed we have seen that this is the case. Why is there such a gendered pay differential across occupations? Barbara Reskin and Patricia Roos (1990) compiled case studies of 11 occupations that experienced shifts in their gender composition. A common pattern across these changing occupations can be understood by thinking about two **queues**: (1) a line of jobs, ranked from best to worst, by prospective employees and (2) a line of applicants ordered according to employers' hiring preferences. Reskin and Roos propose that people filter into jobs as employers move down their list, and applicants accept or reject offers depending on job availability and where each job ranks on their list of preferences. The result is that the highest ranked candidates monopolize the most desirable jobs. All this seems quite rational—why hire a high-school grad when you can get someone with a BA, and why settle for a less desirable job when the one at the top of a job-seeker's queue is offered?

This ranking system becomes questionable, however, when Reskin and Roos factor in gender, race, and other arguably irrelevant inputs from applicants. They summarize the pattern that recurs across the 11 occupations studied: employers' queues incorporate demographic factors into their rankings such that men are preferred over women, whites over racial/ethnic minorities, and so on. This sets up a system wherein people with less desirable (i.e., lower status) demographic profiles move ahead in the employment queue only when more desirable others are unavailable. Thus, when an occupation becomes less lucrative (or jobs within it decline in pay, advancement opportunities, autonomy, etc.), highly ranked workers can move on to other more desirable work leaving a vacuum to be filled by those lower in the queue. Given this logic, women appear disproportionately in low-paying jobs because they start farther down the applicant line than men. At its root, this queueing analysis focuses on gender (and other) biases in hiring patterns.

The segregation of women and men into different occupations certainly plays a significant, if not definitive, role in maintaining the wage gap. When there were some small declines in both occupational segregation and the wage gap across the 1980s, statisticians estimate that about one-third of the earnings gap was accounted for by gender segregation (Cotter, DeFiore, & Hermsen, 1995). This pattern holds up within specialties and employment settings (Bird, 1996; Petersen & Morgan, 1995). However, a recent, provocative study finds a relationship between occupational integration and wages across all occupations such that women who work in metropolitan areas with integrated occupations earn more even if they are employed in female-dominated occupations (Cotter et al., 1997). Although it is not yet clear what mechanisms link occupational integration with enhanced earnings, these findings suggest that genuine occupational integration could have far-reaching effects that indeed might narrow the wage gap.

Competence

If only women . . . were as competent as men. Are women as competent as men? Obviously, if they are not, this would justify the wage gap. This is a complex area, much of which goes beyond our interests and expertise as psychologists. However, psychologists have contributed a piece to this puzzle by considering how subjectivity in evaluations of competence can impact differently on the works produced by women and men.

The piece of research that kicked off this line of thinking was a very simple, yet often misrepresented, study by Philip Goldberg (1968). College women evaluated a series of six brief articles representing fields strongly associated with men (law and city planning), women (elementary school teaching and dietetics), or neither (linguistics and art). The same articles were compiled into two separate booklets, and half were attributed to a fictional male author (John McKay) and the others to a woman (Joan McKay). Which articles were authored by Joan and John were reversed in each booklet so that half the raters evaluated an article on law authored by Joan while the other half rated the same article attributed to John, and so on. Each rater assigned nine ratings to each of the six articles yielding 54 scores. On fully 44 of these, evaluations of articles attributed to male authors exceeded those for female authors. Goldberg (1968) concluded:

> Women . . . are prejudiced against female professionals and, regardless of the actual accomplishments of the professionals, will firmly refuse to recognize them as the equals of their male colleagues (p. 30).

This study spawned a body of research seeking to replicate, extend, and understand this finding. Stimulus materials attributed to women and men expanded beyond Goldberg's written materials to include art work, behaviors, resumés, applications for jobs, and short biographies of the targets. A meta-analysis of 106 of these studies concluded that, overall, women and men are evaluated similarly by both women and men judges (Swim, Borgida, & Maruyama, 1989). However, the analyses suggested that some other factors (moderators) were affecting these findings so that they were not uniform (homogeneous) across studies. Further probing revealed that women's presumed work was denigrated somewhat when the stimulus materials were either masculine or gender neutral. There also was evidence of bias against women when less information was presented about the named originator/author and when the materials judged were resumés or job applications. Other research, controlling for targets' ability, experience, and education, suggests that evaluation bias disadvantages women working in groups of mostly men (Sackett, DuBois, & Noe, 1991).

These findings are consistent with Bernice Lott's (1985) narrative review of this literature. Lott concluded that women's competence was least favorably judged when little information was available about the target person, when the evaluation procedure was real (as opposed to a laboratory simulation), and when a decision had to be made that had consequences for the evaluator (e.g., subsequently working with the person hired). All of these qualifying conditions describe the job hiring process, pinpointing this as a critical area where subjective evaluations of women's competence can work to their unfair disadvantage. Combining this with the preferences of recruiters for gender-appropriate candidates for gender-typed occupations and the queueing proposal, we find serious red flags raised by social scientists about how bias that influences hiring decisions maintains occupational segregation.

Discrimination

This is the only potential cause of the wage gap that cannot be framed from a person-centered perspective focused on deficiencies in women themselves. Although we have seen that situation-centered explanations can be constructed from research findings in many of the areas reviewed above, our focus here will turn to an open consideration of sexist discrimination itself.

A dated but unusually large, longitudinal study rules out all possible human capital explanations, leaving only discrimination as a plausible explanation. James White (1967) followed 1300 women and 1300 men who graduated from law school across the first ten years of their careers. He found that one year after graduation, women averaged $1500 less in salary than men (a lot of money given the dates covered by this study), and that this differential grew to $8300 over ten years. Why? You might consider some possible reasons before reviewing White's data.

If the men were smarter, that could account for the pay difference. But, White purposively matched the women and men in his sample according to their standing in law school. Were the men better trained or more experienced? Again, White matched his participants so that they were from equally prestigious schools and matched for date of graduation. Did the women interrupt their careers more often? Indeed they did, but White's sample was large enough to make comparisons of noninterrupting women with noninterrupting men. He found that the overall patterns of wage differentials remained virtually unchanged. Maybe men went into higher paying private practice in contrast to public work by women? Similarly, maybe women and men might practice different specialties, like high-paying tax and corporate law for men and family law for women? White's sample compared women practicing in private settings with men practicing in comparable settings, and women in specific specialties with men in the same specialty. The discrepant wage patterns persisted.

What plausible explanations remain? Expectations about women being less aggressive as lawyers than men; preferences for men over women by judges, clients, and colleagues; old boys' networks; glass ceilings; etc.? Does a common thread run through these questions? Are these remaining points examples of bias, discrimination, differential treatment . . . ? Whatever you want to call it, there is some subtle, "something-else" that lurks in the background.

Although White's study is dated, his method offers a large sample size and longitudinal design that are hard to find. We can update the findings at bit. Taylor Cox and Celia Harquail (1991) contacted 125 women and 377 men MBAs who graduated from the University of Michigan between 1976–1986. Like White, they found bigger pay increases and hence higher salaries among the men, even though their samples were comparable in years since graduation, training, ethnicity, seniority with their present employer, and even job performance (participants sent their last two formal evaluations to the researchers). Differences in promotion patterns held the key to understanding their wage differential. Women and men reported similar numbers of promotions, but men's promotions tended to be more substantial, involving movement up the management hierarchy, as opposed to titular but empty promotions for women. Men's promotions of substance brought higher pay with them. Parallel research involving a large sample of women and men scientists comes to a similar conclusion (Sonnert & Holton, 1996).

The importance of promotions brings us to the concept of the "glass ceiling." In 1991, the U.S. Department of Labor issued a report that drew on a review of published research as well as intensive data collected from nine randomly selected Fortune 500 companies. They reported that although women represented 37.2% of the

147,179 employees in these companies, women composed only 6.6% of their top executives (assistant vice president or higher). (In fact, these researchers had to reach lower down the organizational hierarchy than they had originally planned to have a sufficient sample of women "top executives.") This report concluded that a **"glass ceiling"** exists, defined as artificial barriers, based on attitudinal or organizational bias, that prevent qualified individuals from advancing upward in their organization. This glass ceiling was bolstered by reliance on upper management's perceptions rather than formal tracking systems; by informal appraisal procedures that often judged women according to how well they got along with coworkers in contrast to men's performance evaluations; by segregation of women into staff functions (e.g., personnel) instead of the line functions that track toward upper management; and by biased and unmonitored hiring practices.

One result of the glass ceiling initiative was the appointment of a Federal Glass Ceiling Commission within the Department of Labor which issued a follow-up report in 1995. This commission concluded:

> A classic *glass ceiling* for women still exists, despite the fact that over the past decade women have moved slowly up the ladder in the largest U.S. corporations. Still, only 3–5 percent of senior positions are held by women—far too few in proportion to their numbers in the labor force (Federal Glass Ceiling Commission, 1995, p. 143).

A key feature of the glass ceiling is its transparency: promotions are cloaked in a guise of fairness so that presumably women cannot see the barriers that are holding them back. This is not the case for many racial and ethnic minorities who realize, quite clearly, that their upward progress is blocked by a combination of sexism and racism. In recognition of this key difference, the Federal Glass Ceiling Commission captured the perceptions of African Americans with the imagery of a **concrete wall**. Testifying in hearings to the commission, one African American woman described this difference:

> Yes, there is a ceiling. That's not news in our community. Indeed, for African Americans, everyone who comments on it seems to call it the concrete ceiling or concrete wall. But for those of us at the [deleted] we say that both of these terms really are descriptions of good, old-fashioned racial discrimination in recruitment, job placement, promotions, performance evaluations, compensation, and other terms and conditions of employment. . . . For Black women it is even worse. They are only three percent of all women managers, and women managers are estimated to be less than two to three percent. So we have a non-existence. We don't even have a wall—no ceiling, no glass to look through. There is nothing (Federal Glass Ceiling Commission, 1995, pp. 68–69).

Overall, large-scale studies controlling for a variety of differences between women and men conclude that a substantial portion of the wage gap is explained by discrimination—as much as 55% (Melamed, 1995b). *If only there wasn't sexist discrimination. . . .*

If there's so much gender-based discrimination out there, why aren't women (and men) outraged? Some are. However, recent research hints that discrimination can remain hidden and thus go unnoticed even by those directly affected by it. Faye Crosby and her associates have conducted a series of studies exploring how comparable instances of discrimination are perceived differently according to how information is presented (Crosby & Clayton, 1986; Rutte et al., 1994). They constructed a hypothetical data set wherein women are substantially undercompensated despite comparable seniority and organizational level to men. They then varied how these data were presented to students, making the differences inconspicuous by avoiding direct comparisons of comparably qualified women and men and by giving piecemeal, case-by-case data, rather than aggregated data. Under these circumstances, students notice the least amount of discrimination, even though, objectively, women are disadvantaged regardless of the presentational method. Given that few people see salary information that directly compares their earnings to equally qualified and situated others and that most of us are privy to only part of an organization's overall wage distributions, it is hard to pinpoint individual wage inequities, even when they exist. Failure to notice discrimination is not a valid signal that it doesn't exist.

CLOSING THE WAGE GAP

We have spent much time in this chapter debunking myths forwarded by human capital theorists to explain women's presumably deficient participation in the workplace. We have eliminated job discontinuities, unwillingness to relocate, turnover, inadequate education, depressed achievement motivation, external attributions for success and the internalization of failure, nonassertiveness, defective leadership style and ineffectiveness, and lack of mentoring and being mentored as plausible justifications for the wage gap. We have asked questions about the effects of family on work and concluded that mixed results require future research focused on the contextual factors that minimize such interference. We noted how stereotyped images of leaders and mentors as men, of assertive women as "bitches," of competence and being a woman as incompatible, and of women's and men's work all serve to bolster workplace inequities. Psychologists have laid to rest many possibilities derived from human capital theory that served to disparage women as workers and have proposed areas for future research focused on contextual factors.

To close the wage gap, we might best ask: *"Who's got the power?"* This question runs throughout all of the above discussion and indeed may explain much of these findings better than gender per se (Reskin, 1988). Where the formal authority and power reside more strongly affects leaders' and subordinates' behaviors than whether the group's leader is a woman or a man (Johnson, 1993). Similarly, the higher status a leader is, the more empowering that individual is perceived to be regardless of her or his gender (Denmark, 1993). Higher-status people are expected to be assertive, to be appropriate for high-status jobs, to be evaluated as competent, and so on.

Most notably for us here, status is linked to being male and to doing masculine work. Jobs ranked as prestigious by students are those jobs described with masculine traits (Glick, 1991). Applicants with mature, not babyish, faces and men were favored for high-status employment (Zebrowitz, Tenenbaum, & Goldstein, 1991), as are applicants wearing masculinizing clothing (Forsythe, 1990). Those with high school as opposed to college degrees were preferred by personnel representatives for lower-status jobs as well as female-stereotyped jobs in an electronics firm (Athey

& Hautaluoma, 1994). Evaluations of a leader's effectiveness were more strongly affected by how powerful the leader was thought to be by subordinates than by the leader's gender (Ragins, 1991). A clear consequence of discrimination is to disempower (Gutek, Cohen, & Tsui, 1996). The recurrent theme across these studies is that if one thinks of men and masculinity, one thinks of power.

This conclusion hits home even more when we consider the fate of most men who elect to do "women's work" and contrast this with what we know about women in male-dominated occupations. Although men in nursing, elementary school teaching, librarianship, and social work do encounter demeaning stereotypes from the outside public, within these occupations, they do not face hiring discrimination, and they benefit from structural advantages (C.L. Williams, 1992). In contrast to the glass ceiling which characterizes women's nontraditional employment experiences, Christine Williams (1992) concludes that men in female-dominated occupations ride a "**glass escalator**" to enhanced pay and advancement. Status and power pay off.

A laboratory simulation I conducted with two graduate students, Tom Schleicher and Tedd McDonald, highlights the hidden but potent effects of power (Yoder, Schleicher, & McDonald, 1998). We told a solo woman that she had been selected by chance to lead a group of 5–7 men doing a masculine decision-making task. This was our analog to a woman working in a male-dominated, masculine occupation. One-third of the women in our study were thus simply appointed to be leader. The other two-thirds arrived before the group session and were trained to do the upcoming task. Our checks of their subsequent individual performance on the task showed that all these women benefited comparably from their training. Half of the trained women were warned not to tell the group about their prior training; the remaining half were openly presented to their groups as trained leaders with special expertise relevant to the task at hand. In this way, we created three types of group leaders: appointed only, trained/appointed, and trained/appointed/legitimated leaders.

We predicted that only the last, the legitimated leaders, had both the knowledge base *and* the power base to effectively influence their group's task performance, and indeed this is what we found. Groups led by legitimated leaders outscored the appointed-only controls. The trained/appointed leaders seemed very frustrated because they knew how to do the task, but the men in the groups discounted their inputs, so that these groups ended up scoring similarly to the appointed-only controls. This study suggests both that being a woman "with all the right stuff" (e.g., leadership position and expertise) may not be enough without power and that organizations can play a role in conveying such legitimacy to women.

How do we enhance women's status and power in the workplace? It is clear that taking a deficiency approach to women doesn't do this. When we dredge up shortcomings in women by asking "if only women . . . " would be more assertive, get better educated, avoid job discontinuities, persuade partners to share housework and childcare, and so on, we are not challenging organizational hierarchies that value some types of work and workers over others. Furthermore, we have seen in this chapter that many of these myths about women workers are based more in stereotypic fiction than in workplace fact.

Rather than arguing that women somehow need to shoulder the burden of redressing workplace inequities, three policy positions have been promoted: affirmative action, equal pay for equal work, and comparable worth (Wittig & Lowe, 1989). Each policy is politically charged, and psychologists have played a role in understanding each of these. **Affirmative action** targets occupational segregation and thus seeks to close the wage gap by assuring women's fair access to high-paying jobs. Psychological approaches to affirmative action are extensively reviewed in the *Journal of Social Issues* (Skedsvold & Mann, 1996).

Equal pay for equal work defines "equal" as "identical," and it is these forms of readily identified discrimination that have been challenged most successfully through legal action (Pinzler & Ellis, 1989). Although this may redress inequities for some women, the entrenched gender segregation of the workforce we have seen in this chapter works against the widespread use of this approach. This is where **comparable worth** comes in, emphasizing the role of job content as the critical determinant of compensation (Aaronson, 1995; Steinberg, 1987; Wittig & Lowe, 1989). Jobs are comparable and should be equally compensated to the degree that, looking across a variety of compensable job content dimensions (e.g., skill, effort, responsibility, and working conditions), their *total* values are equal. Such job evaluation is designed to provide equity in outcomes without demanding identical job participation (i.e., without genuine occupation- and job-level integration). Again, the policy is politically volatile and goes beyond the scope of the present chapter, although psychologists have made significant contributions to this discussion (for example, see the *Journal of Social Issues*, Lowe & Wittig, 1989). Closing the wage gap is not likely to be an easy or quick goal, but psychologists can facilitate efforts toward the realization of this goal by considering the contexts in which women and men work and by working to empower women and men in the workplace.

CHAPTER SUMMARY

Work is experienced almost universally by women and men, even if we narrowly define work in terms of paid employment. Both women and men engage in paid employment for economic reasons, most of which is not optional but necessary as well as to fulfill psychological needs involving personal identity and competence. One of the largest and most influential differences between employed women and men is reflected in the wage gap—the difference between the earnings of full-time, year-long workers. An almost 30% gap between women's and men's earnings persists into the 1990s in the United States. Although no one seriously questions the existence or importance of this gap, there are heated debates about its causes arising from two competing perspectives: human capital and discrimination theories. Human capital theory looks for deficiencies internal to women to explain the gap in contrast to discrimination theory which explores situation-centered possibilities.

Beginning with a person-centered, "if only women . . . ," human capital statement, we reviewed 12 different possible explanations for the wage gap involving job discontinuities, family-work conflict, relocation, turnover, education, achievement motivation, attributions for success, assertiveness, leadership, mentoring, occupational segregation, and competence. In each area, research evidence either debunked the human capital perspective or constructed a *plausible* argument involving contextual factors. In the final subsection focused specifically on discrimination, we argued that sexist discrimination subsumes gendered occupational stereotypes, hiring and promotion biases, and prejudicial attitudes that make the workplace environment and access to it qualitatively different for women and men. Situation-centered policies designed to level the playing field include affirmative action, equal pay for equal work, and comparable worth.

Across Chapters 7 and 8, we have explored the multiple roles that construct women's lives including friendships, romantic attachments, caregiving, and employment. None exists in isolation of the others, nor can any be understood fully without examining a complex interplay of personal, interpersonal, and institutional factors.

NINE

WOMEN'S PHYSICAL HEALTH AND WELL-BEING
Understudied, Mythologized, but Changing

L
ines between physical and mental health have become increasingly blurred as more and more evidence accumulates linking the two. The purpose of this chapter is to take a holistic look at women's physical health and well-being from the perspective of health psychologists who have studied women's sexuality and reproductive health, chronic diseases, and the impact of health care practice and policy on women. Before you read any farther, please complete the checklist in Box 9.1. We'll refer back to this later in the chapter.

BOX 9.1

Put a check next to each of the following signs of stress that you have experienced in the past 4–5 weeks.

Weight gain _____	Insomnia _____
Crying _____	Lowered performance _____
Muscle stiffness _____	Forgetfulness _____
Confusion _____	Take naps _____
Headache _____	Skin disorders _____
Loneliness _____	Feeling of suffocation _____
Orderliness _____	Restlessness _____
Irritability _____	Dizziness, faintness _____
Accidents _____	Decreased efficiency _____
Stay at home _____	Nausea, vomiting _____
Tension _____	Bursts of energy _____
Ringing in ears _____	Chest pains

Source: See footnote 8.

HEALTH PSYCHOLOGY

Taking a Psychological Perspective

More and more evidence is suggesting that conditions typically believed to be largely medical, such as heart disease, cancer, AIDS, and menstruation, are social as well as biological (Travis, 1988a). For example, consider the debate about when to limit medical intervention: when to pull the proverbial "plug" on medical technology. Few people focus exclusively on biological signs of being alive without also considering the "quality of life" a patient is likely to face. At a less dramatic level, whenever dietary and lifestyle changes are indicated for treatment or prevention, the prescription calls for behavioral changes by individuals. Both the definition of health itself and the activities indicated for health maintenance or recovery benefit from the knowledge base amassed by psychologists.

As a case in point, Karen Matthews and her colleagues (1997) describe the research agenda underlying the Women's Health Initiative (WHI), a 15-year project sponsored by the National Institutes of Health targeting 164,500 postmenopausal women. They describe a framework, outlined in Figure 9.1, for studying the rela-

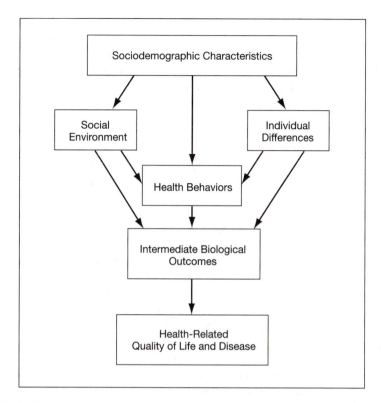

FIGURE 9.1 The general framework being tested by the Women's Health Initiative.
Source: K. A. Matthews et al. (1997). Women's Health Initiative: Why now? What is it? What's new? *American Psychologist, 52,* 101–116. Copyright © 1997 by the American Psychological Association. Reprinted with permission.

tionships among psychological/behavioral states and health outcomes. Note how broad societal sociodemographic characteristics (e.g., economic conditions and race/ethnicity), interpersonal and organizational social environments (e.g., social supports and social integration), and individual differences (e.g., being dispositionally pessimistic or internalizing stress) all combine to affect ultimate health outcomes. Also notice that those health outcomes are defined by more than simple survival—quality of life is key. Thus, psychology plays a significant role in each of these cells.

Focusing on Women: Gender as a Marker

Why do we need a special focus on women's health (Rodin & Ickovics, 1990)? Some health issues disproportionately affect women as compared to men (e.g., osteoporosis and eating disorders) as well as different segments of the population of women (e.g., breast cancer and lupus).[1] Other health concerns are unique to women (e.g., hys-

---

[1] For a good discussion of how ethnicity interacts with gender to affect women's health, see Klonoff, Landrine, and Scott (1995).

terectomy and menstruation). Although interest in women's reproductive health is important, all too often women's health is framed almost exclusively by a myopic focus on these unique capacities of women (Stanton, 1995). Being a healthy woman involves a lot more than being reproductively fit, and as we saw in Chapter 4, life doesn't end when reproductive capacities cease.

The androcentric assumption that men's bodies are normative permeates the field. For example, medical textbooks make disproportionate use of male-specific figures and descriptions, a pattern which has declined a bit since 1890 but which has far from disappeared in 1989 (Lawrence & Bendixen, 1992). This bias has ramifications for prevention, diagnosis, and treatment. For example, two highly publicized studies showing no association between having a daily cup of coffee and heart disease (Grobbee et al., 1990) and linking aspirin usage and reduced heart disease (Shumaker & Smith, 1995) involved large samples of men. Should women drink coffee without concern and take aspirin as a preventive for heart disease? Assuming an affirmative answer literally may prove deadly if women are prescribed the wrong preventives and treatments. Women routinely were excluded from medical research because men are at greater risk of dying younger, because women's variable hormonal levels may confound findings, and because of concerns about pregnancy during clinical trials. Ironically, these same differences may be some of the reasons why findings from men won't readily generalize to women (see Hamilton, 1996, for an overview).

Finally, there's an intriguing paradox about women's health: women generally live longer than men (lower **mortality**) but are sicker (higher **morbidity**). "At every moment across the life span, from conception to death, girls and women are on the average biologically more advantaged and live longer than boys and men" (Strickland, 1988, p. 381). On the one end of the life course, about 125 male embryos are conceived for every 100 female embryos, and 27% more boys than girls die during their first year of life. On the other end of the spectrum, for those who reach 100-years old, only one man is alive for every five women (Rodin & Ickovics, 1990). Overall, a baby born in 1993 is expected to live until *she's* 78.7-years old (79.5 for white women; 73.7 for African American women) or *he's* 72.0-years old (Kranzer, 1995).[2]

The leading causes of death for women and men are similar in that their top ten lists contain the same causes, but their incidence patterns differ somewhat (see Table 9.1). The same is true when races are compared; for example, compare the patterns for African American and white women and men in Table 9.1. Not surprisingly, heart diseases and cancers top the charts for all groups, but note the much higher incidence of death by most causes among men, especially African American men. Accidents rank high for all groups, but their incidence rates are higher for men, especially African American men. Suicide rates are elevated for men, especially for white men.

Overall then there is a mortality gap between women and men that favors women's longevity. Social changes (such as the increased prevalence of smoking[3]

---

[2] The life expectancy for women in the United States is lower than in 15 other developed countries, with Japan topping the list at 82.5 years (Woods, 1995).

[3] In 1991, 23.5% of U.S. women over 18-years old smoked compared with 28.1% of adult men (Ernster, 1993).

TABLE 9.1   Leading Causes of Death for African American and White Women and Men, 1990

Women

African American	White
Heart diseases (168.1)	Cancers (111.1)
Cancers (137.2)	Heart diseases (103.1)
Cerebrovascular disease (42.7)	Cerebrovascular disease (23.8)
Diabetes mellitus (25.4)	Accidents & adverse effects (17.6)
Accidents & adverse effects (20.4)	Pulmonary diseases (15.2)
Pneumonia & influenza (13.7)	Pneumonia & influenza (10.6)
Liver disease & cirrhosis (11.5)	Diabetes mellitus (9.5)
Pulmonary diseases (10.7)	Liver disease & cirrhosis (4.8)
*Septicemia (8.0)	Suicide (4.8)
Suicide (2.4)	*Septicemia (3.1)

Men

African American	White
Heart diseases (275.9)	Heart diseases (202.0)
Cancers (248.1)	Cancers (160.3)
Accidents & adverse effects (62.4)	Accidents & adverse effects (46.4)
Cerebrovascular disease (56.1)	Cerebrovascular disease (27.7)
Pneumonia & influenza (28.7)	Pulmonary diseases (27.4)
Pulmonary diseases (26.5)	Suicide (20.1)
Diabetes mellitus (23.6)	Pneumonia & influenza (17.5)
Liver disease & cirrhosis (20.0)	Liver disease & cirrhosis (11.5)
Suicide (12.4)	Diabetes mellitus (11.3)
*Septicemia (11.6)	*Septicemia (4.2)

* A systemic disease caused by pathogenic organisms or their toxins in the bloodstream.
Note. Numbers in parentheses are deaths per 100,000 in the population.
Source: From THE AMERICAN WOMAN 1994–95: Where We Stand, Women and Health by Cynthia Costello and Anne J. Stone. Copyright © 1994 by The Woman's Research & Education Institute. Reprinted by permission of W.W. Norton. & Co. Inc.

among women which has raised women's incidence of lung cancer) may narrow gaps in incidence rates between women and men. Women's incidence rates also may approach men's, but the timing may be different due to lifespan changes which interact with gender (such as women's increased susceptibility to heart disease as they age). Changes such as these may reduce the mortality gap, but in the wrong way—by lowering women's lifespans rather than by raising men's.

The second half of our medical paradox has to do with being sicker (morbidity). Women are more likely to report illness and to seek medical attention[4]

---

[4]Fully 76% of adult women reported at least one visit to a physician in 1993 compared to 59% of men (Costello & Stone, 1994). Willingness to visit a physician varies within groups of women; for example, delays in seeking medical treatment are common among African American women who express distrust of the medical system (Collins, 1996) and lesbian women who seek to maintain privacy regarding their sexual orientation in response to expected homophobia (Deevey, 1995).

through telephone calls and office visits than are men, although hospitalization rates are similar when childbirth is excluded (Leventhal, 1994; Woods, 1995). In a general health survey, 36% of women and 42% of men rated their health as excellent (Woods, 1995). Does this mean that women are more biologically predisposed to illness than men? Not necessarily; there are a host of other possibilities to explain this difference. Differential socialization about help seeking and admission of weakness, gender stereotypes that fit better with being sick for women than for men, and the stresses of women's roles are just a few examples of how other factors may be confounded with gender. The kinds of complaints women tend to present to their physicians are not life threatening, but rather involve chronic discomfort. It may be more congruent with the feminine gender role to admit these weaknesses, rather than be macho and "tough it out," so that reporting rates may not objectively reflect true incidence.

Other variables beyond gender may influence sickness rates. We saw in Chapter 6 that gender stereotypes vary by race and ethnicity. For example, the stereotype of African American women as strong and long suffering, combined with a common distrust of the medical system, mediates against their use of the medical system and encourages delays in seeking medical treatment (Collins, 1996). On the flip side, the tendency to regard a woman's complaints of physical maladies as "all in her mind," when there is little or no evidence to justify a psychological over a medical diagnosis (referred to as **psychologization**), may interfere with effective treatment of women by the medical system (Goudsmit, 1994).

All this led Elaine Leventhal (1994) to propose that *gender be considered a marker for analysis of health patterns rather than a cause in and of itself.* In this chapter, we will take Leventhal's suggestion and think of gender as a lens through which we can view women's health. The answers won't rest in biology alone, but rather in how being female interacts with other aspects of women's lives. As we have seen in earlier chapters, contextual factors play a significant role in affecting women's attitudes and behaviors. With this in mind, we'll explore what we know about women's sexuality and reproductive health, chronic diseases, and health-care practice and policy.

SEXUALITY AND REPRODUCTIVE HEALTH

Make a list of the medical personnel with whom you interact on a routine basis. You might see a dentist, a general practitioner, an optometrist, and so on. If you are a woman, you probably visit a gynecologist. What's the comparable physician for a man? Unlike men, women are expected to routinely visit two physicians: one to ensure reproductive health and the other to care for "general" health (Clancy & Massion, 1992).

Women's Divided Health: The Case of Cancer

Why do we separate women's health into reproductive and nonreproductive divisions? Cancer presents an ideal opportunity to address this question because it can develop in any body part, including women's and men's reproductive structures. Beth Meyerowitz and Stacey Hart (1995) analyzed the contents of medical and psychological publications reporting cancer research in 1983 and 1992. In the leading medical journal, *Cancer*, more studies focused on breast and reproductive cancers in women than their incidence would warrant. In contrast, for men, studies of reproductive cancers were underrepresented. Paralleling this in the psychology literature, breast cancer survivors dominated samples of research participants, even beyond what we would expect given their optimistic survival rates (5-year survival rates are 77% for breast cancer, 74% for prostate cancer, 56% for colorectal cancer, and only 13% for lung cancer). Medical emphases and research participation rates in psychology both disproportionately stress breast cancer in women. Although breasts indeed are the leading site for cancer in women, the top killer is lung cancer.

Not to diminish the importance of research on breast cancer, we still might ask: why this obsession with breasts? The question itself suggests an answer, but let's go beyond the obvious sexual possibility (see Wilkinson & Kitzinger, 1994). Breast cancer tends to affect a certain segment of the population: older, European/North American, middle- and upper-class, highly educated women who delayed childbearing. One exception is Hawaiian women whose breast cancer rates exceed those of white women (Wang, 1995).

Still, breast cancer is detected most frequently in a select subset of privileged women. This raises questions about the amount of attention afforded breast cancer detection and treatment. Are the women most susceptible to breast cancer as influential as Latina women, for example, who are at highest risk for cervical cancer, a disease that disproportionately strikes Native American (Tom-Orme, 1995) and African American women as well (Leigh, 1995)? Or, what about African American women, of whom almost one of every 250 will struggle with lupus, a blood disorder in which the immune system becomes overactive (Sullivan, 1996)? Furthermore, a questionable belief that may underlie psychologists' apparent obsession with breast cancer assumes that breast vulnerability is especially devastating for women. Research evidence indicates that even complete breast loss, although certainly traumatic, is no more psychologically debilitating than other amputations or serious cancers (Wilkinson & Kitzinger, 1994). The three most common concerns reported by mastectomy patients focus on difficulty in engaging in strenuous activity, fears of reoccurrence of the cancer, and obtaining high quality medical care—none of which deal with breast loss itself.

As you read this chapter, and other texts in the field, you will encounter this division of women's health into reproductive and nonreproductive focuses. Unfortunately, more work to date has accumulated on the former than on the latter topic so that the division remains useful for cataloguing these findings. Note that some recent developments are starting to strain this artificial separation. For example, is AIDS a sexually transmitted disease for women and thus a sexual/reproductive threat? Or, is it a general threat to women's health and well-being? We'll discuss it along with other chronic diseases later. For now, let's turn to women's sexual health and sexuality, then explore a sampling of reproductive concerns including menstruation, pregnancy and miscarriage, and abortion.

Sexuality

Is sexual behavior a natural act? This is a pretty vague question that might better be asked as: Is it useful to think about sexuality as a natural act? On the one hand, thinking about sexuality as a natural act avoids connotations of abnormality. A wide array of sexual behaviors is found in nature so that human participation gains acceptance and sheds inhibitions through such associations. On the other hand, Leonore Tiefer (1994) considers how such thinking can reduce sexuality to biological essentialism—a biological imperative that *drives* people to act. This view overemphasizes the biological and discounts how sexual attitudes and behaviors are shaped within a social context. When that social context changes over time, attitudes and behaviors change, an evolution that sexologists have charted across historical periods. Furthermore, viewing sexuality as a natural drive absolves us of working at being sexual—of teaching it to our children and of making it work as only one aspect of our more-than-biological relationships. Sexuality, like women's health in general, is more than biology; it is filled with social meanings and feelings. The social meaning of menstruation comes through loud and clear in Gloria Steinem's (1978) essay, "If men could menstruate—," excerpts of which are presented in Box 9.2.

BOX 9.2   If Men Could Menstruate—

What would happen, for instance, if suddenly, magically, men could menstruate and women could not?

The answer is clear—menstruation would become an enviable, boast-worthy, masculine event:

Men would brag about how long and how much.

Boys would mark the onset of menses, that longed-for proof of manhood, with religious ritual and stag parties.

Congress would fund a National Institute of Dysmenorrhea to help stamp out monthly discomforts.

Sanitary supplies would be federally funded and free. (Of course, men would still pay for the prestige of commercial brands such as John Wayne Tampons, Muhammad Ali's Rope-a-dope Pads . . .)

Street guys would brag ("I'm a three pad man"). . . .

Lesbians would be said to fear blood and therefore life itself—though probably only because they needed a good menstruating man. . . .

In fact, if men could menstruate, the power justifications could probably go on forever.

If we let them.

Source: G. Steinem, If men could menstruate—. *Ms. Magazine*, 7, Oct. 1978, p. 110. Lang Communications. Reprinted with permission.

"Machines without motors"?   A medicalized view of human sexuality was provided by William Masters and Virginia Johnson (1966) in their pioneering observations and measures of physiological responses during heterosexual activity. They describe four general stages of responsiveness shared by women and men called the **human sexual response cycle**. During the initial **excitement** phase, vasocongestion occurs, increasing blood flow to the genitals and stimulating vaginal lubrication for women and penile erection in men. For women, the lips to the vagina and the clitoris glans swell, and the upper two-thirds of the vagina balloons. The clitoris and head (glans) of the penis are packed with nerve endings so that both are highly sensitive. The clitoris is the only organ of the human body that has no function beyond providing pleasure. Women's nipples harden as muscle fibres contract (myotonia), and heart rate, blood pressure, and rate of breathing accelerate.

At the second, **plateau** phase, vasocongestion and myotonia increase to peak levels with the lower third of the vagina, the orgasmic platform, swelling and tightening so that if a penis is in the vagina, it is gripped tightly, adding to the male's stimulation. The clitoris retracts but remains very sensitive as heart rate, blood pressure, and rate of breathing all elevate. At the third phase, **orgasm** occurs with 3–12 involuntary rhythmic muscular contractions, spaced at about 0.8 second intervals, varying in intensity and number for different women and with different sources of stimulation. At the final **resolution** phase, tension is released throughout the body and blood is expelled from engorged blood vessels. This process is slower in women than in men, and it may be reversed with renewed stimulation. Women return to their unstimulated state in 15–30 minutes, although this may extend to an hour if orgasm was not achieved. The refractory period for men varies widely from a few minutes to 24 hours during which time the man cannot be stimulated to erection and orgasm.

Despite Masters and Johnson's attempts to provide a gender-neutral model of sexuality, critics have pointed to fundamental assumptions that suggest instead that a masculine model of sexuality has been overgeneralized to women (Martin, 1996; Tiefer, 1991a). Although Masters and Johnson do describe detailed physiological reactions to sexual stimulation, they tell us little about the totality of sexuality by ignoring what the person is thinking and feeling. Take another look at the descriptions of the four phases. Does it seem rather mechanical, presenting women and men as two physiologically well-oiled "machines without motors" (feelings) seeking mere physical stimulation? Also, sexuality is implicitly, exclusively, and narrowly defined by genital contact (Christina, 1997; Rothblum, 1994b).

To paint a fuller picture, we need to ask what women and men want from sexuality. Folk wisdom holds that men seek pure pleasure from sexuality in contrast to women who seek emotional connection. Indeed, there is evidence to support this contention (Hatfield et al., 1988). For example, a well-done survey of 445 women and 477 men in San Francisco found that women attached less importance to pure pleasure, conquest, and relief of tension than did men (Leigh, 1989). In contrast to men who ranked pleasure first, women cited emotional closeness as their top reason for engaging in sexual behaviors. Does this mean that men are driven exclusively, or even predominately, by desires for pleasure as our social pundits would lead us to believe? A closer look at the data debunks this purely hedonistic image: men ranked attachment as a close second to pleasure and even considered pleasing their partner more important than did women. These gender differences held across both homosexual and heterosexual respondents.

Attitudes and behaviors: A double standard?   What do women think about sexuality? A meta-analysis of 21 sexual attitudes and behaviors, summarizing 177 usable sources, found that the largest attitudinal difference between women and men involves men's considerably more permissive attitudes toward casual sexual behaviors (Oliver & Hyde, 1993). Does this mean that all women are conservative about sexuality? Recent researchers have argued that there is no monolithic "women's" attitude toward sexuality, but rather that individual differences exist among women.

Attempts to capture these variations classify people into two groups: **erotophilics** who respond favorably to sexuality and who have a sexual self-schema open to sexual experience and free of guilt and **erotophobics** who engage in less sexual activity as well as exhibit negative attitudes and high sexual guilt (Andersen & Cyranowski, 1994; Fisher, Byrne, White, & Kelly, 1989). Variations among women also exist along race and ethnic lines. For example, more Mexican American women espouse a traditional value system (Aneshensel, Fielder, & Becerra, 1989), a perspective that permeates Latina culture in general through the concepts of marianismo (the stereotype of the ideal self-sacrificing, passive, and chaste virgin) and verguenza (shame and embarrassment about sexuality) (Scott et al., 1988).

These attitudinal variations extend to sexual behaviors. Returning to the meta-analysis comparing women's and men's behaviors, the largest gender difference was in the markedly higher rates of masturbation engaged by men (Oliver & Hyde, 1993). Erotophobic women are less likely to perform breast self-exams, seek regular gynecological visits, and use contraceptives when engaging in premarital intercourse (Byrne, 1983). Compared to Anglo women, more Mexican American women experience infrequent intercourse and masturbation and fewer use condoms and birth control pills (Aneshensel et al., 1989; Padilla & O'Grady, 1987).

Is there a sexual double standard? As we saw in Chapter 2, sociobiologists contend that women are more restrictive than men both in their expressions of sexuality and in their sexual attitudes. Looking across the 1960s to 1980s, Mary Oliver and Janet Hyde (1993) conclude that gender differences have narrowed. Although attitudes about women's sexuality may be less restrictive today and women's behaviors reflect this liberation, does that mean that the double standard no longer exists? Not necessarily—some residuals of the double standard may persist.

For example, Gail Wyatt and Monika Riederle (1994) review findings from others' research as well as their own studies of 126 African American and 122 white women, aged 18 to 36, in Los Angeles County. Both possessing adequate sexual knowledge and being able to communicate about sexuality are inhibited by double-standard expectations that women who are informed and assertive are sexually promiscuous ("sluts" as opposed to "studs"). Ironically, deviating from these virginal expectancies is associated with greater sexual satisfaction. Sexually satisfied women initiate sexual contact more often and express their sexual needs clearly in their primary relationships (Hurlbert, Apt, & Rabehl, 1993; Wyatt & Lyons-Rowe, 1990).

When do women violate the double standard? In essence, when they think it's safe to do so. Charlene Muehlenhard and Marcia McCoy (1991) surveyed 403 mostly white college women about being in situations where they wanted to engage in first-time intercourse with a man and either overtly declined or openly acknowledged their desire. The former women assented to the accepted script dictated by the double standard which asserts that men want sexual contact and women, irrespective of their desires, refuse. The researchers included measures of the woman's traditionalism, acceptance of the double standard, and erotophobia-erotophilia. None of these measures predicted how each woman reacted as well as her sense of her partner's belief in the double standard. Women who pursued their desires were more likely to think their partner disavowed the double standard than did women who went along with the double-standard script, despite their desire to do otherwise. This speaks volumes about how women's immediate interpersonal context influences their sexuality above and beyond even their own personalities, attitudes, and desires.

The double standard also continues to influence women's sexual risk-taking behaviors, involving exposure to pregnancy, sexually transmitted diseases, and even AIDS (Wyatt & Riederle, 1994). For example, insisting on condom usage may conflict with some women's beliefs that sexuality is natural and spontaneous, that condoms are uncomfortable for men, and that women should be passive and let men control heterosexual encounters (Worth, 1989). College women report that they failed to plan contraceptive precautions prior to a date because to do so would admit that sexual pursuits are expected (Wright, 1992). Undergraduate women also overrely on partner questioning as a way to reduce HIV risk (Mays & Cochran, 1993). These patterns may be especially true for Latinas, African American women, and childhood abuse survivors, all of whom perceive themselves as being at unrealistically low risk for HIV infection (Mays & Cochran, 1988; Wyatt & Riederle, 1994). These patterns con-

A sexual double standard is alive and well, but it has taken more subtle forms.

verge to suggest that accurate knowledge of adequate prevention alone, without sufficient understanding of the potent role still played by the double standard of sexuality, is not sufficient to reduce sexual risk-taking behaviors (Cochran & Mays, 1993).

Menstruation

What is menstruation? The question sounds simple enough. Before you read on, jot down the *causes* of menstruation in the space below.

Elissa Koff and her colleagues (1990) asked 80 college women, recruited from introductory and intermediate psychology classes, to do what you just did—describe the causes of menstruation. To be graded as correct, an answer must include information that the uterine lining is shed if fertilization has not taken place. How did you do? In the study, only 41% of the answers meet this criterion; 16% mentioned only the lining; and an additional 9% mentioned only the unfertilized egg. Fully 24% provided incorrect or irrelevant information, and the remaining 9% cited vague references to hormones.

Although a sizable proportion of women students were confused about the biological definition of menstruation, there was considerable consensus about the physical and emotional correlates of menstruation (Koff, Rierdan, & Stubbs, 1990). These women attributed four categories of *physical* changes to menstruating—all of them unpleasant: general discomfort (e.g., cramps, aches, and pains); water retention and weight gain; tender or swollen breasts; and a variety of autonomic signs (e.g., nausea and temperature changes). This negativity extended to *emotional* changes focusing on depression, emotional lability (e.g., mood swings), and irritability. Finally, women agreed that there were few, if any, changes in their cognitive or *intellectual* abilities (e.g., reduced concentration) related to menstruation.[5] Interestingly, much of what these women described about the physical and emotional changes associated with menstruation are not really about menstruation itself, but rather the period before the onset of menses, popularly referred to as PMS ("premenstrual syndrome").

"Premenstrual syndrome."   This concentration on the psychology of the presumably unpleasant premenstrual woman is echoed in the popular press where both medical experts and women's testimony are used to establish PMS as a medical malady (Markens, 1996). Joan Chrisler and Karen Levy (1990) analyzed the contents of 81 articles on PMS indexed in the Reader's Guide to Periodical Literature from 1980–1987. Over half the articles mentioned bloating (71%), depression/despair/sad-

---

[5] Similar beliefs were reported by a general sample of women 19- to 52-years old (Cumming, Urion, Cumming, & Fox, 1994).

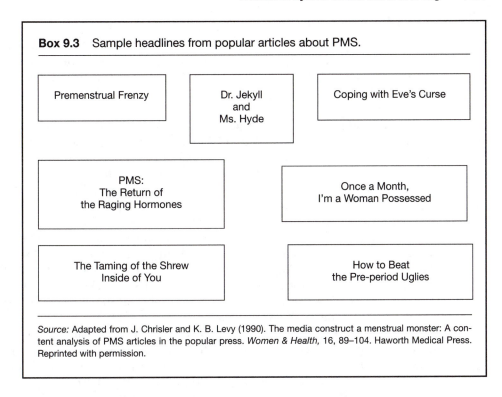

Box 9.3   Sample headlines from popular articles about PMS.

Premenstrual Frenzy

Dr. Jekyll
and
Ms. Hyde

Coping with Eve's Curse

PMS:
The Return of
the Raging Hormones

Once a Month,
I'm a Woman Possessed

The Taming of the Shrew
Inside of You

How to Beat
the Pre-period Uglies

Source: Adapted from J. Chrisler and K. B. Levy (1990). The media construct a menstrual monster: A content analysis of PMS articles in the popular press. *Women & Health,* 16, 89–104. Haworth Medical Press. Reprinted with permission.

ness (72%), irritability (63%), headache (58%), painful/tender breasts (55%), and mood swings (51%). Almost all 75 symptoms listed on the Moos (1968) Menstrual Distress Questionnaire were covered. Of the changes described, only 15% were favorable, citing heightened affection, energy bursts, good concentration, keener sexual excitement, optimism, and euphoria. A great deal of drama is used to convey a generally negative tone about women and PMS—sample some headlines in Box 9.3. The stereotype of maladjusted women comes through loud and clear, with PMS suffering estimated to affect from 5–95% of women according to these articles (with most converging on estimates between 30% and 60%).

We saw what college women think of PMS and what the media tells us. What's real and what's myth? Menstruation is the shedding of the lining of the uterus, approximately 2–3 ounces of menstrual blood and uterine tissue, typically over 3–5 days on a 28-day cycle (Klebanov & Ruble, 1994). The menstrual cycle is characterized by changing hormone levels, the development and release of an ovum by the ovaries, and preparation of the uterus for possible implantation of an ovum, if it is fertilized. If fertilization does not occur, declines in estrogen and progesterone levels signal the shedding of the endometrial lining, or the start of the menstrual flow.

The **menstrual cycle** begins on the first day of menstruation when one of the many immature ovum begins to mature in one of the two ovaries. Over the next two weeks (the **follicular** phase), the follicle grows and matures as a new lining replaces the one just shed. By about the 16th day, estrogen reaches its peak and the ovary releases the fully developed ovum which survives about two days during which it can be fertilized (**ovulation**). Over the remaining two weeks (the **luteal** phase), progesterone levels rise and stimulate the ovaries to release a mucus-like substance to prepare the uterus for a fertilized egg. If fertilization has not occurred on or around the 24th day, estrogen and progesterone decline rapidly, marking the **late luteal** or premenstrual phase, as the uterus again prepares to shed its lining and thus initiate a new menstrual cycle.

It is this last phase of the cycle, generally lasting about 4 days, which has attracted both popular and scientific attention.[6] The assumption underlying much of this attention is that the marked hormonal changes that accompany this *normal* phase of the menstrual cycle account for physical, emotional, and cognitive changes in women—an assumption captured in popular referents to "raging hormones" (Chrisler & Levy, 1990)—although in reality hormone levels are falling. The common discourse for this phase uses the term "premenstrual syndrome" or the more benign term, "premenstrual symptoms" (PMS). The Diagnostic and Statistical Manual of Mental Disorders (DSM) of the American Psychiatric Association (which, in essence, defines abnormality) described Late Luteal Phase Dysphoric Disorder (LLPDD) as a bona fide disorder in its 1987 third edition but renames and relegates "Premenstrual Dysphoric Disorder" (PDD) to the appendix as a syndrome in need of further testing in its 1994 fourth edition (Caplan, 1995).[7]

What is PMS? To be clinically diagnosed with **Premenstrual Dysphoric Disorder**, a woman must present at least one of the first four symptoms listed in Table 9.2, as well as others, with a minimum total of five symptoms during the week before and a few days after the onset of menses (DSM-IV, 1994, p. 717). Furthermore, "the disturbance seriously interferes with work or with usual social activities or relations with others," is not "merely an exacerbation of the symptoms of another disorder . . . ," and is "confirmed by daily self-ratings during at least two symptomatic cycles" (DSM-IV, 1994, p. 718).

For a less clinical diagnosis of PMS, the most commonly used checklist is the Menstrual Distress Questionnaire developed in 1968 by Rudolf Moos. You responded to a subset of items from this scale in Box 9.1 at the beginning of this chapter. How did you fare?[8] My experience with this scale is that even the men in my classes check off many of the symptoms of PMS. How can this be if menstruation and PMS are unique to women?

The literature on PMS gets confusing because researchers have not settled on a clear definition of it (Parlee, 1993). Some researchers focus on the entire luteal phase; others include the late luteal phase plus menstruation itself (perimenstrual); or, most commonly, researchers focus on the four days prior to the onset of menses

---

[6] Carol Tavris (1992, p. 140) reports that researchers' interest in "PMS," "Premenstrual Syndrome," or "Premenstrual Tension" grew from one article in a medical journal in 1964 to 305 articles in medical journals and 120 in psychological journals in 1988-89. How does this attention fit with the emerging women's movement across this same time period?

[7] The popular implications of relegating "PMS" to a mental disorder listed in the DSM are made clear by Heather Nash and Joan Chrisler (1997) who found that people who read the description of PDD as an official psychiatric diagnosis were more likely to view the premenstrual phase as problematic than the uninformed.

[8] Over 150 symptoms have been identified as indicators of PMS (Gurevich, 1995). Box 9.1 selected items from R. H. Moos (1968). The development of a Menstrual Distress Questionnaire. *Psychosomatic Medicine*, Vol. 30, 853–867. Reprinted with permission of Williams & Wilkins.

TABLE 9.2   DSM-IV Symptoms for Premenstrual Dysphoric Disorder

1. markedly depressed mood, feelings of hopelessness, or self-deprecating thoughts
2. marked anxiety, tension, feelings of being "keyed up," or "on edge"
3. marked affective lability (e.g., feeling suddenly sad or tearful or increased sensitivity to rejection)
4. persistent and marked anger or irritability or increased interpersonal conflicts
5. decreased interest in usual activities, e.g., work, school, friends, hobbies
6. subjective sense of difficulty in concentrating
7. lethargy, easy fatigability, or marked lack of energy
8. marked change in appetite, overeating, or specific food cravings
9. hypersomnia or insomnia
10. a subjective sense of being overwhelmed or out of control
11. other physical symptoms, such as breast tenderness or swelling, headaches, joint or muscle pain, a sensation of "bloating," weight gain

Source: Diagnostic and statistical manual of mental disorders: DSM-IV. (4th ed.). (1994). Washington, DC: American Psychiatric Press. Reprinted with permission.

(the late luteal phase) (Gallant & Derry, 1995). Because menstrual cycles vary for individual women, the onset of the late luteal phase is determined retrospectively by counting back from the day menstruation starts. Because of this, some researchers used retrospective reports; others asked participants to keep daily logs; others tried to deal with participants' preconceptions about research on menstruation by disguising the purpose of their studies (unaware groups); a few relied on costly hormonal checks to reliably date the late luteal phase; and a handful included control groups of men or of women using contraceptive pills (which stabilize hormonal levels across the menstrual cycle). Other problems arise from the presumption of change: the key evidence for PMS is change during the late luteal phase such that women are irritable, experience bloating, etc., *more* during this period than others. Even when such change is accurately measured, what makes it symptomatic of a disorder? Typically, documented change must be both distressing and debilitating (Gallant & Derry, 1995).

Given all these caveats, what does a careful reading of this extensive literature tell us about the late luteal phase? Pamela Kato Klebanov and Diane Ruble (1994) conclude that *physical* changes involving pain, water retention, and weight gain have enjoyed consistent support, at least when based on women's self-reports. In a few cases where more objective measures (e.g., actual weight checks) have been employed, the validity of even these effects becomes questionable. On the other hand, in studies where women are given placebos (nonmedicinal, fake pills), reports of physical symptoms persist.[9] Moving from physical to cognitive and *intellectual* consequences, there is no consistent evidence to conclude that women's abilities change across the menstrual cycle.

Conclusions become fuzzier when we focus on *emotional* changes. Hypotheses involving hormones have received, at best, modest support, and linkages with other physiological mechanisms (e.g., neurotransmitters) have not been established convincingly (Klebanov & Ruble, 1994). If we go back to the research framework pre-

---

[9] Because physical indicators are the only "symptoms" of PMS confirmed by research, I elected to discuss this topic here under physical health rather than in the next chapter on mental health.

sented in Figure 9.1, sociodemographic characteristics, social environments, and individual differences among women may each play a role in constructing PMS. In sum, PMS is experienced differently by different women, if at all.

Looking at sociodemographic characteristics, race and ethnicity seem to play a role in PMS reports. For example, none of the African American women nurses studied by Kathryn Lee and Amanda Rittenhouse (1991) reported mood swings, and fewer Asian American women indicated experiencing cramps or weight gain. Controlling for socioeconomic levels, Anglo-Saxon women appear to be at greatest risk for premenstrual symptomatology (Maluf & Ruble, 1993, cited in Klebanov & Ruble, 1994). In a large-scale study of women in 10 countries, patterns and beliefs about menstruation varied widely according to country of residence, religion, literacy, age, work environment, and social status (Severy, Thapa, Askew, & Glor, 1993). Until recently, the impact of gender was not even considered, yet there is evidence that men's general moods cycle too in weekly patterns that may synchronize with women's (Gallant et al., 1991; McFarlane et al., 1988). Although menstruation is unique to women, mood cycles are not.

Turning to women's social environment, stress and social support may affect reports of premenstrual symptomatology. For example, women nurses who acknowledged less satisfaction with their social lives and low levels of social support also tended to report more perimenstrual symptoms (Lee & Rittenhouse, 1992). Heightened exposure to work, familial, and financial stress is related to reports of negative moods during the late luteal phase (Gallant & Derry, 1995). Similarly, more symptomatic women report lower marital quality and less perceived support from their spouses. Interestingly, the relationship between symptomatology and employment is moderated by choice such that homemakers who chose their role reported the lowest symptom ratings in contrast to the highest ratings from women for whom employment was externally imposed and unwanted (Coughlin, 1990).

Personality, attitudes, and expectancies of individual women may influence women's perceptions of premenstrual moods. Although only a few studies have focused on personality correlates with PMS, emotionally symptomatic women may be higher in external locus of control and lower in self-esteem (Gallant & Derry, 1995). Premenarcheal girls, who picked up their attitudes toward menstruation from sources stressing negative aspects, expect more distressed symptomatology (Brooks-Gunn & Ruble, 1982). Finally, researchers tested the hypothesis that expectancies play a role such that women who expect to be moody premenstrually fulfill their prophecy. Pamela Kato Klebanov and John Jemmott (1992) used a fictitious saliva test, presumably measuring hormonal levels, to convincingly persuade premenstrual white women to believe they were premenstrual or in the middle of their cycle. As predicted, although all were premenstrual, those who believed this reported more pain, but the finding did not extend to negative affect (Gallant & Derry, 1995). In reviewing expectancies studies, Sheryle Gallant and Paula Derry (1995) conclude that the role of expectancies remains unresolved.

Looking across the evidence reviewed here, PMS certainly is more than can be accounted for by "raging hormones" (see Davis, 1996, for an overview). But, does it exist at all? Estimates of prevalence vary widely, even in the scientific literature, from a low of 5% to a high of 97% (Gurevich, 1995). These figures inspired Paula Caplan

(1995, p. 122) to pointedly ask: "Do half a million American women go crazy once a month?" Furthermore, if so many women really do experience physical and emotional changes, is PMS really just a normal part of women's cycle? No one intends to dismiss the legitimate complaints of some women, estimated at 8%, who suffer intense perimenstrual symptoms (Klebanov & Ruble, 1994). However, problematizing women's normal cyclicity and placing it within the domains of medicine and psychiatry does not seem advantageous for women, although others like pharmaceutical companies and PMS clinics clearly profit (Gurevich, 1995).[10] Some feminists go so far as to argue that the biological essentialism that underlies many assumptions about PMS serve to deflect women's efforts for social change away from political activities inward and toward individualized clinical treatment (Nicholson, 1995).

Reproductive Health

Childbirth. Health psychologists have contributed to our understanding of the medicalization of childbirth and the postpartum period. Debate has swirled around the medicalization of childbirth, especially with regard to Cesarean sections (Stanton & Danoff-Burg, 1995; Travis, 1993). C-section rates have spiraled upward from 4.5% of births in 1965 to 23.5% in 1991. Although lower infant mortality rates have been attributed, in part, to C-sections, maternal mortality is four times higher for Cesarean than vaginal deliveries. In addition, at least one-third of these women suffer postoperative infections, and almost all experience abdominal pain. The medical justification for many C-sections has been undermined by provocative patterns in their incidence: C-section rates are inflated among women of higher socioeconomic status, among those who are privately insured, and in hospitals with high malpractice claims and employing physicians fearful of legal entanglements. Women having C-sections show no differences in depression, anxiety, or their confidence in mothering, but they do tend to be less satisfied with their delivery experiences. Thus, there appear to be no atypical psychological consequences for mothers delivering by C-section, however, there are medical and pragmatic bases from which to suggest their overuse.

We hear a lot in the popular press about postpartum blues and depression, and unlike their use as synonyms in the media, these refer to different syndromes (Stanton & Danoff-Burg, 1995). **Postpartum blues** may occur in the 10-day period after childbirth during which time the new mother may experience depressed mood, tearfulness, mood swings, anxiety, and other symptoms. Estimates of incidence vary widely from 26% to 85% of new mothers. Comparing these women to other women, there is evidence that mood fluctuations are more pronounced for postpartum women. However, compared to other women who are recovering from elective gynecological surgery, new mothers' symptoms may be milder. Furthermore, an expanded look at women's affect during this period shows heightened positive feelings as well, suggesting that the "blues" exist within a context of enhanced happiness. No definitive link has been established between these so-called blues and hormonal markers.

---

[10] Lander (1988) reports that prescriptions for progesterone can run as high as $200 per month, averaging $60.

Postpartum depression refers to a period of at least two weeks in duration during the first year after giving birth when symptoms of clinical depression appear (Stanton & Danoff-Burg, 1995). Incidence rates of 8% to 26% have been offered, at least for mild depression. Evidence does suggest that rates of mild depression are higher in new mothers than in other women, however, these postpartum levels are no higher, and possibly even lower, than depression levels during pregnancy. No biological markers have been linked to postpartum depression. The predictors for postpartum depression appear no different than those for depression during other periods of women's lives, hence calling into question the usefulness of this concept.

Miscarriage.   About 20% of recognized pregnancies end in miscarriage (Madden, 1994). Reviewing the psychological literature on women's reactions to miscarriage and drawing on interviews with 65 women four months after their miscarriages, Margaret Madden (1994) concludes that reactions are individualized. At the time of the miscarriage, most women reported feeling sad, with frustration, disappointment, anger at one's self, fright, and feeling troubled being expressed by more than one of every five women. Only 10% recalled feeling relieved, and much of this emanated from an end to uncertainties initiated by physical troubles rather than relief to see the pregnancy terminated. One woman summed up these sentiments:

> I was relieved to know it was over with, but I felt a little guilty about being relieved. The uncertainty was settled, even though it wasn't the way I wanted it to be settled (Madden, 1994, p. 98).

As one might expect, immediate emotional distress was more intense when the woman had become attached to the fetus (regardless of the length of the pregnancy), held herself responsible for her loss, and was unable to talk to anyone.

Women's reports at the time of Madden's interviews four months after their miscarriages are a tribute to their resilience. Most felt they were coping well and accepted their miscarriage: "I can take a philosophical view of the miscarriage and feel it was best" (Madden, 1994, p. 99). This does not dismiss their feelings; instead, most expressed concerns about a recurrence, and many described feeling blue on occasion when something triggered their memory, when they were upset about something else, and when they were fatigued. However, these feelings lessened with time and did not dominate their lives. The most frequent emotion expressed by these women was hope and as many women expressed sadness as happiness. In sum, there is no singular set of reactions common to women who miscarry. Because a woman is not devastated with depression and grief, as folk wisdom and the popular media might suggest, does not mean that she is uncaring or even deviant from what most women typically report.

Abortion.[11]   Abortion is a hotly debated moral and political issue[12] which recently extended into the arena of public health policy. It is clear that the legalization of abortion has reduced abortion-related deaths of women in the United States: between 1975 and 1982, mortality from induced abortions declined 89% compared

---

[11] For some ideas about how to teach the topic of abortion, see Greene (1995).

[12] For an excellent description of the contrasting world views of abortion rights and anti-abortion activists, see Kristen Luker's (1984) work.

to a decline in mortality of 35% associated with pregnancy and contraception (Rosenberg & Rosenthal, 1987). The risk of a woman's death from abortion during the first nine weeks of gestation is estimated at one death per half million abortions (National Center for Health Statistics, 1988, cited in Travis, 1993). Based on data such as these, Surgeon General Koop concluded in 1989 that abortion can be a medically safe procedure with no greater health risks than carrying a pregnancy to term (Wilmoth, 1992). His declaration of medical safety shifted interest toward psychology and the possibility of a "postabortion syndrome." Since then, psychologists have addressed questions about who seeks abortions, what the immediate consequences are for women, and the effects of denied abortion on women and children.

Who comes to mind when you picture a woman seeking an abortion? Nancy Felipe Russo and her colleagues (1992; Russo, Horn, & Tromp, 1993) reviewed the characteristics of women, and their reasons for, seeking an abortion. Although women of color are overrepresented among women seeking abortions, the majority are white. The typical profile is of a young (under 25), poor, unmarried woman—is this who you pictured? Still, it would be a mistake to stereotype women seeking abortions along these dimensions. Of all women seeking abortions, almost half are mothers, and about one of every four of these mothers has a child under 2. Although married women have lower abortion rates than would be expected given their sizable representation in the population, they account for one of every five abortion cases. Turning to why women seek abortions, the most common answers include financial constraints, unreadiness to shoulder such responsibility and immaturity, relationship problems or avoidance of single parenting, fear of major life changes, and inadequate spacing between children.

For African American women, considerations about abortion extend beyond control of one's body and the consequences to the fetus and parents (Daniels, 1996). African American women report that their partner's desires for a baby factor into their choices more so than do other women. Some authors interpret this difference as suggesting a stronger relationship between childbearing and solidifying a relationship for Black women. African American women's attitudes often are influenced by fears of abortion as a mechanism for race genocide, fears that are realistically grounded in past practices of coerced sterilization. Strong religious ties also make some African American women more reticent to discuss sexuality and birth-control options publicly. Finally, although economics may be cited by some women as a reason to opt for abortion, many poor women cannot afford an abortion; in 1993, the average first-trimester abortion cost about $100 less than the monthly AFDC (welfare) benefit.

To address questions about psychological responses by women after abortion, Nancy Adler and her colleagues (1990, p. 41) critically reviewed studies they considered methodologically sound and concluded that "legal abortion of an unwanted pregnancy in the first trimester does not pose a psychological hazard for *most* women" (italics added). For example, a study of matched samples of women experiencing early abortions, late abortions, and term births found the three groups to be "startlingly similar" and nonpathological on all subscales of the MMPI (Minnesota Multiphasic Personality Inventory). Who is at risk? Women who struggle with their decision to abort, women who expect abortion to be traumatizing, women who perceive little support from partners and their families, and women who blame their pregnancy on their own characterological deficiencies (e.g., being irresponsible) are at greatest risk for negative psychological consequences (Major & Cozzarelli, 1992; Miller, 1992). Generally, struggles with the decision to abort are more common among African American than white women, accounting for more later term abortions among African American women (Lynxwiler & Wilson, 1994). However, this attitudinal gap may be closing among younger women (Lynxwiler & Gay, 1994).

Turning to alternatives to abortion, research with the small minority (3%) of pregnant adolescents who carry to term and place their infants up for adoption reports that an enduring sense of loss often is experienced by these generally more affluent mothers (Sobol & Daly, 1992). Reviewing the extensive literature on denied abortion, Paul Dagg (1991) concluded that many women who were denied abortions experienced long-term resentments and that their children often encountered social and interpersonal difficulties that persisted into adulthood. In a longitudinal study of 220 children born in Prague between 1961–63 to mothers twice denied abortions for their pregnancy and 220 matched controls, Henry David (1992) found negative psychosocial consequences that widened with age and lasted into early adulthood, even though all children were reared in intact homes. In sum, there is little sound evidence in the psychological literature to support the concept of a postabortion syndrome or to advocate for forced pregnancy over abortion as a way to protect women's health.

In each of the areas we explored in this section including women's sexuality, menstruation, and reproduction, the tendency to biologize each function has detracted from our ability to see each as a normal process that is part of women's broader lives, including their psychological well-being and social and interpersonal contexts. "Raging hormones," alleged to accompany routine menstruation and the postpartum period, lose their force when we consider men's mood cycles and the trauma of any medical procedure, respectively. Presumably devastating miscarriages and "postabortion syndrome" also dissolve when held up to scientific scrutiny. Before considering the next issue, note the patterns that recur throughout each of these discussions. Why is there so much misinformation about women's sexuality and reproductive health?

CHRONIC DISEASES

Chronic diseases affect people's mortality and morbidity. The two leading causes of women's death are cardiovascular diseases (#1) and cancer (#2). As we noted earlier, women's breasts are the leading site of cancer, followed by the colon and rectum, lungs, uterus, and ovaries (Meyerowitz & Hart, 1995). However, the leading cancer killer of women is lung cancer, followed by breast, then colorectal, and ovarian cancers. A wide range of chronic diseases in women has been studied by psychologists including diabetes (Butler & Wing, 1995), autoimmune disorders (Chrisler & Parrett, 1995), and chronic pain (Reading, 1994). Here, we'll take a look at the leading killer of women, cardiovascular disease, and a recent addition to women's list of significant health threats, AIDS.

Cardiovascular Diseases

Cardiovascular diseases, encompassing coronary heart disease, stroke, hypertension, and congestive heart failure, are the leading cause of women's death in the United States (Shumaker & Smith, 1995). The death rate for African American women is 50% higher than that of white women (Leigh, 1995), and cardiovascular heart disease is at the top of the mortality charts for a diversity of women including Chinese Americans, Pacific Islanders (Wang, 1995), Latinas (Zambrana & Ellis, 1995), Native Americans (Tom-Orme, 1995), and whites. Although we tend to think of heart disease as a man's disease, between the ages of 35 and 74, 40% of women's and 46% of men's deaths are accounted for by cardiovascular diseases, with coronary heart disease (56%) leading the pack. Expressing this in numbers, 500,000 U.S. women die each year from coronary heart disease as compared to 90,000 deaths from stroke, 51,000 from lung cancer, and 44,500 from breast cancer. Although gender differences emerge in the presentation, diagnosis, treatment, recovery from, and risk factors related to cardiovascular diseases, heart disease does not discriminate by gender. Unfortunately, researchers have discriminated by excluding women from much research on heart disease, although corrective studies are in progress.

Sally Shumaker and Teresa Rust Smith (1995) review research on cardiovascular diseases in women from the perspective of health psychologists. First, there are differences in who, when, and how women and men present themselves to medical personnel for heart disease. Women tend to be of lower socioeconomic status and possess less formal education than presenting men. African American women are especially prone to hypertension which afflicts about 39% of Black women (compared to 25% of white women) between the ages of 18 and 74 (Crawford-Green, 1996). Related to both hypertension and cardiovascular heart disease for a disproportionate number of African American women is obesity, a common outcome of diets high in fat and low in fruits and vegetables (in other words, "diets of poverty") (Leigh, 1995).

The recognized onset of women's heart disease appears to lag ten years behind that of men, but this could be confounded by differences in presenting symptoms. More men are likely to seek treatment because they suffered a heart attack (myocardial infarction) as compared to the majority of women who initially present with complaints of chest pains (angina pectoris). Follow-ups of women with chest pain are less likely to show narrowing of their arteries, suggesting that this may not be as accurate a marker for heart disease in women as it is for men. Similarly, noninvasive procedures like stress tests may more accurately identify male sufferers than female. When women do present with myocardial infarction, these attacks are more likely to be misdiagnosed and to prove fatal.

The combination of different presenting symptoms, different markers for the disease, and expectations that heart disease is restricted to men (among women themselves, family and friends, as well as physicians) all may lead to misdiagnosis. Once diagnosed, referral and aggressive treatments are more common for men, even controlling for women's older age of diagnosis, their disease severity, and their preoperative status. Looking at prognosis, although a few studies find no gender differences, most studies find higher mortality rates for women following heart attack. There also is limited evidence suggesting that women experience less health-related quality of life and more depression following bypass surgery than men, although this procedure generally is physically beneficial for both.

Finally, turning to risk factors, research currently underway will expand the meager base of information directly ascertained from studies of women to date. For now, research with women has identified coronary-prone behavior, characterized by a sense of time-urgency, hostility, and impatience (Weidner, 1994), being overweight, and cigarette smoking[13] as risk factors. After diagnosis, cardiac rehabilitation programs are equally effective for women and men when they are used, but some researchers suggest that these typically are designed to better accommodate men so that women's participation may be structurally discouraged. Although social supports have proved protective for men, initial research with women suggests that women derive both strain and support from their social networks, possibly making them less beneficial. Finally, lack of exercise, depression, and anxiety have been associated with heightened risk in men but their relationship for women is yet to be understood.

Acquired Immunodeficiency Syndrome (AIDS)[14]

What behaviors put U.S. women at the greatest risk for contracting AIDS? Think about your answer for a few moments.

The HIV virus is a blood-borne virus passed through blood or semen in sexual activity: the surest way to ensure viral transmission of AIDS is to receive one or more pints of these fluids infected with HIV (human immunodeficiency virus), the causative agent for AIDS (Batchelor, 1988). Other clear bodily fluids, like saliva, tears, sweat, and urine, may contain HIV but in such low quantities as to pose virtually no danger of infection. The AIDS virus is fragile and can be killed easily by alcohol, bleach, detergent, hand soap, heat, or drying. HIV damages the immune system by selectively infecting and killing one type of white blood cells, T-4 "helper/inducer" cells, which trigger other cells to launch an attack on invading viruses and infections. By destroying T-4 cells, HIV makes the body susceptible to infections and cancers.

HIV also infects the body directly through the central nervous system and colon, although this typically does not lead directly to death. AIDS came to the attention of the medical community in the United States in 1981 when the Centers for Disease Control noted an unusually high number of requests for an experimental drug to treat a rare form of pneumonia as well as atypically high diagnoses for a rare form of skin cancer.

Given this fundamental background, how is HIV transmitted? HIV is spread through transmission of semen, injections contaminated with infected blood, trans-

---

[13] Although ceasing to smoke may contribute to weight gain, on average this amounts to 4–8 pounds which generally does not enhance the risk associated with being overweight.

[14] For a good primer about AIDS, see Seth Kalichman's (1996) book, "Answering Your Questions About AIDS" (ISBN: 1-55798-339-9) available from the American Psychological Association, Order Department, P.O. Box 2710, Hyattsville, MD 20784-0710, 1-800-374-2721.

fusion of infected blood, and transmission during birth or nursing from an infected mother (Batchelor, 1988). At first, AIDS was confined primarily to sexually active gay men with multiple partners in New York, San Francisco, and Los Angeles. AIDS quickly became labeled as a "gay" disease, and lesbians were misperceived as a high-risk group (even though nonbisexual lesbians are not exposed to semen) (Hamilton, 1988). Muddying the waters further was a 1983 report putting children in high-risk households at heightened risk. Later, these findings were explained by birthing and nursing transmission and their misinterpretation was retracted by the authors, but some public misperception that HIV can be spread through casual contact has persisted.

Given these patterns and this history, we tend to think of AIDS as affecting mostly homosexual and bisexual men, and indeed, in 1988, 70% of diagnosed cases in the United States were attributable to gay male sexual behavior (Batchelor, 1988). However, AIDS is the fourth leading cause of death among women 25- to 44-years old in the United States (Morokoff, Harlow, & Quina, 1995), ranking second for African American, third for Latina, and sixth for white women. From October 1992 through September 1993, women accounted for 15% of adult AIDS cases, up from 6.6% in 1985. The rate of increase for women in 1992–93 (2.40) is higher than that for men (2.05). The majority of these diagnosed women are African American (53%), followed by whites (25%) and Latinas (20%). Looking globally, 1994 estimates count over 6.4 million adult women as HIV infected, representing 40% of adult HIV infections (United Nations, 1995).

Psychologists have played two major roles in dealing with AIDS: devising and implementing models of prevention and helping infected people live with AIDS and its stigma (Morin, 1988). A critical key to prevention is understanding transmission, taking us back to our opening question. Since the leading risk for men, homosexual activity, does not apply to women, what behaviors put women at higher risk for HIV infection? Anal and vaginal heterosexual activity is the likely guess, and indeed this plays an important role. However, the *leading routes of HIV transmission for women in the United States are drug-related* (Morokoff et al., 1995).[15] Almost half the women diagnosed with AIDS were exposed through injected-drug use compared to 35% via heterosexual transmission. Among those exposed through heterosexual activity, fully 55% involved a sexual partner who was also an injected-drug user. This means that fully 69% of women diagnosed with AIDS were exposed through a drug-related route: 76% of Latinas, 71% of African American women, and 61% of white women. For these reasons, and following the lead of others (Stanton & Gallant, 1995), I elected to discuss this topic as a chronic disease rather than as a threat to women's sexual health.

These figures stress that there is no such thing as a protected group. Although researchers used to think in terms of high- and low-risk groups, risk really is measured by the *behaviors* in which one engages (Batchelor, 1988). A monogamous gay man practicing safe sexual behavior is at lower risk than a lesbian injected-drug user who shares needles.

---

[15] Patterns of transmission vary globally with 90% of infected women living in Pattern II areas, including sub-Saharan Africa and some Caribbean countries. In these areas, transmission is predominantly through heterosexual intercourse and perinatal transmission.

How do we cut down on high-risk behaviors? Education is a start, but understanding HIV transmission is not enough to insure protective behavior (Morokoff et al., 1995; Murphy & Kelly, 1994). For poor ethnic-minority women, risks associated with daily living, including exposure to the elements among the homeless, care of dependent children, hunger, drug withdrawal or acquisition, acute illness or trauma resulting from physical or sexual assault, threat of withdrawal of emotional and financial support from sexual partners, and loss of loved ones, often outweigh the risks believed to be associated with HIV-risky behaviors (Mays & Cochran, 1988; Thomas, 1994). To undercut transmission through shared needles, needle exchange programs must be responsive to the special needs of women (Brown & Weissman, 1993), and researchers must be sensitive to gender differences in injection behavior starting with women's greater tendency to share drug paraphernalia (Morokoff et al., 1995).

As for heterosexual transmission, the proper use of *latex* condoms reduces the risk of exposure, however, unflagging condom use is rare, even among women engaged in high-risk behaviors (Morokoff et al., 1995; Thomson & Holland, 1994). A variety of factors are implicated in the inconsistent use of condoms, including race/ethnicity and women's role in the decision-making process (Leonardo & Chrisler, 1992). For example, Spanish-speaking women report having fewer sexual partners as well as reduced condom use (Zambrana & Ellis, 1995). In one study of decision making, if the man made the decision, only 12% of these couples used condoms more than half the time. This figure jumped to 49% when women made the decision and to 32% when both partners decided (Osmond et al., 1993).

Patricia Morokoff, Lisa Harlow, and Kathryn Quina (1995) summarize their review of barriers to condom use: infrequent and irregular usage is associated with being married and monogamous, being less educated, drinking alcohol, sexuality with a main partner rather than a client, beliefs that there is little one can do to protect one's self from sexually transmitted disease, distaste for condoms, and lack of control over decision making. Through all these factors runs a strand of power—the more powerful person, both personally and interpersonally, controls how sexuality is practiced (Amaro, 1995).[16]

Fully 5% of women surveyed for the National AIDS Behavioral Surveys described a high-risk sexual partner (Grinstead et al., 1993). For Latina women, higher education was associated with having a riskier partner while the reverse was true for white women. Fully 17% of women in this study who reported no high-risk behaviors for themselves were unsure of the risk status of their partners. Such uncertainty is especially common among minority women, older women, and less-educated women. In another study of men injected-drug users, half reported a relationship with a woman nonuser who was unaware of the man's drug habit (Rhodes et al., 1990). African American women's heterosexual risk is further aggravated by higher rates of bisexuality among Black as compared to white men (Leigh, 1995).

---

[16] Contrast this need for women's interpersonal empowerment with "The Rules" for dating being espoused in a popular self-help book which promises "Marriage, in the shortest time possible, to a man you love, who loves you even more than you love him" (Fein & Schneider, 1995). This book outlines a set of dating rules for women (e.g., "Don't talk to a man first"; "Don't meet him halfway or go Dutch on a date"; and "Don't accept a Saturday night date after Wednesday") all of which put women in a passive role.

Prevention programs aimed at women must foster women's empowerment in negotiating sexual encounters and in ending those that put them at risk (Croteau et al., 1993). They also must be sensitive to the social context in which risky behavior is enacted, especially regarding cultural differences related to race/ethnicity and socioeconomics (Land, 1994; Shayne & Kaplan, 1991; Weeks et al., 1996). Technological advances, such as the female condom and a microbiocide that kills the HIV virus but that can be used safely as a vaginal gel, foam, or sponge, would give women direct control of their own protection.

The second focus of psychologists studying AIDS-related behaviors has been on women infected with HIV (Semple et al., 1993). For example, delays in seeking medical care, differences in preexisting health, and treatment differences all contribute to lower mean survival times for African Americans after diagnosis (6 months) than for whites (18–24 months) (Leigh, 1995). HIV-infected women commonly struggle with depression, apprehension, sadness, helplessness, anger, and fear (Morokoff et al., 1995). Women report fears of stigmatization (Green, 1995), loss of existing social supports, and forced removal of their children if they disclose their health status. Their subsequent secrecy can result in feelings of isolation and reduced medical care (Eversley, 1993, cited in Morokoff et al., 1995). The role of behavioral changes in day-to-day health care and maintenance is just beginning to be explored, as more and more people are learning to live with HIV infection. Again, the importance of empowering women and of being culturally sensitive are crucial (Daniel, 1996; Williams, 1995). The potential for future psychological research in this area is unbounded.

HEALTH CARE PRACTICE

Although women are disproportionately heavy users of the medical system, the medical system has not been a consistent health promoter for women.[17] We have seen that women have been excluded from research central to their health needs, although women-centered work is in progress. We also have seen that misperceptions of women's bodies that overemphasize reproduction and ignore other symptomatology, such as gender-specific signs of cardiovascular disease, have biased women's interactions with the health care system. Probably the most egregious example of women's questionable treatment centers on surgery.

Surgeries

Leslie Laurence and Beth Weinhouse (1994) detail how current surgical practice affects women's health. They acknowledge that surgery performed appropriately and skillfully saves many lives, and their purpose is not to undermine surgery itself. However, there are patterns of surgical use that raise some very serious questions. Of the top ten inpatient surgeries, three are unique to women: episiotomies (an inci-

---

[17] For a fascinating look at the history of the medical profession in relation to women's health needs and practices, see Barbara Ehrenreich and Deirdre English's (1978) book, "For Her Own Good."

sion between the vagina and rectum meant to speed childbirth), Cesarean sections, and hysterectomies.[18]

Hysterectomy.   Nearly 550,000 hysterectomies are performed in the United States every year, yet experts report that anywhere from 20% to 90% of these are medically unnecessary. Looked at another way, 80–85% of hysterectomies are elective in that other treatment options are available and untried. Only 15% of hysterectomies are performed because of uterine cancer, the most compelling reason for removal. At this rate, it is projected that 40% of American women will have their uteruses removed during their lifetimes; more than one-third will not have their uterus by age 50.

The most common reasons for hysterectomy before age 50 are uterine fibroids and endometriosis (a disease of the uterine lining). Fully one-third of premenopausal women have fibroids, and most naturally shrink as menopause approaches. An American woman is two- to three-times more likely to have a hysterectomy than her counterpart in England, France, or West Germany, and her chances increase if she sees a male physician. Hysterectomy is more likely among poor women, women without a college education, and African American women, and it even was abused as a form of involuntary sterilization for poor Black women. At times, having a hysterectomy worsens one's odds: enlarged uteruses are removed because there is a one in two thousand chance of developing cancer although the death rate for hysterectomy for benign indicators is higher at one in one thousand. There are other complications possible with this surgery that make it a choice that should not be approached casually.

Cosmetic surgery.   We typically think of medicine as health promoting and of surgical procedures as serious, invasive activities with risks made acceptable by pressing health threats. Cosmetic surgery stands in contrast to this image if its outcomes are considered trivial or not worth the risks of intervention. Diana Dull and Candace West (1991) interviewed both cosmetic surgeons and their clients to understand how they reconcile this apparent contradiction. They found that both physicians and their patients justify their involvement by thinking of cosmetic surgery as a form of reconstructive surgery which legitimately is designed to improve physical functioning and minimize disfigurement. If the target of surgery is viewed as deformed and the surgery itself is rationalized as normal and natural, then cosmetic surgery is made to fit within the medical mandate to heal. As one surgeon confided: "If it makes them happy and gives them a boost, then it's no different than going on a two-week vacation as far as I'm concerned" (Dull & West, 1991, p. 56).

Annually, cosmetic surgery is a $300-million-plus industry involving more than a half million people, most of whom are women. It is estimated that about 150,000 women obtain breast implants each year (L. Williams, 1992); in 1994, 51,000 Americans underwent liposuction, making it the most popular aesthetic procedure (Fattrimming, 1995). Liposuction, breast augmentation, breast reduction, and even the surgical tattooing of permanent facial make-up all capitalize on the pressure put upon women to measure up to exacting standards of beauty (Wolf, 1991). Liposuc

---

[18] One of the top ten, prostatectomy, is unique to men.

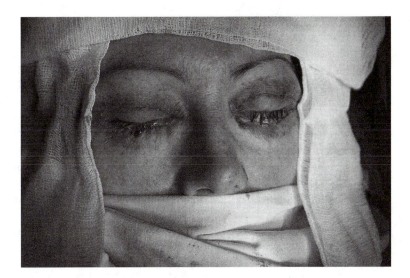

A woman shortly after cosmetic surgery to reduce eye wrinkles.

tion, appealingly advertised as a quick and safe solution to fatty hips and thighs, involves small risks of potential postoperative infection and is itself a violent procedure—a hollow tube is repeatedly forced beneath the skin to loosen and "vacuum" away fat (Laurence & Weinhouse, 1994).

We are just beginning to see the effects of widespread use of silicone breast implants, which the federal Food and Drug Administration banned in April 1992. Amazingly, although silicone implants had been used since 1964, the FDA didn't *request* that manufacturers register reports of serious health problems with implants until 1984 and still didn't *require* manufacturer's safety data until as late as 1991. Such "correction" for small breasts, literally defined as a deformity, seemed to justify unacceptably high rates of capsular contracture (a buildup of scar tissue that made breasts hard and misshapened in as many as 95% of cases), breast and joint pain, excessive fatigue, severe autoimmune reactions, interference with mammography, warnings that silicone is a carcinogen, and so on.

Health Care Policy

All of this leaves us with a very basic question: Does the health care system promote women's health? We know that health care policy in the United States is in crisis and has become a major political issue hotly debated at the federal level. Cheryl Travis, Diane Gressley, and Patricia Adams (1995) review this debate with an eye toward how it affects women and women's health. Two central problems confronted by health-policy reformers focus on cost and access. Fully 38 million Americans (15%) have no medical coverage, and almost 75% of the uninsured are under age 35 and are women, although most of the uninsured have jobs, obligations, and families. Disparities also exist by race and ethnicity; for example, African Americans are 1.8 times more likely to be uninsured than are whites (Leigh, 1995). Underemployment, part-time employment, and employment in small businesses not offering health insurance are associated with being uninsured, and women, especially racial and ethnic minority women, older women, and single heads of households, hold a disproportionate number of these jobs.[19] Most disturbing is the finding that insurance may affect treatment: for example, Travis and her colleagues reviewed 400,000 records of patients with heart disease and found that those with private insurance were twice as likely to receive heart bypass surgery as those on Medicaid [reported in Travis, Gressley, & Adams (1995)].

Health care reform has revolved around three major conceptual strategies: single-payer government-based systems (like Canada's), employer-mandated plans, and market reform (Travis et al, 1995). All strive toward universal coverage at reduced cost. Single-payer systems cover everyone with the government picking up the tab; employer programs require employers to pay into a general public pool (pay) or provide minimum coverage for employees (play); and market reforms rely on tax deductions, credits, or vouchers. Employer plans are especially likely to miss women since coverage is determined by employment in regulated settings.

Travis and her associates conclude that for reform to truly benefit women, health care policy must adequately define what needs and treatments are legitimate; empower individuals to take control of their own health; and value diversity, inclusiveness, and equity in health care provision. Furthermore, it is clear that this debate must be informed by health psychologists.

A recurrent theme that silently hovers in the background of some of the health literature blames women for failing to promote their own health. For example, it is frustrating to find high rates of cervical cancer among groups of women who avoid regular Pap smears; to record late breast-cancer detection rates for women who fail to do routine breast exams and shun mammography;[20] and to find condom avoidance and needle sharing even among those who know better. Who's to blame? It's tempting to point wagging fingers at women, but this reflects the person-blaming perspective we rejected in Chapter 1.

A fuller picture needs to view women within the contexts of their lives, and we saw some examples of this perspective throughout this chapter. Is a poor woman to blame for inadequate gynecological care when 44% of ob/gyns don't accept Medicaid patients (Travis et al., 1995)? Is a woman to blame for not using a condom when the expectation is that women control contraception but its practice depends on a partner's cooperation? Is risk of HIV contraction such a big threat when one lives in a crime-ridden neighborhood and can barely put food on the table? Is liposuction worth the pain and cost if it relieves the shame of being viewed as fat and out-of-control? As the field of health psychology burgeons, a fuller contextual account of

---

[19] A comprehensive report on "Women's Access to Health Insurance" by Y. Yoon, S. Aaronson, H. Hartmann, L. Shaw, and R. Spalter-Roth (1994) is available from the Institute for Women's Policy Research, 1400 20th Street, NW, Suite 101, Washington, DC 20036, (202) 785-5100.

[20] In 1990, 58% of women over 40 years-old reported having a mammogram within the past two years, and 64% had at least one done during their adult lives (Costello & Stone, 1994). Mammogram rates were especially low among African American women, women over age 70, and women with low incomes and less education.

women's lives must be understood to simultaneously empower women to promote their own health and give them the means to do so.

CHAPTER SUMMARY

Psychology plays an indispensable role in understanding and promoting the physical health and well-being of women. A feminist focus on women's health is needed to insure adequate research of those health issues that disproportionately or uniquely affect women; to provide a holistic understanding of women's sexual, reproductive, and general health needs; to counter androcentric assumptions about disease, prevention, and health; and to explore the apparent paradox of women's longer lifespans and greater morbidity. A key to doing this is to consider gender as a marker from which to launch further explorations of health patterns, rather than a cause in and of itself.

Turning to women's sexual well-being, a mechanical view of human sexuality ignores the socioemotional function sexuality plays in the lives of both women and men. Although the residuals of a double standard in sexual attitudes and behaviors persist into the 1990s, there are substantial individual differences, sociodemographic factors, and contextual variations in both, making this a more complex area than simple gender comparisons can capture. Parallel complexities emerge in discussions of menstruation, "PMS," and reproduction, including childbirth, miscarriage, and abortion. Folk wisdom evoking psychological disturbances is debunked, or at least called into question, by growing bodies of research evidence.

Less thoroughly studied than women's reproductive health, women's mortality and morbidity, like men's, are affected by a wide array of chronic diseases with cardiovascular diseases and cancers topping the charts. Beginning research on cardiovascular diseases challenges the simple extension of findings from men to women, beginning with differences as fundamental as onset (later for women), presenting symptoms (e.g., fewer myocardial infarctions), different markers (missed by stress tests and searches for narrowed arteries), expectations (leading to misdiagnosis), and risk factors. AIDS has risen to become the fourth leading cause of death for U.S. women and is most commonly transmitted to women through drug-related routes. Effective prevention strategies need to be sensitive to women's social contexts, including their disempowered status in interpersonal relationships.

The mission of health care practice, to heal, is seriously undermined by questionable patterns in rates of hysterectomy and by the expanding popularity and invasiveness of cosmetic surgery. As health care policy reform continues to be a pressing sociopolitical and economic issue, the input of health psychologists will be integral to the development of women-friendly and inclusive health care policies. The themes that run through each of these areas are that women's health is understudied and mythologized, but this is changing as the impact of feminist transformations of psychology become more pervasive throughout health psychology.

TEN

WOMEN'S MENTAL HEALTH AND WELL-BEING

From "Mental Disorders" to Feminist Practice

W e started this book with the case of Dora, the daughter of a friend of Sigmund Freud's who was brought to therapy by her father. Dora is described as defiant, willful, and disruptive, that is, clinically, "neurotic." Her father wanted her "brought to reason." Evidence, neglected by Freud, suggested that Dora was the target of inappropriate sexual overtures from her father's friend so that her "symptoms" were "normal" reactions to abnormal circumstances. What would happen to Dora today if she elected to visit a therapist?

There is no single answer to this question; different therapists certainly would emphasize different aspects of her case and approach her differently. If Dora's father sought conventional treatment for her, she probably would complete a battery of psychological tests and be classified using the diagnostic criteria outlined in the Diagnostic and Statistical Manual of the American Psychiatric Association (DSM-IV, 1994). Even something as basic as her diagnosis might differ if she visited a feminist therapist. Certainly, her treatment would be very different from Freud's if she did consult a feminist therapist.

In this chapter, we will explore two feminist transformations of clinical psychology since the time of Freud. The first arises from a feminist critique of the DSM and the different patterns of diagnoses its use yields for women and men. This critique challenges definitions of what's normal and pathological; exclusively biological approaches; and an overemphasis on intrapsychic factors to the exclusion of contextual influences. The second transformation comes about by applying feminist theory to practice. Both respond to the long-standing disservice done to women by theory and practice that fail to deal effectively and sensitively with serious and very real psychological pain.

In order to take a critical look at conventional approaches to diagnosis and treatment, we need to understand the DSM and the assumptions inherent in it. Our probing will call into question even the most basic elements of clinical diagnosis, including how we define our subject matter (e.g., DSM's descriptions of "mental disorders"). It also will highlight differences between women and men that are assumed within the DSM's medical model to represent fundamental gender differences rooted within women's and men's biologies or psyches. Embedded within this discussion will be overviews of specific diagnoses with gendered patterns, involving agoraphobia, alcohol and substance abuse, depression,[1] eating disorders, and three personality disorders (borderline, histrionic, and dependent). After critiquing how diagnosis is done within a DSM-based, medical model, we'll take a proactive approach and review the theory of feminist practice.

DIAGNOSIS: THE DSM-IV

Many clinicians' "bible" is the Diagnostic and Statistical Manual of Mental Disorders, which is published by the American *Psychiatric* Association and is now in its fourth edition (DSM-IV, 1994). Here a "**mental disorder**" is defined as:

---

[1] For a good overview of research on women and depression, see the updated report from the APA Task Force on Women and Depression (Sprock & Yoder, 1997).

. . . a clinically significant behavioral or psychological syndrome or pattern that occurs in an individual and that is associated with *present distress* (e.g., a painful symptom) or *disability* (i.e., *impairment* in one of more *important* areas of functioning) or with a significantly increased risk of suffering death, pain, disability or an important loss of freedom. In addition, this syndrome or pattern *must not be merely an expectable and culturally sanctioned response* to a particular event, for example, the death of a loved one. Whatever its original cause, it must currently be considered a manifestation of a behavioral, psychological, or biological dysfunction in the individual. Neither deviant behavior (e.g., political, religious, or sexual) nor conflicts that are primarily between the individual and society are mental disorders unless the deviance or conflict is a symptom of a dysfunction in the individual, as described above (DSM-IV, 1994, p. xxi-xxii, italics added by Caplan, 1995).

Although this definition may sound reasonable and definitive on the face of it, a second look reveals that all the italicized portions are compromised by subjectivity, and therefore vulnerable to biases (Caplan, 1995). For this reason, some therapists have questioned whether we should even think in terms of diagnostic labels.[2] A key question to ask may focus on how labels, once applied, will be *used.* Despite these very serious objections, labeling is at the heart of the DSM; is widely used (over 1 million copies of DSM-III-R were sold in less than six years [Caplan, 1995]); and assumes that a line can be established such that crossing it moves an individual from normality to abnormality (see Chapter 2 of Caplan, 1995, for a good review of definitions of abnormality and their shortcomings.)

In essence, the DSM classifies symptoms into categories of mental disorders: childhood disorders, cognitive disorders, mental disorders due to a medical condition, substance-related disorders, psychotic disorders (e.g., schizophrenia), mood disorders, anxiety disorders, somatoform disorders (physical symptoms not explained by a medical condition), factitious disorders (feigned ailments), dissociative disorders, sexual and gender identity disorders, eating disorders, sleep disorders, impulse-control disorders, adjustment disorders, and personality disorders.

The DSM claims that it classifies symptoms, not people, but in reality, a DSM diagnosis labels a person. Each disorder is assigned a number with decimal (e.g., 302.73 for "Female Orgasmic Disorder") that becomes a handy referent for insurance companies and lends a scientific aura to the diagnosis. A list of diagnostic criteria outlines the symptoms for each disorder usually specifying cut-off points: how many symptoms must be presented to merit each classification and its duration. There even are decision trees at the back of the volume to walk one through the choices possible within a general diagnostic category.

As early as 1977, a task force of the American *Psychological* Association questioned the conceptual basis of the DSM by highlighting its limitations. The DSM reflects a disease-based model extrapolated from medicine; the specific categories are unreliable (and continue to be so with low agreement rates even among trained therapists [Garfield, 1986]); categories are deleted and added based on committee vote with little research backing;[3] the labels can lead to biased treatment; and there

---

[2] Labeling opponents argue that labels are stigmatizing; labeling proponents argue that labels result in the provision of needed services. For a good overview of this debate as well as data linking both lower stigma and high quality services to quality of life and enhanced self-concept, see Rosenfield (1997).

[3] For an insider's look at how the DSM-IV came about, especially regarding Premenstrual Dysphoric Disorder and Self-Defeating Personality Disorder (both of which arguably hurt women), see Caplan (1995).

is little evidence that such categorization facilitates treatments or predicts outcomes (Task Force, 1977, cited in Lerman, 1996).

FEMINIST CRITIQUES OF THE DSM

On its face, the DSM looks thoroughly scientific and benign, but we shall see that feminist analyses of what's in the DSM, and how it is used, are not as value free and supportive of women as we might assume and demand. In trying to demystify the DSM, I am not challenging the existence or severity of psychological problems for women and men; these are indeed real and require serious assistance. However, I am questioning whether or not these needs are best served by the DSM and the medical model it exemplifies.

Use of the DSM has created patterns of diagnoses for some "disorders" that vary for women and men. Are these gender patterns real in that they capture genuine differences between women and men or are they byproducts of the DSM-based model? It is this question which is at the heart of a feminist critique of the DSM. We'll start out this section by pinpointing exactly where rates of diagnosis differ along gender lines, then we'll go on to probe what might cause these differences, exploring three areas: DSM-based definitional explanations, biological possibilities, and social-cultural influences.

Gender Patterns in DSM Diagnoses

Table 10.1 catalogues those disorders identified in DSM-IV as occurring more frequently in one gender than the other. Remember that there are a host of other disorders (such as schizophrenia) which show no gender differences. However, it is clear that boys are more vulnerable than girls; that adult women are more susceptible to major mood, anxiety, and eating disorders; that men dominate in substance-abuse disorders; and that women and men are diagnosed with some different personality disorders. These general patterns are confirmed by two large-scale surveys of the general U.S. population using DSM classifications (Kessler et al., 1994; Robins & Regier, 1991).[4] Interestingly, the lifetime prevalence of disorders overall did not differ for women (47.3% reported at least one disorder across their lifetimes) and men (48.7%) in one study (Kessler et al., 1994); and in the other, men's rates (36%) exceeded women's (30%), with men's excess largely accounted for by alcoholism (Robins & Regier, 1991). *What differs between women and men, girls and boys, then is not so much the occurrence of disorders overall, but rather different patterns for specific disorders.*

The lifetime prevalence of disorders overall appears relatively stable across race

---

[4] These surveys use diagnostic questionnaires that ask questions about symptoms based on DSM classifications and draw on representative samples of segments of the U.S. population. Categorizations of respondents then are made by looking across the criteria for DSM classification. Thus these measures of prevalence are free of reporting influences (i.e., who does and doesn't seek treatment), unlike studies that calculate gender ratios in diagnosed samples. Although speculation that men are unwilling to report psychological symptoms has not been supported (Nolen-Hoeksema, 1987), there is evidence that African Americans are reluctant to use mental-health facilities because they view them as alien and intimidating (Sussman, Robins, & Earls, 1987).

TABLE 10.1   Differential Diagnoses by Gender

The left column lists those diagnoses more common to females than males; the right, diagnoses more common to males than females. Ratios are presented in parentheses when available.

Female	Male
CHILDHOOD	
Selective Mutism	Mental Retardation (1.5:1)
	Reading Disorder
	Language Disorders
	Autistic Disorder
	Attention Deficit/Hyperactivity
	Conduct Disorder
	Oppositional Defiant Disorder
	Feeding Disorder
	Tourette's Disorder (motor/vocal tics)
	Stereotypic Movement Disorder
	Elimination Disorders
ADOLESCENCE AND ADULTHOOD	
Substance-Related Disorders	
	Alcohol Abuse and Dependence (5:1)
	Drug Abuse and Dependence
Mood Disorders	
Major Depression (2:1)	
Dysthymic Disorder (2:1) (long-term depression)	
Anxiety Disorders	
Agoraphobia (3:1)	
Specific Phobia	
Social Phobia	
Somatoform Disorders	
Somatization Disorder	
Conversion Disorder	
Dissociative Disorders	
Dissociative Identity Disorder (3-9:1)	
Eating Disorders	
Anorexia Nervosa (9:1)	
Bulimia Nervosa (9:1)	
Impulse-Control Disorders	
Kleptomania	Intermittent Explosive Disorder
Trichotillomania	Pyromania
(pulling out own hair)	Pathological Gambling (3:1)
Personality Disorders	
Borderline Pers. Disorder (7.5:1)	Paranoid Pers. Disorder
Histrionic Pers. Disorder	Schzoid/Schizotypal Pers. Disorders
Dependent Pers. Disorder	Antisocial Pers. Disorder
	Narcissistic Pers. Disorder
	Obsessive-Compulsive Pers. Disorder

Source: American Psychiatric Association: *Diagnostic and Statistical Manual of Mental Disorders, Fourth Edition.* Washington, DC, American Psychiatric Association, 1994. Reprinted with permission from the Diagnostic and Statistical Manual of Mental Disorders, Fourth edition. Copyright 1994 American Psychiatric Association.

TABLE 10.2   Estimated Lifetime Prevalence Rates in the General U.S. Population for Selected DSM-Defined Disorders

	Major Depression	Alcohol Abuse and Dependence	Panic Disorders
Whites	6.6%		
Women		4.52%	2.17%
Men		23.44%	.58%
African Americans	4.5%		
Women		5.47%	1.93%
Men		23.71%	.57%
Latina/Latinos	5.6%		
Women		3.85%	1.31%
Men		30.02%	.32%

Source: Compiled from L. N. Robins and D. A. Regier (eds.). (1991). *Psychiatric Disorders in America: The Epidemiologic Catchment Area Study.* New York: Free Press. Reprinted with permission.

and ethnicity for women (Robins & Regier, 1991). African American, Latina, and white women share similar prevalence rates within age cohorts with one exception: Black women between the ages of 45–64 years report higher rates of disorders (33%) than do white women (24%). (African American men over 45 years old show a higher prevalence rate than white men in the same cohorts.) However, some patterns differ along racial and ethnic lines for specific disorders (see Table 10.2). Major depression appears most commonly in whites and least in African Americans. Among women, alcohol abuse and dependence is highest for African Americans and lowest for Latinas. Panic disorders are most pronounced for white women and least common among Latina women, and somatization disorders occur more frequently in the lifetimes of non-Black women (.78%) than African American women (.17%).

Summing up, gender differences emerge in a variety of areas. Five of these have attracted the attention of clinical researchers and will be described in this chapter: agoraphobia, alcohol and substance abuse, depression, eating disorders, and a set of three personality disorders (borderline, histrionic, and dependent). Rather than focus on each of these "mental disorders" separately as a DSM-based approach might dictate, our discussion will proceed as a critique of the DSM, using each of these five gendered areas as examples to illustrate points made in this argument. My argument will focus on three areas: (1) on definitions of what is pathological and what is normal; (2) on biological explanations for gender differences in diagnosis; and (3) on problems with exclusively intrapsychic explanations.

DSM Definitions

Janet Williams and DSM-III-R task force head, Robert Spitzer, (1983) argue that the DSM's categories simply reflect reality and thus capture true sex or gender differences (also see Ross, Frances, & Widiger, 1997). A critical problem with this defense is that research looking at prevalence rates frequently relies on the DSM or other similar classification systems to define disorders. Because of this, their evidence relies on a tautology: using the DSM system classifies people in accordance with it and thus confirms its schema. The logic is circular. Paula Caplan (1995) describes how the American Psychiatric Association's membership "votes" on the inclusion of disorders: if enough therapists think a disorder should be included, this is taken as prima facie evidence of its validity.

If the DSMs recorded psychopathologies that exist independent of it, we might expect revisions to be relatively minor. However, the DSMs have grown remarkably over time. The first edition appeared in 1952, was 129 pages long, and described about 79 different diagnostic categories. The most recent version, published in 1994, extends to 886 pages and defines 374 categories (Lerman, 1996). Disorders come and go, take on different names and defining criteria, and move from presumably legitimate status in the text back into the appendices, where they hang in limbo until further research either re-establishes them in the text or removes them. These flip-flops seem most common for disorders involving sexual orientation and gender. In sum, we need to explore what *legitimates* a disorder so that it is included in the DSM, as well as what remains excluded and thus "normal."

What's pathological?   Picture the following client who is being assessed by a therapist:

> Within less than 10 minutes of talking with a therapist, **Terry** is sweating profusely, trembling, having trouble breathing, and feeling lightheaded and out of control. When things settle down, Terry says that fears of these sort of attacks make leaving the house difficult. Terry goes to great lengths to avoid being in a crowd, crossing a bridge, or traveling, preferring to stay home or venture out only occasionally with a companion. Terry always needs to know that escape is possible.

Is Terry a woman or a man? If you slipped a pronoun into the description, was it "she" or "he"?

The description of Terry incorporates the two defining criteria for diagnosing **agoraphobia** with or without a history of panic disorder:

> A. Anxiety about being in places or situations from which escape might be difficult (or embarrassing) or in which help may not be available in the event of having an unexpected or situationally predisposed Panic Attack or panic-like symptoms. Agoraphobic fears typically involve characteristic clusters of situations that include being outside the home alone; being in a crowd or standing in a line; being on a bridge; and traveling in a bus, train, or automobile.

> B. The situations are avoided (e.g., travel is restricted) or else are endured with marked distress or with anxiety about having a Panic Attack or panic-like symptoms or require the presence of a companion (DSM-IV, 1994, p. 396).

In all likelihood, you pictured Terry as a woman. Fully 85-95% of diagnosed agoraphobics are women, the typical age of onset is the mid-twenties to early thirties, and the majority are married (Gelfond, 1991). Prevalence rates for panic disorder are comparable across Latina, African American, and white women (Katerndahl & Realini, 1993). It is estimated that only about one-quarter of phobics seek treatment (Fodor, 1992), and fully 26% of normal college students report experiencing panic attacks in the past year (Brown & Cash, 1990). In a study of average women, 55%

scored at or near the clinical range for agoraphobia (Gelfond, 1988, cited in Gelfond, 1991). These findings suggest that there's a lot more agoraphobia in the general population of women than has been diagnosed. Might some agoraphobia simply be an exaggeration of what most women do in their everyday lives—be careful of where they go alone?[5]

Studies comparing agoraphobic women to others shed some light on this speculation. Agoraphobic women differ from agoraphobic men in that women are more sensitive to others, fear being alone more, and avoid going out alone (Bekker, 1996). Married women's agoraphobia may be sustained by a symptom-supportive spouse (Hafner & Minge, 1989). Thus agoraphobia is expressed by women as fears of solitary and anonymous situations. Agoraphobia also may be easier for women than men to admit—is it compromising for a guy to admit fears of being away from home? (Bekker, 1996). When an antipanic pill was introduced in Holland, signaling that panic was biologically based and hence chemically correctable, significantly more phobic men called a hot line for help and advice than before (Bekker, 1996).

Majorie Gelfond (1991) interviewed, tested, and observed 21 women diagnosed as agoraphobic, 20 average women, and 21 independent women (who scored highest on a measure of autonomy evaluating how often in the past year they traveled more than 50 miles alone, traveled at night, and ate alone in a restaurant). Overall, independent women differed from the other two groupings who had many qualities in common. Agoraphobic and average women shared less instrumental gender-role orientations, were less confident in their way-finding abilities, used less detail in the neighborhood maps they drew, and had restrictive parents (although the agoraphobics' parents were even more anxious; also see Laraia et al., 1994). All women considered home a safe haven, although the agoraphobic women lived in the most highly personalized, carefully decorated houses. All shared similar experiences with crime, but only the independent women were confident in their abilities to respond to criminal occurrences. The overriding finding is that agoraphobic women, although quite different from independent women, weren't that different from women in general.

All this suggests that agoraphobia represents the extreme end of a continuum reflecting many women's concerns about a not-so-women-friendly world. If a continuum of such fears does exist, where do we draw the line between reasonable fears and psychopathology? Also, how much does it help Terry to classify her/him as an agoraphobic? There is no doubt but that Terry is experiencing hardship, but is this ameliorated by labeling this pain as a disorder and suggesting that this deviates significantly from normalcy? We might ask similar questions of other presumably pathological disorders, calling into question the whole basis of the DSM by asking: What's abnormality? There are no definitive answers, but our discussion certainly suggests that these concerns cannot be dismissed lightly.

What's "normal"?   Maybe we can get a better sense of what's pathological by defining what is normal. Again, consider the following profile of a client coming for therapy:

---

[5] For an insightful exploration of the "normalcy" of agoraphobia, see McHugh (1996).

> **Lee** can't stay in a relationship—friends, relatives, and lovers fence Lee in. Lee doesn't like talking about feelings, stays withdrawn from others, and doesn't want to know what others are feeling. Lee thinks there's a place for men and women; feels confident to do anything, especially perform sexually; and thinks others should respect and praise this sexual prowess and omnipotence. Lee is threatened by women who seem more intelligent and derives little, if any, pleasure from helping others.

Did you picture Lee as a woman or a man? If you inserted a pronoun into the description, was it "she" or "he"?

Lee doesn't fit neatly into any of the 374 DSM classifications, so by default, Lee is normal. In contrast, Lee might be labeled as exhibiting "Delusional Dominating Personality Disorder," according to DSM critic Paula Caplan (1995). If Lee sounds like a man, he's meant to. He represents an exaggeration of the masculine stereotype—he can't establish a meaningful relationship; can't be empathetic; uses power, withdrawal, and avoidance to squelch conflict; inflates his own importance; and feels entitled to the services of women. Caplan finds that audiences respond knowingly to this caricature, granting it some legitimacy if we define abnormality by popular acclaim. Expecting to be rebuffed, she submitted it to the DSM committee for consideration where the initial reaction questioned her sincerity. Needless to say, it's unlikely that you'll find this category in a DSM in the near future, although it may indeed represent a harmful personality profile.

Contrast this proposal with **self-defeating personality disorder**. This "mental disorder" appeared in DSM-III, was intended for inclusion in DSM-IV despite serious empirical shortcomings (Caplan & Gans, 1991), but was withdrawn at the last minute in response to a public outcry (Caplan, 1995). In essence, this "disorder" blamed women for being abused: "chooses people and situations that lead to disappointment, failure, or mistreatment . . . "; "rejects or renders ineffective the attempts of others to help him or her"; "incites angry or rejecting responses from others . . . "; "rejects opportunities for pleasure . . ." ; "engages in excessive self-sacrifice"; and so on. Does this description sound like an abused woman? (We'll explore abuse by intimates in Chapter 11.) The inclusion of this category would have provided a sanctioned way to blame people (in most instances, women) for their own victimization.

What I am asking you to think about here is what may be missing from the DSM. Might the columns of Table 10.1 tip in the direction of more disorders ascribed to women because more disorders in the DSM fit women, while those that might describe men are missing? This is the question Paula Caplan is raising with her proposal for a Delusional Dominating Personality Disorder. Although Caplan surely does not want to expand the DSM by adding more "disorders," her proposal does raise questions about what makes the grade and what doesn't.

In conclusion, we raised questions in the preceding section about what is included and excluded from classification in the DSM-IV (also see Kaplan, 1983; Kupers, 1997). In the next two sections, we will examine specific diagnoses within the DSM with an eye to understanding why gendered patterns exist within them. Why is it that more women than men are diagnosed as depressed, eating disordered, and characterologically different with borderline, histrionic, and dependent personality disorders? Why are more men diagnosed for alcohol and substance abuse?

One explanation relies on biological differences; another, on intrapsychic differences which ignore broader contextual influences in women's lives.

Not All Biology

The DSM system best fits with the assumptions of a medical model. Adherents of this model envision mental disorders as similar to physical ones—the role of therapists, paralleling that of physicians, is to catalog symptoms, diagnose, and subsequently treat as the diagnosis dictates. The strongest evidence in support of a medical model comes from explorations of the etiology of disorders in biology. There is evidence that biology plays a role in some disorders, although never an exclusive or even dominant role. Also, as we saw in Chapter 2, it is important to remember that causal relationships between biology and behavior run both ways: biology not only influences behavior but is influenced by it.

For example, in a series of studies with female twins, Kenneth Kendler and his associates found greater concordance rates (both twins exhibiting the disorder) in monozygotic twins (genetically identical) than in dizygotic twins (who are no more genetically similar than siblings), for major depression (Kendler et al., 1992a), generalized anxiety disorder (Kendler et al., 1992b), phobias (Kendler et al., 1992c), and alcoholism (Kendler, Health et al., 1992). Estimating the proportional contribution of genetics to the presence of each disorder (heritability), these researchers calculated heritability rates of 33–45% for depression, 19–30% for anxiety disorders, 39% for agoraphobia, and 56% for alcoholism. A specific genetic marker has not been identified for any of these. Looking beyond genetics, other biological explanations, such as hormonal changes and moods, have not received resounding support (Nolen-Hoeksema, 1987; also see our discussion of premenstrual symptoms in Chapter 9).

Differing patterns across the lifespan, across race and ethnicity, and across cultures suggest that more than biology is at work. Depression rates are comparable for prepubescent girls and boys, then diverge at adolescence (Nolen-Hoeksema & Girgus, 1994). As we saw in Table 10.2, there are some race/ethnicity differences for some diagnoses with general gender differentials. For example, African American women are diagnosed for depression less than white women (Barbee, 1992), although there is some evidence that this pattern is reversed among 18–24 year olds (Somervell et al., 1989). Gender differences in rates of depression seem to disappear in developing countries (Nolen-Hoeksema, 1990), signaling the need for further global studies (Culbertson, 1997).

Focusing on biological causes leads to the treatment of disorders with medical treatments (drugs), the domains of psychiatrists and physicians (not psychologists and other mental health professionals), although these exclusive rights are being challenged. Over half of physician visits where patients are diagnosed with a mental disorder result in a prescription for mood-altering **psychotropic drugs**: tranquilizers, sedatives/hypnotics, antidepressants,[6] and stimulants (Travis, 1988b). Review-

---

[6] Eli Lilly, the producer of the leading antidepressant, Prozac, reported 1996 sales totaling $1.73 billion (Strauch, 1997).

ing psychotropic-drug prescribing for women, Heather Ashton (1991) concluded that throughout Europe and North America, women are prescribed twice as many psychotropic drugs per head than men. People of color are more likely to be prescribed psychotropic drugs and to be given these in lieu of psychotherapy (Jacobsen, 1994). It has been argued that women receive more drug prescriptions because they suffer from more psychiatric distress and are more willing to report psychological symptoms to physicians.

Whatever the validity of these possibilities, psychotropic drugs go hand-in-hand with more physical complaints that are specific to women than to men, a connection that is not readily explained by the physical conditions themselves. This suggests that gender-biased attitudes of physicians play a role, and indeed there is evidence that doctors are more likely to believe that women's physical illnesses encompass a psychological component. There also are reports of physicians dismissing women's complaints of undesirable side effects of medication (Shapiro, 1995). As a personal example, when my husband and I see the same physician for our regular checkups, I am asked if I want prescriptions for "stress" and daily "ups-and-downs" and my husband is not.

Gendered prescribing is further entrenched by advertisements for psychotropic drugs in professional magazines. A frequency analysis of ads for antidepressants published between 1986 and 1988 in the *American Journal of Psychiatry* and the *American Family Physician* found women:men gender ratios of 5:1 and 10:0, respectively (Hansen & Osborne, 1995). Another review of ads for antidepressants in British and American psychiatric journals published between 1989–1991 found that 80% pictured women clients (Prather, 1991). One of these ads, for Prozac, contrasted a photo of a squalid kitchen with the same cleaned kitchen to illustrate how this drug helps women "resume and cope with everyday activities." Beyond blatant sexism, the social problems and situational stresses associated with unipolar depression are rarely, if ever, mentioned (Nikelly, 1995).

Although biology does appear to play some role in the etiology of certain mental disorders, these studies urge us to look beyond biology for a fuller picture. The medical model that underlies the DSM may not foster such expansive exploration. Furthermore, the possible overreliance of medical practitioners on psychotropic drugs to treat women's complaints, both physical and psychological, suggests needs for further research and cautious vigilance on the part of consumers. It also raises questions about the potential psychological treatment of truly physiological maladies—problems that if left untreated could jeopardize women's lives (Brozovic, 1989). All this underscores the need for a feminist approach to psychopharmacology (Marsh, 1995) that considers biochemical treatment as an adjunct to, *not* a replacement for, psychotherapy (Rosewater, 1988).

Not All Intrapsychic

Jeanne Marecek and Rachel Hare-Mustin (1991) argue that the conventional DSM system identifies the individual as the locus of pathology without taking into consideration the gendered contexts of women's and men's lives. This assumption removes the family, the community, and other social factors from consideration in both diagnosis and treatment. Feminist critiques have challenged this exclusive focus on intrapsychic factors presumably internal to and controlled by the client. Alternatively, apparent gender differences in specific diagnoses might result from gender stereotypes, involving both the definition of disorders and therapists' judgments in assigning diagnostic labels, as well as from contextual factors differentially affecting the lives of women and men.

Stereotypes and DSM definitions. Try picturing two more clients seeking therapy:

Over the past two weeks, **Chris** has been depressed most of nearly every day, feeling sad and empty and appearing tearful to others. Chris, who usually isn't like this and who is not experiencing bereavement, doesn't get pleasure from or feel interested in what had been pleasurable activities. Chris doesn't feel like eating, resulting in weight loss across the past month, and wakes up in the middle of the night and can't get back to sleep. Thus Chris is fatigued so that even the smallest tasks, like washing and getting dressed, seem exhausting. Chris appears agitated during the interview, having trouble sitting still, speaks in low, labored tones, and has trouble concentrating. Chris reports feeling worthless and keeps thinking morbid thoughts. What's wrong with Chris?

Pat shows up reeking of alcohol. Pat has been referred for counseling because of repeated driving violations and for picking fights with coworkers. Pat knows that drinking creates problems but feels terrible if a day goes by without a drink—nauseous, agitated, sweating, and just plain nervous. At these times, it seems easier to take a drink (or two, or more—it seems to take more and more to help), even though obtaining and consuming alcohol takes up lots of Pat's time. What's wrong with Pat?

The argument proposed here is that the DSM system, as conceived, draws on gendered stereotypes to define syndromes. For example, is the list of symptoms that defines major depression gender-neutral or does it, at its core, rely on images of women as depressive and thus describes gender-biased versions of this disorder? Chris fits the DSM definition of major depression. Did you imagine her as a woman (specifically a white, middle class woman)? Similarly, does the image of an alcoholic as a man shape how alcohol dependence and abuse are presented in the DSM? Pat presents the symptoms of alcohol abuse and dependence—do you picture "him"? Parallel logic applies to the scenario for Terry, our agoraphobic earlier in the chapter. Hope Landrine (1988; 1989) found these patterns in the responses of students who made consistent determinations regarding the gender of targets diagnosed with depression, dependent personality disorders (white, middle class, married women), and antisocial personality disorders (poor, young men). Stereotypes of these disorders are consistent with gender stereotypes. Go down the list of differential diagnoses presented in Table 10.1 to see if these also fit with gender stereotypes.

Clearly, gender and disorder stereotypes are linked. I have suggested that these DSM classifications are gender biased in that they reflect stereotyped images of women and men. However, if these differences are real such that women indeed are more depressed than men, for example, than these diagnoses simply contain "kernels of truth." But what if individuals with the same diagnosis exhibited different symptoms depending on their gender orientation?

Sarah Oliver and Brenda Toner (1990) compared how college women and men described their own depression on a standard self-report measure (the Beck Depression Inventory). In keeping with gender stereotypes, women described their depression with emotional symptoms, such as crying, in contrast to the somatically oriented problems reported by men (e.g., sleep problems and decreased libido). Focusing on participants who scored as mildly depressed, depressed women were less likely than depressed men to describe sleep disturbances, suicidal thoughts, social withdrawal, and reduced libido and more likely to report feelings of sadness, failure, and tearfulness. So far, both depressed respondents and students in general linked different symptomatology to women and men.

Even more supportive of the association between gender stereotypes and the expression of depression, depressed women with masculine orientations (as measured by the Bem Sex Role Inventory) reported more insomnia, less self-dislike, and less weight loss than feminine women. In other words, masculine women described a masculinized version of depression. Similarly, masculine men reported more social withdrawal than feminine men. In sum, mildly depressed students reported symptoms consistent with their gender-typing (also see Campbell, Byrne, & Baron, 1992; Katz et al., 1993). All of this is consistent with an argument that some DSM diagnoses may not be as gender neutral as we'd expect.

Stereotypes and therapists' judgments.   We have asked many questions about the validity of the DSM itself. Here we will focus on how the DSM is used. Might therapists themselves bring biases to the DSM that are justified, reinforced, and further entrenched by biases within the DSM system so that their combination further compounds the effects of gender stereotypes? In a classic study, Inge Broverman and her colleagues (1970) asked 33 women and 46 men, who were clinically trained psychologists, to rate one of three clients on 122 adjectives, 38 of which used scales designed so that one end was considered feminine (e.g., not at all aggressive) and the other pole, masculine (e.g., aggressive). The person evaluated in the three separate conditions was described as a "healthy, mature, socially competent adult" (1) "man," (2) "woman," or (3) "person." The gender-unspecified person was included to provide a baseline of what therapists regard as healthy, presumably without confounding gender.[7]

There was a lot of agreement in how each of the three targets was rated. In other words, there was consensus among the therapists about what constitutes psychological health for women, for men, and for adults in general, when each was considered separately. However, differences emerged when the three conditions were compared to each other. There was significant overlap between the definitions of a healthy adult and a healthy man. Most relevant to our discussion, this overlap did not extend to women. There was a significant difference between how a healthy woman and a healthy person/man were described. Combining these comparative findings paints a picture of male as normative (androcentrism). The contrast between the ratings of a woman and of a man was explained mostly by male-valued traits,

---

[7] Follow-up research suggests that there is no such thing as a genderless, generic person so that for many of us, when we think of an "adult," we imagine a man (Wise & Rafferty, 1982). This undermines the use of the gender-unspecified target as a neutral baseline, but it does not discredit comparisons of the "man" with the "woman" conditions.

which were not ascribed by therapists to healthy women. Healthy women, relative to men, were portrayed as being more submissive, less independent, less adventurous, more easily influenced, less aggressive, less competitive, more excitable in minor crises, more emotional, more conceited about their appearance, less objective, having their feelings more easily hurt, and disliking math and science—not a very flattering picture of women's mental health.

These findings are dated, and indeed an androgynous blend of traits has emerged in the protocols of therapists in follow-up studies (Thomas, 1985). This may mean that the double standard of mental health has disappeared, that therapists got wise to this rather transparent technique,[8] and/or that bias has gotten more subtle. There is evidence that therapists continue to view others through gendered lenses. A study of gender-typing by 554 psychotherapists found that they typically stereotyped women as more expressive and less instrumental than male targets (Turner & Turner, 1991). Another study of 229 therapists reported that they were more likely to view men's problems with a utilitarian, let's-fix-it approach (Fowers et al., 1996). Both studies suggest that therapists approach male clients expecting a more favorable prognosis.

We saw in Chapter 9 that physicians' expectations about who has heart disease may affect how women are diagnosed. A similar pattern appears here. Marilyn Potts and her colleagues (1991) compared standardized assessments of depression with the clinical assessments of medical and mental health practitioners for 23,101 clients. Among clients who met the standardized criteria for depression, therapists diagnosed it more frequently in women than in men, failing to identify men who broke with feminine expectations for depression. Among those who did not certify as depressed with standard testing, false positives were more common in women than men. Both patterns suggest that gendered expectations about depression influence who is so diagnosed.

Further evidence of therapist bias in the diagnosis of depression comes from a clever analogue study by John Robertson and Louise Fitzgerald (1990). Forty-seven practicing counselors-therapists were shown one of two videos in which the same male actor described symptoms of depression (e.g., poor appetite, boredom, and sleeplessness). In half the tapes, the actor described his marriage as a traditional one in which he was employed as an engineer and his wife was a homemaker and primary caretaker of their children. In the other version, only these segments were altered to describe a nontraditional arrangement in which domestic and employment roles were reversed.

Not surprisingly, practitioners rated the nontraditional client as less masculine (instrumental) on 14 of 20 items of the Bem Sex Role Inventory. Most notably for us, the nontraditional client was diagnosed significantly more frequently with severe mood disorder, and more therapists planned to probe for marital problems as the source of his depression, despite the client's expressed belief that his marital arrangement was satisfactory. This speaks volumes about the mental-health implications of

---

[8] The possibility that therapists' judgments now are affected by social desirability pressures is supported by research finding no difference in the responses of uninformed therapists and those told to answer in socially desirable ways (Lopez et al., 1993).

breaking gendered occupational and domestic norms. More to the point here, depression, with its feminine connotations, was a more likely diagnosis for a less "masculinized" client.

What happens when we look at the opposite scenario: when a woman presents the symptoms of a male-dominated disorder such as **alcohol abuse and dependence**? Alcoholism may not be suspected when it indeed exists (Swett et al., 1991). Examining this androcentric tendency from the perspective of researchers, a review of 90 studies on substance abuse found that fully 65 of the researchers (72%) failed to probe their data for potential gender differences, even though these analyses were feasible (Toneatto, Sobell, & Sobell, 1992). This results in a gap in our understanding of alcoholism (Wilsnack, Wilsnack, & Hiller-Sturmhöfel, 1994) and reinforces male-as-norm bias (Wilke, 1994). Reflecting stronger societal disapproval of drinking by women (Gomberg, 1993), women alcoholics are thought to require more therapy sessions (Hardy & Johnson, 1992). Relatedly, alcoholic women are more likely to be considered co-morbid, combining alcohol abuse with additional diagnoses of mental disorders, most often depression and anxiety (Cornelius et al., 1995; Haver & Dahlgren, 1995). In keeping with these co-diagnoses, women report that they drink to reduce anxiety (Dunne, Galatopoulos, & Schipperheijn, 1993) and alter their moods (Olenick & Chalmers, 1991). This perspective then tends to view women's alcoholism as symptomatic of another underlying disorder.

Most American women (59%) and men (71%) drink alcohol, with 6% of women and 21% of men consuming 2+ drinks daily (Wilsnack et al., 1994). Cross-culturally and across age groups, men drink larger quantities, drink more frequently, and report more drinking-related problems. Young women generally have higher rates of intoxication, drinking problems, heavy episodic drinking, and alcohol dependence than older women, who often are characterized by moderate but more frequent drinking. Alcohol abuse patterns differ among African American and white women. Among Black women, alcoholism rates rise from 18 to 44 years of age and remain high until after 65. In contrast, incidence among white women peaks early (18–29 years), then declines steadily (Caetano, 1994). Patterns of alcohol problems among lesbians, like those of African American women, do not decline with age and are at rates two times higher than those for the general population (Hughes & Wilsnack, 1994).

Factors putting women at risk for drinking-related problems include a family history of problem drinking, depression, trauma, employment in male-dominated occupations, unwanted statuses (e.g., being involuntarily unemployed), stress, and peer and spousal pressure (Gomberg, 1994; Wilsnack et al., 1994). Although linked to marital dissolution for some women with no prior history of alcohol abuse, drinking problems may abate for women who leave reinforcing relationships in which the partner is a heavy drinker (Sandoz, 1995; Wilsnack et al., 1991). There is evidence that women with alcoholic parents will offer more help to an exploitative man, suggesting that high-risk women are prone toward developing nonsupportive relationships (Lyon & Greenberg, 1991). In sum, just as there are male depressives, there are female alcoholics, regardless of gendered stereotypes of these two (and presumably other) disorders.

Neglected contextual factors. The DSM and its use have been criticized for focusing solely on individual causes and expressions of disorders to the exclusion of contextual influences (social forces) (Brown & Ballou, 1992; Kaschak, 1992; Lerman, 1996; Marecek & Hare-Mustin, 1991). For example, in the American Psychological Association's "Task Force Report on Women and Depression" (McGrath et al., 1990), a variety of moderating variables are identified, such as family and employment roles, victimization, and poverty, that may mediate relationships between an individual's personality and depression. To focus on individual personality factors alone implies a personal deficit model that ignores history, human spirit, and a lifespan perspective (Root, 1992).

This individualistic focus is most pronounced in the DSM for personality disorders which are stable over time and hence presumed to be characterological, that is, coming from within the person regardless of external stressors (Brown, 1992). These disorders are afforded heightened attention by "multiaxial assessment" in the DSM-IV whereby clients are assessed over five axes, including Axis II specifically for personality disorders and mental retardation.[9] Looking at Table 10.1, women dominate in the diagnoses of borderline, histrionic, and dependent personality disorders. The most extensively studied differential diagnosis on Axis I (Clinical Disorders) is major depression, estimated as two times more common in women. Each of these disorders will help paint a picture about the importance of contextual factors.

To be classified as having a **major depression**, a client must experience at least two depressive episodes, each of which entails at least five symptoms from a list of nine, present over at least a two-week period, and at least one of which must be either depressed mood or loss of interest or pleasure. (If depression is chronic over a course of at least two years, the diagnosis changes to **dysthymic disorder** which also tips toward great prevalence in women.) The only mention of causes external to the person in this presentation are the disqualifying exceptions of depression due to physiological effects of a substance (e.g., drugs or a medication), a general medical condition, or bereavement. Beyond some biological contributions, external threats to self-esteem, interpersonal stress, body dissatisfaction, physical illness, finances and employment, acculturation, and trauma are ignored.

A link between low self-esteem and depression has been well established (Russo, Green, & Knight, 1993a) and has been accounted for by at least five interrelated models (Woods et al., 1994). Each of these models looks beyond the simple association of low self-esteem with depression to ask what causes the depressive's self-esteem to be low, considering factors outside the woman herself for the root cause of diminished self-esteem. Self-esteem then becomes a mediator in these models (see Figure 10.1).

First, self-in-relation theorists posit that lowered self-esteem, and hence a propensity for depression, results from the devaluation of women's learned desires for interdependency and intimacy. While women seek validation through relationships, our society values the opposite—autonomy. This creates a double bind for women who have to choose between being good, caring women or independent "men." A second, socialization model extends this reasoning to all feminine socialization, arguing that most feminine traits are devalued, causing women who hold these characteristics to feel inadequate relative to the cultural (masculine) ideal.

---

[9] The other axes are: Axis I: Clinical Disorders; Axis III: General Medical Conditions; Axis IV: Psychosocial and Environmental Problems; and Axis V: Global Assessment and Functioning.

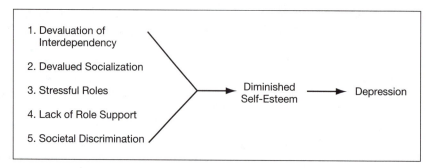

FIGURE 10.1   Five models expand the association between diminished self-esteem and depression.

The third and fourth social role models emphasize the differing roles women and men enact: one model highlights the stresses that accompany women's roles, and the other concentrates on the lack of support afforded women in the fulfillment of their roles.[10] A fifth model argues that women are vulnerable to depressed self-esteem and hence depression because of societal discrimination, which blocks their achievement of personal mastery. The linkage between each of these models to both self-esteem and depression in women has been documented and, although specific patterns may vary by women's race and ethnicity, the associations hold across Asian, African American, and white women (Woods et al., 1994).

Interpersonal stress plays a role in depression for some women and girls—more commonly than for men (Waelde et al., 1994) and boys (Moran & Eckenrode, 1991). Although women typically derive support from their more expansive social networks than do men, these networks also can be sources of interpersonal stress (Turner, 1994) and criticism (Gruen, Gwadz, & Morrobel, 1994). Involvement in conflicted networks is associated with depression for both African American and white women (Woods et al., 1994). The potential supports and risks of social networks is evident in a study of college women who were asked to describe the expressiveness of their families (Cooley, 1992). Women were more prone to depression when their families were more negatively than positively expressive in contrast to depression-resistant women in families showing net positive expressiveness.

We saw in Chapter 6 that some women, mostly white heterosexuals, report greater dissatisfaction with their bodies than do men. Not surprisingly, body dissatisfaction has been linked to depression for women and girls who emphasize the importance of appearance (Koenig & Wasserman, 1995; Ruble et al., 1993). In a study of 300 girls and boys, ages 11, 13, and 15, body image was the single best predictor of girls' depression (Girgus, 1989). Among both depressed outpatients and general college students, body image is the single most influential factor in distinguishing women's from men's depression, as measured by the Beck Depression Inventory (Santor, Ramsay, & Zuroff, 1994). Higher-than-normal weight gain is associated with depression but only for white, not African American, pregnant women (Cameron

---

[10] For example, we saw in Chapter 7 that the bulk of domestic responsibilities fall onto women's shoulders.

et al., 1996). It is no wonder then that depression tends to go along with eating disorders in some women (Fava et al., 1996; Perlick & Silverstein, 1994; Webber, 1994).

Two specific diagnoses compose the category of eating disorders in the DSM-IV. **Anorexia nervosa** is characterized by a refusal to maintain a minimally acceptable body weight. **Bulimia nervosa** is distinguished by recurrent episodes of binge overeating followed by inappropriate compensatory purging behaviors such as self-induced vomiting; laxative, diuretic, or other medicinal abuse; fasting; and/or excessive exercise. An essential feature of both disorders is a disturbance in perception of body shape and weight. Both are described in DSM-IV as disorders with greatest incidence in young women. Researchers narrow these demographics even further to mostly white women (Lucero et al., 1992) and heterosexual women (Herzog et al., 1992).

Characterological approaches emphasize the personality traits associated with eating disorders, including high levels of negative feminine/expressive qualities (Paxton & Sculthorpe, 1991), underidentification with masculine/instrumental qualities (Klingenspor, 1994), adherence to a superwoman ideal (Crago et al., 1996; Hart & Kenny, 1997), and strong desires for perfectionism (Minarik & Ahrens, 1996). A feminist analysis often highlights the influence of a "culture of thinness" which values a thin physique, sets up dieting as normative, links thinness to some athletic and occupational pursuits, and stresses thinness in media and medical advice (White, 1992).[11] There is evidence that associates each of these with being young, white, and female in American culture.

Recent research links the value of a thin physique to desires to attract and please men by showing that body dissatisfaction and eating disorders are related directly to those who share these desires: heterosexual women and gay men (Schneider, O'Leary, & Jenkins, 1995; Siever, 1994). A large-scale survey of dieting to lose weight in the general population confirms that dieting is normative for employed women: fully 75% of women have done this sometime in their lifetimes (as opposed to 47% of men) (Jeffery, Adlis, & Forster, 1991). Eating disorders are most pronounced for girls and women in sports (e.g., gymnastics; see Williamson et al., 1995) and occupations (e.g., modeling; flight attendant; see White, 1992) concerned with body shape and size.

The media contributes to this cycle by stressing weight loss: women's magazines contain 10.5 times as many advertisements and articles promoting weight loss as men's (Andersen & DiDomenico, 1992) and food ads are dominated by weight-loss claims (Klassen, Wauer, & Cassel, 1991). The primary reasons presented for following nutrition and fitness plans are to lose weight and become more attractive (Guillen & Barr, 1994). Even Saturday morning cartoon programming is punctuated with a majority of conflicting ads selling foods and promoting attractiveness enhancement aimed at girls (Ogletree et al., 1990). Women who read fashion magazines distort estimates of their own body size (Waller et al., 1994), and a direct link has been established between exposure to media and eating disorders (Stice et al, 1994). White women exposed to models typifying idealized thin physiques displayed lowered self-

---

[11] An excellent 30-minute video that expands on this point is "Slim Hopes" featuring Jeanne Kilbourne (Media Education Foundation, 26 Center Street, Northhampton, MA 01060, (413) 586-4170).

Former gymnast Christy Henrich is shown at a luncheon fundraiser with her fiance. Henrich died July 26, 1994 after a long battle with two eating disorders that had reduced her to just 60 pounds.

esteem, increased self-consciousness, anxiety about having someone observe their body, and body dissatisfaction (Thornton & Maurice, 1997). This research makes it hard to deny a linkage between what the media portrays and how women feel about their bodies (Kilbourne, 1994). (Personally, I feel a lot better about my own body since I discontinued my subscription to the mail order catalogue of a well-known lingerie purveyor!) The relationship between thinness and health is further aggravated by the health care community, which views fat as pathogenic (Chrisler, 1996; Vandereycken, 1993).

Such evidence of a "culture of thinness" shifts our focus away from characterologically deficient women to sociocultural factors that encourage disordered eating. However, a few recent feminist analyses, although supportive of such refocusing outward, argue that the emphasis on weight, attractiveness, and thinness may have missed the mark for some women with eating disorders. Both anorexia nervosa and bulimia are found in nonwhite women and outside Western culture (Dolan, 1991), although detecting these may be obstructed by stereotypes of who does and doesn't suffer with eating disorders (Root, 1990). Among Asian American (Hall, 1995; Lee, 1995), African American, Latina (Thompson, 1992), and lesbian women (Brown, 1987), eating disorders may be psychological responses, not to body dissatisfaction alone, but to sexual abuse, racism, classism, heterosexism, and poverty. This perspective regards eating disorders as more than seemingly narcissistic attempts to conform to cultural standards of beauty. It regards eating as a way to reassert control; for example, by changing body parts that may be considered responsible for attracting abuse or by turning to food for comfort.

Weight and thinness also may miss the mark as the foci of bodily acceptance or dissatisfaction for some women. For example, skin color, hair texture, and facial features may have a discernible effect on some African American women's views of their physical appearance (Greene, 1994a). For some African American women, skin color can be a symbol of pride, honor, guilt, shame, or oppression (Jenkins, 1993) and can be implicated in familial rivalries (Greene, 1990b). To focus on weight as the sole indicator of bodily regard may reflect assumptions rooted in a dominant racial (white) value system.

We saw in Chapter 9 that more women are likely to struggle with chronic but non-life-threatening illnesses than men. Taking this a step further, it seems reasonable to predict that depression occurs more frequently in women in response to physical discomfort. Indeed, depressed women report more physical complaints and functional limitations than nondepressed women (Betrus, Elmore, & Hamilton, 1995). For African American women, physical health problems were significant predictors of depression (Taylor, Henderson, & Jackson, 1991). Among elderly women, interventions that target physical health and depression together are most effective (Heidrich, 1994).

Also associated with women's depression are financial strain (Jambunathan, 1992; Mendes-de-Leon et al., 1994), poverty (Belle, 1990; McGrath et al., 1990; Sen, 1993), unemployment (Dew, Bromet, & Penkower, 1992; Hauenstein & Boyd, 1994; Osipow & Fitzgerald, 1993), nonemployment (Bromberger & Matthews, 1994), and homelessness (Ingram, Corning, & Schmidt, 1996).[12] These patterns extend to other disorders as well. Alcohol and drug-related problems are exacerbated by poverty (Thomas, 1995) and homelessness (Geissler et al, 1995; Smith, North, & Spitznagel, 1993). Schizophrenia is diagnosed more frequently in people of lower socioeconomic status (Greenwald, 1992). At times these risk factors may be too narrowly defined in line with stereotyped expectancies. For example, Karen Wyche (1993) contends that poor, single-parenting women are overrepresented in applied research exploring factors that affect African American women's lives.

Acculturation of women into American society may create two risks. One results from the added stresses that accompany pressures to blend in. An example is found among some Korean American women who are vulnerable to depression resulting from acculturation pressures (Shin, 1994). The second makes strongly acculturated women more vulnerable to the gendered patterns of disorders that permeate our culture. For example, stronger adoption of American culture has been related to risks of depression among Mexican American women (Masten, Penland, & Nayani, 1994) and of eating disorders among African American women (Pumariega, Gustavson, & Gustavson, 1994).

Finally, there is a growing body of newly focused research linking women's depression to violence and trauma (Cutler & Nolen-Hoeksema, 1991; Hamilton & Jensvold, 1992). This relationship holds across a diversity of women including African American (Barbee, 1992), Asian American (Ho, 1990), and lesbian (Rothblum, 1990) women, although each may express this connection in unique ways (Rosewater, 1990). The neglected role of trauma in women's lives comes through more clearly when we shift our focus to the personality disorders in which women dominate: borderline, histrionic, and dependent (Lerman, 1996).

---

[12] Although more women are economically disadvantaged, income alone cannot account for gender differences in rates of depression (Nolen-Hoeksema, 1987).

Borderline personality disorder is characterized by attention seeking, manipulative behavior, rapidly shifting emotions, self-destructiveness, angry disruptions in close relationships, and chronic feelings of deep emptiness and loss of identity. **Histrionic personality disorder** is distinguished by pervasive and excessive emotionality and attention-seeking behavior. The essential feature of **Dependent personality disorder** is an excessive need to be taken care of, leading to submissive and clinging behaviors and fears of separation. Think of each of these three personality disorders in the context of child sexual abuse, rape, intimate abuse, and so on. Researchers find that sexual and physical abuse occur in women diagnosed with personality disorders at very high rates—as much as 81% (Bryer, Nelson, Miller, & Krol, 1987; Herman, Perry, & van der Kolk, 1989).

Maria Root (1992) distinguishes among three forms of trauma, all of which are stressful. The most obvious forms are **direct trauma**, such as rape and abuse, which are identified by maliciously perpetuated violence. Direct traumas encompass experiences not only of being targeted for, but also of being forced to commit, atrocities (e.g., military orders to kill civilians). **Indirect trauma** is produced through secondary effects, including experiences such as pulling bodies from wreckage, watching one's mother being beaten, and witnessing homicide. **Insidious trauma** results from being devalued because of an individual characteristic intrinsic to one's identity, such as one's gender, race and ethnicity, sexual orientation, physical ability, age, and so on. Examples include women's general fear of rape (Riger & Gordon, 1981), the "terrorism of racism" (Wyatt, 1989), the legacy of racism and sexism (Greene, 1990b), and fears of genocide by children of Holocaust survivors (Danieli, 1985).

DSM-IV includes one diagnosis specifically designed to deal with direct and some indirect trauma survivors: **Posttraumatic Stress Disorder** (PTSD). To meet the diagnostic criteria for PTSD, a person must have been exposed to a traumatic incident in which the "the person experienced, witnessed, or was confronted with an event or events that involved actual or threatened death or serious injury, or a threat to the physical integrity of self or others" and "the person's response involved intense fear, helplessness, or horror" (DSM-IV, 1994, pp. 427–428). For at least one month, the traumatic event is persistently re-experienced in recollections, dreams, flashbacks, symbolic cues, or similar settings and attempts are made to avoid stimuli associated with the trauma. Persistent symptoms of increased arousal are present, such as difficulty falling or staying asleep, irritability or angry outbursts, difficulty concentrating, hypervigilance, and exaggerated startle responses.

PTSD entered the pages of the DSMs in DSM-III, mostly in response to veterans groups and others dealing with the aftermath of military service on young men (Lerman, 1996). It is one of a handful of disorders that recognizes the importance of social factors outside the individual. Needless to say, it immediately became useful to therapists treating women survivors of rape as well as other physical and verbal abuses. In DSM-III, the external stressor triggering PTSD was described as "outside the range of usual human experience" and as "markedly distressing to almost anyone" (quoted in Lerman, 1996, p. 49). This verbiage painted a picture of PTSD as a normal reaction to an abnormal event. This assurance disappeared in the language of DSM-IV where "threat" takes center stage—a tightening of the criteria that some feminists fear may limit its usefulness to women surviving traumatic occurrences that aren't life-threatening, such as most date rape, and that may shift our focus toward justifying the veracity of the threat (Caplan, 1995; Lerman, 1996).

What's in a name? Does it matter so much that an abuse survivor, for example, is labeled as a borderline personality or as experiencing PTSD? The former presumes a characterological deficiency (there's something wrong with the woman) and the latter, especially in its original formulation, sees the abnormality in the precipitating event(s). This plays into how therapists feel about their clients. Hannah Lerman (1996) describes the label of personality disorder as one of the most stigmatizing of the DSM categories, making those who wear it different from everyone else. Therapists typically find clients so classified as difficult to work with, obnoxious, and unlikeable. However, when practitioners recognize that many of these women clients are struggling with traumatic histories, they empathetically come to regard them as distressed and in legitimate need of help. It seems that there's a lot in a name.

Given the importance of labeling, two feminist theorists and practitioners, Laura Brown and Lenore Walker, have proposed alternative classifications to facilitate diagnosis and treatment of abused women (Brown, 1992; Walker, 1986). Both seek to capture the *repetitive exposure* to trauma that differentiates interpersonal violence from the discrete events that presumably underlie PTSD. For example, Abuse and Oppression Artifact Disorder seeks to identify the nature of the stressor by distinguishing between interpersonal (from intimates, acquaintances, or stranger(s)) and cultural environmental stressors (overt, punitive phenomena; covert, systematic phenomena; lack of protection/denial of opportunity). This latter category recognizes the insidious forms of trauma referenced by Maria Root.

Trauma affects more than diagnoses of depression and personality disorders. Histories of sexual abuse and other violence are overrepresented in women in substance abuse programs (Teets, 1995; Woodhouse, 1990), and these have been related to the development of alcoholism (Miller, Downs, Gondoli, & Keil, 1987). Incest rates are higher among alcoholic than nonalcoholic women (Beckman, 1994). In studies of eating disorders, sexual abuse and/or rape are reported in half or more cases, with sexual assault experiences occurring at even higher levels (75%+) in inpatient samples (Root, 1991; also see Miller, 1993; Waller & Ruddock, 1995; Weiner & Stephens, 1993; Wooley, 1994). Sexual abuse has been associated with somatization disorders (Morrison, 1989) and psychotic disorders (Darves-Bornoz et al., 1995). Even when evaluated many years after a physical assault, survivors were more likely to qualify for psychiatric diagnoses than women without such histories (Koss, 1990).

All of this makes a strong case for the importance of factors external to the individual. To consider an individual without considering context confines diagnosis to presenting symptoms. This seems to miss much of what we'd expect follow-up therapy to consider and also to pathologize the person without taking into account the possibility that *normal* people are coping with *pathological* settings. Combined with therapists' biases, the result has been a checkered history of psychiatric treatment of women with egregious examples of misogynous treatment appearing in women's autobiographical accounts. (About 175 of these are thematically reviewed by Jeffrey Geller, 1985.) The remedy to this failure, taking a holistic look at psychological difficulties, has lead some practitioners and scholars to propose feminist approaches to doing therapy.

THE THEORY OF FEMINIST PRACTICE

The above critique of the DSM implies a lot about what feminist therapy should not be, but it doesn't tell us much about what feminist therapy is.[13] We need to explore the theory of feminist therapy—*not* to describe specific techniques of therapy, but rather the conceptual underpinnings of a feminist approach to doing therapy.[14] Guidelines for practicing feminist therapy are outlined, comprehensively and clearly, in a series of 13 principles developed by the American Psychological Association's Committee on Women in Division 17 (Counseling Psychology) (see Fitzgerald & Nutt, 1986). This set of principles has been endorsed by other APA divisions, including Division 35 (Psychology of Women), and it is cited as a resource in the general "Guidelines for the Provision of Counseling Psychological Services" (Guidelines, 1983). For our purposes, these principles encompass most, if not all, of the points developed in other expositions of feminist therapy theory (e.g., Feminist Institute Code of Ethics outlined in Lerman & Porter [1990]; Brown, 1994a; Butler, 1985; Dutton-Douglas & Walker, 1988; Lerner, 1988).

My goal is not to offer a rationale for each of these points,[15] but rather to understand how each is conceptually linked to putting feminism into psychotherapy practice. Each of these points views therapy as a process that is negotiated between therapist and client, not as some technique that is used on a passive recipient.

> Principle 1. Counselors/therapists should be knowledgeable about women, particularly with regard to biological, psychological, and social issues which have impacted on women in general or on particular groups of women in our society.

The key to this opening charge is to take a holistic view of women's lives that draws on biology, psychology, and social issues, or what we have called social forces or context throughout this book. We have seen that individualism without context, assuming that pathology resides in characterological defects within a person, ignores many social forces that have been implicated in women's mental health, such as body dissatisfaction, poverty, acculturation, and trauma.

For example, Julia Boyd (1990) describes the case of a young Southeast Asian woman, recently immigrated, who was ordered by the American courts to therapy for shoplifting. After several nonproductive sessions with a white therapist in which the client refused to detail her reasons for stealing, the therapist remanded her back to the judge with the labels of withdrawn, noncommunicative, and depressed. An Asian paralegal took note of the case and realized that the same product, sanitary napkins, was being stolen repeatedly from the same store. In the context of her culture, her actions didn't reflect depression but rather embarrassment, both from the prospect of publicly purchasing this needed product and from discussing it with strangers. Cultural context, not characterological pathology, explained all.

---

[13] For a helpful brochure on "How to choose a psychologist," contact the American Psychological Association, 750 First Street, NE, Washington, DC 20002-4242, http://www.apa.org.

[14] For an excellent enactment of a feminist therapy session, see "Feminist Therapy" featuring Laura Brown (available from the American Psychological Association's Psychotherapy Videotape Series).

[15] A careful and thorough rationale for each of these principles is offered by Louise Fitzgerald and Roberta Nutt (1986). They also should be evident from much of our earlier discussions throughout this book.

A feminist approach to doing therapy emphasizes making the personal political and vice versa, links gender with other forms of oppression and to power, and privileges women's experiences.

Approaching therapy with the realization that "the personal is political" highlights the view that individual experience does not take place in a vacuum, but rather is informed by the social and cultural context in which it takes place (Brown, 1994a). In this framework, what happens to individual women often reflects broader sociopolitical forces that devalue women and women's experiences, including racism (Comas-Díaz, 1988), ableism (Prilleltensky, 1996), classism, ageism, and so on. Making linkages between individual experiences ("the personal") and general trends that affect many women ("the political") connects women to other women and makes public these common bonds. Consciousness raising becomes a legitimate and important part of individual and group therapy designed to help women relate their personal difficulties to social context (Marecek & Hare-Mustin, 1991).

Although the common bonds that associate one woman's experiences with others' are critical for making connections between the personal and the political, this linkage must be balanced against honoring each client's unique experiences of reality (Brown, 1994a). Just as individualism without context can limit our understanding of women's full lives, so can context without the individual serve to invalidate the personal. Just because other women experience rape, for example, raising serious questions about who has power and how it is used, an individual woman's experience of and coping with such trauma cannot be discounted because of these broader connections. A critical dynamic in feminist therapy is to negotiate this balance.

> Principle 2. Counselors/therapists are aware that the assumptions and precepts of theories relevant to their practice may apply differently to men and women. Counselors/therapists are aware of those theories and models that prescribe or limit the potential of women clients, as well as those that may have particular usefulness for women clients.

We have examined androcentric bias, the assumption that what men do is normative, throughout this book, so that it is no surprise that feminist therapy should react against this as well. A revealing tale of how this bias can infiltrate therapy is told through some uses of psychological tests (Brown, 1994a, Chapter 7). The most widely used psychological test, for example, the Minnesota Multiphasic Personality Inventory (MMPI), routinely overdiagnoses people of color, especially African Americans, as paranoid; raises questions about sexual orientation based on deviations from gender stereotypes; and can label people with progressive political views as pathologically deviant. Although feminist therapists have used the MMPI as a diagnostic tool for uncovering some cases of abuse by intimates (M.A. Dutton, 1992; Rosewater, 1985), some common interpretations can support androcentrism.

Laura Brown (1994a) describes how the MMPI and other male-as-norm biases influenced a custody case of "Alina," a Middle Eastern woman married to a white, American man. Although he had verbally abused both Alina and their children, he came across fine on the MMPI and Rorschach (inkblot) tests; in court he appeared cool, calm, and collected. In contrast, Alina expressed anger that her husband left her for another woman; she tested as a "mixed personality disorder with histrionic and borderline features." The custody case was swinging toward the abusive father. The feminist therapist consulted by Alina convinced the courts to initiate another series of obviously more relevant tests by sending observers to watch parent-children interactions. Even knowing that he was being observed, the father verbally berated his children, disparaged their mother to them, used age-inappropriate language, allowed them to play with potentially dangerous objects, and failed to respond appropriately to their needs. In contrast, the presumably mentally disordered woman behaved as a loving and responsive mother. The court's final judgment favored the mother.

> Principle 3. After formal training, counselors/therapists continue to explore and learn of issues related to women, including the special problems of female subgroups, throughout their professional careers.

The importance of postgraduate training for therapists seems obvious, but a somewhat less obvious point concerns the responsibility of therapists, not clients, to provide such training. Feminist therapists agree that the responsibility for continuing education rests on the shoulders of the therapist, not the client (Porter, 1995). Julia Boyd (1990), an African American therapist, describes the "homework" she did in advance of sessions with a Southeast Asian woman. Her background work paid off as she was able to integrate what the client revealed with what she had learned about the value of family loyalty and harmony between self and nature in Asian culture. The result was a more culturally sensitive and ultimately affected treatment for this client's depression. The availability of a growing body of feminist resources for such training has facilitated this process for therapists (see for example, Brown & Root, 1990; Comas-Díaz & Greene, 1994).

> Principle 4. Counselors/therapists recognize and are aware of all forms of oppression and how these interact with sexism.

Sexism is experienced differently by different women because it combines with other forms of oppression. This point is so central to doing feminist therapy that I have purposively selected examples that incorporate multiple, intertwined forms of oppression.

Consider the case of "Maria," a 30-year-old woman of Cuban American descent involved in a physically abusive relationship with her lesbian partner, "Susana" (Kanuha, 1994). Violence was hard for outsiders to see in this relationship both because the nature of the relationship itself was disguised as nonintimate to avoid homophobic reactions and because women are stereotypically regarded as nonviolent. Susana maintained power over Maria by threatening to "out" her to her employer and family, potentially disrupting the strong family bonds of Maria's Latina culture. Sensitivity to multiple forms of oppression and how they worked together in Maria's life were needed by this therapist to work effectively with her.

> Principle 5. Counselors/therapists are knowledgeable and aware of verbal and nonverbal process variables (particularly with regard to power in the relationship) as these affect women in counseling/therapy so that the counselor/therapist interactions are not adversely affected. The need for shared responsibility between clients and counselors/therapists is acknowledged and implemented.

A key component of feminist therapy revolves around issues of power in the therapist-client relationship itself. The therapist's role encompasses the power to label and to act as an authority, both in reality and symbolically; the well-educated and often relatively affluent position of the therapist may contribute to status differences; and other sociodemographic differences can tip the balance of power. The therapist-client relationship can be used to explore issues of unequal power that then can be generalized to other settings. This may be especially poignant for women with physical disabilities, many of whom experience powerlessness in their interactions with institutional, medical, and bureaucratic settings as well as within interpersonal relationships (Prilleltensky, 1996). Ironically, failure to acknowledge one's power as a therapist can be related to the abuse of this power (Brown, 1994a).

> Principle 6. Counselors/therapists have the capability of utilizing skills that are particularly facilitative to women in general and to particular subgroups of women.

This principle charges feminist therapists to continually expand their repertoire of therapeutic techniques so that they can tailor their use to specific clients. For example, Lillian Comas-Díaz (1994) explores the concept of womanhood for many women of color who define themselves as women, not as autonomous individuals, but rather within the contexts of extended units such as family and community. Given this, she has found family narratives to be a useful therapeutic technique. These cultural stories include family history as well as describe values, lessons, the client's place in the network, and so on. In one example, Comas-Díaz describes a client who reported sudden fears of falling (among other problems), part of which could be traced to a family "lesson" learned from a beloved sister who fell to her death. Part of the therapy process allowed this client to grieve for her sister, and provided reassurances as well about the likely safety of the client's daughter, now the age of the client's sister when she died.

> Principle 7. Counselors/therapists ascribe no preconceived limitations on the direction or nature of potential changes or goals in counseling/therapy for women.

This principle raises serious questions about the goals of therapy and who sets them. Feminist therapists have reacted strongly to a history of misogynous practice wherein women were expected to adjust to oppressive situations rather than work to change them or leave them. The most egregious examples came in settings of abuse where women were urged to "stand by their man," learn not to aggravate him, and, in essence, to be a "good wife." These pressures are especially strong for women of color who want to avoid becoming just another oppressor in their men's already oppressed lives (Greene, 1994b).

What happens when the client's goals conflict with the therapist's (also see Parvin & Biaggio, 1991)? Consider the following woman's disappointment with her therapist:

> One time, after I had recounted a recent incident of my husband's unpredictable and explosive anger, my therapist asked me, "Why do you stay in this relationship?" I explained quite calmly that I had thought about this a lot and decided that in another relationship things could be a lot worse, e.g., substance abuse, violence, physical absence and abandonment, etc. My therapist breathed a deep sigh and almost seemed to bow and shake his head in disgust, disbelief, or sorrow. There was no verbal support for my statement, not even acknowledgment! I felt robbed and cheated. If this was my decision, why didn't I get help to better carry it out? Instead, I felt that I was being castigated by my therapist for not being more independent or assertive in my relationship (Mowbray, 1995, p. 18).

Does this mean that feminist therapists have to accept client's wishes regardless of their beliefs (and arguably, regardless of what many would say are in the best interests of the client)? Additionally, might a therapist's revulsion toward violence conflict with cultural settings which find such behavior "acceptable," or at least widespread enough to be almost normative? Although feminist therapists agree that violence against women is oppressive and intolerable regardless of a women's social or cultural background, therapists' approaches to dealing with it need not be rooted in American, masculine models of self-determination and autonomy (Ho, 1990).

For example, Melba Vasquez (1994) describes how she used a Latina woman's wanting to care for others, not *against* her by labeling her dependent, but *for* her by encouraging her to extend these principles of caring toward herself (and, through herself, toward her children). This approach validated her caring and connection to others and simultaneously enhanced her self-esteem and personal empowerment—necessary ingredients to terminating abuse from within the relationship or by leaving it. Christine Ho (1990) suggests that strong family ties and a hierarchy of elders in Asian communities can be employed to abused women's advantage by drawing on these resources for support and to intercede on their behalf. This paints a much more complex picture of how feminist therapists can work for their clients by working respectfully with, not against, them.

> Principle 8. Counselors/therapists are sensitive to circumstances where it is more desirable for a woman client to be seen by a female or male counselor/therapist.

This guideline raises concerns about the sociodemographic match between a therapist and a client. Some feminist therapy theorists have argued quite persuasively that women clients should see women therapists (Cammaert & Larsen, 1988; Sturdivant, 1980), even arguing that therapists and clients be matched on other qualities, such as sexual orientation and race and ethnicity.[16] Oliva Espín (1994) notes that such specific matches are advantageous because they facilitate firsthand understanding, promote the therapist as a role model, reduce some unequalizing status differences, and heighten the therapist's investment in the client's success. Indeed, she provides a case in point whereby a Latina client was empowered by her Latina therapist's aversion to domestic violence. For this client, having a Latina challenge what the client regarded as a pervasive acceptance of violence in her community benefited her therapeutic progress.

The reality though, acknowledged by Espín, is that matches are not always available nor do they ensure cultural sensitivity. In these cases, feminist therapy must work with these differences. For example, a major obstacle that may stand in the way of white women therapists' effectiveness with clients of color is a misunderstanding of the role of racism in their clients' everyday lives. For many white women, the impact of race on their own lives, while far from nonexistent, is invisible (Frankenberg, 1993; Roman, 1993).[17] For white women therapists to work sensitively with clients of color, they must understand the privileges afforded by their race in American culture, acknowledge the role of racism in their clients' lives, and actively engage in self-education (Espín, 1994; Rave, 1990).

> Principle 9. Counselors/therapists use nonsexist language in counseling/therapy, supervision, teaching, and journal publications.

The primary goal of this principle is to eliminate blatantly sexist treatment beginning with language—a laudable goal. However, nonsexism is far from synonymous with feminism. A nonsexist approach presumably is gender-neutral or gender-inclusive: the gender-neutral ignores gender; the gender-inclusive fails to be responsive to differences between the experiences and social contexts of women and men. In contrast, feminist therapy puts gender front-and-center in our analyses.

Carol Mowbray (1995) uses examples from actual cases contributed by members of a Michigan state committee on women's mental health issues to illustrate how practices by ostensibly *nonsexist* therapists inadvertently can be *nonfeminist* in their effect by ignoring the contexts of women's lives, imbalances of power between therapists and clients, and the importance of self-determination for women. Consider the following woman's frustration with her therapy which ignores the context of her life:

---

[16] Also often implicit in these discussions is the assumption that clients in feminist therapy should be restricted to women, although feminist therapy with men has been described (for example, see Ganley, 1988).

[17] The privilege of white racial status is made very clear in an article by Peggy McIntosh (1995). Her approach can be readily extended to privileges associated with other forms of dominant status, including heterosexuality, able-bodiness, being Christian, and so on. My experience with this approach is that students want to shift discussion away from privilege to oppression, but dogged persistence with the former leads to some eye-opening revelations.

We were a two-career couple. I had a 50-hour a week job that was responsible, stressful, and demanding. Yet, I also had the major responsibility for childcare and family functioning in economic and social arenas. A major part of the communication problems that brought us into marital therapy was a smoldering resentment over these inequities, that kindled into explosive anger in conflicted or stressful circumstances. Yet we never had a discussion in therapy or set goals around redistributing the inequities and lowering my underlying hostility. When I raised these concerns, the discussion always reverted back to how I could better communicate my feelings. Yet, no matter how much I worked on better communication, the inequities in the relationship still did not change (Mowbray, 1995, pp. 15–16).

The structure and function of the family, especially regarding gender roles and power, go unanalyzed and pass without confrontation in this gender-neutral approach. This creates an outcome (maintenance of gendered inequities in this interpersonal relationship) that is far from feminist (Kaschak, 1990). In contrast, a feminist therapist would ask questions that simultaneously challenge the domestic arrangements of this couple, the patriarchal hierarchy that has come to characterize the American family, and the devaluation of household work.

> Principle 10. Counselors/therapists do not engage in sexual activity with their women clients under any circumstances.

The more general point here focuses on setting boundaries in the therapist-client relationship. Although there are egregious examples of boundary violations (such as sexual contact), that are never acceptable within a therapeutic relationship, ethical questions arise about what constitutes appropriate behavior. Is it right to ask a client to take her or his therapist to pick up a car at the repair shop? Should a therapist hug a distraught client? Laura Brown (1994b) explores such boundary confusion by first debunking three myths, concluding instead that (1) there are no clear, universal rules detailing appropriate and inappropriate behavior; (2) that boundary violations are not always easy to detect; and (3) it is possible to violate boundaries even if rigid rules are followed to the letter.

Rather than constructing lists of do's and don'ts, Brown argues that we must understand the basic characteristics of unethical boundary violations to lessen the risks of committing them. Although clients are the ultimate determiners of when lines have been crossed, they are not the sole arbitrators of this decision. Rather, the *responsibility* for maintaining appropriate boundaries rests with therapists.

Boundaries are crossed when the client is objectified, when the therapist acts from impulse, and when the needs of the therapist come before those of the client. Clients can be objectified when they are used by therapists to teach them (for example, about their different cultural experiences), to entertain them, and to listen to the emotional disclosures of the therapist. Therapists act impulsively, not when they draw on intuition, but when they act without diagnostic clarity, that is, without thinking through the impact of their actions on their client.

Regarding therapists' needs, therapists always must play a supporting role in relation to their clients, relinquishing center stage. For example, Julia Boyd (1990) relates how a white woman therapist's preoccupation with her African American woman client's rape alienated the client whose most pressing, immediate concern was the robbery that accompanied her rape and stripped her of her last $25. Brown offers this conceptual analysis of boundaries as a means from which therapists and each of their clients can work together to define and maintain appropriate boundaries specific to their own relationship.

> Principle 11. Counselors/therapists are aware of and continually review their own values and biases and the effects of these on their women clients. Counselors/therapists understand the effects of sex-role socialization upon their own development and functioning and the consequent values and attitudes they hold for themselves and others. They recognize that behaviors and roles need not be sex-based.

This principle, like the others, extends to a full multicultural understanding. For example, the roles of ritual and spirituality in women's lives may be overlooked by some therapists. Teresa LaFromboise and her colleagues (1994) describe how a Navajo woman's interpersonal problems and alcohol abuse declined remarkably after she ritually disposed of her mother's ashes, freeing her mother's as well as her own spirit. Julia Boyd (1990) cites Latina women who return to using their native language, American Indian women who turn to purification rights, and African American women who find solace in religion as sources of personal strength that should not be discounted by feminist therapists.

> Principle 12. Counselors/therapists are aware of how their personal functioning may influence their effectiveness in counseling/therapy with women clients. They monitor their functioning through consultation, supervision, or therapy so that it does not adversely affect their work with women clients.

The point here is not to confuse the issues of the therapist with those of the client. Lillian Comas-Díaz (1994) describes a case in point. A Jewish woman Holocaust survivor as therapist was matched with an American Indian woman as client on the basis of their shared cultural experience as targets of genocide. The client elected not to continue this relationship beyond initial contact because the therapist drew so many parallels between their ethnic commonalties that she failed to acknowledge differences, such as the role alcoholism played in the American Indian woman's community. This therapist did not move beyond her own issues to relate to the uniqueness of those of her client.

> Principle 13. Counselors/therapists support the elimination of sex bias within institutions and individuals.

A central goal for feminist psychotherapy is to empower women—to help women gain control of their lives (Espín, 1994). Such empowerment assists women to be aware of the deleterious effects of sexism and other forms of oppression; to perceive themselves as agents for solving their own problems; to understand how the personal is political; and to work toward broader, societal change. This last part of empowerment moves both the therapist and the client beyond individual change (psychotherapy) to social change. A distinguishing feature of feminist therapy is the realization not only that the personal is political, but that the political is personal.

In other words, with personal empowerment comes the responsibility to actively work for social changes that promote the well-being of women in general. How feminists do this depends on the form of feminism they espouse because there are multiple approaches to doing feminism, as discussed in Chapter 1 (Brown, 1994a). This challenge will be the major focus of the final chapter of this book.

CHAPTER SUMMARY

Throughout this chapter, we have taken a critical look at the existing medical model of "mental disorders" as embodied in the DSM-IV. We saw that this model yields similar overall prevalence rates for women and men, but that gendered patterns emerge for specific diagnoses, including agoraphobia, alcohol and substance abuse, depression, eating disorders, and three personality disorders (borderline, histrionic, and dependent).

In contrast to the assumptions of the DSM which root the causes for these gender differences exclusively in women's and men's biologies or within their psyches, a feminist perspective shifts our focus to consider definitional ambiguities surrounding what is and is not deemed pathological, to move beyond exclusively biological explanations and drug treatments, and to explore extra-psychic influences such as the infiltration of gender stereotypes into definitions of disorders, stereotyped therapists' judgments, and neglected contextual factors. These contextual influences may include threats to women's self-esteem, interpersonal stress, body dissatisfaction, physical illness, finances and employment, acculturation, and direct, indirect, and insidious forms of trauma.

We also reviewed a general feminist approach to practice that encompasses principles explicated by a variety of feminist therapy theorists. Throughout this review of theory of feminist practice and exemplary cases, we have stressed the importance of making the personal political and vice versa, of linking gender with other forms of oppression and to power, and of privileging women's experiences so that they move from the margins of therapy theorizing to center stage. By both critiquing traditional approaches to "mental disorders" and offering an alternative approach (feminist therapy), we are striving to develop theory and practice in psychology that will work effectively and sensitively for all women whose true psychological pain must be considered at the heart of these discussions.

ELEVEN

MALE VIOLENCE AGAINST GIRLS AND WOMEN
Linking Fears of Violence, Harassment, Rape, and Abuse

Anita wants to take a class at a local community college but it's scheduled at night in a neighborhood with which she is unfamiliar and which would require a long bus ride. She calls her friends to see if she can recruit someone to take the class with her, but no one is both available and interested. She decides to take something different (based on Riger & Gordon, 1981).

Barbara was on the subway the other day and a man kept making insulting remarks to her, calling her a snobbish Black slut. He didn't touch her, but Barbara left the train feeling sick, fearful, and disgusted (adapted from Kelly & Radford, 1996, p. 24).

Mary was a freshman science major at a large university. She took a student assistant position in a science department to support herself financially. One of her professors began stopping by her desk, leaning over and touching her breasts "accidentally" while talking about her course work. Fearing for her grade and her job, she remained silent. At the end of the semester she filed a letter of complaint and quietly left school (Quina & Carlson, 1989, p. 8).

Irene recalled, "While I was a little girl of nine, my mom went into the hospital, and it became up to me to run the household. My father drank for the two weeks Mom was away. During this time, my father first began to sexually abuse me. He told me that if I did Mom's work, I had to sleep in her place. This continued until I finally left the house at age eighteen. I tried several times to tell my mom but she never believed me" (Quina & Carlson, 1989, p. 6).

Carol was seventeen, and a virgin. She had dated Andrew for two years when he was drafted into military service. The night before he left, she visited his home. Although she didn't normally drink, he persuaded her to share a "toast." Soon she felt dizzy and had to lie down. With his sister and mother in another part of the house, Andrew raped her (Quina & Carlson, 1989, p. 4).

Elaine married a man she had dated for seven months. He had been rough physically on occasion before they were married, but now he seemed more aggressive. One night, he hid in the house when she came home from work and viciously attacked her. He held a gun while he raped her, saying he "performed better." The next day he was gentle and sweet. This assault was to be repeated every few months until Elaine left him (Quina & Carlson, 1989, p. 4).

A man fired eight bullets at two women backpacking on the Appalachian Trail in south central Pennsylvania in 1988. The lone survivor describes the murderer: "He shot from where he was hidden in the woods 85 feet away, after he stalked us, hunted us, spied on us. . . . He shot us because he identified us as lesbians. He was a stranger with whom we had no connection. He shot us and left us for dead" (Brenner, 1992, p. 12).

On December 6, 1989, a 25-year-old man carrying a hunting rifle burst into an engineering school at the University of Montreal. In some classes, he forced women to line up against one wall; men against another. He clearly expressed his intent to kill feminists. He left a three-page statement blaming feminists for his problems and targeting 15 women, none of whom he found at the school. In the end, he left 14 women dead before he killed himself (Stato, 1993).

Each of the examples above describes some form of psychological, verbal, physical or sexual violence directed against women by men. Each can be subsumed under the working definition of male violence against women used by a task force formed by the American Psychological Association in 1991: "physical, visual, verbal, or sexual acts that are experienced by a woman or girl as a threat, invasion, or assault and that have the effect of hurting her or degrading her and/or taking away her ability to control contact (intimate and otherwise) with another individual" (Koss,

Goodman, Browne, Fitzgerald, Keita, & Russo, 1994). Each involves increasing physical harm ranging from restricted activity for Anita because of fear of violence to the outright murder of women for being women. In between, we find women victimized by other forms of abuse: Barbara by sexist and racist verbal abuse; Mary by sexual harassment at school and work; Irene by childhood sexual abuse; Carol by acquaintance rape; and Elaine by wife abuse and rape. Even mild incidents can escalate suddenly to become more severe forms of violence.

Although each experience is unique to the woman who undergoes it, each of these types of violence against women is linked by common threads that weave a broader tapestry of violence and its consequences for all women. Because of this, violence is not a singular experience; rather it connects all women through their universal vulnerability (Griffin, 1971). This theme of interconnections, among these different forms of violence, among women as targets and potential targets of violence, and between violence and societal-wide male dominance over women, will be echoed throughout this chapter.

We will examine four forms of male violence against women: sexual harassment, rape, male partner abuse, and childhood sexual abuse.[1] We shall see that these are linked by four general themes: (1) problems with defining and talking about male violence against women; (2) debates about incidence and prevalence; (3) invisibility resulting in claims of invalidation; and (4) serious physical and psychological consequences, not only for victims themselves but for women in general.

By limiting our focus to male violence against women, I do not invalidate violence directed at men. However, violence by women against men is not sustained by societal power differences. What happens to individual men does not seep over into men's awareness; it doesn't create general fears of violence and thus restricting their behaviors. Many more women can relate to Anita's experience at the start of this chapter than can men. As for men's victimization of other men, oftentimes this is framed in de-masculinizing ways that "reduce" male victims to "girls"—directly linking such violence with misogyny (woman-hating) and homophobia and therefore with the present discussion.

DEFINING AND TALKING ABOUT VIOLENCE

Before we go on to discuss the complexities of defining and talking about different forms of violence, let's stop for a moment and consider two: sexual harassment and rape. Imagine an incident of each. What are the features of each that make you think of them as examples of sexual harassment and rape?

All forms of male violence against women share some definitional ambiguity where the cutoff between acceptable and abusive behavior is vague. What constitutes sexual harassment, rape, and male partner abuse all have been challenged. These ambiguities carry over into discussions of incidence and prevalence (how often vio-

---

[1] This necessarily is a limited survey of violence targeting women. A more comprehensive, global perspective might include bride burnings, genital mutilation, forced prostitution and trafficking, skewed birth patterns resulting from aborted female fetuses and infanticide, forced sterilization, rape in war, and so on. For an overview of the global health consequences of rape, see Koss, Heise, and Russo (1994).

lence occurs) because without consensus about what constitutes each form of violence, measurement is compromised and discussion gets bogged down in a quagmire of competing definitions. Sexual harassment, rape, and male partner abuse provide good examples of this process. Sexual harassment and rape are most simply approached by attempts to detail specific, verifiable behavioral indicators.

Behavioral Indicators

Sexual harassment on the basis of sex is a violation of Sec. 703 of Title VII of the U.S. Civil Rights Act. According to the Equal Employment Opportunity Commission (EEOC, 1980, cited in Fitzgerald & Ormerod, 1993), sexual harassment involves unwelcome advances, requests for sexual favors, and other verbal or physical contact of a sexual nature when submission is made, implicitly or explicitly, a condition of employment; when submission or rejection affects employment decisions; and when such conduct interferes unreasonably with work performance or creates an intimidating, hostile, or offensive working environment.

This legal definition sets up two distinct types of **sexual harassment**: *quid pro quo,* which is characterized by the dominant power position occupied by the perpetrator who can reward or punish the target, and *hostile work environment,* which involves unwanted behavior that creates a chilling work or educational climate. Seven behavioral indicators of sexual harassment were developed for a major study of federal employees by the U.S. Merit Systems Protection Board (1987): unwanted sexual teasing, jokes, or remarks; unwanted sexual looks or gestures; unwanted deliberate touching; unwanted pressure for dates; pressure for sexual favors; unwanted letters, calls, or sexual materials; and actual or attempted rape or assault. Do these define the incident you imagined as sexually harassing?

The traditional common-law definition of rape is "carnal knowledge of a female forcibly and against her will" (cited in Koss, Goodman et al., 1994, p. 159). In some states in the United States, rape is behaviorally limited to penile-vaginal penetration, but others extend their statutes to include anal and oral intercourse and penetration with objects (Muehlenhard et al., 1992). The definition of **rape** used by the APA Task Force on Male Violence Against Women is: "nonconsensual oral, anal, or vaginal penetration, obtained by force, by threat of bodily harm, or when the victim is incapable of giving consent" (Koss, 1993). All definitions include some notion that the sexual acts are nonconsensual (Muehlenhard et al., 1992).

Perceptions of Violence

The inclusion of "unwanted" and "nonconsensual" elements in definitions of both sexual harassment and rape moves our discussion beyond behaviors themselves to subjective judgments of participants' intentions. This takes us into the realm of perceptions, asking questions about the criteria for establishing nonconsent, the relationship of the victim to the assailant, and who decides whether or not sexual assault has occurred (Muehlenhard et al., 1992).

Regarding criteria for establishing consent in rape, a recent survey of college students finds that the majority support a definition that assumes "yes" until "no" is stated, and that when nonconsent is verbalized, "no" means "no," not "maybe" (Turk & Muehlenhard, 1991, cited in Muehlenhard et al., 1992). As we saw in Chapter 7, the woman's "no" is jeopardized by dating scripts that envision the man as sexual aggressor and the woman as desirous, but virtuously hesitant. Still, other factors can render consent questionable (e.g., intoxication), meaningless (e.g., consent given under duress), or impossible (e.g., a drugged victim).[2]

Turning to the relationship between victim and perpetrator, is marital rape an oxymoron? Consider the 1992 court case of a husband who took videotapes of himself tying up his wife, despite her clear protests, slapping her, taping her eyes and mouth shut, and raping her as she screamed. His attorney told the jury that her screams could be screams of pleasure. They must have agreed because he was found not guilty of rape (Bart & Moran, 1993). The line between marital sexuality and rape may not seem blurry to many feminists, but there still are states which do not outlaw marital rape (but permit assault prosecution, which is a misdemeanor, not a felony) or consider it a lesser offense than the same acts perpetrated by a stranger (Ledray, 1994). This legal ambiguity (reflective of broader social uncertainties) helps cloud definitions of rape when the perpetrator is an intimate or even an acquaintance of the victim.

The third point focuses on who decides whether or not sexual harassment or rape has occurred? Fears of false reporting fuel arguments against relying on victims' claims alone, but there is other, more compelling evidence to call into question such a singular approach. Additionally, what happens when the views of victims and perpetrators conflict? Let's explore how psychologists have addressed each of these still unresolved issues.

Victims know. For various reasons that we'll discuss later, it is not uncommon for victims of violence not to acknowledge their victimization. Women may check off behavioral indicators of sexual harassment but deny having been so victimized (Saunders, 1992, cited in Koss, Goodman et al., 1994). Some battered women also are uncertain about naming their victimization. Michele Fine describes interviews she and her colleagues conducted with women survivors of male battering. Sometimes women distance themselves from researchers' labels:

> Not me. I'm not a battered woman. Battered women have bruises all over their bodies. Two broken legs. And he's not a batterer, not like I seen them. No, he just hits me too much (Fine, 1993, p. 282).

Women may resist being categorized as battered because they do not feel helpless, they hit back, or they are ambivalent about their lover and their relationship—all dis-

---

[2] For example, Rohypnol (pronounced row-hip-nole) is a legally manufactured sedative-hypnotic used for short-term treatment of sleep disorders. Available in the U.S. as a cheap ($2–3/pill) street drug in the 1990s, especially in Florida, California, and Texas, "roachies," "rophies," or "rope" produce, within 20–30 minutes of ingestion, a sedative effect including amnesia, muscle relaxation, and slowing of psychomotor performance that lasts for about 8 hours. Most frequently users take it to simulate or enhance "drunkenness," although its use has been implicated in date rape causing some universities to warn women not to drink from open beverages at group parties. Check out various web sites for more information (e.g., http://www.ocs.mq.edu.au/~korman/feminism/rohypnol.html), or stop by a campus Women's Center.

tinctions that make them dissociate themselves from the stereotype of "battered woman."

A large-scale study of acquaintance rape on college campuses is summarized in a book aptly name, *I Never Called It Rape,* because it is common for victims of rape by known assailants not to name their experiences as rape (Warshaw, 1994). Stereotypes of rape include images of strangers using excessive aggression and force, features which often do not characterize acquaintance rape (Parrot, 1991). Did you imagine a rape at the beginning of this section that involved a "crazed" stranger? In one sample of college students, for example, fully 43% of women who met the behavioral criteria for rape did not label their own experience as such (Koss, 1985). In a vignette study describing physical resistance and intercourse, fully 47% of college students did not label the date's aggressive behavior as rape (Hannon et al., 1996). In a survey with over 3,000 employed women, rates of unacknowledged rape or attempted rape ran as high as 59% (Koss et al., 1996).

Comparing acknowledged and unacknowledged rape victims, no differences were found in dating behaviors; different aspects of the rape experience; reactions; victims' personality; attitudes about rape (Koss, 1985); or resistance strategies (Levine-MacCombie & Koss, 1986). Unacknowledged rape victims are more likely to have been raped by an acquaintance (Koss, 1985) and to possess more violent, stranger-perpetrated rape scripts (Kahn, Mathie, & Torgler, 1994). All this points to the power of rape stereotypes in framing others' and even victims' own perceptions of rape. Extending this logic to marital rape, attitudes about sexuality in marriage that stress husbands' sexual rights and domination further serve to compromise women's acknowledgment of marital rape (Muehlenhard & Schrag, 1991).

Victim-perpetrator discrepancies. Do women and men perceive violence similarly? Generally there is consensus among women and men about harassment that involves severe behaviors and is perpetrated by an authority with power over the victim *(quid pro quo)* (Gutek & O'Connor, 1995). However, definitional ambiguities arise in the murky area of hostile work environment and with milder behaviors. Although there are differences among women and also among men as to how they evaluate specific incidents, men overall tend to hold a narrower definition of what constitutes bona fide harassment (reviewed by Fitzgerald, 1993).

Barbara Gutek and Maureen O'Connor (1995) describe three conditions, relevant to real-life settings, that reduce agreement among observers. First, people who work in sexualized environments tend to become habituated to it so that they label only the most blatant incidents as harassing. This pattern is especially true among higher-status initiators who are oblivious to their power and its effect on others (Bargh & Raymond, 1992). Second, the perceived complicity of the victim decreases consensus. Third, when evaluators aren't cued to think about harassment, more disagreement between women and men arises. All these point to contextual cues that make people more or less sensitive to the possibility of harassment (Fiske & Glick, 1995). Although these contextual cues are likely to distinguish women from men, they certainly do not need to do so. If men are sensitized to what women consider harassing, these contextually created differences could well disappear. Indeed, an educational intervention designed to sensitize participants to incidents of sexual harassment evened out initial gender differences (Bonate & Jessell, 1996).

Parallel reasoning emerges from an analysis of gender differences in acknowledgment of acquaintance rape. Consider the differing perceptions of Bob and Patty in the following scenario:

> BOB: Patty and I were in the same statistics class together. She usually sat near me and was always very friendly. I liked her and thought she liked me, too. Last Thursday I decided to find out. After class I suggested that she come to my place to study for midterms together. She agreed immediately, which was a good sign. That night everything seemed to go perfectly. We studied for a while and then took a break. I could tell that she liked me, and I was attracted to her. I was getting excited. I started kissing her. I could tell that she really liked it. We started touching each other and it felt really good. All of a sudden she pulled away and said "Stop." I figured she didn't want me to think she was "easy" or "loose." A lot of girls think they have to say "no" at first. I knew once I showed her what a good time she could have, and that I would respect her in the morning, it would be OK. I just ignored her protests and eventually she stopped struggling. I think she liked it but afterwards she acted bummed out and cold. Who knows what her problem was?

> PATTY: I knew Bob from my statistics class. He's cute and we are both good at statistics, so when a tough midterm was scheduled, I was glad that he suggested we study together. It never occurred to me that it was anything except a study date. That night everything went fine at first, we got a lot of studying done in a short amount of time, so when he suggested we take a break I thought we deserved it. Well, all of a sudden he started acting really romantic and started kissing me. I liked the kissing but then he started touching me below the waist. I pulled away and tried to stop him but he didn't listen. After a while I stopped struggling; he was hurting me and I was scared. He was so much bigger and stronger than me. I couldn't believe it was happening to me. I didn't know what to do. He actually forced me to have sex with him. I guess looking back on it I should have screamed or done something besides trying to reason with him but it was so unexpected. I couldn't believe it was happening. I still can't believe it did (Hughes & Sandler, 1987, p. 1).

The difference in Bob's and Patty's points of view is substantiated by research showing that men perceive more sexual intent in others than do women (Abbey, 1991; Shotland, 1989).

Naming Violence

Without the right words to describe what has happened, victims can be left without a way to talk, or even think, about their victimization. Indeed the terms we use to name male violence against women are relatively new—no one discussed sexual harassment until the 1980s and marital rape was considered an oxymoron. The terms battered woman, sexual harassment, marital rape, and date rape were all developed in the past 20 or so years to help women label their experiences (McHugh, Frieze, & Browne, 1993).

The language we use to discuss and describe violence also is important to consider. As we saw in Chapter 4, the language we use can shape how we think about a phenomenon. Of key concern to feminists working in this area is how to think about women who are targeted for violence (Koss, Goodman et al., 1994). The term *victim* rightfully places responsibility for violence on the perpetrator and captures the severity of the violence that has occurred. However, it also implies that the recipient is passive and forever damaged by the violation. The term *survivor* overcomes the latter problem, but implies that the violence has passed, ignoring the repetition of violence in some women's lives (e.g., women who are chronically terrorized by their partners) and the long-term consequences of violence. Furthermore, people survive acts of nature as well as acts of violence, but only the violent acts are purposively perpetrated. First, I acknowledge these shortcomings with the terminology. Second, in terms of women's coping with violence, self-labeling that moves from *victim* to *survivor* may be an important step toward recovery (Quina & Carlson, 1989). I will keep this second point in mind throughout the present chapter with my use of these terms.

How we talk about the physical abuse of women by male intimates offers a case in point. Overall, two different approaches to male partner abuse have dominated this literature (Kurz, 1989): the family violence perspective offered by Murray Straus, Richard Gelles, and Suzanne Steinmetz (1980) and a feminist approach (for example, see Stanko, 1985; Yllö & Bograd, 1988; L.E.A. Walker, 1994).

Family violence theorists consider what they call "spouse abuse" or "family violence" to be part of a general pattern involving violence among all family members. Central to their thesis are data suggesting equivalent amounts of violence committed by husbands and wives against each other and toward their children, by children against parents, and among siblings (Straus, 1997). This approach focuses on the family as the central unit of analysis; highlights stresses faced by contemporary families; regards the family as accepting of violence as a means for solving conflict; and cites the power of men over women in the family, as well as in society at large, as a cause of violence. Furthermore, they believe that power in the family can be shared equally by women and men. In support of their proposed relationship between egalitarianism and nonviolence, they cite evidence that abuse occurs least frequently in democratic households. The policy recommendations they offer concentrate on changing societal norms that legitimate and glorify violence—a generally laudable goal.

Feminist refinements to family violence theory have challenged their basic assumptions. Central to this challenge are interpretations of data suggesting equal rates of violence by wives and husbands. These findings rely on surveys of participation rates and measurements of violence using the Conflict Tactics Scale, which simply counts violent acts ranging from swearing to brandishing a gun. Given this framework, a woman who pushes is labeled as violent, just as a man who chokes. Nothing is recorded about intent to harm, amount of harm inflicted, who initiated the exchange, what was done in self-defense, and how much risk was perceived by each (Koss, Goodman et al., 1994; Kurz, 1997). When these qualifiers are factored in, men engage in more severe forms of violence and are more likely to perpetrate multiple aggressive acts; in contrast, women sustain more injuries, feel more threatened, and respond in self-defense. This analysis readily extends to dating violence as well (Sugarman & Hotaling, 1989). Such a feminist reconceptualization of the full context of violence reframes it from a gender-neutral view that focuses on the family as the unit of analysis to one that views men as perpetrators and women as not-so-passive victims. For feminist theorists, male-female power relations are placed front-and-center in their analyses.

This highlighting of gendered relationships raises questions about power dynamics and the use of violence as a means for establishing and maintaining control and dominance. It also questions why women are the more frequent victims of abuse. This reframing moves the discourse about adult abuse by intimates out of the family (where violence against women is thought of as just another example of family violence) into discussions of other forms of male violence against women. Such refocusing paves the way for inclusion of male partner abuse in discussions (such as the present one) focused on rape, sexual harassment, and other forms of social control and male dominance (Kurz, 1989).

The language we use to describe psychological, physical, and sexual abuse in intimate relationships must reflect the basic assumptions of the feminist perspective outlined above. Such a perspective dismisses gender-neutral terms, such as "spousal abuse" and "family violence." An improved (but still far from satisfactory) compromise has been to use the term "wife abuse" to capture both the gendered nature of the violence and its harm. The obvious difficulty with this terminology is that it doesn't include nonmarital abuse in heterosexual cohabiting and dating relationships. This suggests the term "partner abuse" which encompasses lesbian partners. Aggression among lesbian couples is far from nonexistent (estimates as high as 40% have been offered) (Bologna, Waterman, & Dawson, 1987). However, lesbian relationships are free of gendered cultural differences in power that characterize the types of violence reviewed in this chapter, so that violence within lesbian relationships does not produce generalized fears among women (Koss, Goodman et al., 1994).[3] Women do not restrict their behaviors from fear of being attacked by lesbians. For all these reasons throughout this chapter I selected the terminology most representative of the research or ideas being presented, most often using the term "male partner abuse."

Language also can be used to sanitize, and hence minimize, violence that is inflicted against women. Consider the following reports of what ostensibly is the same abuse by a male partner:

> V1. Elizabeth Jones' husband, during their 2 years of marriage, beat her, raped her, and committed acts of gross sexual abuse against her.

> V2. Elizabeth Jones, during her 2 years of marriage, was subjected to beatings, rapes, and acts of gross sexual abuse.

> V3. Elizabeth and Charles Jones, during their 2 years of marriage, had an abusive relationship, in which there were beatings, rapes, and gross acts of sexual abuse (Lamb & Keon, 1995, p. 216).

Which version sounds worse? Version 1 is graphic and presents events in the active voice; version 2 uses passive voice; and version 3 implies shared responsibility for the violence. Both newspaper (Lamb & Keon, 1995) and professional journal articles (Lamb, 1991) most often frame male partner abuse in the third form. This discourse shapes how we perceive the event described. Participants recruited from the general population assigned more lenient punishments to Charles Jones after reading the third version implying shared responsibility (Lamb & Keon, 1995). Such language neutralizes the violence behind terms like battering, covering up the psychological and

---

[3] For reviews of abuse in lesbian relationships, see Stahly and Lie (1995) and Renzetti (1992).

physical harm delivered by pushes, shoves, slaps, kicks, hits, beatings, choking, stabbing, guns and knives, and so on (see Walker, 1979 and 1989a, for blood-chilling, graphic details of real-life terrorism).

Section Summary

One common thread that runs through different forms of male violence against women is definitional ambiguity—what exactly defines sexual harassment, rape, and male partner abuse and who decides that such abuse has occurred. Behaviors alone are insufficient to make these determinations. At an individual level, these uncertainties may interfere with women's ability to name and recover from victimization. They also may be used by perpetrators to excuse their behavior, as in "I didn't sexually harass her; can't she take a joke?" and "I didn't rape her; she liked it." A key to reducing victim-perpetrator misperceptions is to educate and sensitize men and boys about what women and girls regard as sexually threatening behavior and how they react to it. At a societal level, definitional ambiguities cloud discussions and disrupt research on male violence against women, starting with fundamental debates about how widespread each of these forms of violence is.

INCIDENCE AND PREVALENCE

There are two measures of scope that must not be confused: incidence and prevalence. **Incidence** refers to the number of victimizations that occur within a given time period, typically one year. **Prevalence** captures an individual's exposure to at least one assault any time during her lifetime. Extrapolating one from the other can lead to gross misestimates (Muehlenhard et al., 1997).

Although we talk about different forms of male violence against women as conceptually distinct phenomena, they often overlap in women's lives: many women who are raped are also viciously physically assaulted; beaten women may be raped by their male partners; sexually harassed women may be physically threatened, assaulted, and raped; and so on (Koss, Goodman et al., 1994). In real life, different forms of violence co-occur, succeed one another, and blend together to create a pervasive culture of male violence against women. For example, in a survey of wife abuse in San Francisco, 72% of women raped by their husbands were also beaten, and 42% of those who had been beaten were also raped (Russel, 1982).[4] Such **co-occurrences** challenge classification schema that try to sort individuals into discrete, nonoverlapping categories.

Sexual Harassment

Despite definitional challenges, three major studies give us some sense of the prevalence of sexual harassment (Fitzgerald & Ormerod, 1993). The first, best-known study was a large-scale investigation of federal employees conducted by the U.S. Merit Systems Protection Board in 1981 (and replicated in 1987). Fully 42% of all women

---

[4] Subsequent research reviewed by Russel in her 1990 second edition replicates these patterns.

employees checked off exposure to harassing behaviors: 33% reported unwanted sexual remarks; 28%, suggestive looks; 26%, deliberate touching; 15%, pressure for dates; 9%, pressure for sexual favors; 9%, unwanted letters and telephone calls; and 1%, actual or attempted rape or assault.

In an extensive study of the civilian workforce, Barbara Gutek (1985) took a different approach, asking randomly dialed women through a phone interview if they ever experienced incidents at work that they considered harassing. Fully 53% responded affirmatively, citing insulting comments (19.8%), degrading looks and gestures (15.4%), sexual touching (24.2%), and expected sexual activity (7.6%). At two major universities, half of nearly 2,000 women students evidenced harassment, with 35% reporting gender harassment from faculty; 15%, being targeted for sexual behavior; 5%, bribes or threats to secure sexual cooperation; and 9%, sexual imposition ranging from unwanted touching to outright sexual assault.[5]

Although all three studies are not directly comparable because of measurement variations, a consistent pattern does emerge. Louise Fitzgerald (1993; Fitzgerald & Ormerod, 1993) estimates that one of every two women will be subjected to some form of sexual harassment during her academic or working life. Rates of sexual harassment are significantly higher in settings that magnify asymmetrical power relationships, such as those experienced by temporary workers (Rogers & Henson, 1997).

Rape and Sexual Assault

Two major sources of federal statistics on rape incidence are the FBI's Uniform Crime Reports, which compile crimes reported to local authorities, and the Bureau of Justice Statistics' National Crime Victimization Survey (NCVS), which conducts a nationwide, household poll (Koss 1993). The former is heavily jeopardized by the underreporting of rape, considered the most underreported crime of personal violence (Koss, Goodman et al., 1994). The latter relied on an ambiguous question about general attacks and threats to elicit reports of rape and may ask questions in front of other family members, violating confidentiality (Koss, 1992). In 1992–93, NCVS changed their format and instead asked direct questions about rape and sexual assault, following up with questions about whether or not the assailant was known to the victim. The one-year incidence of reported rape doubled from the previous survey to 310,000 cases, fully 80% of which were committed by someone known to the victim (Schafran, 1995). The latter fits with independent surveys which suggest that rape is four times more likely by known than unknown attackers (Koss, 1992).

Turning to prevalence, estimates of rape or sexual assault among adult women typically range from 14–25% (Koss, 1993), although highs of 50% (George, Winfield, & Blazer, 1992) and lows of 8% (Koss, 1993) have been reported. One survey found that up to eight of every ten rape victims reported that the attack occurred before they were 30 years old (National Victims Center, 1992). Using a conservative definition of rape, 14% of ever-married women in a study of 930 adult women reported being raped by a husband or ex-husband at least one time (Russel, 1982). There

---

[5]A review of the sexual harassment literature concludes that fully 73% of women (and 22% of men) were sexually harassed during medical training (Charney & Russell, 1994).

also are regional variations with reports of sexual assault higher in Los Angeles (Sorenson & Siegel, 1992) than in the piedmont of North Carolina (George et al., 1992). The prevalence of sexual assault appears to be equivalent among African American and white women (Wyatt, 1992) and lower among Latinas (Sorenson & Siegel, 1992).

In 1987, Mary Koss conducted an extensive survey of over 3,000 women from 32 colleges and universities across the United States funded by the National Institute for Mental Health and administered with the assistance of the Ms. Foundation (Koss, Dinero, Siebel, & Cox, 1988; Koss, Gidycz, & Wisniewski, 1987; Warshaw, 1994). They found that one in four women was a victim of rape (15.4%) or attempted rape (12.1%); 84% knew their assailant; and 57% happened on dates.[6] Controversy surrounds the involvement of alcohol in Koss's definition of rape,[7] but removing these responses, 9% still reported unwanted sexual intercourse and 6% reported unwanted anal, oral, or object penetration "because a man threatened or used some degree of physical force . . . to make you" (Muehlenhard et al., 1997, p. 245).[8] In one year, 3,187 women reported incidence rates of 328 rapes (as *legally* defined by Ohio law), 534 attempted rapes (again, as *legally* defined), 837 episodes of sexual coercion (intercourse in response to continual pressure), and 2,024 experiences of unwanted fondling, kissing, or petting.

Abuse by a Male Partner

Integrating data from a variety of prominent studies, it is estimated that between 21% and 34% of women in the United States will be physically assaulted—slapped, kicked, beaten, choked, or threatened or attacked with a weapon—by an intimate adult partner (Browne, 1993; also see Straus & Gelles, 1990).[9] Still researchers believe these figures underreport total abuse (Browne, 1993; Dutton, 1988). Fully 52% of women murdered in the first half of the 1980s were killed by their intimate partners (Browne & Williams, 1989), putting women at greater risk for homicide by male partners than by all other categories of murderers combined (Browne & Williams, 1993). Contrast this with the parallel rate for men killed by women intimates: 6% (Federal Bureau of Investigation, 1985).

Rates of violence toward intimates appear comparable for African American and white women (Coley & Beckett, 1988), although African American women are at

---

[6] There is evidence that acquaintance rape on college campuses occurs at similar rates among gay men and lesbian women (Baier, Rosenweig, & Whipple, 1991).

[7] Koss, following Ohio law, included unwanted sexual intercourse "because a man gave you drugs or alcohol," which opens up questions about trading sex for drugs and sexuality that is consensual at the time but later regretted. A broader approach to these problems is offered by Kansas law which includes nonconsensual intercourse "when the victim is incapable of giving consent . . . because of the effect of any alcoholic liquor, narcotic, drug or other substance, which condition was known by the offender or was reasonably apparent to the offender" regardless of the source of these substances (Muehlenhard et al., 1997, p. 245).

[8] These figures also have been questioned regarding the presumed inclusion of responses involving verbal coercion (Gilbert, 1997). However, Koss's estimates do not include these responses, which although important to women's psychological well-being, do not meet legal definitions of rape or attempted rape (Muehlenhard et al., 1997).

[9] These rates are consistent with nationwide surveys in nine other countries which estimate prevalence rates of 17–38% (United Nations, 1995).

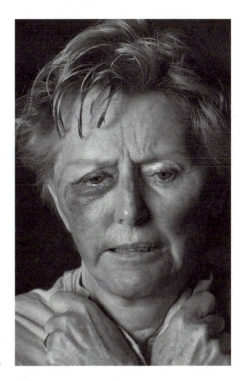

A portrait of an abused woman.

higher risk for lethal violence (Plass & Straus, 1987, cited in McHugh et al., 1993; Stark, 1990). African American women who kill their attackers are more likely to be convicted and serve longer sentences (L.E.A. Walker, 1995). Rates of male partner abuse appear lower among Latina women (Sorenson & Siegel, 1992), although this pattern may be confined to specific subsets of Latinas such as Mexican-born Mexican Americans (Sorenson & Telles, 1991). Christine Ho (1990) warns that low reporting rates by Asian American women may reflect cultural prohibitions against reporting rather than truly lower prevalence rates. Only anecdotal evidence is available presently for Native American women (Allen, 1990). Intimate abuse occurs across social classes (D.G. (1994); Walker, 1979; Sheffield, 1989), and as the photo above shows, its consequences are horrifying.

Childhood Abuse of Girls

Childhood abuse and neglect overall are more widespread than one might think. The National Committee on Child Abuse reported in 1994 that 3.1 million children under 18 in the United States were victims of abuse or neglect, with 1.4 million of these confirmed by physical evidence (Levinson, 1995, cited in Pope and Brown, 1996). This translates into a base rate of 16 *confirmed* cases for every 1,000 children. Their data suggest that almost 90% is perpetrated by parents and other relatives. Turning to women, prevalence rates between 32% and 38% have been reported in community samples (Anderson et al., 1993; Bagley, 1991; Russel, 1986)[10] and between 19% and 34% in college samples (Witchel, 1991). Another national sample cited prevalence rates of 27% for women and 16% for men (Finkelhor et al., 1990). This survey established the median age of onset for girls (9.6 years) and boys (9.9 years), and it noted that the perpetrator was more likely to be a family member for girls and a stranger for boys. Prevalence rates are comparable for African American and white victims (Wyatt, 1985).

INVISIBILITY AND INVALIDATION

These statistics become numbing, but despite attempts to dismiss them as "advocacy numbers" (Gilbert, 1997), the numbers hold (Muehlenhard et al., 1997). At a personal level, it is tempting to ask incredulously, like then-graduate student Katie Roiphe (1993, p. 52): "If 25 percent of my female friends were really being raped, wouldn't I know it?" This asks a question about invisibility and validation—if we don't see something, does it mean it isn't there?

We already have seen that even victims themselves may not define their experiences as sexual harassment, rape, male partner abuse, or childhood abuse, although their experiences meet the criteria for defining these. Might Roiphe's friends—and ours—not share their experiences because they themselves are struggling with their meaning? This highlights the importance of publicizing clear criteria for defining abuse. In addition to having experiences that don't fit with abuse stereotypes, women may fail to name their victimization because of concern for the perpetrator, self-blame and shame, and desires to not think about the events (Parrot, 1991)—processes that are reinforced by sociocultural myths. Many women, especially African American women, don't disclose their victimization even to friends and family (Wyatt, 1992). Finally, women themselves, having internalized societal disregard for their hurt, may come to minimize the severity of their own abuse (Kelly & Radford, 1996). We'll review each of these processes and use different forms of violence to highlight the general point that *invisibility does not invalidate.*

Excusing Perpetrators

It seems hardest to imagine excusing perpetrators of the severest forms of physical and sexual abuse. Both myths and researched data have focused on biological and personality characteristics of individual men who perpetrate these abuses. They paint images of men out of control and responding to their own victimization.

A long-standing myth about male perpetrators of violence against women is that these men are psychopathic. Indeed, a handful of killers are, such as Ted Bundy who targeted attractive, middle-class women, and the less publicized serial killers who brutally murder less protected and less socially valued women (e.g., prostitutes)

---

[10] These prevalence rates are consistent with those found in nationwide studies in Barbados, Canada, the Netherlands, New Zealand, and Norway and are higher than those found in Great Britain (12%) and Germany (17%) (United Nations, 1995).

Our image of a rapist as a crazed maniac (left) often is at odds with real-life images, such as that of Alex Kelly (right) who was convicted of date rape in July 1997 after spending 11 years as a wealthy fugitive in European ski resorts having fled the United States on the eve of the initial rape trial.

(Caputi, 1993). The stereotype of disordered men originated in early studies of convicted rapists who, in reality, represent a very select and small subset of all rapists (Sorenson & White, 1992). It was fostered also by erroneous beliefs that rape is sexually motivated, rather than an expression of male dominance and control (Brownmiller, 1975).

This stereotype of psychopathic rapists is challenged by admissions from men themselves that they would rape a woman if they were assured they wouldn't be caught (studies reviewed by Lonsway & Fitzgerald, 1994). In one of the most recent of these, 69% of 371 male college students reported they would never, under any circumstances, force someone to engage in a sexual act if they were guaranteed not to face reprisals. This leaves fully 31%—that's almost one of every three—to contemplate such an act with or without reprisals! Looked at more behaviorally, of the more than 2,900 men who responded to Koss's survey of college students nationwide, 4.4% admitted to behaviors fulfilling the legal definition of rape, an additional 3.3% attempted these behaviors, 7.2% acknowledged using sexual coercion, and 10.2% admitted to forced or coerced sexual contact such as kissing and petting (Koss, Gidycz, & Wisniewski, 1987).

Furthermore, recent data suggest a great deal of heterogeneity among rapists

(Prentky & Knight, 1991), with only a handful manifesting deviant arousal patterns and personality disorders (Sorenson & White, 1992). Among college students, men who use alcohol, who have an athletic affiliation (Koss & Gaines, 1993), and who are sexually predatory (Kanin, 1985) are more likely to engage in sexual aggression against women, but aggressors certainly are not limited to heavy drinkers, jocks, and flagrant "wolves" (just as all men are not sexually aggressive). In sum, *many rapists appear normal* (Quina & Carlson, 1989).

The gap between cultural mythology and research reality about rapists undermines women's readiness to label their abuser as a rapist. Given this logic, it is no surprise that far more rapes by strangers (estimated at 21%) are reported than are the more common acquaintance rapes (2%) (Koss, Dinero, Siebel, & Cox, 1988). Compound this with the onset of abuse toward women intimates, which is most likely to begin when the couple becomes committed to each other (for 75–85% of abused wives, the abuse didn't start until after they were married), and women often care about the perpetrators of their victimization (Koss, Goodman et al., 1994). Given this, it is not so incredible that some college women report subsequent sexual relations with men who previously had raped them (Koss, 1988).

Other research focuses on the victimization of abusers themselves. Extensive research finds higher rates of witnessing domestic violence or being targeted for childhood abuse among abusive men as compared to nonabusive men (reviewed in Koss, Goodman et al., 1994). However, a distinction needs to be made between being socialized toward violence and excusing responsibility for perpetrating violence (Ptacek, 1988). Not all abusers were socialized toward abuse, and not all of those reared in abusive families grow up to be abusers themselves (Widom, 1989). Similarly, excusing perpetrators because they "lack impulse control" ignores the intended use of violence by many perpetrators as a means for controlling women's behavior (McHugh, Frieze, & Browne, 1993).

Rather than regarding male abusers as rare, obviously pathological, and ultimately unlovable, some researchers focus on the pathology of exaggerations of the male gender role. Taking a macrostructural approach, hypermasculinity was found to be related to higher rape rates across states (Jaffe & Straus, 1987) and across cultures (Sanday, 1981). On an individual level, men who ascribe to more traditional dating scripts—initiating the date, paying all expenses, driving the car—are more likely to report sexual aggressiveness than other men (Muehlenhard & Linton, 1987). Similarly, violent husbands tend to control what the couple does, whose friends they see, and what major household purchases they make (Frieze & McHugh, 1981, cited in McHugh et al., 1993). Researchers have called attention to parallels between domination of a woman and proving one's masculinity (Hansen & Harway, 1993; Quina & Carlson, 1989; L.E.A. Walker, 1984, 1989b, 1994).

Self-Blame and Shame

Sexual harassment, male partner abuse, and rape all share an aura of misunderstanding arising from the misogynous belief that, because of characterological deficiencies, women bring such abuse on themselves and contribute to its continuation.

In no other crime do we heap such blame on the victim. Consider "'The Rape' of Mr. Smith"—the victim of a holdup (Unknown, 1997):

"Mr. Smith, you were held up at gunpoint on the corner of 16th and Locust?"
"Yes."
"Did you struggle with the robber?"
"No."
"Why not?"
"He was armed."
"Then you made a conscious decision to comply with his demands rather than to resist?"
"Yes."
"Did you scream? Cry out?"
"No. I was afraid."
"I see. Have you ever been held up before?"
"No."
"Have you ever given money away?"
"Yes, of course—"
"And did you do so willingly?"
"What are you getting at?"
"Well, let's put it like this, Mr. Smith. You've given away money in the past—in fact, you have quite a reputation for philanthropy. How can we be sure that you weren't *contriving* to have your money taken from you by force?"
"Listen, if I wanted—"
"Never mind. What time did this holdup take place, Mr. Smith?"
"About 11 p.m."
"You were out on the streets at 11 p.m.? Doing what?"
"Just walking."
"Just walking? You know that it's dangerous being out on the street that late at night. Weren't you aware that you could have been held up?"
"I hadn't thought about it."
"What were you wearing at the time, Mr. Smith?"
"Let's see. A suit. Yes, a suit."
"An *expensive* suit?"
"Well—yes."
"In other words, Mr. Smith, you were walking around the streets late at night in a suit that practically *advertised* the fact that you might be a good target for some easy money, isn't that so? I mean, if we didn't know better, Mr. Smith, we might even think you were *asking* for this to happen, mightn't we?"
"Look, can't we talk about the past history of the guy who *did* this to me?"
"I'm afraid not, Mr. Smith. I don't think you would want to violate his rights, now, would you?"

Blaming women for psychological, physical, and sexual abuse encompasses blame both for being targeted and for continuing violence.

Blame for victimization.   The tendency to blame women for bringing on their abuse runs through the common *myths* that surround each form of violence (Sheffield, 1989, p. 14):

Sexual Harassment:
She was seductive.
She misunderstood. I was just being friendly.

Male Partner Abuse:
Some women need to be beaten.
A good kick in the ass will straighten her out.
She needs a punch in the mouth every so often to keep her in line.
She must have done something to provoke him.

Rape:
All women want to be raped.
No woman can be raped if she doesn't want it (you-can't-thread-a-moving-needle argument).
She asked for it.
She changed her mind afterwards.
When she says no she means yes.
If you are going to be raped you might as well enjoy it.

Childhood Sexual Abuse:
The child was the seducer.
The child imagined it.

Acceptance of these myths has not disappeared (Johnson, Kuck, & Schander, 1997). Latina women perceive the most victim-blaming for rape in their communities; white women, the least (Lefley et al., 1993).

Looking across a wide range of rape myths, researchers uncover four distinct themes underlying them: disbelief of rape claims, victim responsibility for rape, rape reports as manipulation of a man by a woman, and the belief that rape happens only to deserving women (Briere, Malamuth, & Check, 1985). All of these undermine the veracity and victimization of the recipient. For those of us who dismiss these myths for the hogwash they are, we may think that we wouldn't blame ourselves if we were so victimized. Indeed, people who read cases of sexual harassment and then are asked to describe what they would do in those situations (analog studies) rarely relate that they would blame themselves (Fitzgerald, 1990). Yet, reports from actual victims provide evidence to the contrary:

> I was ashamed, thought it was my fault, and was worried that the school would take action against me (for "unearned" grades) if they found out about it. . . .

> When I came to, I wanted to die, the guilt and depression were so bad. Your whole sense of worth is tied up with being a successful wife and having a happy marriage. If your husband beats you, then your marriage is a failure, and you're a failure. It's so horribly the opposite of how it is supposed to be (Sheffield, 1989, p. 15).

> I felt guilty. I felt it was my fault because I had been drinking. I felt angry at myself for not having fought or screamed louder (Hanmer & Saunders, 1984, p. 37).

Knowing of this inconsistency between what we think we'd do and what others actually do raises serious questions about what each of us really would do if confronted with these kinds of abuse.

Furthermore, these myths, regardless of their veracity, help to sustain violence. There is well-established evidence linking acceptance of rape myths with the men who perpetrate these acts (Anderson, Cooper, & Okamura, 1997). Surveying various professionals, Colleen Ward (1995) concluded that many doctors, police, and lawyers were misinformed; they accepted these faulty myths, including beliefs that women provoke rape by their dress, that women cannot be believed, and that men are not responsible. On the whole, mental health professionals shared the most women-friendly attitudes and were best informed, although psychiatrists were the most likely to accept rape myths within this generally more progressive group.

Male violence against women does not take place in a vacuum. Rather, it occurs within a sociocultural context that subtly promotes violence or turns away from it. We have seen that exaggerations of the masculine gender role and male-dominant dating scripts help support violence. So does sexualized media violence. When exposed to both X-rated and R-rated materials that portrayed violence directed at women in sexualized contexts, college men expressed callous attitudes toward husband-perpetrated sexual abusiveness and were themselves more aggressive in the laboratory (Donnerstein, Linz, & Penrod, 1987). Similarly, men who watched slasher films showed less sensitivity toward rape victims (Linz, 1989). In general, depictions of sexual violence can promote antisocial attitudes and behavior (Linz, Wilson, & Donnerstein, 1992).

Media violence affects women as well, making college women feel disempowered (Reid & Finchilescu, 1995). Cultural expectations about the influences of alcohol—as a disinhibitor for the man, as an excuse for his behavior, and as a strategy for reducing victims' resistance—also contextually support violence (Koss, Goodman et al., 1994). They send the double messages that "he's not responsible, he was drinking" and "she *is* responsible, *she was drinking*." All of these social factors combine to set up a cultural context that both reflects and reinforces male violence against women.

Blame for "inappropriate" responding. We tend to think of male violence against women as a one-time event. How many women confidently have claimed: "If a man ever hit me, he'd eat my dust"? But much of male violence against women is cyclic. Sexual harassment typically encompasses a long-term barrage of offensive behaviors (Fitzgerald, Swan, & Fischer, 1995). Once the cycle of partner abuse begins, it tends to spiral upward becoming increasingly dangerous for the victim (Morrow & Hawxhurst, 1989). Childhood sexual abuse usually cycles as well (Stanko, 1985).

We have stereotypic images about how women should respond to violence, and these often erroneous stereotypes affect how we react toward victims. The courts have sent a message that victims' behavior will be closely scrutinized in sexual harassment cases and that a "real" victim will speak out against her harassment, both publicly and privately when it is happening (Fitzgerald et al., 1995). Women themselves tend to think hypothetically that if they confronted sexual harassment, they should and would respond assertively to make it stop (Fitzgerald, 1993; Gutek & Koss, 1993). Similarly, we expect abused women to leave their relationships, implying that their failure to do so is indicative of some inexplicable characterological shortcoming. We saw in Chapter 10 that the American Psychiatric Association reified this line of thinking by including a mental disorder in the DSM-III-R to capture these women's pathology: self-defeating personality disorder—also known in psychiatric circles as masochism. (A public outcry removed this classification from the 1994 revision, DSM-IV.) In sum, we have stereotyped images of how genuine victims are supposed to respond.

Why do women tolerate sexual harassment and stay in abusive relationships? Exploring responses to sexual harassment, it is obvious from our discussion above that women must first regard the events as harassing and not blame themselves for them (Jensen & Gutek, 1982). Additional insights come from examining the actual responses of harassment victims and their perceptions.

Louise Fitzgerald and her colleagues (1995) describe two different classes of **coping strategies** used by real-life victims of sexual harassment. **Internally focused** responses include endurance (ignore the situation, pretend it is not happening, not caring); denial (of information, threat, vulnerability, or negative feelings); reattribution (reinterpreting the events as nonharassment, such as, "he was just joking"); illusory control; and detachment. Thus "doing nothing" is a form of responding—one that is used quite frequently by some women, especially if the harassment is less severe.

Externally focused responses include avoidance, appeasement, assertion, seeking social support, and seeking institutional or organizational relief. Of these, avoidance is the most common, followed by appeasement (an attempt to put off the harasser without direct confrontation). The most infrequent response, seeking institutional relief, is probably most effective in terminating the harassment, but unless strong organizational supports exist, targets are fearful of doing this—fearing retaliation, disbelief, harm of one's career, shame, and humiliation. Reviewing the literature, there is substantial evidence to verify that none of these fears is unfounded (Fitzgerald et al., 1995).

Indeed, I remember mustering my own courage to tell the dean about a senior faculty member who threatened to jeopardize the renewal of my one-year appointment as a visiting faculty member if I didn't spend a weekend with him in Mexico. The dean just couldn't believe that his long-time golfing buddy could do such a thing (even though a graduate student overheard and verified the whole exchange). I found another job. Guess what happened to the harasser?

Note how what we think a harassment victim should do (that is, be assertive or report him) differs from what victims really do. Are being a silent tolerator or an instigator-in-kind (someone who appeases harassers by "playing along") forms of consent or forms of coping (Fitzgerald et al., 1995)? Compared to what we stereotypically think victims *should* do, these typical responses look like consent. But, in light of what we have presented here, these responses look more like *coping*. Furthermore, the coping perspective suggests that, rather than concentrate on what *victims* do and don't do to make known their dissent, women would be better served if the burden of demonstrating that sexual overtures were welcomed by a woman in the workplace was put squarely on the shoulders of the *initiator*.

Turning to male partner abuse, escape is oftentimes thwarted by credible threats of escalated violence and even homicide/suicide should the woman try to leave (Browne, 1993; L.E.A. Walker, 1994). Although this may make entrapment understandable, how can we understand a woman who escapes, then returns? One study that followed a group of beaten women across 2.5 years found that 23% were in an abusive relationship at the start and at the end of the study (Campbell et al., 1994). (The average duration of an abusive marriage is 6 years, the same as the average marriage [L.E.A. Walker, 1984]). Reviewing data from a variety of sources, Michael Strube (1988, p. 238) concludes that "about half of all women who seek some form of aid for spouse abuse can be expected to return to their partners." This pattern holds across different races, social classes, marital statuses, educational levels, and the presence of children in the home.

What does seem to distinguish women who don't return from those who do is that the former are more likely to be employed (and thus can afford to leave), are in shorter-term relationships (less committed?), think of themselves as better off financially, are less in love, are less likely to be white (and possibly have wider kinship networks to take them in), and feel they have somewhere to go (Strube & Barbour, 1984). The absence of these facilitators fits with a psychological profile of a returner who feels entrapped; the presence of these facilitators describes women who have less to lose by leaving.

Understanding the cycle of partner abuse also helps frame women's apparent choices to stay and even return. Lenore Walker (1979) in her landmark portrayal of *The Battered Woman*, describes a three-stage **cycle of battering**. In the first phase, **tension builds** as minor battering incidents are seemingly controlled and rationalized by the woman who does her best to avoid "provoking" an outburst. In the second phase, **the acute battering incident**, violence escalates and the woman feels that she has lost control and cannot predict her partner's behavior. The trigger is rarely something the battered woman does, although Walker describes how some women may move things toward this outburst as a way to relieve the intolerable pressure mounting during the tension building phase. (It is during this first phase that Walker, 1989a, reports women are most likely to kill their abusers.) The second phase typically lasts between two and 24 hours, after which most women tend to stay isolated for several days before seeking any help. Phase three can be the hook for many women—after the explosion, the batterer exudes **kindness and contrite, loving behavior**. At the exact time when we would expect the woman to be most motivated to leave, he stops the abuse and steps up the charm. When things return to "normal," tension building begins anew and the cycle continues. Walker describes these women as *survivors* who learn to control inevitable violent outbursts so as to minimize the violence (although their stories are chillingly violent), not as passive victims helplessly out of control.

In sum, both myths about what brings on male violence against women (e.g., women who are "asking for it") and stereotypes of how "genuine" victims should react differ from reality for many women. Until we let go of these false and misleading myths and stereotypes, we will fail to understand many women's victimization and ultimately will contribute to their second victimization as they struggle to cope and survive.[11] At a societal level, these myths and stereotypes help keep alive a culture that accepts violence.

---

[11] Support services for victims of all forms of violence vary by locales. Good resources on college campuses for these services or referrals for services include women's centers, women's studies offices, psychology clinics, and health facilities. Be clear that you are looking for feminist-oriented services.

Cognitive Coping Strategies

Writing this chapter revived memories for me of being sexually harassed over 15 years ago. I can recall many of the details of the three-hour session that took place in my office at a deserted university on a Sunday afternoon. However, I am struck by the fact that I'd have to review a roster of the faculty to remember the name of the senior professor who threatened me (and the idea of doing this is quite unnerving). My feelings parallel those of other women asked to reconstruct their experiences with sexual harassment (Kidder, Lafleur, & Wells, 1995). Denial, avoidance, and numbing are adaptive, especially when the event in question involves a betrayal of trust (Freyd, 1997). Many women have vague, sketchy memories of actual abusive incidents by male partners (Kelly, 1988). Although women certainly remember a past rape experience, their descriptions are characterized by less detail and a numbing of emotion common to memories of other unpleasant experiences—but very different from pleasant memories (Koss et al., 1996).

One of the most controversial areas to explore memories of trauma focuses on recovered memories of childhood sexual abuse (see Pope & Brown, 1996).[12] On the one side, the False Memory Syndrome Foundation, founded in 1992 by accused parents and independent of any recognized organization of mental health professionals, coined a "syndrome" they believe befits DSM-IV as a personality disorder (described in Pope, 1996).[13] People afflicted with this presumed disorder obsess about a false, implanted memory so much that their entire lives revolve around it. They argue that this memory is the product of suggestive psychotherapists who, through naiveté, greed, incompetence, or zealotry, convince the client that she (usually a woman) has been sexually abused by a family member.

The scientific foundation for these claims rests on a series of studies in which a presumably untrue "memory" is suggested by an older family member to research participants who eventually report that they believe the implanted event actually happened. The original procedure created a "memory" of being lost in a shopping mall (Loftus & Ketcham, 1994). Other suggestions tested by researchers have included earaches, trips to the hospital at night, and words that did not appear in a list.

Kenneth Pope (1996) points to some compelling shortcomings in this research. Being lost in a mall is offered as analogous to being sexually abused in that both are arguably traumatic. However, being lost is a more common experience than abuse, contains no sexual content, seems less stressful, and is a singular incident. These differences raise serious questions about the relevance of everyday memory processes toward our understanding of the traumatic memories of childhood abuse (Kristiansen et al., 1996).

A somewhat closer analog may be having a mother give her child an enema. When researchers tried to implant this memory, they were successful with *none* of their participants (Pezdek, 1995, 1996). Also, having an older family member sug-

---

[12] For a good research review of both sides of the recovered memory/false memory debate, see Pezdek and Banks (1996).

[13] For a good feminist analysis of how the foundation and the proposed syndrome continue to distort the prevalence of childhood sexual abuse, see Scott (1997) and Saraga and MacLeod (1997).

gest the false "memory" in these studies is a lot different than having a therapist do so in that only the relative is presumed to have first-hand experience, making her or him more credible. (I know I tell my children lots of stories about their childhoods that they don't recall on their own.) Contrary to the false memory agenda, these studies suggest that if family members can alter their children's memories, then abusers feasibly might convince their victims that "nothing really happened"— or at least insure that they keep events hidden.

We might think of traumas as life-altering events (which indeed they are) that are too powerful to be put aside. However, an approach focused on "recovered" memories asks us to reframe our thinking around the concept of coping. Taking a coping perspective, our expectations change—we expect victims to remember but to do so in ways that let them go on with their lives. Such cognitive adaptation might include talking less about these events, numbing the emotions they engender, and letting go of disturbing details (Koss et al., 1996). There is provocative evidence to support such reframing of our point of view. For example, follow-up studies with women known to have been sexually abused as children (because they were treated in emergency rooms) found that 38% (almost 200 women) were unable to vividly recall the index event. Paralleling these findings, studies of crime victims show that some seem to report hazy memories of even fairly serious attacks (Block & Block, 1984).

Minimization of Violence

Again if we take a coping perspective, it is understandable that some survivors will seek to minimize their abuse (Kelly, 1988). Combine this with the well-documented tendency for abusive men to underreport their violent actions and their impact (reviewed by McHugh et al., 1993), and abuse may be reported by those directly involved as being not as bad as a third-party observer might document. Note the highlighted contradictions in the following examples from British women:

> I was molested by a man who grabbed hold of me and pushed himself against me in the tube when it was crowded. I screamed as loudly as I could. He *slapped my face*, but then got off as we got to a station. I suppose I was lucky that *nothing actually happened*. . . .

> The men in the office are forever having a go—sort of half joke/half propositioning me. They know I don't like it, but they never give up. It's *nothing really*. I can handle it, or I have so far, but it pisses me off. I'm *exhausted by the end of the day*. . . .

> I've been attacked in the library—young white boys fooling around in a threatening and racist way. *Nothing's actually happened* to me, but I've had to *call the police* to have them removed . . . (Kelly & Radford, 1996, p. 26, italics added).

As Liz Kelly and Jill Radford (1996) point out, although these women insist that "nothing really happened," something really did. That something has more to do with women's feelings than with any documented physical hurt per se. The evidence is minimized not only by these women in parts of their stories (and contradicted in other parts), but probably by outsiders as well. Furthermore, these stories illustrate how, when women say "nothing really happened," they may be considering a much worse scenario than what they experienced, such as "he slapped but didn't rape me." In contrast, when the law says "nothing really happened," violation is invalidated.

Section Summary

We have seen that there are a variety of factors that conspire to keep male violence against women hidden, even at times from victims themselves. It is noteworthy that some critics who wish to invalidate women's experiences require that victims appropriately label their abuse before it can be characterized as abuse. Must clients come to therapy calling themselves survivors of childhood abuse to be legitimately treated for its aftermath? Or may conscientious therapists pursue diagnostic leads based on observed signs and testing that may be indicative of abuse?

Even the majority of advocates of a recovered memory model note that clients don't come to therapy without showing any signs of abuse and then spontaneously report it during the course of therapy, as false memory advocates suppose (Polusny & Follette, 1996). Most fundamentally, psychologists are in the habit of assigning labels to people based on their adherence to established criteria, without requiring that they self-report the label given. For example, how many diagnosed alcoholics would we miss if we required self-identification? Similarly, why should a researcher give research participants the Bem Sex Role Inventory if she or he could simply ask them to classify themselves? On close examination, such demands are absurd; yet we seem to accept parallel demands as legitimate for women survivors of abuse.

Even knowing in the abstract why abuse is invisible, at some basic level, I admit to being overwhelmed by these prevalence rates—it's just too depressing to be true. While taking a break from writing this chapter, I bumped into a retired friend, and she asked about my progress with this book. I shared how gut-wrenching this topic was, and she proceeded to tell me about her own experience with attempted date rape—her date ripped her brand new dress then called her the next day oblivious to why she was "acting funny." I was stunned. This nice, white-haired woman recalled vivid images of an attempted date rape that happened over 40 years ago. Somehow this made these prevalence rates more concrete for me. As students and as caring human beings, I urge you to start asking the women you know about their experiences. Sexually assaulted women cope better if they are believed and listened to by others (Ullman, 1996). An author of a tell-all book describes the impact of sharing her experiences as an incest survivor:

> I've learned a great deal by telling my story. I hope other incest victims may experience a similar journey of discovery by reading it. If nothing else, I would wish them to hear in this tale the two things I needed most, but had to wait years to hear: "You are not alone and you are not to blame" (Brady, 1981, p. 253).

We have reviewed different strategies used to invalidate women's experiences, strategies that simultaneously are fueled by the hiddenness of violence as well as ultimately maintain this invisibility. By excusing perpetrators, we place the burden for establishing nonconsent squarely on the shoulders of women victims alone, and we ultimately come to blame victims for bringing about their own victimization. One theme that runs through this section is a call for men to assume responsibility for establishing consent before engaging in sexual relations. At the root of this call is the need to respect and listen to women—a fundamental ingredient that could reduce other forms of violence, like physical assault, as well. A second theme challenges us to replace a victim-blaming perspective with a coping approach to better understand women's responses to violence, including: appearing to play along with sexual harassment; staying and even returning to abusive intimates; denying, avoiding, and numbing; and abuse minimizations.

CONSEQUENCES

Consistent with the previous sections of this chapter, common threads run through what we know about the consequences for women of sexual harassment, rape, male partner abuse, and childhood sexual abuse. Although there are a few noteworthy exceptions (which will be highlighted below), these variations of male violence against women all produce strikingly similar traumatic aftereffects in many women. Here we will explore some immediate and long-term physical and psychological consequences for individual women. We also will explore the resilience of survivors. The patterns we will review come together to argue that the pervasive threat of male violence against women serves to unite all women, differentiates women from men, and is used to maintain social control in a male-dominated, patriarchal society.

Physical Sequelae

Both immediate and long-term physical harm results from all forms of male violence against women. For women coping with sexual harassment, common responses include anxiety attacks, headaches, sleep disturbances, disordered eating, gastrointestinal disorders, nausea, weight loss or gain, and crying spells (Crull, 1982; Gutek, 1985).

One-half to two-thirds of rape survivors escape without physical trauma (Koss & Heslet, 1992), and only half of the injured receive formal medical treatment (Koss, Woodruff, & Koss, 1991). Survivors are more likely to contact a physician than a mental health professional, and gross underfunding of rape crisis-intervention programs has limited their utility (Koss, 1993). Although sexually transmitted diseases result for 4%–30% of women, a 1992 national sample found that no AIDS testing was reported by fully 73% of acknowledged survivors nor was pregnancy testing or precautionary intervention offered to 60% (National Victims Center, 1992). Physical problems persist for a disproportionate number of women beyond the immediate aftermath. Survivors report more physical health problems, perceive their health less favorably, and visit physicians twice as often as women in general (Koss, 1993).

The most obvious consequences of male partner abuse are physical, yet the range of violent acts is stunning. Lenore Walker (1979) sums up the stories of 120 women:

> Major physical assaults included: slaps and punches to the face and head; kicking, stomping, and punching all over the body; choking to the point of consciousness loss; push-

ing and throwing across a room, down the stairs, or against objects; severe shaking; arms twisted or broken; burns from irons, cigarettes, and scalding liquids; injuries from thrown objects; forced shaving of pubic hair; forced violent sexual acts; stabbing and mutilation with a variety of objects, including knives and hatchets; and gunshot wounds. The most common physical injuries reported are those inflicted by the man's hands and feet to the head, face, back, and rib areas. Broken ribs and broken arms, resulting from the woman's raising her arm to defend herself, are the most common broken bones.

Several women in this sample have suffered broken necks and backs, one after being flung against objects in the room. One woman suffered the loss of a kidney and severe injury to her second kidney when she was thrown against a kitchen stove. Others suffered serious internal bleeding and bruises. Swollen eyes and nose, lost teeth, and concussions were all reported. Surgery was required in a large number of cases. Women were often knocked unconscious by these blows. Many others were choked nearly unconscious (pp. 79–80).

Male partner abuse produces more injuries to women in one year in the United States than reported rape, car accidents, and muggings combined (Stark & Flitcraft, 1988). Approximately 21% of all women using emergency surgical services are victims of partner-perpetrated physical abuse (Browne, 1993). While it is typical for adults to make one injury visit to an emergency service in their lifetime, abused wives average more than one such visit each year (Stark & Flitcraft, 1996). Emergency-room personnel tend to medicalize and disembody women's abuse so that they treat the injury without recognition of or concern for the cause (Warshaw, 1989). In a clinical study of 691 pregnant women, 17% reported physical and sexual abuse during their pregnancy (MacFarlane et al., 1992), and 25% of women using a community-based family practice reported injuries inflicted by an intimate (Hamberger, Saunders, & Hovey, 1992).

Psychological Sequelae

Given our premise that different forms of male violence against women are linked, it comes as no surprise that survivors' reactions to such victimization share much in common (but with a few noteworthy exceptions). All violence poses threats to normal psychological well-being and challenges survivors' fundamental beliefs about the world.

Disrupted psychological well-being.   Throughout these explorations, what is cause and what is effect often have been confused. For example, low self-esteem characterizes victims of male partner abuse. For those who assume that women's low self-esteem predated their abuse, presumed helplessness has been cited as a preexisting characterological flaw in women that exacerbates their vulnerability to battering. However, researchers who have questioned this causal chain have concluded instead that low self-esteem, like other signs of helplessness and entrapment, results from the abuse itself (Hotaling & Sugarman, 1986; Margolin, 1988; Romero, 1985; L.E.A. Walker, 1984). *The psychological aftermath we will describe here is more accurately conceptualized as a result of the trauma these women experienced rather than as something that was germinating in these survivors prior to their assault.*

Targets of sexual harassment describe fear, anger, anxiety, depression, self-questioning, and self-blame (Koss, 1990). To date, a state-of-the-art prospective study of the impact of sexual harassment on women's mental health does not exist, but Louise Fitzgerald and Alayne Ormerod (1993) provide some guidelines for designing such a study. Future research should work to integrate and explain victims' responses and outcomes by exploring the harassing event, victim characteristics, and organizational context.

We know much more about the psychological consequences of rape survival. Generally, women's responses change over time (Koss, 1993). For many survivors, distress levels are severely elevated during the first week then peak in severity by about three weeks. For an average of 12 days after a rape, fully 94% of survivors meet the criteria for posttraumatic stress disorder (PTSD). This continues at an elevated level for about the next month, then begins to diminish. By two to three months postassault, many differences between survivors and women in general disappear, with the exceptions of persistent reports of fear, anxiety, self-esteem problems, and sexual dysfunction among survivors. Fully 46% still meet the criteria for PTSD three months afterwards. These patterns appear to hold for Latina, African American, and white women (Wyatt, 1992).

When does a rape survivor go back to her preassault self? Possibly never. Even years after a rape, survivors are more likely to be diagnosed for major depression, alcohol and drug abuse and dependence, generalized anxiety, obsessive-compulsive disorder, and PTSD (Koss, 1993). Independent of whether or not a date-rape survivor acknowledges her rape, from 31% to 48% of survivors eventually will seek professional help (Koss & Burkhart, 1989). It is critical that this help integrate issues of race, ethnicity, and class into effective counseling (Holzman, 1996). Compared to victims of other criminal assaults, survivors of rape (and even attempted rape) exhibit disproportionately high levels of suicidal thoughts, attempted suicide, and "nervous breakdowns" (Kilpatrick et al., 1985). Anti-lesbian rape, targeting lesbians and designed to degrade lesbian sexuality, often threatens women's general sense of safety, independence, and well-being (Garnets, Herek, & Levy, 1993).

For women survivors of male partner abuse, reactions of shock, denial, withdrawal, confusion, psychological numbing, and fear are common (Browne, 1987; D.G. Dutton, 1992). These survivors frequently are characterized by high levels of depression, suicide ideation, and suicide attempts (McGrath et al., 1990). Chronic fatigue and tension, intense startle reactions, disturbed sleep and eating patterns, and nightmares also may result (Goodman, Koss, & Russo, 1993; Herman, 1992). More severe symptomatology is likely for women who experience more violent forms of abuse (Gelles & Harrop, 1989) and for victims of both physical and sexual aggression (Browne, 1987).

The psychological effects of childhood sexual abuse may be long-term for survivors. Given the hidden nature of this form of victimization, it is hard to gauge its consequences. However, it is estimated that fully 40% of survivors will need therapy sometime during their adulthood (Browne & Finkelhor, 1986). Documented sequelae include depression, self-destructive behavior, feelings of isolation and stigma, poor self-esteem, sexual maladjustment, difficulty trusting others, PTSD symptoms, and symptoms of dissociation (Browne & Finkelhor, 1986; Roesler & McKenzie, 1994).

Disrupted world views.   We all possess views of how the world works—who can be trusted, what's fair, and who deserves what (Lerner, Miller, & Holmes, 1975), as well as hopes expressed by "it just can't happen to me" (Janoff-Blumen & Frieze, 1983). A woman's fundamental beliefs about the world, including feelings of safety, power or efficacy, trust, esteem, and intimacy, may be challenged by experiencing rape (Koss, 1993). For many lesbians raped by a man, recovery is complicated by feelings of violation of one's self as a lesbian, by revival of internalized feelings of homophobia, and by disruption of the coming out process (Garnets et al., 1993). For women survivors of date rape and male partner abuse, heightened feelings of self-blame and betrayal further impede recovery (Roth, Wayland, & Woolsey, 1990; Browne, 1991). These may be aggravated for beaten women who rely on their abusive partners for shelter and financial support (Browne, 1991). We might intuit that date and marital rape would be less physically threatening for women; however, large-scale surveys find that fear of injury or death is just as high for women raped by husbands and dates as by survivors of stranger rape (Koss, 1993).

Diagnosis.   A common diagnosis for victims/survivors of sexual and male partner abuse is posttraumatic stress disorder (PTSD). As we saw in Chapter 10, PTSD has advantages over characterological diagnoses, like borderline and histrionic personality disorders, because PTSD focuses diagnosis and hence treatment on traumatic events outside the individual. However, PTSD was developed for war survivors and, as such, has several noteworthy limitations (Koss, Goodman et al., 1994). First, responses to sexual assault go beyond PTSD's focus on fear and anxiety, missing common violence aftereffects such as relational disturbances, isolation, and sexual dysfunction. Second, PTSD ignores the cognitive disruptions we examined above to survivors' views of the world, as well as the chronic and seemingly inescapable risks inherent in many women's daily lives (e.g., living in violent neighborhoods or with abusive partners). Third, PTSD responds better to single traumatic events rather than the recurrent ones that tend to characterize male partner abuse and childhood sexual abuse. Finally, one might philosophically ponder why the DSM-IV considers victimization a mental disorder while perpetrating such violence, except in egregious cases, goes undiagnosed.

Resilience

Although there are few known reliable predictors of what facilitates resilience after rape (Koss, 1993), women who resisted rape by using forceful physical strategies exhibit less postassault depression than other survivors (Bart & O'Brien, 1993). Nonsupportive behavior from significant others predicts poorer adjustment, suggesting that social support is a potential facilitator (Davis, Brickman, & Baker, 1991). Practical advice is found in *Recovering from Rape* (1994) by Linda Ledray (a clinical psychologist and registered nurse).[14] This book is an excellent compendium of

---

[14]For a good resource for people who are helping a loved one cope with her or his history of abuse, see Davis (1991).

advice for survivors. It can be used effectively by a supportive confidant of a victim as well as by victims who choose to report or not and who have been raped recently or in the past. As for therapy, key features of an effective approach include avoidance of blaming the victim; a nonstigmatizing view that regards rape as criminal victimization; support to overcome cognitive and behavioral avoidance; information about the normality of trauma reactions; and expectations that symptoms will improve (Resick & Markaway, 1991).

The resilience of some abuse survivors is attested to in in-depth interviewers conducted by Linda DiPalma (1994). In childhood, some girls imagined sunny but realistic futures to relieve their pain and escape their victimization. Some put their energy into academic success to obtain personal validation; others drew on creative outlets such as writing, drama, and music. Their stories testify to their unflagging determination and inner strength.

> Being a survivor means being able to feel again, not to repress, not to forget, not to run away from, but to be able to stand still, remember what happened, claim all of that experience, claim the feelings, and still be able to hang on to this new person that I am (DiPalma, 1994, p. 87).

Unique Consequences

Although there are many commonalties across women's responses to violence, some consequences are unique to specific types of violence. For example, sexual harassment produces work- or education-related consequences not directly attributable to other forms of violence. One study found that fully half the women who filed a formal sexual harassment complaint in California were fired, and an additional 25% resigned because of pressures related to the harassment itself and/or retaliation for filing (Coles, 1986; also see Crull, 1982; U.S. Merit Systems, 1987). Other outcomes include lowered morale and higher absenteeism (U.S. Merit Systems, 1981), decrements in work quality and quantity, and disrupted interpersonal relationships (Bandy, 1989). College students describe dropping courses and changing academic majors (Fitzgerald et al., 1988).

There is a myth unique to long-term abuses (e.g., childhood and adult abuses by intimates): once a victim, always a victim. As we've seen, 23% of abused wives at the start of a study were still in abusive relationships over two years later (Campbell et al., 1994), and we examined the factors that mediate such persistence. However, these data also highlight the majority who successfully changed their lives. The myth that battered women simply will trade one abusive relationship for another was discredited many years ago (Walker, 1979).

A different pattern of perpetuation emerges for survivors of childhood sexual abuse. There is evidence that such victimization can encourage patterns of risky behavior that elevate *some* survivors' chances for further victimization. Survivors of childhood abuse are 2.4 times more likely to be assaulted again as adults than nonvictims (Wyatt, Guthrie, & Notgrass, 1992). Although comparisons of rape survivors and nonvictims generally find no victim characteristics that might predispose women to rape, a minority (10%), with twice the general risk, possess liberal sexual attitudes, higher-than-average alcohol use, and more sexual partners. Provocatively, this minority of high-risk women also is more likely to include survivors of childhood sexual abuse, and the three risk behaviors just noted are regarded as likely traumatic after-effects of sexual abuse (Koss & Dinero, 1989). Pulling this together, childhood abuse may combine with antecedent risk behaviors to put these survivors at heightened risk for falling into a continuing cycle of victimization.

Consequences for All Women

The consequences of male violence against women are not limited to the women who survive these attacks. All women are affected, every day of their lives, by the threat of psychological, physical, and sexual abuse. Every time a woman restricts her activities because of fear, sits in a locked car in sweltering heat, feels her heart beat faster as someone runs up behind her, wears clothes that restrict her means of escape, drops a course when a professor points her out as the only woman in the class . . . , she is reacting to her fear of attack and vulnerability created by the simple fact that she is a woman in a patriarchal culture. These consequences are what distinguish male violence against women from women-perpetrated violence and what link some forms of male violence against men to this discussion.

Fully one-third of urban women reported fear of physical harm, especially rape, as their most common concern (Gordon & Riger, 1989). Although women are less likely than men to be victimized by violent crime overall, more than half of the women surveyed admit to using self-isolation as a form of protection in stark contrast to only 10% of men in the same neighborhoods who admitted to taking steps to reduce their vulnerability to crime. These fears are exaggerated for older women who often are more vulnerable because they are considered "easy" targets (Davis & Brody, 1979). *Living with the burden of threat of physical and sexual violation unites all women and is limited to them* (Thompson & Norris, 1992).

One of the strongest forms of social control is not force itself, but the threat of it (Wrong, 1979, p. 43). In this way, every example we read at the beginning of this chapter, from fear of rape through femicide, is a form of social control (Koss, Goodman et al., 1994). This logic extends to *racial* control for women of color who survive sexual abuse from white men or live with the persistent threat of it (Donat & D'Emilio, 1992) and to lesbian women who are targets of hate crimes (von Schulthess, 1992).

CHAPTER SUMMARY

The major point I have argued throughout this chapter is that the threat of male violence against women and its various realized forms are connected so that each reinforces the others. For example, consider the myths in Table 11.1 that are concocted for sexual harassment, rape, and male partner abuse—there is a variant of each overriding message tailored for each form of violence. (You should be able to argue knowledgeably against each of these now.) As we have seen, sexual harass-

TABLE 11.1 Common Myths and Stereotypes about Male Violence against Women

Myth	Harassment	Rape	Male Partner Abuse
Victim Masochism They enjoy/want it.	It wasn't harassment, only teasing. Women invite it and feel flattered by the attention.	It wasn't rape, only "rough sex." Women say no when they mean yes. Some women enjoy rape.	Some women are masochistic, seeking out violent men. Women don't leave so it can't be that bad.
Victim Precipitation They ask for/deserve it.	Women invite it by flirting or the way they dress, by working late or traveling on business trips.	Women provoke men by the way they dress, by "leading men on." They take risks by going out alone, accepting lifts.	Women provoke men by nagging, not fulfilling household "duties," refusing sex.
It only happens to certain types of women/in certain kinds of families.	Paranoid women; women with an ax to grind; women who behave inappropriately in the workplace.	Women who live in poor areas; women who are sexually active; women who take risks; women who have previously been abused.	Working-class women; women who are "bad" housewives; women who saw or experienced violence as children.
Victim Fabrication They tell lies/ exaggerate.	Disgruntled workers or women who are scorned file harassment charges.	Women make false reports for revenge, to protect their "reputation."	It wasn't violence, only a fight. Women exaggerate to get a quick divorce.
Men are justified in their behavior or not responsible for unintentional effects.	He's just expressing his interest in her, she should be flattered; he's just trying to be nice to her; he didn't mean it.	He paid for her date; he had to release his sexual "tension"; he didn't mean it.	He was punishing her for unwifely behavior; he had a bad day at the office; he didn't mean it.
The acts are not really harmful.	He didn't hurt her; she didn't lose her job or promotion.	She wasn't a virgin; there were no bruises.	She didn't break any bones; she'll heal.
The acts are very unusual or deviant.	He was drinking and not himself; he's under a lot of stress and needs help.	He was drinking and not himself; he must be sick or under stress and needs help and understanding.	He was drinking and not himself; he must be sick or under stress and needs help and understanding.

Source: M. P. Koss, L. A. Goodman et al. (1994). *No Safe Haven: Male violence against women at home, at work, and in the community.* Washington, DC: American Psychological Association. Copyright © 1994 by the American Psychological Association, University of Minnesota Press, and the Federation of Behavioral, Psychological, and Cognitive Services. Reprinted with permission.

ment, rape, male partner abuse, and childhood sexual abuse all are linked by definitional ambiguities, language that masks their severity, high prevalence rates, invisibility and efforts to invalidate women's experiences so that they remain hidden, and serious immediate and long-term consequences that extend beyond direct victims to all women.

In the final chapter, we explore what can be done to reduce male violence against women, as well as respond to the other challenges introduced throughout this book.

PA1. I think that most women will feel most fulfilled by being a wife and a mother.

strongly disagree　　disagree　　neither agree nor disagree　　agree　　strongly agree

R2. I used to think that there isn't a lot of sex discrimination, but now I know how much there really is.

strongly disagree　　disagree　　neither agree nor disagree　　agree　　strongly agree

EE3. Being a part of a women's community is important to me.

strongly disagree　　disagree　　neither agree nor disagree　　agree　　strongly agree

S4. Some of the men I know are more feminist than some of the women I know.

strongly disagree　　disagree　　neither agree nor disagree　　agree　　strongly agree

AC5. I want to work to improve women's studies.

strongly disagree　　disagree　　neither agree nor disagree　　agree　　strongly agree

PA6. I've never really worried or thought about what it means to be a woman in this society.

strongly disagree　　disagree　　neither agree nor disagree　　agree　　strongly agree

R7. It only recently occurred to me that I think it's unfair that men have the privileges they have in this society simply because they are men.

strongly disagree　　disagree　　neither agree nor disagree　　agree　　strongly agree

EE8. My social life is mainly with women these days, but there are a few men I wouldn't mind having a nonsexual friendship with.

strongly disagree　　disagree　　neither agree nor disagree　　agree　　strongly agree

S9 While I am concerned that women be treated fairly in life, I do not see men as the enemy.

strongly disagree　　disagree　　neither agree nor disagree　　agree　　strongly agree

AC10. I have a lifetime commitment to working for social, economic, and political equality for women.

strongly disagree　　disagree　　neither agree nor disagree　　agree　　strongly agree

PA11. If I were married to a man and my husband was offered a job in another state, it would be my obligation to move in support of his career.

strongly disagree　　disagree　　neither agree nor disagree　　agree　　strongly agree

R12. It makes me really upset to think about how women have been treated so unfairly in this society for so long.

strongly disagree　　disagree　　neither agree nor disagree　　agree　　strongly agree

EE13. I share most of my social time with a few close women friends who share my feminist values.

strongly disagree　　disagree　　neither agree nor disagree　　agree　　strongly agree

S14. I feel that some men are sensitive to women's issues.

    strongly   disagree   neither agree   agree   strongly
    disagree   nor disagree   agree

AC15. I feel that I am a very powerful and effective spokesperson for the women's issues I am concerned with right now.

    strongly   disagree   neither agree   agree   strongly
    disagree   nor disagree   agree

PA16. I am not sure what is meant by the phrase "women are oppressed under patriarchy."

    strongly   disagree   neither agree   agree   strongly
    disagree   nor disagree   agree

R17. When I see the way most men treat women, it makes me so angry.

    strongly   disagree   neither agree   agree   strongly
    disagree   nor disagree   agree

EE18. Especially now, I feel that the other women around me give me strength.

    strongly   disagree   neither agree   agree   strongly
    disagree   nor disagree   agree

S19. Although many men are sexist, I have found that some men are supportive of women and feminism.

    strongly   disagree   neither agree   agree   strongly
    disagree   nor disagree   agree

AC20. I am very committed to a cause that I believe contributes to a more fair and just world for all people.

    strongly   disagree   neither agree   agree   strongly
    disagree   nor disagree   agree

PA21. I think that rape is sometimes the woman's fault.

    strongly   disagree   neither agree   agree   strongly
    disagree   nor disagree   agree

R22. When you think about most of the problems in the world—the threat of nuclear war, pollution, discrimination—it seems to me that most of them are caused by men.

    strongly   disagree   neither agree   agree   strongly
    disagree   nor disagree   agree

EE23. If I were to paint a picture or write a poem, it would probably be about women or women's issues.

    strongly   disagree   neither agree   agree   strongly
    disagree   nor disagree   agree

S24. I evaluate men as individuals, not as members of a group of oppressors.

    strongly   disagree   neither agree   agree   strongly
    disagree   nor disagree   agree

AC25. I am willing to make certain sacrifices to effect change in this society in order to create a nonsexist, peaceful place where all people have equal opportunities.

    strongly   disagree   neither agree   agree   strongly
    disagree   nor disagree   agree

PA = Passive Acceptance
R = Revelation
EE = Embeddedness-Emanation
S = Synthesis
AC = Active Commitment

Source: See p. 24.

TWELVE

MAKING A DIFFERENCE
Transforming Ourselves, Our Relationships, and Our Society

Before you start reading this chapter, complete the questionnaire that comes before it. It might look familiar, because you filled in this scale after reading Chapter 1, but don't consult your previous answers yet. Answer the questions, then read on. We'll come back to this survey later in this chapter.

As we look back over this book, there are at least four major themes that recur. The first overriding theme is that psychology has been irrevocably transformed by feminist questions that critique, refine, and expand what we do, how we do it, what we've found, and how we interpret our findings. My approach throughout this book has been designed to encourage questions and critical thinking so that research does not stand unchallenged or in isolation, but rather comes together to support a cohesive argument. Oftentimes we have seen that alternative arguments and the research supporting them critically challenge myths that actively disparage women and girls. All this argues that we "do" psychology as a discipline, that is, the field of psychology is socially constructed. It does not exist independent of our values and our lives. Rather, a transformed psychology is constructed by psychologists who have explored their values. It is related to people's lives and is valued for its resonance, and it relies on systematic research that is inclusive of all people and draws on a wide variety of methodologies and disciplines to take a holistic approach to understanding a problem. It is this approach to doing psychology that gives us a vantage from which to better understand women and gender.

A second repeated theme across these chapters is that a holistic approach to understanding women and gender must draw on biological, socialization, and personality explanations, as well as on social contextual factors. Focusing on context helps us view gender as socially constructed. This situation-centered perspective takes us beyond causes internal to people as explanations for differences between women and men to explore moderators linked with gender such as social status and power. This moves us away from an androcentric, deficit model that blames women for their presumed shortcomings and lays the groundwork for social activism directed at eliminating unfair external constraints. It also opens up a wide array of possibilities for individuals who are not limited by gendered stereotypes or prescriptions dictating what they "should" do as women and as men.

Our third point takes our contextual analysis beyond gender to consider other markers of social status and power including race and ethnicity, physical (dis)ability, sexual orientation, socioeconomic class, religion, age, and so on. Each of these is enmeshed with gender so that how one plays out her or his gender is inseparably and always intertwined with these other social markers. Additionally, these social indicators cannot be left unexplored as final explanations for differences. For example, when race and ethnic differences are found, a full analysis must examine the cultural settings that are related to these markers. We cannot simply accept race and ethnicity itself as an explanation; rather we need to "do" difference as part of "doing" gender. This book only begins this process by focusing mostly on gender.

Our fourth recurrent theme centers on *why* we do what we do as psychologists. We have seen that a variety of feminisms and feminist viewpoints give meaning to the work we do as psychologists by directing its purpose—to end sexist oppression and thus work toward social justice. Certainly we have reviewed masses of research which compose the scholarship of this burgeoning field, but the ultimate value of our efforts will be judged by their usefulness in contributing to feminist goals for women and men. The purpose of this final chapter is to explore some concrete ways we can use what we've learned throughout this book to "make a difference."

The hope I expressed for this book in the first chapter was that when you finished it, you would take something important away from it. This book would fall short of its usefulness in a movement toward social justice if we didn't examine its impact on you and what you can do with what you've learned and considered. Feminist psychologists have looked at making a difference in three realms: (1) within ourselves as individuals, (2) within our relationships, and (3) throughout our society through social activism. Each is informed by our general understanding of power and empowerment. We first will take a close look at how psychologists in general, and feminist psychologists in particular, have approached the concepts of power and empowerment, then we'll go on to discuss how we can become empowered individually and in relationships, as well as simultaneously work toward social change as activists.

POWER AND EMPOWERMENT

Feminist psychologists have had an uneasy relationship with the concept of power. Traditionally, psychologists have conceptualized power as dominance, control, or influence over others (see Unger, 1986, for a review of social-psychological approaches to studying power). From this tradition emerged six distinct bases of **direct power**: reward, coercive, expert, information, legitimate authority (derived from one's position), and referent (derived from others wanting to emulate or identify with the powerful person) (French & Raven, 1959). Stereotypes of men's power conform to these direct forms of expressing power in contrast to stereotypes of women's power which describe indirect attempts to influence (e.g., whining and nagging) (Johnson, 1976). Additionally, women ascribe these forms of direct power to men and think of them as fitting with a general, societal definition of power (Miller & Cummins, 1992).

It is these forms of direct power that underlie feminist analyses of male dominance or patriarchy—ending sexist oppression ultimately means righting unjust power relationships. Yet Celia Kitzinger (1991) points to the paradoxes accompanying such a feminist critique of power in psychology (and in feminism as a whole). In psychology, the concept of power is rarely mentioned, and when it is used, it often summarizes power differentials in gender relationships without explaining how those differences arose. Although power may be as invisible and all-encompassing as the air we breathe (Henley, 1977), this description does little to inform us about what it is. Joan Griscom (1992) details four components of a good definition of power: power must involve more than coercion or dominance; it must be understood as relational (i.e., one has power over another—it cannot exist in isolation of others); it is sustained at an individual and relational level by broader societal forces; and it is a process that dynamically changes over time (rather than exists as a stable trait).

In addition to defining what power is, feminist analyses of male dominance necessarily portray women as powerless, engendering disempowered feelings in women who acknowledge the extent and pervasiveness of their oppression:

> My entry into the women's movement has led to feelings of vulnerability, despair, and shock. That cannot be denied. For identifying with women, instead of men, means taking on, in part, the notion of one's powerlessness, victimisation, and lack of resources. In my own head, for example, I was much less exposed to the danger of rape when I believed that the women who were raped contributed to it in some way, for after all there was no way *I* would provoke or initiate such an attack. Recognising now that *all* women are potentially rape victims, that most rapists are known to their victims, that the object of rape is domination, I no longer have that (false) security that it won't happen to me (Spender, 1984, p. 211).

Attributing the powerlessness of women to conditioning or socialization ultimately underestimates the power of male dominance by suggesting that if only women understood they were free, they would be, ignoring the social consequences of deviance and the strong normative pressures that enforce conformity (Kitzinger, 1991). Paradoxically, a feminist analysis of power that defines power solely in terms of dominance and control and that assigns such power exclusively to (some) men renders women both powerless and blame-worthy.

One potential solution to this quandary is a reconceptualization of power as empowerment or **power-to,** rather than **power-over** (Yoder & Kahn, 1992). This approach regards empowerment as more of a process than a thing, focusing on power as energy, potential, and competence, not as domination, coercion, and competition (Browne, 1995). Such an analysis of power recognizes the forces of patriarchal domination *and* turns to the empowerment of women and men not only to empower themselves (develop personal agency) but also to change broader social structures (activism) (Kitzinger, 1991). This form of empowerment is articulated by Colette Browne (1995) as:

> . . . a process of liberation of self and others, as a life force, a potential, a capacity, growth, and energy, where one works toward community and connection responsibly as opposed to working primarily toward one's individual good (p. 360).

Note that this definition meets all four of Griscom's (1992) criteria: power is more than coercion, is relational, is sustained by societal forces, and is a dynamic process.

Although psychological emphases on empowerment all too often focus exclusively on personal agency without concern for activism (Kitzinger, 1991), activism may be enhanced to the degree one has developed personal agency. We will start by exploring what psychologists can tell us about developing feminist personal empowerment. Keep in mind that such an individualistic approach must be complemented with activism to meet the criteria for feminist action that we have regarded as fundamental throughout this text. This will become clearer when we consider empowerment in women's relationships with men. The following is far from an exhaustive list of what psychologists have done and could do to better understand the development of empowerment in individuals and relationships, but it does give us the general flavor of what each area is like.

PERSONAL EMPOWERMENT

Our emphasis in this section will be on empowering individuals. We saw in Chapter 10 that individual empowerment is a primary goal of feminist therapy so we begin by examining empowered psychological well-being. We have seen throughout this book that inflexible adherence to gender-role prescriptions constrains the full expression of human thinking, feeling, and acting in both women and men. Next we explore gender-role transcendence as an alternative to such rigidity. Finally, we look at the development of a feminist identity which has been related to individual empowerment and has been linked to some positive outcomes for both women and men.

Well-Being

Clinical and counseling psychologists view personal empowerment or agency as a step toward enhanced psychological well-being (Gibbs & Fuery, 1994; Worell & Remer, 1992). As we saw in Chapter 4, what originally was interpreted as masculinity (as measured by the Bem Sex Role Inventory or Personal Attributes Questionnaire) has been reconceptualized as instrumentality or personal agency. Using these measures, there is extensive empirical evidence relating agency and well-being: agency has been associated with reduced depression, lower anxiety, elevated self-esteem, fewer health complaints, and decreased distress (reviewed by Helgeson, 1994). The other facet measured by these scales, expressiveness or communion, shows either weaker or little relation to these aspects of psychological adjustment. Although both facets are exhibited by both women and men, more men score high in instrumentality (personal agency); more women score high in expressiveness (communion). This suggests a link between being male and mental health that is moderated by enhanced agency and that is consistent with a gendered view of mental health (see Chapter 10).

If we take this a step farther, a picture of well-being emerges that stresses autonomy, self-control, and independence from others. Feminist critiques of this model uncover some significant cracks in this reasoning. Such a model is Euro-centric, heterosexist, and nonfeminist. In African American communities (King & Ferguson, 1996) and lesbian relationships (Green, 1990), communal relations are stressed. A collective orientation is more likely to be espoused by women who report high levels of feminist identity development (Ng, Dunne, & Cataldo, 1995).

This androcentric model defines well-being exclusively in individualistic terms, ignoring the relationship aspects of psychological health. A feminist reassessment enlarges the scope of what defines mental health to include self and others. Descriptions by 51 feminist women of a fully functioning woman integrate both individualistic independence and communal interdependence—women who feel empowered in and by themselves and their relationships (Crowley-Long & Long, 1992).

Consistent with this perspective, Vicki Helgeson (1994) finds that unmitigated agency (extreme agency stripped of communion) is related to negative mental and physical health outcomes. She also reviews the extensive research evidence linking communion to positive relationship outcomes, including social self-esteem, sociability-congeniality, marital satisfaction, and social support. Similarly, she finds unfavorable linkages between unmitigated communion and mental health. Taken together, these findings argue for a blending of instrumental and expressive empowerment in more comprehensive, feminist definitions of empowered well-being for both women and men.

Gender-Role Transcendence

Strict adherence to gender-role prescriptions limits the full expression of human behavior in both women and men (Philpot et al., 1997). As we saw in Chapter 3, gender-schematic thinking that holds fast to gendered stereotypes constrains thinking and social interaction. We also explored in Chapter 3 some ways to counteract sexist socialization processes; however, we noted that this approach was compromised by the pervasiveness of sexist societal influences. It also gives up on adults whose childhood socialization is complete. A supplement to gender-aschematic socialization is offered by gender-role transcendence—an approach that views people simply as people who often operate in gender-laden contexts.

Gender-role transcendence does not ignore gender, rather it reflects the final stage in a developmental progression that grapples with gendered norms in increasingly complex ways (Eccles, 1987; Rebecca, Hefner, & Olenshansky, 1976). At the simplest stage, people are undifferentiated by gender. A person who ignores gender might claim to treat individuals without regard to their sex, claiming to be gender "blind." Such a stance avoids grappling with sexist oppression and ultimately is a form of passive resistance to feminism. It defines a starting point for the development of gender-role transcendence, not its endpoint.

In response to repeated exposure to a classification system that divides people into female and male, a polarized view emerges that regards the sexes as opposite and distinct. This polarization may mellow somewhat, but gendered stereotypes continue to have a prescriptive quality by defining what women, girls, men, and boys *should* do. Both gender-neutrality and gender-polarized thinking must be rejected to move toward true gender role transcendence.

For this movement to happen, four psychological shifts are critical (Eccles, 1987, p. 236). First, we must break the link between gender identity and gender stereotypes so that our gender identity is independent from what is culturally prescribed. Here is a trivial personal example: I harbored a distaste for pink clothing for a long time in reaction to the feminizing quality it represented. My feminist identity was somehow compromised by the thought of wearing this color, even though I knew at a fundamental level that my self-concept need not be so fragile.

This relates to the second necessary ingredient for gender-role transcendence— the differentiation of the descriptive (what is) and prescriptive (what should be) functions of stereotypes. Pink may describe some women's clothes, but it need not prescribe or dictate these. Men's clothes can be pink, and women's can vary endlessly (although I still recoil from putting pink on a baby, probably because it is used to demarcate the gender of infants). On a more substantial level, nursing describes more women's than men's employment, but it certainly need not be this way.

Understanding the difference between description and prescription, the third step is to question the validity of the prescriptive functions of stereotypes, both for individuals and for society at large. Why should women be nurses and not surgeons; and why should men be surgeons and not nurses? On the face of it, these questions seem simplistic, but when we dig deep to explore them, they open up lots of challenges to gendered stereotypes, beginning with who benefits and who loses out from such restrictions. They also bring forward a host of social factors that channel women and men in different directions.

The fourth shift in thinking toward gender-role transcendence moves away from gender as a defining property of one's self-image and evaluations of others, refocusing our understanding of gender outward to social, contextual factors that influence women's and men's lives. This takes us beyond feeling secure as a woman or man (gender identity) to how we feel about ourselves as people, about others, and about the settings in which we live. Here we would think it's appropriate for a person to be tender toward a baby, directive with subordinates, warm and expressive with friends, cool and detached with opponents, and so on. The situation, not gender, would dictate the appropriateness of a full range of behaviors—what is prescribed is situationally, not gender related. This fits well with our discussion of gender-aschematicity in Chapter 3.

Summing up, gender-role transcendence is the opposite of rigid gender polarization, including hypermasculinity and hyperfemininity. It also rejects gender-neutrality and gender-"blindness." Throughout this book, we have seen the pitfalls of exaggerations of stereotypes, both feminine (e.g., vulnerability to agoraphobia, Ch. 10) and masculine (e.g., tendencies toward violence, Ch. 11). However, gender-role transcendence can take us only so far toward social change. Even if we each manage to better understand the role gender plays in our own lives and in our interactions with others, we often will be opposing broad societal norms and will face the not-so-trivial consequences of deviance (remember the sexist discrimination of Chapters 6 and 8).

Feminist Identity

Definition. One psychological approach to conceptualizing feminist identity has been offered by Patricia Gurin (1985; Gurin & Markus, 1989; Gurin & Townsend, 1986). Feminist consciousness[1] encompasses seven aspects:

Collective orientation	involves understanding that feminists must work together to bring about changes
Common fate	recognizes that women share a common fate based on their gender
Discontent	deals with how much influence women feel they have in American life and politics

---

[1] Gurin wrote mainly about "gender consciousness" aimed specifically at women. I have adapted her ideas to talk about feminist consciousness because it brings in men as profeminists and because subsequent research shows that women's identification with feminists, not just women in general, is more strongly related to group consciousness (Henderson-King & Stewart, 1994). For a good history of feminist consciousness, see Lerner (1993).

Legitimacy of disparities	recognizes that women are treated less favorably than men
Identification	measures the degree to which an individual identifies as a feminist
Cognitive centrality	refers to how salient one's feminist orientation is
Feminist attitudes	encompasses beliefs about women's and men's roles in society

How generalizable is this definition? For example, can men develop a feminist identity? One approach to men and masculinity, often acclaimed in the popular media (e.g., poet Robert Bly's 1990 *Iron John*—a book which spent 35 weeks on the bestseller list in 1991), mimics the claims of the women's movement by lamenting the oppression of men vis-à-vis the restrictions of the masculine gender role (Allen, 1997). The fundamental goal of this movement of "weekend warriors" is to de-feminize, then re-masculinize, men and boys (Kimmel & Kaufman, 1997). At its heart, it is a defensive reaction to the presumed male-bashing of the feminist movement. (As we will see in our model of feminist identity development, male-bashing may be a stage through which some pass in moving toward a more advanced feminist identity that brings in men as partners in activism.) At its core, this approach fails to recognize the privileges attached to the masculine gender role, seeks to reaffirm it, and is thus fundamentally antifeminist.

A second strand of men's studies emerges from a profeminist stance (Brod, 1987a; Clatterbaugh, 1990; Messner, 1997). From this perspective, men's lives become a focal point for study because leaving men's lives unexamined ignores male privilege (Brod, 1987b, p. 57). For example, an often-cited drawback of the masculine stereotype is the demand for strength that eschews weakness (operationalized as not being

How is it that we intuitively know the sex of the person in the closet? Who has more power in this exchange?

able to cry and express emotions). A profeminist perspective would approach this gendered expectation to see if its enactment privileges men and boys in some ways—for example, by empowering them by hiding vulnerability and withholding information (Brod, 1987a, p. 8). Such a perspective envisions an end to sexist oppression that ultimately liberates both women and men, rather than a re-entrenchment of male-dominance. It also provides a framework from which men can join women in developing feminist identities.

Others have questioned whether models of feminist identity and its development apply to only a subset of women—white, middle-class, well-educated, heterosexual, relatively privileged women. For example, Janet Helms (1990) explores the concept of "**womanist identity**" (E.B. Brown, 1989) for African American women, proposing that gender and racial identity development are intertwined. She outlines a model which describes different feminist identities for African American and white women. Both incorporate racial influences—Black identity for African American women and anti-racism for white women. Re-examine the seven aspects of feminist identity with an eye to adding both racial awareness and anti-racism. A parallel integration of class issues in gender consciousness has been forwarded for working-class women (Brewer, 1996), and the interaction of gender, race, class, and culture has been explored for Asian American women (Chow, 1987).

Measurement and changes.   Now is the time to return to the questionnaire you completed both at the start of this chapter and at the end of Chapter 1. Compare your "before" and "after" answers; are there any changes? Do you have some information to back up your answers for some items that you didn't have before reading this text? In a study following the same procedure we replicated here, changes were found in individual students' answers from before to after taking a women's studies course. Furthermore, those taking a feminist course differed from a control group taking other courses at the end, but not at the beginning, of the semester (Bargad & Hyde, 1991).

The questionnaire you completed contains selected items from the "Feminist Identity Development Scale" (FIDS) (Bargad & Hyde, 1991). It was designed to assess five dimensions of feminist identity development projected from a model proposed by Nancy Downing and Kristin Roush (1985). According to this model, respondents high in **passive acceptance** are either unaware of or deny individual, institutional, and cultural prejudice and discrimination against women (PA items on the FIDS). These people believe that traditional roles are advantageous for women and men and that men are superior. On the FIDS, passive acceptors would agree that marriage and motherhood fulfill most women (item PA1), would worry little about being a woman (PA6), readily would relocate for a husband's job (PA11), would not understand oppression and patriarchy (PA16), and would accept a rape myth (PA21). After taking a women's studies course, students were likely to disagree with these items both more than before taking the course and more than control students taking other courses (Bargad & Hyde, 1991). Do you see changes in yourself on these items?

A second dimension involves **revelation**—a series of crises or contradictions disrupt one's passive acceptance so that ignoring and denying are no longer possible. Potential disruptions include this book and the course you are taking (as well as other women's studies classes). These typically result in open questioning of one's self and one's roles, often accompanied by feelings of anger and guilt. Often this stage is characterized by dualistic thinking in which women are seen as positive and men are vilified. You can see these themes running through the five items I selected from the FIDS. Again, students surveyed by Adena Bargad and Janet Hyde (1991) agreed with these revelation items after taking a feminist course—more than they did beforehand and more than control students.

Nancy Downing and Kristin Roush (1985) drew upon a model of racial-identity development (Cross, 1971) that projected stages of development. A central assumption of stagewise models is that individuals pass through and resolve prior stages before moving to more advanced stages in a stepwise progression. Such a progression is evident from passive acceptance to revelation as earlier attitudes are rejected in the face of an intervening crisis. However, moving from revelation to some resolution does not seem to follow a simple, linear progression from rudimentary to more advanced forms of feminist identity as Downing and Roush originally theorized. A better conceptualization based on subsequent research considers the next three configurations as dimensions of feminist identity that co-exist in many post-revelation people (Worell, 1996) and through which an individual may recycle (Henderson-King & Stewart, 1997). For our purposes, you probably will see various parts of each of the remaining three dimensions in your own post-revelation identity.

In the third dimension of the model, **embeddedness-emanation**, feminists immerse themselves in feminist culture, seeking both affirmation and strengthening of their new identity. The new-found feminist identity that first emerges may be somewhat rigid, but openness to alternative viewpoints develops. A more relativistic approach to men appears—it may be worthwhile to engage in cautious interaction with a select few. In the fourth, **synthesis** dimension, people are able to transcend traditional gender roles, celebrate and value the positive aspects of femininity, make choices based on personal values, and evaluate men on an individual, not a stereotyped, basis. The final dimension emphasizes **active commitment**, integrating personal feminist identity with plans for meaningful and effective action aimed at social change. Men are viewed as equal to, but not the same as, women. These five dimensions are summarized in Table 12.1.

Each of these last three dimensions is captured in the items of the FIDS I selected. Furthermore, each dimension was affected by taking a women's studies course such that students expressed stronger agreement with each dimension after taking a course than they did beforehand (Bargad & Hyde, 1991). As one student commented:

> I feel I have a better understanding of feminist issues so I can argue for the feminist cause more effectively, making me more confident in identifying myself as a feminist (Bargad & Hyde, 1991, p. 193).

Other studies have documented the positive influence of psychology of women and other women's studies classes on students' feminist attitudes (Jones & Jacklin, 1988), performance self-esteem and occupational aspirations (Stake & Gerner, 1987), activism (Stake & Rose, 1994; Stake et al., 1994), and self-concept and assertiveness

TABLE 12.1   Feminist Identity Development According to Downing and Roush

Passive Acceptance	Revelation	Embeddedness-Emanation	Synthesis	Active Commitment
Passive acceptance of traditional gender roles and discrimination; belief that traditional roles are advantageous; men are considered superior.	Catalyzed by a series of crises, resulting in open questioning of self and roles and feelings of anger and guilt; dualistic thinking; men are perceived as negative.	Characterized by connectedness with other select women, affirmation and strengthening of new identity. Eventually more relativistic thinking and cautious interaction with men.	Development of an authentic and positive feminist identity; gender-role transcendence; "flexible truce" with the world; evaluate men on an individual basis.	Consolidation of feminist identity; commitment to meaningful action; to a nonsexist world. Actions are personalized and rational. Men are considered equal but not the same as women.

Source: N. E. Downing and K. L. Roush. From passive acceptance to active commitment: A model of feminist identity development for women. *The Counseling Psychologist,* 13, pp. 695–709, copyright © 1985 by Sage Publications, Inc. Reprinted by Permission of Sage Publications, Inc.

(O'Connell, 1989). All of this research predicts that this book and the course you are taking are likely to have had some impact on how you think, feel, and act toward feminism and feminist psychology.

Correlates.   What value is there in having a well-developed feminist identity? Studies of feminist identity in women find that women with strong feminist identities are personally empowered and see the world through feminist lenses. College women who scored high on the feminist identity scale followed less traditional dating scripts than did women high on passive acceptance (Rickard, 1989). Women's feminist views influenced political voting choices when candidates held divergent views on feminist issues (Cook, 1993); predicted perceptions of gender discrimination on a college campus (Fischer & Good, 1994) and in general (Kobrynowicz & Branscombe, 1997); and eliminated evaluation bias such that feminist college women did not devalue the work of women artists (Rickard, 1990). A feminist orientation can affect occupational aspirations: feminist adolescent girls exhibited enhanced confidence in their abilities to pursue career-related tasks (Ahrens & O'Brien, 1996), and feminist African American women placed greater value on blending career and family (Weathers et al., 1994). Nonbulimic women were more likely to endorse a feminist ideology than bulimics (Brown, Cross, & Nelson, 1990), and women who identified with feminist values reported less body dissatisfaction, fewer bulimic symptoms, and strengthened feelings of effectiveness (Snyder & Hasbrouck, 1996). Women with strong feminist identities certainly appear empowered.

Feminist values may serve as an antidote to male violence against women. Men who endorsed feminist ideology tested as possessing a lower proclivity to perpetrate sexual harassment (Bartling & Eisenman, 1993) and reported less acceptance of interpersonal violence overall (Truman, Tokar, & Fischer, 1996). Feminist adult women survivors of childhood sexual abuse expressed more anger toward their parents in therapy and, relatedly, were less likely to blame themselves for bringing on their own abuse (Newman & Peterson, 1996).

What does an individual do with a feminist identity? As we saw, a strong feminist identity involves both a sense of personal empowerment and a commitment to social activism. We also argued in Chapter 1 of this book that a psychology of women was valuable to the extent that it is useful—that it works *for* women. It is clear that effective activism relies on individual empowerment. However, we shall see that personal empowerment without social activism falls short of an active commitment to social change and hence misses the mark of this final dimension of feminist identity development. Too often, psychologists have focused on personal empowerment without making this necessary connection to social activism (Kravetz & Marecek, 1996; Marecek & Hare-Mustin, 1991; Parvin & Biaggio, 1991). Although we will begin here by exploring personal empowerment, this section cannot stand alone without the one that follows later on social activism. The need for this broader definition of empowerment becomes even clearer when we consider empowerment in women's relationships with men.

EMPOWERED RELATIONSHIPS

A general model for how gender is enacted in interpersonal exchanges was proposed by Kay Deaux and Brenda Major (1987). They think of gender as one aspect of ongoing relationships in which one member expects certain behaviors from another, the other member negotiates her or his own identity, and the context in which the interaction occurs shapes what behaviors are emitted. Given this model, we would expect to find lots of stereotype-confirming behavior if both parties in an interaction hold traditional beliefs, and these are activated by the situation.

For example, consider a manager who has two subordinates, Joan and John. If that manager held traditional beliefs about the male-appropriateness of leadership, those beliefs might prompt the manager to describe a performance appraisal exercise quite differently to the two employees: say as an opportunity for John to take charge and for Joan to display cooperative skills. To further maximize the gender-typing here, assume that Joan and John have different histories and expectations about leadership that also conform to gender stereotypes. Combine these with what the manager conveys (either openly or subtly), and an observable gender difference between the behaviors of Joan and John is likely to result: John is likely to take charge and Joan is likely to work cooperatively with her group.

Consider the same scenario with all components working synchronously to *minimize* gender differences. We would expect to find few differences between the behaviors of Joan and John if (1) the manager believed that women and men enact leadership similarly; (2) gender-related beliefs were not activated in the manager; (3) Joan and John thought similarly about leadership and shared similar past experiences; and (4) similar schema about leadership were activated in Joan and John.

We saw in Chapter 6 that gender expectations can become self-fulfilling (what we expect to happen actually happens). This model can both explain how this happens, and offer an alternative scenario to short-circuit the process. The important point here is that *gendered enactments are dependent on ourselves, the others with whom we interact, and the context in which this occurs.* With this in mind, we'll explore empowerment in heterosexual dating, marital, and working relationships, and in responses to violence. We saw in Chapter 7 that gendered issues of imbalanced power are influential in heterosexual intimate relationships so our discussion here is purposively confined to heterosexual dating and marriage.

Heterosexual Dating

One intervention designed for high-school girls and college women in abusive heterosexual dating relationships formed support groups to help empower them (Rosen & Bezold, 1996). Participants report that the groups were effective in providing a safe environment to share experiences; in encouraging thoughtful consideration of their relationship; in inspiring self-efficacy; in developing communication, problem-solving, and assertiveness skills; and in recognizing their own personal rights. The heterosexual dating scripts we saw in Chapter 7 were associated with dating violence in Chapter 11 in part because these scripts serve to disempower women. Support groups such as this, as well as the development of a feminist identity (noted above, Rickard, 1989), serve to better balance these power dynamics.

Marriage

A similar effect of women's empowerment emerges from our discussion in Chapter 7 of the division of domestic labor. We saw that there is some evidence, although far from conclusive, that the balance of power in a heterosexual relationship may make a difference. We also saw that egalitarian attitudes do not automatically translate into domestic sharing. Some clues regarding how to empower women and men in marriage (and other intimate heterosexual relationships) can be gleaned from studies of feminist couples.

In one such study, Karen Blaisure and Katherine Allen (1995) conducted in-depth interviews with 10 self-identified feminist married couples. All participants stressed the importance of **vigilance** and the dynamic nature of their exchanges as they *continually worked* to define and redefine their participation in their marriages. All couples monitored their relationship in three ways. First, they spent time together exploring the sexism faced by women in their everyday lives. They analyzed life events from a feminist framework:

> DAN: I was mad because I felt Barb wasn't valued for what she was. She worked just as hard as anyone else, and she wasn't appreciated. It made me more supportive of her (Blaisure & Allen, 1995, p.11).

Second, they worked hard to demonstrate publicly their concern for the wife's status in marriage, most often through different last names and joint involvement in financial decisions:

> LARRY: Well, the world we're in still expects to see the male making all the decisions about what the family is going to do. So people ranging from a car salesman to everything else expect me to make any decision that is confronting what we should do. They talk to me, and I don't like that. I don't want them to talk to me, I want them to talk to both of us (Blaisure & Allen, 1995, p. 12).

Third, all participants stressed the importance of supporting the woman's activities, including employment and feminist activism.

Six of the ten couples interviewed justified their unequal division of household labor by pointing to either gendered (e.g., cooking is women's work) or personality (e.g., she enjoys cooking) explanations. In contrast, four claimed to share equally in domestic responsibilities, and only these four reported two additional processes of vigilance. First, the equal-contributing subset continually monitored their contributions:

> PATRICK: I think it is really possible to have equality or a nonoppressive marriage but it is not something that sort of happens and you say "Zap, now we got it" and you go on. You have to constantly communicate and sometimes it swings a little bit more toward the other. . . . You have to ensure that equality maintains itself (Blaisure & Allen, 1995, p. 13).

Second, although all couples noted the importance of feeling close to their partner, the four equal-sharers worked together to meet each other's emotional needs:

> MIRIAM: He's my soul mate, and I know I would never find anyone as perfect for me as he is. Other friends are for spice, for variety, for flavor, for a fuller emotional range (Blaisure & Allen, 1995, p. 15).

The message that comes through loud and clear is that equal sharing is not a given, but rather reflects a continual process of vigilance and painstaking work to bring feminist ideology to life in everyday practice.[2]

On the Job

Almost all of what we discussed in Chapter 8 points to broad macrostructural factors (e.g., occupational segregation) and more narrow microstructural factors (e.g., tokenism) that work together to restrict women's and men's participation in the workforce. One small form of personal empowerment that emerged from this discussion focused on using individuating information on job resumes, most notably by masculinizing an applicant's background for a male-defined job. Others have noted the value of making earnings public to highlight, and ultimately undermine, wage inequities (Steinem, 1983). Beyond the individual worker, I believe that it is important for employers to ask what they can do to level the playing field, for example, by training and legitimating women leaders (Yoder, Schleicher, & McDonald, 1998).

Responses to Violence

Feminists have discussed personal empowerment as a component of violence prevention and as an impetus for recovery. Both themes appear in discussions of sex-

---

[2]For sound, practical advice on how to realize gender equality in dual career relationships, see Lucia Gilbert's work (1993).

ual harassment (Anonymous, 1991; Charney & Russell, 1994), male partner abuse (Dutton-Douglas, 1992; Frieze & McHugh, 1992; Webb, 1992), and childhood sexual abuse (Liem, O'Toole, & James, 1992: Nelson, 1991). To illustrate the role empowerment plays in discussions of violence, we'll consider the example of rape avoidance and prevention here.

Rape resistance and avoidance. What should an individual woman do if attacked by a stranger? Comparisons of women who were raped by a stranger with those who escaped focus on situational characteristics, offender aggression, and victim resistance. Higher completion rates have been found when the rape takes place indoors, when environmental interruptions (e.g., someone driving by) are absent, when a weapon is present, when the attack occurs at night, and when it is a blitz attack (i.e., a surprise physical assault) (reviewed by Ullman & Knight, 1993). These findings are summarized in Table 12.2.

Offender aggression can fall into one of four categories: nonviolent verbal aggression (the attacker tells the victim what to do); violent verbal aggression (the perpetrator yells and/or swears at the victim); violent physical aggression (using physical assault or a weapon); and use of other items (e.g., blindfolds, ropes, and sticks) (Ullman & Knight, 1991). Victim resistance can be classified as none; nonforceful verbal (e.g., pleading or crying); forceful verbal (e.g., screaming); physical (e.g., pushing, wrestling, striking, and biting); and fleeing (Zoucha-Jensen & Coyne, 1993). The effectiveness (defined as rape escape, minimal physical harm, and less sexual abuse) of each of these depends on the type of offender aggression and on some situational characteristics.

Sarah Ullman and Raymond Knight (1991; 1993) found that forceful verbal and physical responses were equally efficacious across all rape locations. In contrast, nonforceful verbal strategies were ineffective in escaping rape in both dangerous and less dangerous situations. Forceful verbal, physical, and fleeing responses were

TABLE 12.2   Summary of Factors Mediating Stranger-Rape Escape

Situational Characteristics	Offender Aggression	Victim Resistance
location (indoors; outside*)	nonviolent verbal	none
environmental interruptions (no; yes*)	violent verbal***	nonforceful verbal
weapon (present; absent*)	violent physical**	forceful verbal*
time of day (night; day*)	use of other items	physical*
surprise (yes; no*)		fleeing*

 * Enhance escape
 ** Increase physical injury to victim
*** Aggravate sexual assault
Source: Compiled from S. E. Ullman & R. A. Knight (1991). A multivariate model for predicting rape and physical injury outcomes during sexual assaults. *Journal of Consulting and Clinical Psychology, 59,* 724–731. Printed with permission of the American Psychological Association.

most effective for escaping rape, especially in dangerous settings. Physical resistance proved effective in thwarting a rape attempt even in the presence of a weapon, although more rapes are completed with the presence of a weapon (Bart & O'Brien, 1993).

Physical injury to the victim resulted more from the offender's violent physical aggressiveness than from the physicality of the victim's resistance. In other words, most physical injury appears to result from the sexual assault itself, not the victim's resistance. Women tend to confine their use of physical resistance to offenders who use violent physical aggressiveness (so it is hard to say if this would work with other forms of attack). Sexual abuse was most severe when the assailant used violent verbal aggression or executed a con assault (in which the victim was duped into trusting her more sadistic attacker) or stalker-like assault. In sum, crying and pleading don't seem to help; rather meeting the offender's violence with an equal level of resistance is generally most effective (also see Siegel et al., 1989; for a clear overview see Bart & O'Brien, 1993).

The above discussion was generated by research with survivors of stranger rape and attempted rape, ignoring a more likely threat to women from acquaintances and intimates. Recognizing this, Joyce Levine-MacCombie and Mary Koss (1986) compared college women who either escaped date rape or were victimized. All reported feeling angry during the attack, but only successful resistors recalled less fear and guilt during the attack. Women who succeeded in escaping rape retrospectively perceived their assault as less violent, and they reported running away and screaming for help more often than unsuccessful resistors.

This resistance pattern parallels what we saw above with stranger rape. Quarreling with the offender contributed significantly to the completion of date rape, making this a strategy to avoid. In contrast to stranger escape, women who escaped date rape reported that crying and reasoning contributed to their success, probably because they had some relationship with the attempted perpetrator. However, these nonforceful verbal strategies were less effective than more active patterns of resistance—still making screaming, physical attacking, and fleeing the most effective responses.

Ironically, these effective response strategies involve actions many women have been socialized to avoid as "unfeminine," "impolite," and hurtful (Rozee, 1996; Quina & Carlson, 1989). This is where empowerment programs come in. Women completing a self-defense class decreased their perceived vulnerability to assault, reduced their incidence of negative thinking and avoidance behaviors, and felt more self-efficacious (Ozer & Bandura, 1990). As we have seen in heterosexual dating relationships, communication and assertiveness skills are linked to successful date-rape resistance (Rosen & Bezold, 1996).

Some avoidance advice argues for developing "assertive wariness," whereby women recognize risky behaviors and plan alternative escape and avoidance strategies (Quina & Carlson, 1989). An example is carrying one's purse tucked securely under one's arm rather than holding it loosely—a strategy that reflects "street savvy" (Riger & Gordon, 1981). Although tips on day-to-day protective strategies can reduce risk (Cummings, 1992), they also fail to challenge the faulty ideas that women alone are responsible for preventing violence; that women who are unsuccessful at resisting rape are blame-worthy; that confine rape scenarios to the less likely occurrence of stranger-rape; and that (taken to an extreme) fit with the pattern of borderline agoraphobia we examined in Chapter 10.

Successfully escaping rape and avoiding rape attempts are positive outcomes, the importance of which should not be minimized for individual women. However, an avoidance approach is fundamentally individualistic; it does not protect women in general (Lonsway, 1996). Rapists tend to seek out vulnerable women so that the success of one woman in deterring rape is offset by the likely victimization of another. Because of this, no matter how well trained women are in avoidance, escape, and self-defense, they remain vulnerable to sexual assault to the extent that men continue to commit these acts (Schewe & O'Donohue, 1993). It is this key point that distinguishes rape avoidance from rape prevention.

Rape prevention. Rape prevention focuses on men as the perpetrators of these acts and on cultural beliefs and institutions that, intentionally or not, support the victimization of women. Kimberly Lonsway (1996) reviewed educational programs, not simply inclusive of men but designed specifically for them, with an eye toward identifying programming characteristics that have been demonstrated to be effective preventatives. Targeting the misinformation of rape mythology is a widely used technique of educational programs that has been linked to desirable attitude change. Similarly, participant interaction, typically in the forms of group discussion, role play, and interactive dramatic performances, generally is found to co-occur with favorable attitude change.

Improved communication skills appear effective only when they incorporate explicit understandings of gender roles and the subordinated status of women. Simple enhancements to dyadic exchanges without these broader, societal linkages indeed may make communication clearer, but men who perpetrate sexual aggression seem to ignore, not misunderstand (Hanson & Gidycz, 1993). Evidence about the effectiveness of getting men to empathize with their targets and of previous experiences with either victimization or perpetration is inconclusive, warranting further research. Finally, confrontational approaches induce alienation and defensiveness, both of which run contrary to prevention. It is clear that educational programs using effective approaches are likely to encourage positive attitude change. However, a causal link between rape-rejecting attitudes and reduced sexually aggressive behavior has not been established definitively, although these factors clearly are correlated (Lonsway & Fitzgerald, 1994).

Box 12.1 lists some clear things men can do to reduce violence against women beyond the obvious solution of not directly assaulting women (Mahlstedt & Kohat, 1991; Men against rape, 1979/80; Warshaw, 1994; also see Funk, 1993). I have argued that violence is more than acts confined to individual women and men; for this reason, solutions must look beyond individuals as well. Some broader possibilities include supporting and participating in "take back the night" events (where supporters march in unison in settings individual women usually find disturbing); pressuring organizations to establish policies and set up an atmosphere in which they'll be enforced (Bravo & Cassedy, 1992); boycotting products that rely on violent advertising; raising nonviolent children; making violence visible by speaking out (Quina & Carlson,

---

BOX 12.1   What a Man Can Do to Help Stop Violence against Women

---

- Attend events that raise your consciousness about violence against women.
- Confront men who use sexist language or make jokes degrading to women.
- Be aware of your own behavior which may be threatening to women. (For example, on a quiet street at night, realize that walking behind a woman may be threatening to her. Crossing to the other side of the street would relieve this threat.)
- Be willing to examine your defensiveness when listening to the expression of feminist ideas.
- Do not confuse mere friendliness with sexual invitation.
- Discuss issues related to sexism and violence with your male and female friends.
- Be aware of sexism in advertising and the media that depicts women in degrading ways.
- Be responsible for your actions when drinking. Do not use alcohol as an excuse or reason for acting violently.
- If you suspect or directly experience physical or verbal abuse directed toward a woman (or man), take appropriate action.

1989); educational programs targeting young children (Tulloch & Tulloch, 1992) and college students (Berkowitz, 1994; Earle & Nies, 1994); interventions designed for male batterers (Dutton, 1988) and rape perpetrators (Pollard, 1994); multifaceted community-based programs and services for incest survivors (Wisconsin Coalition Against Sexual Assault, 1989) and campus rape (Adams & Abarbanel, 1988; Bohmer & Parrot, 1993); organizations for men against rape (see the appendix of Beneke, 1992, for a beginning list), including fraternities (Egidio & Robertson, 1981); expanded feminist coverage of violence against women in the media (Stone, 1993); and so on.

ACTIVISM

In each of the examples of personal and relationship empowerment we explored here, we saw that the picture was incomplete if we didn't expand our vision beyond the individual or dyadic levels. Gender-role transcendence indeed moves individuals away from gendered-typed thinking and behaviors, but when enacted within a gender-schematic societal context, different behaviors easily can be regarded as deviant, rather than as models for social change. Similar scenarios emerged from our discussions of empowerment in heterosexual dating, marital, and working relationships, empowered well-being, and violence avoidance. Individual solutions cannot exist alone without consideration of broader societal forces. Here's where activism enters the scene.

Definition and History

What constitutes feminist activism? In the 1970s and through the defeat of the Equal Rights Amendment (ERA) in 1982, it was clear what the mainstream, large-scale feminist issues were. Feminist organizations, like the National Organization for Women, National Abortion Rights Action League, Women's Equity Action League, Women's Legal Defense Fund, and the National Women's Political Caucus, flourished as did grass-roots consciousness raising and political and social action groups (e.g., battered women's shelters, rape-crisis centers, and job-training programs). Women's Studies programs spread on college campuses, the Supreme Court's 1973 *Roe v. Wade* decision seemed to protect abortion rights, the Equal Rights Amendment[3] sailed through both houses of Congress after a long dormancy (it was first introduced in 1923) and racked up the support of 35 of 38 states (needing just three more for final ratification), affirmative action laws passed, and so on. Doing feminist activism seemed clear during this period, considered the heyday of the contemporary wave of feminism (Ryan, 1992; Taylor & Whittier, 1993).

After the defeat of the ERA, some political analysts argued that feminism died (offering contradictory arguments that it both outlived its usefulness and succumbed to its whimsy). It is not uncommon to now hear about a "post-feminist" period. Indeed the 1980s saw a decline in both formal and informal feminist organizations, and the political climate shifted away from values of equality, human rights, and social justice, igniting a backlash directed against feminism and its gains during the 1970s (Faludi, 1991; Taylor & Whittier, 1993). Recognizing all this, feminist analysts, like Verta Taylor and Nancy Whittier (1993), are not so pessimistic (or so naively optimistic to think that a feminist agenda is no longer necessary). Instead, they describe a post-heyday period of abeyance.

Taylor and Whittier (1993) argue that social movements go into **abeyance** in order to hold out during periods of hostility toward their ideology. Applied to contemporary feminism, this is reflected in the lower profile recently adopted by many feminists, although there have been significant exceptions (e.g., the 300,000-600,000 person-strong march in Washington in 1989 to protest restrictions on abortion). Feminism in the 1990s has established strong links to other political causes (ranging from peace to environmental, gay and lesbian, AIDS, anti-violence, etc., movements) (Paul, 1993). It offers within each an approach that includes and empowers women and men. Consciousness-raising activities continue in classes, in books such as this one, and from one generation to the next. Additionally, some of the tenets of feminism have so permeated our culture that we barely notice them, taking for granted everything from married couples with different last names and separable

---

[3] The full text of the ERA states: "Equality of rights under the law shall not be denied or abridged by the United States or by any state on account of sex. The Congress shall have the power to enforce, by appropriate legislation, the provisions of this article. The amendment shall take effect two years after the date of ratification."

Feminist issues infuse movements not directly connected to feminism such as the "million-women" march of African American women which drew crowds of over 300,000 people to Philadelphia on October 25, 1997.

credit ratings to the viability of women political candidates. Feminism isn't dead; it's just not as visible as it was at other times. With a little digging, feminist activism comes within one's reach.

Being an Activist

Who *does* feminist activism? There are committed feminists who devote their lives to feminist causes, but most of us are everyday folks with everyday lives. Comparing rank-and-file feminist activists to nonactivists, activists tend to be better educated, not live in the South, belong to voluntary organizations, work in the labor force, have fewer children, and believe in nontraditional political roles for women, abortion rights, the importance of women's rights, and the trustworthiness of others (Dauphinais, Barkan, & Cohn, 1992). Interestingly in this study, there were a few activists who weren't strongly committed feminists, but rather who were pulled into supporting the women's movement by friends, their affiliation with voluntary organizations, and their experiences in the workforce.

What can we each do to contribute to feminist activism? First steps obviously involve developing, expanding, and refining our own feminist identity and personal empowerment. Part of this includes adopting the simple label of feminist to describe one's self. As we saw in Chapter 1, there are some strongly negative cultural stereotypes that can make this a risky proclamation. Women's feminist identity is threatened by homophobia, which links feminism with homosexuality as a means to disparage both (Frye, 1992); by stereotypes predicting family-role failure for feminist activists (Rickabaugh, 1995); and by justifiable fears that claiming a feminist identity will make one an outsider in some contexts (Griffin, 1994). This is offset by becoming an insider in feminist contexts. Women who take notice of discrimination are women who are willing to risk losing social approval (Kobrynowicz & Branscombe, 1997). For men, feminist identification is undermined by de-masculinizing stereotypes, but these may be counteracted by expectancies that feminist men will be favorably oriented toward family (Connell, 1993; Rickabaugh, 1995).

Gloria Steinem (1983) offers an amazingly empowering, yet simple strategy for individuals to do—engage in "outrageous acts and everyday rebellions" for the cause of social justice. She contends, and I agree, that having done one act, the world will seem different and you'll want to do more. She gives some examples to get the ball rolling (e.g., making public your salary; challenging some bit of woman-hating, homophobic, or racist humor), but feel free to brainstorm and try out your own. For example, my husband routinely irritates sexists by putting my name before his (most ostensibly on our car titles and income-tax returns) and by directing a server to have *me* taste a freshly opened bottle of wine. A resource for such ideas is Donna Jackson's (1992) intriguing book, *How to Make the World a Better Place for Women in Five Minutes a Day*.

There are plenty of outrageous acts you can do as a student. In psychology, some examples include doing a paper on a "forgotten" woman psychologist for your history course; giving a presentation on sexist bias in therapy in a psychopathology course; joining a professional organization for women (see Chapter 1 for ideas); and generally resisting the aspects of the discipline that run counter to feminist ideology and practice (see Kitzinger, 1990). By taking women's studies classes, you cast a vote for their inclusion in the curriculum (Coulson & Bhavnani, 1990). Challenge the discipline of psychology, as well as the general academic curriculum, to be feminist (see Ussher, 1990). As you can see, many of these acts are simple things that don't consume time or financial resources. Rather, they simply require some attention to details in your everyday life that can make a difference.

A major point repeated throughout this chapter is the need to see activism beyond the individual level to encompass the collective. Often the unification of feminists is compromised by diversity among feminists, and indeed the heyday of American feminism was remiss in acknowledging and learning from differences among feminist women and men (Taylor & Whittier, 1993). Since then, feminists have learned that the paradox of difference is that an awareness of diversity can lead to better understandings and, ultimately, to unity (Collins, 1986; Dill, 1983; hooks, 1984; MacPherson & Fine, 1995). It also is this understanding that makes feminism more of an approach, a way of seeing the world, that can permeate many arenas—personal, political, social, economic, educational, organizational, and so on. There are a wide range of examples of how women working together change things (see for example, Bookman and Morgen, 1988). This is true in psychology as well (Tiefer, 1991b; Wilkinson, 1990). My challenge to you (and for me as well) is to be a "welder":

The Welder*
Cherríe Moraga

I am a welder.
Not an alchemist.
I am interested in the blend
of common elements to make
a common thing.

No magic here.
Only the heat of my desire to fuse
what I already know
exists. Is possible.

We plead to each other,
we all come from the same rock
we all come from the same rock
ignoring the fact that we bend
at different temperatures
that each of us is malleable
up to a point.

Yes, fusion *is* possible
but only if things get hot enough—
all else is temporary adhesion,
patching up.

It is the intimacy of steel melting
into steel, the fire of our individual
passion to take hold of ourselves
that makes sculpture of our lives,
builds buildings.

And I am not talking about skyscrapers,
merely structures that can support us
without fear
of trembling.

For too long a time
the heat of my heavy hands
has been smoldering
in the pockets of other
people's business—
they need oxygen to make fire.

I am now
coming up for air.
Yes, I *am*
picking up the torch.

---

*C. Moraga (1981). The Welder. In C. Moraga and G. Anzaldua (eds.), *This bridge called my back: Writings by radical women of color.* New York: Kitchen Table: Women of Color Press, pp. 219–220. Reprinted with permission.

I am the welder.
I understand the capacity of heat
to change the shape of things.
I am suited to work
within the realm of sparks
out of control.

I am the welder.
I am taking the power
into my own hands.

REFERENCES

Aaronson, S. (1995, January). *Pay equity and the wage gap: Success in the states.* Washington, DC: Institute for Women's Policy Research.

AAUW. (1992). *The AAUW report: How schools shortchange girls.* Washington, DC: The American Association of University Women Educational Foundation.

AAUW. (1996). *Girls in the middle: Working to succeed in school.* Washington, DC: AAUW Sales Office.

Abbey, A. (1991). Misperception as an antecedent of acquaintance rape: A consequence of ambiguity in communication between women and men. In A. Parrot & L. Bechhofer (Eds.), *Acquaintance rape: A hidden crime* (pp. 96–112). New York: Wiley.

Acitelli, L.K., & Antonucci, T.C. (1994). Gender differences in the link between marital support and satisfaction in older couples. *Journal of Personality and Social Psychology, 67,* 688–698.

Adams, A., & Abarbanel, G. (1988). *Sexual assault on campus: What colleges can do.* Santa Monica, CA: Rape Treatment Center of Santa Monica Hospital Medical Center.

Adelman, C. (1991). *Women at thirtysomething: Paradoxes of attainment* (Report No. OR 91-530). Washington, DC: Department of Education.

Adelmann, P.K. (1994a). Multiple roles and physical health among older adults: Gender and ethnic comparisons. *Research on Aging, 16,* 142–166.

Adelmann, P.K. (1994b). Multiple roles and psychological well-being in a national sample of older adults. *Journals of Gerontology, 49,* S277–S285.

Adler, D.N., & Johnson, S.B. (1994). Sample description, reporting, and analysis of sex in psychological research: A look at APA and APA division journals in 1990. *American Psychologist, 49,* 216–218.

Adler, N.E., David, H.P., Major, B.N., Roth, S.H., Russo, N.F., & Wyatt, G.E. (1990). Psychological responses after abortion. *Science, 248,* 41–44.

Adolph, M.R. (1993). The myth of the golden years: One older woman's perspective. *Women & Therapy, 14,* 55–66.

AFL-CIO. (1997). *Ask a working woman: Executive summary.* Washington, DC.

Ahrens, J.A., & O'Brien, K.M. (1996). Predicting gender-role attitudes in adolescent females: Ability, agency, and parental factors. *Psychology of Women Quarterly, 20,* 409–417.

Ainsworth, M.D.S., Blehar, M.L., Waters, E., & Wall, S.C. (1978). *Patterns of attachment: A psychological study of the strange situation.* Hillsdale, NJ: Erlbaum.

Akan, G.E., & Grilo, C.M. (1995). Sociocultural influences on eating attitudes and behaviors, body image, and psychological functioning: A comparison of African-American, Asian-American, and Caucasian college women. *International Journal of Eating Disorders, 18,* 181–187.

Alessandri, S.M., & Lewis, M. (1993). Parental evaluation and its relation to shame and pride in young children. *Sex Roles, 29,* 335–344.

Allan, J.D., Mayo, K., & Michel, Y. (1993). Body size values of White and Black women. *Research in Nursing and Health, 16,* 323–333.

Allan, K., & Coltrane, S. (1996). Gender display in television commercials: A comparative study of television commercials in the 1950s and 1980s. *Sex Roles, 35,* 185–203.

Allen, L., Hines, M., Shryne, J., & Gorski, R. (1989). Two sexually dimorphic cell groups in the human brain. *Journal of Neuroscience, 9,* 497–506.

Allen, M. (1997). We've come a long way, too, baby. And we've still got a ways to go. So give us a break! In M.R. Walsh (Ed.), *Women, men, and gender: Ongoing debates* (pp. 402–405). New Haven, CT: Yale.

Allen, P.G. (1990). Violence and the American Indian woman. *The speaking profits us: Violence in the lives of women of color.* Seattle, WA: SAFECO Insurance Company.

Alper, J.S. (1985). Sex differences in brain asymmetry: A critical analysis. *Feminist Studies, 11,* 7–37.

Amaro, H. (1995). Love, sex, and power. *American Psychologist, 50,* 437–447.

Andersen, A.E., & DiDomenico, L. (1992). Diet vs. shape content of popular male and female magazines: A dose-response relationship to the incidence of eating disorders? *International Journal of Eating Disorders, 11,* 283–287.

Andersen, B.L., & Cyranowski, J.M. (1994). Women's sexual self-schema. *Journal of Personality and Social Psychology, 67,* 1079–1100.

Anderson, D., & Shapiro, D. (1996). Racial differences in access to high-paying jobs and the wage gap between Black and white women. *Industrial and Labor Relations Review, 49,* 273–286.

Anderson, J., Martin, J., Mullen, P., Romans, S., et al. (1993). Prevalence of childhood sexual abuse experiences in a community sample of women. *Journal of the American Academy of Child and Adolescent Psychiatry, 32,* 911–919.

Anderson, K.B., Cooper, H., & Okamura, L. (1997). Individual differences and attitudes toward rape: A meta-analytic review. *Personality and Social Psychology Bulletin, 23,* 295–315.

Aneshensel, C.S., Fielder, E.P., & Becerra, R.M. (1989). Fertility and fertility-related behavior among Mexican-American and non-Hispanic white female adolescents. *Public Opinion Quarterly, 53,* 548–562.

Angier, N. (1994, June 21). Feminists and Darwin: Scientists try closing the gap. *The New York Times,* pp. B7, B12.

Ankney, C.D. (1995). Sex differences in relative brain size: The mismeasure of woman, too?. *Personality and Intelligence, 16,* 329–336.

Anonymous. (1991). Sexual harassment: A female counseling student's experience. *Journal of Counseling and Development, 69,* 502–506.

Anzaldua, G. (1987). *Borderlands: The new mestiza.* San Francisco, CA: Aunt Lute Books.

Appleby, Y. (1994). Out in the margins. *Disability and Society, 9,* 19–32.

Applegate, J.S., & Kaye, L.W. (1993). Male elder caregivers. In C.L. Williams (Ed.), *Doing "women's work": Men in nontraditional occupations* (pp. 152–167). Newbury Park, CA: Sage.

Arber, S., & Ginn, J. (1994). Women and aging. *Reviews in Clinical Gerontology, 4,* 349–358.

Archer, C.J. (1984). Children's attitudes toward sex-role division in adult occupational roles. *Sex Roles, 10,* 1–10.

Archer, D., Iritani, B., Kimes, D.D., & Barrios, M. (1983). Face-ism: Five studies on sex differences in facial prominence. *Journal of Personality and Social Psychology, 45,* 725–735.

Army says women can compete in military. (1996, January 30). *Milwaukee Journal Sentinel,* p. 3.

Aronson, J. (1992). Women's sense of responsibility for the care of old people: "But who else is going to do it?" *Gender & Society, 6,* 8–29.

Arvey, R.D., Landon, T.E., Nutting, S.M., & Maxwell, S.E. (1992). Development of physical ability tests for police officers: A construct validation approach. *Journal of Applied Psychology, 77,* 996–1009.

Aryee, S. (1993). Dual-earner couples in Singapore: An examination of work and nonwork sources of their experienced burnout. *Human Relations, 46,* 1441–1468.

Asch, S.E. (1956). Studies of independence and conformity: I. A minority of one against a unanimous majority. *Psychological Monographs, 70(9,* Whole No. 416), 1–70.

Ashmore, R.D. (1990). Sex, gender, and the individual. In L.A. Pervin (Ed.), *Handbook of personality: Theory and research* (pp. 486–526). New York: Guilford Press.

Ashton, H. (1991). Psychotropic-drug prescribing for women. *British Journal of Psychiatry, 158* (suppl. 10), 30–35.

Atchley, R.C. (1994). *Social forces and aging: An introduction to social gerontology* (7th ed.). Belmont, CA: Wadsworth.

Athey, T.R., & Hautaluoma, J.E. (1994). Effects of applicant overeducation, job status, and job gender stereotype on employment decisions. *Journal of Social Psychology, 134,* 439–452.

Auerbach, J.D. (1990). Employer-supported child care as a women-responsive policy. *Journal of Family Issues, 11,* 384–400.

Aukofer, F.A., & Gunn, E. (1991, March 20). Johnson Controls loses case: U.S. Supreme Court strikes down fetal-protection policy. *Milwaukee Journal,* p. 1.

Baber, K.M., & Monaghan, P. (1988). College women's career and motherhood expectations: New options, old dilemmas. *Sex Roles, 19,* 189–203.

Baenninger, M., & Newcombe, N. (1989). The role of experience in spatial test performance: A meta-analysis. *Sex Roles, 20,* 327–344.

Bagley, C. (1991). The prevalence and mental health sequels of child sexual abuse in a community sample of women aged 18 to 27. *Canadian Journal of Community Mental Health, 10,* 103–116.

Bahniuk, M.H., Dobos, J., & Hill, S.K. (1990). The impact of mentoring, collegial support, and information adequacy on career success: A replication. *Journal of Social Behavior and Personality, 5,* 431–452.

Baier, J., Rosenzweig, M., & Whipple, E. (1991). Patterns of sexual behavior, coercion, and victimization of university students. *Journal of College Student Development, 32,* 310–322.

Bailey, J.M., & Pillard, R. (1991). A genetic study of male sexual orientation. *Archives of General Psychiatry, 48,* 1089–1096.

Bailey, J.M., & Pillard, R.C. (1997). The innateness of homosexuality. In M.R. Walsh (Ed.), *Women, men, and gender: Ongoing debates* (pp. 184–187). New Haven, CT: Yale.

Bailey, J.M., Pillard, R.C., Neale, M.C., & Agyei, Y. (1993). Hereditable factors influence sexual orientation in women. *Archives in General Psychiatry, 50,* 217–223.

Bailey, J.M., & Zucker, K.J. (1995). Childhood sex-typed behavior and sexual orientation: A conceptual analysis and quantitative review. *Developmental Psychology, 31*, 43–55.

Bailey, W.T. (1991). Knowledge, attitude, and psychosocial development of young and old adults. *Educational Gerontology, 17*, 269–274.

Bailey, W.T., Harrell, D.R., & Anderson, L.E. (1993). The image of middle-aged and older women in magazine advertisements. *Educational Gerontology, 19*, 97–103.

Banaji, M.R., & Greenwald, A.G. (1994). Implicit stereotyping and prejudice. In M.P. Zanna & J.M. Olson (Eds.), *The psychology of prejudice: The Ontario symposium* (Vol. 7, pp. 55–76). Hillsdale, NJ: Erlbaum.

Bandura, A., & Walters, R.H. (1963). *Social learning and personality development.* New York: Holt, Rinehart & Winston.

Bandy, N. (1989). *Relationships between male and female employees at Southern Illinois University.* Unpublished doctoral dissertation, College of Education, Southern Illinois University, Chicago.

Bank, B.J. (1994). Effects of national, school, and gender cultures on friendships among adolescents in Australia and the United States. *Youth and Society, 25*, 435–456.

Bank, B.J. (1995). Friendships in Australia and the United States: From feminization to a more heroic image. *Gender & Society, 9*, 79–98.

Banks, A., & Gartrell, N.K. (1995). Hormones and sexual orientation: A questionable link. *Journal of Homosexuality, 28*, 247–268.

Barak, A., Feldman, S., & Noy, A. (1991). Traditionality of children's interests as related to their parents' gender stereotypes and traditionality of occupations. *Sex Roles, 24*, 511–524.

Barash, D. (1979). *The whisperings within.* New York: Harper & Row.

Barbee, E.L. (1992). African American women and depression: A review and critique of the literature. *Archives of Psychiatric Nursing, 6*, 257–265.

Barer, B.M. (1994). Men and women age differently. *International Journal of Aging and Human Development, 38*, 29–40.

Bargad, A., & Hyde, J.S. (1991). Women's studies: A study of feminist identity development in women. *Psychology of Women Quarterly, 15*, 181–201.

Bargh, J., & Raymond, P. (1992). *An automatic power-sex association in men likely to be sexual harassers.* Paper presented at the meeting of the Society for Experimental Social Psychology, San Antonio, TX.

Barker, K. (1993). Changing assumptions and contingent solutions: The costs and benefits of women working full- and part-time. *Sex Roles, 28*, 47–71.

Barnas, M.V., & Cummings, E.M. (1994). Caregiver stability and toddlers' attachment-related behavior towards caregivers in day care. *Infant Behavior and Development, 17*, 141–147.

Barnett, E.A. (1988). La Edad Critica: The positive experience of menopause in a small Peruvian town. In P. Whelehan (Ed.), *Women and health: Cross-cultural perspectives.* Granby, MA: Bergin & Garvey Publishers.

Barnett, R.C. (1997). How paradigms shape the stories we tell: Paradigm shifts in gender and health. *Journal of Social Issues, 53*(2), 351–368.

Barnett, R.C., & Marshall, N.L. (1992). Worker and mother roles, spillover effects, and psychological distress. *Women and Health, 18*, 9–40.

Barnett, R.C., Marshall, N.L., & Sayer, A. (1992). Positive-spillover effects from job to home: A closer look. *Women and Health, 19*, 13–41.

Barnett, R.C., Marshall, N.L., & Singer, J.D. (1992). Job experiences over time, multiple roles, and women's mental health: A longitudinal study. *Journal of Personality and Social Psychology, 62*, 634–644.

Barrett, M. (1988). *Women's oppression today: The Marxist/feminist encounter* (rev. ed.). London: Verso.

Barry, H., III, Bacon, M.K., & Child, I.L. (1957). A cross-cultural survey of some sex differences in socialization. *Journal of Abnormal and Social Psychology, 55*, 327–332.

Bart, P.B., & Moran, E.G. (Eds.). (1993). *Violence against women: The bloody footprints.* Newbury Park, CA: Sage.

Bart, P.B., & O'Brien, P.H. (1993). Stopping rape: Effective avoidance strategies. In L. Richardson & V. Taylor (Eds.), *Feminist Frontiers III* (pp. 413–424). New York: McGraw-Hill.

Barth, R.J., & Kinder, B.N. (1988). A theoretical analysis of sex differences in same-sex friendships. *Sex Roles, 19*, 349–363.

Bartling, C.A., & Eisenman, R. (1993). Sexual harassment proclivities in men and women. *Bulletin of the Psychonomic Society, 31*, 189–192.

Baruch, G.K., & Barnett, R. (1986). Role quality, multiple role involvement, and psychological well-being in midlife women. *Journal of Personality and Social Psychology, 51*, 578–585.

Basow, S.A., & Howe, K.G. (1987). Evaluations of college professors: Effects of professors' sex-type and sex, and students' sex. *Psychological Reports, 60*, 671–678.

Basow, S.A., & Kobrynowicz, D. (1993). What is she eating? The effects of meal size on impressions of a female eater. *Sex Roles, 28*, 335–344.

Batchelor, W.F. (1988). AIDS 1988: The science and the limits of science. *American Psychologist, 43*, 853–858.

Baxter, J. (1992). Power attitudes and time: The domestic division of labour. *Journal of Comparative Family Studies, 23*, 165–182.

Bazzini, D.G., McIntosh, W.D., Smith, S.M., Cook, S., & Harris, C. (1997). The aging woman in popular film: Underrepresented, unattractive, unfriendly, and unintelligent. *Sex Roles, 36*, 531–543.

Becker, G., & Nachtigall, R.D. (1994). "Born to be a mother": The cultural construction of risk in infertility treatment in the U.S. *Social Science and Medicine, 39*, 507–518.

Becker, J., & Breedlove, S.M. (1992). Introduction to behavioral endrocrinology. In J.B. Becker, S.M. Breedlove, & D. Crews (Eds.), *Behavioral endocrinology* (pp. 3–37). Cambridge, MA: MIT Press.

Beckman, L.J. (1994). Treatment needs of women with alcohol problems. *Alcohol Health and Research World, 18*, 206–211.

Beckwith, J.B. (1992). Stereotypes and reality in the division of household labor. *Social Behavior and Personality, 20*, 283–288.

Beere, C.A. (1990). *Gender roles: A handbook of tests and measures.* New York: Greenwood.

Beggs, J.M., & Doolittle, D.C. (1993). Perceptions now and then of occupational sex typing: A replication of Shinar's 1975 study. *Journal of Applied Social Psychology, 23*, 1435–1453.

Bekker, M.H.J. (1996). Agoraphobia and gender: A review. *Clinical Psychology Review, 16*, 129–146.

Bellas, M.L. (1992). The effects of marital status and wives' employment on the salaries of faculty men: The (house) wife bonus. *Gender & Society, 6*, 609–622.

Belle, D. (1990). Poverty and women's mental health. *American Psychologist, 45*, 385–389.

Belsky, J., & Rovine, M.J. (1988). Nonmaternal care in the first year of life and the security of infant-parent attachment. *Child Development, 59*, 157–167.

Bem, D.J. (1996). Exotic becomes erotic: A developmental theory of sexual orientation. *Psychological Review, 103*, 320–335.

Bem, S.L. (1974). The measurement of psychological androgyny. *Journal of Consulting and Clinical Psychology, 42*, 155–162.

Bem, S.L. (1975). Sex-role adaptability: One consequence of psychological androgyny. *Journal of Personality and Social Psychology, 31*, 634–643.

Bem, S.L. (1977). On the utility of alternative procedures for assessing psychological androgyny. *Journal of Consulting and Clinical Psychology, 45*, 196–205.

Bem, S.L. (1981). Gender schema theory: A cognitive account of sex-typing. *Psychological Review, 88*, 354–364.

Bem, S.L. (1985). Androgyny and gender schema theory: A conceptual and empirical integration. In T.B. Sonderegger (Ed.), *Nebraska Symposium on Motivation, 1984: Psychology and gender* (pp. 179–226). Lincoln, NE: University of Nebraska Press.

Bem, S.L. (1989). Genital knowledge and gender constancy in preschool children. *Child Development, 60,* 649–662.

Bem, S.L. (1993). *The lenses of gender: Transforming the debate on sexual inequality.* New Haven, CT: Yale.

Bem, S.L. (1996). Transforming the debate on sexual inequality: From biological difference to institutionalized androcentrism. In J.C. Chrisler, C. Golden, & P.D. Rozee (Eds.), *Lectures on the psychology of women* (pp. 9–21). New York: McGraw-Hill.

Bem, S.L., & Bem, D.J. (1973). Does sex-biased job advertising "aid and abet" sex discrimination? *Journal of Applied Social Psychology, 3,* 6–18.

Benbow, C.P. (1988). Sex differences in mathematical reasoning ability in intellectually talented preadolescents: Their nature, effects, and possible causes. *Behavioral and Brain Sciences, 11,* 169–132.

Benbow, C.P., & Stanley, J.C. (1980). Sex differences in mathematical ability: Fact or artifact? *Science, 210,* 1262–1264.

Beneke, T. (1992). *Men on rape: What they have to say about sexual violence.* New York: St. Martin's Press.

Benin, M., & Keith, V.M. (1995). The social support of employed African American and Anglo mothers. *Journal of Family Issues, 16,* 275–297.

Beren, S.E., Hayden, H.A., Wilfley, D.E., & Striegel-Moore, R.H. (1997). Body dissatisfaction among lesbian college students: The conflict of straddling mainstream and lesbian cultures. *Psychology of Women Quarterly, 21,* 431–445.

Berendsen, L., & Yoder, J.D. (1997). *Racial similarities and differences in measures of women's gender attitudes and identities.* Unpublished manuscript. University of Wisconsin-Milwaukee.

Berenstain, S., & Berenstain, J. (1974). *He bear, she bear.* New York: Random House.

Bergen, D.J., & Williams, J.E. (1991). Sex stereotypes in the United States revisited: 1972–1988. *Sex Roles, 24,* 413–423.

Bergquist, W.H., Greenberg, E.M., & Klaum, G.A. (1993). *In our fifties: Voices of men and women reinventing their lives.* San Francisco, CA: Jossey-Bass.

Berkowitz, A.D. (1994). A model acquaintance rape prevention program for men. In A. Berkowitz (Ed.), *Men and rape: Theory, research, and prevention programs in higher education* (pp. 35–42). San Francisco, CA: Jossey-Bass.

Betrus, P.A., Elmore, S.K., & Hamilton, P.A. (1995). Women and somatization: Unrecognized depression. *Health Care for Women International, 16,* 287–297.

Bettencourt, B.A., & Miller, N. (1996). Gender differences in aggression as a function of provocation: A meta-analysis. *Psychological Bulletin, 119,* 422–447.

Betz, N.E. (1993). Women's career development. In F.L. Denmark & M.A. Paludi (Eds.), *Psychology of women: A handbook of issues and theories.* Westport, CT: Greenwood Press.

Betz, N.E., & Fitzgerald, L.F. (1987). *The career psychology of women.* Orlando, FL: Academic Press.

Betz, N.E., Mintz, L., & Speakmon, G. (1994). Gender differences in the accuracy of self-reported weight. *Sex Roles, 30,* 543–552.

Bielawska-Batorowicz, E. (1993). Maternal perception of an infant during the first month after birth. *Journal of Reproductive and Infant Psychology, 11,* 235–242.

Biernat, M., & Wortman, C.B. (1991). Sharing of home responsibilities between professionally employed women and their husbands. *Journal of Personality and Social Psychology, 60,* 844–860.

Bilimoria, D., & Piderit, S.K. (1994). Board committee membership: Effects of sex-based bias. *Academy of Management Journal, 37,* 1453–1477.

Binion, V.J. (1990). Psychological androgyny: A Black female perspective. *Sex Roles, 22,* 487–507.

Bird, C.E. (1996). An analysis of gender differences in income among dentists, physicians, and veterinarians in 1987. *Research in the Sociology of Health Care, 13,* 31–61.

Bittman, M., & Lovejoy, F. (1993). Domestic power: Negotiating an unequal division of labor within a framework of equality. *Australian and New Zealand Journal of Sociology, 29,* 302–321.

Björkqvist, K. (1994). Sex differences in physical, verbal, and indirect aggression: A review of recent research. *Sex Roles, 30,* 177–188.

Black, S.M., & Hill, C.E. (1984). The psychological well-being of women in their middle years. *Psychology of Women Quarterly, 8,* 282–292.

Blain, J. (1994). Discourses of agency and domestic labor: Family discourse and gendered practice in dual-earner families. *Journal of Family Issues, 15,* 515–549.

Blair, S.L., & Lichter, D.T. (1991). Measuring the division of household labor: Gender segregation of housework among American couples. *Journal of Family Issues, 12,* 91–113.

Blaisure, K.R., & Allen, K.R. (1995). Feminists and the ideology and practice of marital equality. *Journal of Marriage and the Family, 57,* 5–19.

Bleier, R. (1984). *Science and gender: A critique of biology and its theories on women.* New York: Pergamon.

Bleier, R. (1986). Sex differences research: Science or belief? In R. Bleier (Ed.), *Feminist approaches to science.* New York: Pergamon.

Bleier, R. (1991). Gender ideology and the brain: Sex differences research. In M.T. Notman & C.C. Nadelson (Eds.), *Women and men: New perspectives in gender differences.* Washington, DC: American Psychiatric Press.

Blinde, E.M., & Taub, D.E. (1992). Women athletes as falsely accused deviants: Managing the lesbian stigma. *Sociological Quarterly, 33,* 521–533.

Block, C.R., & Block, R.L. (1984). Crime definition, crime measurement, and victim surveys. *Journal of Social Issues, 40(1),* 137–160.

Blood, P., Tuttle, A., & Lakey, G. (1995). Understanding and fighting sexism: A call to men. In M.L. Andersen & P.H. Collins (Eds.), *Race, class, and gender: An anthology* (2nd ed) (pp. 154–161). Belmont, CA: Wadsworth.

Bly, R. (1990). *Iron John.* Reading, MA: Addison-Wesley.

Bock, B.C., & Kanarek, R.B. (1995). Women and men are what they eat: The effects of gender and reported meal size on perceived characteristics. *Sex Roles, 33,* 109–119.

Bohan, J.S. (1990). Contextual history: A framework for re-placing women in the history of psychology. *Psychology of Women Quarterly, 14,* 213–227.

Bohan, J.S. (1993). Regarding gender: Essentialism, constructionism, and feminist psychology. *Psychology of Women Quarterly, 17,* 5–21.

Bohmer, C., & Parrot, A. (1993). *Sexual assault on campus: The problem and the solution.* New York: Lexington.

Bolger, N., DeLongis, A., Kessler, R.C., & Wethington, E. (1989). The contagion of stress across multiple roles. *Journal of Marriage and the Family, 51,* 175–183.

Bologna, M.J., Waterman, C.K., & Dawson, L.J. (1987, July). *Violence in gay male and lesbian relationships: Implications for practitioners and policy makers.* Paper presented at the Third National Conference for Family Violence Researchers, Durham, NH.

Bonate, D.L., & Jessell, J.C. (1996). The effects of educational intervention on perceptions of sexual harassment. *Sex Roles, 35,* 751–764.

Bond, R., & Smith, P.B. (1996). Culture and conformity: A meta-analysis of studies using Asch's (1952b, 1956) line judgment task. *Psychological Bulletin, 119,* 111–137.

Bond, S., & Cash, T.F. (1992). Black beauty: Skin color and body images among African-American college women. *Journal of Applied Social Psychology, 22,* 874–888.

Bookman, A., & Morgen, S. (Eds.). (1988). *Women and the politics of empowerment.* Philadelphia, PA: Temple.

Borofsky, G.L., Stollak, G.E., & Messé, L.A. (1971). Sex differences in bystander reactions to physical assault. *Journal of Experimental Social Psychology, 7,* 313–318.

Bosscher, R.J., Van De Aa, H., Van Dasler, M., Deeg, D.J., et al. (1995). Physical performance and physical self-efficacy in the elderly: A pilot study. *Journal of Aging and Health, 7,* 459–475.

Boston Women's Health Book Collective. (1969). *Our bodies, ourselves.* New York: Simon & Schuster.

Boyd, J.A. (1990). Ethnic and cultural diversity: Keys to power. In L.S. Brown & M.P.P. Root (Eds.), *Diversity and complexity in feminist therapy* (pp. 151–167). New York: Harrington Park Press.

Brabant, S., & Mooney, L.A. (1997). Sex role stereotyping in the Sunday comics: A twenty year update. *Sex Roles, 37,* 269–281.

Bradbard, M.R., Brown, E.G., & Bischoff, R. (1992). Developing the day care checklist for parents of school-age children. *Early Child Development and Care, 83,* 77–91.

Brady, K. (1981). *Father's days: A true story of incest.* New York: Dell.

Branscombe, N.R., & Smith, E.R. (1990). Gender and racial stereotypes in impression formation and social decision-making processes. *Sex Roles, 22,* 627–647.

Bravo, E., & Cassedy, E. (1992). *The 9 to 5 guide to combating sexual harassment.* New York: Wiley.

Brenner, C. (1992). Survivor's story: Eight bullets. In G.M. Herek & K.T. Berrill (Eds.), *Hate crimes: Confronting violence against lesbian and gay men* (pp. 11–15). Newbury Park, CA: Sage.

Brenner, O.C., Tomkiewicz, J., & Schein, V.E. (1989). The relationship between sex role stereotypes and requisite management characteristics revisited. *Academy of Management Journal, 32,* 662–669.

Brett, J.M., Stroh, L.K., & Reilly, A.H. (1993). Pulling up roots in the 1990s: Who's willing to relocate? *Journal of Organizational Behavior, 14,* 49–60.

Brewer, S. (1996). The political is personal: Father-daughter relationships and working-class consciousness. *Feminism & Psychology, 6,* 401–410.

Bridgeman, B., & Lewis, C. (1995). Gender differences in college mathematics grades and SAT-M scores: A reanalysis of Wainer and Steinberg. *Educational Testing Service Reports,* ETS-RR-95-7, 34pp.

Bridges, J. (1993). Pink or blue: Gender-stereotypic perceptions of infants as conveyed by birth congratulations cards. *Psychology of Women Quarterly, 17,* 193–205.

Bridges, J.S., & Etaugh, C. (1995). College students' perceptions of mothers: Effects of maternal employment-childrearing pattern and motive for employment. *Sex Roles, 32,* 735–751.

Briere, J., & Lanktree, C. (1983). Sex-role related effects of battering: Attitudes and childhood experience. *Journal of Research in Personality, 21,* 62–69.

Briere, J., Malamuth, N., & Check, J.V.P. (1985). Sexuality and rape-supportive beliefs. *International Journal of Women's Studies, 8,* 398–403.

Brod, H. (Ed.). (1987a). *The making of masculinities: The new men's studies.* Boston, MA: Unwin.

Brod, H. (1987b). The case for men's studies. In H. Brod (Ed.), *The making of masculinities: The new men's studies* (pp. 39–62). Boston, MA: Unwin.

Brody, C.M. (1990). Women in a nursing home: Living with hope and meaning. *Psychology of Women Quarterly, 14,* 579–592.

Brody, J.E. (1997, Nov. 4). Girls and puberty: The crisis years. *The New York Times,* p. B8.

Bromberger, J.T., & Matthews, K.A. (1994). Employment status and depressive symptoms in middle-aged women: A longitudinal investigation. *American Journal of Public Health, 84,* 202–206.

Bronstein, P., & Pfenning, J. (1988). Misperceptions of women and affirmative action principles in faculty hiring: Response to Elliott's comment on Bronstein et al. *American Psychologist, 43,* 668–669.

Brooks-Gunn, J., & Ruble, D.N. (1982). The development of menstrual-related behaviors during early adolescence. *Child Development, 53,* 1567–1577.

Broverman, I.K., Broverman, D.M., Clarkson, F.E., Rosenkrantz, P.S., & Vogel, S.R. (1970). Sex-role stereotypes and clinical judgments of mental health. *Journal of Consulting and Clinical Psychology, 34,* 1–7.

Brown, A., Goodwin, B.J., Hall, B.A., & Jackson-Lowman, H. (1985). A review of psychology of women textbooks: Focus on the Afro-American woman. *Psychology of Women Quarterly, 13,* 445–458.

Brown, E.B. (1989). Womanist consciousness: Maggie Lena Walker and the Independent Order of St. Luke. *Signs, 14,* 610–633.

Brown, J.A., Cross, H.J., & Nelson, J.M. (1990). Sex-role identity and sex-role ideology in college women with bulimic behavior. *International Journal of Eating Disorders, 9,* 571–575.

Brown, L.M., & Gilligan, C. (1993). Meeting at the crossroads: Women's psychology and girls' development. *Feminism & Psychology, 3,* 11–35.

Brown, L.S. (1987). Lesbians, weight, and eating: New analyses and perspectives. In Boston Lesbian Psychologies Collective (Eds.), *Lesbian psychologies* (pp. 294–309). Urbana, IL: University of Illinois Press.

Brown, L.S. (1989). New voices, new visions: Toward a lesbian/gay paradigm for psychology. *Psychology of Women Quarterly, 13,* 445–458.

Brown, L.S. (1992). A feminist critique of the personality disorders. In L.S. Brown & M. Ballou (Eds.), *Personality and psychopathology: Feminist reappraisals* (pp. 206–228). New York: Guilford.

Brown, L.S. (1994a). *Subversive dialogues: Theory in feminist therapy.* New York: Basic.

Brown, L.S. (1994b). Boundaries in feminist therapy: A conceptual formulation. *Women & Therapy, 15,* 29–38.

Brown, L.S., & Ballou, M. (Eds.). (1992). *Personality and psychopathology: Feminist reappraisals.* New York: Guilford.

Brown, L.S., & Root, M.P.P. (Eds.). (1990). *Diversity and complexity in feminist therapy.* New York: Harrington Park Press.

Brown, T.A., & Cash, T.F. (1990). The phenomenon of nonclinical panic: Parameters of panic, fear, and avoidance. *Journal of Anxiety Disorders, 4,* 15–29.

Brown, V., & Weissman, G. (1993). Women and men injection drug users: An updated look at gender differences and risk factors. In B.S. Brown & G.M. Beschner (Eds.), *Handbook of risk of AIDS: Injection drug users and sexual partners* (pp. 173–194). Westport, CT: Greenwood Press.

Browne, A. (1987). *When battered women kill.* New York: Macmillan/Free Press.

Browne, A. (1991). The victim's experience: Pathways to disclosure. *Psychotherapy, 28,* 150–156.

Browne, A. (1993). Violence against women by male partners: Prevalence, outcomes, and policy implications. *American Psychologist, 48,* 1077–1087.

Browne, A., & Finkelhor, D. (1986). The impact of child sexual abuse: A review of the research. *Psychological Bulletin, 99,* 66–77.

Browne, A., & Williams, K.R. (1989). Exploring the effects of resource availability and the likelihood of female-perpetrated homicides. *Law and Society Review, 23,* 75–94.

Browne, A., & Williams, K.R. (1993). Gender, intimacy, and lethal violence: Trends from 1976 through 1987. *Gender & Society, 7,* 78–98.

Browne, C.V. (1995). Empowerment in social work practice with older women. *Social Work, 40,* 358–364.

Brownmiller, S. (1975). *Against our will: Men, women and rape.* New York: Simon & Schuster.

Brozovic, M. (1989). With women in mind. *British Medical Journal, 299,* 689.

Bryant, B.K. (1985). The neighborhood walk: Sources of support in middle childhood. *Monographs of the Society for Research in Child Development, 50,* 11985.

Bryer, J.B., Nelson, B.A., Miller, J.B., & Krol, P.A. (1987). Childhood sexual and physical abuse as factors in adult psychiatric illness. *American Journal of Psychiatry, 144,* 1426–1430.

Buchanan, C.M., Eccles, J.S., & Becker, J.B. (1992). Are adolescents the victims of raging hormones? Evidence for activational effects of hormones on moods and behavior at adolescence. *Psychological Bulletin, 111,* 62–107.

Burke, H.L., & Yeo, R.A. (1994). Systematic variations in callosal morphology: The effects of age, gender, hand preference, and anatomic asymmetry. *Neuropsychology, 8,* 563–571.

Burke, R.J., & McKeen, C.A. (1995). Do managerial women prefer women mentors? *Psychological Reports, 76,* 688–690.

Burr, C. (1996). *A separate creation: The search for the biological origins of sexual orientation.* New York: Hyperion.

Bushy, A. (1990). Rural determinants in family health: Considerations for community nurses. *Family and Community Health, 12,* 29–38.

Buss, D.M. (1995). Psychological sex differences: Origins through sexual selection. *American Psychologist, 50,* 164–168.

Bussey, K., & Bandura, A. (1984). Influence of gender constancy and social power on sexlinked modeling. *Journal of Personality and Social Psychology, 47,* 1292–1302.

Butler, B.A., & Wing, R.R. (1995). Women with diabetes: A lifestyle perspective focusing on eating disorders, pregnancy, and weight control. In A.L. Stanton & S.J. Gallant (Eds.), *The psychology of women's health: Progress and challenges in research and application* (pp. 85–116). Washington, DC: American Psychological Association.

Butler, M. (1985). Guidelines for feminist therapy. In L.B. Rosewater & L. Walker (Eds.), *Handbook of feminist therapy* (pp. 32–38). New York: Springer.

Bybee, J., Glick, M., & Zigler, E. (1990). Differences across gender, grade level, and academic track in the content of the ideal self-image. *Sex Roles, 22,* 349–358.

Byrne, D. (1983). The antecedents, correlates, and consequences of erotophobia-erotophilia. In C.M. Davis (Ed.), *Challenges in sexual science: Current theoretical issues and research advances* (pp. 53–75). Lake Mills, IA: Graphic.

Caetano, R. (1994). Drinking and alcohol-related problems among minority women. *Alcohol Health and Research World, 18,* 333–341.

Caldwell, M.A., & Peplau, L.A. (1982). Sex differences in same-sex friendship. *Sex Roles, 8,* 721–732.

Cameron, R.P., Grabill, C.M., Hobfoll, S.E., Crowther, J.H., et al. (1996). Weight, self-esteem, ethnicity, and depressive symptomatology during pregnancy among inner-city women. *Health Psychology, 15,* 293–297.

Cammaert, L.P., & Larsen, C.C. (1988). In M.A. Dutton-Douglas & L.E. Walker (Eds.), *Feminist psychotherapies: Integration of therapeutic and feminist systems* (pp. 12–36). Norwood, NJ: Ablex.

Campbell, J.C., Miller, P., Cardwell, M.M., & Belknap, R. (1994). Relationship status of battered women over time. *Journal of Family Violence, 9,* 99–111.

Campbell, K.T., & Evans, C. (1993, November). *Gender issues and the math/science curricula: Effects on females.* Paper presented at the annual meeting of the Mid-South Educational Research Association, New Orleans, LA.

Campbell, T.L., Byrne, B.M., & Baron, P. (1992). Gender differences in the expression of depressive symptoms in early adolescents. *Journal of Early Adolescence, 12,* 326–338.

Cann, A. (1993). Evaluative expectations and the gender schema: Is failed inconsistency better? *Sex Roles, 28,* 667–678.

Cannings, K. (1991). An interdisciplinary approach to analyzing the managerial gender gap. *Human Relations, 44*, 679–695.

Caplan, P.J. (1995). *They say you're crazy: How the world's most powerful psychiatrists decide who's normal.* Reading, MA: Addison-Wesley.

Caplan, P.J., & Gans, M. (1991). Is there empirical evidence for the category of "self-defeating personality disorder"? *Feminism & Psychology, 1*, 263–278.

Caplan, P.J., MacPherson, G.M., & Tobin, P. (1985). Do sex-related differences in spatial abilities exist? *American Psychologist, 40*, 786–799.

Caputi, J. (1993). The sexual politics of murder. In P.B. Bart & E.G. Moran (Eds.), *Violence against women: The bloody footprints* (pp. 5–25). Newbury Park, CA: Sage.

Carli, L.L. (1990). Gender, language, and influence. *Journal of Personality and Social Psychology, 59*, 941–951.

Carlo, G., Koller, S.H., Eisenberg, N., & DeSilva, M.S. (1996). A cross-national study on the relations among prosocial moral reasoning, gender role orientations, and prosocial behaviors. *Developmental Psychology, 32*, 231–240.

Carter, D.B., & Levy, G.D. (1988). Cognitive aspects of children's early sex-role development: The influence of gender schemas on preschoolers' memories and preferences for sex-typed toys and activities. *Child Development, 59*, 782–793.

Carter, D.B., & Levy, G.D. (1991). Gender schemas and the salience of gender: Individual differences in nonreversal discrimination learning. *Sex Roles, 25*, 555–568.

Cash, T.F., & Henry, P.E. (1995). Women's body images: The results of a national survey in the U.S.A. *Sex Roles, 33*, 19–28.

Cataldi, S. (1995). Reflections on "male bashing." *National Women's Studies Association Journal, 7*, 76–85.

Caughy, M.O., DiPietro, J.A., & Strobino, D.M. (1994). Day-care participation as a protective factor in the cognitive development of low-income children. *Child Development, 65*, 457–471.

Cesarone, B. (1994). *Video games and children.* Urbana, IL: ERIC Clearinghouse on Elementary and Early Childhood Education.

Chan, C.S. (1987). Asian-American women: Psychological responses to sexual exploitation and cultural stereotypes. *Women & Therapy, 6*, 33–38.

Chang, C.F., & White-Means, S.I. (1991). The men who care: An analysis of male primary caregivers who care for frail elderly at home. *The Journal of Applied Gerontology, 10*, 343–358.

Charney, D.A., & Russell, R.C. (1994). An overview of sexual harassment. *American Journal of Psychiatry, 151*, 10–17.

Cheever, S. (November 14, 1996). Twiggy: A stick figure. *The New York Times Magazine*, p. 74.

Cherry, F., & Deaux, K. (1978). Fear of success versus fear of gender-inappropriate behavior. *Sex Roles, 4*, 97–101.

Chesler, P. (1991). Mothers on trial: The custodial vulnerability of women. *Feminism and Psychology, 1*, 409–425.

Chester, N.L. (1990). Achievement motivation and employment decisions: Portraits of women with young children. In H.Y. Grossman & M.L. Chester (Eds.), *The experience and meaning of work in women's lives* (pp. 83–101). Hillsdale, NJ: Lawrence Erlbaum.

Chester, N.L., & Grossman, H.Y. (1990). Introduction: Learning about women and their work through their own accounts. In H.Y. Grossman & M.L. Chester (Eds.), *The experience and meaning of work in women's lives* (pp. 1–9). Hillsdale, NJ: Lawrence Erlbaum.

Chipman, S.F., & Thomas, V.G. (1985). Women's participation in mathematics: Outlining the problem. In S.F. Chipman, L.R. Brush, & D. M. Wilson (Eds.), *Women and mathematics: Balancing the equation* (pp. 1–24). Hillsdale, NJ: Erlbaum.

Chodorow, N. (1978). *The reproduction of mothering.* Berkeley, CA: University of California Press.

Chow, E.N. (1987). The development of feminist consciousness among Asian American women. *Gender & Society, 1,* 284–299.

Chrisler, J.C. (1996). Politics and women's weight. In S. Wilkinson & C. Kitzinger (Eds.), *Representing the other: A Feminism & Psychology reader* (pp. 94–96). Thousand Oaks, CA: Sage.

Chrisler, J.C., & Ghiz, L. (1993). Body image issues of older women. *Women & Therapy, 14,* 67–75.

Chrisler, J.C., & Levy, K.B. (1990). The media construct a menstrual monster: A content analysis of PMS articles in the popular press. *Women & Health, 16,* 89–104.

Chrisler, J.C., & Parrett, K.L. (1995). Women and autoimmune disorders. In A.L. Stanton & S.J. Gallant (Eds.), *The psychology of women's health: Progress and challenges in research and application* (pp. 171–195). Washington, DC: American Psychological Association.

Christina, G. (1997). Are we having sex yet? In M. Crawford & R. Unger (Eds.), *In our own words: Readings on the psychology of women and gender.* New York: McGraw-Hill.

Clance, P.R., Dingman, D., Reviere, S.L., & Stober, D.R. (1995). Impostor phenomenon in an interpersonal/social context: Origins and treatment. *Women & Therapy, 16,* 79–96.

Clance, P.R., & O'Toole, M.A. (1987). The impostor phenomenon: An internal barrier to empowerment and achievement. *Women & Therapy, 6,* 51–64.

Clancy, C.M., & Massion, C.T. (1992). American women's health care: A patchwork quilt with gaps. *Journal of the American Medical Association, 268,* 1918–1920.

Clark, M.L. (1986). Predictors of scientific majors for Black and White college students. *Adolescence, 21,* 205–213.

Clarke-Stewart, K.A. (1989). Infant day care: Maligned or malignant? *American Psychologist, 44,* 266–273.

Clatterbaugh, K. (1990). *Contemporary perspectives on masculinity: Men, women, and politics in modern society.* Boulder, CO: Westview.

Clay, R.A. (1996, September). Psychology continues to be a popular degree. *APA Monitor,* p. 53.

Clopton, N.A., & Sorell, G.T. (1993). Gender differences in moral reasoning: Stable or situational? *Psychology of Women Quarterly, 17,* 85–102.

Coats, M. (1994). *Women's education: The cutting edge series.* Bristol, PA: Society for Research in Higher Education and Open University Press.

Cochran, S.D., & Mays, V.M. (1993). Applying social psychological models to predicting HIV-related sexual risk behaviors among African Americans. *Journal of Black Psychology, 19,* 142–154.

Cogan, J.C., Bhalla, S.K., & Sefa-Dedeh, A. (1996). A comparison of the United States and African students on perceptions of obesity and thinness. *Journal of Cross-Cultural Psychology, 27,* 98–113.

Cohen, A.G., & Gutek, B.A. (1991). Sex differences in the career experiences of members of two APA divisions. *American Psychologist, 46,* 1292–1298.

Cohen, J. (1977). *Statistical power analysis for the behavioral sciences* (Rev. ed.). San Diego, CA: Academic Press.

Cohn, L.D. (1991). Sex differences in the course of personality development: A meta-analysis. *Psychological Bulletin, 109,* 252–266.

Cohn, L.D., & Adler, N.E. (1992). Female and male perceptions of ideal body shapes: Distorted views among Caucasian college students. *Psychology of Women Quarterly, 16,* 69–79.

Cole, E., & Rothblum, E. (1990). Commentary on "Sexuality and midlife woman." *Psychology of Women Quarterly, 14,* 509–512.

Cole, J.R., & Zuckerman, H. (1987). Marriage, motherhood and research performance in science. *Scientific American, 256,* 119–125.

Coleman, M.T. (1988). The division of household labor: Suggestions for future empirical consideration and theoretical development. *Journal of Family Issues, 9*, 473–490.

Coles, F.S. (1986). Forced to quit: Sexual harassment complaints and agency response. *Sex Roles, 14*, 81–95.

Coley, S.A., & Beckett, J.O. (1988). Black battered women: A review of empirical literature. *Journal of Counseling and Development, 66*, 266–270.

Collin, C.A., DiSano, F., & Malik, R. (1994). Effects of confederate and subject gender on conformity in a color classification task. *Social Behavior and Personality, 22*, 355–364.

Collins, C.F. (Ed.). (1996). *African-American women's health and social issues.* Westport, CT: Auburn House.

Collins, P.H. (1986). Learning from the outsider within: The sociological significance of Black feminist thought. *Social Problems, 33*, S14–S32.

Collins, P.H. (1989). The social construction of Black feminist thought. *Signs, 14*, 745–773.

Collins, P.H. (1994). The meaning of motherhood in Black culture. In R. Staples (Ed.), *The Black family* (5th ed.). Belmont, CA: Wadsworth.

Comas-Díaz, L. (1988). Feminist therapy with Hispanic/Latina women: Myth or reality? *Women & Therapy, 6*(4), 39–61.

Comas-Díaz, L. (1994). An integrative approach. In L. Comas-Díaz & B. Greene (Eds.), *Women of color: Integrating ethnic and gender identities in psychotherapy* (pp. 287–318). New York: Guilford.

Comas-Díaz, L., & Greene, B. (Eds.) (1994). *Women of color: Integrating ethnic and gender identities in psychotherapy.* New York: Guilford.

Committee on Lesbian and Gay Concerns. (1991). Avoiding heterosexist bias in language. *American Psychologist, 46*, 973–974.

Connell, R.W. (1987). *Gender and power: Society, the person, and sexual politics.* Stanford, CA: Stanford University Press.

Connell, R.W. (1993). Men and the women's movement. *Social Policy, 23*(4), 72–78.

Conner, J.M., & Serbin, L.A. (1985). Visual-spatial skill: Is it important for mathematics? Can it be taught? In S.F. Chipman, L.R. Brush, & D.M. Wilson (Eds.), *Women and mathematics: Balancing the equation* (pp. 151–174). Hillsdale, NJ: Erlbaum.

Conner, J.M., Schackman, M., & Serbin, L.A. (1978). Sex-related differences in response to practice on a visual-spatial test and generalization to a related test. *Child Development, 49*, 24–29.

Connidis, I.A., & McMullin, J.A. (1993). To have or have not: Parent status and the subjective well-being of older men and women. *Gerontologist, 33*, 630–636.

Contarello, A., & Volpato, C. (1991). Images of friendship: Literary depictions through the ages. *Journal of Social and Personal Relationships, 8*, 49–75.

Conway, M., Pizzamiglio, M.T., & Mount, L. (1996). Status, communality, and agency: Implications for stereotypes of gender and other groups. *Journal of Personality and Social Psychology, 71*, 25–38.

Cook, E.A. (1993). Feminist consciousness and candidate preference among American women, 1972–1988. *Political Behavior, 15*, 227–246.

Cooke, R.A., & Rousseau, D.M. (1984). Stress and strain from family roles and work-role expectations. *Journal of Applied Psychology, 69*, 252–260.

Cooley, E.L. (1992). Family expressiveness and proneness to depression among college women. *Journal of Research in Personality, 26*, 281–287.

Cornelius, J.R., Jarrett, P.J., Thase, M.E., & Fabrega, H., et al. (1995). Gender effects on the clinical presentation of alcoholics at a psychiatric hospital. *Comprehensive Psychiatry, 36*, 435–440.

Costello, C., & Krimgold, B.K. (Eds.). (1996). *The American woman, 1996–97.* New York: Norton.

Costello, C., & Stone, A.S. (Eds.). (1994). *The American woman 1994–95: Women and health.* New York: Norton.

Cota, A.A., Reid, A., & Dion, K.L. (1991). Construct validity of a diagnostic ratio measure of gender stereotypes. *Sex Roles, 25,* 225–235.

Cotter, D.A., DeFiore, J.M., & Hermsen, J.M. (1995). Occupational gender desegregation in the 1980s. *Work and Occupations, 22,* 3–21.

Cotter, D.A., DeFiore, J., Hermsen, J.M., Kowalewski, B.M., & Vannerman, R. (1997). All women benefit: The macro-level effect of occupational integration on gender earnings equality. *American Sociological Review, 62,* 714–734.

Coughlin, P.C. (1990). Premenstrual syndrome: How marital satisfaction and role choice affect symptom severity. *Social Work, 35,* 351–355.

Coulson, M., & Bhavnani, K. (1990). Making a difference—questioning women's studies. In E. Burman (Ed.), *Feminists and psychological practice* (pp. 62–75). Newbury Park, CA: Sage.

Coverman, S. (1989). Women's work is never done: The division of domestic labor. In J. Freeman (Ed.), *Women: A feminist perspective* (4th ed.), pp. 356–370. Mountain View, CA: Mayfield.

Covey, L.A., & Feltz, D.L. (1991). Physical activity and adolescent female psychological development. *Journal of Youth and Adolescence, 20,* 463–474.

Cowan, G., & Hoffman, C.D. (1986). Gender stereotyping in young children: Evidence to support a concept-learning approach. *Sex Roles, 14,* 211–224.

Cox, T.H., & Harquail, C.V. (1991). Career paths and career success in the early career stages of male and female MBAs. *Journal of Vocational Behavior, 39,* 54–75.

Coyle, J.M. (1989). *Women and aging: A selected, annotated bibliography.* Westport, CT: Greenwood.

Crabb, P.B., & Bielawski, D. (1994). The social representation of material culture and gender in children's books. *Sex Roles, 30,* 69–79.

Crago, M., Yates, A., Fleischer, C.A., Segerstrom, B., & Gray, N. (1996). The superwoman ideal and other risk factors for eating disturbances in adolescent girls. *Sex Roles, 35,* 801–810.

Craig, R.S. (1992). The effect of television day part on gender portrayals in television commercials: A content analysis. *Sex Roles, 26,* 197–211.

Crawford, M., & English, L. (1984). Generic versus specific inclusion of women in language: Effects on recall. *Journal of Psycholinguistic Research, 13,* 373–381.

Crawford, M., & Marecek, J. (1989). Psychology reconstructs the female, 1968–1988. *Psychology of Women Quarterly, 13,* 147–166.

Crawford-Green, C. (1996). Hypertension and African-American women. In C.F. Collins (Ed.), *African-American women's health and social issues* (pp. 59–73). Westport, CT: Auburn House.

Crosby, F.J. (Ed.). (1987). *Spouse, parent, worker: On gender and multiple roles.* New Haven, CT: Yale.

Crosby, F.J. (1991). *Juggling: The unexpected advantages of balancing career and home for women and their families.* New York: Free Press.

Crosby, F.J., & Clayton, S. (1986). Introduction: The search for connections. *Journal of Social Issues, 42*(2), 1–10.

Cross, W.E. (1971). Negro-to-Black conversion experience: Toward a psychology of Black liberation. *Black World, 20*(9), 13–27.

Croteau, J.M., Nero, C.I., & Prosser, D.J. (1993). Social and cultural sensitivity in group-specific HIV and AIDS programming. *Journal of Counseling and Development, 71,* 290–296.

Crouter, A.C., & Crowley, M.S. (1990). School-age children's time alone with fathers in single- and dual-earner families: Implications for the father-child relationship. *Journal of Early Adolescence, 10,* 296–312.

Crowley-Long, K., & Long, K.J. (1992). Searching for models of fully functioning women. *Women & Therapy, 12,* 213–225.

Crull, P. (1982). Stress effects of sexual harassment on the job: Implications for counseling. *American Journal of Orthopsychiatry, 52,* 539–544.

Culbertson, F.M. (1997). Depression and gender: An international review. *American Psychologist, 52,* 25–31.

Cumming, C.E., Urion, C., Cumming, D.C., & Fox, E.E. (1994). "So mean and cranky, I could bite my mother": An ethnosemantic analysis of women's descriptions of premenstrual change. *Women & Health, 21,* 21–41.

Cummings, N. (1992). Self-defense training for college women. *Journal of American College Health, 40,* 183–188.

Cunningham, M.R., Roberts, A.R., & Barbee, A.P. (1995). "Their ideas of beauty are, on the whole, the same as ours": Consistency and variability in the cross-cultural perception of female physical attractiveness. *Journal of Personality and Social Psychology, 68,* 261–279.

Cutler, S.E., & Nolen-Hoeksema, S. (1991). Accounting for sex differences in depression through female victimization: Childhood sexual abuse. *Sex Roles, 24,* 425–438.

Dagg, P.K.B. (1991). The psychological sequelae of therapeutic abortion—Denied and completed. *American Journal of Psychiatry, 148,* 578–585.

Dan, A.J., Wilbur, J., Hedricks, C., O'Connor, E., & Holm, K. (1990). Lifelong physical activity in middle and older women. *Psychology of Women Quarterly, 14,* 531–542.

Dancey, C.P. (1990). The influence of familial and personality variables on sexual orientation in women. *Psychological Record, 40,* 437–449.

Dancey, C.P. (1992). The relationship of instrumentality and expressiveness to sexual orientation in women. *Journal of Homosexuality, 23,* 71–82.

Daniel, R.B. (1996). Allowing illness in order to heal: Sojourning African-American women and the AIDS pandemic. In C.F. Collins (Ed.), *African-American women's health and social issues* (pp. 13–24). Westport, CT: Auburn House.

Danieli, Y. (1985). The treatment and prevention of long-term effects and intergenerational transmission of victimization: A lesson from Holocaust survivors and their children. In C.R. Figley (Ed.), *Trauma and its wake: The study and treatment of post-traumatic stress disorder* (pp. 295–313). New York: Brunner/Mazel.

Daniels, S. (1996). Reproductive rights: Who speaks for African-American women? In C.F. Collins (Ed.), *African-American women's health and social issues* (pp. 187–197). Westport, CT: Auburn House.

Darves-Bornoz, J.M., Lemperiere, T., Degiovanni, A., & Gaillard, P. (1995). Sexual victimization in women with schizophrenia and bipolar disorder. *Social Psychiatry and Psychiatric Epidemiology, 30,* 78–84.

Dauber, S.L., & Benbow, C.P. (1990). Aspects of personality and peer relations of extremely talented adolescents. *Gifted Child Quarterly, 34,* 10–15.

Dauphinais, P.D., Barkan, S.E., & Cohn, S.F. (1992). Predictors of rank-and-file feminist activism: Evidence from the 1983 General Social Survey. *Social Problems, 39,* 332–344.

Davenport, D.S., & Yurich, J.M. (1991). Multicultural gender issues. *Journal of Counseling & Development, 70,* 64–71.

David, H.P. (1992). Born unwanted: Long-term developmental effects of denied abortion. *Journal of Social Issues, 48*(3), 163–181.

Davis, D. (1996). The cultural constructions of the premenstrual and menopausal syndromes. In C.F. Sargent & C.B. Brettell (Eds.), *Gender and health: An international perspective* (pp. 57–86). Upper Saddle River, NJ: Prentice Hall.

Davis, L. (1991). *Allies in healing: When a person you love was sexually abused as a child.* New York: Harper Perennial.

Davis, L.D., & Brody, E.M. (1979). *Rape and older women: A guide to prevention and protection.* Washington, DC: National Institute of Mental Health.

Davis, R.C., Brickman, E., & Baker, T. (1991). Supportive and unsupportive responses of others to rape victims: Effects on concurrent victim adjustment. *American Journal of Community Psychology, 19,* 443–451.

Davis, S. (1990). Men as success objects and women as sex objects: A study of personal advertisements. *Sex Roles, 23,* 43–50.

Dawkins, R. (1976). *The selfish gene.* New York: Oxford.

Dean, A., Kolody, B., Wood, P., & Matt, G.E. (1992). The influence of living alone on depression in elderly persons. *Journal of Aging and Health, 4,* 3–18.

Deater-Deckard, K., Scarr, S.S., McCartney, K., & Eisenberg, M. (1994). Paternal separation anxiety: Relationships with parenting stress, child-rearing attitudes, and maternal anxieties. *Psychological Science, 5,* 341–346.

Deaux, K. (1993). Commentary: Sorry, wrong number—A reply to Gentile's call. *Psychological Science, 4,* 125–126.

Deaux, K., & Emswiller, T. (1974). Explanations of successful performance on sex-linked tasks: What is skill for the male is luck for the female. *Journal of Personality and Social Psychology, 29,* 80–85.

Deaux, K., & Kite, M. (1993). Gender stereotypes. In F.L. Denmark & M.A. Paludi (Eds.), *Psychology of women: A handbook of issues and theories* (pp. 107–139). Westport, CT: Greenwood.

Deaux, K., & Lewis, L.L. (1984). Structure of gender stereotypes: Interrelationships among components and gender label. *Journal of Personality and Social Psychology, 46,* 991–1004.

Deaux, K., & Major, B. (1987). Putting gender into context: An interactive model of gender-related behavior. *Psychological Bulletin, 94,* 369–389.

Deaux, K., Winton, W., Crowley, M., & Lewis, L.L. (1985). Level of categorization and content of gender stereotypes. *Social Cognition, 3,* 145–167.

Deevey, S. (1995). Lesbian health care. In C.I. Fogel & N.F. Woods (Eds.), *Women's health care: A comprehensive handbook* (pp. 189–206). Thousand Oaks, CA: Sage.

de Klerk, V., & Bosch, B. (1996). Nicknames as sex-role stereotypes. *Sex Roles, 35,* 525–541.

de Lacoste, C., & Holloway, R. (1982, June 25). Sexual dimorphism in the human corpus callosum. *Science, 216,* 1431–1432.

de Lacoste, C., Horvath, D.S., & Woodward, D.J. (1991). Possible sex differences in the developing human fetal brain. *Journal of Clinical and Experimental Neurobiology, 13,* 831–846.

deLeon, B. (1993). Sex role identity among college students: A cross-cultural analysis. *Hispanic Journal of Behavioral Sciences, 15,* 476–489.

De Lisi, R., & Soundranayagam, L. (1990). The conceptual structure of sex role stereotypes in college students. *Sex Roles, 23,* 593–611.

DeLouth, T.N.B., Pirson, B., & Hitchcock, D. (1995). Gender and ethnic role portrayals: Photographic images in three California newspapers. *Psychological Reports, 76,* 493–494.

Denmark, F.L. (1993). Women, leadership, and empowerment. *Psychology of Women Quarterly, 17,* 343–356.

Denmark, F.L., Russo, N.F., Frieze, I.H., & Sechzer, J.A. (1988). Guidelines for avoiding sexism in psychological research: A report of the ad hoc committee on nonsexist research. *American Psychologist, 43,* 582–585.

Denton, T.C. (1990). Bonding and supportive relationships among Black professional women: Rituals of restoration. *Journal of Organizational Behavior, 11,* 447–457.

Desmond, D.W., Glenwick, D.S., Stern, Y., & Tatemichi, T.K. (1994). Sex differences in the representation of visuospatial functions in the human brain. *Rehabilitation Psychology, 39,* 3–14.

Desrochers, S. (1995). What types of men are most attractive and most repulsive to women? *Sex Roles, 32*, 375–391.

Deutsch, F.M., LeBaron, D., & Fryer, M.M. (1987). What is a smile? *Psychology of Women Quarterly, 11*, 341–351.

Deutsch, F.M., Zalenski, C.M., & Clark, M.E. (1986). Is there a double standard of aging? *Journal of Applied Social Psychology, 16*, 771–785.

Dew, M.A., Bromet, E.J., & Penkower, L. (1992). Mental health effects of job loss in women. *Psychological Medicine, 22*, 751–764.

D.G. (1994, Sept./Oct.). What's love got to do with it? *Ms.*, V(2), 34–37.

Diagnostic and statistical manual of mental disorders: DSM-IV. (4th ed.). (1994). Washington, DC: American Psychiatric Association.

Dickson, L. (1993). The future of marriage and the family in Black America. *Journal of Black Studies, 23*, 472–491.

Dill, B.T. (1983). Race, class and gender: Prospects for an all-inclusive sisterhood. *Feminist Studies, 9*, 131–150.

Dindia, K., & Allen, M. (1992). Sex differences in self-disclosure: A meta-analysis. *Psychological Bulletin, 112*, 106–124.

Dion, K., & Cota, A.A. (1991). The Ms. stereotype: Its domain and the role of explicitness in title preference. *Psychology of Women Quarterly, 15*, 403–410.

Dion, K.L., & Schuller, R.A. (1990). Ms. and the manager: A tale of two stereotypes. *Sex Roles, 22*, 569–577.

Dionne, M., Davis, C., Fox, J., & Gurevich, M. (1995). Feminist ideology as a predictor of body dissatisfaction in women. *Sex Roles, 33*, 277–287.

DiPalma, L.M. (1994). Patterns of coping and characteristics of high-functioning incest survivors. *Archives of Psychiatric Nursing, 8*, 82–90.

Dodd, D.K., Harcar, V., Foerch, B.J., & Anderson, H.T. (1989). Face-ism and facial expressions of women in magazine photos. *Psychological Record, 39*, 325–331.

Dodds, P. (1997, April 6). Day care closes for moms to stay home. *Milwaukee Journal-Sentinel*, p. 18A.

Dodge, K.A., Gilroy, F.D., & Fenzel, L.M. (1995). Requisite management characteristics revisited: Two decades later. *Journal of Social Behavior and Personality, 10*, 253–264.

Dolan, B. (1991). Cross-cultural aspects of anorexia nervosa and bulimia: A review. *International Journal of Eating Disorders, 10*, 67–79.

Dolgin, K.G., Meyer, L., & Schwartz, J. (1991). Effects of gender, target's gender, topic, and self-esteem on disclosure to best and midling friends. *Sex Roles, 25*, 311–329.

Donat, P.L.N., & D'Emilio, J. (1992). A feminist redefinition of rape and sexual assault: Historical foundations and change. *Journal of Social Issues, 48(1)*, 9–22.

Donnerstein, E., Linz, D., & Penrod, S. (1987). *The question of pornography: Research findings and policy implications.* New York: Free Press.

Dougherty, D.M., Cherek, D.R., & Bennett, R.H. (1996). The effects of alcohol on the aggressive responding of women. *Journal of Studies on Alcohol, 57*, 178–186.

Douthitt, R.A. (1989). The division of labor within the home: Have gender roles changed? *Sex Roles, 20*, 693–704.

Dovidio, J.F., Ellyson, S.L., Keating, C.F., Heltman, K., & Brown, C.E. (1988). The relationship of social power to visual displays of dominance between men and women. *Journal of Personality and Social Psychology, 54*, 233–242.

Dovidio, J.F., & Gaertner, S.L. (1986). *Prejudice, discrimination, and racism.* New York: Academic Press.

Dowling, C. (1981). *The Cinderella complex: Women's hidden fear of independence.* New York: Summit.

Downing, N.E., & Roush, K.L. (1985). From passive acceptance to active commitment: A model of feminist identity development for women. *The Counseling Psychologist, 13*, 695–709.

Doyle, A., & Somers, K. (1978). The effects of group and family day care on infant attachment behaviours. *Canadian Journal of Behavioural Science, 10*, 38–45.

Dreher, G.F., & Ash, R.A. (1990). A comparative study of mentoring among men and women in managerial, professional, and technical positions. *Journal of Applied Psychology, 75*, 539–546.

Dreher, G.F., & Cox, T.H., Jr. (1996). Race, gender, and opportunity: A study of compensation attainment and the establishment of mentoring relationships. *Journal of Applied Psychology, 81*, 297–308.

Drentea, P. (1995, August). *Consequences of men's and women's formal and informal job search methods for employment in female-dominated jobs.* Paper presented at the meeting of the American Sociological Association, Washington, DC.

Driesen, N.R., & Raz, N. (1995). The influence of sex, age, and handedness on corpus callosum morphology: A meta-analysis. *Psychobiology, 23*, 240–247.

DSM-IV: Diagnostic and statistical manual of mental disorders. (1994). (4th ed.). Washington, DC: American Psychiatric Association.

Duck, S., & Wright, P.H. (1993). Re-examining gender differences in same-gender friendships: A close look at two kinds of data. *Sex Roles, 28*, 709–727.

Duke at center of fire department tension. (1996, December 9). *Milwaukee Journal Sentinel*, p. 5A.

Dull, D., & West, C. (1991). Accounting for cosmetic surgery: The accomplishment of gender. *Social Problems, 38*, 54–70.

Dunkle, J.H., & Francis, P.L. (1990). The role of facial masculinity/femininity in the attribution of homosexuality. *Sex Roles, 23*, 157–167.

Dunn, L. (1993). Ratio and group size in day care programs. *Child and Youth Care Forum, 22*, 193–226.

Dunne, F.J., Galatopoulos, C., & Schipperheijn, J.M. (1993). Gender differences in psychiatric morbidity among alcohol misusers. *Comprehensive Psychiatry, 34*, 95–101.

Dutton, D.G. (1988). *The domestic assault of women: Psychological and criminal justice perspectives.* Boston, MA: Allyn and Bacon.

Dutton, D.G. (1992). Assessment and treatment of PTSD among battered women. In D. Foy (Ed.), *Treating PTSD: Cognitive and behavioral strategies* (pp. 69–98). New York: Guilford.

Dutton, M.A. (1992). *Empowering and healing the battered woman.* New York: Springer.

Dutton-Douglas, M.A. (1992). Treating battered women in the aftermath stage. *Psychotherapy in Private Practice, 10*, 93–98.

Dutton-Douglas, M.A., & Walker, L.E. (Eds.). (1988). *Feminist psychotherapies: Integration of therapeutic and feminist systems.* Norwood, NJ: Ablex.

Eagan, T. (1995, May 31). If juveniles break law, town is charging the parents, too. *The New York Times*, pp. A1, C19.

Eagly, A.H. (1987). *Sex differences in social behavior: A social-role interpretation.* Hillsdale, NJ: Erlbaum.

Eagly, A.H. (1994). II. On comparing women and men. *Feminism & Psychology, 4*, 513–522.

Eagly, A.H. (1995a). The science and politics of comparing women and men. *American Psychologist, 50*, 145–158.

Eagly, A.H. (1995b). Reflections on the commenters' views. *American Psychologist, 50*, 169–171.

Eagly, A.H., & Carli, L.L. (1981). Sex of researcher and sex-typed communications as determinants of sex differences in influenceability: A meta-analysis of social influences studies. *Psychological Bulletin, 90*, 1–20.

Eagly, A.H., & Crowley, M. (1986). Gender and helping behavior: A meta-analytic review of the social psychological literature. *Psychological Bulletin, 100,* 283–308.

Eagly, A.H., & Johnson, B.T. (1990). Gender and leadership style: A meta-analysis. *Psychological Bulletin, 108,* 233–256.

Eagly, A.H., & Karau, S.J. (1991). Gender and the emergence of leaders: A meta-analysis. *Journal of Personality and Social Psychology, 60,* 685–710.

Eagly, A.H., Karau, S.J., & Makhijani, M.G. (1995). Gender and the effectiveness of leaders: A meta-analysis. *Psychological Bulletin, 117,* 125–145.

Eagly, A.H., Makhijani, M.G., & Klonsky, B.G. (1992). Gender and the evaluation of leaders: A meta-analysis. *Psychological Bulletin, 111,* 3–22.

Eagly, A.H., & Mladinic, A. (1989). Gender stereotypes and attitudes toward women and men. *Personality and Social Psychology Bulletin, 15,* 543–558.

Eagly, A.H., & Steffen, V.J. (1986). Gender and aggressive behavior: A meta-analytic review of the social psychological literature. *Psychological Bulletin, 100,* 309–330.

Earle, J.P., & Nies, C.T. (1994). Resources for developing acquaintance rape prevention programs for men. In A. Berkowitz (Ed.), *Men and rape: Theory, research, and prevention programs in higher education* (pp. 73–82). San Francisco, CA: Jossey-Bass.

Eccles, J.S. (1987). Adolescence: Gateway to gender-role transcendence. In D.B. Carter (Ed.), *Current conceptions of sex roles and sex typing: Theory and research* (p. 225–241). New York: Praeger.

Eccles, J.S. (1989). Bringing young women to math and science. In M. Crawford & M. Gentry (Eds.), *Gender and thought* (pp. 36–58). New York: Springer-Verlag.

Eccles, J.S. (1994). Understanding women's educational and occupational choices: Applying the Eccles et al. model of achievement-related choices. *Psychology of Women Quarterly, 18,* 585–609.

Eccles, J.S., & Harold, R.D. (1992). Gender differences in educational and occupational patterns among the gifted. In N. Colangelo, S.G. Assouline, & D.L. Ambroson (Eds.), *Talent development: Proceedings from the 1991 Henry B. and Jocelyn Wallace National Research Symposium on Talent Development* (pp. 3–29). Unionville, NY: Trillium Press.

Eccles, J.S., & Jacobs, J.E. (1986). Social forces shape math attitudes and performance. *Signs, 11,* 367–380.

Eccles, J.S., Wigfield, A., Harold, R.D., & Blumenfeld, P. (1993). Ontogeny of children's self-perceptions and subjective task values across activity domains during the early elementary school years. *Child Development, 64,* 830–847.

Eckert, E.D., Bouchard, T.J., Bohlen, J., & Heston, L.L. (1986). Homosexuality in monozygotic twins reared apart. *British Journal of Psychiatry, 148,* 421–425.

Eckes, T. (1994). Explorations in gender cognition: Content and structure of female and male subtypes. *Social Cognition, 12,* 37–60.

Eckes, T. (1996). Linking female and male subtypes to situations: A range-of-situation-fit effect. *Sex Roles, 35,* 401–426.

Eckholm, E. (1991, December 1). A tough case for Dr. Healy. *The New York Times Magazine,* pp. 67,68, 122–124.

Eckholm, E. (1992, October 6). Finding out what happens when mothers go to work. *The New York Times,* pp. A1, A12.

Edwards, G.H. (1992). The structure and content of the male gender role stereotype: An exploration of subtypes. *Sex Roles, 27,* 533–551.

Egidio, R.K., & Robertson, D.E. (1981). Rape awareness for men. *Journal of College Student Development, 22,* 455–456.

Ehrenreich, B., & English, D. (1978). *For her own good: 150 years of the experts' advice to women.* New York: Anchor.

Ehrhardt, A.A., & Meyer-Bahlburg, H.F.L. (1981). Effects of prenatal sex hormones on gender-related behavior. *Science, 211,* 1312–1318.

Eisenhart, M.A., & Holland, D.C. (1992). Gender constructs and career commitment: The influence of peer culture on women in college. In T.L. Whitehead & B.V. Reid (Eds.), *Gender constructs and social issues* (pp. 142–180). Urbana, IL: University of Illinois Press.

Eldridge, N.S., & Gilbert, L.A. (1990). Correlates of relationship satisfaction in lesbian couples. *Psychology of Women Quarterly, 14,* 43–62.

Eliason, M., Donelan, C., & Randall, C. (1992). Lesbian stereotypes. *Health Care for Women International, 13,* 131–144.

Eliason, S.R. (1995). An extension of the Sorensen-Kalleberg theory of the labor market matching and attainment processes. *American Sociological Review, 60,* 247–271.

Ellis, J. (1993). Supporting giftedness in girls in the classroom. *Proceedings of the Society for the Advancement of Gifted Education Annual Conference, EC 303,* 142.

Ely, R.J. (1995). The power in demography: Women's social constructions of gender identity at work. *Academy of Management Journal, 38,* 589–634.

Emmerich, W., & Shepard, K. (1984). Cognitive factors in the development of sex-typed preferences. *Sex Roles, 11,* 997–1008.

England, E.M. (1992). College student gender stereotypes: Expectations about the behavior of male subcategory members. *Sex Roles, 27,* 699–716.

Epstein, C.F. (1988). *Deceptive distinctions: Sex, gender and the social order.* New Haven, CT: Yale.

Epstein, S. (1987). Gay politics, ethnic identity: The limits of social constructionism. *Socialist Review, 17,* 9–53.

Erdle, S., Sansom, M., Cole, M.R., & Heapy, N. (1992). Sex differences in personality correlates of helping behavior. *Personality and Individual Differences, 13,* 931–936.

Erdwins, C.J., & Buffardi, L.C. (1994). Different types of child care and their relationship to maternal satisfaction, perceived support, and role conflict. *Child & Youth Care Forum, 23,* 41–54.

Erikson, E. (1959). *Identity and the life cycle.* New York: Norton.

Erikson, E.H. (1968). Womanhood and the inner space. In E.H. Erikson (Ed.), *Identity: Youth and crisis* (pp. 261–294). New York: Norton.

Ernster, V.L. (1993). Women and smoking. *American Journal of Public Health, 83,* 1202–1203.

Espín, O. (1994). Feminist approaches. In L. Comas-Díaz & B. Greene (Eds.), *Women of color: Integrating ethnic and gender identities in psychotherapy* (pp. 265–286). New York: Guilford.

Etaugh, C. (1993). Women in the middle and later years. In F.L. Denmark & M.A. Paludi (Eds.), *Psychology of women: A handbook of issues and theories* (pp. 213–246). Westport, CT: Greenwood.

Etaugh, C., & Duits, T. (1990). Development of gender discrimination: Role of stereotypic and counterstereotypic gender cues. *Sex Roles, 23,* 215–222.

Etaugh, C., & Liss, M.B. (1992). Home, school, and playroom: Training grounds for adult gender roles, *Sex Roles, 26,* 129–147.

Etaugh, C., & Nekolny, K. (1990). Effects of employment status and marital status on perceptions of mothers. *Sex Roles, 23,* 273–280.

Etaugh, C., & Poertner, P. (1991). Effects of occupational prestige, employment status, and marital status on perceptions of mothers. *Sex Roles, 24,* 345–353.

Etaugh, C., & Study, G.G. (1989). Perceptions of mothers: Effects of employment status, marital status, and age of child. *Sex Roles, 20,* 59–70.

Eyer, D.E. (1992). *Mother-infant bonding: A scientific fiction.* New Haven, CT: Yale.

Fagot, B.I. (1985). A cautionary note: Parents' socialization of boys and girls. *Sex Roles, 12,* 471–476.

Fagot, B.I., Hagen, R., Leinbach, M.D., & Kronsberg, S. (1985). Differential reactions to assertive and communicative acts of toddler boys and girls. *Child Development, 56,* 1499–1505.

Fagot, B.I., & Leinbach, M.D. (1995). Gender knowledge in egalitarian and traditional families. *Sex Roles, 32,* 513–526.

Falk, P.J. (1993). Lesbian mothers: Psychosocial assumptions in family law. In L.D. Garnets & D.C. Kimmel (Eds.), *Psychological perspectives on lesbian and gay male experiences* (pp. 420–436). New York: Columbia.

Faludi, S. (1991). *Backlash: The undeclared war against American women.* New York: Doubleday.

Fat-trimming method may replace liposuction. (1995, Oct. 22). *Milwaukee Journal-Sentinel,* p. 25A.

Fausto-Sterling, A. (1992). *Myths of gender* (2nd ed.). New York: Basic.

Fausto-Sterling, A. (1993, March/April). The five sexes: Why male and female are not enough. *The Sciences,* p. 20–24.

Fava, M., Abraham, M., Alpert, J., Nierenberg, A.A., et al. (1996). Gender differences in Axis I comorbidity among depressed outpatients. *Journal of Affective Disorders, 38,* 129–133.

Feagans, L.V., Fendt, K., & Farran, D.C. (1995). The effects of day care intervention on teacher's ratings of the elementary school discourse skills in disadvantaged children. *International Journal of Behavioral Development, 18,* 243–261.

Feather, N.T., & Simon, J.G. (1975). Reactions to male and female success and failure in sex-linked occupations: Impressions of personality, causal attributions, and perceived likelihood of different consequences. *Journal of Personality and Social Psychology, 31,* 20–31.

Federal Bureau of Investigation. (1985). *Uniform crime reports.* Washington, DC: U.S. Department of Justice.

Federal Glass Ceiling Commission. (1995, March). *Good for business: Making full use of the nation's human capital.* Washington, DC: U.S. Department of Labor.

Fein, E., & Schneider, S. (1995). *The rules: Time-tested secrets for capturing the heart of Mr. Right.* New York: Warner.

Feingold, A. (1988). Cognitive gender differences are disappearing. *American Psychologist, 43,* 95–103.

Feingold, A. (1990). Gender differences in effects of physical attractiveness on romantic attraction: A comparison across five research paradigms. *Journal of Personality and Social Psychology, 59,* 981–993.

Feingold, A. (1995). The additive effects of differences in central tendency and variability are important in comparisons between groups. *American Psychologist, 50,* 5–13.

Feiring, C., & Lewis, M. (1987). The child's social network: Sex differences from three to six years. *Sex Roles, 17,* 621–636.

Feldman, D.C. (1994). The decision to retire early: A review and conceptualization. *Academy of Management Review, 19,* 285–311.

Feldman-Summers, S., & Kiesler, S.B. (1974). Those who are number two try harder: The effect of sex on attributions of causality. *Journal of Personality and Social Psychology, 30,* 846–855.

Felmlee, D.H. (1994). Who's on top? Power in romantic relationships. *Sex Roles, 31,* 275–295.

Field, T. (1991). Quality infant day care and grade school behavior and performance. *Child Development, 62,* 863–870.

Findlay, B.M., & Lawrence, J.A. (1991). Who does what? Gender-related distribution of household tasks for couples and their families of origin and their ideals. *Australian Journal of Marriage and Family, 12,* 3–11.

Fine, M. (1985). Reflections on a feminist psychology of women: Paradoxes and prospects. *Psychology of Women Quarterly, 9,* 167–183.

Fine, M. (1989). Coping with rape: Critical perspectives on consciousness. In R.K. Unger (Ed.), *Representations: Social construction of gender* (pp. 186–200). Amityville, NY: Baywood.

Fine, M. (1991, March). *Women with disabilities.* Paper presented at the meeting of the Association for Women in Psychology, Hartford, CT.

Fine, M. (1993). The politics of research and activism: Violence against women. In P.B. Bart & E.G. Moran (Eds.), *Violence against women: The bloody footprints* (pp. 278–287). Newbury Park, CA: Sage.

Fine, M., & Asch, A. (1988). Disability beyond stigma: Social interaction, discrimination, and activism. *Journal of Social Issues, 44*(1), 3–21.

Finegan, J., Bartleman, B., & Wong, P.Y. (1989). A window for the study of prenatal sex hormones influences on postnatal development. *Journal of Genetic Psychology, 150,* 101–112.

Finkelhor, D., Hotaling, G., Lewis, I.A., & Smith, C. (1990). Sexual abuse in a national survey of adult men and women: Prevalence characteristics and risk factors. *Child Abuse and Neglect, 14,* 19–28.

Firth, M. (1982). Sex discrimination in job opportunities for women. *Sex Roles, 8,* 891–901.

Fischer, A.R., & Good, G.E. (1994). Gender, self, and others: Perceptions of the campus environment. *Journal of Counseling Psychology, 41,* 343–355.

Fish, M., Gross, A., & Sanders, J. (1986). The effect of equity strategies on girls' computer usage in school. *Computers in Human Behavior, 2,* 127–184.

Fisher, B., & Galler, R. (1988). Friendship and fairness: How disability affects friendship between women. In M. Fine & A. Asch (Eds.), *Women with disabilities* (pp. 172–194). Philadelphia, PA: Temple.

Fisher, C.S., & Oliker, S.J. (1983). A research note on friendship, gender and the life cycle. *Social Forces, 62,* 124–133.

Fisher, W.A., Byrne, D., White, L.A., & Kelley, K. (1989). Erotophobia-erotophilia as a dimension of personality. *Journal of Sex Research, 25,* 123–151.

Fiske, S.T. (1993). Social cognition and social perception. *Annual Review of Psychology, 44,* 155–194.

Fiske, S.T., Bersoff, D.N., Borgida, E., Deaux, K., & Heilman, M.E. (1991). Social science research on trial: Use of the sex stereotyping research in *Price Waterhouse v. Hopkins. American Psychologist, 46,* 1049–1060.

Fiske, S.T., & Glick, P. (1995). Ambivalence and stereotypes cause sexual harassment: A theory with implications for organizational change. *Journal of Social Issues, 51*(1), 97–115.

Fiske, S.T., & Stevens, L.E. (1993). What's so special about sex? Gender stereotyping and discrimination. In S. Oskamp & M. Castanzo (Eds.), *Gender issues in contemporary society: Applied social psychology annual* (pp. 173–196). Newbury Park, CA: Sage.

Fiske, S.T., & Taylor, S.E. (1991). *Social cognition* (2nd ed.). New York: McGraw-Hill.

Fiske, S.T., & Von Hendy, H.M. (1992). Personality feedback and situational norms can control stereotyping processes. *Journal of Personality and Social Psychology, 62,* 577–596.

Fitzgerald, L.F. (1990). Sexual harassment: The definition and measurement of a construct. In M. Paludi (Ed.), *Ivory power: Sexual harassment on campus* (pp. 21–44). Albany, NY: State University of New York Press.

Fitzgerald, L.F. (1993). Sex harassment: Violence against women in the workplace. *American Psychologist, 48,* 1070–1076.

Fitzgerald, L.F., & Nutt, R. (1986). The Division 17 Principles Concerning the Counseling/Psychotherapy of Women: Rationale and implementation. *The Counseling Psychologist, 14,* 180–216.

Fitzgerald, L.F., & Ormerod, A.J. (1993). Breaking the silence: The sexual harassment of women in academia and the workplace. In F.L. Denmark & M.A. Paludi (Eds.), *Psychology of women: A handbook of issues and theories* (pp. 553–581). Westport, CT: Greenwood.

Fitzgerald, L.F., Shullman, S.L., Bailey, N., Richards, M., Swecker, J., Gold, A., Ormerod, A.J.,

& Weitzman, L. (1988). The incidence and dimensions of sexual harassment in academia and the workplace. *Journal of Vocational Behavior, 32*, 152–175.

Fitzgerald, L.F., Swan, S., & Fischer, K. (1995). Why didn't she just report him? The psychological and legal implications of women's responses to sexual harassment. *Journal of Social Issues, 51*(1), 117–138.

Fivush, R. (1989). Exploring sex differences in the emotional content of mother-child conversations about the past. *Sex Roles, 20*, 675–691.

Flint, M., & Samil, R.S. (1990). Cultural and sub-cultural meanings of the menopause. In M. Flint, F. Kronenberg, & W. Utian (Eds.), *Multidisciplinary perspectives on menopause. Annals of the New York Academy of Sciences, 592*, 134–155.

Florentine, R. (1988). Increasing similarity in the values and life plans of male and female college students? Evidence and implications. *Sex Roles, 18*, 143–158.

Floyd, K. (1995). Gender and closeness among friends and siblings. *Journal of Psychology, 129*, 193–202.

Fodor, I.G. (1992). The agoraphobic syndrome: From anxiety neurosis to panic disorder. In L.S. Brown & M. Ballou (Eds.), *Personality and psychopathology: Feminist reappraisals* (pp. 177–205). New York: Guilford.

Forsythe, S.M. (1990). Effect of applicant's clothing on interviewer's decision to hire. *Journal of Applied Social Psychology, 20*, 1579–1595.

Fowers, B.J. (1991). His and her marriage: A multivariate study of gender and marital satisfaction. *Sex Roles, 24*, 209–221.

Fowers, B.J., Applegate, B., Tredinnick, M., & Slusher, J. (1996). His and her individualisms? Sex bias and individualism in psychologists' responses to case vignettes. *Journal of Psychology, 130*, 159–174.

Fox, M., & Hesse-Bibr, S. (1984). *Women at work*. Palo Alto, CA: Mayfield.

Fox, M.F., & Ferri, V.C. (1992). Women, men, and their attributions for success in academe. *Social Psychology Quarterly, 55*, 257–271.

Frable, D.E.S., & Bem, S.L. (1985). If you're gender-schematic, all members of the opposite sex look alike. *Journal of Personality and Social Psychology, 49*, 459–468.

Frances, L., & Wozniak, P.H. (1989). Children's television viewing with family members. *Psychological Reports, 65*, 395–400.

Frankel, M.T., & Rollins, H.A., Jr. (1983). Does Mother know best? Mothers and fathers interacting with preschool sons and daughters. *Developmental Psychology, 19*, 694–702.

Frankenberg, R. (1993). *White women, race matters: The social construction of whiteness*. Minneapolis, MN: University of Minnesota Press.

Franks, M.M., & Stephens, M.P. (1992). Multiple roles of middle-generation caregivers: Contextual effects and psychological mechanisms. *Journals of Gerontology, 47*, S123–S129.

Franzoi, S.L. (1995). The body-as-object versus the body-as-process: Gender differences and gender considerations. *Sex Roles, 33*, 417–437.

Franzoi, S.L. (1996). *Social psychology*. Madison, WI: Brown & Benchmark.

French, J.R.P., & Raven, B. (1959). The bases of social power. In D. Cartwright (Ed.), *Studies in social power* (pp. 150–167). Ann Arbor, MI: Institute for Social Research, University of Michigan.

Freud, S. (1969). *An outline of psycho-analysis* (J. Strachey, Trans.) (Rev. ed.). New York: Norton.

Freud, S. (1990). Femininity. In S. Ruth, *Issues in feminism: An introduction to women's studies* (2nd ed.). Mountain View, CA: Mayfield.

Freyd, J.J. (1997). Violations of power, adaptive blindness and betrayal trauma theory. *Feminism & Psychology, 7*, 22–32.

Friedman, W.J., Robinson, A.B., & Friedman, B.L. (1987). Sex differences in moral judgments? *Psychology of Women Quarterly, 11*, 37–46.

Frieze, I.H., & McHugh, M.C. (1992). Power and influence strategies in violent and nonviolent marriages. *Psychology of Women Quarterly, 16,* 449–465.

Frieze, I.H., & McHugh, M.C. (Eds.). (1997). Measuring beliefs about appropriate roles for women and men [Special issue]. *Psychology of Women Quarterly, 21*(1).

Frye, M. (1992). Willful virgin or do you have to be a lesbian to be a feminist? In *Willful virgin: Essays in feminism* (pp. 124–137). Freedom, CA: Crossing Press.

Fulton, S.A., & Sabornie, E.J. (1994). Evidence of employment inequality among females with disabilities. *Journal of Special Education, 28,* 149–165.

Funk, R.E. (1993). *Stopping rape: A challenge for men.* Philadelphia, PA: New Society Publishers.

Furey, E.M. (1994). Sexual abuse of adults with mental retardation: Who and where. *Mental Retardation, 32,* 173–180.

Furnham, A., & Baguma, P. (1994). Cross-cultural differences in the evaluation of male and female body shapes. *International Journal of Eating Disorders, 15,* 81–89.

Furnham, A., & Bitar, N. (1993). The stereotyped portrayal of men and women in British television. *Sex Roles, 29,* 297–310.

Furnham, A., Hester, C., & Weir, C. (1990). Sex differences in the preferences for specific female body shapes. *Sex Roles, 22,* 743–754.

Furumoto, L., & Scarborough, E. (1986). Placing women in the history of psychology: The first American women psychologists. *American Psychologist, 41,* 35–42.

Gackenbach, J. (1978). The effect of race, sex, and career goal differences on sex role attitudes at home and at work. *Journal of Vocational Behavior, 12,* 93–101.

Galambos, N.L., & Walters, B.J. (1992). Work hours, schedule inflexibility, and stress in dual-earner spouses. *Canadian Journal of Behavioral Science, 24,* 290–302.

Galinsky, E., & Bond, J.T. (1996). Work and family: The experiences of mothers and fathers in the U.S. labor force. In C. Costello & B.K. Krimgold (Eds.), *The American woman, 1996–97* (pp. 79–103). New York: Norton.

Galinsky, E., Bond, J.T., & Friedman, D.E. (1996). The role of employers in addressing the needs of employed parents. *Journal of Social Issues, 52*(1), 111–136.

Gallant, S.J., & Derry, P.S. (1995). Menarche, menstruation, and menopause: Psychosocial research and future directions. In A.L. Stanton & S.J. Gallant (Eds.), *The psychology of women's health: Progress and challenges in research and application* (pp. 199–259). Washington, DC: American Psychological Association.

Gallant, S.J., Hamilton, J.A., Popiel, D.A., Morokoff, P.J., & Chakraborty, P.K. (1991). Daily moods and symptoms: Effects of awareness of study focus, gender, menstrual-cycle phase, and day of week. *Health Psychology, 10,* 180–189.

Ganley, A.L. (1988). Feminist therapy with male clients. In M.A. Dutton-Douglas & L.E. Walker (Eds.), *Feminist psychotherapies: Integration of therapeutic and feminist systems* (pp. 186–205). Norwood, NJ: Ablex.

Gannon, L.R. (1985). *Menstrual disorders and menopause: Biological, psychological and cultural research.* New York: Praeger.

Gannon, L.R., Luchetta, T., Rhodes, K., Pardie, L., & Segrist, D. (1992). Sex bias in psychological research: Progress or complacency? *American Psychologist, 47,* 389–396.

Ganong, L.H., & Coleman, M. (1995). The content of mother stereotyping. *Sex Roles, 32,* 495–512.

Garfield, S.L. (1986). Problems in diagnostic classification. In T. Millon & G.L. Klerman (Eds.), *Contemporary directions in psychotherapy: Toward DSM-IV* (pp. 99–114). New York: Guilford.

Garnets, L.D. (1996). Life as a lesbian: What does gender have to do with it? In J.C. Chrisler, C. Golden, & P.D. Rozee (Eds)., *Lectures on the psychology of women* (pp. 137–151). New York: McGraw-Hill.

Garnets, L.D., Herek, G.M., & Levy, B. (1993). Violence and victimization of lesbians and gay men: Mental health consequences. In L.D. Garnets & D.C. Kimmel (Eds.), *Psychological perspectives on lesbian & gay male experiences* (pp. 577–597). New York: Columbia University Press.

Gaskill, L.R. (1991). Women's career success: A factor analytic study of contributing factors. *Journal of Career Development, 17,* 167–178.

Gastil, J. (1990). Generic pronouns and sexist language: The oxymoronic character of masculine generics. *Sex Roles, 23,* 629–643.

Geis, F.L., Brown, V., Jennings, J., & Porter, N. (1984). TV commercials as achievement scripts for women. *Sex Roles, 10,* 513–525.

Geissler, L.J., Bormann, C.A., Kwiatkowski, C.F., Braucht, G.N., & Reichardt, C.S. (1995). Women, homelessness, and substance abuse: Moving beyond the stereotypes. *Psychology of Women Quarterly, 19,* 65–83.

Gelfond, M. (1991). Reconceptualizing agoraphobia: A case study of epistemological bias in clinical research. *Feminism & Psychology, 1,* 247–262.

Geller, J.L. (1985). Women's accounts of psychiatric illness and institutionalization. *Hospital and Community Psychiatry, 36,* 1056–1062.

Gelles, R., & Harrop, J.W. (1989). Violence, battering, and psychological distress among women. *Journal of Interpersonal Violence, 4,* 400–420.

George, L.K. (1996). Missing links: The case for a social psychology of the life course. *The Gerontologist, 36,* 248–255.

George, L.K., Winfield, I., & Blazer, D.G. (1992). Sociocultural factors in sexual assault: Comparison of two representative samples of women. *Journal of Social Issues, 48*(1), 105–126.

Gergen, K.J. (1985). The social constructionist movement in modern psychology. *American Psychologist, 40,* 255–265.

Gergen, M.M. (1990). Finished at 40: Women's development within the patriarchy. *Psychology of Women Quarterly, 14,* 471–494.

Gerson, K. (1985). *Hard choices: How women decide about work, career and motherhood.* Berkeley, CA: University of California Press.

Gerson, K. (1993). *No man's land: Men's changing commitments to family and work.* New York: Basic.

Gerstel, N., & Gallagher, S. (1993). Kinkeeping and distress: Gender, recipients of care and work-family conflict. *Journal of Marriage and the Family, 55,* 598–608.

Gerstel, N., & Gallagher, S. (1994). Caring for kith and kin: Gender, employment, and the privatization of care. *Social Problems, 41,* 519–539.

Gervasio, A.H., & Crawford, M. (1989). Social evaluations of assertiveness: A critique and speech act reformulation. *Psychology of Women Quarterly, 13,* 1–25.

Gettys, L.D., & Cann, A. (1981). Children's perceptions of occupational sex stereotypes. *Sex Roles, 7,* 301–308.

Gibbs, J.T., & Fuery, D. (1994). Mental health and well-being of Black women toward strategies of empowerment. *American Journal of Community Psychology, 22,* 559–582.

Gibbs, N. (1992, March 9). The war against feminism. *Time,* pp. 50–57.

Gilbert, L.A. (1993). *Two careers/one family.* Newbury Park, CA: Sage.

Gilbert, L.A., & Rossman, K.M. (1992). Gender and the mentoring process for women: Implications for professional development. *Professional Psychology Research and Practice, 23,* 233–238.

Gilbert, N. (1997). Advocacy research exaggerates rape statistics. In M.R. Walsh (Ed.), *Women, men, and gender: Ongoing debates* (pp. 236–242). New Haven, CT: Yale.

Gillem, A.R. (1996). Beyond double jeopardy: Female, biracial, and perceived to be Black. In J.C. Chrisler, K. Golden, & P.D. Rozee (Eds)., *Lectures on the psychology of women* (pp. 199–209). New York: McGraw-Hill.

Gilligan, C. (1979). Woman's place in man's life cycle. *Harvard Educational Review, 49,* 431–446.

Gilligan, C. (1982). *In a different voice: Psychological theory and women's development.* Cambridge, MA: Harvard.

Girgus, J. (1989, October). Body image in girls pushes rate of depression up. *APA Monitor,* Washington, DC.

Gjerdingen, D.K., Froberg, D.G., & Fontaine, P. (1990). A causal model describing the relationship of women's postpartum health to social support, length of leave, and complications of childbirth. *Women and Health, 16,* 71–87.

Glass, D. (1964). Changes in liking as a means of reducing cognitive discrepancies between self-esteem and aggression. *Journal of Personality, 32,* 531–549.

Glass, J. (1990). The impact of occupational segregation on working conditions. *Social Forces, 68,* 779–796.

Glick, P. (1991). Trait-based and sex-based discrimination in occupational prestige. *Sex Roles, 25,* 351–378.

Glick, P. (1997, October). *Allport's afterthought: Why prejudice cannot be defined as an antipathy.* Paper presented at the meeting of the Society of Experimental Social Psychology, Toronto.

Glick, P., Diebold, J., Bailey-Werner, B., & Zhu, L. (1997). The two faces of Adam: Ambivalent sexism and polarized attitudes toward women. *Personality and Social Psychology Bulletin, 23,* 1334–1344.

Glick, P., & Fiske, S.T. (1996). The Ambivalent Sexism Inventory: Differentiating hostile and benevolent sexism. *Journal of Personality and Social Psychology, 70,* 491–512.

Glick, P., & Fiske, S.T. (1999). Sexism and other "isms": Interdependence, status, and the ambivalent content of stereotypes. In W.B. Swann, Jr., J. Langlois, & L.A. Gilbert (Eds.), *Sexism and stereotypes in modern society: Essays in honor of Janet Taylor Spence.* Washington, DC: American Psychological Association.

Glick, P., Zion, C., & Nelson, C. (1988). What mediates sex discrimination in hiring decisions? *Journal of Personality and Social Psychology, 55,* 178–186.

Goh, S.C. (1991). Sex differences in perceptions of interpersonal work style. *Sex Roles, 24,* 701–710.

Gold, D., Crombie, G., & Noble, S. (1987). Relations between teachers' judgments of girls' and boys' compliance and intellectual competence. *Sex Roles, 16,* 351–358.

Goldberg, E., Podell, K., Harner, R., Riggio, S., & Lovell, M. (1994). Cognitive bias, functional cortical geometry, and the frontal lobes: Laterality, sex, and handedness. *Journal of Cognitive Neuroscience, 63,* 276–296.

Goldberg, P. (1968, April). Are women prejudiced against women? *Trans-action, 5,* 28–30.

Goldberg, W.A., Greenberger, E., Hamill, S., & O'Neil, R. (1992). Role demands in the lives of employed single mothers with preschoolers. *Journal of Family Issues, 13,* 312–333.

Goldfield, A, & Chrisler, J.C. (1995). Body stereotyping and stigmatization of obese persons by first graders. *Perceptual and Motor Skills, 81,* 909–910.

Golding, J.M. (1990). Division of household labor, strain, and depressive symptoms among Mexican Americans and non-Hispanic Whites. *Psychology of Women Quarterly, 14,* 103–117.

Goldman, J.D.G., & Goldman, R.J. (1983). Children's perceptions of parents and their roles: A cross-national study in Australia, England, North America, and Sweden. *Sex Roles, 9,* 791–812.

Golombok, S., & Tasker, F. (1996). Do parents influence the sexual orientation of their children? Findings from a longitudinal study of lesbian families. *Developmental Psychology, 32,* 3–11.

Gomberg, E.L. (1993). Women and alcohol: Use and abuse. *Journal of Nervous and Mental Disease, 181,* 211–219.

Gomberg, E.S.L. (1994). Risk factors for drinking over a woman's life span. *Alcohol Health and Research World, 18,* 220–227.

Gomez, M.J., & Fassinger, R.E. (1994). An initial model of Latina achievement: Acculturation, biculturalism, and achieving styles. *Journal of Counseling Psychology, 41*, 205–215.

Goodenow, C., & Gaier, E.L. (1990, August). *Best friends: The close reciprocal friendships of married and unmarried women.* Paper presented at the meeting of the American Psychological Association, Washington, D.C.

Goodman, L.A., Koss, M.P., & Russo, N.F. (1993). Violence against women: Physical and mental health effects: Part 1. Research findings. *Applied and Preventive Psychology, 2*, 79–89.

Goodnow, J.J., & Bowes, J.M. (1994). *Men, women and household work.* New York: Oxford.

Goodwin, R., & Lee, I. (1994). Taboo topics among Chinese and English friends: A cross-cultural comparison. *Journal of Cross-Cultural Psychology, 25*, 325–338.

Goossens, F.A., & van Ijzendoorn, M.H. (1990). Quality of infants' attachments to professional caregivers: Relation to infant-parent attachment and day-care characteristics. *Child Development, 61*, 550–567.

Gordon, M.T., & Riger, S. (1989). *The female fear.* New York: Free Press.

Gorman, C. (1992, January 20). Sizing up the sexes. *Time*, pp. 42–51.

Gorski, R., et al. (1978). Evidence for a morphological sex difference within the medial preoptic area of the rat brain. *Brain Research, 148*, 333–346.

Goudsmit, E.M. (1994). All in her mind! Stereotypic views and the psychologisation of women's illness. In S. Wilkinson & C. Kitzinger (Eds.), *Women and health: Feminist perspectives* (pp. 7–12). London: Taylor & Francis.

Gould, S.J. (1981). *The mismeasure of man.* New York: Norton.

Grady, K.E. (1981). Sex bias in research design. *Psychology of Women Quarterly, 5*, 628–636.

Graham, A. (1975). The making of a nonsexist dictionary. In B. Thorne & N. Henley (Eds.), *Language and sex: Difference and dominance.* Rowley, MA: Newbury House.

Grambs, J.D. (1989). *Women over forty: Visions and realities* (Rev. ed.). New York: Springer.

Gratch, L.V., Bassett, M.E., & Attra, S.L. (1995). The relationship of gender and ethnicity to self-silencing and depression among college women. *Psychology of Women Quarterly, 19*, 509–515.

Green, G. (1995). Attitudes towards people with HIV: Are they as stigmatizing as people with HIV perceive them to be? *Social Science and Medicine, 41*, 557–568.

Green, G.D. (1990). Is separation really so great? *Women & Therapy, 9*, 87–104.

Greene, B. (1990a). Sturdy bridges: The role of African American mothers in the socialization of their children. *Women & Therapy, 10*, 205–225.

Greene, B. (1990b). What has gone before: The legacy of racism and sexism in the lives of black mothers and daughters. *Women & Therapy, 9*, 207–230.

Greene, B. (1994a). Diversity and difference: The issue of race in feminist therapy. In M.P. Mirkin (Ed.), *Women in context: Toward a feminist reconstruction of psychotherapy* (pp. 333–351). New York: Guilford.

Greene, B. (1994b). African American women. In L. Comas-Díaz & B. Greene (Eds.), *Women of color: Integrating ethnic and gender identities in psychotherapy* (pp. 10–29). New York: Guilford.

Greene, E. (1995). Teaching about psychological perspectives on abortion. *Teaching of Psychology, 22*, 202–204.

Greenwald, D. (1992). Psychotic disorders with emphasis on schizophrenia. In L.S. Brown & M. Ballou (Eds.), *Personality and psychopathology: Feminist reappraisals* (pp. 144–176). New York: Guilford.

Griffin, C. (1989). "I'm not a women's libber, but...": Feminism, consciousness and identity. In S. Skevington & D. Baker (Eds.), *The social identity of women* (pp. 173–193). London: Sage.

Griffin, G. (1994). The desire for change and the experience of women's studies. In G. Griffin (Ed.), *Changing our lives: Doing women's studies* (pp. 13–45). Boulder, CO: Pluto Press.

Griffin, S. (1971). Rape: The all-American crime. *Ramparts, 10,* 26–35.

Griffith, W.I., Sell, J., & Parker, M.J. (1993). Self-interested versus third-party allocations of rewards. *Social Psychology Quarterly, 56,* 148–155.

Grinstead, O.A., Faigeles, B., Binson, D., & Eversley, R. (1993). Sexual risk for human immunodeficiency virus infection among women in high-risk cities. *Family Planning Perspectives, 25,* 252–256, 277.

Griscom, J.L. (1992). Women and power: Definition, dualism, and difference. *Psychology of Women Quarterly, 16,* 389–414.

Grobbee, D.E., Rimm, E.B., Giovannucci, E., Colditz, G., Stampfer, M., & Willett, W. (1990). Coffee, caffeine, and cardiovascular disease in men. *New England Journal of Medicine, 323,* 1026–1032.

Gross, J. (1991, June 16). More young single men hang on to apron strings. *The New York Times,* pp. 1,18.

Gruen, R.J., Gwadz, M., & Morrobel, D. (1994). Support, criticism, emotion and depressive symptoms: Gender differences in the stress-depression relationship. *Journal of Social and Personal Relationships, 11,* 619–624.

Guarino, M., Fridrich, P., & Sitton, S. (1994). Male and female conformity in eating behavior. *Psychological Reports, 75,* 603–609.

Gue, S. (1985). A cross-cultural study of the relation between degree of American acculturation and androgyny. *Asian American Psychological Association Journal,* 40–51.

Guidelines for the Provision of Counseling Psychological Services. (1983). Washington, DC: American Psychological Association.

Guillen, E.O., & Barr, S.I. (1994). Nutrition, dieting, and fitness messages in a magazine for adolescent women, 1970–1990. *Journal of Adolescent Health, 15,* 464–472.

Gullette, M.M. (1997). *Declining to decline: Cultural combat and the politics of midlife.* Charlottesville, VA: University Press of Virginia.

Gurevich, M. (1995). Rethinking the label: Who benefits from the PMS construct? *Women & Health, 23,* 67–98.

Gurin, P. (1985). Women's gender consciousness. *Public Opinion Quarterly, 49,* 143–163.

Gurin, P., & Markus, H. (1989). Cognitive consequences of gender identity. In S. Skevington & D. Baker (Eds.), *The social identity of women* (pp. 152–172). Newbury Park, CA: Sage.

Gurin, P., & Townsend, A. (1986). Properties of gender identity and their implications for gender consciousness. *British Journal of Social Psychology, 25,* 139–148.

Gutek, B.A. (1985). *Sex and the workplace.* San Francisco, CA: Jossey-Bass.

Gutek, B.A., Cohen, A.G., & Tsui, A. (1996). Reactions to perceived sex discrimination. *Human Relations, 49,* 791–813.

Gutek, B.A., & Koss, M.P. (1993). Changed women and changed organizations: Consequences of and coping with sexual harassment. *Journal of Vocational Behavior, 42,* 28–48.

Gutek, B.A., & O'Connor, M. (1995). The empirical basis for the reasonable woman standard. *Journal of Social Issues, 51*(1), 151–166.

Gutek, B.A., Repetti, R.L., & Silver, D.L. (1988). Nonwork roles and stress at work. In C.L. Cooper & R. Payne (Eds.), *Causes, coping, and consequences of stress at work* (pp. 141–174). New York: Wiley.

Guthrie, R.V. (1976). *Even the rat was white: A historical view of psychology.* New York: Harper & Row.

Gutmann, D. (1987). *Reclaimed powers: Toward a new psychology of men and women in later life.* New York: Basic.

Hackett, G., & Byars, A.M. (1996). Social cognitive theory and the career development of African American women. *Career Development Quarterly, 44,* 322–340.

Haddock, G., & Zanna, M.P. (1994). Preferring "housewives" to "feminists": Categorization and the favorability of attitudes toward women. *Psychology of Women Quarterly, 18,* 25–52.

Hafner, R.J., & Minge, P.J. (1989). Sex role stereotyping in women with agoraphobia and their husbands. *Sex Roles, 20,* 705–711.

Hagekull, B., & Bohlin, G. (1995). Day care quality, family and child characteristics and socioe-motional development. *Early Childhood Research Quarterly, 10,* 505–526.

Hall, C.C.I. (1995). Asian eyes: Body image and eating disorders of Asian and Asian American women. *Eating Disorders: The Journal of Treatment and Prevention, 3,* 8–19.

Hall, C.C.I, & Crum, M.J. (1994). Women and "body-isms" in television beer commercials. *Sex Roles, 31,* 329–337.

Hall, D.T. (1972). A model of coping with role conflict: The role behavior of college educated women. *Administrative Science Quarterly, 17,* 471–486.

Hall, J.A. (1984). *Nonverbal sex differences: Communication accuracy and expressive style.* Baltimore, MD: Johns Hopkins University Press.

Hall, J.A., & Halberstadt, A.G. (1997). Subordination and nonverbal sensitivity: A hypothesis in search of support. In M.R. Walsh (Ed.), *Women, men, & gender: Ongoing debates* (pp. 120–133). New Haven, CT: Yale.

Hall, R. (1996). Sweating it out: The good news and the bad news about women and sport. In J.C. Chrisler, C. Golden, & P.D. Rozee (Eds.), *Lectures on the psychology of women* (pp. 75–89). New York: McGraw-Hill.

Hall, R., & Rose, S. (1996). Friendships between African-American and white lesbians. In J. Weinstock & E. Rothblum (Eds.), *Lesbian friendships* (pp. 165–191). New York: New York University Press.

Halpern, D.F. (1994). III. Stereotypes, science, censorship and the study of sex differences. *Feminism & Psychology, 4,* 523–530.

Halpern, D.F. (1997). Sex differences in intelligence: Implications for education. *American Psychologist, 52,* 1091–1102.

Hamberger, L.K., Saunders, D.G., & Hovey, M. (1992). The prevalence of domestic violence in community practice and rate of physical inquiry. *Family Medicine, 24,* 283–287.

Hamilton, J.A. (1992). Biases in women's health research. *Women & Therapy, 12*(4), 91–101.

Hamilton, J.A. (1996). Women and health policy: On the inclusion of females in clinical trials. In C.F. Sargent & C.B. Brettell (Eds.), *Gender and health: An international perspective* (pp. 292–325). Upper Saddle River, NJ: Prentice Hall.

Hamilton, J.A., & Jensvold, M. (1992). Personality, psychopathology, and depressions in women. In L.S. Brown & M. Ballou (Eds.), *Personality and psychopathology: Feminist reappraisals* (pp. 116–143). New York: Guilford.

Hamilton, M.C. (1988). Masculine generic terms and misperception of AIDS risk. *Journal of Applied Social Psychology, 18,* 1222–1240.

Hamilton, M.C. (1991). Masculine bias in the attribution of personhood: People = male, male = people. *Psychology of Women Quarterly, 15,* 393–402.

Hamilton, M.C., & Henley, N.M. (1982, March). *Detrimental consequences of generic masculine usage: Effects on the reader/hearer's cognitions.* Paper presented at the meeting of the Western Psychological Association, Sacramento, CA.

Hanmer, J., & Saunders, S. (1984). *Well founded fear.* London: Hutchinson.

Hanna, W.J., & Rogovsky, E. (1991). Women with disabilities: Two handicaps plus. *Disability, Handicap and Society, 6,* 49–63.

Hanna, W.J., & Rogovsky, E. (1992). On the situation of African-American women with physical disabilities. *Journal of Applied Rehabilitation Counseling, 23,* 39–45.

Hannon, R., Kuntz, T., Van Laar, S., Williams, J., & Hall, D.S. (1996). College students' judgments regarding sexual aggression during a date. *Sex Roles, 35,* 765–780.

Hansen, C., & Hansen, R.D. (1988). How rock music videos can change what is seen when boy meets girl: Priming stereotypic appraisal of social interactions. *Sex Roles, 19,* 287–316.

Hansen, F.J., & Osborne, D. (1995). Portrayal of women and elderly patients in psychotropic drug advertisements. *Women & Therapy, 16(1)*, 129–141.

Hansen, M. & Harway, M. (Eds.). (1993). *Battering and family therapy: A feminist perspective.* Newbury Park, CA: Sage.

Hanson, K., & Gidycz, C.A. (1993). Evaluation of a sexual assault prevention program. *Journal of Consulting and Clinical Psychology, 61*, 1046–1052.

Hanson, K., & Wapner, S. (1994). Transition to retirement: Gender differences. *International Journal of Aging and Human Development, 39*, 189–208.

Harding, S. (1986). *The science question in feminism.* Ithaca, NY: Cornell.

Hardy, D.M., & Johnson, M.E. (1992). Influence of therapist gender and client gender, socioeconomic status and alcohol status on clinical judgments. *Journal of Alcohol and Drug Education, 37*, 94–102.

Hardy, M.A., & Hazelrigg, L.E. (1995). Gender, race/ethnicity, and poverty in later life. *Journal of Aging Studies, 9*, 43–63.

Hare-Mustin, R.T. (1983). An appraisal of the relationship between women and psychotherapy: 80 years after the case of Dora. *American Psychologist, 38*, 593–601.

Hare-Mustin, R.T., & Marecek, J. (1988). The meaning of difference: Gender theory, postmoderism, and psychology. *American Psychologist, 43*, 455–464.

Hare-Mustin, R.T., & Marecek, J. (1994). IV. Asking the right questions: Feminist psychology and sex differences. *Feminism & Psychology, 4*, 531–537.

Harris, A.C. (1994). Ethnicity as a determinant of sex role identity: A replication study of item selection for the Bem Sex Role Inventory. *Sex Roles, 31*, 241–273.

Harris, M.B. (1995). Ethnicity, gender, and evaluators of aggression. *Aggressive Behavior, 21*, 343–357.

Harris, M.B., Begay, C., & Page, P. (1989). Activities, family relationships, and feelings about aging in a multicultural elderly sample. *International Journal of Aging and Human Development, 29*, 103–117.

Harris, S. (1994). Racial differences in predictors of college women's body image attitudes. *Women and Health, 21*, 89–104.

Hart, K., & Kenny, M.E. (1997). Adherence to the super woman ideal and eating disorder symptoms among college women. *Sex Roles, 36*, 461–478.

Hartl, D.L. (1983). *Human genetics.* New York: Harper & Row.

Hartmann, H.I. (1976). Capitalism, patriarchy, and job segregation by sex. *Signs, 1*, 137–167.

Harway, M., & Hansen, M. (1993). Therapist perceptions of family violence. In M. Hansen & M. Harway (Eds.), *Battering and family therapy: A feminist perspective* (pp. 42–53). Newbury Park, CA: Sage.

Hatch, L.R. (1991). Informal support patterns of older African-American and white women: Examining effects of family, paid work, and religious participation. *Research on Aging, 13*, 144–170.

Hatfield, E., Sprecher, S., Pillemer, J.T., Greenberger, D., et al. (1988). Gender differences in what is desired in the sexual relationship. *Journal of Psychology and Human Sexuality, 1*, 39–52.

Hauenstein, E.J., & Boyd, M.R. (1994). Depressive symptoms in young women of the Piedmont: Prevalence in rural women. *Women & Health, 21*, 105–123.

Haver, B., & Dahlgren, L. (1995). Early treatment of women with alcohol addiction (EWA): A comprehensive evaluation and outcome study: I. Patterns of psychiatric comorbidity at intake. *Addiction, 90*, 101–109.

Hawkins, A.J., Marshall, C.M., & Meiners, K.M. (1995). Exploring wives' sense of fairness about family work: An initial test of the distributive justice framework. *Journal of Family Issues, 16*, 693–721.

Hawkins, J.W., & Aber, C.S. (1993). Women in advertisements in medical journals. *Sex Roles, 28,* 233–242.

Healey, S. (1993). Confronting ageism: A MUST for mental health. *Women & Therapy, 14,* 41–54.

Hebl, M.R. (1995). Gender bias in leader selection. *Teaching of Psychology, 22,* 186–188.

Heidrich, S.M. (1993). The relationship between physical health and psychological well-being in elderly women: A developmental perspective. *Research in Nursing & Health, 16,* 123–130.

Heidrich, S.M. (1994). The self, health, and depression in elderly women. *Western Journal of Nursing Research, 16,* 544–555.

Heidrich, S.M., & Ryff, C.D. (1992). How elderly women cope: Concern and strategies. *Public Health Nursing, 9,* 200–208.

Heister, G., Landis, T., Regard, M., & Schroeder-Heister, P. (1989). Shift of functional cerebral asymmetry during the menstrual cycle. *Neuropsychologia, 27,* 871–880.

Helgeson, V.S. (1994). Prototypes and dimensions of masculinity and femininity. *Sex Roles, 31,* 653–682.

Helgeson, V.S. (1994). Relation of agency and communion to well-being: Evidence and potential explanations. *Psychological Bulletin, 116,* 412–428.

Heller, C.W. (1996). A paradox of silence: Reflections of a man who teaches women's studies. In K.J. Mayberry (Ed.), *Teaching what you're not: Identity politics in higher education* (pp. 228–237). New York: New York University Press.

Helms, J.E. (Ed.). (1990). *Black and white racial identity: Theory, research, and practice.* New York: Greenwood.

Helson, R. (1992). Women's difficult times and the rewriting of the life story. *Psychology of Women Quarterly, 16,* 331–347.

Helson, R., & Wink, P. (1992). Personality change in women from the early 40s to the early 50s. *Psychology and Aging, 7,* 46–55.

Henderson-King, D.H., & Stewart, A.J. (1994). Women or feminists? Assessing women's group consciousness. *Sex Roles, 31,* 505–516.

Henderson-King, D.H., & Stewart, A.J. (1997). Feminist consciousness: Perspectives on women's experiences. *Personality and Social Psychology Bulletin, 23,* 415–426.

Henley, N.M. (1977). *Body politics: Power, sex, and nonverbal communication.* Englewood Cliffs, NJ: Prentice Hall.

Henley, N.M. (1989). Molehill or mountain? What we do know and don't know about sex bias in language. In M. Crawford & M. Gentry (Eds.), *Gender and thought* (pp. 59–78). New York: Springer-Verlag.

Henley, N.M. (1995). Ethnicity and gender issues in language. In H. Landrine (Ed.), *Bringing cultural diversity to feminist psychology: Theory, research, and practice* (pp. 361–395). Washington, DC: American Psychological Association.

Henley, N.M., & Freeman, J. (1989). The sexual politics of interpersonal behavior. In J. Freeman (Ed.), *Women: A feminist perspective* (4th ed.) (pp. 457–469). Mountain View, CA: Mayfield.

Henretta, J.C., O'Rand, A.M., & Chan, C.G. (1993). Gender differences in employment after spouse's retirement. *Research on Aging, 15,* 148–169.

Herdt, G.H., & Davidson, J. (1988). The Sambra "Turnim-man": Sociocultural and clinical aspects of gender formation in male pseudohermaphrodites with 5-alpha-reductase deficiency in Papua New Guinea. *Archives of Sexual Behavior, 17,* 33–56.

Herek, G.M. (1988). Heterosexuals' attitudes toward lesbians and gay men: Correlates and gender differences. *Journal of Sex Research, 25,* 451–477.

Herman, J.L. (1992). *Trauma and recovery.* New York: Basic.

Herman, J.L., Perry, J.C., & van der Kolk, B.A. (1989). Childhood trauma in borderline personality disorder. *American Journal of Psychiatry, 146,* 490–495.

Herz, D.E., & Wootton, B.H. (1996). Women in the workforce: An overview. In C. Costello & B.K. Krimgold (Eds.), *The American woman, 1996–97* (pp. 44–78). New York: Norton.

Herzog, D.B., Newman, K.L., Yeh, C.J., & Warshaw, M. (1992). Body image satisfaction in homosexual and heterosexual women. *International Journal of Eating Disorders, 11,* 391–396.

Hessing, M. (1994). More than clockwork: Women's time management in their combined workload. *Sociological Perspectives, 37,* 611–633.

Hessler, R.M., Jia, S., Madsen, R., & Pazaki, H. (1995). Gender, social networks and survival time: A 20-year study of the rural elderly. *Archives of Gerontology and Geriatrics, 21,* 291–306.

Hewlett, S.A. (1986). *A lesser life: The myth of women's liberation in America.* New York: Morrow.

Hibbard, J.H., & Pope, C.R. (1991). Effect of domestic and occupational roles on morbidity and mortality. *Social Science and Medicine, 32,* 805–811.

Higginbotham, E.B. (1992). African-American women's history and the metalanguage of race. *Signs, 17,* 251–274.

Hill, M. (1987). Child-rearing attitudes of Black lesbian mothers. In Boston Lesbian Psychologies Collective (Eds.), *Lesbian psychologies* (pp. 215–225). Urbana, IL: University of Illinois Press.

Himes, C.L. (1992). Future caregivers: Projected family structures of older persons. *Journals of Gerontology, 47,* S17–S26.

Hines, M., & Kaufman, F.R. (1994). Androgen and the development of human sex typical behavior: Rough-and-tumble play and sex of preferred playmates in children with cogenital adrenal hyperplasia (CAH). *Child Development, 65,* 1042–1053.

Ho, C.K. (1990). An analysis of domestic violence in Asian American communities: A multicultural approach to counseling. In L.S. Brown & M.P.P. Root (Eds.), *Diversity and complexity in feminist therapy* (pp. 129–150). New York: Harrington Park Press.

Hochschild, A.R. (1989). *The second shift: Working parents and the revolution at home.* New York: Viking.

Hoffman, C., & Hurst, N. (1990). Gender stereotypes: Perception or rationalization? *Journal of Personality and Social Psychology, 58,* 197–208.

Hoffman, L.W. (1989). Effects of maternal employment in the two-parent family. *American Psychologist, 44,* 283–292.

Holcomb, L.P., & Giesen, C.B. (1995). Coping with challenges: College experiences of older women and women with disabilities. In J.C. Chrisler & A.H. Hemstreet (Eds.), *Variations on a theme: Diversity and the psychology of women* (pp. 175–199). Albany, NY: SUNY Press.

Hollander, E.P., & Yoder, J.D. (1980). Some issues comparing women and men as leaders. *Journal of Basic and Applied Social Psychology, 1,* 267–280.

Holloway, W. (1994). V. Beyond sex differences: A project for feminist psychology. *Feminism & Psychology, 4,* 538–546.

Holmes, D.S., & Jorgensen, B.W. (1971). Do personality and social psychologists study men more than women? *Representative Research in Social Psychology, 2,* 71–76.

Holtzen, D.W., & Agresti, A.A. (1990). Parental responses to gay and lesbian children: Differences in homophobia, self-esteem, and sex-role stereotyping. *Journal of Social and Clinical Psychology, 9,* 390–399.

Holzman, C.G. (1996). Counseling adult women rape survivors: Issues of race, ethnicity and class. *Women & Therapy, 19,* 47–62.

hooks, b. (1984). *Feminist theory: From margin to center.* Boston, MA: South End Press.

Horner, M.S. (1970). Femininity and successful achievement: A basic inconsistency. In J.M. Bardwick, E. Douvan, M.S. Horner, & D. Gutman (Eds.), *Feminine personality and conflict* (pp. 45–74). Belmont, CA: Brooks/Cole.

Horney, K. (1926). The flight from womanhood. *International Journal of Psychoanalysis, 7,* 324–339.

Horney, K. (1966). *New ways in psychoanalysis.* New York: Norton.

Hornstein, G.A., & Wapner, S. (1985). Modes of experiencing and adapting to retirement. *International Journal of Aging and Human Development, 21,* 548–571.

Hossain, Z., & Roopnarine, J.L. (1993). Division of household labor and child care in dual-earner African-American families with infants. *Sex Roles, 29,* 571–583.

Hotaling, G.T., & Sugarman, D.B. (1986). An analysis of risk markers in husband to wife violence: The current state of knowledge. *Violence and Victims, 1,* 101–124.

Howe, K.G. (1989). Telling our mother's story: Changing daughters' perceptions of their mothers in a women's studies course. In R.K. Unger (Ed.), *Representations: Social constructions of gender* (pp. 45–60). Amityville, NY: Baywood.

Howes, C. (1990). Can the age of entry and the quality of infant child care predict adjustment in kindergarten? *Developmental Psychology, 26,* 292–303.

Howes, C. (1991). Caregiving environments and their consequences for children: The experience in the United States. In E.C. Melhuish & P. Moss (Eds.), *Day care for young children: International perspectives* (pp. 185–198). New York: Tavistock/Routledge.

Hoyenga, K.B., & Hoyenga, K.T. (1993). *Gender-related differences: Origins and outcomes.* Boston, MA: Allyn & Bacon.

Hubbard, R. (1990). *The politics of women's biology.* New Brunswick, NJ: Rutgers.

Hughes, J.O., & Sandler, B.R. (1987). *"Friends" raping friends: Could it happen to you?* Washington, DC: Association of American Colleges.

Hughes, T.L., & Wilsnack, S.C. (1994). Research on lesbians and alcohol: Gaps and implications. *Alcohol Health and Research World, 18,* 202–205.

Hurlbert, D.F., & Apt, C. (1993). Female sexuality: A comparative study between women in homosexual and heterosexual relationships. *Journal of Sex and Marital Therapy, 19,* 315–327.

Hurlbert, D.F., Apt, C., & Rabehl, S.M. (1993). Key variables to understanding female sexual satisfaction: An examination of women in nondistressed marriages. *Journal of Sex and Marital Therapy, 19,* 154–165.

Huston, A.C., Greer, D., Wright, J.C., Welch, R., & Ross, R. (1984). Children's comprehension of televised formal features with masculine and feminine connotations. *Developmental Psychology, 20,* 707–716.

Hyde, J.S. (1984a). Children's understanding of sexist language. *Developmental Psychology, 20,* 697–706.

Hyde, J.S. (1984b). How large are gender differences in aggression? A developmental meta-analysis. *Developmental Psychology, 20,* 722–736.

Hyde, J.S. (1990). Meta-analysis and the psychology of gender differences. *Signs, 16,* 55–73.

Hyde, J.S. (1994a). I. Should psychologists study gender differences? Yes, with some guidelines. *Feminism & Psychology, 4,* 507–512.

Hyde, J.S. (1994b). Can meta-analysis make feminist transformations in psychology? *Psychology of Women Quarterly, 18,* 451–462.

Hyde, J.S., & Essex, M.J. (Eds.). (1991). *Parental leave and child care: Setting a research and policy agenda.* Philadelphia, PA: Temple.

Hyde, J.S., Fennema, E., & Lamon, S.J. (1990). Gender differences in mathematics performance: A meta-analysis. *Psychological Bulletin, 107,* 139–155.

Hyde, J.S., & Frost, L.A. (1993). Meta-analysis in the psychology of women. In F.L. Denmark & M.A. Paludi (Eds.), *Psychology of women: A handbook of issues and theories* (pp. 67–103). Westport, CT: Greenwood.

Hyde, J.S., Klein, M.H., Essex, M.J., & Clark, R. (1995). Maternity leave and women's mental health. *Psychology of Women Quarterly, 19,* 257–285.

Hyde, J.S., Krajnik, M., & Skuldt-Niederberger, K. (1991). Androgyny across the life span: A replication and longitudinal follow-up. *Developmental Psychology, 27*, 516–519.

Hyde, J.S., & Linn, M.C. (1988). Gender differences in verbal ability: A meta-analysis. *Psychological Bulletin, 104*, 53–69.

Hyde, J.S., & Plant, E.A. (1995). Magnitude of psychological gender differences: Another side of the story. *American Psychologist, 50*, 159–161.

Idle, T., Wood, E., & Desmarais, S. (1993). Gender role socialization in toy play situations: Mothers and fathers with their sons and daughters. *Sex Roles, 28*, 679–691.

Imperato-McGinley, J., Peterson, R.E., Gautier, T., & Sturla, E. (1979). Androgens and the evolution of male gender identity among male pseudohermaphrodites with a 5-alpha-reductase deficiency. *New England Journal of Medicine, 300*, 1236–1237.

Ingram, K.M., Corning, A.F., & Schmidt, L.D. (1996). The relationship of victimization experiences to psychological well-being among homeless women and low-income housed women. *Journal of Counseling Psychology, 43*, 218–227.

Innes, J.M., Dormer, S., & Lukins, J. (1993). Knowledge of gender stereotypes and attitudes towards women: A preliminary report. *Psychological Reports, 73*, 1005–1006.

Institute for Gay and Lesbian Strategic Studies. (1996, July). *Economic issues for lesbian and bisexual women.* Washington, DC.

Institute for Women's Policy Research. (1997, February). *Research in brief: The wage gap: Women's and men's earnings.* Washington, DC.

Ishii-Kuntz, M., & Coltrane, S. (1992). Predicting the sharing of household labor: Are parenting and housework distinct? *Sociological Perspectives, 35*, 629–647.

Izraeli, D.N. (1994). Money matters: Spousal incomes and family/work relations among physician couples in Israel. *Sociological Quarterly, 35*, 69–84.

Jacklin, C.N., & McBride-Chang, C. (1991). The effects of feminist scholarship on developmental psychology. *Psychology of Women Quarterly, 15*, 549–556.

Jackson, D. (1992). *How to make the world a better place for women in five minutes a day.* New York: Hyperion.

Jackson, L. (1992). *Physical appearance and gender: Sociobiological and sociocultural perspectives.* Albany, NY: SUNY Press.

Jackson, L.A., & Ervin, K.S. (1991). The frequency and portrayal of Black females in fashion advertisements. *Journal of Black Psychology, 18*, 67–70.

Jackson, L.A., Fleury, R.E., & Lewandowski, D.A. (1996). Feminism: Definitions, support, and correlates of support among female and male college students. *Sex Roles, 34*, 687–693.

Jackson, L.A., & McGill, O.D. (1996). Body type preferences and body characteristics associated with attractive and unattractive bodies by African American and Anglo Americans. *Sex Roles, 35*, 295–307.

Jackson, L.A., & Sullivan, L.A. (1990). Perceptions of multiple role participants. *Social Psychology Quarterly, 53*, 274–282.

Jackson, P.B., Thoits, P.A., & Taylor, H.F. (1995). Composition of the workplace and psychological well-being: The effects of tokenism on America's Black elite. *Social Forces, 74*, 543–557.

Jacobs, J.A. (1985). Sex segregation in American higher education. *Women and Work, 1*, 191–214.

Jacobs, J.A. (1989). Long-term trends in occupational segregation by sex. *American Journal of Sociology, 95*, 160–173.

Jacobs, J.A., & Lim, S.T. (1992). Trends in occupational and industrial sex segregation in 56 countries, 1960–1980. *Work and Occupations, 19*, 450–486.

Jacobs, R.L., & McClelland, D.C. (1994). Moving up the corporate ladder: A longitudinal study of the leadership motive pattern and managerial success in women and men. *Consulting Psychology Journal: Practice and Research, 46*, 32–41.

Jacobsen, F.M. (1994). Psychopharmacology. In L. Comas-Díaz & B. Greene (Eds.), *Women of color: Integrating ethnic and gender identities in psychotherapy* (pp. 319–338). New York: Guilford.

Jaffe, D., & Straus, M.A. (1987). Sexual climate and reported rape: A state-level analysis. *Archives of Sexual Behavior, 16*, 107–124.

Jaggar, A. (1983). Political philosophies of women's liberation. In L. Richardson & V. Taylor (Eds.), *Feminist frontiers: Rethinking sex, gender, and society* (pp. 322–329). New York: Random House.

Jambunathan, J. (1992). Sociocultural factors in depression in Asian Indian women. *Health Care for Women International, 13*, 261–270.

James, J.B. (1990). Women's employment patterns and midlife well-being. In H.Y. Grossman & M.L. Chester (Eds.), *The experience and meaning of work in women's lives* (pp. 103–120). Hillsdale, NJ: Lawrence Erlbaum.

James, J.B. (1997). What are the social issues involved in focusing on *difference* in the study of gender? *Journal of Social Issues, 53*(2), 213–232.

James, J.B., Lewkowicz, C., Libhaber, J., & Lachman, M. (1995). Rethinking the gender identity crossover hypothesis: A test of a new model. *Sex Roles, 32*, 185–207.

Janman, K. (1989). One step behind: Current stereotypes of women, achievement, and work. *Sex Roles, 21*, 209–230.

Janoff-Bulman, R., & Frieze, I.H. (1983). A theoretical perspective for understanding reactions to victimization. *Journal of Social Issues, 39*(2), 1–17.

Jaschik, S. (1990, June 27). Report says NIH ignores own rules on including women in its research. *The Chronicle of Higher Education*, p. A27.

Jeffrey, R.W., Adlis, S.A., & Forster, J.L. (1991). Prevalence of dieting among working men and women: The healthy worker project. *Health Psychology, 10*, 274–281.

Jeffreys, S. (1985). *The spinster and her enemies: Feminism and sexuality, 1880–1930.* London: Pandora.

Jenkins, S.R. (1996). Self-definition in thought, action, and life path choices. *Personality and Social Psychology Bulletin, 22*, 99–111.

Jenkins, Y. (1993). African American women: Ethnocultural variables and dissonant expectations. In J.L. Chin, V. De La Cancela, & Y. Jenkins (Eds.), *Diversity in psychotherapy: The politics of race, ethnicity and gender* (pp. 117–136). Westport, CT: Praeger.

Jensen, I., & Gutek, B.A. (1982). Attributions and assignment of responsibility for sexual harassment. *Journal of Social Issues, 38*(4) 121–136.

John, B.A., & Sussman, L.E. (1989). Initiative taking as a determinant of role-reciprocal organization. In R.K. Unger (Ed.), *Representations: Social constructions of gender* (pp. 259–272). Amityville, NY: Baywood.

John, D., & Shelton, B.A. (1997). The production of gender among Black and white women and men: The case of household labor. *Sex Roles, 36*, 171–193.

John, D., Shelton, B.A., & Luschen, K. (1995). Race, ethnicity, gender, and perceptions of fairness. *Journal of Family Issues, 16*, 357–379.

Johnson, B.E., Kuck, D.L., & Schander, P.R. (1997). Rape myth acceptance and sociodemographic characteristics: A multidimensional analysis. *Sex Roles, 36*, 693–707.

Johnson, C. (1993). Gender and formal authority. *Social Psychology Quarterly, 56*, 193–210.

Johnson, C.L., & Troll, L.E. (1994). Constraints and facilitators to friendships in late life. *Gerontologist, 34*, 79–87.

Johnson, J.S., Kellen, J., Seibert, G., & Shaughnessy, C. (1996). No middle ground? Men teaching feminism. In K.J. Mayberry (Ed.), *Teaching what you're not: Identity politics in higher education* (pp. 85–103). New York: New York University Press.

Johnson, P. (1976). Women and power: Toward a theory of effectiveness. *Journal of Social Issues, 32*(3), 99–110.

Johnson, W.B., & Hayes, D. (1993). "Cadism": Odd man out. *American Psychologist, 48*, 689.

Jolly, E.J., & O'Kelly, C.G. (1980). Sex-role stereotyping in the language of the deaf. *Sex Roles, 6*, 285–292.

Jones, G.P., & Jacklin, C.N. (1988). Changes in sexist attitudes towards women during introductory women's and men's studies courses. *Sex Roles, 18*, 611–622.

Jones, R.W., Abelli, D.M., & Abelli, R.B. (1994, August). *Ratio of female:male characters and stereotyping in educational programming.* Paper presented at the annual meeting of the American Psychological Association, Los Angeles, CA.

Joseph, J. (1987). Warning. In S. Marts (Ed.), *When I am an old woman I shall wear purple.* Watsonville, CA: Papier-Mache.

Joseph, R. (1992). *Right brain and the unconscious: Discovering the stranger within.* New York: Plenum.

Jozefowicz, D.M., Barber, B.L., & Eccles, J.S. (1993, March). *Adolescent work-related values and beliefs: Gender differences and relation to occupational aspirations.* Paper presented at biennial meeting of the Society for Research on Child Development, New Orleans, LA.

Jump, T.L., & Haas, L. (1987). Fathers in transition: Dual-career fathers participate in child care. In M.S. Kimmel (Ed.), *Changing men: New directions in research on men and masculinity* (pp. 98–114). Newbury Park, CA: Sage.

Jussim, L. (1986). Self-fulfilling prophecies: A theoretical and integrative review. *Psychological Review, 93*, 429–445.

Kahn, A.S., & Gaeddert, W.P. (1985). From theories of equity to theories of justice: The liberating consequences of studying women. In V.E. O'Leary, R.K. Unger, & B.S. Wallston (Eds.), *Women, gender, and social psychology* (pp. 129–148). Hillsdale, NJ: Erlbaum.

Kahn, A.S., & Gibson, P.R. (1993). The psychology of women: Maturing of the field. *Contemporary Psychology, 38*, 1175–1177.

Kahn. A.S., Mathie, V.A., & Torgler, C. (1994). Rape scripts and rape acknowledgment. *Psychology of Women Quarterly, 18*, 53–66.

Kahn, A.S., & Yoder, J.D. (1989). The psychology of women and conservatism: Rediscovering social change. *Psychology of Women Quarterly, 13*, 417–432.

Kalichman, S.C. (1996). *Answering your questions about AIDS.* Washington, DC: American Psychological Association.

Kalin, R., & Hodgins, D.C. (1984). Sex bias in judgements of occupational suitability. *Canadian Journal of Behavioral Science, 16*, 311–325.

Kamen, P. (1991). *Feminist fatale.* New York: Donald I. Fine.

Kamerman, S.B., & Kahn, A.J. (1995). Innovations in toddler day care and family support services: An international overview. *Child Welfare, 74*, 1281–1300.

Kamo, Y. (1994). Division of household work in the United States and Japan. *Journal of Family Issues, 15*, 348–378.

Kane, M.J., & Stangl, J.M. (1991). Employment patterns of female coaches in men's athletics: Tokenism and marginalization as reflections of occupational sex-segregation. *Journal of Sport and Social Issues, 15*, 21–41.

Kanin, E.J. (1985). Date rapists: Differential sexual socialization and relative deprivation. *Archives of Sexual Behavior, 14*, 219–231.

Kanter, R.M. (1977). *Men and women of the corporation.* New York: Basic.

Kantrowitz, B. (May 16, 1994). Men, women & computers. *Newsweek*, pp. 48–55.

Kanuha, V. (1994). Women of color in battering relationships. In L. Comas-Díaz & B. Greene (Eds.), *Women of color: Integrating ethnic and gender identities in psychotherapy* (pp. 428–454). New York: Guilford.

Kaplan, M. (1983). A woman's view of the DSM-III. *American Psychologist, 38*, 786–792.

Karp, D.A. (1988). A decade of reminder: Changing age consciousness between fifty and sixty years old. *The Gerontologist, 28*, 727–738.

Karraker, K.H., Vogel, D.A., & Lake, M.A. (1995). Parents' gender-stereotyped perceptions of newborns: The eye of the beholder revisited. *Sex Roles, 33*, 687–701.

Kaschak, E. (1990). How to be a failure as a family therapist: A feminist perspective. In H. Lerman & N. Porter (Eds.), *Feminist ethics in psychotherapy* (pp. 70–81). New York: Springer.

Kaschak, E. (1992). *Engendered lives: A new psychology of women's experience.* New York: Basic.

Kaslow, F.W., Hansson, K., & Lundblad, A.M. (1994). Long term marriages in Sweden: And some comparisons with similar couples in the United States. *Contemporary Family Therapy: An International Journal, 16*, 521–537.

Katerndahl, D.A., & Realini, J.P. (1993). Lifetime prevalence of panic states. *American Journal of Psychiatry, 150*, 246–249.

Katz, M.M., Wetzler, S., Cloitre, M., Swann, A., et al. (1993). Expressive characteristics of anxiety in depressed men and women. *Journal of Affective Disorders, 28*, 267–277.

Kaufert, P.L. (1990). Methodological issues in menopause research. In M. Flint, F. Kronenberg, & W. Utian (Eds.), *Multidisciplinary perspectives on menopause. Annals of the New York Academy of Sciences, 592*, 114–122.

Kaye, L.W., & Applegate, J.S. (1990). Men as elder caregivers: Building a research agenda for the 1990s. *Journal of Aging Studies, 4*, 289–298.

Keating, N., & Jeffrey, B. (1983). Work careers of ever married and never married women. *Gerontologist, 23*, 416–421.

Keddy, B., Cable, B., Quinn, S., & Melanson, J. (1993). Interrupted work histories: Retired women telling their stories. *Health Care for Women International, 14*, 437–446.

Kehl, D.G. (1985). Thalia meets Tithonus: Gerontological wit and humor in literature. *The Gerontologist, 25*, 539–544.

Keith, V.M. (1993). Gender, financial strain, and psychological distress among older adults. *Research on Aging, 15*, 123–147.

Kelly, L. (1988). *Surviving sexual violence.* Minneapolis, MN: University of Minnesota Press.

Kelly, L., & Radford, J. (1996). "Nothing really happened": The invalidation of women's experiences of sexual violence. In M. Hester, L. Kelly, & J. Radford (Eds.), *Women, violence and male power* (pp. 19–33). Bristol, PA: Open University Press.

Kendler, K.S., Heath, A.C., Neale, M.C., Kessler, R.C., & Eaves, L.J. (1992). A population-based twin study of alcoholism in women. *JAMA: Journal of the American Medical Association, 268*, 1877–1882.

Kendler, K.S., Neale, M.C., Kessler, R.C., Heath, A.C., & Eaves, L.J. (1992a). A population-based twin study of major depression in women. *Archives of General Psychiatry, 49*, 257–266.

Kendler, K.S., Neale, M.C., Kessler, R.C., Heath, A.C., & Eaves, L.J. (1992b). Generalized anxiety disorder in women. *Archives of General Psychiatry, 49*, 267–272.

Kendler, K.S., Neale, M.C., Kessler, R.C., Heath, A.C., & Eaves, L.J. (1992c). The genetic epidemiology of phobias in women. *Archives of General Psychiatry, 49*, 273–281.

Kerber, L.K. (1986). Some cautionary words for historians. *Signs, 11*, 304–310.

Kessler, R.C., McGonagle, K.A., Zhao, S., Nelson, C.B., Hughes, M., Eshleman, S., Wittchen, H., & Kendler, K.S. (1994). Lifetime and 12-month prevalence of the DSM-III-R psychiatric disorders in the United States: Results from the National Comorbidity Survey. *Archives of General Psychiatry, 51*, 8–19.

Kidder, L.H., Lafleur, R.A., & Wells, C.V. (1995). Recalling harassment: Reconstructing experience. *Journal of Social Issues, 51*(1), 53–67.

Kiesler, S., Sproull, L., & Eccles, J.S. (1985). Pool halls, chips, and war games: Women in the culture of computing. *Psychology of Women Quarterly, 9*, 451–462.

Kilbourne, J. (1994). Still killing us softly: Advertising and the obsession with thinness. In P. Fallon, M.A. Katzman, & S.C. Wooley (Eds.), *Feminist perspectives on eating disorders* (pp. 395–418). New York: Guilford.

Kilpatrick, D.G., Best, C.L., Veronen, L.J., Amick, A.E., Villeponteaux, L.A., & Ruff, G.A. (1985).

Mental health correlates of criminal victimization: A random community survey. *Journal of Consulting and Clinical Psychology, 53,* 866–873.

Kimball, M. (1981). Women and science: A critique of biological theories. *International Journal of Women's Studies, 4,* 318–338.

Kimmel, E.B. (1989). The experience of feminism. *Psychology of Women Quarterly, 13,* 133–146.

Kimmel, M.S., & Kaufman, M. (1997). Weekend warriors: The new men's movement. In M.R. Walsh (Ed.), *Women, men, and gender: Ongoing debates* (pp. 406–420). New Haven, CT: Yale.

King, T.C., & Ferguson, S.A. (1996). "I am because we are": Clinical interpretations of communal experience among African American women. *Women & Therapy, 18,* 33–45.

Kinsler, K., & Zalk, S.R. (1996). Teaching is a political act: Contextualizing gender and ethnic voices. In K.F. Wyche & F. Crosby (Eds.), *Women's ethnicities: Journeys through psychology* (pp. 27–48). Boulder, CO: Westview.

Kite, M.E., Deaux, K., & Miele, M. (1991). Stereotypes of young and old: Does age outweigh gender? *Psychology and Aging, 6,* 19–27.

Kite, M.E., & Johnson, B.T. (1988). Attitudes toward older and younger adults: A meta-analysis. *Psychology and Aging, 3,* 233–244.

Kitzinger, C. (1987). *The social constructionism of lesbianism.* London: Sage.

Kitzinger, C. (1990). Resisting the discipline. In E. Burmna (Ed.), *Feminists and psychological practice* (pp. 119–139). Newbury Park, CA: Sage.

Kitzinger, C. (1991). Feminism, psychology, and the paradox of power. *Feminism & Psychology, 1,* 111–129.

Kitzinger, C. (1994). Editor's introduction: Sex differences: Feminist perspectives. *Feminism & Psychology, 4,* 501–506.

Kitzinger, C., & Wilkinson, S. (1995). Transitions from heterosexuality to lesbianism: The discursive production of lesbian identities. *Developmental Psychology, 31,* 95–104.

Klassen, M.L., Wauer, S.M., & Cassel, S. (1991). Increases in health and weight loss claims in food advertising in the eighties. *Journal of Advertising Research, 30,* 32–37.

Klebanov, P.K., & Jemmott, J.B., III. (1992). Effects of expectations and bodily sensations on self-reports of premenstrual symptoms. *Psychology of Women Quarterly, 16,* 289–310.

Klebanov, P.K., & Ruble, D.N. (1994). Toward an understanding of women's experience of menstrual symptoms. In V.J. Adesso, D.M. Reddy, & R. Fleming (Eds.), *Psychological perspectives on women's health* (pp. 183–221). Washington, DC: Taylor & Francis.

Kline, S. (1993). *Out of the garden: Toys, TV, and children's culture in the age of marketing.* New York: Verso.

Klingenspor, B. (1994). Gender identity and bulimic eating behavior. *Sex Roles, 31,* 407–431.

Klinkenberg, D., & Rose, S. (1994). Dating scripts of gay men and lesbians. *Journal of Homosexuality, 26,* 23–35.

Klonoff, E.A., Landrine, H., & Scott, J. (1995). Double jeopardy: Ethnicity and gender in health research. In H. Landrine (Ed.), *Bringing cultural diversity to feminist psychology: Theory, research, and practice* (pp. 335–360). Washington, DC: American Psychological Association.

Kobrynowicz, D., & Branscombe, N.R. (1997). Who considers themselves victims of discrimination? Individual difference predictors of perceived gender discrimination in women and men. *Psychology of Women Quarterly, 21,* 347–363.

Koenig, L.J., & Wasserman, E.L. (1995). Body image and dieting failure in college men and women: Examining links between depression and eating problems. *Sex Roles, 32,* 225–249.

Koenigsberg, J., Garet, M.S., & Rosenbaum, J.E. (1994). The effect of family on the job exits of young adults: A competing risk model. *Work and Occupations, 21,* 33–63.

Koff, E., Rierdan, J., & Stubbs, M.L. (1990). Conceptions and misconceptions of the menstrual cycle. *Women & Health, 16,* 119–136.

Kohlberg, L. (1966). A cognitive-developmental analysis of children's sex-role concepts and attitudes. In E.E. Maccoby (Ed.), *The development of sex differences* (pp. 82–173). Stanford, CA: Stanford University Press.

Kohlberg, L. (1981). *The philosophy of moral development: Essays on moral development* (Vols. I & II). San Francisco, CA: Harper & Row.

Kolata, G. (February 29, 1995). Man's world, woman's world? Brain studies point to differences. *The New York Times*, pp. B5–6.

Kolb, B. (1989). Brain development, plasticity, and behavior. *American Psychologist, 44*, 1203–1212.

Kontos, S., Hsu, H.C., & Dunn, L. (1994). Children's cognitive and social competence in child care centers and family day-care homes. *Journal of Applied Developmental Psychology, 15*, 387–411.

Kopp, R.G., & Ruzicka, M.F. (1993). Women's multiple roles and psychological well-being. *Psychological Reports, 72*, 1351–1354.

Kortenhaus, C.M., & Demarest, J. (1993). Gender role stereotypes in children's literature: An update. *Sex Roles, 28*, 219–232.

Koslow, R.E. (1987). Sex-related differences and visual-spatial mental imagery as factors affecting symbolic motor skill acquisition. *Sex Roles, 17*, 521–528.

Koss, M.P. (1985). The hidden rape victim: Personality, attitudinal, and situational characteristics. *Psychology of Women Quarterly, 9*, 193–212.

Koss, M.P. (1988). Hidden rape: Sexual aggression and victimization in a national sample of students in higher education. In A.W. Burgess (Ed.), *Rape and sexual assault* (Vol. 2) (pp. 3–25). New York: Garland.

Koss, M.P. (1990). The women's mental health research agenda: Violence against women. *American Psychologist, 45*, 374–380.

Koss, M.P. (1992). The underdetection of rape. *Journal of Social Issues, 48*(1), 63–75.

Koss, M.P. (1993). Rape: Scope, impact, interventions, and public policy responses. *American Psychologist, 48*, 1062–1069.

Koss, M.P., & Burkhart, B.R. (1989). A conceptual analysis of rape victimization. *Psychology of Women Quarterly, 13*, 27–40.

Koss, M.P., & Dinero, T.E. (1989). Discriminant analysis of risk factors for sexual victimization among a national sample of college women. *Journal of Consulting and Clinical Psychology, 57*, 242–250.

Koss, M.P., Dinero, T.E., Siebel, C., & Cox, S. (1988). Stranger, acquaintance, and date rape: Is there a difference in the victim's experience? *Psychology of Women Quarterly, 12*, 1–24.

Koss, M.P., Figueredo, A.J., Bell, I., Tharan, M., & Tromp, M. (1996). Traumatic memory characteristics: A cross-validated mediational model of response to rape among employed women. *Journal of Abnormal Psychology, 105*, 1–12.

Koss, M.P., & Gaines, J.A. (1993). The prediction of sexual aggression by alcohol use, athletic participation, and fraternity affiliation. *Journal of Interpersonal Violence, 8*, 94–106.

Koss, M.P., Gidycz, C.A., & Wisniewski, N. (1987). The scope of rape: Incidence and prevalence of sexual aggression and victimization in a national sample of higher education students. *Journal of Consulting and Clinical Psychology, 55*, 162–170.

Koss, M.P., Goodman, L.A., Browne, A., Fitzgerald, L.F., Keita, G.P., & Russo, N.F. (1994). *No safe haven: Male violence against women at home, at work, and in the community.* Washington, DC: American Psychological Association.

Koss, M.P., Heise, L., & Russo, N.F. (1994). The global health burden of rape. *Psychology of Women Quarterly, 18*, 509–537.

Koss, M.P., & Heslet, L. (1992). Somatic consequences of violence against women. *Archives of Family Medicine, 1*, 53–59.

Koss, M.P., Woodruff, W.J., & Koss, P. (1991). Criminal victimization among primary care medical patients: Prevalence, incidence, and physician usage. *Behavioral Sciences and the Law, 9,* 85–96.

Kossek, E.E., & Nichol, V. (1992). The effects of on-site child care on employee attitudes and performance. *Personnel Psychology, 45,* 485–509.

Kram, K.E. (1983). Phases of the mentor relationship. *Academy of Management Journal, 26,* 608–625.

Kram, K.E. (1985). *Mentoring at work: Developmental relationships in organizational life.* Glenview, IL: Scott, Foresman.

Kramer, P., & Lehman, S. (1990). Mismeasuring women: A critique of research on computer ability and avoidance. *Signs, 16,* 158–172.

Kranzer, S. (1995). U.S. longevity unchanged. *Statistical Bulletin, 76,* 12–22.

Krause, N., & Keith, V. (1989). Gender differences in social support among older adults. *Sex Roles, 21,* 609–628.

Kravetz, D., & Marecek, J. (1996). The personal is political: A feminist agenda for group psychotherapy research. In B. DeChant (Ed.), *Women and group psychotherapy: Theory and practice* (pp. 351–369). New York: Guilford.

Krefting, L.A., Berger, P.K., & Wallace, M.J., Jr. (1978). The contribution of sex distribution, job content, and occupational classification to job sextyping: Two studies. *Journal of Vocational Behavior, 13,* 181–191.

Kristiansen, C.M., Felton, K.A., & Hovdestad, W.E. (1996). Recovered memories or child abuse: Fact, fantasy or fancy? *Women & Therapy, 19,* 47–59.

Kupers, T.A. (1997). The politics of psychiatry: Gender and sexual preference in DSM-IV. In M.R. Walsh (Ed.), *Women, men, and gender: Ongoing debates* (pp. 340–347). New Haven, CT: Yale.

Kurdek, L.A. (1993). The allocation of household labor in gay, lesbian, and heterosexual married couples. *Journal of Social Issues, 49*(3), 127–139.

Kurdek, L.A. (1995). Developmental changes in relationship quality in gay and lesbian cohabiting couples. *Developmental Psychology, 31,* 86–94.

Kurz, D. (1989). Social science perspectives on wife abuse: Current debates and future directions. *Gender & Society, 3,* 489–505.

Kurz, D. (1997). Physical assaults by male partners: A major social problem. In M.R. Walsh (Ed.), *Women, men, and gender: Ongoing debates* (pp. 222–231). New Haven, CT: Yale.

Lachar, D. (1974). *The MMPI: Clinical assessment and automated interpretation.* Los Angeles, CA: Western Psychological Services.

LaFromboise, T.D., Berman, J.S., & Sohi, B.K. (1994). American Indian women. In L. Comas-Díaz & B. Greene (Eds.), *Women of color: Integrating ethnic and gender identities in psychotherapy* (pp. 30–71). New York: Guilford.

Lakoff, R. (1990). *Talking power: The politics of language.* New York: Basic.

Lamb, C.S., Jackson, L.E., Cassiday, P.B., & Priest, D.J. (1993). Body figure preferences of men and women: A comparison of two generations. *Sex Roles, 28,* 345–358.

Lamb, S. (1991). Acts without agents: An analysis of linguistic avoidance in journal articles on men who batter women. *American Journal of Orthopsychiatry, 61,* 250–257.

Lamb, S., & Keon, S. (1995). Blaming the perpetrator: Language that distorts reality in newspaper articles on men battering women. *Psychology of Women Quarterly, 19,* 209–220.

Land, H. (1994). AIDS and women of color. *Families in Society, 75,* 355–361.

Lander, L. (1988). *Images of bleeding: Menstruation as ideology.* New York: Orlando Press.

Landrine, H. (1985). Race x class stereotypes of women. *Sex Roles, 13,* 65–75.

Landrine, H. (1988). Depression and stereotypes of women: Preliminary empirical analyses of the gender-role hypothesis. *Sex Roles, 19,* 527–541.

Landrine, H. (1989). The politics of personality disorder. *Psychology of Women Quarterly, 13,* 325–339.

Lang-Takac, E., & Osterweil, Z. (1992). Separateness and connectedness: Differences between the genders. *Sex Roles, 27,* 277–289.

Laraia, M.T., Stuart, G.W., Frye, L.H. & Lydiard, R.B. (1994). Childhood environment of women having panic disorder with agoraphobia. *Journal of Anxiety Disorders, 8,* 1–17.

Larose, H., Tracy, J., & McKelvie, S.J. (1993). Effects of gender on the physical attractiveness stereotype. *Journal of Psychology, 127,* 677–680.

Larsen, K.S. (1990). The Asch conformity experiment: Replication and transhistorical comparisons. *Journal of Social Behavior and Personality, 5,* 163–168.

Lasher, K.P., & Faulkender, P.J. (1993). Measurement of aging anxiety: Development of the Anxiety about Aging Scale. *International Journal of Aging and Human Development, 37,* 247–259.

Lauer, R.H., Lauer, J.C., & Kerr, S.T. (1990). The long-term marriage: Perceptions of stability and satisfaction. *International Journal of Aging and Human Development, 31,* 189–195.

Laurence, L., & Weinhouse B. (1994). *Outrageous practices: The alarming truth about how medicine mistreats women.* New York: Fawcett.

Lawrence, S.C., & Bendixen, K. (1992). His and hers: Male and female anatomy in anatomy texts for U.S. medical students, 1890–1989. *Social Science and Medicine, 35,* 925–934.

Lawrie, L., & Brown, R. (1992). Sex stereotypes, school subject preferences and career aspirations as a function of single/mixed-sex schooling and presence/absence of an opposite sex sibling. *British Journal of Educational Psychology, 62,* 132–138.

Leaper, C. (1995). The use of "masculine" and "feminine" to describe women's and men's behavior. *The Journal of Social Psychology, 135,* 359–369.

Leaper, C., Leve, L., Strasser, T., & Schwartz, R. (1995). Mother-child communication sequences: Play activity, child gender, and marital status effects. *Merrill Palmer Quarterly, 41,* 307–327.

Ledray, L.E. (1994). *Recovering from rape* (2nd ed.). New York: Holt.

Lee, K.A., & Rittenhouse, C.A. (1991). Prevalence of perimenstrual symptoms in employed women. *Women & Health, 17,* 17–32.

Lee, K.A., & Rittenhouse, C.A. (1992). Health and perimenstrual symptoms: Health outcomes for employed women who experience perimenstrual symptoms. *Women & Health, 19,* 65–78.

Lee, S. (1995). Self-starvation in context: Towards a culturally sensitive understanding of anorexia nervosa. *Social Science and Medicine, 41,* 25–36.

Lefley, H.P., Scott, C.S., Llabre, M., & Hicks, D. (1993). Cultural beliefs about rape and victims' response in three ethnic groups. *American Journal of Orthopsychiatry, 63,* 623–632.

LeGuin, U.K. (1994). *The left hand of darkness.* New York: Walker.

Lehr, U. (1984). The role of women in the family generation context. In V. Garms-Homolova, E.M. Hoerning, & D. Schaeffer (Eds.), *Intergenerational relationships* (pp. 125–132). Lewiston, NY: C.J. Hogrefe.

Leiblum, S.R. (1990). Sexuality and the midlife woman. *Psychology of Women Quarterly, 14,* 495–508.

Leigh, B.C. (1989). Reasons for having and avoiding sex: Gender, sexual orientation, and relationship to sexual behavior. *Journal of Sex Research, 26,* 199–209.

Leigh, W.A. (1995). The health of African American women. In D.L. Adams (Ed.), *Health issues for women of color: A cultural diversity perspective* (pp. 112–132). Thousand Oaks, CA: Sage.

Lemkau, J.P. (1979). Personality and background characteristics of women in male-dominated occupations: A review. *Psychology of Women Quarterly, 4,* 221–240.

Lennon, M.C. (1987). Is menopause depressing? An investigation of three perspectives. *Sex Roles, 17,* 1–16.

Lennon, M.C., & Rosenfield, S. (1994). Relative fairness and the division of housework: The importance of options. *American Journal of Sociology, 100,* 506–531.

Leonard, D.K., & Jiang, J. (1995, April). *Gender bias in the college predictors of the SAT.* Paper presented at the annual meeting of the American Educational Research Association, San Francisco.

Leonardo, C., & Chrisler, J.C. (1992). Women and sexually transmitted diseases. *Women & Health, 18,* 1–15.

Leone, C., & Robertson, K. (1989). Some effects of sex-linked clothing and gender schema on the stereotyping of infants. *Journal of Social Psychology, 129,* 609–619.

Lerman, H. (1986). From Freud to feminist personality theory: Getting here from there. *Psychology of Women Quarterly, 10,* 1–18.

Lerman, H. (1996). *Pigeonholing women's misery: A history and critical analysis of the psychodiagnosis of women in the twentieth century.* New York: Basic.

Lerman, H., & Porter, N. (Eds.). (1990). *Feminist ethics in psychotherapy.* New York: Springer.

Lerner, G. (1992). Placing women in history: Definitions and challenges. In J.S. Bohan (Ed.), *Re-placing women in psychology: Readings toward a more inclusive history* (pp. 31–43). Dubuque, IA: Kendall/Hunt.

Lerner, G. (1993). *The creation of feminist consciousness: From the middle ages to eighteen-seventy.* New York: Oxford.

Lerner, H.G. (1988). *Women in therapy.* Northvale, NJ: Jason Aronson.

Lerner, M.J., Miller, D.T., & Holmes, J.G. (1975). Deserving versus justice: A contemporary dilemma. In L. Berkowitz & E. Walster (Eds.), *Advances in experimental social psychology* (Vol. 12). New York: Academic Press.

LeVay, S. (1991, August 30). A difference in hypothalamic structure between heterosexual and homosexual men. *Science, 253,* 1034–1037.

Leventhal, E.A. (1994). Gender and aging: Women and their aging. In V.J. Adesso, D.M. Reddy, & R. Fleming (Eds.), *Psychological perspectives on women's health* (pp. 11–35). Washington, DC: Taylor & Francis.

Levine, R., Sato, S., Hashimoto, T., & Verma, J. (1995). Love and marriage in eleven cultures. *Journal of Cross-Cultural Psychology, 26,* 554–571.

Levine-MacCombie, J., & Koss, M.P. (1986). Acquaintance rape: Effective avoidance strategies. *Psychology of Women Quarterly, 10,* 311–320.

Levy, G.D. (1994). High and low gender schematic children's release from proactive interference. *Sex Roles, 30,* 93–108.

Levy, G.D., & Carter, D.B. (1989). Gender schema, gender constancy, and gender-role knowledge: The roles of cognitive factors in preschoolers' gender-role stereotype attributions. *Developmental Psychology, 25,* 444–449.

Lewin, T. (1994, Oct. 12). Men whose wives work earn less, studies show. *The New York Times,* pp. A1, A15.

Lewin, T. (1997, Sept. 15). Wage difference between women and men widens. *The New York Times,* p. A1.

Li, P.S., & Currie, D. (1992). Gender differences in work interruptions as unequal effects of marriage and childrearing: Findings from a Canadian national survey. *Journal of Comparative Family Studies, 23,* 217–229.

Liem, J.H., O'Toole, J.G., & James, J.B. (1992). The need for power in women who were sexually abused as children: An exploratory study. *Psychology of Women Quarterly, 16,* 467–480.

Lightdale, J., & Prentice, D.A. (1994). Rethinking sex differences in aggression: Aggressive behavior in the absence of social roles. *Personality and Social Psychology Bulletin, 20,* 34–44.

Lindner, M.A., Ryckman, R.M., Gold, J.A., & Stone, W.F. (1995). Traditional vs. nontraditional women and men's perceptions of the personalities and physiques of ideal women and men. *Sex Roles, 32,* 675–690.

Linn, M.C., & Petersen, A.C. (1985). Emergence and characterization of sex differences in spatial ability: A meta-analysis. *Child Development, 56,* 1479–1498.

Linz, D. (1989). Exposure to sexually explicit materials and attitudes toward rape: A comparison of study results. *Journal of Sex Research, 26,* 50–84.

Linz, D., Wilson, B.J., & Donnerstein, E. (1992). Sexual violence in the mass media: Legal solutions, warnings, and mitigation through education. *Journal of Social Issues, 48*(1), 145–172.

Lipsey, M.W., & Wilson, D.B. (1993). The efficacy of psychological, educational, and behavioral treatment: Confirmation from meta-analysis. *American Psychologist, 48,* 1181–1209.

Llewellyn, C. (1981). Occupational mobility and the use of the comparative method. In H. Roberts (Ed.), *Doing feminist research* (pp. 129–158). Boston, MA: Routledge.

Lloyd, M. (1992). Does she boil eggs? Towards a feminist model of disability. *Disability, Handicap and Society, 7,* 207–221.

Lobel, T.E. (1994). Sex typing and the social perception of gender stereotypic and non-stereotypic behavior: The uniqueness of feminine males. *Journal of Personality and Social Psychology, 66,* 379–385.

Locher, P., Unger, R.K., Sociedade, P., & Wahl, J. (1993). At first glance: Accessibility of the physical attractiveness stereotype. *Sex Roles, 28,* 729–743.

Loevinger, J. (1976). *Ego development: Conceptions and theories.* San Francisco, CA: Jossey-Bass.

Loftus, E.F., & Ketcham, K. (1994). *The myth of repressed memory: False memories and allegations of abuse.* New York: St. Martins Press.

Logue, B.J. (1991). Women at risk: Predictors of financial stress for retired women workers. *Gerontologist, 31,* 657–665.

Lonsdale, S. (1992). *Women and disability.* New York: St. Martin's Press.

Lonsway, K.A. (1996). Preventing acquaintance rape through education: What do we know? *Psychology of Women Quarterly, 20,* 229–265.

Lonsway, K.A., & Fitzgerald, L.F. (1994). Rape myths: In review. *Psychology of Women Quarterly, 18,* 133–164.

Lopez, S.R., Smith, A., Wolkenstein, B.H., & Charlin, V. (1993). Gender bias in clinical judgment: An assessment of the analogue method's transparency and social desirability. *Sex Roles, 28,* 35–45.

Lorber, J. (1994). *Paradoxes of gender.* New Haven, CT: Yale University Press.

Lorde, A. (1984). Age, race, class, and sex: Women redefining difference. In A. Lorde, *Sister outsider* (pp. 114–123). Trumansburg, NY: Crossing Press.

Lorde, A. (1995). Man child: A Black lesbian feminist's response. In M.L. Andersen & P.H. Collins (Eds.), *Race, class, and gender: An anthology* (2nd ed.) (pp. 275–281). Belmont, CA: Wadsworth.

Lott, B. (1985). The devaluation of women's competence. *Journal of Social Issues, 41*(4), 43–60.

Lott, B. (1989). Sexist discrimination as distancing behavior: II. Primetime television. *Psychology of Women Quarterly, 13,* 341–355.

Lott, B. (1991). Social psychology: Humanist roots and feminist future. *Psychology of Women Quarterly, 15,* 505–520.

Lott, B. (1995). Distancing from women: Interpersonal sexist discrimination. In B. Lott & D. Maluso (Eds.), *The social psychology of interpersonal discrimination* (pp. 12–49). New York: Guilford.

Lott, B. (1997). The personal and social correlates of a gender difference ideology. *Journal of Social Issues, 53*(2), 279–298.

Lott, B., Lott, A.J., & Fernald, J.L. (1990). Individual differences in distancing responses to women on a photo choice task. *Sex Roles, 22,* 97–110.

Lott, B., & Maluso, D. (1993). The social learning of gender. In A.E. Beall & R.J. Sternberg (Eds.), *The psychology of gender* (pp. 99–123). New York: Guilford.

Lottes, I.L. (1993). Nontraditional gender roles and the sexual experiences of heterosexual college students. *Sex Roles, 29,* 645–669.

Lowe, R.H., & Wittig, M.A. (Eds). (1989). Approaching pay equity through comparable worth. *Journal of Social Issues, 45(4).*

Luborsky, M.R. (1994). The cultural adversity of physical disability: Erosion of full adult personhood. *Journal of Aging Studies, 8,* 239–253.

Luce, C., & Russo, N.F. (1996). Research on the psychology of women: 1995 highlights. *Psychology of Women Newsletter, 23(1),* 15–18.

Lucero, K., Hicks, R.A., Bramlette, J., Brassington, & Welter, M.G. (1992). Frequency of eating problems among Asian and Caucasian college women. *Psychological Reports, 71,* 255–258.

Luecke, A.D., Anderson, D.R., Collins, P.A., & Schmitt, K.L. (1995). Gender constancy and television viewing. *Developmental Psychology, 31,* 773–780.

Luker, K. (1984). *Abortion & the politics of motherhood.* Berkeley, CA: University of California Press.

Lundberg, U. (1996). Influence of paid and unpaid work on psychophysiological stress responses of men and women. *Journal of Occupational Health Psychology, 1,* 117–130.

Lykes, M.B., & Stewart, A.J. (1986). Evaluating the feminist challenge to research in personality and social psychology: 1963–1983. *Psychology of Women Quarterly, 10,* 393–412.

Lynn, D.B. (1966). The process of learning parental and sex-role identification. *Journal of Marriage and the Family, 28,* 466–470.

Lynn, R. (1994). Sex differences in intelligence and brain size: A paradox resolved. *Personality and Individual Differences, 17,* 257–271.

Lynxwiler, J., & Gay, D. (1994). Reconsidering race differences in abortion attitudes. *Social Science Quarterly, 75,* 67–84.

Lynxwiler, J., & Wilson, M. (1994). A case study of race differences among late abortion patients. *Women & Health, 21,* 43–56.

Lyon, D., & Greenberg, J. (1991). Evidence of codependency in women with an alcoholic parent: Helping out Mr. Wrong. *Journal of Personality and Social Psychology, 61,* 435–439.

Lytton, H., & Romney, D.M. (1991). Parents' differential socialization of boys and girls: A meta-analysis. *Psychological Bulletin, 109,* 267–296.

Maccoby, E.E. (1990). Gender and relationships: A developmental account. *American Psychologist, 45,* 513–520.

Maccoby, E.E., & Jacklin, C.N. (1974). *The psychology of sex differences.* Stanford, CA: Stanford University Press.

MacCorquodale, P., & Jensen, G. (1993). Women in the law: Partners or tokens? *Gender & Society, 7,* 582–593.

MacFarlane, J., Parker, B., Soeken, K., & Bullock, L. (1992). Assessing for abuse during pregnancy: Severity and frequency of injuries associated with entry into prenatal care. *Journal of American Medical Association, 267,* 3176–3178.

MacKinnon, C.A. (1982). Feminism, Marxism, method, and the state: An agenda for theory. *Signs, 7,* 515–544.

MacKinnon, J. (1978). *The ape within us.* New York: Holt.

MacPherson, P., & Fine, M. (1995). Hungry for an us: Adolescent girls and adult women negotiating territories of race, gender, class and difference. *Feminism & Psychology, 5,* 181–200.

Madden, M.E. (1994). The variety of emotional reactions to miscarriage. *Women & Health, 21,* 85–104.

Magee, M., & Miller, D.C. (1992). "She foreswore her womanhood": Psychoanalytic views of female homosexuality. *Clinical Social Work Journal, 20,* 67–87.

Mahlstedt, D., & Kohat, K. (1991, August). *Fraternity violence education project: When men take action.* Paper presented at the meeting of the American Psychological Association, San Francisco.

Major, B. (1993). Gender, entitlement, and the distribution of family labor. *Journal of Social Issues, 49*(3), 141–159.

Major, B., & Cozzarelli, C. (1992). Psychosocial predictors of adjustment to abortion. *Journal of Social Issues, 48*(3), 121–142.

Mansfield, P.K., & Voda, A.M. (1993). From Edith Bunker to the 6:00 news: How and what midlife women learn about menopause. *Women & Therapy, 14,* 89–104.

Marecek, J. (1989). Introduction to special issue: Theory and method in feminist psychology. *Psychology of Women Quarterly, 13,* 367–378.

Marecek, J., & Hare-Mustin, R.T. (1991). A short history of the future: Feminism and clinical psychology. *Psychology of Women Quarterly, 15,* 521–536.

Margolin, G. (1988). Interpersonal and intrapersonal factors associated with marital violence. In G.T. Hotaling, D. Finkelhor, J.T. Kirkpatrick, & M.A. Straus (Eds.), *Family abuse and its consequences: New directions for research* (pp. 203–217). Newbury Park, CA: Sage.

Markens, S. (1996). The problematic of "experience": A political and cultural critique of PMS. *Gender & Society, 10,* 42–58.

Markides, K.S. (1989). Consequences of gender differentials in life expectancy for Black and Hispanic Americans. *International Journal of Aging and Human Development, 29,* 95–102.

Markson, E.W. (1983). *Older women: Issues and prospects.* Lexington, MA: D.C. Heath.

Markson, E.W., & Taylor, C.A. (1993). Real versus reel world: Older women and the Academy Awards. *Women & Therapy, 14,* 157–172.

Marsh, M. (1995). Feminist psychopharmacology: An aspect of feminist psychiatry. *Women & Therapy, 16(1),* 73–84.

Martin, C.L. (1990). Attitudes and expectations about children with nontraditional and traditional gender roles. *Sex Roles, 22,* 151–165.

Martin, C.L. (1993). New directions for investigating children's gender knowledge. *Developmental Review, 13,* 184–204.

Martin, C.L., & Halverson, C.F. (1983). The effects of sex-typing schemas on young children's memory. *Child Development, 61,* 1427–1439.

Martin, C.L., & Little, J.K. (1990). The relation of gender understanding to children's sex-typed preferences and gender stereotypes. *Child Development, 61,* 1427–1439.

Martin, C.L., & Parker, S. (1995). Folk theories about sex and race differences. *Personality and Social Psychology Bulletin, 21,* 45–57.

Martin, C.L., Wood, C.H., & Little, J.K. (1990). The development of gender stereotypes components. *Child Development, 61,* 1891–1904.

Martin, E. (1996). The egg and the sperm: How science has constructed a romance based on stereotypical male-female roles. In C.F. Sargent & C.B. Brettell (Eds.), *Gender and health: An international perspective* (pp. 29–43). Upper Saddle River, NJ: Prentice Hall.

Martin, S.E. (1994). "Outsider within" the station house: The impact of race and gender on Black women police. *Social Problems, 41,* 383–400.

Martinez, M. (1992). Interest enhancements to science experiments: Interactions with student gender. *Journal of Research in Science Teaching, 29,* 167–177.

Martinez, R., & Dukes, R.L. (1991). Ethnic and gender differences in self-esteem. *Youth and Society, 22,* 318–338.

Martinko, M.J., & Gardner, W.L. (1983). A methodological review of sex-related access discrimination problems. *Sex Roles, 9,* 825–839.

Mason, C., & Kahle, J.B. (1988). Student attitudes toward science and science-related careers: A program designed to promote a stimulating gender-free learning environment. *Journal of Research in Science Teaching, 26,* 25–39.

Masson, J.M. (1985). *The assault on truth: Freud's suppression of the seduction theory.* New York: Penguin.

Masten, W.G., Penland, E.A., & Nayani, E.J. (1994). Depression and acculturation in Mexican-American women. *Psychological Reports, 75,* 1499–1503.

Masters, M.S., & Sanders, B. (1993). Is the gender difference in mental rotation disappearing? *Behavior Genetics, 23,* 337–341.

Masters, W.H., & Johnson, V.E. (1966). *Human sexual response.* Boston: Little Brown.

Matsui, T., Ohsawa, T., & Onglatco, M. (1995). Work-family conflict and the stress-buffering effects of husband support and coping behavior among Japanese married working women. *Journal of Vocational Behavior, 47,* 178–192.

Matthews, K.A., Shumaker, S.A., Bowen, D.J., Langer, R.D., Hunt, J.R., Kaplan, R.M., Klesges, R.C., & Ritenbaugh, C. (1997). Women's Health Initiative: Why now? What is it? What's new? *American Psychologist, 52,* 101–116.

Mayne, T.J., Norcross, J.C., & Sayette, M.A. (1994). Admission requirements, acceptance rates, and financial assistance in clinical psychology programs: Diversity across the practice-research continuum. *American Psychologist, 49,* 806–811.

Mays, V., & Cochran, S.D. (1988). Issues in the perception of AIDS risk and risk reduction activities by Black and Hispanic/Latina women. *American Psychologist, 43,* 949–957.

Mays, V.M., & Cochran, S.D. (1993). Ethnic and gender differences in beliefs about sex partner questioning to reduce HIV risk. *Journal of Adolescent Research, 8,* 77–88.

Mazzella, C., Durkin, K., Cerini, E., & Buralli, P. (1992). Sex role stereotyping in Australian television advertisements. *Sex Roles, 26,* 243–259.

McAninch, C.B., Milich, R., Crumbo, G.B., & Funtowicz, M.N. (1996). Children's perception of gender-role-congruent and -incongruent behavior in peers: Fisher-Price meets Price Waterhouse. *Sex Roles, 35,* 619–638.

McClintock, M.K. (1971). Menstrual synchrony and suppression. *Nature, 229,* 244–245.

McCreary, D.R. (1990). Self-perceptions of life-span gender-role development. *International Journal of Aging and Human Development, 31,* 135–146.

McFarland, C., & Ross, M. (1982). Impact of causal attributions on affective reactions to success and failure. *Journal of Personality and Social Psychology, 43,* 937–946.

McFarlane, J., Martin, C.L., & Williams, T.M. (1988). Mood fluctuations: Women versus men and menstrual versus other cycles. *Psychology of Women Quarterly, 12,* 201–223.

McGlone, J. (1980). Sex differences in human brain asymmetry: A critical survey. *The Behavioral and Brain Sciences, 3,* 215–263.

McGrath, E., Keita, G.P., Strickland, B.R., & Russo, N.F. (Eds.). (1990). *Women and depression: Risk factors and treatment issues.* Washington, DC: American Psychological Association.

McHugh, M.C. (1996). A feminist approach to agoraphobia: Challenging traditional views of women at home. In J.C. Chrisler, C. Golden, & P.D. Rozee (Eds.), *Lectures on the psychology of women* (pp. 339–357). New York: McGraw-Hill.

McHugh, M.C., Frieze, I.H., & Browne, A. (1993). Research on battered women and their assailants. In M. Paludi & F. Denmark (Eds.), *Handbook on the psychology of women* (pp. 513–552). New York: Greenwood Press.

McHugh, M.D., Koeske, R.D., & Frieze, I.H. (1986). Issues to consider in conducting non-sexist psychological research: A guide for researchers. *American Psychologist, 41,* 879–890.

McIntosh, P. (1995). White privilege and male privilege: A personal account of coming to see correspondences through work in Women's Studies. In M.L. Andersen & P.H. Collins, *Race, class, and gender: An anthology* (2nd ed.) (pp. 76–87). Belmont, CA: Wadsworth.

McKinley, N.M., & Hyde, J.S. (1996). The Objectified Body Consciousness Scale: Development and validation. *Psychology of Women Quarterly, 20,* 181–215.

McMahan, I.D. (1982). Expectancy of success on sex-linked tasks. *Sex Roles, 8,* 949–958.

McNamara, J.R., & Grossman, K. (1991). Initiation of dates and anxiety among college men and women. *Psychological Reports, 69*, 252–254.

McRae, M.B. (1994). Influence of sex role stereotypes on personnel decisions of Black managers. *Journal of Applied Psychology, 79*, 306–309.

Medcalf-Davenport, N.A. (1993). A comparative study of the general world knowledge and language development of pre-kindergarten children from either day care or in-home care. *Early Child Development and Care, 93*, 1–14.

Mednick, M.T. (1989). On the politics of psychological constructs: Stop the bandwagon, I want to get off. *American Psychologist, 44*, 1118–1123.

Mednick, M.T., & Thomas, V.G. (1993). Women and the psychology of achievement: A view from the eighties. In F.L. Denmark & M.A. Paludi (Eds.), *Psychology of women: A handbook of issues and theories*. Westport, CT: Greenwood Press.

Melamed, T. (1995a). Career success: The moderating effect of gender. *Journal of Vocational Behavior, 47*, 35–60.

Melamed, T. (1995b). Barriers to women's career success: Human capital, career choices, structural determinants, or simply sex discrimination. *Applied Psychology: An International Review, 44*, 295–314.

Men against rape. (1979/80, Winter). *M. Gentle Men for Gender Justice*. Madison, WI, p. 4.

Mendes-de-Leon, C.F., Rapp, S.S., & Kasl, S.V. (1994). Financial strain and symptoms of depression in a community sample of elderly men and women: A longitudinal study. *Journal of Aging and Health, 6*, 448–468.

Merritt, R.D., & Kok, C.J. (1995). Attribution of gender to a gender-unspecified individual: An evaluation of the people=male hypothesis. *Sex Roles, 33*, 145–157.

Merton, R.K. (1957). *Social theory and social structure*. New York: Free Press.

Messner, M.A. (1997). *Politics of masculinities: Men in movements*. Thousand Oaks, CA: Sage.

Meyer, S., Murphy, C.M., Cascardi, M., & Birns, B. (1991). Gender and relationships: Beyond the peer group. *American Psychologist, 46*, 537.

Meyerowitz, B.E., & Hart, S. (1995). Women and cancer: Have assumptions about women limited our research agenda? In A.L. Stanton & S.J. Gallant (Eds.), *The psychology of women's health: Progress and challenges in research and application* (pp. 51–84). Washington, DC: American Psychological Association.

Micevych, P., & Ulibarri, C. (1992). Development of the limbic-hypothalamic cholecystokinin circuit: A model of sexual differentiation. *Developmental Neuroscience, 14*, 11–34.

Miller, B.A., Downs, W.R., Gondoli, D.M., & Keil, A. (1987). The role of childhood sexual abuse in the development of alcoholism in women. *Violence Victims, 2*, 157–172.

Miller, C.L., & Cummins, A.G. (1992). An examination of women's perspectives on power. *Psychology of Women Quarterly, 16*, 415–428.

Miller, D.T., & Turnbull, W. (1986). Expectancies and interpersonal processes. *Annual Review of Psychology, 37*, 233–256.

Miller, J.B. (1986). *Toward a new psychology of women* (2nd ed.). Boston, MA: Beacon Press.

Miller, K.J. (1993). Prevalence and process of disclosure of childhood sexual abuse among eating-disordered women. *Eating Disorders: The Journal of Treatment and Prevention, 1*, 211–225.

Miller, W.B. (1992). An empirical study of the psychological antecedents and consequences of induced abortion. *Journal of Social Issues, 48*(3), 67–93.

Millet, K. (1969). *Sexual politics*. New York: Ballantine Books.

Minarik, M.L., & Ahrens, A.H. (1996). Relations of eating and symptoms of depression and anxiety to the dimensions of perfectionism among undergraduate women. *Cognitive Therapy and Research, 20*, 155–169.

Mindel, C.H. (1995). The long term impact of a "relationship-centered" child care program on public school performance. *Child and Youth Care Forum, 24*, 247–259.

Mitchell, V., & Helson, R. (1990). Women's prime of life: Is it the 50s? *Psychology of Women Quarterly, 14,* 451–470.

Mize, J., & Freeman, L.C. (1989). Employer-supported child care: Assessing the need and potential support. *Child and Youth Care Quarterly, 18,* 289–301.

Mobley, G.M., Jaret, C., Marsh, K., & Lim, Y. (1994). Mentoring, job satisfaction, gender, and the legal profession. *Sex Roles, 31,* 79–98.

Moen, P., & Forest, K.B. (1990). Working parents, workplace supports, and well-being: The Swedish experience. *Social Psychology Quarterly, 53,* 117–131.

Moen, P., Dempster-McClain, D., & Williams, R.M. (1989). Social integration and longevity: An event history analysis of women's roles and resilience. *American Sociological Review, 54,* 635–647.

Money, J., & Ehrhardt, A. (1972). *Man & woman, boy & girl.* Baltimore, MD: Johns Hopkins University Press.

Monroe, P.A. (1996). *Left-brain finances for right-brain people: A guide for the creatively inclined.* Naperville, IL: Sourcebooks.

Monsour, M., Harris, B., Kurzweil, N., & Beard, C. (1994). Challenges confronting cross-sex friendships: "Much ado about nothing?" *Sex Roles, 31,* 55–77.

Mooney, K.M. & Lorenz, E. (1997). The effects of food and gender on interpersonal perceptions. *Sex Roles, 36,* 639–653.

Moore, D. (1995). Gender role attitudes and division of labor: Sex or occupation-type differences? An Isreali example. *Journal of Social Behavior and Personality, 10,* 215–234.

Moos, R.H. (1968). The development of a Menstrual Distress Questionnaire. *Psychosomatic Medicine, 30,* 853–867.

Moraga, C. (1981). The welder. In C. Moraga & G. Anzaldúa (Eds.), *This bridge called my back: Writings by radical women of color* (pp. 219–220). New York: Kitchen Table: Women of Color Press.

Moran, P.B., & Eckenrode, J. (1991). Gender differences in the costs and benefits of peer relationships during adolescence. *Journal of Adolescent Research, 6,* 396–409.

Morawski, J.G. (1987). The troubled quest for masculinity, femininity, and androgyny. *Review of Personality and Social Psychology: Sex and Gender, 7,* 44–69.

Morin, S.F. (1988). AIDS: The challenge to psychology. *American Psychologist, 43,* 838–842.

Morokoff, P.J., Harlow, L.L., & Quina, K. (1995). Women and AIDS. In A.L. Stanton & S.J. Gallant (Eds.), *The psychology of women's health: Progress and challenges in research and application* (pp. 117–169). Washington, DC: American Psychological Association.

Morris, J. (1992). Personal and political: A feminist perspective on researching physical disability. *Disability, Handicap and Society, 7,* 157–166.

Morrison, J. (1989). Childhood sexual histories of women with somatization disorder. *American Journal of Psychiatry, 146,* 239–241.

Morrow, S.L., Gore, P.A., Jr., & Campbell, B.W. (1996). The application of a sociocognitive framework to the career development of lesbian women and gay men. *Journal of Vocational Behavior, 48,* 136–148.

Morrow, S.L., & Hawxhurst, D.M. (1989). Lesbian partner abuse: Implications for therapists. *Journal of Counseling and Development, 68,* 58–62.

Mowbray, C.T. (1995). Nonsexist therapy: Is it? *Women & Therapy, 16(4),* 9–30.

Muehlenhard, C.L., & Linton, M.A. (1987). Date rape and sexual aggression in dating situations: Incidence and risk factors. *Journal of Counseling and Psychology, 34,* 186–196.

Muehlenhard, C.L., & McCoy, M.L. (1991). Double standard/double bind: The sexual double standard and women's communication about sex. *Psychology of Women Quarterly, 15,* 447–461.

Muehlenhard, C.L., Highby, B.J., Phelps, J.L., & Sympson, S.C. (1997). Rape statistics are not exaggerated. In M.R. Walsh (Ed.), *Women, men, and gender: Ongoing debates* (pp. 243–246). New Haven, CT: Yale.

Muehlenhard, C.L., Powch, I.G., Phelps, J.L., & Giusti, L.M. (1992). Definitions of rape: Scientific and political implications. *Journal of Social Issues, 48*(1), 23–44.

Muehlenhard, C.L., & Schrag, J. (1991). Nonviolent sexual coercion. In A. Parrot & L. Bechhofer (Eds.), *Acquaintance rape: The hidden crime* (pp. 115–128). New York: Wiley.

Mueller, K.A., & Yoder, J.D. (1997). Gendered norms for family size, employment, and occupation: Are there personal costs for violating them? *Sex Roles, 36*, 207–220.

Mukerjee, M. (1995). Sexual and other abuse may alter a brain region. *Scientific American, 273*, 14–20.

Murphy, D.A., & Kelly, J.A. (1994). Women's health: The impact of the expanding AIDS epidemic. In V.J. Adesso, D.M. Reddy, & R. Fleming (Eds.), *Psychological perspectives on women's health* (pp. 285–312). Washington, DC: Taylor & Francis.

Murphy, D.G.M., DeCarli, C., McIntosh, A.R., Daly, E., et al. (1996). Sex differences in human brain morphometry and metabolism: An in vivo quantitative magnetic resonance imaging and position emission tomography study on the effect of aging. *Archives of General Psychiatry, 53*, 585–594.

Murphy-Berman, V.A., Berman, J.J., Singh, P., & Pandy, J. (1992). Cultural variations in sex typing: A comparison of students in the United States, Germany, and India. *Journal of Social Psychology, 132*, 403–405.

Murray, B. (1996, February). Psychology remains top college major. *APA Monitor*, pp. 1, 42.

Mussen, P.H., Conger, J.J., Kagan, J., & Huston, A.C. (1990). *Child development and personality* (7th ed.). New York: Harper & Row.

Mwangi, M.W. (1996). Gender roles portrayed in Kenyan television commercials. *Sex Roles, 34*, 205–214.

Nash, H.C., & Chrisler, J.C. (1997). Is a little (psychiatric) knowledge a dangerous thing? The impact of premenstrual dysphoric disorder on perceptions of premenstrual women. *Psychology of Women Quarterly, 21*, 315–322.

National Victims Center. (1992). *Rape in America: A report to the nation.* Arlington, VA: Author.

National Women's Health Network (1989). *Taking hormones and women's health: Choices, risks, benefits.* (Available from NWHN, 1325 G Street, NW, Washington, DC 20005).

Nelson, C., & Watson, J.A. (1990–91). The computer gender gap: Children's attitudes, performance, and socialization. *Journal of Educational Technology Systems, 19*, 345–353.

Nelson, D.L., Quick, J.C., Hitt, M.A., & Moesel, D. (1990). Politics, lack of career progress, and work-home conflict: Stress and strain for working women. *Sex Roles, 23*, 169–185.

Nelson, M. (1991). Empowerment of incest survivors: Speaking out. *Families in Society, 72*, 618–624.

Nelson, T.E., Acker, M., & Manis, M. (1996). Irrepressible stereotypes. *Journal of Experimental Social Psychology, 32*, 13–38.

Newcombe, N., Bandura, M.M., & Taylor, D.G. (1983). Sex differences in spatial ability and spatial activities. *Sex Roles, 9*, 377–386.

Newman, A.L., & Peterson, C. (1996). Anger of women incest survivors. *Sex Roles, 34*, 463–474.

Newt sticks neck out on gender and giraffes. (1995, January 19). *The Milwaukee Journal Sentinel*, p. A7.

Ng, S.H., Dunne, M., & Cataldo, M. (1995). Feminist identities and preferred strategies for advancing women's positive self-concept. *Journal of Social Psychology, 135*, 561–572.

Nicholson, P. (1995). The menstrual cycle, science and femininity: Assumptions underlying menstrual cycle research. *Social Science Medicine, 41*, 779–784.

Niemann, Y.F., Jennings, L., Rozelle, R.M., Baxter, J.C., & Sullivan, E. (1994). Use of free responses and cluster analysis to determine stereotypes of eight groups. *Personality and Social Psychology Bulletin, 20*, 379–390.

Niemela, P., & Lento, R. (1993). The significance of the 50th birthday for women's individuation. *Women & Therapy, 14,* 117–127.

Nigro, G.N., Hill, D.E., Gelbein, M.E., & Clark, C.L. (1988). Changes in the facial prominence of women and men over the last decade. *Psychology of Women Quarterly, 12,* 225–235.

Nikelly, A.G. (1995). Drug advertisements and the medicalization of unipolar depression in women. *Health Care for Women International, 16,* 229–242.

Nolen-Hoeksema, S. (1987). Sex differences in unipolar depression: Evidence and theory. *Psychological Bulletin, 101,* 259–282.

Nolen-Hoeksema, S. (1990). *Sex differences in depression.* Stanford, CA: Stanford University Press.

Nolen-Hoeksema, S., & Girgus, J.S. (1994). The emergence of gender differences in depression during adolescence. *Psychological Bulletin, 115,* 424–443.

Novak, M., & Thacker, C. (1991). Satisfaction and strain among middle-aged women who return to school: Replication and extension of findings in a Canadian context. *Educational Gerontology, 17,* 323–342.

Nurmi, J.E. (1991). How do adolescents see their future? A review of the development of future orientation and planning. *Developmental Review, 11,* 1–59.

Nye, W.P. (1993). Amazing grace: Religion and identity among elderly Black individuals. *International Journal of Aging and Human Development, 36,* 103–114.

Ochman, J.M. (1996). The effects of nongender-role stereotyped, same-sex role models in storybooks on the self-esteem of children in grade three. *Sex Roles, 35,* 711–735.

O'Connell, A.N. (1989). Psychology of women students' self-concepts, attitudes, and assertiveness: A decade of research. *Teaching of Psychology, 16,* 178–181.

O'Connell, A.N., & Russo, N.F. (Eds.). (1990). *Women in psychology: A bio-bibliographic sourcebook.* New York: Greenwood.

O'Connell, A.N., & Russo, N.F. (Eds.). (1991). Women's heritage in psychology: Origins, development, and future directions [Special Issue]. *Psychology of Women Quarterly, 15*(4).

O'Connor, J.J. (1989, June 6). What are commercials selling to children? *The New York Times,* p. 28.

Offer, D., & Schonert-Reichl, K.A. (1992). Debunking the myths of adolescence: Findings from recent research. *Journal of the American Academy of Child and Adolescent Psychiatry, 31,* 1003–1014.

Offermann, L.R., & Beil, C. (1992). Achievement styles of women leaders and their peers: Toward an understanding of women and leadership. *Psychology of Women Quarterly, 16,* 37–56.

Ogletree, S.M., Williams, S.W., Raffeld, P., Mason, B., & Fricke, K. (1990). Female attractiveness and eating disorders: Do children's television commercials play a role? *Sex Roles, 22,* 791–797.

O'Keefe, E.S.C., & Hyde, J.S. (1983). The development of occupational sex-role stereotypes: The effects of gender stability and age. *Sex Roles, 9,* 481–492.

Olenick, N.L., & Chalmers, D.K. (1991). Gender-specific drinking styles in alcoholics and nonalcoholics. *Journal of Studies on Alcohol, 52,* 325–330.

Oliver, M.B., & Hyde, J.S. (1993). Gender differences in sexuality: A meta-analysis. *Psychological Bulletin, 114,* 29–51.

Oliver, S.J., & Toner, B.B. (1990). The influence of gender role typing on the expression of depressive symptoms. *Sex Roles, 22,* 775–790.

Olson, J.E., Frieze, I.H., & Detlefsen, E.G. (1990). Having it all? Combining work and family in a male and a female profession. *Sex Roles, 23,* 515–533.

O'Meara, J.D. (1989). Cross-sex friendship: Four basic challenges of an ignored relationship. *Sex Roles, 21,* 525–543.

Orenstein, P. (1994). *School Girls: Young women, self-esteem, and the confidence gap.* New York: Anchor.

Orosan, P.G., & Schilling, K.M. (1992). Gender differences in college students' definitions and perceptions of intimacy. *Women and Therapy, 12,* 201–212.

Osipow, S.H., & Fitzgerald, L.F. (1993). Unemployment and mental health: A neglected relationship. *Applied and Preventive Psychology, 2,* 59–63.

Osmond, M.W., Wambach, K.G., Harrison, D.F., Byers, J., Levine, P., Imershein, A., & Quadagno, D.M. (1993). The multiple jeopardy of race, class, and gender for AIDS risk among women. *Gender & Society, 7,* 99–120.

O'Sullivan, L.F., & Byers, E.S. (1992). College students' incorporation of initiator and restrictor roles in sexual dating interactions. *Journal of Sex Research, 29,* 435–446.

Outtz, J.H. (1996). *Are Mommies dropping out of the labor force?* Washington, DC: Institute for Women's Policy Research.

Ozer, E.M. (1995). The impact of childcare responsibility and self-efficacy on the psychological health of professional working mothers. *Psychology of Women Quarterly, 19,* 315–335.

Ozer, E.M., & Bandura, A. (1990). Mechanisms governing empowerment effects: A self-efficacy analysis. *Journal of Personality and Social Psychology, 58,* 472–486.

Padilla, E.R., & O'Grady, K.E. (1987). Sexuality among Mexican Americans: A case of sexual stereotyping. *Journal of Personality and Social Psychology, 52,* 5–10.

Palladino, D., & Stephenson, Y. (1990). Perceptions of the sexual self: Their impact on relationships between lesbian and heterosexual women. *Women and Therapy, 9,* 231–253.

Palmerton, P.R., & Judas, J. (1994, July). *Selling violence: Television commercials targeted to children.* Paper presented at the annual meeting of the International Communication Association, Sydney, New South Wales, Australia.

Paludi, M.A. (1992). *The psychology of women.* Dubuque, IA: Brown & Benchmark.

Paradise, S.A. (1993). Older never married women: A cross-cultural investigation. *Women & Therapy, 14,* 129–139.

Parasuraman, S., Purohit, Y.S., & Godshalk, V.M. (1996). Work and family variables, entrepreneurial career success and psychological well-being. *Journal of Vocational Behavior, 48,* 275–300.

Parker, S., & de Vries, B. (1993). Patterns of friendship for women and men in same and cross-sex relationships. *Journal of Social and Personal Relationships, 10,* 617–626.

Parlee, M.B. (1993). Psychology of menstruation and premenstrual syndrome. In F.L. Denmark & M.A. Paludi (Eds.), *Psychology of women: A Handbook of issues and theories* (pp. 325–377). Westport, CT: Greenwood Press.

Parlee, M.B., & Rajagopol, J. (1974). Sex differences on the embedded-figures test: A cross-cultural comparison of college students in India and in the United States. *Perceptual and Motor Skills, 39,* 1311–1314.

Parrot, A. (1991). Institutionalized response: How can acquaintance rape be prevented? In A. Parrot & Bechhofer (Eds.), *Acquaintance rape: The hidden crime.* New York: Wiley.

Parsons, T., & Bales, R. (1955). *Family, socialization, and inter-action process.* Glencoe, IL: Free Press.

Parvin, R., & Biaggio, M.K. (1991). Paradoxes in the practice of feminist therapy. *Women & Therapy, 11(2),* 3–12.

Patterson, C.J. (1992). Children of lesbian and gay parents. *Children Development, 63,* 1025–1042.

Paul, E. (1993). The women's movement and the movement of women. *Social Policy, 23(4),* 44–50.

Paxton, S.J., & Sculthorpe, A. (1991). Disordered eating and sex role characteristics in young women: Implications for sociocultural theories of disturbed eating. *Sex Roles, 24,* 587–598.

Peirce, K. (1993). Socialization of teenage girls through teen-magazine fiction: The making of a new woman or an old lady? *Sex Roles, 29,* 59–68.

Penning, M.J., & Strain, L.A. (1994). Gender differences in disability, assistance, and subjective well-being in later life. *Journals of Gerontology, 49,* S202–S208.

Peplau, L.A., & Conrad, E. (1989). Beyond nonsexist research: The perils of feminist methods in psychology. *Psychology of Women Quarterly, 13,* 379–400.

Pepper, S.C. (1970). *World hypotheses.* Berkeley, CA: University of California Press.

Percy, C., & Kremer, J. (1995). Feminist identification in a troubled society. *Feminism & Psychology, 5,* 201–222.

Perkins, K. (1993). Working class women and retirement. *Journal of Gerontological Social Work, 20,* 129–146.

Perlick, D., & Silverstein, B. (1994). Faces of female discontent: Depression, disordered eating, and changing gender roles. In P. Fallon, M.A. Katzman, & S.C. Wooley (Eds.), *Feminist perspectives on eating disorders* (pp. 77–93). New York: Guilford.

Peters, D.K., & Cantrell, P.J. (1993). Gender roles and role conflict in feminist lesbian and heterosexual women. *Sex Roles, 28,* 379–392.

Petersen, A.C. (1988). Adolescent development. *Annual Review of Psychology, 39,* 583–607.

Petersen, T., & Morgan, L.A. (1995). Separate and unequal: Occupation-establishment sex segregation and the gender wage gap. *American Journal of Sociology, 101,* 329–365.

Pezdek, K. (1995, November). *What types of false childhood memories are not likely to be suggestively implanted?* Paper presented at the annual meeting of the Psychonomic Society, Los Angeles, CA.

Pezdek, K. (1996, November). *False memories are more likely to be planted if they are familiar.* Paper presented at the annual meeting of the Psychonomic Society, Chicago, IL.

Pezdek, K., & Banks, W.P. (Eds.). (1996). *The recovered memory/false memory debate.* San Diego, CA: Academic Press.

Pfost, K.S., & Fiore, M. (1990). Pursuit of nontraditional occupations: Fear of success or fear of not being chosen? *Sex Roles, 23,* 15–24.

Pharr, S. (1988). The common elements of oppression. In S. Pharr, *Homophobia: A weapon of sexism* (pp. 53–64). Inverness, CA: Chardon Press.

Phillips, B.S. (1990). Nicknames and sex role stereotypes. *Sex Roles, 23,* 281–289.

Phillips. D.A., Voran, M., Kisker, E., Howes, C., & Whitebook, M. (1994). Child care for children in poverty: Opportunity or inequity? *Child Development, 65,* 472–492.

Philpot, C.L., Brooks, G.R., Lusterman, D., & Nutt, R.L. (1997). *Bridging separate gender worlds: Why men and women clash and how therapists can bring them together.* Washington, DC: American Psychological Association.

Piaget, J. (1954). *The construction of reality in the child.* New York: Basic.

Piedmont, R.L. (1995). Another look at fear of success, fear of failure, and test anxiety: A motivational analysis using the five-factor model. *Sex Roles, 32,* 139–158.

Pies, C.A. (1989). Lesbians and the choice to parent. *Marriage and Family Review, 14,* 137–154.

Piliavin, I.M., Piliavin, J.A., & Rodin, J. (1975). Costs, diffusion, and the stigmatized victim. *Journal of Personality and Social Psychology, 32,* 429–438.

Pingitore, R., Dugoni, B.L., Tindale, R.S., & Spring, B. (1994). Bias against overweight job applicants in a simulated employment interview. *Journal of Applied Psychology, 79,* 909–917.

Pinzler, I.K., & Ellis, D. (1989). Wage discrimination and comparable worth: A legal perspective. *Journal of Social Issues, 45*(4), 51–65.

Pleck, J.H. (1975). Masculinity-femininity: Current and alternate paradigms. *Sex Roles, 1,* 161–178.

Pleck, J.H. (1985). *Working wives/working husbands.* Beverly Hills: Sage.

Pohl, J.M., & Boyd, C.J. (1993). Ageism within feminism. *Images: Journal of Nursing Scholarship, 25,* 199–203.

Polit, D.F. (1978). Stereotypes relating to family-size status. *Journal of Marriage and the Family, 40(1),* 105–114.

Pollard, J.W. (1994). Treatment for perpetrators of rape and other violence. In A. Berkowitz

(Ed.), *Men and rape: Theory, research, and prevention programs in higher education* (pp. 51–66). San Francisco, CA: Jossey-Bass.

Polusny, M., & Follette, V. (1996). Remembering childhood sexual abuse: A national survey of psychologists' clinical practices, beliefs, and personal experiences. *Professional Psychology: Research and Practice, 27,* 41–52.

Pomazal, R.J., & Clore, G.L. (1973). Helping on the highway: The effects of dependency and sex. *Journal of Applied Social Psychology, 3,* 150–164.

Poole, M.E., & Langan-Fox, J. (1992). Conflict in women's decision-making about multiple roles. *Australian Journal of Marriage and Family, 13,* 2–18.

Pope, K.S. (1996). Memory, abuse, and science: Questioning claims about the false memory syndrome epidemic. *American Psychologist, 51,* 957–974.

Pope, K.S., & Brown, L.S. (1996). *Recovered memories of abuse: Assessment, therapy, forensics.* Washington, DC: American Psychological Association.

Porter, N. (1995). Supervision of psychotherapists: Integrating anti-racist, feminist, and multicultural perspectives. In H. Landrine (Ed.), *Bringing cultural diversity to feminist psychology: Theory, research, and practice* (pp. 163–175). Washington, DC: American Psychological Association.

Posner, J.K., & Vandell, D.L. (1994). Low-income children's after-school care: Are there beneficial effects of after-school programs? *Child Development, 65,* 440–456.

Potts, M.K., Burnam, M.A., & Wells, K.B. (1991). Gender differences in depression detection: A comparison of clinician diagnosis and standardized assessment. *Psychological Assessment, 3,* 609–615.

Poulin-Dubois, D., Serbin, L.A., Kenyon, B., & Derbyshire, A. (1994). Infants' intermodal knowledge about gender. *Developmental Psychology, 30,* 436–442.

Powell, A.D., & Kahn, A.S. (1995). Racial differences in women's desires to be thin. *International Journal of Eating Disorders, 17,* 191–195.

Prather, J.E. (1991). Decoding advertising: The role of communications studies in explaining the popularity of minor tranquilizers. In J. Gabe (Ed.), *Understanding tranquilizer use* (pp. 112–135). London: Tavistock/Routledge.

Prentky, R.A., & Knight, R.A. (1991). Identifying critical dimensions for discriminating among rapists. *Journal of Consulting and Clinical Psychology, 59,* 643–661.

Prilleltensky, I. (1989). Psychology and the status quo. *American Psychologist, 44,* 795–802.

Prilleltensky, O. (1996). Women with disabilities and feminist therapy. *Women & Therapy, 18,* 87–97.

Ptacek, J. (1988). Why do men batter their wives? In K. Yllö & M. Bograd (Eds.), *Feminist perspectives on wife abuse* (pp. 133–157). Newbury Park, CA: Sage.

Publication manual of the American Psychological Association (4th ed.). (1994). Washington, DC: American Psychological Association.

Pugh, M.D., & Wahrman, R. (1983). Neutralizing sexism in mixed-sex groups: Do women have to be better than men? *American Journal of Sociology, 88,* 746–762.

Pumariega, A.J., Gustavson, C.R., & Gustavson, J.C. (1994). Eating attitudes in African-American women: The Essence Eating Disorders Survey. *Eating Disorders: The Journal of Treatment and Prevention, 2,* 5–16.

Purcell, P. & Stewart, L. (1990). Dick and Jane in 1989. *Sex Roles, 22,* 177–185.

Pyke, K., & Coltrane, S. (1996). Entitlement, obligation, and gratitude in family work. *Journal of Family Issues, 17,* 61–82.

Quam, J.K., & Whitford, G.S. (1992). Adaptation and age-related expectations of older gay and lesbian adults. *The Gerontologist, 32,* 367–374.

Quina, K., & Carlson, N.L. (1989). *Rape, incest, and sexual harassment: A guide for helping survivors.* New York: Praeger.

Rabinowitz, V., & Sechzer, J.A. (1993). Feminist perspectives on research methods. In F.L. Denmark & M.A. Paludi (Eds.), *Psychology of women: Handbook of issues and theories.* Westport, CT: Greenwood.

Rafaeli, A. (1989). When clerks meet customers: A test of variables related to emotional expression on the job. *Journal of Applied Psychology, 74*, 385–393.

Ragins, B.R. (1991). Gender effects in subordinate evaluations of leaders: Real or artifact? *Journal of Organizational Behavior, 12*, 259–268.

Ragins, B.R., & Cotton, J.L. (1991). Easier said than done: Gender differences in perceived barriers to gaining a mentor. *Academy of Management Journal, 34*, 939–951.

Ragins, B.R., & Cotton, J.L. (1993). Gender and willingness to mentor in organizations. *Journal of Management, 19*, 97–111.

Ragins, B.R., & McFarlin, D.B. (1990). Perceptions of mentor roles in cross-gender mentoring relationships. *Journal of Vocational Behavior, 37*, 321–339.

Ragins, B.R., & Scandura, T.A. (1994). Gender differences in expected outcomes of mentoring relationships. *Academy of Management Journal, 37*, 957–971.

Raley, R.K. (1995). Black-White differences in kin contact and exchange among never married adults. *Journal of Family Issues, 16*, 77–103.

Ramey, F.H. (1995). Obstacles faced by African American women administrators in higher education: How they cope. *Western Journal of Black Studies, 19*, 113–119.

Ramist, L., & Arbeiter, S. (1986). *Profiles, college-bound seniors, 1985.* New York: College Entrance Examination Board.

Randle, N. (1992, July 5). Their time at bat. *Chicago Tribune Magazine*, pp. 11–15.

Rankin, E.D. (1993). Stresses and rewards experienced by employed mothers. *Health Care for Women International, 14*, 527–537.

Ransome, W. (1993). *What every girl in school needs to know.* Concord, MA: National Coalition of Girls' Schools.

Rasi, R.A., & Rodriguez-Nogues, L. (Eds.). (1995). *Out in the workplace: The pleasures and perils of coming out on the job.* Los Angeles, CA: Alyson Publications.

Ratcliff, K.S., & Bogdan, J. (1988). Unemployed women: When social support is not supportive. *Social Problems, 35*, 54–63.

Raup, J.L., & Myers, J.E. (1989). The empty nest syndrome: Myth or reality? *Journal of Counseling and Development, 68*, 180–183.

Rave, E.J. (1990). White feminist therapists and anti-racism. In L.S. Brown & M.P.P. Root (Eds.), *Diversity and complexity in feminist therapy* (pp. 313–326). New York: Harrington Park Press.

Reading, A.E. (1994). Pain. In V.J. Adesso, D.M. Reddy, & R. Fleming (Eds.), *Psychological perspectives on women's health* (pp. 223–246). Washington, DC: Taylor & Francis.

Reardon, P., & Prescott, S. (1977). Sex as reported in a recent sample of psychological research. *Psychology of Women Quarterly, 2*, 157–161.

Rebecca, M., Hefner, R., & Oleshansky, B. (1976). A model of sex-role transcendence. *Journal of Social Issues, 32*(3), 197–206.

Reid, G.M. (1994). Maternal sex-stereotypes of newborns. *Psychological Reports, 73*, 1443–1450.

Reid, G.M. (1995). Children's occupational sex-role stereotyping in 1994. *Psychological Reports, 76*, 1155–1165.

Reid, P., & Finchilescu, G. (1995). The disempowering effects of media violence against women on college women. *Psychology of Women Quarterly, 19*, 397–411.

Reid, P.T. (1985). Sex-role socialization of Black children: A review of theory, family, and media influences. *Academic Psychology Bulletin, 7*, 211–212.

Reid, P.T. (1993). Poor women in psychological research: Shut up and shut out. *Psychology of Women Quarterly, 17*, 133–150.

Reid, P.T., & Comas-Díaz, L. (1990). Gender and ethnicity: Perspectives on dual status. *Sex Roles, 22*, 397–408.

Reid, P.T., Haritos, C., Kelly, E., & Holland, N.E. (1995). Socialization of girls: Issues of ethnicity in gender development. In H. Landrine (Ed.), *Bringing cultural diversity to feminist psychology: Theory, research, and practice* (pp. 93–111). Washington, DC: American Psychological Association.

Reid, P.T., & Paludi, M. (1993). Girls' development: Conception to adolescence. In F.L. Denmark & M.A. Paludi (Eds.), *Psychology of women: A handbook of theories and issues.* Westport, CT: Greenwood.

Reinharz, S. (1992). *Feminist methods in social research.* New York: Oxford University Press.

Reis, H.T., Senchak, M., & Solomon, B. (1985). Sex differences in the intimacy of social interaction: Further examination of potential explanations. *Journal of Personality and Social Psychology, 48*, 1204–1217.

Reisman, J.M. (1990). Intimacy in same-sex friendships. *Sex Roles, 23*, 65–82.

Reitzes, D.C., & Multran, E.J. (1994). Multiple roles and identities: Factors influencing self-esteem among middle-aged working men and women. *Social Psychology Quarterly, 57*, 313–325.

Renzetti, C. (1987). New wave or second stage? Attitudes of college women toward feminism. *Sex Roles, 16*, 265–278.

Renzetti, C. (1992). *Violent betrayal: Partner abuse in lesbian relationships.* Newbury Park, CA: Sage.

Resick, P.A., & Markaway, B.K. (1991). Clinical treatment of adult female victims of sexual assault. In C.R. Hollin & K. Howells (Eds.), *Clinical approaches to sex offenders and their victims* (pp. 261–284). New York: Wiley.

Reskin, B.F. (1988). Bringing the men back in: Sex differentiation and the devaluation of women's work. *Gender & Society, 2*, 58–81.

Reskin, B.F. (1993). Sex segregation in the workplace. *Annual Review of Sociology, 19*, 241–270.

Reskin, B.F., & Padavic, I. (1994). *Women and men at work.* Thousand Oaks, CA: Pine Forge Press.

Reskin, B.F., & Roos, P.A. (1990). *Job queues, gender queues: Explaining women's inroads into male occupations.* Philadelphia, PA: Temple.

Rhodes, F., Corby, N.H., Wolitski, R.J., Tashima, N., Crain, C., Yankovich, D.R., & Smith, P.K. (1990). Risk behaviors and perceptions of AIDS among street injection drug users. *Journal of Drug Education, 20*, 271–288.

Rich, M.K., & Cash, T.F. (1993). The American image of beauty: Media representations of hair color for four decades. *Sex Roles, 29*, 113–124.

Rickabaugh, C.A. (1995). College students' stereotypes of gender and political activism. *Basic and Applied Social Psychology, 16*, 319–331.

Rickard, K.M. (1989). The relationship of self-monitored dating behaviors to level of feminist identity on the feminist identity scale. *Sex Roles, 20*, 213–226.

Rickard, K.M. (1990). The effect of feminist identity level on gender prejudice toward artists' illustrations. *Journal of Research in Personality, 24*, 145–162.

Riger, S. (1992). Epistemological debates, feminist voices: Science, social values, and the study of women. *American Psychologist, 47*, 730–740.

Riger, S. (1997). From snapshots to videotape: New directions in research on gender differences. *Journal of Social Issues, 53*(2), 395–408.

Riger, S., & Galligan, P. (1980). Women in management: An exploration of competing paradigms. *American Psychologist, 35*, 902–910.

Riger, S., & Gordon, M.T. (1981). The fear of rape: A study in social control. *Journal of Social Issues, 37*(4), 71–92.

Rindfuss, R.R., Swicegood, C.G., & Rosenfeld, R.A. (1987). Disorder in the life course: How common and does it matter? *American Sociological Review, 52*, 785–801.

Risman, B.J. (1987). Intimate relationships from a microstructural perspective: Men who mother. *Gender & Society, 1*, 6–32.

Rix, S.E. (Ed.). (1988). *The American Woman 1988–89.* New York: Norton.

Robertson, J., & Fitzgerald, L.F. (1990). The (mis)treatment of men: Effects of client gender role and life-style on diagnosis and attribution of pathology. *Journal of Counseling Psychology, 37*, 3–9.

Robins, L.N., & Regier, D.A. (Eds.). (1991). *Psychiatric disorders in America: The Epidemiologic Catchment Area Study.* New York: Free Press.

Robinson, J.P. (1988). Who's doing the housework? *American Demographics, 10*, 24–28, 63.

Robinson, J., & Spitze, G. (1992). Whistle while you work? The effect of household task performance on women's and men's well-being. *Social Science Quarterly, 73*, 844–861.

Robinson, M.B. (1989, May 11). Women bear the burden of caregiving, study finds. *Morning Call,* p. A8.

Rodin, J., & Ickovics, J.R. (1990). Women's health: Review and research agenda as we approach the 21st century. *American Psychologist, 45*, 1018–1034.

Roesler, T.A., & McKenzie, N. (1994). Effects of childhood trauma on psychological functioning in adults sexually abused as children. *Journal of Nervous and Mental Disease, 182*, 145–150.

Rogers, A. (1993). Voice, play, and practice of ordinary courage in girls' and women's lives. *Harvard Education Review, 63*, 265–295.

Rogers, J.K., & Henson, K.D. (1997). "Hey, why don't you wear a shorter skirt?": Structural vulnerability and the organization of sexual harassment in temporary clerical employment. *Gender & Society, 11*, 215–237.

Roiphe, K. (1993). *The morning after: Sex, fear, and feminism on campus.* Boston, MA: Little, Brown.

Rolandelli, D.R. (1991). Gender role portrayal analysis of children's television programming in Japan. *Human Relations, 44*, 1273–1299.

Roll, S., McClelland, G., & Abel, T. (1996). Differences in susceptibility to influence in Mexican American and Anglo females. *Hispanic Journal of Behavioral Sciences, 18*, 13–20.

Roman, L.G. (1993). White is a color! White defensiveness, postmodernism, and anti-racist pedagogy. In C. McCarthy & W. Crichlow (Eds.), *Race identity and representation in education* (pp. 71–88). New York: Routledge.

Romero, M. (1985). A comparison between strategies used on prisoners of war and battered wives. *Sex Roles, 13*, 537–547.

Roos, P.A., & Reskin, B.F. (1992). Occupational desegregation in the 1970s: Integration and economic equity? *Sociological Perspectives, 35*, 69–91.

Root, M.P.P. (1990). Disordered eating in women of color. *Sex Roles, 22*, 525–536.

Root, M.P.P. (1991). Persistent, disordered eating as a gender-specific, post-traumatic stress response to sexual assault. *Psychotherapy, 28*, 96–102.

Root, M.P.P. (1992). Reconstructing the impact of trauma on personality. In L.S. Brown & M. Ballou (Eds.), *Personality and psychopathology: Feminist reappraisals* (pp. 229–265). New York: Guilford.

Rose, S. (1995). Women's friendships. In J.C. Chrisler & A.H. Hemstreet (Eds.), *Variations on a theme: Diversity and the psychology of women* (pp. 79–105). Albany, NY: SUNY Press.

Rose, S. (1996). Who to let in: Women's cross-race friendships. In J.C. Chrisler, C. Golden, & P.D. Rozee (Eds.), *Lectures on the psychology of women* (pp. 211–226). New York: McGraw-Hill.

Rose, S., & Frieze, I.H. (1993). Young singles' contemporary dating scripts. *Sex Roles, 28*, 499–509.

Rose, S., & Serafica, F.C. (1986). Keeping and ending casual, close and best friendships. *Journal of Social and Personal Relationships, 3,* 275–288.

Rosen, E.F., et al. (1993). African-American males prefer a larger female body silhouette than do Whites. *Bulletin of the Psychonomic Society, 31,* 599–601.

Rosen, K.H., & Bezold, A. (1996). Dating violence prevention: A didactic support group for young women. *Journal of Counseling Development, 74,* 521–525.

Rosenberg, M.J., & Rosenthal, S.M. (1987). Reproductive mortality in the United States: Recent trends and methodologic considerations. *American Journal of Public Health, 77,* 833–836.

Rosenbluth, S.C., & Steil, J.M. (1995). Predictors of intimacy for women in heterosexual and homosexual couples. *Journal of Social and Personal Relationships, 12,* 163–175.

Rosenfield, S. (1997). Labeling mental illness: The effects of received services and perceived stigma on life satisfaction. *American Sociological Review, 62,* 660–672.

Rosenthal, R. (1991). Meta-analysis: A review. *Psychosomatic Medicine, 53,* 247–271.

Rosewater, L.B. (1985). Feminist interpretation of traditional testing. In L.B. Rosewater & L.E.A. Walker (Eds.), *Handbook of feminist therapy: Women's issues in psychotherapy* (pp. 266–273). New York: Springer.

Rosewater, L.B. (1988). Feminist therapies with women. In M.A. Dutton-Douglas & L.E.A. Walker (Eds.), *Feminist psychotherapies: Integration of therapeutic and feminist systems* (pp. 137–155). Norwood, NJ: Ablex.

Rosewater, L.B. (1990). Diversifying feminist theory and practice: Broadening the concept of victimization. In L.S. Brown & M.P.P. Root (Eds.), *Diversity and complexity in feminist therapy* (pp. 299–311). New York: Harrington Park Press.

Rosnow, R.L., & Rosenthal, R. (1989). Statistical procedures and the justification of knowledge in psychological science. *American Psychologist, 44,* 1276–1284.

Ross, L. (1977). The intuitive psychologist and his shortcomings: Distortions in the attribution process. In L. Berkowitz (Ed.), *Advances in experimental social psychology,* Vol. 10 (pp. 174–221). New York: Academic Press.

Ross, L., Anderson, D.R., & Wisocki, P.A. (1982). Television viewing and adult sex-role attitudes. *Sex Roles, 8,* 589–592.

Ross, R., Frances, A., & Widiger, T.A. (1997). Gender issues in DSM-IV. In M.R. Walsh (Ed.), *Women, men, and gender: Ongoing debates* (pp. 348–357). New Haven, CT: Yale.

Rost, D.H., & Hanses, P. (1994). The possession and use of toys in elementary-school boys and girls: Does giftedness make a difference? *Educational Psychology, 14,* 181–194.

Rostosky, S.S., & Travis, C.B. (1996). Menopausal research and the dominance of the biomedical model 1984–1994. *Psychology of Women Quarterly, 20,* 285–312.

Roth, S., Wayland, K., & Woolsey, M. (1990). Victimization history and victim-assailant relationship as factors in recovery from sexual assault. *Journal of Traumatic Stress, 3,* 169–180.

Rothblum, E.D. (1990). Depression among lesbians: An invisible and unresearched phenomenon. *Journal of Gay and Lesbian Psychotherapy, 1,* 67–87.

Rothblum, E.D. (1994a). Lesbians and physical appearance: Which model applies? *Contemporary Perspectives in Lesbian and Gay Psychology, 1,* 84–97.

Rothblum, E.D. (1994b). Transforming lesbian sexuality. *Psychology of Women Quarterly, 18,* 627–641.

Rountree, C. (1993). *On women turning 50: Celebrating mid-life discoveries.* San Francisco, CA: Harper.

Rozee, P.D. (1996). Freedom from fear of rape: The missing link in women's freedom. In J.C. Chrisler, C. Golden, & P.D. Rozee (Eds.)., *Lectures on the psychology of women* (pp. 309–322). New York: McGraw-Hill.

Rubin, D.L., & Greene, K.L. (1991). Effects of biological and psychological gender, age cohort, and interviewer gender on attitudes toward gender-inclusive language. *Sex Roles, 24,* 391–412.

Ruble, D.N., Greulich, F., Pomerantz, E.M., & Gochberg, B. (1993). The role of gender-related processes in the development of sex differences in self-evaluation and depression. *Journal of Affective Disorders, 29,* 97–128.

Rucker, C.E., & Cash, T.F. (1992). Body images, body-size perceptions, and eating behaviors among African-American and White college women. *International Journal of Eating Disorders, 12,* 291–299.

Rudman, L.A., & Borgida, E. (1995). The afterglow of construct accessibility: The behavioral consequences of priming men to view women as sexual objects. *Journal of Experimental Social Psychology, 31,* 493–517.

Rushton, J.P. (1994). Cranial capacity related to sex, rank, and race in a stratified random sample of 6,325 military personnel. *Intelligence, 16,* 401–413.

Russel, D.E.H. (1982). *Rape in marriage.* New York: Macmillan.

Russel, D.E.H. (1986). *The secret trauma: Incest in the lives of girls and women.* New York: Basic.

Russell, S. (1985). Social dimensions of disability: Women with MS. *Resources for Feminist Research, 14,* 56–58.

Russo, N.F. (1979). Overview: Roles, fertility and the motherhood mandate. *Psychology of Women Quarterly, 4,* 7–15.

Russo, N.F., & Denmark, F.L. (1987). Contributions of women to psychology. *Annual Review of Psychology, 38,* 279–298.

Russo, N.F., Green, B.L., & Knight, G. (1993). The relationship of gender, self-esteem, and instrumentality to depressive symptomatology. *Journal of Social and Clinical Psychology, 12,* 218–236.

Russo, N.F., Horn, J.D., & Schwartz, R. (1992). U.S. abortion in context: Selected characteristics and motivations of women seeking abortions. *Journal of Social Issues, 48*(3) 183–202.

Russo, N.F., Horn, J.D., & Tromp, S. (1993). Childspacing intervals and abortion among Blacks and whites: A brief report. *Women & Health, 20,* 43–51.

Russo, N.F., & Jansen, M.A. (1988). Women, work, and disability: Opportunities and challenges. In M. Fine & A. Asch (Eds.), *Women with disabilities: Essays in psychology, culture, and politics* (pp. 229–244). Philadelphia, PA: Temple.

Russo, N.F., Kelly, R.M., & Deacon, M. (1991). Gender and success-related attributions: Beyond individualistic conceptions of achievement. *Sex Roles, 25,* 331–350.

Rust, P.C. (1993). "Coming out" in the age of social constructionism: Sexual identity formation among lesbian and bisexual women. *Gender & Society, 7,* 50–77.

Rutte, C.G., Diekmann, K.A., Polzer, J.T., Crosby, F.J., & Messick, D.M. (1994). Organization of information and the detection of gender discrimination. *Psychological Science, 5,* 226–231.

Ruuskanen, J.M., & Ruoppila, I. (1994). Physical activity and psychological well-being among people aged 65–84 years. *Journal of Gerontology, 49,* 292–296.

Ryan, B. (1992). *Feminism and the women's movement: Dynamics of change in social movement, ideology and activism.* New York: Routledge.

Ryan, W. (1972). *Blaming the victim.* New York: Vintage.

Ryujin, D.H., & Herrold, A.J. (1989). Cross-sex comparisons: A word of caution. *Sex Roles, 20,* 713–719.

Sackett, P.R., DuBois, C.L.Z., & Noe, A.W. (1991). Tokenism in performance evaluation: The effects of work group representation on male-female and white-Black differences in performance ratings. *Journal of Applied Psychology, 76,* 263–267.

Sadker, M., & Sadker, D. (1994). *Failing at fairness: How America's schools cheat girls.* New York: Macmillan.

Sampson, E.E. (1978). Scientific paradigms and social values: Wanted—a scientific revolution. *Journal of Personality and Social Psychology, 36*, 1332–1343.

Sanday, P.R. (1981). The socio-cultural context of rape: A cross-cultural study. *Journal of Social Issues, 37*(4), 5–27.

Sandoz, C.J. (1995). Gender issues in recovery from alcoholism. *Alcoholism Treatment Quarterly, 12*, 61–69.

Sang, B.E. (1993). Existential issues of midlife lesbians. In L.D. Garnets & D.C. Kimmel (Eds.), *Psychological perspectives on lesbian and gay male experiences* (pp. 500–516). New York: Columbia University Press.

Santor, D.A., Ramsay, J.O., & Zuroff, D.C. (1994). Nonparametric item analyses of the Beck Depression Inventory: Evaluating gender item bias and response option weights. *Psychological Assessment, 6*, 255–270.

Saraga, E., & MacLeod, M. (1997). False memory syndrome: Theory of defence against reality? *Feminism & Psychology, 7*, 46–51.

Sattel, J.W. (1976). Men, inexpressiveness, and power. In L. Richardson & V. Taylor (Eds.), *Feminist frontiers: Rethinking sex, gender, and society* (pp. 242–246). New York: Random House.

Sayers, J. (1982). *Biological politics: Feminist and anti-feminist perspectives.* New York: Tavistock.

Scarborough, E., & Furumoto, L. (1987). *Untold lives: The first generation of American women psychologists.* New York: Columbia University Press.

Scarr, S., & Eisenberg, M. (1993). Child care research: Issues, perspectives, and results. *Annual Review of Psychology, 44*, 613–644.

Scarr, S., Eisenberg, M., & Deater-Deckard, K. (1994). Measurement of quality in child care centers. *Early Childhood Research Quarterly, 9*, 131–151.

Scarr, S., Phillips, D., & McCartney, K. (1989). Working mothers and their families. *American Psychologist, 44*, 1402–1409.

Schafran, L.H. (1995, August 26). Rape is still underreported. *The New York Times*, p. 15.

Schaie, K.W. (1988). Ageism in psychological research. *American Psychologist, 43*, 179–183.

Schein, V.E. (1973). The relationship between sex role stereotypes and requisite management characteristics. *Journal of Applied Psychology, 57*, 95–105.

Schein, V.E., & Mueller, R. (1992). Sex role stereotyping and requisite management characteristics: A cross-cultural look. *Journal of Organizational Behavior, 13*, 439–447.

Schein, V.E., Mueller, R., & Jacobson, C. (1989). The relationship between sex role stereotypes and requisite management characteristics among college students. *Sex Roles, 20*, 103–110.

Schein, V.E., Mueller, R., Lituchy, T., & Lui, J. (1996). Think manager—think male: A global phenomenon? *Journal of Organizational Behavior, 17*, 33–41.

Schewe, P., & O'Donohue, W. (1993). Rape prevention: Methodological problems and new directions. *Clinical Psychology Review, 13*, 667–682.

Schiebinger, L.L. (1992). The gendered brain: Some historical perspectives. In A. Harrington (Ed.), *So human a brain: Knowledge and values in the neurosciences* (pp. 110–120). Boston, MA: Birkhauser.

Schneer, J.A., & Reitman, F. (1993). Effects of alternate family structures on managerial career paths. *Academy of Management Journal, 36*, 830–843.

Schneider, J.A., O'Leary, A., & Jenkins, S.R. (1995). Gender, sexual orientation, and disordered eating. *Psychology and Health, 10*, 113–128.

Schroeder, K.A., Blood, L.L., & Maluso, D. (1992). An intergenerational analysis of expectations for women's career and family roles. *Sex Roles, 26*, 273–291.

Schwabacher, S. (1972). Male vs. female representation in psychological research: An examination of the *Journal of Personality and Social Psychology*, 1970, 1971. *JSAS: Catalog of Selected Documents in Psychology, 2*, 20–21.

Schwartz, F.N. (1989, Jan.-Feb.). Management women and the new facts of life. *Harvard Business Review, 89,* 65–75.

Schwartz, L.A., & Markham, W.T. (1985). Sex stereotyping in children's toy advertisements. *Sex Roles, 12,* 157–170.

Scott, C.S., Shifman, L., Orr, L., Owen, R.G., & Fawcett, N. (1988). Hispanic and Black American adolescents' beliefs relating to sexuality and contraception. *Adolescence, 23,* 667–688.

Scott, S.E. (1997). Feminists and false memories: A case of postmodern amnesia. *Feminism & Psychology, 7,* 33–38.

Sears, D.O. (1986). College sophomores in the laboratory: Influences of a narrow data base on social psychology's view of human nature. *Journal of Personality and Social Psychology, 51,* 515–530.

Seccombe, K., & Ishii-Kuntz, M. (1994). Gender and social relationships among the never-married. *Sex Roles, 30,* 585–603.

Segura, D. (1994). Working at motherhood: Chicana and Mexican immigrant mothers and employment. In E.N. Glenn, G. Chang, & L.R. Forcey (Eds.), *Mothering: Ideology, experience, and agency.* New York: Routledge.

Segura, D.A., & Pierce, J.L. (1993). Chicana/o family structure and gender personality: Chodorow, familism, and psychoanalytic sociology revisited. *Signs, 19,* 62–91.

Selkow, P. (1984). Effects of maternal employment on kindergarten and first-grade children's vocational aspirations. *Sex Roles, 11,* 677–690.

Semple, S.J., Patterson, T.L., Temoshok, L.R., McCutchan, J.A., Straits-Troster, K.A., Chandler, J.L., & Grant, I. (1993). Identification of psychobiological stressors among HIV-positive women. *Women & Health, 20,* 15–36.

Sen, K.R. (1993). Factors predicting depression among Korean-American women in New York. *International Journal of Nursing Studies, 30,* 415–423.

Serbin, L.A., Powlishta, K.K., & Gulko, J. (1993). The development of sex typing in middle childhood. *Monographs for the Society for Research in Child Development, 58*(2, Serial No. 232).

Severy, L.J., Thapa, S., Askew, I., & Glor, J.E. (1993). Menstrual experiences and beliefs: A multicountry study of relationships with fertility and fertility regulating methods. *Women & Health, 20,* 1–20.

Seyler, D.L., Monroe, P.A., & Garand, J.C. (1995). Balancing work and family: The role of employer-supported child care benefits. *Journal of Family Issues, 16,* 170–193.

Shacher, R. (1991). His and her marital satisfaction: The double standard. *Sex Roles, 25,* 451–467.

Shakin, M., Shakin, D., & Sternglanz, S.H. (1985). Infant clothing: Sex labeling for strangers. *Sex Roles, 12,* 955–964.

Shapiro, B.A. (1995). The dismissal of female clients' reports of medication side effects: A first hand account. *Women & Therapy, 16(1),* 113–127.

Shapiro, J., & Kroeger, L. (1991). Is life just a romantic novel? The relationship between attitudes about intimate relationships and the popular media. *American Journal of Family Therapy, 19,* 226–236.

Sharps, M.J., Price, J.L., & Williams, J.K. (1994). Spatial cognitions and gender: Instructional and stimulus influences on mental image rotation performance. *Psychology of Women Quarterly, 18,* 413–426.

Sharps, M.J., Welton, A.L., & Price, J.L. (1993). Gender and task in the determination of spatial cognitive performance. *Psychology of Women Quarterly, 17,* 71–83.

Shaw, S.M. (1992). Dereifying family leisure: An examination of women's and men's everyday experiences and perceptions of family time. *Leisure Sciences, 14,* 271–286.

Shayne, V.T., & Kaplan, B.J. (1991). Double victims: Poor women and AIDS. *Women & Health, 17,* 21–37.

Shaywitz, B.A., Shaywitz, S.E., Pugh, K.R., Constable, R.T., Skudlarski, P., Fulbright, R.K., Bronen, R.A., Fletcher, J.M., Shankweiler, D.P., Katz, L., & Gore, J.C. (1995). Sex differences in the functional organization of the brain for language. *Nature, 373*, 607–609.

Shea, G.F. (1994). *Mentoring: Helping employees reach their full potential.* New York: American Management Association.

Sheffield, C.J. (1989). Sexual terrorism. In J. Freeman (Ed.), *Women: A feminist perspective* (4th ed.) (pp. 3–19). Mountain View, CA: Mayfield.

Shelton, B.A. (1990). The distribution of household tasks: Does wife's employment status make a difference? *Journal of Family Issues, 11*, 115–135.

Sherif, C.W. (1979). Bias in psychology. In J.A. Sherman & E.T. Beck (Eds.), *The prism of sex* (pp. 93–133). Madison, WI: University of Wisconsin Press.

Sherman, J.A. (1978). *Sex-related cognitive differences: An essay on theory and evidence.* Springfield, IL: Charles C Thomas.

Sherman, J.A., & Fennema, E. (1978). Distribution of spatial visualization and mathematical problem solving scores: A test of Stafford's *x*-linked hypothesis. *Psychology of Women Quarterly, 3*, 157–167.

Sherrod, D. (1987). The bonds of men: Problems and possibilities in close male relationships. In H. Brod (Ed.), *The making of masculinities: The new men's studies.* Boston, MA: Unwin Hyman.

Shields, S.A. (1975). Functionalism, Darwinism, and the psychology of women: A study in social myth. *American Psychologist, 30*, 739–754.

Shin, K.R. (1994). Psychosocial predictors of depressive symptoms in Korean-American women in New York City. *Women & Health, 21*, 73–82.

Shmurak, C.B. (1993, April). *Career patterns of women graduates of independent schools: A comparison of coeducational and all-girls high schools.* Paper presented at the annual meeting of the American Educational Research Association, Atlanta, GA.

Shotland, R.L. (1989). A model of the causes of date rape in developing and close relationships. In C. Hendrick (Ed.), *Close relationships* (pp. 247–270). Newbury Park, CA: Sage.

Shotland, R.L., & Craig, J.M. (1988). Can men and women differentiate between friendly and sexually interested behavior? *Social Psychology Quarterly, 51*, 66–73.

Shumaker, S.A., & Hill, D.R. (1991). Gender differences in social support and physical health. *Health Psychology, 10*, 102–111.

Shumaker, S.A., & Smith, T.R. (1995). Women and coronary heart disease: A psychological perspective. In A.L. Stanton & S.J. Gallant (Eds.), *The psychology of women's health: Progress and challenges in research and application* (pp. 25–49). Washington, DC: American Psychological Association.

Shye, D., Mullooly, J.P., Freeborn, D.K., & Pope, C.R. (1995). Gender differences in the relationship between social network support and mortality: A longitudinal study of an elderly cohort. *Social Science and Medicine, 41*, 935–947.

Siegel, J.M., Sorenson, S.B., Golding, J.M., Burnam, M.A., & Stein, J.A. (1989). Resistance of sexual assault: Who resists and what happens? *American Journal of Public Health, 79*, 27–31.

Siegel, R.J. (1993). Between midlife and old age: Never too old to learn. *Women & Therapy, 14*, 173–185.

Siegel, R.J., Choldin, S., & Orost, J.H. (1995). The impact of three patriarchal religions on women. In J.C. Chrisler & A.H. Hemstreet (Eds.), *Variations on a theme: Diversity and the psychology of women* (pp. 107–144). Albany, NY: SUNY Press.

Siever, M.D. (1994). Sexual orientation and gender as factors in socioculturally acquired vulnerability to body dissatisfaction and eating disorders. *Journal of Consulting and Clinical Psychology, 62*, 252–260.

Signorielli, N. (1989). Television and conceptions about sex roles: Maintaining conventionality and the status quo. *Sex Roles, 21*, 341–360.

Signorielli, N., & Lears, M. (1992). Children, television, and conceptions about chores: Attitudes and behaviors. *Sex Roles, 27*, 157–170.

Silver, H. (1993). Homework and domestic work. *Sociological Forum, 8*, 181–204.

Silverstein, L.B. (1991). Transforming the debate about child care and maternal employment. *American Psychologist, 46*, 1025–1032.

Silverstein, M., & Waite, L.J. (1993). Are Blacks more likely than whites to receive and provide social support in middle and old age? Yes, no, and maybe so. *Journals of Gerontology, 48*, S212–S222.

Simon, R.W. (1995). Gender, multiple roles, role meaning, and mental health. *Journal of Health and Social Behavior, 36*, 182–194.

Simoni, J. (1996). Confronting heterosexism in the teaching of psychology. *Teaching of Psychology, 23*(4), 220–226.

Singer, J.D. (1993). Once is not enough: Former special educators who return to teaching. *Exceptional Children, 60*, 58–72.

Singh, D. (1994). Body fat distribution and perception of desirable female body shape by young Black men and women. *International Journal of Eating Disorders, 16*, 289–294.

Skedsvold, P.R., & Mann, T.L. (Eds.). (1996). Linking research, policy and implementation in affirmative action programs. *Journal of Social Issues, 52*(4).

Skinner, B.F. (1948). *Walden Two.* New York: Macmillan.

Sklover, B. (1997). Women and sports: The 25th anniversary of Title IX. *AAUW Outlook, 90*, 12–17.

Skrypnek, B.J., & Snyder, M. (1982). On the self-perpetuating nature of stereotypes about women and men. *Journal of Experimental Social Psychology, 18*, 277–291.

Slaby, R.G., & Frey, K.S. (1975). Development of gender constancy and selective attention to same-sex models. *Child Development, 46*, 849–856.

Smith, A. (1992, December 13). Toy catalog teaches kids outdated lessons in gender behavior. *The Milwaukee Journal*, G2.

Smith, D. (1987). *The everyday world as problematic.* Boston, MA: Northeastern University Press.

Smith, E.M., North, C.S., & Spitznagel, E.L. (1993). Alcohol, drugs, and psychiatric comorbidity among homeless women: An epidemiologic study. *Journal of Clinical Psychiatry, 54*, 82–87.

Smith, J.E., Waldorf, V.A., & Trembath, D.L. (1990). "Single White male looking for thin, very attractive..." *Sex Roles, 23*, 675–685.

Smith, W., & Erb, T.O. (1986). Effect of women science career role models on early adolescents' attitudes toward scientists and women in science. *Journal of Research in Science Teaching, 23*, 664–676.

Snodgrass, S.E. (1985). Women's intuition: The effects of subordinate role on interpersonal sensitivity. *Journal of Personality and Social Psychology, 49*, 146–155.

Snodgrass, S.E. (1992). Further effects of role versus gender on interpersonal sensitivity. *Journal of Personality and Social Psychology, 62*, 154–158.

Snyder, R., & Hasbrouck, L. (1996). Feminist identity, gender traits, and symptoms of disturbed eating among college women. *Psychology of Women Quarterly, 20*, 593–598.

Sobol, M.P., & Daly, K.J. (1992). The adoption alternative for pregnant adolescents: Decision making, consequences, and policy implications. *Journal of Social Issues, 48*(3), 143–161.

Sokoloff, N.J. (1988). Evaluating gains and losses by Black and white women and men in the professions, 1960–1980. *Social Problems, 35*, 36–53.

Somervell, P.D., Leaf, P.J., Weissman, M.M., Blazer, D.G., & Bruce, M.L. (1989). The prevalence of major depression in Black and White adults in 5 United States Communities. *American Journal of Epidemiology, 130*, 725–735.

Sommers-Flanagan, R., Sommers-Flanagan, J., & Davis, B. (1993). What's happening on music television? A gender role content analysis. *Sex Roles, 28*, 745–753.

Sonnert, G., & Holton, G. (1996). Career patterns of women and men in the sciences. *American Scientist, 84*, 63–71.

Sorenson, S.B., & Siegel, J.M. (1992). Gender, ethnicity, and sexual assault: Findings from a Los Angeles study. *Journal of Social Issues, 48*(1), 93–104.

Sorenson, S.B., & Telles, C.A. (1991). Self-reports of spousal violence in a Mexican-American and non-Hispanic white population. *Violence and Victims, 6*, 3–15.

Sorenson, S.B., & White, J.W. (1992). Adult sexual assault: Overview of research. *Journal of Social Issues, 48*(1), 1–8.

Sparks, E.E. (1996). Overcoming stereotypes of mothers in the African American context. In K.F. Wyche & F.J. Crosby (Eds.), *Women's ethnicities: Journeys through psychology* (pp. 67–86). Boulder, CO: Westview.

Spelman, E. (1988). *The inessential woman: Problems of exclusion in feminist thought.* Boston, MA: Beacon.

Spence, J.T., & Hahn, E.D. (1997). The Attitudes toward Women Scale and attitude change in college students. *Psychology of Women Quarterly, 21*, 17–34.

Spence, J.T., & Helmreich, R. (1978). *Masculinity and femininity: Their psychological dimensions, correlates, and antecedents.* Austin, TX: University of Texas Press.

Spence, J.T., & Helmreich, R.L. (1972). The Attitudes Toward Women Scale: An objective instrument to measure attitudes toward the rights and roles of women in contemporary society. *Catalog of Selected Documents in Psychology, 2*, 66. (Ms No. 153).

Spence, J.T., & Helmreich, R.L. (1980). Masculine instrumentality and feminine expressiveness: Their relationships with sex-role attitudes and behaviors. *Psychology of Women Quarterly, 5*, 147–163.

Spender, D. (1984). In R. Rowland (Ed.), *Women who do and women who don't join the women's movement.* London: Routledge & Kegan Paul.

Spigelman, M., & Schultz, K. (1981, June). *Attitudes toward obesity.* Paper presented at the annual convention of the Canadian Psychological Association, Toronto.

Spitzack, C. (1990). *Confessing excess: Women and the politics of body reduction.* Albany, NY: State University of New York Press.

Sprecher, S., & Duck, S. (1994). Sweet talk: The importance of perceived communication for romantic and friendship attraction experienced during a get-acquainted date. *Personality and Social Psychology Bulletin, 20*, 391–400.

Sprock, J., & Yoder, C.Y. (1997). Women and depression: An update on the report of the APA Task Force. *Sex Roles, 36*, 269–303.

Squire, C. (1994). Empowering women? The *Oprah Winfrey Show. Feminism & Psychology, 4*, 63–79.

Stack, C. (1986). The culture of gender: Women and men of color. *Signs, 11*, 321–324.

Stack, C., & Burton, L.M. (1993). Kinscripts. *Journal of Comparative Family Studies, 24*, 157–170.

Stahly, G.B., & Lie, G. (1995). Women and violence: A comparison of lesbian and heterosexual battering relationships. In J.C. Chrisler & A.H. Hemstreet (Eds.), *Variations on a theme: Diversity and the psychology of women* (pp. 51–78). Albany, NY: State University of New York Press.

Staines, G., Tavris, C., & Jayaratne, T.E. (1974, January). The queen bee syndrome. *Psychology Today*, pp. 55–58, 60.

Stake, J.E., & Gerner, M.A. (1987). The women's studies experience: Personal and professional gains for women and men. *Psychology of Women Quarterly, 11*, 277–283.

Stake, J.E., Roades, L., Rose, S., Ellis, L., & West, C. (1994). The women's studies experience: Impetus for feminist activism. *Psychology of Women Quarterly, 18*, 17–24.

Stake, J.E., & Rose, S. (1994). The long-term impact of women's studies on students' personal lives and political activism. *Psychology of Women Quarterly, 18,* 403–412.

Standing, T.S., & Glazer, G. (1992). Attitudes of low-income clinic patients toward menopause. *Health Care for Women International, 13,* 271–280.

Stanko, E. (1985). *Intimate intrusions.* London: Routledge & Kegan Paul.

Stanton, A.L. (1995). Psychology of women's health: Barriers and pathways to knowledge. In A.L. Stanton & S.J. Gallant (Eds.), *The psychology of women's health: Progress and challenges in research and application* (pp. 3–21). Washington, DC: American Psychological Association.

Stanton, A.L., & Danoff-Burg, S. (1995). Selected issues in women's reproductive health: Psychological perspectives. In A.L. Stanton & S.J. Gallant (Eds.), *The psychology of women's health: Progress and challenges in research and application* (pp. 261–305). Washington, DC: American Psychological Association.

Stanton, A.L., & Gallant, S.J. (Eds.). (1995). *The psychology of women's health: Progress and challenges in research and application.* Washington, DC: American Psychological Association.

Stark, E. (1990). Rethinking homicide: Violence, race and the politics of gender. *International Journal of Health Services, 20,* 3–27.

Stark, E., & Flitcraft, A. (1988). Violence among intimates: An epidemiological review. In V.B. Van Hasselt, R.L. Morrison, A.S. Bellack, & M. Hersen (Eds.), *Handbook of family violence* (pp. 293–317). New York: Plenum.

Stark, E., & Flitcraft, A. (1996). *Women at risk: Domestic violence and women's health.* Thousand Oaks, CA: Sage.

Starrels, M.E. (1994). Husbands' involvement in female gender-typed household chores. *Sex Roles, 31,* 473–491.

Stato, J. (1993). Montreal gynocide. In P.B. Bart & E.G. Moran (Eds.), *Violence against women: The bloody footprints* (pp. 132–133). Newbury Park, CA: Sage.

Steele, C. (1996, August). *A Burden of Suspicion: The Role of Stereotypes in Shaping Intellectual Identity.* Master lecture presented at the meeting of the American Psychological Association, Toronto, Canada.

Steele, J., & Barling, J. (1996). Influence of maternal gender-role beliefs and role satisfaction on daughters' vocational interests. *Sex Roles, 34,* 637–648.

Steiger, T., & Reskin, B.F. (1990). Baking and baking off: Deskilling and changing sex make-up of bakers. In B.F. Reskin & P.A. Roos, *Job queues, gender queues: Explaining women's inroads into male occupations* (pp. 257–274). Philadelphia, PA: Temple.

Steil, J.M., & Weltman, K. (1991). Marital inequality: The importance of resources, personal attributes, and social norms on career valuing and the allocation of domestic responsibilities. *Sex Roles, 24,* 161–179.

Steinberg, R. (1987). Radical challenges in a liberal world: The mixed success of comparable worth. *Gender & Society, 1,* 466–475.

Steinem, G. (1978, October). If men could menstruate—. *Ms, 7,* 110.

Steinem, G. (1983). Far from the opposite shore. In *Outrageous acts and everyday rebellions* (pp. 341–362). New York: Holt.

Steinem, G. (1994, March/April). Womb envy, testyria, and breast castration anxiety. *Ms,* pp. 48–56.

Steinke, J., & Long, M. (1995, May). *A lab or her own? Portrayals of female characters on children's educational science programs.* Paper presented at the annual meeting of the International Communication Association, Albuquerque, NM.

Steinmetz, H., et al. (1995). Corpus callosum and brain volume in women and men. *Neuroreport: An International Journal for the Rapid Communication of Research in Neuroscience, 6,* 1002–1004.

Stericker, A. (1981). Does this "he or she" business really make a difference? The effect of masculine pronouns as generics on job attitudes. *Sex Roles, 7,* 637–641.

Stern, M., & Karraker, K.H. (1989). Sex stereotyping of infants: A review of gender labeling studies. *Sex Roles, 20,* 501–522.

Stevens, J., Sumanyika, S.K., & Keil, J.E. (1994). Attitudes toward body size and dieting: Differences between elderly Black and White women. *American Journal of Public Health, 84,* 1322–1325.

Stewart, A.J., & Healy, J.M. (1989). Linking individual development and social changes. *American Psychologist, 44,* 30–42.

Stewart, A.J., & Malley, J.E. (1987). Role combination in women: Mitigating agency and communion. In F.J. Crosby (Ed.), *Spouse, parent, worker: On gender and multiple roles* (pp. 42–62). New Haven, CT: Yale.

Stice, E., Schupak-Neuberg, E., Shaw, H.E., & Stein, R.I. (1994). Relation of media exposure to eating disorder symptomology: An examination of mediating mechanisms. *Journal of Abnormal Psychology, 103,* 836–840.

Stimpson, C.R. (1987, July-August). The "F" word. *Ms, 16,* p. 80.

Stoddart, T., & Turiel, E. (1985). Children's concepts of cross-gender activities. *Child Development, 56,* 1241–1252.

Stohs, J.H. (1995). Predictors of conflict over the household division of labor among women employed full-time. *Sex Roles, 33,* 257–275.

Stoller, E. P. (1994). Teaching about gender: The experiences of family care of frail elderly relatives. *Educational Gerontology, 20,* 679–697.

Stone, S.D. (1993). Getting the message out: Feminists, the press and violence against women. *Canadian Review of Sociology and Anthropology, 30,* 377–400.

Stone, S.D. (1995). The myth of bodily perfection. *Disability and Society, 10,* 413–424.

Stoneman, Z., Brody, G.H., & MacKinnon, C.E. (1986). Same-sex and cross-sex siblings: Activity choices, role behavior, and gender stereotypes. *Sex Roles, 15,* 495–511.

Strauch, B. (1997, Aug. 10). Drug companies seeking approval of anti-depressants for children. *Milwaukee Journal Sentinel,* p. 9A.

Straus, M.A. (1997). Physical assaults by women partners: A major social problem. In M.R. Walsh (Ed.), *Women, men, and gender: Ongoing debates* (pp. 210–221). New Haven, CT: Yale.

Straus, M.A., & Gelles, R.J. (1990). *Physical violence in American families: Risk factors and adaptation to violence in 8,145 families.* New Brunswick, NJ: Transaction.

Straus, M.A., Gelles, R.J., & Steinmetz, S. (1980). *Behind closed doors: Violence in the American family.* Garden City, NY: Anchor Press.

Street, S., Kimmel, E.B., & Kromrey, J.D. (1995). Revisiting university student gender role perceptions. *Sex Roles, 33,* 183–201.

Stricker, L.J., Rock, D.A., & Burton, N.W. (1993). Sex differences in predictions of college grades from Scholastic Aptitude scores. *Journal of Educational Psychology, 85,* 710–718.

Strickland, B.R. (1988). Sex-related differences in health and illness. *Psychology of Women Quarterly, 12,* 381–399.

Striegel-Moore, R.H., Tucker, N., & Hsu, J. (1990). Body image dissatisfaction and disordered eating in lesbian college students. *International Journal of Eating Disorders, 9,* 493–500.

Stroeher, S.K. (1994). Sixteen kindergartners' gender-related views of careers. *Elementary School Journal, 95,* 95–103.

Stroh, L.K., Brett, J.M., & Reilly, A.H. (1992). All the right stuff: A comparison of female and male managers' career progression. *Journal of Applied Psychology, 77,* 251–260.

Stroh, L.K., Brett, J.M., & Reilly, A.H. (1996). Family structure, glass ceiling, and traditional explanations for the differential rate of turnover of female and male managers. *Journal of Vocational Behavior, 49,* 99–118.

Strube, M.J. (1988). The decision to leave an abusive relationship: Empirical evidence and theoretical issues. *Psychological Bulletin, 104*, 236–250.

Strube, M.J., & Barbour, L.S. (1984). Factors related to the decision to leave an abusive relationship. *Journal of Marriage and the Family, 46*, 837–844.

Struthers, N.J. (1995). Differences in mentoring: A function of gender or organizational rank? *Journal of Social Behavior and Personality, 10*, 265–272.

Stunkard, A.J., Sorenson, T., & Schlusiner, F. (1980). Use of the Danish adoption register for the study of obesity and thinness. In S. Kety, L.P. Rowland, R.L. Sidman, & S.W. Matthysse (Eds.), *The genetics of neurological and psychiatric disorders*. New York: Raven Press.

Sturdivant, S. (1980). *Therapy with women: A feminist philosophy of treatment*. New York: Springer.

Sugarman, D.B., & Hotaling, G.T. (1989). Dating violence: Prevalence, context, and risk markers. In M.A. Pirog-Good & J.E. Stets (Eds.), *Violence in dating relationships* (pp. 2–31). New York: Praeger.

Suitor, J.J., & Reavis, R. (1995). Football, fast cars, and cheerleading: Adolescent gender norms, 1978–1989. *Adolescence, 30*, 265–272.

Sullivan, E.G. (1996). Lupus: The silent killer. In C.F. Collins (Ed.), *African-American women's health and social issues* (pp. 25–35). Westport, CT: Auburn House.

Surra, C.A., & Longstreth, M. (1990). Similarity of outcomes, interdependence, and conflict in dating relationships. *Journal of Personality and Social Psychology, 59*, 501–516.

Sussman, L.K., Robins L.N., & Earls, F. (1987). Treatment-seeking for depression by Black and White Americans. *Social Science Medicine, 24*, 187–196.

Sutton, R.E. (1991). Equity and computers in the schools: A decade of research. *Review of Educational Research, 61*, 475–503.

Swacker, M. (1975). The sex of the speaker as a sociolinguistic variable. In B. Thorne & N. Henley (Eds.), *Language and sex: Difference and dominance*. Rowley, MA: Newbury House.

Swan, K. (1995, April). *Saturday morning cartoons and children's perceptions of social reality*. Paper presented at the annual meeting of the American Educational Research Association, San Francisco, CA.

Swett, C., Cohen, C., Surrey, J., Compaine, A., et al. (1991). High rates of alcohol use and history of physical and sexual abuse among women outpatients. *American Journal of Drug and Alcohol Abuse, 17*, 49–60.

Swim, J.K. (1994). Perceived versus meta-analytic effect sizes: An assessment of the accuracy of gender stereotypes. *Journal of Personality and Social Psychology, 66*, 21–36.

Swim, J.K., Aikin, K.J., Hall, W.S., & Hunter, B.A. (1995). Sexism and racism: Old-fashioned and modern prejudices. *Journal of Personality and Social Psychology, 68*, 199–214.

Swim, J.K., Borgida, E., Maruyama, G., & Myers, D.G. (1989). Joan McKay versus John McKay: Do gender stereotypes bias evaluations? *Psychological Bulletin, 105*, 409–429.

Swim, J.K., & Sanna, L.J. (1996). He's skilled, she's lucky: A meta-analysis of observed attributions for women's and men's successes and failures. *Personality and Social Psychology Bulletin, 22*, 507–519.

Symons, D. (1979). *The evolution of human sexuality*. New York: Oxford.

Talaga, J.A., & Beehr, T.A. (1995). Are there gender differences in predicting retirement decisions? *Journal of Applied Psychology, 80*, 16–28.

Tangri, S.S., & Jenkins, S.R. (1997). Why expecting conflict is good. *Sex Roles, 36*, 725–746.

Tannen, D. (1990). *You just don't understand: Women and men in conversations*. New York: Ballantine.

Tavris, C. (1992). *The mismeasure of woman*. New York: Simon & Schuster.

Taylor, C.R., Lee, J.Y., & Stern, B.B. (1995). Portrayals of African, Hispanic, and Asian Americans in magazine advertising. *American Behavioral Scientist, 38*, 608–621.

Taylor, J., Henderson, D., & Jackson, B.B. (1991). A holistic model for understanding and predicting depressive symptoms in African-American women. *Journal of Community Psychology, 19,* 306–320.

Taylor, J.M., Gilligan, C., & Sullivan, A.M. (1995). *Between voice and silence: Women and girls, race and relationship.* Cambridge, MA: Harvard.

Taylor, S.E., & Fiske, S.T. (1975). Point of view and perceptions of causality. *Journal of Personality and Social Psychology, 32,* 439–445.

Taylor, V., & Whittier, N. (1993). The new feminist movement. In L. Richardson & V. Taylor (Eds.), *Feminist Frontiers III* (pp. 533–548). New York: McGraw-Hill.

Teets, J.M. (1995). Childhood sexual trauma of chemically dependent women. *Journal of Psychoactive Drugs, 27,* 231–238.

Teicher, M.H., Glod, C.A., Surrey, J., & Swett, C. (1993). Early childhood abuse and limbic system ratings in adult psychiatric outpatients. *Journal of Neuropsychiatry and Clinical Neurosciences, 5,* 301–306.

Tenbrunsel, A.E., Brett, J.M., Maoz, E., Stroh, L.K. et al. (1995). Dynamic and static work-family relationships. *Organizational Behavior and Human Decision Processes, 63,* 233–246.

Tesch, B.J., Osborne, J., Simpson, D.E., Murray, S.F., et al. (1992). Women physicians in dual-physician relationships compared with those in other dual-career relationships. *Academic Medicine, 67,* 542–544.

Tetenbaum, T.J., & Pearson, J. (1989). The voices in children's literature: The impact of gender on the moral decisions of storybook characters. *Sex Roles, 20,* 381–395.

Tetlock, P. (1992). The impact of accountability on judgment and choice: Toward a social contingency model. In M.P. Zanna (Ed.), *Advances in Experimental Social Psychology* (Vol. 25, pp. 331–376). New York: Academic Press.

Thomas, C. (1985). The age of androgyny: The new views of psychotherapists. *Sex Roles, 13,* 381–392.

Thomas, J.R., & French, K.E. (1985). Gender differences across age in motor performance: A meta-analysis. *Psychological Bulletin, 98,* 260–282.

Thomas, S. (1995). Planning the prevention of alcohol and other drug-related problems among women. *Drug and Alcohol Review, 14,* 7–15.

Thomas, V. (1994). Using feminist and social structural analysis to focus on the health of poor women. *Women & Health, 22,* 1–15.

Thompson, B.W. (1992). "A way outa no way": Eating problems among African-American, Latina, and White women. *Gender & Society, 6,* 546–561.

Thompson, C. (1964). *On women.* New York: New American Library.

Thompson, M.P., & Norris, F.H. (1992). Crime, social status, and alienation. *American Journal of Community Psychology, 1,* 97–119.

Thompson, S.H., Sargent, R.G., & Kemper, K.A. (1996). Black and white adolescent males' perceptions of ideal body size. *Sex Roles, 34,* 391–406.

Thompson, T.L., & Zerbinos, E. (1995). Gender roles in animated cartoons: Has the picture changed in 20 years? *Sex Roles, 32,* 651–673.

Thompson, T.L., & Zerbinos, E. (1997). Television cartoons: Do children notice it's a boy's world? *Sex Roles, 37,* 415–432.

Thomson, R., & Holland, J. (1994). Young women and safer (hetero)sex: Context, constraints and strategies. In S. Wilkinson & C. Kitzinger (Eds.), *Women and health: Feminist perspectives* (pp. 13–32). London: Taylor & Francis.

Thorne, Y.M. (1995). Achievement motivation in high achieving Latina women. *Roeper Review, 18,* 44–49.

Thornton, B., & Maurice, J. (1997). Physique contrast effect: Adverse impact of idealized body images for women. *Sex Roles, 37,* 433–439.

Thurer, S.L. (1994). *The myths of motherhood: How culture reinvents the good mother.* Boston: Houghton Mifflin.

Tiedje, L.B., & Darling-Fisher, C.S. (1993). Factors that influence fathers' participation in child care. *Health Care for Women International, 14*, 99–107.

Tiefer, L. (1991a). Historical, scientific, clinical and feminist criticisms of "the human sexual response cycle" model. *Annual Review of Sex Research, 2*, 1–23.

Tiefer, L. (1991b). A brief history of the Association for Women in Psychology: 1969–1991. *Psychology of Women Quarterly, 15*, 635–649.

Tiefer, L. (1994). *Sex is not a natural act and other essays.* Boulder, CO: Westview.

Tijerina-Jim, A. (1993). Three Native American women speak about the significance of ceremony. *Women & Therapy, 14*, 33–39.

Tognoli, J., Pullen, J., & Lieber, J. (1994). The privilege of place: Domestic and work locations of characters in children's books. *Children's Environments, 11*, 272–280.

Tom-Orme, L. (1995). Native American women's health concerns: Toward restoration of harmony. In D.L. Adams (Ed.), *Health issues for women of color: A cultural diversity perspective* (pp. 27–41). Thousand Oaks, CA: Sage.

Tomkiewicz, J., & Adeyemi-Bello, T. (1995). A cross-sectional analysis of the attitudes of Nigerians and Americans toward women as managers. *Journal of Social Behavior and Personality, 10*, 189–198.

Toneatto, A., Sobell, L.C., & Sobell, M.B. (1992). Gender issues in the treatment of abusers of alcohol, nicotine, and other drugs. *Journal of Substance Abuse, 4*, 209–218.

Top, T.J. (1991). Sex bias in the evaluation of performance in the scientific, artistic, and literary professions: A review. *Sex Roles, 24*, 73–106.

Towson, S.M.J., Zanna, M.P., & MacDonald, G. (1989). Self-fulfilling prophecies: Sex role stereotypes as expectations for behavior. In R.K. Unger (Ed.), *Representations: Social constructions of gender* (pp. 97–107). Amityville, NY: Baywood.

Traustadottir, R. (1991). Mothers who care: Gender, disability, and family life. *Journal of Family Issues, 12*, 211–228.

Travis, C.B. (1988a). *Women and health psychology: Biomedical issues.* Hillsdale, NJ: Lawrence Erlbaum.

Travis, C.B. (1988b). *Women and health psychology: Mental health issues.* Hillsdale, NJ: Lawrence Erlbaum.

Travis, C.B. (1993). Women and health. In F.L. Denmark & M.A. Paludi (Eds.), *Psychology of women: A Handbook of issues and theories* (pp. 283–323). Westport, CT: Greenwood Press.

Travis, C.B., Gressley, D.L., & Adams, P.L. (1995). Health care policy and practice for women's health. In A.L. Stanton & S.J. Gallant (Eds.), *The psychology of women's health: Progress and challenges in research and application* (pp. 531–565). Washington, DC: American Psychological Association.

Trepagnier, B. (1994). The politics of White and Black bodies. *Feminism & Psychology, 4*, 199–205.

Trepanier, M.L., & Romatowski, J.A. (1985). Attributes and roles assigned to characters in children's writing: Sex differences and sex-role perceptions. *Sex Roles, 13*, 263–272.

Truman, D.M., Tokar, D.M., & Fischer, A.R. (1996). Dimensions of masculinity: Relations to date rape supportive attitudes and sexual aggression in dating situations. *Journal of Counseling and Development, 74*, 555–562.

Tuck, B., Rolfe, J., & Adair, V. (1994). Adolescents' attitude toward gender roles within work and its relationship to gender, personality type, and parental occupation. *Sex Roles, 31*, 547–558.

Tulloch, M.I., & Tulloch, J.C. (1992). Attitudes to domestic violence: School students' responses to a television drama. *Australian Journal of Marriage and Family, 13*, 62–69.

Turgeon, M. (1993). *Right brain-left brain reflexology: A self-help approach to balancing life energies with color, sound, and pressure-point techniques.* Rochester, VT: Inner Traditions.

Turner, B.F., & Turner, C.B. (1991). Bem Sex-Role Inventory stereotypes for men and women varying in age and race among National Register psychologists. *Psychological Reports, 69,* 931–944.

Turner, H.A. (1994). Gender and social support: Taking the bad with the good? *Sex Roles, 30,* 521–541.

Turner, P.J., & Gervai, J. (1995). A multidimensional study of gender typing in preschool children and their parents: Personality, attitudes, preferences, behavior, and cultural differences. *Developmental Psychology, 31,* 759–779.

Turner, P.J., Gervai, J., & Hinde, R.A. (1993). Gender-typing in young children: Preferences, behaviour and cultural differences. *British Journal of Developmental Psychology, 11,* 323–342.

Turner-Bowker, D.M. (1996). Gender stereotyped descriptors in children's picture books: Does "Curious Jane" exist in the literature? *Sex Roles, 35,* 461–488.

U.S. Bureau of the Census. (1995, September). *Statistical abstracts of the United States: 1995* (115th ed.). Washington, DC.

U.S. Department of Education, National Center for Education Statistics. (1996). *Digest of Educational Statistics 1996,* NCES 96–133. Washington, DC: U.S. Government Printing Office.

U.S. Department of Labor. (1991). *A report on the glass ceiling initiative* (#91-656-P). Washington, DC: Government Printing Office.

U.S. Department of Labor. (1995, May). *Twenty facts on women workers.* Washington, DC: Women's Bureau of the Department of Labor.

U.S. Merit Systems Protection Board. (1981). *Sexual harassment of federal workers: Is it a problem?* Washington, DC: U.S. Government Printing Office.

U.S. Merit Systems Protection Board. (1987). *Sexual harassment of federal workers: An update.* Washington, DC: U.S. Government Printing Office.

Udry, J.R. (1988). Biological predispositions and social control in adolescent sexual behavior. *American Sociological Review, 53,* 709–722.

Ullman, L.P., Freedland, K.E., and Warmsun, C.H. (1978). Sex and ethnic group effects on attitudes toward women. *Bulletin of the Psychonomic Society, 11,* 179–180.

Ullman, S.E. (1996). Social reactions, coping strategies, and self-blame attributions in adjustment to sexual assault. *Psychology of Women Quarterly, 20,* 505–526.

Ullman, S.E., & Knight, R.A. (1991). A multivariate model for predicting rape and physical injury outcomes during sexual assaults. *Journal of Consulting and Clinical Psychology, 59,* 724–731.

Ullman, S.E., & Knight, R.A. (1993). The efficacy of women's resistance strategies in rape situations. *Psychology of Women Quarterly, 17,* 23–38.

Unger, R.K. (1979). Toward a redefinition of sex and gender. *American Psychologist, 34,* 1085–1094.

Unger, R.K. (1982). Advocacy versus scholarship revisited: Issues in the psychology of women. *Psychology of Women Quarterly, 7,* 5–17.

Unger, R.K. (1983). Through the looking glass: No wonderland yet! (The reciprocal relationship between methodology and models of reality). *Psychology of Women Quarterly, 8,* 9–32.

Unger, R.K. (1986). Looking toward the future by looking at the past: Social activism and social history. *Journal of Social Issues, 42*(1), 215–227.

Unger, R.K. (1988). Psychological, feminist, and personal epistemology. In M.M. Gergen (Ed.), *Feminist thought and the structure of knowledge* (pp. 124–141). New York: New York University Press.

Unger, R.K., & Crawford, M. (1993). Commentary: Sex and gender—The troubled relationship between terms and concepts. *Psychological Science, 4,* 122–124.

United Nations. (1991). *The world's women: Trends and statistics, 1970–1990.* New York: United Nations Publications.

United Nations. (1995). *The world's women 1995: Trends and statistics.* New York: United Nations Publications.

Unknown. (1997). "The rape" of Mr. Smith. In M. Crawford & R. Unger (Eds.), *In our own words: Readings on the psychology of women and gender* (pp. 129–130). New York: McGraw-Hill.

Useem, M. (1976). Government influence on the social science paradigm. *The Sociological Quarterly, 17,* 146–161.

Ussher, J. (1990). Choosing psychology or not throwing the baby out with the bathwater. In E. Burman (Ed.), *Feminists and psychological practice* (pp. 47–61). Newbury Park, CA: Sage.

Uttal, L. (1996). Custodial care, surrogate care, and coordinated care: Employed mothers and the meaning of child care. *Gender & Society, 10,* 291–311.

Vandell, K., & Dempsey, S.B. (1991). *Stalled agenda: Gender equity and the training of educators.* Washington, DC: American Association of University Women.

Vandereycken, W. (1993). The sociocultural roots of the fight against fatness: Implications for eating disorders and obesity. *Eating Disorders: The Journal of Treatment and Prevention, 1,* 7–16.

Vanderkolk, B.S., & Young, A.A. (1991). *The work and family revolution: How companies can keep employees happy and business profitable.* New York: Facts on File.

Vandewater, E.A., Ostrove, J.M., & Stewart, A.J. (1997). Predicting women's well-being in midlife: The importance of personality development and social role involvements. *Journal of Personality and Social Psychology, 72,* 1147–1160.

Vasquez, M.J.T. (1994). Latinas. In L. Comas-Díaz & B. Greene (Eds.), *Women of color: Integrating ethnic and gender identities in psychotherapy* (pp. 114–138). New York: Guilford.

Vasta, R., Knott, J.A., & Gaze, C.E. (1996). Can spatial training erase the gender differences on the water-level task? *Psychology of Women Quarterly, 20,* 549–568.

Vazquez-Nuttall, E., Romero-Garcia, I., & De Leon, B. (1987). Sex roles and perceptions of femininity and masculinity of Hispanic women. *Psychology of Women Quarterly, 11,* 409–425.

Vega, W.A. (1990). Hispanic families in the 1980s: A decade of research. *Journal of Marriage and the Family, 52,* 1015–1024.

Vernon, J.A., Williams, J.A., Jr., Phillips, T., & Wilson, J. (1991). Media stereotyping: A comparison of the way elderly women and men are portrayed on prime-time television. *Journal of Women & Aging, 2,* 55–68.

Villimez, C., Eisenberg, N., & Carroll, J.L. (1986). Sex differences in the relation of children's height and weight to academic performance and others' attributions of competence. *Sex Roles, 15,* 667–681.

von Schulthess, B. (1992). Violence in the streets: Anti-lesbian assault and harassment in San Francisco. In G.M. Herek & K.T. Berrill (Eds.), *Hate crimes: Confronting violence against lesbian and gay men* (pp. 65–75). Newbury Park, CA: Sage.

Waelde, L.C., Silvern, L., & Hodges, W.F. (1994). Stressful life events: Moderators of the relationships of gender and gender roles to self-reported depression and suicidality among college students. *Sex Roles, 30,* 1–22.

Wagner, H.L., & Smith, J. (1991). Facial expression in the presence of friends and strangers. *Journal of Nonverbal Behavior, 15,* 201–214.

Wagner, R. (1987). Changes in the friend network during the first year of single parenthood for Mexican American and Anglo women. *Journal of Divorce, 11,* 89–109.

Waldron, I., & Jacobs, J.A. (1989). Effects of multiple roles on women's health: Evidence from a national longitudinal study. *Women and Health, 15,* 3–19.

Walker, K. (1994). Men, women, and friendship: What they say, what they do. *Gender & Society, 8,* 246–265.

Walker, K. (1995). "Always there for me": Friendship patterns and expectations among middle- and working-class men and women. *Sociological Forum, 10,* 273–296.

Walker, L.E.A. (1979). *The battered woman.* New York: Harper & Row.

Walker, L.E.A. (1984). The battered woman syndrome. New York: Springer.

Walker, L.E.A. (1986, August). *Diagnosis and politics: Abuse disorders.* Paper presented at the meeting of the American Psychological Association, Washington, DC.

Walker, L.E.A. (1989a). *Terrifying love: Why battered women kill and how society responds.* New York: Harper.

Walker, L.E.A. (1989b). Psychology and violence against women. *American Psychologist, 44,* 695–708.

Walker, L.E.A. (1994). *Abused women and survivor therapy: A practical guide for the psychotherapist.* Washington, DC: American Psychological Association.

Walker, L.E.A. (1995). Racism and violence against women. In J. Adleman & G. Enguídanos (Eds.), *Racism in the lives of women: Testimony, theory, and guides to antiracist practice* (pp. 239–250). New York: Haworth.

Walker, L.J. (1984). Sex differences in the development of moral reasoning: A critical review. *Child Development, 55,* 677–691.

Waller, G., & Ruddock, A. (1995). Information-processing correlates of reported sexual abuse in eating-disordered and comparison women. *Child Abuse and Neglect, 19,* 745–759.

Waller, G., Shaw, J., Hamilton, K., Baldwin, G., et al. (1994). Beauty is in the eye of the beholder: Media influences on the psychopathology of eating problems. *Appetite, 23,* 287.

Wallston, B.S., & Grady, K.E. (1985). Integrating the feminist critique and the crisis in social psychology. In V.E. O'Leary, R.K. Unger, & B.S. Wallston (Eds.), *Women, gender and social psychology* (pp. 7–34). Hillsdale, NJ: Erlbaum.

Wang, G.M. (1995). Health issues for Asian/Pacific Island women: A brief overview. In D.L. Adams (Ed.), *Health issues for women of color: A cultural diversity perspective* (pp. 71–77). Thousand Oaks, CA: Sage.

Ward, C.A. (1995). *Attitudes toward rape: Feminist and social psychological perspectives.* Thousand Oaks, CA: Sage.

Warshaw, C. (1989). Limitations of the medical model in the care of battered women. *Gender & Society, 3,* 506–517.

Warshaw, R. (1994). *I never called it rape.* New York: Harper Perennial.

Weathers, P.L., Thompson, C.E., Robert, S., & Rodriguez, J. (1994). Black college women's career values: A preliminary investigation. *Journal of Multicultural Counseling and Development, 22,* 96–105.

Webb, W. (1992). Treatment issues and cognitive behavior techniques with battered women. *Journal of Family Violence, 7,* 205–217.

Webber, E.M. (1994). Psychological characteristics of binging and nonbinging obese women. *Journal of Psychology, 128,* 339–351.

Wechsler, D. (1981). *WAIS-R Manual: Wechsler Adult Intelligence Scale-Revised.* San Antonio, TX: The Psychological Corporation, Harcourt Brace Jovanovich.

Weeks, M.R., Singer, M., Grier, M., & Schensul, J.J. (1996). Gender relations, sexuality, and AIDS risk among African American and Latina women. In C.F. Sargent & C.B. Brettell (Eds.), *Gender and health: An international perspective* (pp. 338–370). Upper Saddle River, NJ: Prentice Hall.

Weidner, G. (1994). Coronary risk in women. In V.J. Adesso, D.M. Reddy, & R. Fleming (Eds.), *Psychological perspectives on women's health* (pp. 57–81). Washington, DC: Taylor & Francis.

Weiner, E.J., & Stephens, L. (1993). Sexual barrier weight: A new approach. *Eating Disorders: The Journal of Treatment and Prevention, 1,* 241–249.

Weisstein, N. (1971). Psychology constructs the female. In V. Gornick & B.K. Moran (Eds.), *Woman in sexist society* (pp. 133–146). New York: Signet.

Weitz, R., & Gordon, L. (1993). Images of Black women among Anglo college students. *Sex Roles, 28,* 19–34.

Weitzman, L.M. (1994). Multiple-role realism: A theoretical framework for the process of planning to combine career and family roles. *Applied & Preventive Psychology, 3,* 15–25.

Weitzman, N., Birns, B., & Friend, R. (1985). Traditional and nontraditional mothers' communication with their daughters and sons. *Child Development, 56,* 894–898.

Welch, R.L., Huston-Stein, A., Wright, J.C., & Plehal, R. (1979). Subtle sex-role cues in children's commercials. *Journal of Communications, 29,* 202–209.

Weller, A., & Weller, L. (1992). Menstrual synchrony in female couples. *Psychoneuroendocrinology, 17,* 171–177.

Wells, C.G. (1991). *Right-brain sex: How to reach the heights of sensual pleasure by releasing the erotic power of your mind.* New York: Avon.

Werner, P.D., & LaRussa, G.W. (1985). Persistence and change in sex-role stereotypes. *Sex Roles, 12,* 1089–1100.

West, C., & Fenstermaker, S. (1995). Doing difference. *Gender & Society, 9,* 8–37.

West, C., & Zimmerman, D.H. (1987). Doing gender. *Gender & Society, 1,* 125–151.

West, J., Wright, D., & Hausken, E.G. (1995, October). *Child care and early educational program participation of infants, toddlers, and preschoolers* (NCES 95–824). Washington, DC: National Center for Education Statistics.

Westman, M., & Etzion, D. (1990). The career success/personal failure phenomenon as perceived in others: Comparing vignettes of male and female managers. *Journal of Vocational Behavior, 37,* 209–224.

Whitbourne, S.K. (1985). The psychological construction of the life span. In J.E. Birren & K.W. Schaie (Eds.), *Handbook of the psychology of aging* (pp. 594–618). New York: Van Nostrand Reinhold.

Whitbourne, S.K., & Hulicka, I.M. (1990). Ageism in undergraduate psychology texts. *American Psychologist, 45,* 1127–1136.

Whitbourne, S.K., & Powers, C.B. (1994). Older women's constructs of their lives: A quantitative and qualitative exploration. *International Journal of Aging and Human Development, 38,* 293–306.

White, J. (1967, April). Women in the law. *Michigan Law Review, 65,* 1053.

White, J.H. (1992). Women and eating disorders, Part I: Significance and sociocultural risk factors. *Health Care for Women International, 13,* 351–362.

White, J.W., & Kowalski, R.M. (1994). Deconstructing the myth of the nonaggressive woman: A feminist analysis. *Psychology of Women Quarterly, 18,* 487–508.

Whiting, B.B., & Edwards, C.P. (1988). *Children of different worlds: The formation of social behavior.* Cambridge, MA: Harvard University Press.

Widom, C.S. (1989). Does violence beget violence? A critical examination of the literature. *Psychological Bulletin, 106,* 3–28.

Wilke, D. (1994). Women and alcoholism: How a male-as-norm bias affects research, assessment, and treatment. *Health and Social Work, 19,* 29–35.

Wilkie, J.R. (1993). Changes in U.S. men's attitudes toward the family provider role, 1972–1989. *Gender & Society, 7,* 261–279.

Wilkinson, S. (1990). Women organizing within psychology. In E. Burman (Ed.), *Feminists and psychological practice* (pp. 140–151). London: Sage.

Wilkinson, S., & Kitzinger, C. (1994). Towards a feminist approach to breast cancer. In S. Wilkinson & C. Kitzinger (Eds.), *Women and health: Feminist perspectives* (pp. 124–140). London: Taylor & Francis.

Williams, C.L. (1992). The glass escalator: Hidden advantages for men in the "female" professions. *Social Problems, 39,* 253–267.

Williams, J.B.W., & Spitzer, R.L. (1983). The issue of sex bias in DSM-III: A critique of "A woman's view of DSM-III" by Marcie Kaplan. *American Psychologist, 38,* 793–798.

Williams, J.E., & Best, D.L. (1982). *Measuring sex stereotypes: A thirty-nation study.* Beverly Hills: Sage.

Williams, J.E., & Best, D.L. (1990). *Measuring sex stereotypes: A multination study.* Newbury Park, CA: Sage.

Williams, J.H. (1987). *Psychology of women: Behavior in a biosocial context* (3rd ed.). New York: Norton.

Williams, J.K. (1995). Afro-American women living with HIV infection: Special therapeutic interventions for a growing population. *Social Work in Health Care, 21,* 41–53.

Williams, K.J., & Alliger, G.M. (1994). Role stressors, mood spillover, and perceptions of work-family conflict in employed parents. *Academy of Management Journal, 37,* 837–868.

Williams, K.J., Suls, J., Alliger, G.M., Learner, S.M., & Wan, C.K. (1991). Multiple role juggling and daily mood states in working mothers: An experience sampling study. *Journal of Applied Psychology, 76,* 664–674.

Williams, L. (1992, Feb. 6). Women's image in a mirror: Who defines what she sees? *The New York Times,* pp. A1, B7.

Williamson, D.A., Netemeyer, R.G., Jackman, L.P., Anderson, D.A., et al. (1995). Structural equation modeling of risk factors for the development of eating disorder symptoms in female athletes. *International Journal of Eating Disorders, 17,* 387–393.

Willis, F.N., & Carlson, R.A. (1993). Singles ads: Gender, social class, and time. *Sex Roles, 29,* 387–404.

Willis, S.L., & Schaie, K.W. (1988). Gender differences in spatial ability in old age: Longitudinal and intervention findings. *Sex Roles, 18,* 189–204.

Wilmoth, G.H. (1992). Abortion, public health policy, and informed consent legislation. *Journal of Social Issues, 48*(3), 1–17.

Wilsnack, S.C., Klassen, A.D., Schur, B.E., & Wilsnack, R.W. (1991). Predicting onset and chronicity of women's problem drinking: A five-year longitudinal analysis. *American Journal of Public Health, 81,* 305–318.

Wilsnack, S.C., Wilsnack, R.W., & Hiller-Sturmhöfel, S. (1994). How women drink: Epidemiology of women's drinking and problem drinking. *Alcohol Health and Research World, 18,* 173–181.

Wilson, E.O. (1978). *On human nature.* Cambridge, MA: Harvard.

Wine, J. (1985). Models of human functioning: A feminist perspective. *International Journal of Women's Studies, 8,* 183–192.

Wisconsin Coalition Against Sexual Assault. (1989). *Encouraging communities to respond to incest survivors and their needs.* Madison, WI.

Wise, E., & Rafferty, J. (1982). Sex bias and language. *Sex Roles, 8,* 1189–1196.

Wiseman, C.V., Gray, J.J., Mosimann, J.E., & Ahrens, A.H. (1992). Cultural expectations of thinness in women: An update. *International Journal of Eating Disorders, 11,* 85–89.

Witchel, R.I. (1991). College-student survivors of incest and other child sexual abuse. *New Directions for Student Services, 54,* 63–76.

Witkin, H.A., Mednick, S.A., Schulsinger, F., Bakkestrom, E., Christiansen, K.O., Goodenough, D.R., Hirschhorn, K., Lundsteen, C., Owen, D.R., Philip, J., Rubin, D.B., & Stocking, M. (1976). Criminality in XXY and XYY men. *Science, 193,* 547–555.

Wittig, M.A., & Lowe, R.H. (1989). Comparable worth theory and policy. *Journal of Social Issues, 45*(4), 1–21.

Wolf, N. (1991). *The beauty myth: How images of beauty are used against women.* New York: Doubleday.

Women's Programs Office. (1993). *Graduate faculty interested in the psychology of women*. Washington, DC: American Psychological Association.

Women's Programs Office. (1995). *Women in the American Psychological Association: 1995*. Washington, DC: American Psychological Association.

Woo, D. (1995). The gap between striving and achieving: The case of Asian American women. In M.L. Andersen & P.H. Collins (Eds.), *Race, class, and gender: An anthology* (2nd ed.) (pp. 218–227). Belmont, CA: Wadsworth.

Wood, F.B., Flowers, D.L., & Naylor, C.E. (1991). In F.L. Kitterle (Ed.), *Cerebral laterality: Theory and research* (pp. 103–115). Hillsdale, NJ: Lawrence Erlbaum.

Woodhouse, L.D. (1990). An exploratory study of the use of life history methods to determine treatment needs for female substance abusers. *Response to the Victimization of Women and Children, 13*, 12–15.

Woods, N. (1982). Menopausal distress: A model for epidemiologic investigation. In A.M. Voda, M. Dinnerstein, & S.R. O'Donnell (Eds.), *Changing perspectives on menopause* (pp. 220–238). Austin, TX: University of Texas Press.

Woods, N.F. (1995). Women and their health. In C.I. Fogel & N.F. Woods (Eds.), *Women's health care: A comprehensive handbook* (pp. 1–22). Thousand Oaks, CA: Sage.

Woods, N.F., Lentz, M., Mitchell, E., & Oakley, L.D. (1994). Depressed mood and self-esteem in young Asian, Black, and White women in America. *Health Care for Women International, 15*, 243–262.

Wooley, S.C. (1994). Sexual abuse and eating disorders: The concealed debate. In P. Fallon, M.A. Katzman, & S.C. Wooley (Eds.), *Feminist perspectives on eating disorders* (pp. 171–211). New York: Guilford.

Worell, J. (1988). Women's satisfaction in close relationships. *Clinical Psychology Review, 8*, 477–498.

Worell, J. (1996). Feminist identity in a gendered world. In J.C. Chrisler, C. Golden, & P.D. Rozee (Eds.), *Lectures on the psychology of women* (pp. 358–370). New York: McGraw-Hill.

Worell, J., & Remer, P. (1992). *Feminist perspectives in therapy: An empowerment model for women*. New York: Wiley.

Worth, D. (1989). Sexual decision-making and AIDS: Why condom promotion among vulnerable women is likely to fail. *Studies in Family Planning, 20*, 297–307.

Wright, D. (1992). Impediments to safer heterosexual sex: A review of research with young people. *AIDS Care, 4*, 11–23.

Wright, E.O., Shire, K., Hwang, S., Dolan, M., & Baxter, J. (1992). The non-effects of class on the gender division of labor in the home: A comparative study of Sweden and the United States. *Gender & Society, 6*, 252–282.

Wright, P.H. (1982). Men's friendships, women's friendships and the alleged inferiority of the latter. *Sex Roles, 8*, 1–20.

Wright, P.H., & Scanlon, M.B. (1991). Gender role orientations and friendship: Some attenuation, but gender differences abound. *Sex Roles, 24*, 551–566.

Wrong, D.H. (1979). *Power: Its forms, bases and uses*. New York: Harper Colophon Books.

Wyatt, G.E. (1985). The sexual abuse of Afro-American and white American women in childhood. *Child Abuse and Neglect, 9*, 507–519.

Wyatt, G.E. (1989, August). *The terrorism of racism*. Paper presented at the meeting of the American Psychological Association, New Orleans, LA.

Wyatt, G.E. (1992). The sociocultural context of African American and white American women's rape. *Journal of Social Issues, 48*(1), 77–92.

Wyatt, G.E., Guthrie, D., & Notgrass, C.M. (1992). Differential effects of women's child sexual abuse and subsequent sexual revictimization. *Journal of Consulting and Clinical Psychology, 60*, 167–173.

Wyatt, G.E., & Lyons-Rowe, S. (1990). Afro-American women's sexual satisfaction as a dimension of their sex roles. *Sex Roles, 22,* 509–524.

Wyatt, G.E., & Riederle, M.H. (1994). Reconceptualizing issues that affect women's sexual decision-making and sexual functioning. *Psychology of Women Quarterly, 18,* 611–625.

Wyche, K.F. (1993). Psychology and African-American women: Findings from applied research. *Applied and Preventive Psychology, 2,* 115–121.

Ying, Y. (1991). Marital satisfaction among San Francisco Chinese-Americans. *International Journal of Social Psychiatry, 37,* 201–213.

Yllö, K., & Bograd, M. (Eds.). (1988). *Feminist perspectives on wife abuse.* Newbury Park, CA: Sage.

Yoder, J.D. (1989). Women at West Point: Lessons for token women in male-dominated occupations. In J. Freeman (Ed.), *Women: A feminist perspective* (4th ed.). Mountain View, CA: Mayfield.

Yoder, J.D. (1991). Rethinking tokenism: Looking beyond numbers. *Gender & Society, 5,* 178–192.

Yoder, J.D., Adams, J., & Prince, H.T. (1983). The price of a token. *Journal of Political and Military Sociology, 11,* 325–337.

Yoder, J.D., Adams, J., Grove, S., & Priest, R.F. (1985). To teach is to learn: Overcoming tokenism with mentors. *Psychology of Women Quarterly, 9,* 119–131.

Yoder, J.D., & Aniakudo, P. (1997). "Outsider within" the firehouse: Subordination and difference in the social interactions of African American women firefighters. *Gender & Society, 11,* 324–341.

Yoder, J.D., & Kahn, A.S. (1992). Toward a feminist understanding of women and power. *Psychology of Women Quarterly, 16,* 381–388.

Yoder, J.D., & Kahn, A.S. (1993). Working toward an inclusive psychology of women. *American Psychologist, 48,* 846–850.

Yoder, J.D., & Schleicher, T.L. (1996). Undergraduates regard deviation from occupational gender stereotypes as costly for women. *Sex Roles, 34,* 171–188.

Yoder, J.D., Schleicher, T.L., & McDonald, T.W. (1998). Empowering token women leaders: The importance of organizationally legitimated credibility. *Psychology of Women Quarterly, 22,* 209–222.

Yoder, J.D., & Winegarden, B.J. (1993). The psychology of women: No passing fad. *Contemporary Psychology, 38,* 1178–1179.

Young, D.J., & Fraser, B.J. (1992, April). *Sex differences in science achievement: A multilevel analysis.* Paper presented at the annual meeting of the American Research Association, San Francisco, CA.

Young, I.M. (1992). Five faces of oppression. In T.E. Wartenberg (Ed.), *Rethinking power* (pp. 174–195). Albany, NY: State University of New York Press.

Young, T., & Harris, M.B. (1996). Most admired women and men: Gallup, Good Housekeeping, and gender. *Sex Roles, 35,* 363–375.

Yukie, A., & Falbo, T. (1991). Relationships between marital satisfaction, resources, and power strategies. *Sex Roles, 24,* 43–56.

Zambrana, R.E., & Ellis, B.K. (1995). Contemporary research issues in Hispanic/Latino women's health. In D.L. Adams (Ed.), *Health issues for women of color: A cultural diversity perspective* (pp. 42–70). Thousand Oaks, CA: Sage.

Zebrowitz, L.A., Tenenbaum, D.R., & Goldstein, L.H. (1991). The impact of job applicants' facial maturity, gender, and academic achievement on hiring recommendations. *Journal of Applied Social Psychology, 21,* 525–548.

Zepplin, H., Sills, R.A., & Heath, M.W. (1987). Is age becoming irrelevant? An exploratory study of perceived age norms. *International Journal of Aging and Human Development, 24,* 241–256.

Zimmer, L. (1988). Tokenism and women in the workplace: The limits of gender-neutral theory. *Social Problems, 35*, 64–77.

Zoucha-Jensen, J.M., & Coyne, A. (1993). The effects of resistance strategies on rape. *American Journal of Public Health, 83*, 1633–1634.

Zucker, K.J., Wilson-Smith, D.N., Kurita, J.A., & Stern, A. (1995). Children's appraisals of sex-typed behavior in their peers. *Sex Roles, 33*, 703–725.

Zuckerman, D.M. (1980). Self-esteem, self-concept, and the life goals and sex-role attitudes of college students. *Journal of Personality, 48*, 149–162.

Zuckerman, D.M. (1981). Sex-role related goals and attitudes of minority students: A study of Black college women and re-entry students. *Journal of College Student Personnel, 22*, 23–30.

Zuckerman, M., & Kieffer, S.C. (1994). Race differences in face-ism: Does facial prominence imply dominance? *Journal of Personality and Social Psychology, 66*, 86–92.

PHOTO CREDITS

INDEX

Psychoanalysis *(con't.)*
  androcentrism, 53–54
    biological essentialism, 54–55
    moral reasoning, 55–58
Psychological aggression, 138
Psychological consequences of violence, 326–28
Psychological well-being, gender and, 121–22
Psychologization of women's physical maladies, 246
Psychology, feminist transformations of. *See* Feminist transformations of psychology
Psychology of Sex Differences, The (Maccoby and Jacklin), 129
Psychology of Women Quarterly, 14
Psychopathic rapists, stereotype of, 314–15
Psychosexual development, 44
Psychotropic drugs, 279–80
PsycLIT, 116, 117, 198*n*
Pugh, M.D., 223

Q

Quality of day care, 204
"Queen bee syndrome," 226–27
Questions, questioning, 3–7
Quid pro quo sexual harassment, 304, 306
Quina, Kathryn, 264

R

Race and ethnicity. *See also specific races and ethnicities*
  cardiovascular diseases and, 261
  cross-race friendships, 188
  health insurance and, 268
  male partner abuse and, 312–13
  occupational segregation within, 229
  premenstrual syndrome and, 256
  prevalence of mental disorders and, 275
Racism, 188
Radford, Jill, 323
Rape, 304
  acquaintance, 306, 307, 316
  date, 305*n*, 328, 350
  disrupted world view and, 328
  excusing perpetrator of, 314–16
  incidence and prevalence of, 311–12
  marital, 305, 306, 328
  myths about, 318–19
  perceptions of, 304–5, 306
  physical consequences of, 325
  prevention of, 351–52
  psychological consequences of, 327
  resistance and avoidance of, 349–51
Reactive role behavior, 181
Reactivity of research participants, 19–20
Reasoning, moral, 55–58

Recall, gender-schematic vs. gender-aschematic patterns of, 73
Recovered memories of childhood sexual abuse, 322–23
Recovering from Rape (Ledray), 328–29
Recruiting strategies, gender-typing of work and, 95–97
Reforms, 5
Reis, Harry, 186
Reitman, Freida, 217
Relational, nurturing orientation, 55
Relationships, close. *See* Close relationships
Relationship satisfaction, 183–84, 192
Relocation, wage gap and, 218
Reproduction of Mothering, The (Chodorow), 54
Reproductive health, 257–60
Research
  initial decision to do, 19
  objectivity of, feminist critique of, 18–20
  single-gender, 10–11, 12
  systematic, 18–20
Resilience, 328–29
Reskin, Barbara, 227, 233
Resolution phase of sexual response cycle, 249
Retirement, 105–6
Revelation, 343–44, 345
Revolutions, 5
Riederle, Monika, 251
Rights reasoning, 57
Risman, Barbara, 200
Rittenhouse, Amanda, 256
Ritual in women's lives, role of, 299
Robertson, John, 283
Roe v. *Wade*, 353
Rogers, Annie, 92
Rohypnol, 305*n*
Role behaviors, gender stereotypes of, 152–57
Role conflict, 179
Role meaning, 180–81
Role-modeling function of women mentors, 226
Role overload, 178, 179
Role quality, 180
Roles
  gender, 52
  multiple. *See* Multiple roles
Roll, Samuel, 137
Romantic attachments, 183, 188–96
  being partnered, 191–96
    lesbian relationships, 191–92
    marital relationships, 192–96
  dating, 189–91, 264*n*, 347
Roos, Patricia, 233
Root, Maria, 290, 291
Rose, Suzanna, 188, 189
Roush, Kristin, 343, 344